PROMOTION IN THE MERCHANDISING ENVIRONMENT

SECOND EDITION

PROMOTION IN THE MERCHANDISING ENVIRONMENT

SECOND EDITION

Kristen K. Swanson

NORTHERN ARIZONA UNIVERSITY

Judith C. Everett

NORTHERN ARIZONA UNIVERSITY

Fairchild Publications, Inc.

New York

Director of Sales and Acquisitions: Dana Meltzer-Berkowitz
Executive Editor: Olga T. Kontzias
Senior Development Editor: Jennifer Crane
Development Editor: Barbara Chernow
Art Director: Adam B. Bohannon
Production Manager: Ginger Hillman
Senior Production Editor: Elizabeth Marotta
Photo Researcher: Christi De Larco and Erin Fitzsimmons
Copyeditor: Aimee E. Chevrette

Cover Design: Adam B. Bohannon
Text Design: Dutton & Sherman Design

Second Edition, Copyright © 2007 Fairchild Publications, Inc.
Fairchild Fashion Group
A Division of Condé Nast Publications

First Edition, Copyright © 2000 Fairchild Publications, Inc.

Library of Congress Catalog Card Number: 2007923705

ISBN-13: 978-1-56367-551-5

GST R 133004424

Printed in Canada

CH01, TP14

─○ contents

Chapter 2 · CONSUMER BEHAVIOR   33

Chapter 3 · PROMOTION ORGANIZATION   63

PART TWO   *Promotion Mix*

Chapter 8 · ADVERTISING AND THE CREATIVE PROCESS   222

Promotion is everywhere. We see it. We hear it. Sometimes we welcome it into our homes and businesses, and at other times it invades our world without our permission. Promotion is exciting and creative, entertaining and informative, and influences us every day consciously and unconsciously. That is just as true today as it was when we wrote the first edition of *Promotion in the Merchandising Environment.* The purpose of the second edition remains the same, to explain the process of promotion and to describe the promotion mix tools available for creating successful campaigns. This book focuses on the comprehensive nature of promotion in the merchandising environment of fashion-related goods and emphasizes the evolving nature of promotion in a global marketplace.

Several themes are evident throughout this text. The first theme is the concept of integrated marketing communications (IMC). In an IMC environment, all promotion elements are thought of as a single communication system with each element supporting the objectives of every other element. Advertising, direct marketing and interactive media, sales promotion, public relations, special events, fashion shows, visual merchandising, and personal selling work together to communicate the same message about the merchandise, brand, or organization to the end user. IMC is reinforced in each chapter with industry examples.

A second theme, which is a thread through the text, is the global nature of promotion. In today's society, promotion is undeniably global. With advanced communication and transportation technologies, companies have the ability to locate nearly anywhere in the world, and recognition of international brands is very evident. While much promotion is still at the local or national level, manufacturers, designers, and retailers must be able to communicate to consumers around the world. The global nature of promotion was even more obvious as we wrote the second edition. Examples of international promotions are included throughout this text.

Changes in technology are driving communication and promotion, the third theme of this book. Technological changes include the rapid increase in the use of the Internet and the interactive transfer of data by industry and consumers. Promotion strategies that once were limited to live performances, print, or broadcast formats must now consider more innovative means of communication. Additionally, communication technologies are revolutionizing the way we send and receive promotional information. Promotion tools now include satellite, cable, fiber-optic electronic devices, and personal communication tools, such as BlackBerries and wireless Internet connections. When we wrote the first edition, the World Wide Web was just starting to have influence on our society. At that time we felt it was important to provide Web addresses for important retailers, manufacturers, forecasting services, media groups, professional organizations, and so forth. That is not the case today. The Internet has become a good research resource, and it is so easy to find information about people, products, and services that providing Web addresses is no longer a priority.

This book focuses on the merchandising environment. We consider merchandising to include forecasting what customers want to buy, investigating where to find that merchandise in the marketplace, determining the price the customer is willing to pay, and making it available through retail stores or other merchandising outlets where the customer is willing to buy the merchandise. Promotion is a key element at each step of the process. In the merchandising environment, promotion is twofold. It is an essential information source for end users to keep abreast of the global marketplace. It is also a fundamental strategy to fulfill the merchandising task for manufacturers, designers, and retailers. This text features examples from all levels of the distribution channel to explain the role of promotion in the merchandising field.

The authors believe that fashion is evident in many product categories beyond clothing and accessories, and therefore, although the majority of examples in this text are from clothing and related categories, we have included appropriate examples to broaden students' thinking about promotion. Promotion extends to fields beyond fashion. This text is written to teach techniques that can be used in a fashion setting or transferred to other product categories.

The skills necessary to become a promotion practitioner are stressed throughout this book. Photographs, illustrations, checklists, and real-world examples are part of every chapter to encourage creativity in those readers who will eventually produce promotion campaigns. To engage the reader in thinking beyond the boundaries of the text, each chapter features readings on the topic that provide perspective. The readings range from how-to discussions to case studies, to discussions from professionals in the industry. Articles, tables, figures, and examples are updated in each chapter of the second edition. Other features of the text include chapter objectives and summaries, highlighted key terms, questions for discussion, additional resources, and a comprehensive glossary.

This text is written to give a logical and informative order to promotion, from basic concepts to specific activities. After teaching from this book, we have decided to reorganize information in the second edition. The first part of the text covers basic concepts and tools relevant to all types of promotion methods. The global nature of promotion is introduced, followed by an updated discussion about consumer behavior, promotion organization, promotional aspects of fashion forecasting, along with planning and budgeting promotion methodologies. The second section of the book covers each of the promotion mix elements in depth. We discuss advertising and the creative process, print media, broadcast media, direct marketing and interactive media, sales promotion, public relations, special events, fashion shows, visual merchandising, and personal selling. The methods for measuring and evaluating each promotion mix activity is now included with each chapter.

As teachers and authors, we realize that course curricula are not always prepared according to a text. It has been our goal in writing this book to provide the instructor who teaches all promotion mix aspects in one course with enough information to adequately cover each of the subjects. We also realize that some instructors pull out certain topics, such as fashion forecasting, fashion shows, or visual merchandising, and teach those as independent courses with textbooks specific to that topic. Therefore, this book is written with the understanding that each chapter may be used independently or collectively as part of the entire promotion industry.

Promotion is fun, exciting, and changing daily. When we started writing the first edition of this text, electronic retailing and other technologies were in their infancy stages. As we finish writing the second edition, use of interactive technologies is commonplace. We can only guess what new technologies will emerge in the future. We hope you will find promotion as exciting as we do. We watch television, listen to the radio, read fashion magazines and newspapers, and surf the Internet, always finding new and creative promotions along with unique methods for sending information.

ACKNOWLEDGMENTS

In the second edition, we would like to thank all of our students who have offered input, suggestions, and recommendations for this revision. Additional thanks go to Heather Madrill, Heather Shoup, Suzanne Barr, and Mark Swanson. We also acknowledge Donna Cunningham, a lecturer of advertising and public relations, for her recommendations about the practice of public relations.

From the first edition, we thank the following individuals for their assistance with this text: Rebecca Pierson of Union Bay; Carmela Carratie and David Wolfe of the Doneger Group; Katherine Flintoff of Mervyn's; Christine Walker of Walker Media; Helen Atkins of Pretty Polly; and Pam Esser of Esser Designs.

Reviewers selected by the publisher were also helpful. They include: Cindi Baker, Berkeley College; Barbara Frazier, Western Michigan University; Ruth Glock, Iowa State University; Michele Granger, Southwest Missouri State University; Shelley Harp, Texas Tech University; Patricia Huddleson, Michigan State University; Frances Huey, ICM School of Business; Kim K.P. Johnson, University of Minnesota; Gloria Johnston, Fashion Institute of Design and Merchandising; Jamie Kridler, East Tennessee University; Suzanne Marshall, California State University—Long Beach; Barbara Oliver, Colorado State University; Lynda Gamans Poloian, New Hampshire College; Carolyn Predmore, Manhattan College; William Rogers, University of Arizona; Tom Sands, Nassau Community College; Nancy Stanforth, Oklahoma State; and Carol Tuntland, California State University—Los Angeles.

Without Olga Kontzias of Fairchild Books neither edition of this book would exist. Olga's sense of humor and encouragement made the process enjoyable. We offer her a special thanks and to her able staff as well. We worked with Sylvia Weber on the first edition and with Joseph Miranda, Jennifer Crane, Elizabeth Marotta, and Christi De Larco on the second edition.

A special and personal thank you is extended to James Power and Christopher Everett. Without your encouragement, patience, and support, we could not devote the effort to our writing projects.

During the writing of the first edition of this book, there was a popular television advertisement for a packaging service. It went something like this: "Up on the top floor, the marketing guru is giving a lecture on *thinking outside the box*. Meanwhile, you are down in shipping concerned with *what's in the box*." Even though that commercial no longer runs, we hope this book gives you a good foundation for *working within the box* and at the same time causes you to think *outside the box*.

Kristen Swanson
Judith Everett

part one

Role and Structure of Promotion

FIGURE 1.1 Kanye West performing at a Fendi launch party in Tokyo.

CHAPTER 1

Promotion: A Global Perspective

Taking a different tack with the Japanese market, Fendi hosted the hottest hip-hop-flavored fashion party in town, with Japanese streetwear ringleader Nigo—not Karl Lagerfeld or Silvia Venturini Fendi—calling the creative shots for the night.

The immediate occasion was the global launch of a range of leather goods by Venturini Fendi called B. Mix. But the overarching goal was to start speaking to Japanese customers in a new way and keep fanning Fendi's global momentum.

"It's about a different way of seeing Western fashion," Michael Burke, Fendi's chief executive officer, said in an interview just before the event, which featured performances by Kanye West, and the Teriyaki Boys in a giant tent in Tokyo's National Stadium, which Nigo chose as a wink to the Colosseum in Rome. "The formula used to be: Duplicate your Milanese runway and they'll be happy."

But in Burke's estimation, it's time to take notice of how Japanese consumers are changing: Diversifying their spending and paying more attention to local fashion heroes.

". . . I think we're going to have to be much more in tune with the customer. . . . The solution is to stay relevant with these consumers rather than screaming one monolithic message."

And how. Trendy young Tokyoites came out in force.

In an interview, Nigo, the man behind the cult Bathing Ape label, said he appreciated Fendi's initiative, which allowed him to give the event a local flavor, from the mix of the 1,000 guests he assembled to the red makeup slashed across the eyes of the female string quartet that backed up West.

Source: Socha, M. (2006, December 4). Fendi's hip-hop take on Japan. *Women's Wear Daily*, p. 4.

> **After you have read this chapter, you should be able to:**
>
> Explain the roles of promotion and its function in a global society.
>
> Distinguish promotion from marketing and merchandising.
>
> Recognize the significance of communication in making consumers aware of products and services.
>
> Identify the essential components of the promotion mix within the merchandising environment.
>
> Define integrated marketing communications (IMC) and explain why it is becoming increasingly important in planning and implementing a coordinated promotional mix.

ENDI'S RADICAL LAUNCH PROVIDES an excellent example of how to effectively promote a product or service. Recognizing a preference among its potential Japanese consumers for Nigo over Lagerfeld, the fashion designer replaced an old formula, which it recognized as stale, with a fresh concept that appealed to trendy young Tokyoites. A closer examination of the essential terms and concepts of promotion in the academic and professional worlds will show how companies like Fendi reach new customers and increase their appeal in the global marketplace.

As it is used in this book, **promotion** is a comprehensive term for all of the communication activities initiated by the seller to inform, persuade, and remind the consumer about products, services, and/or ideas offered for sale. The goal of the seller is to have consumers respond by purchasing what is offered. Although some authors feel that promotion involves only nonpersonal approaches to influence consumers to buy products, this book looks at both personal methods, such as personal selling, and nonpersonal techniques, such as advertising and public relations, to achieve the goals of promotional communication.

Messages created by sellers are intended to attract, inform, and urge buyers to action. Domestic and foreign firms have generated billions of dollars' worth of expenditures on various promotional activities. These messages are extremely significant to a firm's complete marketing and merchandising communication program, proof of which may be demonstrated by the dollars spent on advertising and by predictions for its continued growth.

Robert Coen, Senior Vice President, Director of Forecasting at Universal McCann, details the position of advertising expenditures and forecasts the upcoming year in an annual report presented in December of each year. Coen makes comparisons of the health of advertising in relation to the health of the general economy. In 1980 expenditures on advertising in the United States totaled $53 billion, and $49 billion was spent on such sales promotion techniques as allowances and discounts to retailers, contests, coupons, premiums, product samples, rebates, and sweepstakes. By 2005 advertising expenditures at the local and national levels had increased to over $276 billion, whereas sales promotion programs had grown to nearly $300 billion (2005). Coen also reports that promotional expenditures in international markets outside of the United States have grown significantly from $55 billion in 1980 to nearly $294 billion in 2005, bringing total worldwide advertising expenditures to nearly $570 billion.

Advertising spending is closely watched because it is believed to be a reliable indicator of the general health of the economy. According to Coen, although a leak in the Internet bubble occurred in late 2000, growth in advertising spending continued, outshining the growth in the gross domestic product (GDP) (2005). In 2001, the entire economy slumped with no growth, and advertising was disastrously impacted with a decline in spending. The impact of the events of September 11, 2001 was felt through all sectors of the economy. A gradual improvement in the economy took place in 2002 and 2003, but advertising sales continued to lag behind expected growth. By 2004, the economic recovery strengthened, as did ad spending. One key promotional area with significant increases in 2004 and 2005 was direct mail advertising, which was positively affected by the "do not call" restrictions placed upon telemarketing in 2004 (2005). Many advertisers have turned to the Internet, contributing to a slump in demand for traditional media time and space in local media.

The changes in top and secondary product categories are also documented in the annual report. Coen states (2005) that toiletries and cosmetics, which are considered to be part of the top product categories, increased advertising expenditures 4 percent overall, with the greatest growth in spot television (17 percent increase) and in magazines (14 percent increase). Apparel is considered a secondary product category with an increase in advertising spending of 7 percent in general, increasing advertising primarily in national television and magazines (2005).

This chapter serves as the foundation for studying promotion by defining essential terms used in both academic and professional worlds. Because promotion means different things to different people, the chapter begins by comparing the role of promotion in today's domestic and global society. The global perspective of promotion is a key theme that starts here and is carried throughout the text, because many firms are crossing international borders. Next, the fundamental terms *marketing, merchandising,* and *communication* are considered. The chapter then briefly defines the individual tools of promotion used to disseminate messages—advertising, direct marketing and interactive media, sales promotion, public relations, personal selling, special events, fashion shows, and visual merchandising. Chapter 1 concludes with a discussion about integrated marketing communications.

———o THE ROLES OF PROMOTION

Promotion means different things to different people. To some people, promotion is strictly a business activity. Individuals or firms involved in both public and private sectors use promotional messages to communicate with their target markets. Advertising agencies create promotional situations, and retail stores use promotion to create interest in their products and sales environment. These communications are critical to the success of a company. Messages can be presented in the form of advertisements or transmitted through other promotional methods such as direct mail or fashion show productions.

To other people, promotion may be thought of as a social phenomenon. Nearly everyone in the contemporary world is affected by various forms of promotion. This force can be found in social, legal, and ethical environments. Advertising and other promotional activities may be used to promote various causes. Retailers might encourage high school art students to participate in a poster design contest, demonstrating a safety concern, prevention of illegal activities, or ways to protect the environment. By displaying their works of art, the retailer may gain recognition as a responsible citizen of the community and may attract new customers. Political candidates use the public media to promote their economic, environmental, social, or political points of view.

To still others, promotion is a basic element of a free enterprise system. It helps manufacturers and merchandisers make consumers aware of the products and services that are available. Billions of dollars are spent annually to inform customers of the opening of a new store or the specifications of a new and better computer software application or hardware design.

Various techniques or strategies of promotion may be viewed as a positive force accelerating change or as an unnecessary expense influencing people to purchase unwanted products. No matter how these activities are viewed, promotion remains an important element in the global marketplace.

———o GLOBAL NATURE OF PROMOTION

The term *global* is used when referring to something with worldwide implications. In business, **globalization** is the integration of international trade and foreign investment, resulting in worldwide trade of merchandise and resources. As the 21st century begins, the world's economies are roughly as intertwined as they were in 1913 (Uchitelle, 1998b). Despite two world wars and the Great Depression that attempted to dismantle global integration during the 20th century, advanced communication and transportation technologies have created multiple worldwide consumer markets and sources for producing or acquiring merchandise. Today, companies are able to locate almost anywhere in the world, aided by information technology that vastly increases the speed of transactions across borders. Multinational firms, such as IBM, Royal Dutch/Shell, and Imperial Chemical Industries, have led the way for other firms by integrating revenues, research, finances, stockholders, and management over many countries.

While a borderless global economy has been the goal of some individuals and companies, others have disagreed with this movement. Despite interest in overseas sales and investment, nationality binds firms to their home countries. "What we have is United States, European, and Japanese corporations trying to dress in global clothing," according to William W. Keller, executive director of the Center for International Studies at the Massachusetts Institute of Technology (Uchitelle, 1998a).

Despite differences of opinions about the strengths and weaknesses of international trade, we are moving quickly in the direction of a global economy. With no slowdown in international trade anticipated, understanding world cultures and economies are essential tools for individuals doing business and providing communication and promotional messages to consumers in the 21st century.

The fashion industry has been reshaped by globalization. Manufacturing of fashion goods has moved from the United States to offshore production sites. This movement has played a role in helping underdeveloped countries become industrialized. This shift has helped create greater consumer demand for products than ever before.

The economy of a country is often defined by its **gross domestic product (GDP)**, which is the amount of goods and services produced by a country in one year. This is the output of products and services produced within a nation, without consideration of the country's imports or exports. This figure is an important indicator of a nation's wealth.

As countries become more developed, the interest in fashion becomes stronger as well. When we first considered the international nature of fashion in the 20th century, we concentrated on western European countries. As the innovators of high fashion, France, Italy, and Great Britain were the trendsetters. Now we must consider the widespread nature of fashion. It is not unusual to look at Australia, Brazil, Thailand, China, and India as sources of fashion inspiration and manufacturing or as consumers of fashion.

The economies of both China and India are growing as this edition is being written. ACNielsen, a market research firm, did a survey of the most coveted global fashion brands (Hall, 2006). Although many of the fashion brands identified were not yet physically available in China or India, consumers were well aware of them. According to Bhawani Singh, the managing director of consumer research at ACNielsen Europe, "awareness remains quite high because of international television, fashion magazines, and the Internet" (Hall, 2006, p. 12). Table 1.1 compares the top fashion brands that consumers

TABLE 1.1   *Far East Fashion-Forward Brands*

China			India		
Rank	Brand	%	Rank	Brand	%
1*	Chanel	38	1	Gucci	42
2*	Versace	38	2	Giorgio Armani	38
3	Louis Vuitton	32	3	Christian Dior	35
4	Giorgio Armani	26	4	Versace	34
5	Christian Dior	22	5	Louis Vuitton	29
6	Gucci	20	6	Ralph Lauren	25
7	Givenchy	16	7	Yves Saint Laurent	20
8	Prada	10	8*	Chanel	17
9*	Max Mara	9	9*	Prada	17
10*	Ralph Lauren	9	10*	DKNY	17

*Indicates a tie.

Adapted from: Hall, C. (2006, June 1). The WWD list: Far East fashion-forward. *Women's Wear Daily*, p. 12.

in China and India would buy, if money were no object. It is interesting to note that all of the brands originate in France, Italy, or America.

Transitioning to a Global Perspective

Promotional activities—along with other aspects of marketing—are global in their reach, as demonstrated at the beginning of the chapter by Fendi's hip-hop fashion party in Tokyo. Several important factors have contributed to the trend toward international-ization. Kitty Dickerson, professor and chair of the Department of Textile and Apparel Management at the University of Missouri—Columbia, identified five reasons for the shift to a global perspective in the textile and apparel industries. The following have been among the most influential developments of the 20th century causing this change:

1. **Economic growth.** Sustained growth of global economies after World War II resulted in increased international trade. Although there have been economic fluctuations, trade has increased because (a) consumers have had the means to purchase products from various parts of the world, (b) companies have been able to add capacity under the assumption that foreign consumers would be able to sustain demand, and (c) fewer restrictions have typically been applied to imports when the economy has been flourishing.
2. **Improved economic status of developing countries.** In recent years, developing nations have been exporting manufactured products such as apparel rather than exporting agricultural products and minerals. Thus, these developing nations have taken steps toward more economic and industrial expansion, especially in the fields of textiles and apparel.
3. **Increased global communication with emerging communication technologies.** Communication technologies such as satellite transmissions and fiber optics were intro-duced in the 20th century, reducing time and distance for international trade. These advances in communication technologies allow importers (individuals or companies that bring merchandise into a country) and exporters (individuals or companies that send merchandise to another country) to conduct business more quickly than ever before. Videoconferencing has been used by such firms as J.C. Penney to broadcast buyers' meetings showing new fashion lines and informing branch managers about promo-tional activities. Additionally, worldwide communication efforts have stimulated demand for products in various parts of the globe where demand never existed before.

   Demonstrating the impact of increased international communication, a visit to The Gap Internet home page offers viewers from anywhere in the world product infor-mation, news, advertising updates, company information, and a store locator service (Fig. 1.2). This firm enables a potential customer to find the nearest international store location or purchase products via the website.
4. **Improved transportation systems.** Transportation systems including airplanes, ships, and trains have made it easier for buyers to access areas almost anywhere in the world. Transportation systems permit individuals to travel farther and faster today than they did even a decade or two ago, contributing to a shrinking world.
5. **Institutional arrangements by business and government.** Various institutional innovations have been implemented to facilitate the exchange of goods and services and the transfer of funds for the payment of those goods and services (Dickerson, 1999).

Passage of various trade agreements, including the North American Free Trade Agreement (NAFTA) in 1994 and the World Trade Organization (WTO) in 1995, has broken down traditional trade barriers and led to global expansion of traditional U.S.

FIGURE 1.2 The Gap website offers viewers an opportunity to locate stores near their homes or to make virtual visits to stores at various locations around the world.

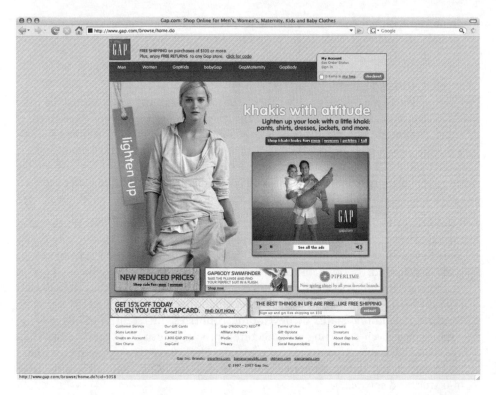

retail stores. Despite economic uncertainty in both Mexico and Canada in 1994, by the end of the decade their economies had improved. Now, the majority of fashion and apparel items sold in the United States are imported. As of 2004, China, followed by Mexico, provided the highest percentage of imports of apparel into the United States (American Apparel and Footwear Association, 2004).

As we have seen so far, breaking down trade barriers and increased interest in foreign products are just a couple of the reasons why retailers have entered into global arrangements. English firms such as Burberry's have had a presence in the United States for many years. Americans visiting London or Paris are just as likely to see a Gap store, or find Clinique or MAC at the British or French department stores. Although Gap stores originated in San Francisco, branches of the retail giant can be found throughout the United States, as well as in the United Kingdom, France, Germany, and Japan. Highlighting this trend, a special report, compiled by Deloitte & Touche, on the *Global Powers of Retailing* is presented annually as a supplement to *Stores* magazine. Table 1.2 describes the top global retailers. With retailers, manufacturers, and designers taking a more global approach, the field of promotion must look beyond national borders.

In major U.S. retail organizations such as Sears, J.C. Penney, and Wal-Mart, the international reach of promotional activities is the norm. Brands such as Revlon and Maybelline are no longer simply domestic products; international product usage demands global product awareness.

Thinking Globally, Acting Locally

Merchandise brands and retail store identities have become international. Today, a consumer can purchase a "Big Mac" in Moscow or a "Maharaja Mac" in New Delhi, or a

Table 1.2 *Top 10 Global Retailers*

Rank	Country of Origin	Company Name	Formats	2004 Retail Sales (US$ mil)
1	United States	Wal-Mart	Cash & Carry/Warehouse Club, Discount Department, Hypermarket/Supercenter/Superstore, Supermarket	285,222
2	France	Carrefour	Cash & Carry/Warehouse Club, Convenience/ Forecourt, Discount Store, Hypermarket/Supercenter/ Superstore, Supermarket	89,568
3	United States	The Home Depot	Home Improvement	73,094
4	Germany	Metro AG	Cash & Carry/Warehouse Club, Discount Department, Electronics Specialty, Home Improvement, Hypermarket/Supercenter/Superstore, Other Specialty, Supermarket	69,781
5	United Kingdom	Tesco	Convenience/Forecourt, Hypermarket/Supercenter/ Superstore, Supermarket	62,505
6	United States	Kroger	Convenience/Forecourt, Discount Store, Hypermarket/ Supercenter/Superstore, Other Specialty Supermarket	56,434
7	United States	Costco	Cash & Carry/Warehouse Club	47,146
8	United States	Target	Discount Department Store, Hypermarket/ Supercenter/Superstore	45,682
9	Netherlands	Aldi	Discount Store, Supermarket	42,908
10	Germany	Schwarz Unternehmens Treuhand	Discount Store, Hypermarket/Supercenter/Superstore	42,793

Adapted from: 2006 Global Powers of Retailing. (2006, January). *Stores* (Section 2), p. G16.

"Chanel suit" in Paris, San Francisco, or Tokyo. McDonald's has recognized the need to practice **glocalization.** The term, coined by Hans Hijlkema, former president and founder of European Marketing Confederation, refers to a combination of global branding practices and localized marketing (Miller, 1996). McDonald's acted locally by customizing the traditional burger to a culture like the one in India that does not eat beef. Since the residents of New Delhi consider cows sacred, McDonald's introduced a two-mutton patty sandwich with special sauce, lettuce, cheese, pickles, and onions on a sesame seed bun (1996).

In the sports apparel industry, Nike tailored its ads to fit the interests of specific geographic target markets. Nike, a big sponsor of soccer events, did not want to offend its European consumers by featuring the top soccer players from only one or two countries. Instead, the sponsor selected highly rated players from several European teams for its European television commercials based on the premise of a soccer match against the devil. Thus, Nike did not offend any particular nationality. At the same time these soccer commercials were running in Europe, Nike featured American basketball stars in ads produced for the audience in the United States. Sports stars wearing Nike products were the common international theme, but the firm chose to present them in a manner that would be understood by the local consumer. See Box 1.1 for a localized strategy for fashion in the Middle East.

Standardized Strategy

Many people think that the citizens of the modern world, especially in industrialized countries, have become so similar that a standard approach will work throughout the

BOX 1.1

Looking for Fashion in the Muslim World

For as long as he can remember, Villa Moda founder Majed Al-Sabah has been flipping through Middle Eastern fashion magazines—and wincing with pain.

In a typical magazine, Chanel ads sit next to ones for Head & Shoulders, Louis Vuitton spreads appear alongside ones for cleaning detergent, photos are pixilated, and stories are cut and pasted from Western titles without any regard for copyright. And he's not taking it anymore.

For fall, Al-Sabah will launch his own magazine, to be called *Alef: A New Language of Beauty*. "We want to become the fashion magazine of record in the Middle East," said Al-Sabah over a cup of tea at the Berkeley Hotel here. "We want to position ourselves as a must-read for fashion insiders."

Al-Sabah said he's creating the magazine mostly out of necessity. "I have franchises to look after now, and they have ad budgets, but there's no place to put the ads—except for the cut-and-paste magazines," he said. "And that's money down the drain."

Alef, which is the letter A in Arabic, will bow with a September issue and come out four times a year. Al-Sabah, whose money is behind the project, hopes eventually to ramp the number of issues up to ten a year. He's named Sameer Reddy, formerly of hintmag.com and *Bidoun Magazine*, as *Alef's* editor and publisher. Paul de Zwart, cofounder and former publisher of *Wallpaper**, is consultant publisher. Edward Jowdy is creative director, Sam Shahid is editor at large, and contributors include Samira Nasr and Horacio Silva.

"It wouldn't take much to raise that bar on magazines in the Middle East," said Reddy with a laugh, "but we do want to show the rest of the world that we can produce a respectable creative title."

The time is certainly ripe for a high-end magazine: Climbing oil prices are fueling an economic boom in the Persian Gulf, fashion brands such as Giorgio Armani and Versace are opening luxury hotels in the region, and department stores like Saks Fifth Avenue and Harvey Nichols are opening franchised stores there.

Reddy said he plans to fill the magazine with fashion, beauty, design, food, film, music, and celebrity coverage. About 70 percent of *Alef* will be devoted to Middle Eastern culture, he said, even though the magazine will be published out of

New York and have a satellite office in Kuwait. Stories will also focus on hot gallerists and philanthropists, regional celebrities and royals. Al-Sabah said he's hoping his name and position in the Middle East (he hails from a big Kuwaiti family) will help the magazine gain access to VIPs' homes.

"A lot of Middle Eastern people are afraid of the tabloids, afraid of exposing their lives to strangers. If they know I'm behind it, they may be more willing," suggested Al-Sabah.

Reddy said the magazine wants to have a mix of internationally known photographers and local talent. "But, don't worry, it's not going to become an affirmative action program for the locals," he said.

Reddy said he doesn't see the Middle East's more conservative social mores as a barrier to a hip fashion title. "I'm more interested in working to find innovative ways to express sensuality and beauty instead of resorting to the lowest common denominator of sex to create a strong image," he said. "And I think the major photographers with whom we're speaking are inspired by the challenge of pioneering a new kind of fashion aesthetic that doesn't rely on nudity and overt sexuality to make a convincing image."

Alef will have an initial print run of 60,000 to 70,000, small by American standards, and will be distributed at newsstands, in hotels, and on partner airlines in the Middle East, and on newsstands in major U.S., European, and Southeast Asian cities. The copy will be in English, with Arabic subtitles. The cover price is still being determined, although Reddy said it will be £4.00 in the Middle East and £5.00 in the West, or $6.96 to $8.70.

The launch issue will be slightly more than 200 pages, and advertisers will include major luxury brands, said Reddy, although he declined to reveal any names.

Al-Sabah said he hopes *Alef* will play another role as well. "I want the magazine to be an ambassador from the Middle East, something that reflects the beauty of the region and shows that it's not only about Osama bin Laden, Saddam Hussein, and terrorism."

Source: Conti, S. (2006, February 24). Looking for fashion in the Muslim world. *Women's Wear Daily*, p. 18.

FIGURE 1.3 IKEA stores are found in Europe, North America, the Middle East, and Asia Pacific countries.

world. This means that a **standardized strategy,** which uses one approach for multiple markets, can be used in most countries. This would allow the firm to benefit from economies of scale, because it would not have to put out the considerable amount of time and expense of creating a separate strategy in each culture. This is also called a global strategy, because it focuses on commonalities across cultures, reflecting beliefs about the culture as viewed by outsiders.

IKEA, the Swedish-based furniture business, employs a standardized strategy throughout the world. A customer in Copenhagen, Denmark, will find the same types of goods as a customer in Tempe, Arizona. The store layout, product mix, as well as promotional strategies, are similar in the United States to the ones used in Denmark, France, Kuwait, or Japan. Figure 1.3 shows all of the international locations where IKEA stores can be found.

Lands' End offers websites in both the United Kingdom and the United States. Apparel and shoes available on the Lands' End site are similar for each nationality.

Many companies that use a standardized or global strategy are vertically integrated, which means that the company owns different levels in the production and distribution channels. Vertically integrated firms manufacture goods at self-owned factories and sell through self-owned retail stores. Most of the merchandise is private label, with the firm's name as the brand.

Localized Strategy

As we opened the section on Thinking Globally and Acting Locally, we introduced the approach by fast-food giant McDonald's. This specialization of the product, focusing on the cultural variations to meet the needs of the local market, is a **localized strategy.** Marketing specialists who endorse a localized strategy recognize that each culture is unique, with its own norms, value systems, conventions, and regulations. Any strategy must be tailored to meet the sensibilities and needs of each specific country.

This type of approach requires the firm to modify the product, as McDonald's does, or position the product to make it acceptable to the local tastes.

Amazon.com operates websites in several countries, from the original in the United States to Canada, China, France, Germany, Japan, and the United Kingdom. While the layout of each website is similar in each country, the books, music, and other products are targeted to its American, Canadian, Chinese, French, German, Japanese, or British audience. *Harry Potter* or *The Da Vinci Code* might be available at each of the international sites, but products unique to each culture are more likely to be featured.

Customers of the future will be better educated, quality oriented, and budget conscious. They will require sophisticated promotional strategies to meet their ever-growing demands. To better understand the nature of the promotional process and to have a common frame of reference, it is helpful to define the basic terms of the industry and their relationships.

——o Marketing

The marketing process represents how a product is conceived and moved through various channels from producer to consumer. Marketing holds various expectations within American culture. Many individuals use the terms *marketing* and *sales* synonymously. Some professionals believe marketing is simply the process of selling. Others take marketing a step further to include the elements of business, such as product research and development, pricing, and advertising. Marketing involves all of these operations and many more. To prevent confusion, the American Marketing Association approved the following definition of **marketing** in 1985: "the process of planning and executing the conception, pricing, promotion, and distribution of ideas, goods, and services to create exchanges that satisfy individual and organizational objectives" (AMA Board, 1985).

Marketing activities involve product design and development, distribution of products through marketing channels, pricing, and promotion. The entire marketing process must recognize the interdependence of the marketing activities. Firms that are marketing oriented plan operations around satisfaction of consumer wants and needs (see Box 1.2).

The **marketing mix** involves the coordination of the four P's—product, price, place, and promotion. Contemporary professionals have replaced promotion with communication. Analysts look at the needs of consumers and determine the demand for the product. The price must meet the expectations for quality and value. By offering the needed product at a particular and convenient location, the manufacturer can inform the consumer where to find the product. The fundamental challenge for marketing is to synthesize these four elements into a program that will lead to exchange in the marketplace.

Focus on Exchange

Exchange is a concept fundamental to marketing. For exchange to occur, there must be two or more participants with something of value to each other. The participants must have the ambition and interest to give up something in exchange for something else. This goes beyond simple communication. Promotion enables one party to inform another about a product or service and to persuade the party that the item will satisfy his or her wants or needs.

Not all marketing transactions involve exchange of tangible goods or services for money; some may also involve intangible feelings of philanthropy and altruism. Nonprofit firms often look to charitable donations to provide services. Goodwill Industries International is an example of a nonprofit organization that offers training and employment services to disabled and disadvantaged populations. In order to achieve these goals,

Goodwill retail stores accept used goods as donations. These items are resold and "profits" are used for training and development. Nonprofit organizations also look to people to provide cash donations. Although many people donate cash or used clothing and household items to such organizations, individuals may not see any tangible gains. The benefits come from the sense of social and psychological fulfillment that humanitarianism and charity produce.

Global Marketing

Marketing activities, once strictly aimed at domestic markets, are evident in virtually every corner of the world. The purpose of domestic and **global marketing** is the same; the difference between the two is created by the external conditions faced by an international or multinational firm. Differences from one country to another can be attributed to culture, language, buying power, education, geography, politics, government regulations, and religion, to mention just a few variables. These factors influence what is acceptable or inappropriate in terms of marketing activities.

American designers, manufacturers, and retailers have used marketing and advertising to make their names known throughout the world. Calvin Klein, Ralph Lauren, Donna Karan, and Tommy Hilfiger have become well known in Europe, Asia, and Mexico because of their huge advertising and marketing campaigns.

Additional evidence of the influence of global marketing is shown by increased participation of foreign press and buyers at the New York Fashion Week. Representatives from Milan, Paris, London, Tokyo, Mexico City, and Berlin attend the semiannual events to introduce new American fashion designs. American retailers and media are just as likely to attend ready-to-wear shows in London, Paris, or Milan. Denmark, Germany, Spain, and Brazil are emerging as fashion centers as well. Next, we look at the role of merchandising.

———o MERCHANDISING

Similar to marketing and promotion, the term *merchandising* means different things to different people. There are as many definitions of merchandising in print as there are in common practice. To some people, merchandising refers simply to retail selling. Others see merchandising as a product planning and retail distribution process. Academics and practitioners have struggled to develop a functional definition of merchandising for years. The classic definition of merchandising for the retail industry was originally developed by Paul Mazur as the planning involved in marketing the right merchandise at the right place at the right time in the right quantities at the right price (1927).

Merchandising Definition

Merchandising has evolved to take into consideration practices in both retail and manufacturing sectors. Recognizing the need to look at this changing nature of the industry, Kean (1987) proposed the following definition: "merchandising is the analysis and response to the changes (transformations) and processes (advances) which occur in the planning, negotiation, acquisition, and selling of products/services from their inception to their reception and use by the target customer" (p. 10). Kean viewed merchandising as just one part of the marketing continuum.

Grace Kunz proposed the Behavioral Theory of the Apparel Firm (BTAF) (Glock &

BOX 1.2

Gap Blitz Begins: TV, Outdoor, Radio to Tout Icon's Overhaul

Gap is pulling out all the stops in what will be a pivotal fall season.

As pressure for change mounts, amid slumping sales and investor impatience, Gap brand executives say their $6.8 billion business (the largest division of the $16 billion Gap Inc.) is about to climb out of its hole and that they are reworking just about every aspect of the operation to show a difference this fall.

Among the maneuvers is one of the company's most complex and ambitious advertising campaigns. It kicks off July 20 and is marked by a return to TV advertising after over a year's absence. There's also radio advertising, which hasn't been done since the late nineties, outdoor ads for the first time in two years, and print ads. It will be supported by in-store events at key locations, including live bands, shopping parties with stylists, customized T-shirts and redesigned shopping bags.

The message centers on what executives called the "reinvention of Gap iconic items" in updated silhouettes, styles, colors and fits. And for the first time, the advertising will unfold in three different installments during the fall season, and for holiday, there will be two installments of the campaign. In the past, Gap would sustain a single theme through an entire season, even if it grew tired fast. For this fall, however, there's one for denim kicking off next week, apropos for back-to-school. Four weeks later, ads focus on T-shirts, and four weeks after that, it's all about cropped black pants.

Although complicated in its development, the ads are reminiscent of past Gap campaigns, with familiar elements such as dancing, heavy use of black-and-white portraiture, the focus on a single item and a mix of celebrities and models in poses that seem intimate and personal. Among those in the upcoming ads are actors Jeremy Piven and Mia Farrow, singer Natasha Bedingfield and model Eva Herzigova.

There is also subtle use of the seventies slogan "fall into the Gap," which hasn't been seen in about a decade, with the same melody. Discretely on the bottom of some ads, psychedelic wavy doodling will reappear, another signature from the seventies.

"This is a real return to the whole concept of individuality applied to an item," said Trey Laird, of Laird + Partners, Gap's creative agency. "The Gap is really great at surrounding such simple things as T-shirts and jeans with [an aura] of sophistication, coolness and a sense of style."

Along with the marketing buildup, Gap has been accelerating store remodels that started with prototypes in Denver and have spread to 60 sites this year. They feature better lighting and outfit display, and sharper demarcation between items and women's and men's wear. Sixty units will get overhauled next year. Another 200 key stores are getting spruced up, with new paint, mannequins and display tables, and adding "dedicated" visual display associates, as a prelude to full remodeling. The stores are being remerchandised with shop concepts to make stronger statements in T-shirts, jeans, activewear. The idea is to focus on categories, rather than the entire collection.

At the moment, windows have been darkened as a teaser for the launch of the campaign.

The company also has been equipping sales associates with greater product knowledge and training them to better engage customers.

On the product side, executives said improvements have been made on fit, color and fabrics. With jeans, for example, "there's no one hero silhouette," Laird said, referring to how Gap merchandised in past seasons. Instead, there's a much greater variety, including skinny jeans, trouser jeans, straight legs and skirt jeans, among others, getting equal attention. While reviving the cropped black pant, it's with a front zipper instead of the side zipper. It's also slightly lower on the waist, but not low-waisted.

"It's a very pivotal season. The investor community places high urgency on it," said Mark Montagna, analyst at CL King & Associates. "Paul Pressler [Gap Inc. president and chief executive officer] has pretty much laid down the line saying they will get it right this fall. This time people are really going to hold him to it."

"This is a very critical fall for them and especially for Pressler," said Robert Kerson, of the executive search firm bearing his name. "He has to just do it, and do less talking about it. The analysts are tired of waiting. It will force changes if Gap doesn't have a good fall. The company must show some increases and show shareholder value. You will hear a drumbeat right after back-to-school. They will know certainly by the early part of October how fall is going."

In a related development, Old Navy, the company's second-largest division, also is reworking product and adding some higher price points, as well as developing a new store design.

The Gap brand's new advertising is one of the biggest and most complex campaigns ever developed by Gap. It's the first season to reflect the combined efforts of several new players on the teams, including Cynthia Harriss, president, and Charlotte Neuville, executive vice president of Gap adult design and product development.

In the initial "Jeans Take Shape" TV ads, filmed by director Francis Lawrence, female dancers wear skinny jeans, miniskirts, and long-sleeved shirts; the men wear dark, straight-leg jeans and jackets. As each person dances, their look transitions from one outfit to another, illustrating a range of denim silhouettes. The 30-second spot will run on network and cable TV through August 17 on shows including *Grey's Anatomy* and *The O.C.*

The print campaign, photographed by David Simms, mirrors the TV ads by highlighting denim silhouettes in pops of denim blue colors against a black-and-white background, and blue graphics that illustrate the names of different fits including "the skinny" and "the boyfriend." Print ads will run in August issues of magazines including *Vanity Fair*, *Vogue*, *In Style*, *GQ*, and *Rolling Stone*. Radio ads run in select markets July 19–30.

"We need to give our customers something new and something to talk about on a monthly basis," said Kyle Andrew, vice president of Gap marketing. "We must keep them engaged more than four times a year."

Andrew characterized the upcoming campaign as "celebration of a return to iconic categories. We're celebrating denim, celebrating our T-shirts, celebrating our hoodies. We are making a big deal of the product we always loved and our customers always loved. We will always evolve and keep our product current and fresh, but we also want to make sure we have the best hoodies, the perfect pair of jeans, the perfect pair of black pants. You should always be able to find that at the Gap, and we will have great new product campaigns to back them up on a much more frequent basis."

Andrew added, "In the past, we have done a good job of introducing new product or a new campaign, or educating our sales force team. There was more of an emphasis on certain things" at the expense of others. "This fall we have really gone after every aspect of our business that touches our customer. Every touch point has to be great. Gap can't just come out with great product and have an unsatisfactory store experience. We want to provide a holistic experience on every aspect. This fall, we have gone after everything. There is a sense of urgency. We also have a new team," led by Harriss, who became president last year, as well as Neuville, who joined last fall. Andrew said it's the new team's first real expression of the brand.

She declined to specify the cost of the ad campaign, but said: "It's not so much about the spend. We are spending in line with what we spent in the past. It's more about the amount of messages."

While fall will have three campaigns, holiday will have two. Previously, both would have just one. "We will definitely make a big impact every month. We need news all the time. . . . Our teams are working like crazy."

Source: Moin, D. (2006, July 13). Gap blitz begins: TV, outdoor, radio to tout icon's overhaul. *Women's Wear Daily*, pp. 1, 15.

Kunz, 2005). BTAF identifies marketing and merchandising as two of the five constituencies necessary to operate an apparel firm. Rather than seeing merchandising as a subset of marketing, Kunz saw merchandising and marketing as interactive yet equivalent functions. Along with Ruth Glock, Kunz developed the following definition of merchandising, reflecting behavioral theory: "the planning, developing, and presenting of product line(s) for identified target market(s) with regard to pricing, assortment, styling, and timing" (p. 63).

This text takes the position that merchandising should be considered in the broad context. Thus, **merchandising** involves forecasting what customers want to buy, investigating where to find that merchandise in the marketplace, determining the price the customer is willing to pay, and making it available through the retail store or other outlets where the customer is willing to buy the merchandise. This practice involves market research, preparing buying plans, selecting specific products, promoting those products to the consumer, and selling the products or services at a profit.

The Merchandising Environment

The application of marketing processes frequently involves a wide range of products and services. Marketing executives and academics use all types of products as a part of their practices and studies. It would be just as common to analyze and develop strategies for automobile and beer manufacturers as it would be to do the same for a telephone company or a soap detergent producer.

The **merchandising environment** incorporates all of the products and services relating to personal and home surroundings. These goods are also known as fashion products. These products are often considered to be the soft goods lines, such as apparel for the entire family, home furnishings, cosmetics, and related merchandise that enhances personal attractiveness. Many individuals consider these products to be the rapidly changing lines rather than hard product lines like appliances or automobiles. Consumers wait to buy expensive hard goods until they need a replacement, as they do for basic soft goods. However, fashion features influence the selection of the new purchase.

This book emphasizes the products and services associated with the merchandising environment. It covers the promotional strategies utilized in the fashion manufacturing and retailing sectors of the global enterprise system. Knowledge of the basic terms of business, including marketing and merchandising, is necessary to make promotional activities in this environment successful. An understanding of the role of communication, our next topic, is also necessary.

──o communication

By definition, **communication** is a transmission or exchange of information and/or messages. A basic knowledge of communication and communication theory is a necessity for anyone involved in promotion. For communication to occur, there must be some common thinking between the message sender and the message receiver. An understanding of information passed from one person or group to another establishes that common bond. Reaching this common bond is not easy; many attempts to communicate are thwarted by obstacles.

The Communication Process

A model of the communication process will help to explain the difficulties. In this model (Fig. 1.4), the communication process involves a sender encoding a message and sending that information to a receiver, who decodes the message and provides a response through feedback.

Communication begins with the sender or the source of the information. This may be an individual or an organization with a message to transmit to other individuals or organizations. This individual may be a salesperson, spokesperson, celebrity, or an organization such as a retailing, manufacturing, or advertising firm. The sender selects a combination of words or symbols to be presented orally or in written/visual form. This arrangement of the words and/or symbols is termed **encoding.** A major challenge to promotion experts is to develop messages and images that are easily understood by all target audiences.

The encoded message is conveyed to the receiver through various **channels**, the methods by which the message is translated. Personal selling channels include direct or face-to-face communication. This may also be called **word-of-mouth** communication. The opposite channel, nonpersonal selling, is often referred to as mass communication. The message is sent to many people at once through widely viewed broadcast or print media. Broadcast media consist of television, radio, and some forms of electronic technology. Print media include newspapers, magazines, direct mail, billboards, or any other two-dimensional print designs.

Once the message has been sent, the receiver must **decode** the message or transform

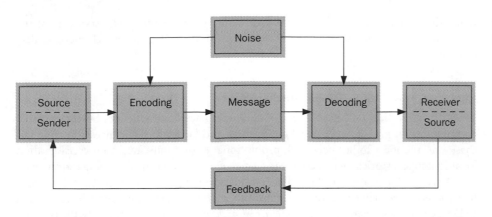

FIGURE 1.4 Communication process model.

it back into thought. This step forces the receiver to interpret what he or she believes the sender wanted the receiver to know and is dependent upon the receiver's frame of reference, or past experiences. Attitudes, values, perceptions, and cultural background are among the characteristics that help the receiver understand or misinterpret the message.

Noise refers to any outside factors that may interfere with the reception of the information or lead to some distortion of the message. Distortion may occur as the information is encoded or during the transmission or interpretation of the message. One way of thinking about noise is as if it were some technical difficulty experienced while broadcasting a television program. Part of the message may be eliminated or changed through signal distortion. Lack of common experiences could lead to similar problems in communication. Miscommunication may take place because of failure to understand the symbols presented in advertisements. The message sent by the advertiser for a popcorn popper could be misunderstood if the receiver views the salt box, used as a prop, as the main product being promoted.

When the receiver sends back some type of response or **feedback**, the sender will know if the intent of the message has been understood. Response may come in many forms, from simple recognition in a face-to-face interaction to the purchase of a product through a toll-free number advertised in a magazine or a sudden increase in sales after a billboard sign is put up. Feedback can close the loop of communication, letting the source know whether or not the message has been accurately sent, decoded, and acted upon.

Promotion Communication Audience

Promotion communication is commonly directed toward a particular type of audience. The nature and purpose of promotional communication differs from one situation to another. Some firms aim messages to the audience of ultimate consumers, the people who will buy and use the merchandise or services. These promotion messages are sent to people who consume the goods and services, and the audience is considered to be a **consumer market.**

In other situations, firms want to build awareness, heighten an image for the company, generate leads for its sales force, or strengthen buyer confidence in purchasing from the firm. In this case, the message is being sent from one business to another and this is called a **business-to-business market,** also known as a **trade market.** Communication is targeted to individuals who purchase raw materials to be converted into saleable products or finished products that will eventually be sold to ultimate consumers. Business-to-business and trade promotion communication is targeted to members of the marketing channel, such as wholesalers, distributors, or retailers. The sponsors of the communication hope other firms will stock, promote, sell, and restock merchandise offered by the message sponsor.

Communication in the Global Marketplace

The communication process in the global marketplace has challenges beyond normal communication problems. Cultural experiences and language differences contribute to these uncertainties. To be successful, promotional efforts must take into consideration local customs, historical perspectives, and language. Consider the following examples.

A cosmetic firm attempted to sell its products to Japanese consumers by presenting a television commercial that featured a statue of the ancient Roman emperor Nero coming to life, as a pretty woman wearing the firm's lipstick walked by. Unfortunately, the product introduction was not accepted because the Japanese women resented the hard sell approach and had no idea who Nero was. In this case, if the firm had wanted to use a historical figure, it should have selected a figure known within the local culture (Ricks, 2006).

After a shipment of wool weighed less than the paperwork indicated, Iranians accused a Taiwanese textile firm of cheating and refused to pay. After a long and expensive investigation, no deception by the shipper was discovered. The wool came from a humid climate and weighed more in Taiwan than it did in the dry climate of Iran (Ricks, 2006).

Product and company names can cause problems for firms in global expansion. When American retailer Sears, which originally was known as Sears Roebuck, wanted to open in Spain, the firm was forbidden to use its name. Although Sears had a good reputation, there was confusion. The locals speak Castillian Spanish and pronunciation of Sears sounds like *Seat*, which is the name of Spain's largest car manufacturer. Seat forced Sears to incorporate the name Roebuck on all of its products (Ricks, 2006).

Nike desired a global image and attempted to show that image in a television commercial broadcast in the United States. The company asked people from around the world to say Nike's slogan, *Just do it*, in their native language. Nike was embarrassed by an African Samburu tribesman who really said, "I don't want these shoes, give me big shoes" (Ricks, 2006, p. 55). After a competitor pointed out the error, Nike was forced to admit that it did not really know what people were saying. Nike and other companies will, more than likely, want to confirm what people say in the future.

In the global marketplace, English has become the common language. In the business world, many nonnative speakers use English to communicate with other nonnative users—for example, Japanese with Koreans, Koreans with Germans, Germans with Indonesians, Indonesians with Greeks, Greeks with Portuguese, and so forth. Although English is the common denominator, misunderstandings are still common.

Promotional blunders in the global marketplace can be avoided by taking several important steps.

- Conduct research about the intended consumers, especially in foreign markets, taking into consideration customs and culture in addition to language.
- Select a good translator. It is not enough that the translator use grammatically correct language; he or she must also be intimately familiar with the second language to understand its nuances, colloquialisms, slang, and idioms.
- Solicit feedback through retranslating and local input.

These steps will help prevent mistakes and misunderstandings.

──o PROMOTION MIX

The basic tools used for achieving a firm's communication and marketing goals are referred to as the **promotion mix.** In the merchandising environment these promotion mix categories include advertising, direct marketing and interactive media, sales promotion, public relations, personal selling, special events, fashion shows, and visual merchandising (Fig. 1.5). These elements take on various forms and have specific advantages and disadvantages. Each of the promotion mix elements is discussed in a separate chapter in Part II of this text.

Advertising

Advertising is any nonpersonal message paid for, placed in the mass media, and controlled by the sponsoring organization. This communication contains information about the organization, product, service, or idea created by the sponsoring firm to influence sales. The information is normally featured in public media such as newspapers, magazines, radio, television, direct mail, or other similar vehicles. Figure 1.6 shows a Norwegian magazine advertisement for a Danish-made product.

The *paid* concept of advertising indicates that the sponsoring agency must purchase either space in the print media or time in the electronic media. The *nonpersonal* element of advertising requires the message to be transmitted through the mass media. Television, radio, newspapers, or magazines are typical mass media through which an advertising message may be sent to a large group of people. Because of the nonpersonal nature of the communication channel, the ability of the sender to assess the effectiveness of the message is limited. There is no chance to obtain immediate feedback. Before developing and sending an advertising message, the sender must consider how the public will comprehend and react to the message.

Advertising is considered to be one of the most effective methods of distributing information to a large audience at an effective cost. It remains a primary element of the promotion mix. The general topic of advertising is discussed more fully in Chapter 8, while print media is the subject of Chapter 9 and broadcast media is the topic of Chapter 10.

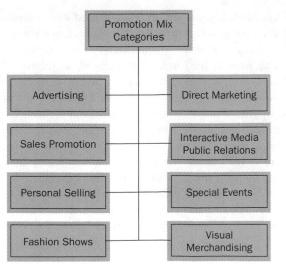

FIGURE 1.5 Promotion mix categories used in the merchandising environment.

FIGURE 1.6 Danish-produced Ecco shoes are advertised in a Norwegian magazine.

Direct Marketing and Interactive Media

Direct marketing describes the marketing process by which organizations communicate directly with target customers to generate a response or transaction. This communication normally uses a set of **direct-response media** such as mail, telephone, magazines, the Internet, radio, or television with messages aimed directly to the target consumer.

One of the big changes in direct marketing happened in 2004. Consumers were tired of and unhappy receiving unsolicited telemarketing phone calls and demanded that the government listen to their concerns. A national "Do Not Call" list was implemented. A valuable direct marketing tool was virtually eliminated. In response, there was an increase in the number of direct mail pieces distributed. In the first half of 2005, the number of mail items sent at regular standard mail rates increased nearly 5 percent, resulting in an annualized estimate of nearly 10 billion more pieces of mail sent in 2005 compared to 2004 (Coen, 2005).

Direct marketing has not always been considered a part of the traditional promotion mix. Direct marketing may have started with direct mail and mail-order catalogs, but today it has expanded to include many other areas. Growth and popularity of the Internet have led to direct marketing opportunities unheard of in the past.

Direct marketing techniques range from the simple postcard or sales letter to elaborate sales presentations on CD-ROMS and DVDs. These materials may be developed and distributed via traditional distribution channels and electronic media, or through a personal sales force hired by the marketer.

Since the first edition of this book was written, interactive media have created the biggest and most revolutionary changes in promotion, compared with any other promotion mix activity. These changes result from the dramatic transformation and improvements in technology, enhanced by the forward progress of the Internet. **Interactive media** allow for a back-and-forth flow of information whereby users can participate in and modify the form and content of the information they receive in real time (Belch & Belch, 2007). This is significantly different from traditional forms of promotion, such as advertising or earlier forms of direct marketing, which involved one-way message sponsorship. These conventional formats did not encourage the audience to respond or alter the messages to fit their needs, make inquiries, respond to questions, and make purchases. Interactive media provide information about products and services to potential purchasers, and they provide information back to the producers to make the product or service more relevant and more desirable. Interactive television, kiosks, and cell phones are other forms of technology that make interactive communication possible.

Text messaging, once thought of as a form of communication between young cell phone users, has entered into the promotional mix. Today it is not unusual to receive a personalized text message alerting the consumer that the latest Kate Spade handbag or Teva shoe has arrived at the nearest store or is available from the company's website.

Retailers, such as eBags.com, ICE.com, TowerRecords.com, and others, are experimenting with another new interactive media technique. **Really simple syndication,** known more commonly as **R.S.S.,** is a method used to send product alerts to Internet users who have set up personalized Web pages on Yahoo, Google, and other sites (Tedeschi, 2006). In the case of eBags, consumers who visit the firm's regular or shoe site will see an R.S.S. icon near the site's products. Messages offer the users regular updates on those particular products. If a user indicates a preference for a size 10 Cole Haan loafer by clicking on the R.S.S. icon, information will be sent to his personal page. The user confirms the request by signing into that page. When a new product or promotion related to the specified items occurs, eBags sends the user an alert with an item description and a photo. R.S.S. is being used by retailers with a fashion-forward product mix and customers who are enthusiastic about new products. Direct marketing and interactive media are more fully explored in Chapter 11.

Sales Promotion

Sales promotion refers to activities that provide extra value or incentives to the sales force, distributors, or ultimate consumer. It is a set of paid marketing endeavors, other than advertising and personal sales, taken on to immediately stimulate sales. Some professionals refer to the entire promotion industry as sales promotion, which may lead to confusion in the advertising and promotion business. This book uses the term *promotion* as the broader umbrella term that encompasses *all* of the elements of the promotion mix, not just sales promotion. As previously defined, promotion is the element of the marketing mix used by firms to communicate with their potential customers.

Sales promotion may be consumer or trade oriented. The ultimate consumer or product user is the target of consumer-oriented sales promotion. These activities include: contests, coupons, gift-with-purchase, purchase-with-purchase, point-of-sale displays, refunds, rebates, sweepstakes, and sampling, among others. Such activities encourage prompt purchase of products and can improve short-term sales.

Trade-oriented sales promotion is directed to the distribution intermediaries such as wholesalers, distributors, and retailers. Activities aimed at the trade include promotional and merchandising allowances, price deals, sales contests, special counter displays or sales fixtures, and trade show discounts, among others. The topic of sales promotion is explored in Chapter 12.

Public Relations

Although many people use the terms *advertising, publicity,* and *public relations* interchangeably, there is a distinction between them. Advertising depends upon paid sponsorship in the media, while publicity and public relations do not require payment for space or time. This text adopts the terminology most commonly used within the promotion industry.

Many different definitions for public relations have been presented by various communication and marketing professionals over the years. Key elements that are common to most definitions of public relations include:

- It is a function of an organization's management team.
- It is grounded in two-way communication between the organization and its stakeholders (the public).
- It is designed to foster mutually beneficial relationships.
- It monitors and identifies policies, procedures, and actions and analyzes the impact they have upon public opinions that conflict with or support general public interests and for the sponsoring organization's survival.
- It produces measurable changes in awareness, opinions, attitudes, and behavior inside and outside the organization.

The definition we use in this book comes from Cutlip, Center, and Broom: "**public relations (PR)** is the management function that establishes and maintains mutually beneficial relationships between an organization and the public on whom its success or failure depends" (2006, p. 5). The role of public relations is broad, and involves planning and distributing information that will control and manage the image of a firm. It is much more encompassing than publicity, which is a term confusingly used by some to mean public relations. Publicity is a tool used by public relations specialists.

Public Relations Tools

Tools used by public relations practitioners include development, internal relations, investor relationships, issues management, lobbying, press agentry, public affairs, and publicity. All of the tools used by public relations specialists are discussed in Chapter 13, where we look at public relations in depth.

Publicity

Journalists reporting messages through mass media get a lot of their information from public relations sources. Because public relations specialists do not pay for placement in the media, PR specialists cannot control *if* the information will be used, *when* it is used, or *how* it is used, or misused. **Publicity** is information with news value, information that is uncontrolled by the source because the source does not pay the media for placement, and is provided by public relations specialists to be used in the mass media. Information is provided as a news story, editorial, or announcement through a news release or media kit. Like advertising, publicity involves nonpersonal communication being presented to a mass audience. But publicity differs from advertising because placement in a print or electronic medium is not paid by the source of the information, nor is the presentation of its original content guaranteed.

Part of the confusion about the relationship between publicity and public relations may be due to the fact that public relations uses publicity and a variety of other tools to achieve its goals. Some of the other tools that public relations specialists use to manage a company's image include creating special publications, participating in community activities, fund-raising, and other public relations activities.

Although public relations and PR tools have not been traditional elements of the promotion mix and integrated marketing communication, these tools are more frequently being used by advertising and marketing companies. Now many of these firms are using public relations as an integral part of the promotion mix and as part of the integrated marketing communications package. Public relations is discussed further in Chapter 13.

Personal Selling

Personal selling is the direct interaction between the customer and the seller for the purpose of making a sale. This interpersonal communication enables the seller to assist or influence the buyer to purchase a product or service or act upon an idea.

Most people think of personal sales taking place only in the retail environment, but personal sales can also take place as part of business-to-business communication. This promotion mix method allows the seller to see or hear the potential buyer's reaction. This feedback allows the seller to adapt the message to meet the needs of the client. Personal selling allows more direct and accurate feedback about the sales message than any other promotion mix technique. A more complete look at personal selling may be found in Chapter 17.

Special Events

A **special event** is a one-time occurrence with planned activities, focused on a specific purpose—to bring attention to a brand, manufacturer, retailer, or organization, or to influence the sale of merchandise. Special events are created to bring people together at a specific time and place to share an experience. The range of event categories is almost endless, including such attractions as celebrity appearances; product demonstrations or sampling; museum exhibits; gallery displays; and musical, theatrical, or sports performances. These activities are sponsored to attract new or existing customers; recognize the contributions of employees or volunteers; or celebrate performances by artists, designers, or students.

Many special events reoccur, but each event is unique. For example, the fragrance divisions of Coty or Inter Parfums introduce a number of new scents, such as Phat Farm Atman and Burberry London for Men, each year. Every time a celebrity or high-profile new product comes on the market, a launch event occurs. The launch for Phat Farm Atman, which means "spirit of man," promotes the fact that Russell Simmons's personal proceeds will be donated to charities selected by him. Simmons will be on hand to introduce the product at various locations. On the other side of the ocean, Burberry London for Men is launched as a crossover between the worlds of fashion and fragrance in England. The bottle is wrapped in a swatch of the Burberry signature plaid fabric and features the clothing label on the outer packaging. In addition to television ads, Burberry will provide samples in two-milliliter vials and scent strips to worldwide consumers. Many of these samples will be presented at in-store events at the time the commercials start airing on television. This shows two different ways to launch a product with celebrity appearances and product sampling. A more in-depth look at special events is in Chapter 14.

Although some practitioners may not view special events as an element of the promotion mix, special events are frequently used to build interest and increase traffic in retail stores. Special events can be as simple as product sampling or as complex as a merchandising event cosponsored by a fashion magazine and retail store. It is easy to think of examples of product sampling at a grocery store. Samples of food items are offered as an incentive to purchase that product. This practice is also common in department and specialty store environments. "Fragrance models" walk through the store offering samples of perfumes or other cosmetics. Fragrances as well as cosmetic samples are used to encourage the purchase of full-size products. Magazines such as *Glamour*, *Seventeen*, or *Vogue* may provide an editor of the magazine as the commentator for a fashion show or beauty makeover, for an audience of retail store customers.

Fashion Shows

A **fashion show** is the presentation of apparel, accessories, and other products to enhance personal attractiveness on live models to an audience. This form of promotion communication transmits the message about fashionable attire through physical images as an informal show, formal runway show, production show, or as a video production. The target audience may consist of consumers or trade professionals. Although some individuals may not view the fashion show as a traditional promotion mix element, this book looks at fashion shows as a promotional tool commonly used within the merchandising environment.

The popularity of the fashion show as a promotional activity increases or decreases at various times. Fashion shows have become hot news items in the 21st century, covered by the entertainment media as well as the traditional fashion media, such as magazines and newspapers. Interest in the personalities of the designers, models, and production teams seems almost as great as the interest in the fashions being featured. Fashion shows are the topic of Chapter 15.

Visual Merchandising

Visual merchandising is the physical presentation of products in a nonpersonal approach. Typically products are presented in window displays, store interior merchandise presentations, or remote displays. Figure 1.7 shows the store design for Urban Outfitters in London. Store design and merchandise presentation were used as a part of the promotional strategy in the British expansion of this hip American retailer of women's and men's wear and home furnishings aimed at the 18- to 30-year-old fashion customer.

FIGURE 1.7 Store layout and design are part of the promotional strategy for Urban Outfitters.

FIGURE 1.8 The exhibit *Balenciaga in Paris* featured 170 garments that were borrowed from collections in Japan, England, Spain, France, and the United States.

The merchandising environment encourages the creative use of merchandise presentation to generate interest and sales of fashion products. Small "mom-and-pop" retailers may rely on window displays and interior merchandise presentation as their only method of promotion. However, an attractive physical space with interesting merchandise presentation is an inexpensive promotional technique, especially popular with retailers that have limited promotional budgets.

Museum exhibits of historical and contemporary fashions have become popular exhibits throughout the world, drawing thousands of people to art museums. In this text such exhibits are considered to be a type of visual merchandising, whereas the opening gala and media attention are considered to be a function of special events and public relations.

The Costume Institute of the Metropolitan Museum of Art in New York offers an annual exhibit of fashion. These popular Costume Institute exhibits have included *Anglo-Mania: Tradition and Transgression in British Fashion; CHANEL Fashion, from Coco Chanel to Karl Lagerfeld;* and *Bravehearts: Men in Skirts*. Regional museums also have launched popular historical costume exhibits. The Philadelphia Museum of Art paid tribute to Grace Kelly by displaying *Art for a Princess: Grace Kelly's Wedding Dress*. The Phoenix Art Museum in Arizona presented fashions with wide-ranging themes, from *Rudi Gernreich* and *Judith Leiber Handbags* to *Trench Coat* and *Motorcycle Jacket*.

Internationally, the Museum of Fashion and Textiles in Paris presented *Balenciaga in Paris*, an exhibition of garments, covering nearly 70 years. Garments from Cristobal Balenciaga to Nicolas Ghesquière were shown. Figure 1.8 shows looks from the Balenciaga exhibit that opened when the haute couture fashion shows took place in Paris. A more complete look at visual merchandising is provided in Chapter 16.

○ INTEGRATED MARKETING COMMUNICATIONS

Marketing and merchandising executives have realized that the wide range of promotional activities can be more effective when the various elements of the promotional mix are

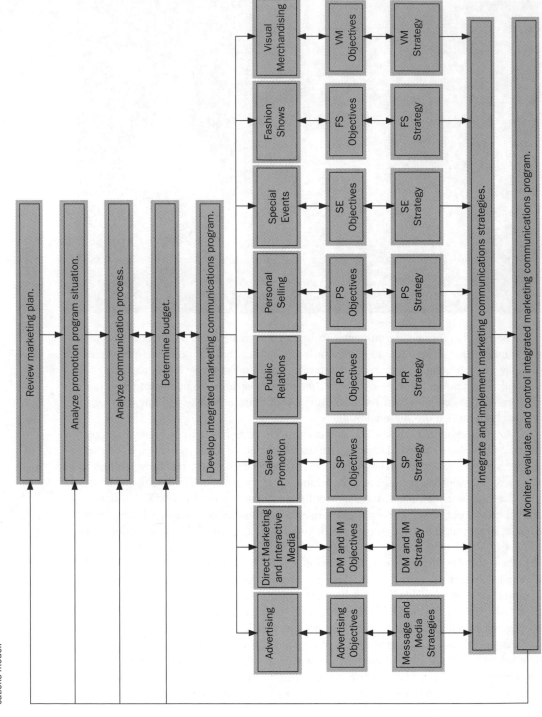

FIGURE 1.9 Integrated marketing communi-cations model.

coordinated. The American Association of Advertising Agencies has recognized that agencies and practitioners need to become more active in developing skills beyond those traditionally used in marketing communications. Promotional mix tools have been coordinated in an attempt to more successfully communicate to target customers by presenting a consistent image. Many companies have moved toward an integrated marketing communications concept, which involves coordination of the various promotional elements with other marketing activities that communicate to the firm's customers and stakeholders, or interested third parties, such as critics, designers, and members of the press.

The American Association of Advertising Agencies defines **integrated marketing communications (IMC)** as: "a concept of marketing communications planning that recognized the added value of a comprehensive plan that evaluates the strategic roles of a variety of communication disciplines—for example, general advertising, direct response, sales promotion, and public relations—and combines these disciplines to provide clarity, consistency, and maximum communications impact" (Schultz, 1993, p. 17).

IMC requires an umbrella or big-picture approach to planning promotion. It also dictates coordination of the various communications, marketing, and promotion functions. True integration occurs when all aspects of the product, from product development, package design, and brand name creation to price and type of sales location, are coordinated. IMC attempts to project a consistent impression about the product in the marketplace. Figure 1.9 shows the IMC planning model.

An IMC approach was used as an efficient way to introduce Rouge Idole, indelible lipcolor products. Consumers indicated they wanted a lipstick that would not wear off too quickly, so Lancôme created a product to stay on the lips for an extended period of time. The firm took product design, packaging, brand name, advertising message, and the image of the stores where the product would be sold into consideration as it developed a communication program to introduce the product.

Lancôme also uses an IMC approach. The company aggressively advertises its fragrance and cosmetic products in fashion magazines and newspapers (see Figure 1.10). The company then is able to negotiate for store selling space in the prime traffic aisles. The themes used in advertising are repeated in promotional displays, gift-with-purchase, and purchase-with-purchase sales promotions.

This chapter provides basic definitions for promotion, marketing, merchandising, and communication. It introduces the promotion mix methods, the techniques used by professionals to distribute information about products and services to individuals and groups throughout the world. Integrated marketing communications, the process that enables senders to expose consumers or other interested parties to their message, brings a variety of these promotional methods together into a coordinated effort. These terms and concepts, which are fundamental to the field of promotion, are explored in depth throughout the book. Global themes are featured throughout this text. The promotional mix tools included advertising, direct marketing, sales promotion, and public relations. Figure 1.11 shows how the products are advertised for target audiences in Brazil and Italy.

summary

- Promotion is a comprehensive term for all activities initiated by the seller or sponsor to inform, persuade, and remind the consumer about goods and services available.
- Billions of dollars are spent yearly, domestically and internationally, to promote products, services, or societal causes. The expenditures for promotional activities are anticipated to continue to grow in the 21st century.

FIGURE 1.10 There are
strong similarities between the
ads for Lancome's lipstick
in French and American
magazines, reflecting a global
promotional approach.

FIGURE 1.11 Product advertisements from Brazil and Italy are global in approach.

- Marketing involves research and development, distribution and sales, and promotion of products and ideas to fulfill consumer demand for all types of products. Exchange is an essential component of marketing. Participants must have the desire and ability to substitute something of value for something else.
- Merchandising involves forecasting what customers want to buy, investigating where to find that merchandise in the marketplace, determining the price the customer is willing to pay, and making it available through the retail store or other merchandising outlets where the customer is willing to buy the merchandise. Fashion merchandising focuses on styles and products that are popular at a given period of time.
- The merchandising environment emphasizes goods that are considered fashion or soft lines, characteristically apparel, home furnishings and decor, and other merchandise to improve an individual's appearance or well-being.
- Communication involves the transmission or exchange of information. Communication theory assists marketing and merchandising executives in accomplishing their professional goals.
- The promotion mix defines the various activities used by the seller to achieve its goals. Promotion mix elements in the merchandising environment include: advertising, direct marketing and interactive media, sales promotion, public relations, personal selling, special events, fashion shows, and visual merchandising. Integrated marketing communications (IMC) involves the coordination of the various promotional techniques with other marketing activities.

key terms

advertising
business-to-business market
channels
communication
consumer market
decode
direct marketing
direct-response media
encoding
exchange
fashion show
feedback
global marketing

globalization
glocalization
gross domestic product
integrated marketing
    communications
interactive media
localized strategy
marketing
marketing mix
merchandising
merchandising
    environment
noise

personal selling
promotion
promotion mix
public relations
publicity
really simple syndication
    (R.S.S.)
sales promotion
special event
standardized strategy
trade market
visual merchandising
word-of-mouth

questions for discussion

1. What is the importance of a global society to the distribution and promotion of products in the merchandising environment?
2. What is the role of communication in the promotional process?
3. How do the elements of the promotional mix relate?
4. What is the role of integrated marketing communications? Why is it important to promotion?

Additional resources

Belch, G.E., & Belch M.A. (2007). *Advertising and promotion: An integrated marketing communications perspective* (7th ed.). New York: McGraw-Hill Irwin.

Clow, K.E., & Baack, D. (2007). *Integrated advertising, promotion and marketing communications* (3rd ed.). Upper Saddle River, N.J.: Pearson Prentice-Hall.

Kunz, G.I., & Garner, M.B (2006). *Going global: The textile and apparel industry.* New York: Fairchild Books.

Annual publications

Coen, R.J. (Published annually in December). *Insider's report: Robert Coen presentation on advertising expenditures.* New York: Universal McCann.com/pdf/Insiders1205.pdf.

Deloitte Touche Tohmatsu & Stores (Eds.). (Published annually in January). Global powers of retailing, *Stores.* (Section 2).

references

American Apparel and Footwear Association. (2004). *Trends annual.* Retrieved June 6, 2006, from https://www.apparelandfootwear.org/UserFiles/File/Statistics/Trends2004Annual.pdf

AMA board approves new marketing definition. (1985, March 1). *Marketing News,* p.1.

Belch, G.E., & Belch, M.A. (2007). *Advertising and promotion: An integrated marketing communications perspective* (7th ed.). New York: McGraw-Hill Irwin.

Coen, R.J. (2005). *Insider's report: Robert Coen presentation on advertising expenditures.* New York: Universal McCann. Retrieved June 4, 2006, from http://www.universalmccann.com/pdf/Insiders1205.pdf

Cutlip, S.M., Center, A.H., and Broom, G.M. (2006). *Effective public relations* (9th ed.). Upper Saddle River, NJ: Pearson Prentice Hall.

Dickerson, K.G. (1999). *Textiles and apparel in the global economy* (3rd ed.). Upper Saddle River, NJ: Pearson Prentice Hall.

Glock, R.E., and Kunz, G.I. (2005). *Apparel manufacturing: Sewn product analysis* (4th ed.). Upper Saddle River, NJ: Pearson Prentice Hall.

Hall, C. (2006, June 1). The WWD list. Far East fashion-forward, *Women's Wear Daily,* p. 12.

Kean, R.C. (1987). Definition of merchandising: Is it time for a change? In R.C. Kean (Ed.), *Theory building in apparel merchandising.* (pp. 8–11). Lincoln: University of Nebraska-Lincoln.

Mazur, P. (1927). *Principles of organization applied to modern retailing.* New York: Harper & Brothers.

Miller, C. (1996, December 2). World leaders acknowledge hurdles to uniform market, chasing global dream, *Marketing News,* p. 1.

Ricks, D.A. (2006). *Blunders in international business* (4th ed.). Cambridge, MA: Blackwell.

Schultz, D. (1993, January 18). Integrated marketing communications: Maybe definition is in the point of view, *Marketing News,* p. 17.

Tedeschi, B. (2006, March 6). Your personal shopper with the initials R.S.S., *New York Times,* p. C4.

Uchitelle, L. (1998a, April 30). Globalization has not severed corporations' national links, *New York Times.* Retrieved May 5, 1998, from http://www.nytimes.com

Uchitelle, L. (1998b, April 30). World economy is as interconnected today as in 1913, *New York Times.* Retrieved May 5, 1998, from http://www.nytimes.com

FIGURE 2.1 The exterior and interior of a store.

CHAPTER 2

Consumer Behavior

For a time three years ago, AEO lost sight of its objectives and business suffered as a result. Calling it a "painful" lesson, Susan McGalla, president and chief merchandising officer for the $2 billion specialty store chain, said the company found out what could happen when it lost that "connection with our customer."

Looking back on this "bump in the road," she said, taught the retailer that although businesses tend to "hang onto ideas," they need instead to look to the customer for a "report card" and be willing to abandon ill-fated strategies.

Turning to the retailer's new Aerie division, McGalla said this subbrand of intimates and dormwear for women arose out of the company's desire to respond to customer needs. "We've offered intimates and dormwear for over seven years, and what she was telling us is that she wanted to walk into an environment that felt private, that she could have fun in, that she could come in with her girlfriends."

The result was two standalone Aerie stores and an additional 10 units where the collection is merchandised side by side with an American Eagle store and shares an entrance.

So far, McGalla said AEO is pleased with the results it has achieved with Aerie but that there are no plans to expand the brand into men's wear. "We have dormwear for men, but it seems to exist best in the environment with the sportswear. They're not quite the same shopaholics with the same shopping patterns," she said.

Source: Palmieri, J.E. (2006, November 15). American Eagle's team spirit. *Women's Wear Daily* (Section II) p. 20.

> **After you have read this chapter, you should be able to:**
>
> Describe the role of the consumer in merchandise promotion.
>
> Understand the concept of market segmentation and the importance of target markets.
>
> Identify and describe demographic, behavioristic, and psychographic bases for segmentation of a population.
>
> Explain behavior characteristics of global consumers.

AEO TURNED ITS BUSINESS AROUND by basing its promotional programs on the behavior of its consumers. The retailer noted that college women preferred to shop for dormwear in a space that felt private and comfortable where they could bring their girlfriends, not unlike an actual women's dorm room. College men, on the other hand, liked their dormwear with their sportswear. So the company created new spaces for its female clientele and left the guys alone. A closer look at how companies study consumer behavior and act on the findings will show specifically how AEO managed to reconnect with its customers.

In this chapter we explore the role of consumer behavior as it applies to promotion programs. The chapter begins with a discussion of the consumption process consumers typically follow to purchase new or replacement items. Consumption is based on consumer motivation which is discussed next. Acquisition of a fashion item is illustrated using the fashion life cycle, which is also discussed here. We then briefly explore research, which is a necessary tool to understand the consumer. Finally, the chapter focuses on the importance of segmenting consumers into target markets. Demographic, geographic, psychographic, behavioristic, and benefit segmentation approaches are discussed.

─o consumer behavior in promotion

Consumer behavior is the study of consumers' decision-making processes, as they acquire, consume, and dispose of goods and services. Successful promotions rely on a clear understanding of the consumer. How do consumers behave? What will ultimately shift them toward a specific product? Marketers are obliged to familiarize themselves with the behavior of consumers—how they think, what motivates them, and the environment in which they live. Understanding the consumer is complicated by the fact that consumer behaviors are constantly changing. Just when a marketer has figured out a pattern of behavior on which to build a promotion, a new piece of information is introduced to consumers and their behavior changes. Complicating matters further is the fact that consumers and fashion marketers perceive promotion in very different ways.

As we pointed out in Chapter 1, nearly everyone in the contemporary world is affected by promotion. While promotion specialists spend considerable time analyzing the best promotional techniques to communicate with the consumer, the consumer does not differentiate among techniques. To a consumer, everything an organization does to promote itself is considered advertising, whether or not it was paid for by the sponsoring organization (Schultz & Barnes, 1995). Every time consumers come in contact with a brand, they are exposed to promotion. Exposure may be planned, such as store signage, event sponsorship, or paid advertising, or unplanned, such as seeing shopping bags in the hands of customers at a mall, hearing word-of-mouth experiences from friends, viewing a news story on television, or seeing litter in the street with the identifiable brand. Because consumers associate every contact they make with a brand to be "advertising," it is important that the marketing team coordinate promotion functions using the integrated marketing communications (IMC) approach introduced in Chapter 1. All aspects of the product—brand image, packaging, advertising, sales promotion, and the like—should project a consistent message to the consumer. Understanding the behaviors of consumers can assist marketers in planning promotions from the viewpoint of the consumer.

Consumption

Consumption is the process of acquiring, using, and discarding products. Figure 2.2 is a flow chart that illustrates consumer acquisition, use, and disposal of products and services. All products follow the same consumption process. The process begins with product acquisition, moves through product use, and finishes with product disposal.

Acquisition

Before most purchases are made, consumers become aware of the need for a new or replacement product. We may read a fashion magazine and become aware of a new trend, or through use, realize that we need to replace a good. Upon recognition of the need, we begin to search for information about the product. **Product acquisition** is the process of searching, evaluating, and choosing among alternative items. Information is gathered (through advertisements, promotional materials, the Internet, personal references, and other means) and alternatives are evaluated for benefits and limitations.

Impulse buying occurs when no previous need recognition has taken place before the purchase is made. Many goods are purchased as impulse buys as a result of the feeling gained by the purchase rather than the utilitarian purpose of the good. Point-of-purchase displays for magazines, candy, and personal care products make impulse buying effortless for the consumer.

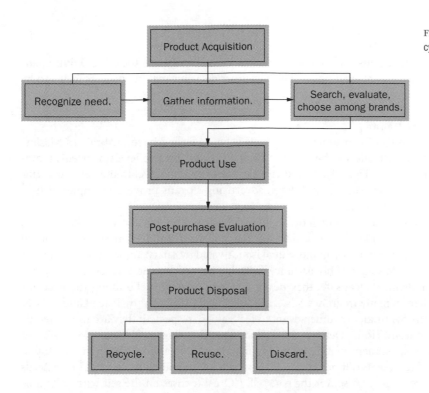

FIGURE 2.2 Consumption cycle model.

Use

Using the information we have gathered, we evaluate the alternatives and make a decision. The product is purchased and put into service for its useful life. The useful life of a product may be once, as with picnic supplies; over a season, as with fashion trend items; or extended over many years, as with a home appliance. Just because we make a purchase does not mean we stop evaluating alternatives. During product use, we make post-purchase evaluations. We may question whether we made the right decision based on the information and the alternatives available at the time. Continual evaluation after the purchase hopefully reinforces that our purchase was the correct decision.

Disposal

At some point, we conclude that we no longer need or want the product. It may be worn out, a replacement product with a new feature may have become available in the market-place, or the fashion trend may have passed. Product disposal is the decision by the consumer to discard the product once use is complete. Consumers are becoming very concerned with how a product can be disposed of as landfills and other refuse areas are filling up. The practice of reusing and/or recycling both goods and the packaging they come in is becoming standard practice among many consumers and retailers. Origins, a maker of environmentally friendly cosmetics, favors packaging that is easily recyclable. North Face, an outdoor manufacturer, promotes apparel products made from recycled milk containers.

Promotion is used at each stage of the consumption cycle. Promotion is used to plant the seed in consumers' minds to buy a new item. Promotion educates consumers about various products and reinforces their choice after the purchase. Finally, promotion convinces consumers when and how to dispose of products.

Consumer Motivation

Motives are the reasons consumers buy. Motives are described as the drives within people that stimulate wants and needs. The consumer decision-making process is driven by a consumer's motive to solve a problem.

Hierarchy of Needs

The understanding of consumer motivations is based on work from Abraham Maslow and his **hierarchy of needs theory.** The theory is based on five levels of needs, represented by a pyramid (Fig. 2.3). An individual passes from one level to the next upon fulfillment of the prior need. At each level, advertising slogans provide examples of how each consumer need is met.

At the base of the pyramid, individuals seek basic physiological needs of food, water, and shelter. "Got Milk?" by the California Dairy Council fulfills a basic physiological need for nourishment. Next, an individual is motivated by safety. Yoplait directly appeals to consumer's safety against breast cancer with its "Save Lids to Save Lives" campaign.

Once individuals feel safe, they desire love and belonging. Fulfilling the need for love is evident in many fragrance ads, including "Beautiful Love" by Estée Lauder. Near the top of the pyramid, consumers want to feel valued, respected; they are motivated by a need for esteem. Home Depot, with its long-standing slogan "You can do it. We can help™" gives consumers confidence and fulfills their motivation for esteem. The top of the pyramid represents self-actualization, in which an individual has met all lower needs and is now reaching to discover the true self. L'Oréal focuses on the self with its tagline "Because you're worth it."

The fashion industry depends on consumer motivations to acquire, use, and dispose of fashion merchandise each season. Fashion merchandise moves through a life cycle based on consumer acceptance. In the next section, we illustrate how acquisition of a fashion item moves through the fashion cycle.

The Fashion Cycle

The **fashion cycle** describes the process of acceptance of a trend or fashion item. When the cycle is graphed, it appears as a bell-shaped curve (Fig. 2.4). The fashion cycle has three major stages: innovation, culmination, and decline. Each stage is represented by two groups of consumers: earlier adopters and later adopters.

Innovation

The first stage in the fashion cycle—innovation—is marked by two phases, introduction and rise. Early adopters, called **fashion innovators,** will adopt a trend at the very earliest opportunity. Fashion innovators represent 2 percent of the buying public. They desire distinction and high fashion and are the very first consumers to identify a trend. **Fashion leaders,** later adopters in the innovation stage, will accept the trend as it begins to rise in popularity. Fashion leaders, who represent 14 percent of consumers, purchase sophisticated items and appreciate what is new and in good taste.

Fashion innovators and fashion leaders purchase goods in the innovation stage through designers or very exclusive stores, paying high prices to own exclusive and novel items. Retail buyers for stores that market to these consumers purchase limited quantities, simultaneously testing many styles and new trends.

At the innovation stage, retail selling precedes actual consumer use. Promotion and

FIGURE 2.3 Hierarchy of needs model.

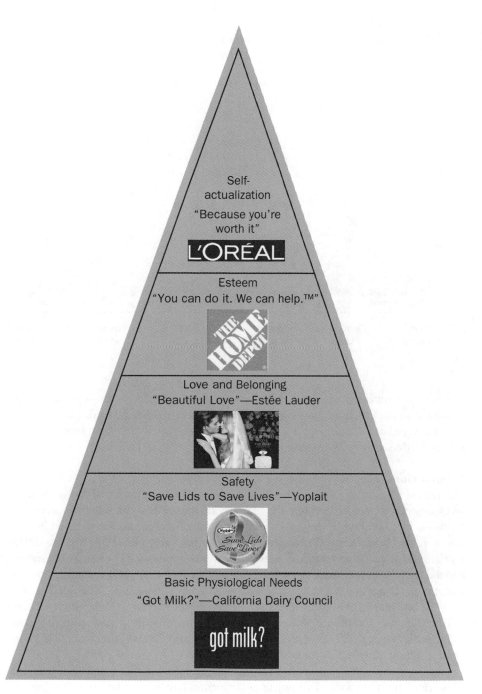

FIGURE 2.4 The fashion
cycle.

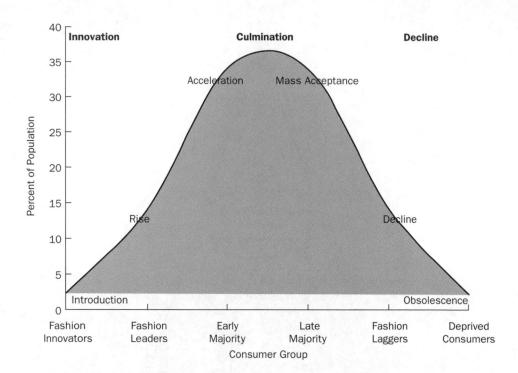

FIGURE 2.4 The fashion cycle.

advertising campaigns consist of informational, institutional, or prestige ads. Visual merchandise presentations appear at the front of a store or in window displays to introduce the very latest trends. Figure 2.5 is a prestige ad targeted to fashion innovators and fashion leaders during the innovation stage.

Culmination

The second stage of the fashion life cycle—culmination—comprises the two phases of acceleration and mass acceptance. The majority of consumers—slightly more than two-thirds—adopt a product during the culmination stage. These consumers purchase items in season for immediate use. Consumers who are in the **early majority** purchase during acceleration of the fashion trend. The early majority accounts for 34 percent of consumers, and they purchase fashionable items used as wardrobe builders. These consumers are very receptive to change and generally make purchases at department and specialty stores.

The **late majority** of consumers, also 34 percent of the population, purchase items during the mass acceptance phase of a trend. The late majority have a desire to look fashionable but realize that practicality and durability are also important. They purchase goods at all types of stores.

Retail buyers who represent stores that target culmination stage consumers purchase maximum stocks and complete assortments. During acceleration, they reorder "hot" items. Promotions are persuasive, informing consumers of regular price lines and special limited offers. Product ads are abundant, and displays are centered at high-traffic areas within the middle of the store.

Decline

The final stage in the fashion life cycle—decline—is divided between decline and obsolescence phases. The earlier adopters within this stage are called **fashion laggers** and represent 14 percent of consumers. As a fashion trend declines, consumers are motivated to purchase strictly by economic values. They make purchases at discount houses, chain stores, or at special sales. Later adopters in this stage, representing 2 percent of the population, make purchases when a fashion has reached obsolescence. These financially **deprived consumers** are value-oriented and purchase items at clearance and close-out outlets. Fashion laggers are acquiring merchandise at the same time fashion innovators are disposing of the same styles.

Retail buyers do not purchase items for the decline stage; rather, they reduce stock with markdowns or purchase special quantity items from other vendors. Advertising is produced as clearance reminders. Promotions state reduced prices, clearance, or close-out merchandise (Fig. 2.6). Visual merchandising is very limited, promoting price reduction. Displays change from artistic presentations to sized distributions on sale tables or rounders.

An understanding of where consumers fall within the fashion cycle allows promotion specialists to create the right marketing mix, matching the needs of the consumer with the sales objectives of the business. Using the fashion cycle stages is one way businesses can differentiate consumers into relatively homogeneous groups. In the next section, we discuss market segmentation, the different ways in which consumers can be grouped to identify current and potential customers. A business that can correctly identify its intended target market is able to tailor the promotion mix in a very effective manner.

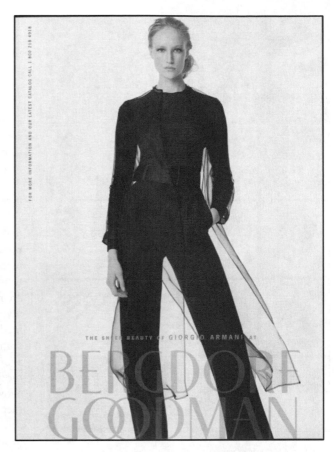

FIGURE 2.5 A prestige ad targeted to consumers in the innovation stage of the fashion cycle. This cooperative advertisement promotes the designer Giorgio Armani and specialty retailer Bergdorf Goodman.

——○ Market Segmentation

On a typical trip to the mall, are you likely to visit one store or many stores? If you are like many consumers, you shop at many specialty stores. Specialty stores have gained popularity because they cater to a narrowly defined group of consumers determined through the process of market segmentation. Promotion planners, as we will see in Chapter 5, segment and target the market to effectively promote the right message to the right audience.

Segmentation divides the market into groups of people who have similar characteristics. **Targeting** identifies the group that is most likely to respond to communication messages and therefore be profitable. These subsets of consumers are called **target markets** or **market segments.** Fashion businesses use segmentation to better understand the attitudes, characteristics, and behaviors of their customers to better meet their needs.

A **mass market** is a large group of consumers with similar needs. A **niche market** is a small group of consumers with characteristics noticeably different from the mass market. The **primary market** is the essential target group identified for communication. A **secondary market** is an auxiliary target group with potential values to the message sponsor.

FIGURE 2.6 Advertisement produced as a clearance reminder for the decline phase of the fashion cycle.

The primary market for children's clothing is typically parents. Grandparents constitute the secondary market using different purchase criteria when making choices.

Research

Segmentation is achieved through research. Research is conducted numerous times for numerous reasons throughout the promotion process. Research is carried out to develop a fashion forecast. The situation analysis is developed through research. Later, research is used to evaluate the effectiveness of promotion strategies and tactics.

Research is the investigation of a subject in order to understand it in a detailed, accurate manner. **Market research** is the investigation of product, price, promotion, place, and other details in order to understand the environment in which a product or service competes. Results are reported in the marketing plan. **Advertising research** investigates all elements of advertising including message, media, and evaluation. Consumer behavior relies on **consumer research**, the investigation of people who want a product or service in terms of their characteristics, motives, attitudes, and interests. Consumer research allows executives to determine appropriate market segments in which to direct promotion strategies.

Good research is based on the **scientific method,** a decision-making process focused on objective and orderly testing of ideas before they are accepted. The opposite of the scientific method is **intuition,** basing decisions on subjective feelings or instinct. Using the scientific method, researchers use insight or observation to develop hypotheses. A **hypothesis** is an educated guess about the relationship between things, or predictions about the future. Hypotheses are tested before final decisions are made.

For example, a beauty business wants to introduce a new line of lip colors. A business that relies on executive intuition will develop the lip colors based on assumptions that the consumer wants new lip colors and then *hopes* the consumer will buy the new colors. A business that relies on the scientific method will first ask consumers what motivates them to buy lip colors, what colors they desire, what other benefits they gain from lip color, and so on, *then* develop a product that meets these desires. All solid research is grounded in the scientific method.

Primary Research

Research data is obtained from two sources—primary or secondary. **Primary research** is original research carried out by the company in order to answer a very specific question. Fashion businesses use four types of primary research:

1. **Qualitative** or **exploratory research.** Used in psychographic segmentation to better define the problem, the market, or the consumer.
2. **Quantitative** or **descriptive research.** The most widely used type of research used in demographic segmentation to describe a problem, market, or consumer.

3. **Experimental research.** Widely used in new product research consisting of laboratory testing in which a cause-and-effect relationship is sought. Textile companies use experimental research to create new fibers and finishes or to test durability.
4. **Performance evaluation.** Often used to evaluate the effects of a program, such as promotion, or a product, such as textiles.

Primary data sources include observing and questioning. During observation, equipment such as videotapes and scanners are used to look at what consumers do and how they behave. Envirosell is an example of a behavioral market research and consulting company that does primary observation research for retail stores, banks, restaurants, and other businesses throughout the world to understand consumer shopping behavior. Box 2.1 provides more details about companies researching consumer habits.

The wearable video is another type of observation research. Actionspeak, a qualitative marketing research company, uses tiny cameras about the size of a quarter, positioned on the consumer to conduct behavior research. The company only conducts research in environments where clients explicitly give permission to implement the camera approach, using the cameras as memory tools (2005).

Fashion Count. A **fashion count** is an observation method. The fashion count is an organized plan for counting and classifying fashion components. By counting components, a researcher can show the relative importance of different styles, colors, and fabrics worn by the specified group. Current fashion looks can be identified using a fashion count. Repeated at frequent intervals, a fashion count shows which styles, colors, or other trends are nearing the innovation, culmination, or decline stages of the fashion cycle.

○ BOX 2.1

Primping for the Cameras in the Name of Research

The quest for the holy grail of beauty begins in a stark white bathroom, where a middle-aged strawberry blonde primps her freshly washed and blown hair under the relentless gaze of two overhead cameras. Steps away, a researcher checks a flickering computer screen, toggling controls to zoom in on the woman, who has just sampled unmarked bottles of shampoo and conditioner.

This bathroom laboratory near the Place de la Concorde in Paris is a shiny ceramic war room for one of the leading international beauty giants, L'Oréal, and one the company is reproducing around the world. In France alone, researchers are examining the mixed population of the Paris region to create what is called an "atlas for the human hair," with test subjects reflecting European and Western and Central African roots to compare with volunteers in Beijing and Shanghai.

Like its major rivals, Procter & Gamble and Unilever, L'Oréal, based in Paris, is battling for advantage in a fiercely competitive $231 billon market for cosmetics and grooming products. In the business of beauty, growth is powered by alluring hawkers like the actress Scarlett Johansson and glamour novelties like "phototonic" eye shadow intended to refract light like butterfly wings, or new cosmetic lines suited for aging skin and the color palette of baby boomers. L'Oréal, with sales last year of 14 billion euros ($16.9 billion), is spending heavily on research, devoting 507 million euros, or more than 3 percent of revenue, to it.

Crucial to that effort is the search for differences that could help build a brand in critical emerging markets like India and China. L'Oréal has an expanding network of 13 evaluation centers around the world created to observe grooming and ponder a variety of burning questions: Do national differences exist in primping styles? Would women in Japan and Europe, for instance, stroke on mascara with the same lavish hand? (The answer is that in Japan, women apply mascara with an average of 100 brushstrokes compared with Europeans, who are satisfied with 50, a difference noted by ethnologists for L'Oréal.)

It was observations like these that ultimately affected how the company made and marketed its mascara or developed the foaming quality of its shampoos. "We are far from understanding everybody everywhere. It takes time," said Fabrice Aghassian, director of international product evaluation for L'Oréal, which is seeking to map the world's beauty routines in a landscape the company calls geocosmetics. "When we know the behaviors of people, we know what unexpressed expectations we do have to consider."

The beauty of China's 451 million women ages 15 to 64 is of particular interest these days to industrial ethnologists; the nation's cosmetics market has almost doubled in the last five years, to $7.9 billion, according to Euromonitor, and with rising affluence, the market could come close to $13 billion by 2009.

In November, Estée Lauder opened a sleek new research center in Shanghai with the aim of developing local raw materials inspired by traditional Chinese medicine. Other multinational beauty companies are making similar moves. Elizabeth Arden purchased Leroy, a distribution company based there, and last year L'Oréal created the Pudong L'Oréal Research Center on the outskirts of the city to study the properties of Chinese hair and skin and botanical materials used in Chinese medicine.

China is a critical engine of growth for these companies, which have struggled with weak sales in Europe and rising prices for petroleum, an important ingredient in many cosmetics.

"As a global company with headquarters in New York, the Estée Lauder companies bring a different flavor versus our mainly French and Japanese competition in the market," said Michel Grunberg, who supervises the Lauder regional offices out of Shanghai. The company has introduced brands like Bobbi Brown, Aramis, Clinique, and Tommy Hilfiger in the region.

China is driving the growth of Estée Lauder; the company's most recent report in September indicated that sales in Europe, the United States, the Middle East, and Africa were flat compared with a year earlier, but Asia-Pacific sales gained 5 percent, to $198.6 million.

L'Oréal, which renders its name in Mandarin as "Oulayia" and translates that as "elegance from Europe," had revenue of 290 million euros in China in 2004, a 58 percent rise from a year earlier, after much stronger growth in the previous two years.

To fathom the tastes of the Chinese, the company interviews about 35,000 women a year, among them, a woman in Shanghai with hair about 13 feet long who is under contract to study the aging of hair fiber.

Consumer habits vary significantly in China according to the seasons, with women washing their hair more frequently in the summer and switching products and textures according to the climate, Mr. Aghassian said.

Besides studies in laboratory bathrooms, house calls offer an even more realistic view. From home visits, Mr. Aghassian and his researchers learned that many Chinese wash themselves and shampoo over a bowl to conserve water in cities where the water supply is frequently interrupted.

That information "is essential since the qualities in use constitute major competitive advantages," he noted. One result was to formulate a local variety of shampoo that rinses easily.

In 2003, L'Oréal opened a multimillion-dollar research and development laboratory in Chicago, which the company says was the first lab to focus specifically on the beauty needs of people of color. The company is lavishing even more resources on marketing and promotion, spending about 30 percent of its revenue to promote its products.

It recently hired Ms. Johansson and another actress, Eva Longoria of the television series *Desperate Housewives*, to pitch its cosmetics, and it has signed a two-year deal with the moviemaking Weinstein Company of product placements in films and to be a cohost corporation at high-wattage events like parties for the Golden Globes and Academy Awards.

But amid all this spending Michael Steib, an analyst for Morgan Stanley in London, has reservations on L'Oréal's shares, given the multinational crowd jostling for the same business. "Innovation is one of the key strengths of L'Oréal," he said. "There are a lot of competitive changes in the industry, and there are a lot more aggressive players."

With the merger of Procter & Gamble with Gillette last fall, some $20 billion of P. & G.'s sales are now competing with L'Oréal, he said, noting that other beauty companies like Beiersdorf and Henkel have growing ambitions tied to innovation in products.

Mr. Steib also said he expected that growth in emerging markets would become more costly for all the companies pursuing expansion. Beiersdorf, the maker of the Nivea, Juvena, and Eucerin brands, is planning more investment in China.

Amid all the competition, vital bathroom laboratory research presses forward. How else would the world learn that South Korean women use no fewer than 9 to 12 products for their morning beauty routine? And that does not include nail polish, mascara, and lipstick.

Source: Carvajal, D. (2006, February 7). Primping for the cameras in the name of research. *New York Times*. p. C6. Copyright 2006 The New York Times Company.

Fashion counts sum the components worn by consumers, or the number of times a component is featured in a fashion magazine.

The use of a fashion count is varied. For example, a Denver skiwear manufacturer was interested in forecasting style elements and color combinations for future skiwear. Forecasting teams were sent to three different Colorado ski resorts on the same weekend to take fashion counts of the skiwear being worn on the slopes. The three ski resorts were selected based on the different clientele each resort targeted. The first was a lower-price resort, frequented by the local skiing population and college students. The second resort was a midpriced resort, visited by families for a ski holiday. The third resort was high priced, exclusive to celebrities and the wealthy. The manufacturer and research team determined the variables that were to be counted, and a tabulation sheet was formulated. The fashion count was taken, tabulated, and results returned to the manufacturer for evaluation. The three ski resorts provided quite different results based on their target customers. The manufacturer, who produced moderate-priced clothing, used the results from the high-priced resort to project what new apparel combinations and color combinations would trickle down to the mass market the following year. The manufacturer also determined what color combinations and apparel items were at the end of the product life cycle based on results from the lower-price-pointed resort.

Focus Group. This type of questioning involves in-depth and focused group interviews, panel discussions, and personal surveys done online or conducted through the mail. A **focus group** is a carefully planned discussion designed to obtain perceptions on a defined area of interest in a nonthreatening environment. Focus groups are commonly used to collect psychographic information from consumers, reflecting their true attitudes, opinions, and interests about the product or service in question.

Figure 2.7 is a flow chart illustrating the steps that a market researcher uses to conduct a focus group. Focus groups are generally composed of seven to 10 participants who do not know one another. Participants are selected purposely, not randomly, because of their common interest in the topic of the focus group. A moderator facilitates the focus group and creates an atmosphere that nurtures different perceptions and points of view without an intended bias. Group members may influence each other by responding to ideas and comments in the discussion. Participants are not encouraged to reach consensus. The focus group is conducted several times with different participants to identify trends and patterns in perceptions. Careful and systematic analyses follow the focus group to determine how a product or service is perceived.

Additional research methodologies are discussed in Chapter 8.

Secondary Research

Secondary research is data that is already available, having been collected by someone else. Secondary data can come from inside or outside the company. Internal data includes company files, reports, marketing information, employee and sales data, or other pieces of relevant information. Secondary data from outside the company may come from the Internet, libraries, government agencies, trade associations, universities, private research organizations, and other sources. An example of a government source for secondary data is the U.S. Census Bureau, which collects census data and allows others to access and use the data. Examples of private research organizations that collect research data are listed in Chapter 8.

Research can be used in a number of ways to segment the marketplace based on consumer characteristics and buying situations. Five broad categories for segmentation are as follows:

FIGURE 2.7 Focus group flow chart.

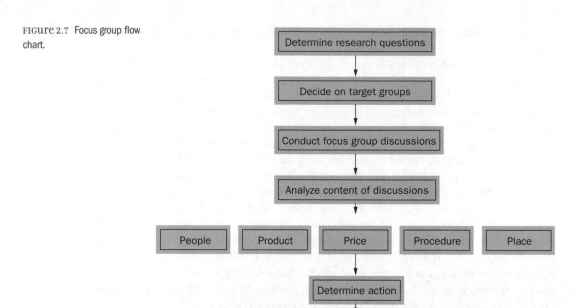

- **Demographic segmentation**—dividing the market using statistical characteristics of the population
- **Geographic segmentation**—dividing the market using location characteristics
- **Psychographic segmentation**—dividing the market based on attitudes, opinions, and lifestyle patterns, among other characteristics
- **Behavioristic segmentation**—dividing the market based on product category and brand usage
- **Benefit segmentation**—dividing the market based on consumer needs or problems and the benefits they will derive from buying products

These categories will be the focus of the remaining sections of this chapter.

Demographic Segmentation

Demographics are the statistics used to study a population. These statistics provide an easy tool for comparison among groups. Demographic segmentation allows fashion marketers to conceptualize their target market using readily available statistics (secondary data) and review the target market over time to determine patterns of change. The common demographic characteristics used to describe an individual include age, gender, education, income, occupation, race and ethnicity, and family size and structure. The combination of these individual characteristics creates a composite of relatively homogeneous market segments within the population.

Age

Age is a driving force in promotion. Consumers of different ages have different needs. Strategies and tactics must be geared to the target audience's age in order to be effective. The largest age group, and often the most targeted, is 20- to 44-year-olds (Fig. 2.8). In

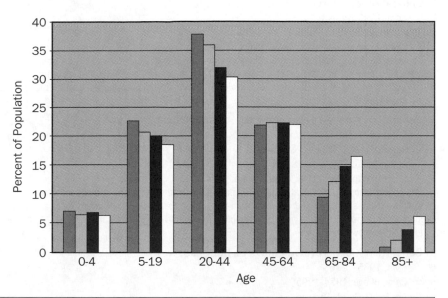

FIGURE 2.8 Projected population percentages of the United States by age and sex, 2000 and 2050.

2000 this group represented 36.9 percent of the total population (U.S. Census, 2004). Projections indicate that in 2050 this group will decrease to 31.2 percent of the population but will remain the largest age demographic in the United States.

The time period in which a consumer is born creates a bond with many other consumers born during the same time period. These groups are called **age cohorts** because they have grown up with others with similar experiences. Currently, eight age cohorts coexist in our culture. Figure 2.9 gives a brief snapshot of each cohort. These cohorts were identified in the mid-1990s and still have relevance today.

Recently researchers have broadened definitions of the age cohorts to comprise four generations, each working and purchasing goods in the contemporary marketplace creating generational differences. The four generations are Traditionalists, Baby Boomers, Generation X, and Generation Y. Generations may easily coexist in fashion businesses: A Baby Boomer manager hires Generation X and Generation Y employees to provide products to all four generations.

In 2005, as part of a joint initiative between the American Society of Newspaper Editors (ASNE) and the Newspaper Association of America (NAA), a report was published showing media usage from a generational perspective (Audience, 2005). Table 2.1, from that report, shows the evolution of media available to the four generations. With the exception of newspapers, magazines, and broadcast radio, all other media types were invented after Traditionalists were born. In contrast, most media formats have always been around for Generation Y. Understanding the four generations is a starting point to help promotion specialists target the correct audience with correct media choices.

Traditionalists. This generation was born between 1900 and 1945 and numbered 41 million in 2005 (Audience, 2005). In 2010, the youngest of this group will be age 65. The oldest members of this generation reached young adulthood during great economic and political turmoil and believed it was very important to stay informed. They obtained

FIGURE 2.9 Characteristics of the generations.

Age Cohorts

Generation Z cohort
Born: 1995–present
Age in 2010: 15+
Share of population: 17.7%, 49 million people

Characteristics shaping this cohort include a wider mix of backgrounds—race and family structure—along with more varied experiences than previous cohorts. Marketers predict that consumers from this age cohort with eventually have a lot of knowledge, power, and money but can't yet predict what they will spend it on.

Generation Y cohort (also know as echo boomers)
Born: 1977–1994
Came of age: 1995 +
Age in 2010: 16–33
Share of population: 16%, 44 million people

This cohort is shaped by digital media—i.e., never being without it. Many in this cohort have grown up with two-income families and are accustomed to having many material things. They are very optimistic about spending power and earning power. Many hold credit cards and believe they can afford the lifestyle they grew up in.

Generation X cohort (also known as baby-busters)
Born: 1965–1976
Came of age: 1984–1995
Age in 2010: 34–45
Share of population: 15%, 42 million people

Called latchkey kids, this is the first generation to be marked by divorce and day care. These individuals are looking for anchors. These consumers have a "what's-in-it-for me" attitude and a mind-set that is confused about many things. Their perception of money is spend? Save? What?

Boomers II cohort (also known as zoomers)
Born: 1955–1964
Came of age: 1973–1983
Age in 2010: 46–55
Share of population: 16%, 44 million people

This cohort is marked by Watergate. The naive enthusiasm of youth disappeared. Instead, this cohort became self-absorbed, preoccupied with themselves, which manifested itself in everything from self-help movements to self-deprecation in the media. Changes in the economy had a profound effect on the group. Debt as a means of maintaining a lifestyle made sense.

Boomers I cohort (also know as the Woodstock generation)
Born: 1946–1954
Came of age: 1963–1972
Age in 2010: 56–64
Share of population: 12%, 34 million people

Baby boomers I and II collectively make up 38% of the total population. The two baby boomer cohorts are separated by the end of the Vietnam conflict. The assassinations of John F. Kennedy, Martin Luther King Jr., and Robert Kennedy marked the end of the era in which people felt comfortable and secure. However, cohort I continued to experience good economic times and wants a lifestyle at least as good as the one experienced by earlier cohorts. Both baby boom cohorts believe in spending, then borrowing, then spending some more.

Post-war cohort (also known as the silent generation)
Born: 1928–1945
Came of age: 1946–1963
Age in 2010: 65–82
Share of population: 15%, 42 million people

Members of this cohort grew up during a long period of economic growth and expectation of good times. While the Cold War and threat of nuclear power have caused some uncertainty with these adults, they enjoy feeling comfortable, secure, and familiar. This cohort believes in spending some and saving some.

FIGUre 2.9 (*Continued*)

World War II cohort (also known as the Depression generation)
    Born: 1922–1927
    Came of age: 1940–1945
    Age in 2010: 83–88
    Share of population: 5.2%, 14.4 million people
People in this cohort came of age during the 1940s and World War II. Postponement shaped this cohort while military personnel were away and loved ones were at home. This cohort is also intensely romantic resulting from the war ending. This cohort believes in spending a little as long as you save a lot.

Depression cohort (also known as the G.I. generation)
    Born: 1912–1921
    Came of age: 1930–1939
    Age in 2010: 89–98
    Share of population: 1.5%, 4.1 million people
These consumers were shaped by the Great Depression. They were anxious growing up and have continued to be anxious concerning issues of spending, saving, and debt, and believe it is better to save money than spend money. This cohort was the first cohort to be influenced by contemporary media—radio and motion pictures.

Adapted from: Meredith, G., & Schewe, C.; Paul, P.; Solomon, M. R., & Rabolt, N,J. U.S. Census Bureau; and Wellner, A.

TaBLe 2.1   *Evolution of Media Availability Among the Generations*

	Traditionalist (Born before 1946)	Baby Boomers (Born 1946–1964)	Generation X (Born 1965–1976)	Generation Y (Born 1977–1994)
Newspapers				
Magazines				
Broadcast Radio				
Broadcast Television	X			
Transistor Radio	X			
8-Track Tapes	X	X		
Walkman Radio	X	X		
Video Games	X	X		
VCRs	X	X		
Cable Television	X	X		
Personal computers	X	X	X	
Satellite Television	X	X	X	
Internet	X	X	X	
Cell phones	X	X	X	
Online News	X	X	X	
DVD Players	X	X	X	X
Satellite Radio	X	X	X	X
MP3 Players	X	X	X	X
TiVo	X	X	X	X
iPod Video Player	X	X	X	X

Key:

A blank box indicates the technology/media format was "always there"

"X" indicates the technology/media format was invented during the generation's time

Adapted from: Audience Development Initiative. (2005) *Growing audience, media usage: A generational perspective*. www.growingaudeince.com

news from newspapers, broadcast radio, and national magazines. The youngest members of this group saw broadcast television, network news, and mass-market television shows come into their parents' homes before they graduated from high school. Members of this group are heavy consumers of news, loyal newspaper readers, and the fastest growing demographic online (Audience, 2005).

This market has rapidly changed as the life span beyond retirement has increased. Younger members of this group feel free to spend money on themselves rather than leaving an estate to their children. These consumers spend money on entertainment, travel, recreation, adult education, and convenience- and experience-oriented products and services (Reda, 1998). Promotion strategies and tactics that portray Traditionalists as attractive, active, healthy, and affluent consumers have the most potential for success.

Baby Boomers.   This generation, born between 1946 and 1964, has always been the largest age segment of the U.S. population, over 80 million in 2005 (Audience, 2005). In 2010, the youngest Baby Boomers will be 46. Because of their size, their consumption choices have made them continuous market and social trendsetters. As Baby Boomers have moved through the life cycle, they have caused specific product category sales to grow and then decline in a predictable pattern.

Younger Baby Boomers (cohort II) are more likely to borrow money for purchases, because they measure progress in life by the possession of things. Older Baby Boomers (cohort I) are typically characterized as high-income, free-spending individuals whose purchase motives are directed at quality, durability, and variety. This generation is often sandwiched between taking care of their Traditionalist parents and their Generation X or Y children at the same time.

Baby Boomers differ from Traditionalists in two important ways: They are not as loyal to newspapers and they adapt to new media technologies faster (Audience, 2005). Older Baby Boomers turned to network television for news and entertainment and younger Baby Boomers saw the advent of the VCR, which allowed time-shift television programs. This generation was also the first to enjoy music anywhere and anytime with the introduction of the Walkman cassette player. When the youngest Baby Boomers entered the workforce after college, many businesses were changing over to computer systems.

Adult consumers see themselves as 10 to 15 years younger than their chronological age. Age-based communication strategies that promote messages to the *psychological age* of consumers have a greater acceptance by the target market. Promotions that do not refer to age are more likely to be accepted by Baby Boomers.

Generation Xers.   Members of this generation were born between 1965 and 1976. While this group had the shortest time span (11 years), they number 47 million, roughly the size of Traditionalists (Audience, 2005). In 2010, the youngest members of this generation will be 34. This group also has been called Latchkey Kids because they had to take care of themselves during their youth while both parents worked.

The consumer behavior of this generation has been shaped by divorce, diversity, and declining incomes (Ritchie, 1995). Many in this generation were responsible for household shopping and had a major influence on the products and brands that were brought into the home as they were growing up. They have more expertise in electronic equipment, computers, and automobiles than their parents. They have also remained members of the household longer and kept closer ties with family than earlier generations. This generation redefined the extended family to include close friends, stepparents, adopted and half siblings, live-in partners, and other relations shaped by divorce. Items such as cell phones that allow this generation to stay in touch with family are considered necessities, not luxuries (Ritchie, 1995).

This generation learned to be independent at a very early age and incorporated electronic gadgets such as CD players and home computers rather than traditional media into their lifestyle. They were influenced by broadcast and cable television and increasingly sophisticated video games, which they used as after-school entertainment (Audience, 2005). They also grew up during high inflation and economic difficulties of the 1980s and are therefore described as economically conservative. They are online shoppers who like to research facts. They are also skeptics because they are the first generation to not expect to achieve a lifestyle equal or better than their parents, although they feel they deserve one.

Generation Xers have grown up with commercials and dislike advertisements that are stupid, misleading, offensive, or boring. They are attracted to promotions that show diversity, avoiding negative stereotypes and offensiveness. The diversity of this generation will remain a formidable challenge. Generation X target markets are defined as many diverse groups, all equally important.

Generation Y. This generation was born between 1977 and 1994. The youngest will be 16, just in time to drive, in 2010. They are the children of Baby Boomers and also known as *Echo Boomers.* In 2005 they were nearly the same size as Baby Boomers, 77 million (Audience, 2005).

These individuals were born into households with more media choices than any previous demographic segment. Raised in a decade of global access and knowledge, unavailable to generations before them, they use media and the computer as their playground. This generation is called the "Linked Generation," never having known a world without digital media (Audience, 2005).

Media serves several functions for Generation Y. For the very young, it serves as a developmental toy. As children, digital media have become the "virtual hearth" at home. Digital media is set up in a public room and many digital activities are shared by family members, making it the center of family life (Levere, 1999). It also serves as a library, giving Generation Y tremendous access to information, causing this generation to be more visually and verbally sophisticated than previous generations.

Generation Y is impatient and wants information fast. They have embraced communication technology, personalizing it to meet their media needs for entertainment, news, and information. They are the first generation to have consumption habits that trickle up, influencing media consumption patterns of older generations. The youngest members of this group (born between 1987 and 1994) are called *Millennials* and "the world and everyone they know is located in their computers and cell phone directories" (Audience, 2005, p. 28).

Promotions delivered to Generation Y need to be smart, sophisticated messages that empower youth (Levere, 1999). It is also important to develop brand building *with* them instead of *for* them. This generation tunes out promotions that sound too young. Many members of this generation have grown up in two-income households and are accustomed to having many material things. They also have sufficient income to spend on themselves, buying clothing, entertainment, food, personal care items, and sporting goods, among other items. Box 2.2 details the challenges of appealing to the Millennials.

Gender

Second only to age, **gender** (sexual identity) is the most popular statistic used to segment populations. Within the population of the United States, gender is nearly balanced—49.1

○ BOX 2.2

Brands' Challenge: Bridging Gap with Young People

The Millennials' penchant for individualism, along with the proliferation of generation-based marketing, are making it more difficult for brands to connect with youths and young adults.

More than 30 years ago, the Vietnam war was a polarizing issue, widening a generation gap between Baby Boomers and their parents, and creating some solid turf for marketers to claim in early, generation-based messages. The early Nineties brought a significant increase in generation-driven marketing, at that time focusing on Gen-Xers. So now, shouldn't the stage be set for generational appeals to the latest wave of youths and young adults, the Millennials?

Author/generation expert William Strauss answers that question with a resounding no. Since the onslaught of marketing aimed at Xers, the pop culture landscape has changed, Strauss said. Along with fellow generation expert Neil Howe, Strauss authored "Millennials and the Pop Culture: Strategies for a New Generation of Consumers" (Life Course Associates, $49).

Today's landscape is populated with teens and twentysomethings who are thinking more independently, changing their minds more frequently and partaking of media that are mobile and messages that are instant, making them a tough group to influence, Strauss said in an interview.

"Pop culture purveyors feel they're [relating to] the styles and attitudes of the Millennials, but they're expecting too much similarity [among them]," Strauss said of a generation he defines as those 23 and younger. At a time when marketers are willing participants in the country's celebrity-drenched culture, Strauss and Howe write, "Today's teenage consumers tell pollsters they are six times more likely to trust parents than pop celebrities on important issues."

In fact, when asked in 2003 how important it is for the brands they use to have various attributes, only 7 percent cited celebrity advertising, 12th among 12 characteristics. "Something my parents wouldn't like" ranked 11th, seen as important by 10 percent, while "worth the money spent" topped the list (86 percent) and high quality was second (83 percent).

A protective, close bond between parents and Millennial teens that evokes the Twenties and Thirties, teens' collective upbeat attitudes and their desire to do things in groups reflect the value youths are placing on sharing, Strauss said. This plays out in different ways, from teens going to movies in big groups to their staging of large-scale musicals. It's no coincidence that Disney's "High School Musical" has recently been

the country's top-selling CD, for instance.

In such an environment, the portrayal of romance and wholesome fun are cards marketers ought to play if they expect to score with sizable numbers of tweens, teens, and twentysomethings, Strauss advised. Images that could resonate, he said, range from teens and twentysomethings engaged in courtship rituals or making the grand gesture, to mixed-company partying and just having a good time. "The occasional adult in the picture would be good, too," he added.

Polo Jeans, Original Zinc, Adidas, Dooney & Bourke, American Girl, J.C. Penney, and Macy's are brands Strauss believes are effectively building connections with Millennials, via the brands' websites and ads in magazines like *Teen Vogue* and *Elle Girl*. He cited the Penney ads for "upbeat, confident, look-you-in-the-eye" models; Original Zinc for "a bit of a pull-back from the sexuality of the clothing"; and Polo Jeans' G.I.V.E. campaign, his favorite, for showing "smartly dressed young women who do smart things, too."

Fashion players proffering ad imagery that is less likely to hit a winning note with most Millennials, Strauss said, include Abercrombie & Fitch, Calvin Klein, Gucci, and Christian Dior. Referring to recent ads from Gucci and Dior showing women behind sunglasses, looking slightly away, for example, Strauss said the images of "hyperaffluence at a distance" are contrary to the Millennials' sensibilities. "Millennials don't like to reveal much affluence, for the most part," the author said. Affluent Millennials, he said, "don't like to set themselves apart" from contemporaries or others who are not as well off.

Informed that Strauss sees an "emphasis on the physicality of models" in Abercrombie campaigns as unappealing to many Millennials, Sam Shahid, president and creative director at Shahid & Co., which counts A&F as a client, responded: "We don't think in terms of appealing to a particular generation. It's just about being fabulous, beautiful, healthy, and optimistic."

Much as the Millennials gravitate toward forming groups and share a sense of optimism about the future, Strauss anticipates they will increasingly rally around big brands rather than niche names. "Over the next few years, just as the raucous '20s morphed into the swing '30s, the edgy youth styles of the '90s will become just a memory," Strauss and Howe predict in "Millennials and the Pop Culture." Target and Wal-Mart, the authors note, already have "enjoyed post-9/11 boosts in teen buying," while mass fads and a lower-profile commercial style are perceived by the duo as poised for a comeback.

These dynamics stand in contrast to Boomers' and Xers' continued inclination to push the edge. For instance, Strauss said, a recent *Newsweek* cover showed a nude, middle-aged woman as seen through reading glasses. "It's hard to imagine something like that being done with collegians," he said. "Having grown up with Howard Stern and Bill Clinton, their tendency is to pull back and create a sense of personal, physical decorum."

"Baby Boomers always wanted to fashion something new, reinvent things, which informed the generation gap with their parents," Strauss said. "Millennials have rejected the Boomers' rejection."

Source: Seckler, V. (2006, April 12). Brands' challenge: Bridging gap with young people. *Women's Wear Daily,* pp. 10–11.

percent male and 50.9 percent female (U.S. Census, 2004). Projections indicate that by 2050 gender will be even more balanced; the male population will increase to 49.2 percent while that female population will decrease to 50.8 percent. Demographically, a relationship exists between age and gender. As indicated in Figure 2.8, males are a larger proportion of the population under age 44; females are a larger portion of the population age 45 and over.

Fashion businesses have long used gender segmentation for clothing, cosmetics, and toiletries categories. Traditionally marketers have made distinctions between female- and male-dominated purchases and created campaigns to attract the identified gender. Female purchases include food, clothing, and household items. Male-dominated purchases include investments and insurance. These distinctions are diminishing, however, as men and women assume equal roles at work and in home and family life.

Ugg Australia, among other brands, has begun promoting across gender lines to position the brand and products as unisex must-haves (Thompson, 2006). Traditional men's advertising in the luxury market generally has featured the product. Ugg is featuring men and women together to make the gender crossover and become an all-encompassing brand like Ralph Lauren and Cole Haan.

Within the last decade, a new demographic related to gender has emerged as an important target market—the gay, lesbian, bisexual, and transgender (GLBT) market. In 2005, the size of the U.S. gay community was approximately 15 million people, with spending power over $610 billion (Haley, 2005). In 2004, it was reported that for the first time, the majority (59 percent) of all ads in national gay publications used creative material specifically targeted to gay consumers. Additionally, it was reported that 150 Fortune 500 brands are actively promoted in the gay market, up from only 72 in 2001.

The GLBT community is a desirable demographic because a large proportion of this group is either single or in double-income, no-kids relationships and has more disposable income than the average family (Ward, 2006). Additionally, this target market tends to be early adopters of trends and is very technologically savvy.

Promotion strategies and tactics can focus on the dedicated GLBT press and/or mainstream press. When pitching an advertising campaign to gay media, it is better to have a gay angle (Ward, 2006). When trying to reach GLBT audiences through mainstream media, it is better to have an appealing story, and focus on publications with high gay readership. These promotions should be inclusive, not just with homosexual references. Promotions should not be pitched toward gay men and lesbians together; they have different interests. Use gay and lesbian agencies that understand the demographic to help craft promotion strategies and tactics. And, according to Ward (2006), do not ignore gay parents. There are many new opportunities for forward-thinking companies with parenting and children's products.

Education

Demographic statistics on education attainment have been gathered since 1940. Education levels of the United States population have increased each decade and are reaching an all-time high (Fig. 2.10). Of the population 25 years and older, 80 percent have a high school diploma and 24 percent have completed at least a bachelor's degree (U.S. Census, 2006). In general, younger people are more likely to have completed higher educational levels than older people because of the opportunities afforded them to attend school and the expectation by society that one should go to college. The number of college-educated Americans is expected to increase with continued educational opportunities.

Professional, college-educated individuals are a profitable market, but they are hard to keep. They have greater financial ability, which allows them to take greater purchase risks and causes them to be less brand loyal. Promotional strategies aimed at this target group should involve emerging technologies and innovations because this group reads more, watches less television, and requests more information about products and services than target groups with less education. In today's society, educational attainment is correlated with a higher income.

Income

Businesses often look at household incomes to make statistical generalizations about members of the household. An individual's personal income is comprised of **disposable income**, money available after taxes; and **discretionary income**, money available after taxes and necessities such as food and housing have been paid for. A household income of $50,000 will reflect quite different spending probabilities for a single female with no children versus a married couple with two children.

Income can be reported as mean or median income. **Mean income** is the average value of all incomes within the sample. Mean income will include very small and very large incomes, distorting a true picture of the market segment. For an accurate picture, businesses look at the **median income** of their potential target segment. This is the middle value in the income distribution with an equal number of incomes above and below

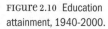
FIGURE 2.10 Education attainment, 1940-2000.

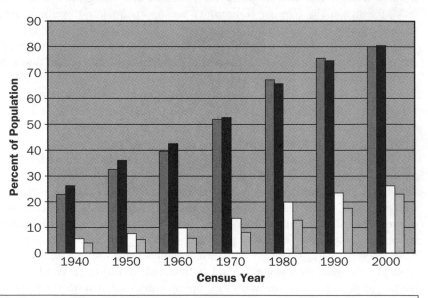

the midpoint. Pricing strategies that look only at mean incomes may miss the target market to whom the promotion is aimed.

Members of society positioned socioeconomically between the lower working class and the wealthy are considered the **middle class.** Middle class is determined on the basis of annual household after-tax income and is the portion of the population grouped around the national average. The middle class may be proportionally smaller today than it was decades ago, but it has not disappeared. The middle class, which in the past included nearly everyone, is no longer growing in terms of population or purchasing power but instead swelling at the top and bottom ends (Leonhardt, 1997). The shrinking of the middle class has caused marketers to adopt a new strategy that encourages companies to tailor their products and promotions to two different target markets divided along economic, educational, and technological lines. This strategy is called two-tier marketing.

Occupation

The occupation of an individual will influence his or her income. Occupation is the vocation that serves as one's regular source of income. Occupational trends that began in the 1970s continue to have an impact during the 21st century. Information-based occupations, such as lawyers, doctors, and engineers, have replaced the industrial occupations of farming and private household workers. Record numbers of women have entered the job market. Blue-collar occupations have been progressively replaced with white-collar occupations.

Changing occupational trends have influenced the content and media choice of promotional campaigns. For example, advertisements provide a higher degree of technical information to the consumer than in past decades. In addition to the information presented as part of the campaign, it is common practice to broadcast or print a website address to direct the consumer to more information about the product or service. Characters within promotion campaigns are nearly always white-collar professional and increasingly female (Wells et al., 1998).

Race and Ethnicity

Race is the biological heritage of an individual. Black and Caucasian are examples of races. **Ethnicity** is the description of a group bound together by ties of cultural homogeneity and is often based around national origins. "Hispanic" is an ethnicity, not a race. The term refers to people whose ancestry is from Spanish-speaking countries of South and Central America. A Hispanic person will also be designated as a member of the Caucasian, Black, American Indian, or other racial designation.

Ethnic diversity is changing the market segments of the United States. As shown in Fig. 2.11, population estimates indicate that between 2000 and 2050, Hispanic people of any race will almost double in percentage of the population from 12.6 percent to 24.4 percent (U.S. Census, 2004). Additionally, the Asian population will have increased from 3.8 percent to 8.0 percent, and the black population will have smaller increases from 12.7 percent to 14.6 percent. People who self-identify as other races, including American Indian and Alaska Native alone, Native Hawaiian and Other Pacific Islander alone, and Two or More Races, will increase from 2.5 percent to 5.3 percent. It is projected that the white population will decrease in percentage from 81.0 percent in 2000 to 72.1 percent in 2050.

Retailers who understand the ethnic differences among potential customers are offering product lines that compliment the appropriate target market. Merchandise selection and promotion activities are influenced by the ethnic mix of the primary and secondary target markets. The race of a potential target group may determine merchan-

FIGURE 2.11 Projected population percentages of the United States by race and Hispanic origin, 2000 to 2050.

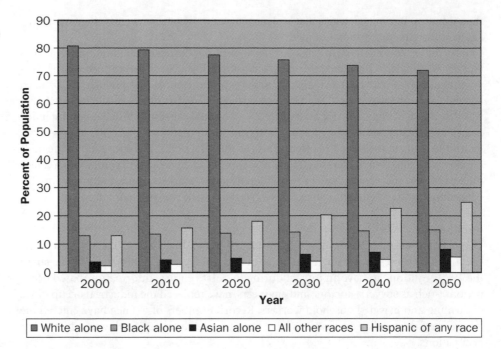

Year

■ White alone   ■ Black alone   ■ Asian alone   □ All other races   ■ Hispanic of any race

dise selection, for instance, cosmetic and beauty products that meet the needs of ethnic consumers (Fig. 2.12). The physical build of the ethnic group that predominates among a store's customers may influence its merchandise assortment. For example, Asian-American females are typically smaller in build than members of some other ethnic groups. Retailers targeting this market segment should have a larger selection of petite and small sizes. Grocers look at the ethnic mix of potential customers to determine the specific food offerings to be sold at different branches and promote these grocery offerings in media appropriate to the target market.

Ethnic groups will continue to grow in number and purchasing power. Promotion specialists need to pay close attention to creating advertising that is ethnically targeted. Rabin (1994) articulated several ideas to assist sponsors in communicating with racial and ethnic groups in a multicultural society. The ideas are still relevant and include understanding:

• Social values, methods of communication, and common interests that cross cultural boundaries.
• How religion may shape the way an ethnic group thinks and communicates.
• The existence of bilingual communication among minority populations who work and live among white populations, allowing these populations to speak and understand messages in both cultures.
• The distinct tastes in media that exist among cultural groups.

Rabin suggested creating advertising and promotional messages that consist of universal messages addressing the commonalities and differences within target markets. Use a mix of broadcast and print media to present messages blending words and pictures that have strong oral and strong written communication traditions to attract both cultures. He also suggested seeking permission from community leaders before attempting to open communication channels within ethnic target groups. The most important element in designing a promotion campaign targeted to ethnic groups is to avoid reinforcing racial and ethnic stereotypes.

Family Size and Structure

Another demographic statistic useful in determining target markets is family size and structure. The perception of the household as "parents with children" is no longer realistic. Fig. 2.13 illustrates the composition of households according to the 2000 census. Just a little over half (52 percent) of all households are married couples (U.S. Census, 2003). One-person households make up 26 percent of households, while two or more people living together but not married make up 12 percent of households.

Certain age groups reflect certain types of households. The majority of single men who live alone are under age 45, while the largest number of single women who live alone are over age 65. Additionally, young people are more likely than older adults to live in a cohabitating or unrelated roommate household.

Contemporary households are composed of few children and are unlikely to involve a member of the extended family. Single-parent households and empty nesters also make up a larger number of households than in the past. Whereas in the past, large economy sizes were the trend in packaging many hard-line goods such as food, manufacturers are now bringing back smaller-sized containers to accommodate smaller households in smaller spaces.

FIGURE 2.12 A skin care advertisement targeted to an ethnic consumer.

Geographic Segmentation

Dividing the market using location characteristics is the focus of geographic segmentation. National advertisers often use geographic segmentation to position themselves in regional target markets. Typical geographic breakdowns include regions, metropolitan statistical area (MSA) size, density of population, and climate. Regional zip codes are a common geographic segmentation tool based on the first digit or first three digits of the zip code. Metropolitan statistical areas have a population over 250,000 people. Urban, suburban, or rural populations may be geographic targets or differentiation may be based on climate. The geographic unit may be large, encompassing several states, or small, limited to streets within a neighborhood.

National fashion magazines use distinctive advertisements to promote regional trends and styles and highlight the availability of the trend at regional stores. In each case, marketers determine the benefit of boosting local market shares with the additional costs needed for production of the regional issue. *Vogue* used the cover of its magazine to emphasize geographic segmentation when it distributed the same issue under three separate covers, featuring New York, Texas, or Los Angeles (Fig. 2.14).

FIGURE 2.13 Percentages of different household types.

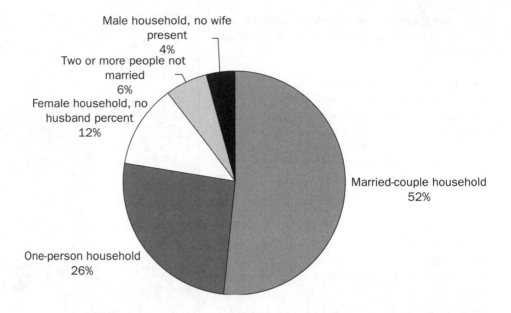

Male household, no wife present
4%

Two or more people not married
6%

Female household, no husband percent
12%

Married-couple household
52%

One-person household
26%

Psychographic Segmentation

FIGURE 2.14 The cover of *Vogue* targeted to three different geographic areas of the country.

Have you ever filled out the consumer questionnaire included in the packaging of a consumer good? If you have, you participated in psychographic segmentation by that particular manufacturer. Demographic and behavioristic information does not always provide adequate information to target a specific market. Although demographics give a retailer a basic description of its customers, a better predictor of consumer behavior may be found in the lifestyle profile of the consumer through psychographics. Psychographic segmentation profiles the lifestyle of consumers based upon activities, interests, and opinions.

Obtaining information on activities, interests, and opinions is more complex than collecting demographic information. While demographic information is exact, psychographic information is subjective and indirect in meaning. There are no commonly accepted definitions for terms frequently used in psychographic questions such as "satisfaction" with a product, or how the product makes you "feel." As a result, psychographic information is more difficult to compare.

Lifestyle information is usually gained through a questionnaire asking consumers what they do, how they spend their time, what they buy, and why they buy it. Interests are obtained by asking about hobbies, travel, and leisure time. Consumers are also asked their views on social issues, world events, economic situations, and values to determine their opinions. Based upon the profile, advertisers develop themes for promotions and select the appropriate media in which to transmit the promotions. For example, very specific questions about activities, interests, and opinions help an advertiser determine the effectiveness of using one magazine over another when placing an ad.

Questionnaires or online surveys distributed to a random sample are common methods used to obtain psychographic information. However, the wording of the question, no matter how carefully presented, may influence the type of answer received. Consumers, while saying one thing, may do something else. Many consumers surveyed have shown widespread interest in recycling, for example, but this interest is not reflected in the purchase of products made from recycled materials.

VALS

A popular psychographic segmentation tool is VALS. The basic theory behind VALS is that people express their personalities through their behaviors. The original VALS system was built by consumer futurist Arnold Mitchell to explain changing values and lifestyles in the 1970s in the United States. The Stanford Research Institute (SRI) refined the research tool and now uses VALS to help businesses segment the consumer marketplace on the basis of personality traits.

VALS has identified eight distinct personality types: Innovators, Thinkers, Achievers, Experiencers, Believers, Strivers, Makers, and Survivors. "The personality traits are the motivation—the cause. Buying behavior becomes the effect—the observable, external behavior prompted by an internal driver" (SRI, 2006, para 2), The VALS survey and a complete discussion of the personality types can be found at www.sric-bi.com/VALS. Many companies use VALS to segment markets for promotion purposes.

VALS is only one of many psychographic segmentation tools available to market researchers. Each lifestyle system developed and marketed has the potential to segment consumers in a new and creative way. Any list of systems provided in this textbook would be out of date as soon as the list was written. However, it is very easy for students and promotion planners to find psychographic lifestyle systems over the Internet and determine the system with the most potential to analyze consumers and retailers for promotion effectiveness.

The Global Consumer

As the population increases, businesses and researchers are becoming more concerned with broadening consumer research beyond the traditional considerations of demographic and psychographic bases of segmentation and targeting their customer at a deeper, more emotional level. They are taking a more global view of consumer understanding and finding that consumers around the world are not that different. In the first study of its kind to describe the global consumer, Roger Starch Worldwide, a New York–based research firm, interviewed 35,000 consumers in 35 countries to identify shared values that cross national borders. The purpose of the study, according to Tom Miller, group senior vice president and director for international operations, was to put into place a globally comparable system of gathering consumer intelligence and predicting consumer trends around the world (Elliott, 1998).

The study identified six distinct global value groups based on belief systems that define worldwide adult consumers long term (Elliott, 1998). The six groups are strivers, devouts, altruists, intimates, fun seekers, and creatives.

- *Strivers* represent 23 percent of the population and consider material things extremely important. They value wealth, status, ambition, and power. Strivers are more likely to be middle-aged males from developed or developing nations like Japan and the Philippines and will use the newspaper as their primary media source.
- *Devouts* are adults with more traditional values like faith, duty, obedience, and respect for elders. Devouts represent 22 percent of the population and are concentrated in Africa, Asia, and the Mideast. This group is the least involved with the media and least likely to want Western brands.
- *Altruists* are very outer-focused and interested in social issues and causes. They are generally well-educated females and represent 18 percent of the population. Altruists are often found in Latin America and Russia.
- *Intimates* are worldwide adult consumers who are "people-people" focusing on relationships very close to home such as spouses, family, colleagues, and friends. They make up 15 percent of the population and are frequently found in Britain, Hungary, the Netherlands, and the United States. Intimates are heavy users of media that can be shared to create a common bond with others, such as television, movies, and radio, which people watch or listen to and discuss with others the next day.
- *Fun seekers* are the youngest group of consumers and prize values such as pleasure, excitement, adventure, and looking good. They represent 15 percent of the population and are high users of electronic media.
- *Creatives* are the smallest group at 10 percent, but the highest consumers of media including books, magazines, and newspapers. Creatives value knowledge and technology and are considered global trendsetters in owning a PC or surfing the Web.

Businesses willing to use this information to identify appropriate promotion campaigns will be able to attract the global customer.

There are two equally important but seemingly opposite points of view that should direct advertising and promotion aimed at the global consumer. On the one hand, communication is readily available around the world with the use of computers, satellite communications, and other technologies; therefore, it should be assumed that consumers from many countries will see the message. On the other hand, messages aimed at the global consumer should be customized to the customer profile of the intended audience. More viewers are starting to perceive mass media messages as noise, not intended for them, and are ignoring the message. According to Schultz and Barnes (1995), advertising is moving from a focus on efficiency to a focus on effectiveness. Promotion planning should target the best customers worldwide instead of the most customers. Identification of the best customers is achieved only through very sophisticated market segmentation and development of an IMC strategy that is focused on the best customers.

Behavioristic Segmentation

While demographic characteristics provide a researcher with basic statistical information to determine target groups, this information does not address the behavioral patterns of consumers, which may tell us more about them than their age, income, or ethnic identity. Consumers in the marketplace can also be segmented based on their behavior.

Think about an item you recently purchased. How often do you buy this item? Did you wait until you needed to replace it, or did you buy it to have it on hand? When you replaced it, did you buy the same brand or an alternative brand? Do you always purchase this item at the same store, or do you purchase it wherever you happen to be? Were you influenced by sales promotions surrounding the item? All of these questions relate to your behavior as a consumer.

Behaviorist segmentation is a method of segmenting markets based on consumer usage, loyalty, or buying responses to a product or service. Researchers who use behavior segmentation look at what consumers actually do in the marketplace as opposed to what consumers say they do in the marketplace.

Behaviorist segmentation includes the degree of use a consumer exhibits toward a product. Consumer usage patterns define users as regular users, first-time users, prospective users, ex-users, or nonusers. Consumer usage patterns also define consumers as light users, moderate users, or heavy users. Promotions are designed with the type of user in mind. Advertisers may direct promotions to consumers who are very familiar with, and intend to buy, the product, as well as to consumers who are completely unfamiliar with the product and have no information on which to base a decision. A new product may be promoted to attract the prospective user. Promotions may be created to convince the light user to become a moderate user, or moderate users to become heavy users.

Behavioristic segmentation may be used to determine consumer segments based on brand loyalty. Consumers may insist on certain brands or reject certain brands. Recognition of a specific brand or nonrecognition of all brands may influence buying behavior. Brand familiarity may influence a regular or potential user's intention to buy. Many sales promotion techniques are designed to reinforce brand loyalty to consumers. Behaviors such as buying activity and store preference may also be used to determine segmentation bases. Are consumers most likely to purchase a product at a convenience store, a department store, or a specialty shop? Do consumers comparison shop at several stores before making the purchase or do they purchase the product randomly wherever they happen to be? Behavior segmentation plays an important role in analyzing effective sales promotion techniques, as will be discussed in Chapter 12.

Benefit Segmentation

The last type of segmentation fashion businesses use is benefit segmentation, which divides the market based on consumer needs or problems and the benefits they will derive from buying products. Fashion marketers differentiate target markets and develop promotion campaigns that focus on the benefits a consumer will gain by purchasing a specific product or brand. Benefits may include features unique to the product or brand, or may fulfill such needs as quality, service, or value. A complete discussion of product benefits is included in positioning strategies in Chapter 5.

Because an accurate promotion mix does not just happen, marketers must combine all elements into a marketing program that will encourage positive exchange between consumers and the reseller using consumer research and information. Although product, price, and place are important, manufacturers and retailers can have the greatest influence on consumers by coordinating a promotion plan that communicates the marketing strategy of the company to the consumer. This communication can only be effective if all parts of the promotional effort—including advertising, direct marketing, personal sales, public relations, and others—work together in an integrated marketing communications strategy.

summary

- Consumer behavior is the study of decision-making processes involved in acquiring, using, and disposing of goods and services.
- Consumption consists of need recognition, information search, alternative evaluation, post-purchase evaluation, and disposal evaluation.
- Impulse buying occurs when no formal need recognition is identified before the purchase is made.
- Motives are reasons consumer buy. Understanding motives is based on the hierarchy of needs theory.
- The fashion cycle describes the process of acceptance of a fashion item or trend through innovation, culmination, and decline of an item.
- Market segmentation is the subdivision of the marketplace into relatively homogeneous subsets of consumers, called target markets or market segments.
- Demographics such as age, gender, education, income, occupation, race and ethnicity, and family size and structure can be used to segment markets.
- Behavioristic segmentation is a method of segmenting markets based on consumer usage, loyalty, or buying responses to a product or service.
- Psychographic segmentation examines consumer activities, interests, and opinions.
- Global consumers can be segmented into six distinct global value groups, Strivers, Devouts, Altruists, Intimates, Fun Seekers, and Creatives.

key terms

advertising research
age cohorts
behavioristic segmentation
benefit segmentation
consumer behavior
consumer research
consumption
demographic segmentation
deprived consumer
descriptive research
discretionary income
disposable income
early majority
ethnicity
experimental research
exploratory research
fashion count
fashion cycle

fashion innovators
fashion laggers
fashion leaders
focus group
gender
geographic s
   egmentation
hierarchy of needs theory
hypothesis
impulse buying
intuition
late majority
market research
market segment
mass market
mean income
median income
middle class

motives
niche market
performance evaluation
primary market
primary research
product acquisition
psychographic
   segmentation
qualitative research
quantitative research
race
research
scientific method
secondary market
secondary research
segmentation
target market
targeting

QUESTIONS FOR DISCUSSION

1. Identify contemporary fashion trends. What makes each a trend? What promotion tools help you determine the importance of the trend?
2. What age cohort are you a member of? Your parents? Your grandparents? Can you identify differences among your family members based on their cohort?
3. Discuss the role of segmentation in creating promotion strategies.
4. How are global consumers different and similar to one another?
5. Discuss particular demographic aspects of your community with regard to age, income levels, family structure, and cultural diversity. What promotional strategies are most likely to be effective in your community?
6. Discuss bases of segmentation other that those listed in this chapter that might help to describe a population.

ADDITIONAL RESOURCES

Underhill, P. (1999). *Why we buy: The science of shopping*. New York: Simon & Schuster.
Underhill, P. (2004). *Call of the mall*. New York: Simon & Schuster.

DATA SOURCE

Census Bureau Home Page. (Continual updates). http://www.census.gov/.

REFERENCES

Actionspeak. (2005). *Wearable video*. Retrieved June 20, 2006, from http://actionspeak.com/approach/wearablevideo.html
Audience Development Initiative. (2005). *Growing audience*. Retrieved May 21, 2007, from http://www.growingaudience.com
Elliott, S. (1998, June 25). Research finds consumers worldwide belong to six basic groups that cross national lines. *New York Times*. Retrieved June 15, 2006, from the LexisNexis Academic database.
Haley, K. (2005, June). Queer eye for the marketing guy, *Multichannel News*, 29.
Leonhardt, D. (1997, March 17). Two-tier marketing. *Business Week*, 82–87, 90.
Levere, J. L. (1999, January 29). A generation shaped by digital media presents fresh marketing challenges, a study finds. *New York Times*. Retrieved June 3, 2006, from the LexisNexis Academic database.
Rabin, S. (1994). How to sell across cultures. *American Demographics, 16*(3), 56. Retrieved June 5, 2006, from the Academic Search Premier database.
Reda, S. (1998, March). Reaching the aging boomers, *Stores*, 22–24, 26.
Ritchie, K. (1995). Marketing to generation X. *American Demographics, 17*(4), 34. Retrieved June 3, 2006, from the Academic Search Premier database.
Schultz, D. E., & Barnes, B. E. (1995). *Strategic brand communication campaigns* (5th ed.). Lincolnwood, IL: NTC Business Books.
SRI Consulting Business Intelligence. (2006). *Welcome to VALS*™. Retrieved June 15, 2006, from http://www.sric-bi.com/VALS
Thompson, S. (2006). Ugg, others take a shot at gender bending. *Advertising Age, 77*(21), S4–S6. Retrieved June 3, 2006, from the Academic Search Premier database.
U.S. Census Bureau. (2003). *Married-couple and unmarried-partner households: 2000*. Retrieved June 15, 2006, from http://www.census.gov/prod/2003pubs/censr-5.pdf
U.S. Census Bureau (2004). *U.S. Projections by age, sex, race and Hispanic origin*. Retrieved June 15, 2006, from http://www.census.gov/ipc/www/usinterimproj/
U.S. Census Bureau.(2006). *A half-century of learning: Historical statistics on educational attainment in the United States, 1940 to 2000*. Retrieved June 15, 2006, from http://www.census.gov/population/www/socdemo/education/introphct41.html
Ward, D. (2006, May 29) PR technique: Reaching out to the GLBT market, *PR Week*. Retrieved June 3, 2006, from the InfoTrack OneFile database.
Wells, W., Moriarty, S., & Burnett, J. (2006). *Advertising principles and practice* (7th ed.). Upper Saddle River, NJ: Pearson Prentice Hall.

FIGURE 3.1 The Prince's Charities is a group of not-for-profit organizations of which the Prince of Wales is president.

CHAPTER 3
Promotion Organization

"Luxury is competing across a variety of sectors nowadays. Aston Martin competes in the automobile and the luxury market, for example," said Suki Larson, chief executive officer of Provenance, and a former consultant at McKinsey & Co.

"The solution for luxury brands is never one-size-fits-all, and it's not necessarily a print or TV ad," Larson related. "It might be a new logo or new packaging. For some brands, customers may even be best reached through viral marketing."

Larson is the first to admit that Provenance can learn from relatively smaller luxury players that have been able to establish a significant presence, as have Jimmy Choo, Rupert Sanderson, and the Mandarin Oriental hotel chain.

Shoe designer Rupert Sanderson often hosts private, in-store events for high-spending customers and personally visits magazine editors in key markets. Aside from having no real ad budget, Sanderson, a former ad executive, believes print and TV ads aren't necessary for true luxury brands.

"Word of mouth is a very old-fashioned—and valid—strategy, and most importantly, it relies on the quality of the product," Sanderson said. "Once you expose people to a quality product, they'll tell other people. Traditional media is about reaching quantities of people, but the point about luxury is that it's exclusive."

Provenance counts among its clients Coutts, the exclusive bank that serves Britain's royal family; RF Hotels, the group founded by Sir Rocco Forte; and the Prince's Charities, run by Prince Charles.

Source: Conti, S. (2006, May 31). Provenance: Solving luxe riddle. *Women's Wear Daily*, p. 13.

After you have read this chapter you should be able to:

Explain the roles and functional responsibilities of various people involved in merchandise promotion.

Distinguish the organizational relationships of the promotion division of retail stores, manufacturers, advertising agencies, and specialized services.

Decide whether to use an in-house division or outside agency for promotion assistance.

Determine how to evaluate an advertising agency or promotion department.

Recognize professional behavior.

Distinguish professional and academic organizations.

S UCCESSFUL PROMOTION REQUIRES knowing your product and its market. Having served with a top management consulting firm like McKinsey & Co., Suki Larson knows that a wide range of professional resources are available. She might choose a no-budget, word-of-mouth strategy like Rupert Sanderson's or opt for an expensive print and media campaign. What will do for a Jimmy Choo shoe might fit too tightly around a hotel chain. The key is to know your way around the organizational structure and resources that serve the business of promotion.

The purpose of this chapter is to analyze the organizational structure that retail and manufacturing firms use for promotion. First, we discuss the participants of promotion. Next, the organizational formats for retailing and manufacturing firms are presented. In-house promotion units are considered in relation to other functional areas, followed by a discussion of the operating divisions of promotion agencies. Methods of evaluating performance and how agencies attract new clients are also analyzed. The chapter concludes with a discussion of successful promotion personnel, professionalism, and awards.

———o PROMOTION PARTICIPANTS

Four categories of participants are involved in promotion: clients, promotion division or agency employees, media representatives, and suppliers. All four groups are necessary when producing promotion activities.

Clients are persons seeking recognition for their products or services. They may be identified as advertisers, sponsors, or marketers. Designers such as Ralph Lauren, manufacturing companies such as VF Corporation, and retailing firms such as Macy's are examples of clients or advertisers seeking consumer acceptance for their products. Designers and manufacturing firms also seek acceptance by promoting to each other and by promoting to retailers or the media. The Cotton Incorporated advertisement shown in Figure 3.2 is part of a long-standing campaign, "The Fabric of Our Lives," promoting cotton fibers and fabrics. The clay models are regular features in the print advertising campaign and appear in ads aimed at the trade customer in publications such as *Women's Wear Daily*.

Organizations that assist clients in achieving promotional goals are in-house **promotion divisions** or outside **advertising agencies**. The in-house promotion division includes personnel employed by the designer, manufacturer, or retailer. A large corporation may set up an advertising agency that is owned and operated as an independent division of the corporation. Alternatively, the client may choose to plan, create, and implement a promotion strategy by hiring an outside or autonomous promotion agency specializing in these activities.

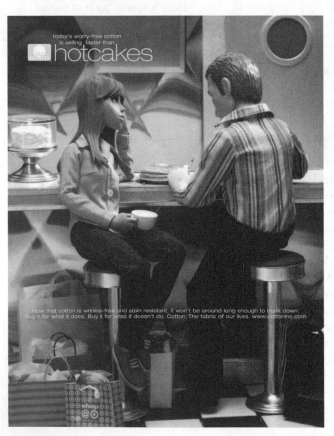

FIGURE 3.2 An advertisement directed to the trade customer.

Asprey, a luxury goods firm based in London, is an example of a company that develops promotions in-house. In 2006, the firm appointed its first creative director (Conti, 2006). The creative director reports directly to the chief executive and is in charge of design, marketing, advertising, promotion, and visual merchandising. Before the position was developed, promotion duties were still conducted in-house—split among the ready-to-wear, jewelry, and home accessories design teams.

The third category of participants is **media representatives** for print, broadcast, and interactive media. Print representatives sell space in newspapers, magazines, or out-of-home media, while broadcast and interactive media representatives sell time on television and radio or space on the Internet to carry the advertiser's broadcast message to the consumer. **Media organizations,** such as the *San Francisco Examiner,* CNN, and *Time* magazine, are major participants in the promotion process, functioning primarily as providers of information or entertainment to their subscribers, viewers, or readers. These media organizations provide the mechanism for communication messages distributed to large audiences.

The last category of promotion participants is **suppliers**. Suppliers assist clients and promotion departments or agencies in preparing materials.

Activities of suppliers contribute creatively to the finished product. These suppliers include photographers, graphic designers, audio and/or video production personnel, printers, and other similar personnel. Suppliers may be specialists or generalists who provide support to the clients, agencies or departments, and media representatives.

The structure of promotion organizations is varied. A small firm may be run by one individual with responsibility for all aspects of promotion. The promotion division of a huge corporation or a large advertising agency may be a multiperson operation with specialists in every area of research, planning, creating, and evaluation. The significance given to promotion depends upon the size of the company, the type of products or services it produces, competitive and current economic environments, and the commitment of the owner or top management.

───o TASKS OF PROMOTION

Certain functions are necessary for the successful operation of a promotion department or agency. These functions encompass administration, planning, budgeting, coordination, and creation. **Administration** is the management of personnel and programs based upon the company's marketing plans and budgets. This management requires analysis of the current situation, evaluation of current promotion activities and personnel, and direction of people and procedures.

Planning is a continual process of defining, refining, and explaining promotional goals and objectives. A formal planning process typically takes place once or twice each year in large companies. This task provides significant input to the success of any promotion and is discussed in detail in Chapter 5. This preparation leads to **budgeting** determining how much to spend on promotion activities in relationship to anticipated income, the topic of Chapter 6.

Coordination, balancing all activities and personnel, is necessary to make sure that functional areas of the firm are working toward the same goals and objectives. The buyer for a retail store must have purchased the shoes that are to be advertised in the newspaper. While the copywriter, who is responsible for verbal content, and the graphic designer, who is responsible for the visual component, create the advertisement, warehouse personnel must have the items ticketed and out on the sales floor. As the media buyer places the ad in the newspaper, the visual merchandisers create displays for customers to locate the merchandise. Coordination is needed between merchandising and promotion personnel in order for this promotion to be successful. **Creation** is the process of development and implementation of the unique and inventive promotional program.

───o RETAIL ORGANIZATION

Regardless of the size or category of the firm, retailers have specific business functions that are necessary for the operation of the firm. Merchandise must be purchased and delivered to the store before it is priced, ticketed, and placed on the sales floor where customers are able to purchase it. The products must be visually presented or promoted in some manner so that customers know what it is and where it is available. Stores must keep records of what has come into the inventory and what has sold. Information must be collected and distributed to the company owners as well as state and federal agencies. Employees need to be hired, fired, trained, and paid. Store security and comfort must be maintained. All of these functions are required for successful retailing operations. A clearly defined organizational structure will designate the appropriate division for handling these responsibilities most efficiently. An **organizational chart** is a visible blueprint of the structure of a firm. It shows how responsibilities and authority are delegated within a firm. The organizational structure may vary broadly depending on the size of the firm.

Responsibility gives an individual the obligation to perform certain duties and tasks. In order to assure that responsibilities are carried through, the individual must also be given the authority or power to use physical and human resources to accomplish the duties and tasks. The organizational chart clearly demonstrates the person in charge of the responsibilities and the chain of command, or lines of authority, within a company.

The most commonly used retail organizational plan was developed by Paul Mazur (1927). Mazur was commissioned by the National Retail Dry Goods Association, now known as the National Retail Federation, to develop a model for retail organizational structure. His plan consisted of four major functional divisions: merchandising, financial control, operations, and promotion.

Although this model was created decades ago, the organizational chart developed by Mazur still remains at the core of modern retailing. The growth of multibranch or chain retailers and the development of computer technology have stimulated expansion of the model to include two additional functional divisions: branch operations and information technology. The **branch operations division** supervises the multistore operations in various regions or districts. The area managing technology and computer applications is the **information technology division**. The functional areas of a contemporary large retailing organization are shown in Figure 3.3.

Merchandising Division

The **merchandising division** of the retail store is responsible for locating, buying, and reselling products. Buyers are given the primary authority for these activities. This division supervises and administers sales associates, department managers, assistant buyers, buyers, divisional merchandise managers, and general merchandise managers. The head of the merchandise division is the vice president of merchandising.

Operations Division

The branch of the store responsible for sales support functions such as facilities management, security, customer service, merchandise processing, and warehousing is called the **operations division.** The head of the division is the vice president of operations.

Human Resources Division

In Mazur's original plan, personnel responsibilities were part of the operations division. Personnel, which was renamed **human resources,** has become so significant it is now a separate functional division. The human resources division is responsible for hiring, training, monitoring legal issues, and, if necessary, firing personnel. The executive responsible for the management of this division is the vice president of human resources.

Financial Control Division

The **financial control division** has the responsibility for administering the budget in addition to handling all of the financial functions, such as payroll, accounts receivable, accounts payable, and inventory control. Auditing is used to check and verify that

FIGURE 3.3 Organization chart for a contemporary retailing organization.

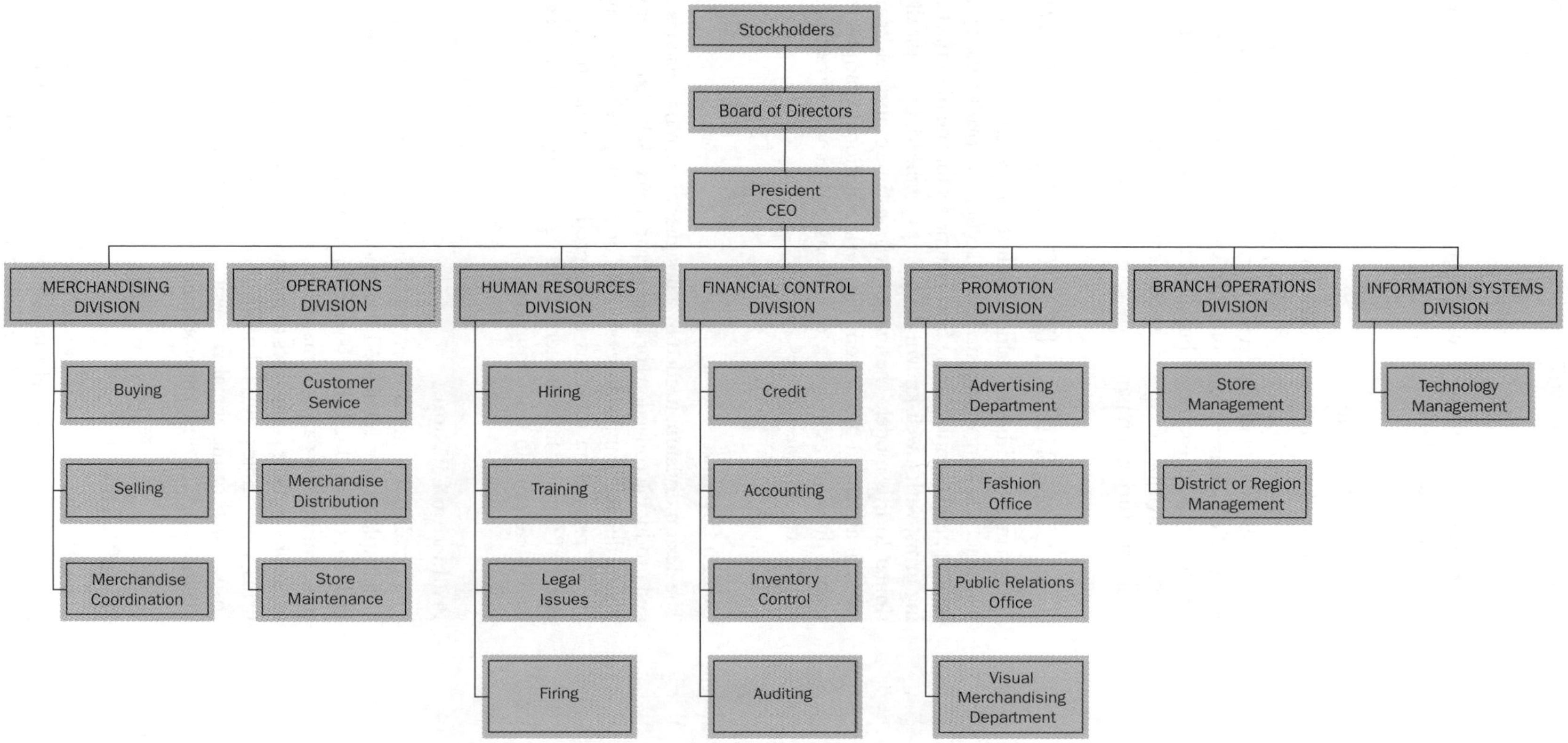

information is accurate. The head of this division is the vice president of finance or corporate controller.

Promotion Division

Originally, Mazur named the division responsible for stimulating sales through advertising, fashion coordination, and display the sales promotion division. Since sales promotion has evolved to imply a type of promotion mix activity, one that encourages sales by means of coupons or point-of-sale displays, the use of the term has changed. In modern retailing this division may be called the promotion, advertising, marketing, or public relations division, led by a vice president. Next, we look at the organizational structure of a manufacturing company.

───o MANUFACTURING ORGANIZATION

The garment and home fashions industries are characterized by both small and large manufacturing organizations. In this section, we profile the organizational structure of a large apparel manufacturing firm as a model for the manufacturing sector. Manufacturing firms, with a well-known designer as the head, are typically organized in a manner similar to this model. The major divisions in an apparel firm are design, production, sales, finance, and promotion (Fig. 3.4). Traditional manufacturers maintain all fundamental divisions as in-house operations, but some contract production and promotion activities to outside agencies.

Design Division

The **design division,** headed by a designer or merchandiser, is responsible for designing and producing collections or lines of garments each year. After garments are created, the design department produces samples or prototypes. These samples are used by the sales and/or promotion divisions to sell products to retail buyers and to make the media aware of the new lines of merchandise. A nonapparel manufacturing firm may call this activity new product development.

Production Division

The **production division** is responsible for mass-producing merchandise and filling orders placed by retailers. Production in an apparel company consists of pattern-making, cutting, bundling, sewing, finishing, and maintaining quality control. Although some traditional garment manufacturers produce their own merchandise, many other firms hire outside companies to perform specific processes. This system of hiring outside firms to assemble goods is known as contracting. To take advantage of lower production costs, much of the actual garment construction has moved to foreign countries. This practice is called offshore production.

Sales Division

The **sales division** has the responsibility of selling the line or collection. Sales may take place in a showroom, a sales facility located in a major market center, or through personal sales at the retail buyer's office. Sales personnel are known as representatives or sales reps.

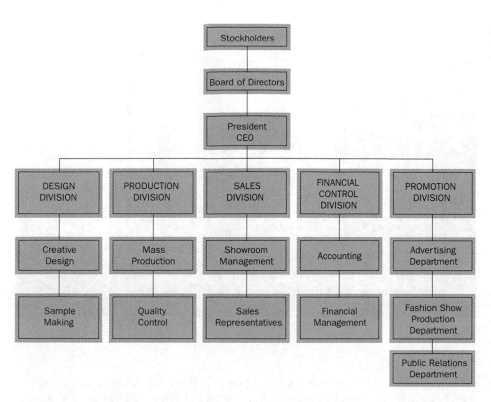

FIGURE 3.4 Organization chart for an apparel manufacturing organization.

Financial Control Division

The financial control division in the manufacturing environment has similar responsibilities for financial management as it does in retailing. One additional consideration in garment manufacturing is the role of the **factor**, a finance company that buys a manufacturer's accounts receivables. These receivables consist of retailers' orders that have not yet been paid for and delivered. The finance company takes a commission as a percentage of the total dollar payment and gives the manufacturer the balance of the money. This type of transaction gives the manufacturer cash necessary to operate while the garments are being made and shipped. Sometimes the factor will take over the billing and financial management of the manufacturing firm.

Promotion Division

The promotion division of a manufacturer or fashion design firm plans and implements a range of services that include direct-marketing materials, merchandise catalogs, advertisements, fashion show production, and special event sponsorship coordination. Although some manufacturing firms hire outside agencies to handle promotion activities, several apparel producers including Calvin Klein maintain an in-house promotion division. Calvin Klein Incorporated uses its own in-house agency, CRK advertising. Figure 3.5 is an advertisement created by CRK advertising. Both the company and the in-house agency worked closely together to create a campaign that focused less on product and more on artistic images (Karimzadeh, 2006). The creative director for Calvin Klein Collection women's apparel had significant influence on the message and worked directly with the CRK advertising creative director to create concepts for the set and the styling. As the creative

director of Calvin Klein, Francisco Costa explained, "When you design a collection, you want to put forth an image that relates to it . . . it's naturally how it should go. All the inspiration of the pictures comes from when we started the collection" (p. 14). If a manufacturing or retailing company maintains promotion in-house, it is managed as a separate division of the corporation. Next, we consider the organization of an in-house promotion division.

⎯o PROMOTION DIVISION ORGANIZATION

The promotion division of a large retailing or manufacturing corporation is managed by a top executive with the title of vice president of promotion or creative director. This person may also be known as the vice president of marketing, fashion, or advertising, depending upon how the firm identifies this division. Although the titles of the functional division, as well as management designations, are not consistent from one firm to another, this vice president or creative director has the ultimate authority for any activities used by the company to stimulate the sale of products or services.

Typical promotion mix activities used by retail stores include advertising, fashion shows, special events, public relations, and visual merchandising. The promotion division communicates information about the store, its fashion image, and the products and/or services available to the public. The intent is to create awareness and interest so potential customers will come into the store.

The promotion division of a retail store is generally divided into four departments: advertising, fashion, public relations, and visual merchandising (Fig 3.6). The **advertising department** is responsible for planning, creating, placing the advertising in the media, and evaluating the effectiveness of ads. Depending upon the size of the retail firm, some or all of the creative aspects of advertising may be handled by store personnel. If the company is small or desires specialized work, the retail store may hire an advertising agency or media specialist. Most large retail corporations handle their own print ads.

FIGURE 3.6 Organization chart for the promotion division of a retail store.

The **fashion department** is involved in developing the fashion image for the company. The manager in charge of this department may have the title of fashion director or special events coordinator. Again, the titles may differ from one retail company to another. The job may differ slightly, but this individual and their staff cover all of the designer line openings and analyze the important trends for a season.

Once fashion trends are identified and purchased, the employees are informed about the trends and trained to sell them by members of the fashion office. These activities may be accomplished through training bulletins, in-store fashion shows featuring store employees, or video productions. Fashion shows and special events are then developed by the fashion staff to disseminate the current fashion message to potential consumers.

The **public relations department** has the responsibility for developing broad-range policies and programs to create a favorable public opinion of the firm. The public relations director uses publicity as one of the tools to create a positive public image. News releases are sent to the media to report community involvement. Working with a local charity to raise money for breast cancer research, by hosting a celebrity performance or using merchandising and design students for an annual fashion show, helps generate a favorable public image. The public relations office works on these types of projects.

Visual presentation of the store image and its merchandise is the primary function of the **visual merchandising department.** This department is involved in creating window and interior displays, developing signs and visual identity by presenting merchandise presentation in a particular style, and selecting merchandise fixtures and showcases. The responsibilities for the store planning, layout, and design are also assigned to this department. The director of visual merchandising heads the visual merchandising department.

The breakdown of the promotion division as outlined is typical for a large retail corporation. In smaller stores, all of the promotional functions as well as the other retail functions may be handled by the owner or manager. The size and complexity of the firm will demand versatility or require specialization of the personnel involved.

Promotion mix activities used by manufacturers also typically include advertising, direct marketing and interactive media, fashions shows, special events, and public relations. The organization of the promotion division of a large manufacturing organization would be similar to the organization of a large retailing firm with the exception of visual merchandising. That function is the responsibility of the showroom staff as part of the sales division.

Advantages of In-house Promotion

There any many reasons why retailing, manufacturing, or design companies maintain in-house promotion departments. One of the primary reasons is to maintain control over the creative message. Some companies believe that no outside firm can understand product or retail characteristics as well as the company producing or selling them.

Containing costs associated with promotion activities also contributes to the decision to maintain in-house divisions. Firms with large advertising expenditures pay large media commissions to outside agencies. With internal control, the commissions go to the in-house department or agency.

In-house agencies are able to focus on the specific market with greater clarity because of their familiarity with the company mission as well as its day-to-day operations. Promotion personnel are not distracted by working on promotion for another client's product. In addition, there are time savings, assured with tight control over the various processes.

Bad experiences with outside agencies in the past are another reason for maintaining in-house control. Problems may have occurred because of negligence or lack of proper follow-through. Other negative perceptions may have resulted after promotions planned by outside agencies did not live up to expectations. Whatever the reason for a bad experience, it may be impossible to overcome a negative opinion.

Cost savings, time savings, greater control, and coordination are all reasons firms cite for maintaining an in-house staff. Some companies simply believe that they are capable of doing a better job than an outside agency.

Advantages of Outside Agencies

Critics of the in-house system say that the promotion department cannot give the client an objective opinion of the promotional process and may not be able to provide the scope of services available from an outside agency. Agencies may have highly talented experts. They can provide a varied viewpoint with greater flexibility. In-house staff may become stale, working on the same products and services. Since the agency has a staff with a variety of backgrounds, it is able to create fresh and original approaches. Also, the outside agency can be terminated if the firm is not satisfied.

After weighing the pros and cons, the retailing or manufacturing firm may choose to use the services of an outside agency rather than maintaining an in-house promotion staff. In that case, the firm would hire an agency to handle the creative development and execution of promotion. It may also choose to hire a specialized marketing communications services firm, such as a professional fashion show production crew or public relations firm, to take care of those particular promotion needs. Next, we discuss the organization of advertising agencies and other types of specialized services available to clients.

──○ PROMOTION AGENCY ORGANIZATION

Advertising agencies are extremely varied in size and in the range of services provided. Some agencies are small one-person businesses, offering specific assistance. Other advertising agencies are huge companies with thousands of employees in several cities. This section looks at various types of agencies, types of services offered, and how they are organized. A full discussion of how agencies are compensated is in Chapter 6.

The world's top marketing organizations are featured in Table 3.1. As shown by the

TABLE 3.1   *Top 10 Worldwide Marketing Organizations*

Rank				Worldwide Gross Income		% Change
2005	**2004**	**Organization**	**Headquarters**	**2005**	**2004**	**2005–2004**
1	1	Omnicom Group	New York	$10,481.1	$9,747.2	7.5
2	2	WWP Group	London	10,032.2	9,645.1	4.0
3	3	Interpublic Group of Cos.	New York	6,274.3	6,387.0	−1.8
4	4	Publicis Groupe	Paris	5,107.2	4,777.3	6.9
5	5	Dentsu	Tokyo	2,887.8	2,940.6	−1.8
6	6	Havas	Suresnes (France)	1,808.0	1,866.0	−3.1
7	7	Aegis Group	London	1,577.6	1,373.6	14.9
8	8	Hakuhodo DY Holdings	Tokyo	1,364.0	1,372.4	−0.6
9	9	Asatsu-DK	Tokyo	444.8	473.3	−6.0
10	11	MDC Partners	Toronto/New York	443.5	316.7	40.0

Note: Revenue in millions of U.S. dollars.

Adapted from: Endicott, R., & Wylie, K. (2006, May 1). Agency report. *Advertising Age*, 77 (18). Retrieved June 26, 2006, from Business Source Premier database. Reprinted with permission. Copyright, Crain Communications, Inc., 2006.

data, much of the activity in marketing communications is conducted by four top marketing organizations with consistent rankings. Table 3.2 shows the world's top multicultural organizations. Rankings show movement indicating continuing market potential for Hispanic, African-American, and Asian-American promotion agencies.

Full-Service Agencies

A firm that offers a full range of marketing, communication, and promotion services is known as a **full-service agency.** This type of agency is involved in planning, creating, and producing advertising; selecting and buying media time or space; and evaluating advertising effectiveness. In addition to these primary advertising activities, the full-service agency is capable of handling such services as long-term strategic planning; production of sales promotion materials; sales personnel training; and design of packaging, trade show and exhibit space, and materials. Developing public relations programs and publicity materials can also be accomplished by this type of organization.

A full-service agency is made up of various departments that focus on the needs of the client. Most full-service agencies are organized around five basic functions: management and finance, creative services, media, research, and account management. Each functional division reports to the agency owner, president, or board of directors. A high degree of coordination among the functional areas is necessary for an agency to be successful, since many of the operations are interdependent. An example of an organizational chart for a full-service advertising agency is provided in Figure 3.7.

TABLE 3.2   *Top Multicultural Agencies*

Rank				Worldwide Gross Income		
2005	2004	Organization	Headquarters	2005	2004	% Changes 2005–2004
Hispanic						
1	1	Bromley Communications (Publicis)	San Antonio, Texas	$40,000	$39,000	1.3
2	2	Bravo Group (WPP)	New York, New York	39,400	37,500	5.1
3	4	GlobalHue (Interpublic)	Southfield, Michigan	36,260	32,120	12.9
4	3	Dieste, Harmel & Partners (Omnicom)	Dallas, Texas	35,000	31,000	12.9
5	11	Vidal Partnership	New York, New York	23,950	13,000	84.2
African-American						
1	1	GlobalHue (Interpublic)	Southfield, Michigan	$34,780	$29,630	17.5
2	NA	Carol H. Williams Advertising	Oakland, California	33,000	NA	NA
3	2	Burrell Communication Group (Publicis)	Chicago, Illinois	32,200	28,000	15.0
4	3	Uniworld Group (WWP)	New York, New York	14,309	12,826	11.6
5	8	Matlock Advertising & Public Relations	Atlanta, Georgia	8,532	4,960	72.0
Asian-American						
1	3	PanCom International	Los Angeles, California	$10,533	$8,500	23.9
2	1	Kang & Lee (WPP)	New York, New York	10,100	9,400	7.4
3	2	A Partnership	New York, New York	8,996	8,774	2.5
4	4	Admerasia	New York, New York	7,900	7,200	9.7
5	5	InterTrend Communications	Long Beach, California	7,170	7,015	2.2

Note: Revenue in millions of U.S. Dollars.

Adapted from: Endicott, R., & Wylie, K. (2006, May 1). Agency report. *Advertising Age*, 77(18). Retrieved June 26, 2006, from Business Source Premier database. Reprinted with permission. Copyright, Crain Communications, Inc., 2006.

Management and Finance Division

The **management and finance division** handles commercial operations similar to the responsibilities of the operations, finance, and control divisions of a retail store. This division deals with the internal business affairs including managing the office, billing clients, making payments to the various media, and controlling personnel issues. In addition to the basic administrative functions, the management and finance division is involved in generating new business by soliciting new clients.

Creative Services Division

The **creative services division** is the heart of a full-service agency. It is responsible for the creation and execution of the advertisements. Creating advertisements may involve many different people with very specific skills. In large full-service agencies with a number of clients, it takes a great deal of coordination to put together the creative services.

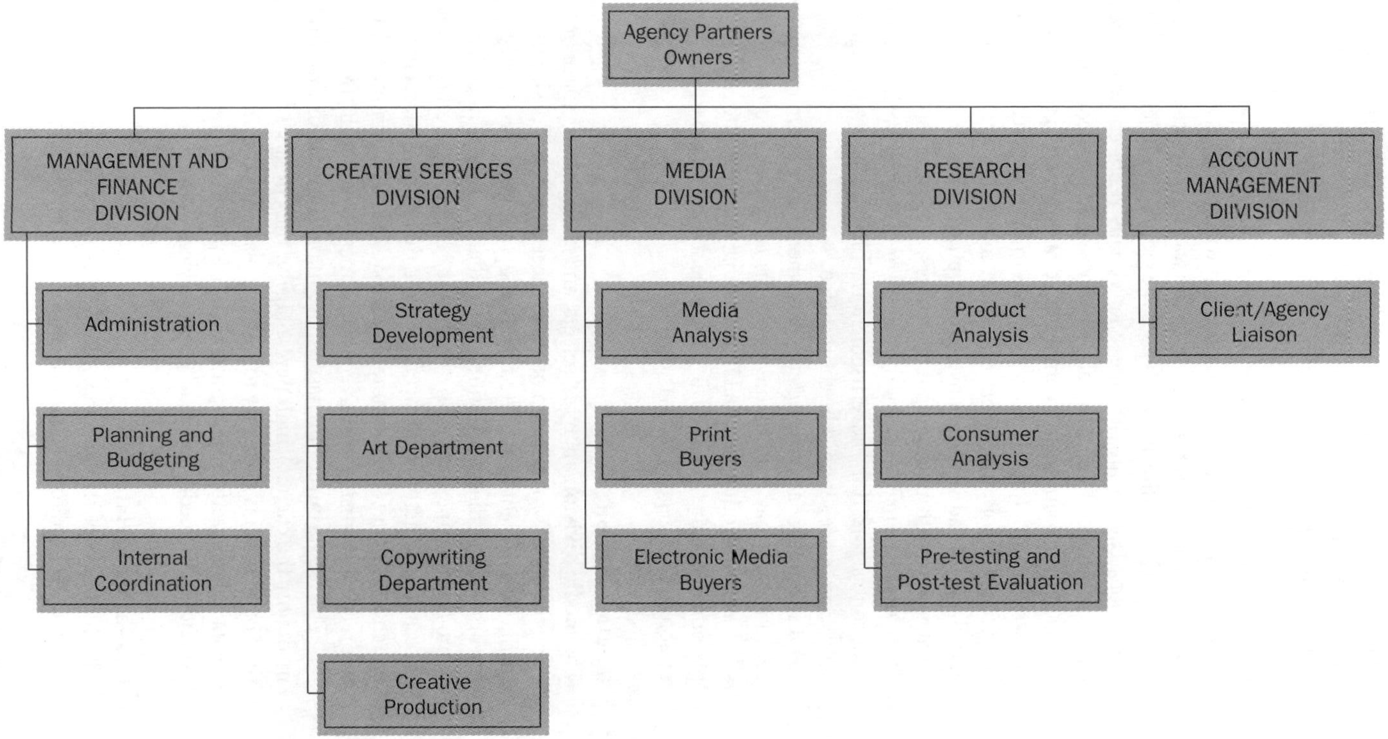

FIGURE 3.7 Organization chart for a full-service advertising agency.

```
                              Agency Partners
                                  Owners
                                     |
   ┌─────────────┬─────────────┬─────────────┬─────────────┬─────────────┐
   |             |             |             |             |             |
MANAGEMENT    CREATIVE       MEDIA        RESEARCH      ACCOUNT
AND FINANCE   SERVICES      DIVISION      DIVISION    MANAGEMENT
DIVISION      DIVISION                                 DIVISION
   |             |             |             |             |
Administration  Strategy     Media       Product      Client/Agency
               Development   Analysis     Analysis      Liaison
   |             |             |             |
Planning and   Art         Print        Consumer
Budgeting      Department   Buyers       Analysis
   |             |             |             |
Internal       Copywriting  Electronic   Pre-testing and
Coordination   Department   Media        Post-test Evaluation
               |            Buyers
               Creative
               Production
```

The creative services division is managed by the creative director, who sets the creative philosophy of the firm. He or she is directly involved in the creation of ads for the agency's most important clients.

The creative services area is generally divided into two functional areas: verbal and visual. Copywriters are responsible for the verbal communication message. They are involved in envisioning the message and writing the headlines, subheads, and body copy. The art department is responsible for the way the advertisement looks; this is the visual part of the ad. The art director supervises the graphic designers or artists in the development of the layouts. Layouts are drawings that visually represent what the advertisement will look like. For broadcast commercials, a storyboard is the equivalent of the layout, a series of frames or boxes similar to a comic strip that represents the commercial in still form. Artists and writers work together to develop ads to meet the creative strategy for a client.

Once the copy and layout have been completed and approved by the creative director and client, the ad is turned over to the production department. The production department works with photographers, printers, and other specialists to produce finished ads. These suppliers may work for the agency or they may work on a freelance basis as independent contractors. If the advertisement is a broadcast commercial, a video production crew, actors, and stage set must be coordinated.

In very large advertising agencies where there are many clients and types of projects, coordination may be difficult. These firms may have a **traffic department**, to organize all phases of production, making sure that the deadlines for creative services and media placement are met. The traffic department may be a part of the creative services, media, or account management division.

Media Division

The **media division** analyzes, selects, and contracts for space or time in the media, delivering the client's message. In order to meet the client's desire to reach a target market, the media department is expected to develop an appropriate media plan. Media specialists research the media to determine the audience and the rates. They review information on demographics, newspaper or magazine readership, radio listenership, television audience, and interactive audience. Knowing this information enables the media specialist to match the client with the suitable media. This division may also have the responsibility to pretest advertising effectiveness and measure overall effectiveness.

The media buyer purchases space in print media or time on broadcast or interactive media for the client. A high percentage of the client's advertising budget is spent buying time or space. It is necessary to justify a plan that communicates the message in the right media in a cost-effective manner. Box 3.1 provides an example of a traditional publisher expanding its media and marketing services.

Research Division

The function of the **research division** is to gather, analyze, and interpret information that will be used to develop promotional activities as was discussed in Chapter 2.

Account Management Division

The **account management division** provides the link between the client and the agency. The account executive is the agency representative who works with the client, interpreting the client's needs to agency personnel. He or she coordinates agency activities and presents the agency's ideas to the client. Once the client approves the plan, the agency puts that plan into action.

*Meredith to Buy Interactive-Ad Agencies: Purchases
to Augment Publisher's New Focus on Marketing Services*

In a sign of how the once-sharp dividing line between the media world and Madison Avenue is disappearing, publisher and broadcaster Meredith Corp. today announced its acquisition of two interactive-marketing agencies, giving it a significant presence in the ad world.

Meredith, whose magazine titles include *Better Homes and Gardens, Family Circle,* and *Ladies' Home Journal,* is spending an undisclosed sum to acquire Los Angeles-based digital-ad agency Genex and Arlington, Va., word-of-mouth-marketing firm New Media Strategies.

The acquisitions follow Meredith's purchase of Los Angeles-based interactive-marketing agency O'Grady Meyers, whose clients include Nestlé. The latest deals are the strongest signal to date that Meredith—confronting slowing growth in its core publishing and television businesses—is broadening its focus to include marketing services, one of the fastest-growing parts of the advertising industry. Even after these purchases, the Des Moines, Iowa, company is still on the prowl for other acquisitions to round out its marketing-services offerings, says Stephen Lacy, Meredith's president and chief executive.

"We believe the marketing services area will have a faster growth rate than either of the two traditional-media businesses," Mr. Lacy says. Meredith owns 26 magazines and 14 TV stations; publishing accounted for about 80% of the company's $1.6 billion in revenue.

The strategy pits Meredith against most of the big ad-holding companies, such as Omnicom Group and WPP Group, which lately have been pouring resources into services such as digital marketing and in-store advertising. Such services are increasingly demanded by advertisers, who are trying new techniques in response to changes in media. Meredith plays down its competitive threat to ad agencies, saying it won't enter the creative side of advertising.

Still, there used to be a clear division between media outlets such as newspapers, magazines and TV stations—which sold ad time or space—and ad agencies, which designed and placed the ads on behalf of marketers. One reason: the potential for conflicts of interest if an ad agency owned by a media company was seen to be unfairly directing ads to its sibling media outlets.

But the line has been fading for some time. Publishers such as Condé Nast, with *Vogue* magazine, and Wenner Media, with *Rolling Stone,* have in recent years started in-house ad units to lure more advertising dollars to their titles. Growth of the Internet has blurred the line more. New-media outlets such as Google have expanded aggressively into ad sales, while newspaper giant Gannett acquired Internet advertising technology firm PointRoll Inc.

For their part, Madison Avenue firms have taken tentative steps into new media. Last year, WPP Group invested in Wild Tangent, an online-game publisher with advertising capabilities, and Interpublic Group acquired a minority stake in Facebook, the online social network.

As advertisers spend more money online, they are increasingly open to being served by a new host of players, says Seth Alpert, managing director of AdMedia Partners, an investment bank that represented both Genex and New Media Strategies in the Meredith acquisitions.

Meredith began the transition in the late 1990s, producing custom and Internet-related publications for companies that include clothing retailer Charming Shoppes, Daimler-Chrysler, Carnival Cruise Lines and Century 21. These publications are largely marketing tools. For Charming Shoppes, for instance, owner of the Lane Bryant, Fashion Bug and Catherine's retail stores, Meredith produces a magazine for plus-sized women called *Figure.* Eventually Meredith realized it could do more for those clients in the new-media area if it acquired an agency. "With (Meredith's) custom publishing business, these guys are asking themselves, 'What is this business really? Isn't that marketing?' " Mr. Alpert says.

At the same time, Meredith's traditional business was encountering choppy conditions. Ad pages at *Better Homes and Gardens,* Meredith's flagship publication, fell 8.2% last year, according to the Publishers Information Bureau, although some other titles showed increases.

The expansion into marketing services already has begun to pay dividends. After Meredith acquired O'Grady Meyers, the agency began working with Charming Shoppes to create an online component for *Figure.* The site, to launch this spring, will include a community aspect, polls and blogs.

The three agencies together give Meredith a broad array of clients—O'Grady is strong in food, packaged goods and health care, whereas Genex's clients are predominantly in the automotive, financial-services and technology sectors. It also gives Meredith a full suite of interactive-marketing services, including Web-site development and word-of-mouth marketing, that will allow the company to compete on pitches for both traditional and digital work.

Building these capabilities internally would have taken a long time, "so we committed ourselves to the buy," says Jack Griffin, president of Meredith Publishing Group. He adds that the move into advertising won't create conflicts for Meredith's traditional business because the focus of the agencies is on creating websites and word-of-mouth campaigns rather than buying space in traditional media.

For the interactive agencies, becoming part of Meredith helps them compete with bigger ad companies. "The business is changing. You are no longer having a consistent client that wants independent nonintegrated services—they want integrated services that can cross all media," says Walter Schild, founder and CEO of Genex.

Source: Steel, E. (2007, January 10). Meredith to buy interactive-ad agencies. Copyright 2007 *Wall Street Journal*, p. 83.

──o OTHER TYPES OF SPECIALIZED SERVICES

Not every potential advertiser wants or can afford a full-service advertising agency. Many small agencies specialize in specific services. Alternatives to full-service agencies are as varied as the imaginations of the personnel involved.

Creative Boutiques

A **creative boutique** is an agency that provides only creative services, such as innovative layout, logo, or graphic design. A business that has an in-house promotion department may seek the spark of creative inspiration from an outside source. Sometimes a full-service agency may contract a creative services boutique to supplement its own departments when they are extremely busy. A creative boutique can be used on a fee-for-service basis, saving the agency, retailer, or manufacturer the cost of hiring additional temporary personnel.

Direct Marketing and Interactive Media Agencies

Direct marketing, one of the fastest-growing areas in integrated marketing communications (IMC) promotion, is communication by firms with their target audience through telemarketing, direct mail, interactive media, or other forms of direct-response promotion. As the interest in this form of promotion has grown, direct marketing agencies have been created to meet the advertisers' needs. **Direct marketing agencies** furnish an assortment of services including research, database management, creative assistance, direct mail, media services, and production capabilities. Database development and administration is one of the most significant roles for a direct marketing firm. Database marketing enables a firm to identify new customers and develop loyalty with existing customers. In addition to these services, some of the direct marketing agencies have expanded into production of infomercials.

The typical direct marketing agency consists of three divisions: account management, creative services, and media services. In some of the firms a fourth division focuses on database management. Similar to a full-service agency, the account management division works with clients to develop a direct-response program. The creative division is responsible for creating the direct-response message through its creative personnel, including copywriters, artists, and other members of the production team. The media division is in charge of media placement.

Direct marketing agencies are similar to full-service advertising agencies. They must seek new clients and provide satisfactory completion of projects. These agencies may be paid on a fee-for-service basis or by a commission.

Fashion Show Production Agencies

Fashion show production agencies provide the services necessary to present fashion shows. Organizations or retail stores may wish to utilize these services when they determine that it is not beneficial to maintain an in-house staff to complete these tasks. Frequently a modeling agency or modeling school has a division for fashion show production. Services may include any or all of the following: selecting and supervising models; reserving the show location; setting up the stage; hiring the lighting, music, and backstage personnel; and hiring the caterers. Services are normally paid on a contract basis.

Market Research Companies

While some advertisers maintain their own research departments, many do not. In that case they hire **market research companies** to help them understand the client's target customers. The research firm will gather objective information that will enable the advertiser to plan and evaluate its advertising and promotion programs.

Some firms with their own research divisions may actually hire a marketing research firm. The in-house staff may not have appropriate expertise to complete the analysis, or the advertiser may wish to have an outside opinion. Market research firms use such data-gathering techniques as in-depth interviews, focus groups, and market surveys.

Media Buying Services

Media buying services are independent firms that exclusively handle purchasing media time, primarily for radio and television. The nature of television has changed dramatically in the past few years. Not only does an advertiser need to consider local stations and major national networks, it must also consider the large number of independent networks and cable channels. Media buying services have found a niche, analyzing and purchasing media to meet the needs of their clients. Both full-service agencies and independent advertisers use media buying agencies. Because media buying services purchase large blocks of time and space, they are able to receive discounts. These price reductions can save small agencies or advertisers money on media purchases. Media buying services are paid a fee or commission on their work.

Public Relations Firms

In addition to the services of an advertising agency, a client may seek the services of a public relations firm. It is the responsibility of a **public relations firm** to manage the client's public image, the client's relationships with consumers, and other services. The task of the public relations firm is to evaluate the relationship between the client and the relevant publics, which might include some or all of the following: stockholders, suppliers, employees, government, labor groups, and the general public. Once the public relations firm has evaluated the appropriate constituents, it is able to determine how the client's operation impacts the public, develop public relations strategies and approaches, put these programs into action, and evaluate their effectiveness.

Typical tools and activities of a public relations firm involve conducting research, generating publicity, participating in community events, lobbying public affairs, preparing news releases and other communication information, designing and managing special events, handling crisis management, and supervising all areas of communication. As advertisers move to an IMC model, public relations is combined into the marketing communications mix. This helps to increase message credibility and save media costs. Public relations firms are frequently paid on a contract basis.

Sales Promotion Agencies

Sales promotion agencies specialize in developing and managing sales promotion programs, such as contests, refunds or rebates, premium or incentive offers, sweepstakes, or sampling programs. Although some large full-service advertising agencies have created their own sales promotion divisions, many independent sales promotion agencies serve the needs of their clients.

Sales promotion agencies will work with a client's advertising or direct marketing firm to coordinate sales promotion efforts with the advertising and/or direct marketing efforts. Services provided by a sales promotion agency might include research, planning, creative services, tie-in coordination, premium design and management, catalog development, and contest or sweepstakes management. Sales promotion agencies are generally compensated on a fee-for-service basis.

——o AGENCY EVALUATION

Because so much money is spent on promotion annually, the client is constantly evaluating the performance of its agency. Regular reviews of the agency's performance are necessary to prove accountability for the expenditures.

Unfortunately agency evaluation is often done on a subjective or informal basis. When sales go down or fail to meet expectations, it is easy to say it is the fault of the advertising agency. The next step is to fire the agency without considerations of the manufacturer's distribution problems or of prices that are out of line with the competition. A formal assessment system can help firms justify that their money is being spent efficiently and effectively.

A formal assessment system may simply look at the planning goals and objectives and how well these were met. However, market share or sales goals may not be the only criteria on which a firm is evaluated. Creative development, market research and ideas, cost controls, or effectiveness of a partnership relationship may also be tools to measure the agency/client relationship. As financial controls tighten and clients require more accountability, firms will require formal evaluation procedures. Figure 3.8 is a sample agency performance review based on a model from the Institute of Canadian Advertisers. Only after a client has conducted an objective evaluation of its promotion division or advertising agency should the decision to eliminate the division or fire the agency be considered. Understanding the reasons why advertisers switch or fire advertising agencies can help agencies avoid potential problems. Some of the most commonly cited reasons include:

- **Poor performance.** The client becomes unhappy with the caliber of the advertisement and/or the quality of service rendered.
- **Poor communication.** The account executive responsible for communication from the agency to the client does not work at supporting a positive working relationship hard enough.
- **Personnel changes.** The client hires a new manager who wants to work with an advertising firm that he or she has worked with in the past, or an account executive leaves an agency, taking the client along.
- **Interpersonal conflict.** Rapport between the account executive and client is insufficient

STRICTLY CONFIDENTIAL

Agency: _____ Evaluator: _____ Date: _____

1. CLIENT SERVICING

1.1 Agency Management Group

	Better Than Expected	As Expected	Below Expectations
Interest and knowledge of account			
Strategic output			
Response to issues			

Comments _____

1.2 Account Group
Strategic involvement

	Better Than Expected	As Expected	Below Expectations
Knowledge of market, competition			
Ability to interpret data			
Ability to provide sound recommendations			
Ability to communicate effectively			
Open-mindedness, objectivity			
Initiative, proactivity			
Quality of contributions from both cultures			

Comments _____

Operational involvement

	Better Than Expected	As Expected	Below Expectations
Coordination of Account Management teams			
Availability			
Promptness, accuracy in ongoing reports			
Effective, punctual meetings			
Efficient management of hours reports			
Sensitivity to budgets			

Comments _____

2. CREATIVE

2.1 Senior Management

	Better Than Expected	As Expected	Below Expectations
Establish structure to facilitate cultural synergy			
Interest, knowledge of account			
Strategic input			

Comments _____

FIGUre 3.8 A sample agency performance review.

2.2 Assigned Personnel
Creative development

	Better Than Expected	As Expected	Below Expectations
Working proactively within strategy			
Knowledge of market, competition			
Cultural team synergy in creative development			
Providing practical, expandable plans			
Ability to capitalize on research			
Well-organized presentation			
Quality of work:			
Copy			
Art			
Production			
Clearly defined lines of authority			
Accepting ideas, feedback in positive fashion			

Comments _____

3. MEDIA
3.1 Senior Management

	Better Than Expected	As Expected	Below Expectations
Interest, knowledge of account			
Strategic input			
Responses to issues, requests			

Comments _____

3.2 Assigned Personnel
Strategic involvement

	Better Than Expected	As Expected	Below Expectations
Knowledge of market, audiences, products/services, objectives			
Use of media research			
Strategic input			
Providing innovative, imaginative media plans			
Keeping advertiser up to date on media trends, developments			

Comments _____

4. OVERALL ASSESSMENT OF AGENCY

	Better Than Expected	As Expected	Below Expectations

Agency's major strengths:

_____

Areas that require improvement:

_____

FIGURE 3.8 (*continued*)

for them to continue working together. Personality differences and dissimilar work styles have led to friction.

- **Conflicts of interest.** As many industries including corporate retailing undergo significant changes in ownership due to mergers and acquisitions, accounts are lost due to a conflict of interests.
- **Declining sales.** Perhaps the most common reason for leaving an agency is static or weakening sales. Advertising and promotion are blamed for the problems and a new agency is hired to bring in a new approach.

The agency should be looking for signs in a changing marketplace and be able to adjust plans to meet current conditions and demands. Some of the conditions may be avoidable; others may be beyond the control of the agency. Those conditions that can be controlled require attention by the agency; however, sometimes a change may become necessary. The agency or the client may discontinue the associations, leaving both companies to seek new affiliations.

───○ HOW AGENCIES GAIN NEW CLIENTS

A business relationship between a client and an agency may be initiated by either party. An advertiser may wish to change to a new agency for any of the reasons listed earlier. An agency seeks new clients through the following methods:

- **Referrals.** Many agencies obtain new clients by recommendations from existing clients, media representatives, suppliers, or other agencies unable to handle additional business. By providing good service to the various people involved in promotion, agencies gain recognition and new clients.
- **Solicitations.** Agencies directly request the business of a new client. The head of the agency or a new business development group within an agency searches for and establishes contact with potential clients using solicitation letters, making cold calls, and following up on leads. Solicitations may be conducted through advertising in trade publications.
- **Presentations.** A potential client invites an agency to make a speculative presentation. This allows the agency to present information about its experience, personnel, capabilities, operating procedures, and previous work. In this formal presentation, the agency proposes a tentative communication program after investigating the client's current situation. Because these types of presentations are expensive in terms of time and preparation, without any guarantee of obtaining any new business, agencies are not fond of competing for clients in this manner. Nevertheless, many agencies participate in this form of appeal for new business by choice or competitive necessity.
- **Public relations.** Agencies provide pro bono (at cost or free) services to civic, social, or charitable organizations to gain respect within the community. Participation in these activities can lead to new business contacts.
- **Image and reputation.** Agencies that create successful campaigns are respected and are often approached by potential clients because of this reputation. Entering contests and winning awards are other methods of gaining recognition and enhancing the image of the agency. Box 3.2 details how an agency with a quirky reputation is attracting new clients.

───○ PROFESSIONALISM

According to *Webster's New World Dictionary*, a **professional** is engaged in a profession worthy of high standards. Thus, **professionalism** implies work of the highest quality or

BOX 3.2

A Mainstream Brand Tiptoes Toward the Quirky

Mix blue and red and you get purple. But what happens when you mix navy, as in the retailer Old Navy, with strawberry, as in an agency named StrawberryFrog?

That is the question Madison Avenue has been asking since June, when the Old Navy division of Gap announced that it had hired the New York office of StrawberryFrog to create a major part of its big back-to-school marketing campaign. The StrawberryFrog work, aimed at parents and teenagers, is now appearing on television and in magazines.

Old Navy is the first well-known American client for StrawberryFrog, which was founded in Amsterdam six years ago by Scott Goodson, a Canadian. Mr. Goodson, president and creative partner at StrawberryFrog, has been evangelistic in his belief that new types of agencies—more nimble and Web-based, less bureaucratic and hierarchical—are needed to help mainstream marketers to reach consumers in new ways.

"I've been talking about it for years," Mr. Goodson said in an interview. "There's definitely an understanding now that there's a changing landscape."

"It's not the soup du jour," he added. "It's a fundamental shift, both in what clients are looking for and how agencies are working."

StrawberryFrog was among the first in a new wave of smaller, mostly independently owned agencies remaking the advertising landscape. They specialize in campaigns that are distinctive creatively, often quirky, and that typically extend beyond traditional media like television commercials. Some of the agencies, like StrawberryFrog, bear distinctive names meant to signal their different approach; others in that vein include Amalgamated, Mother and Taxi. Other new wave agencies carry more traditional names, like Crispin Porter & Bogusky, McGarry Bowen and Shepardson Stern & Kaminsky.

Whatever they are called, the new agencies have a couple of things in common. One is their focus on business as unusual. The other is their growing success, often at the expense of mainline agencies that find themselves sharing clients with the upstarts—or worse yet, losing assignments to them.

Take Old Navy. For more than a year, the retailer had used the Marina del Rey, California, office of Deutsch, part of the Interpublic Group of Companies, as its lead creative agency. But in June, Old Navy executives said they would switch to a portfolio approach, working with a changing roster of agencies rather than a sole creative agency of record.

"We're looking to have a small group of highly creative agencies that we can pull ideas from," said Susan Wayne, executive vice president for marketing at Old Navy in San Francisco. "It's a better model to have a steady stream of new thinking, new ideas." Other large marketers taking similar tacks include Anheuser-Busch and Coca-Cola.

StrawberryFrog "has been one of the agencies gaining attention for creativity," Ms. Wayne said, which led Old Navy to meet with Mr. Goodson and other executives and decide "to partner with them on a project basis."

StrawberryFrog, which opened its New York office last year, was assigned the tasks of producing "mainline TV ads for moms and teens," Ms. Wayne said, while Deutsch was assigned duties that included creating commercials to run in movie theaters, online ads, and CD-ROMs.

Subsequent assignments will also be made on a similar basis, she added. She declined to discuss a report in the trade publication *Adweek* that Deutsch had been awarded the duties to create a campaign for the holiday shopping season.

The first Old Navy commercial from StrawberryFrog, which began running July 28, departs significantly from the retailer's recent style of focusing spots on popular songs. The commercial is set in a diner whose only customers are mothers with children.

As the commercial unfolds, viewers soon realize it is not a typical diner: The cooks and waitresses are serving up children's back-to-school clothing, not food, which is being delivered on plates and trays as if it were meat loaf or mashed potatoes.

"It's based on the look and feel of a classic American diner, but with an Old Navy spin on it, a wink and a twist," Ms. Wayne said.

Asked how much she and other Old Navy executives liked the StrawberryFrog idea for the commercial, she replied, "We obviously liked it enough to produce it and put it on air for back-to-school." This is an important time of year for Old Navy, which has been struggling in recent months to stimulate flat or declining sales.

A second Old Navy commercial from StrawberryFrog, aimed at teenagers, is scheduled to start running Thursday. Print ads are already appearing, in September issues of magazines like *Cosmo Girl, Elle Girl, Teen People,* and *Teen Vogue,* in the form of four-page inserts promoting a line of pants called Big Color Cords.

Old Navy is among several familiar brands that StrawberryFrog was recently named to handle, joining a client lineup that includes Asics Tiger, Ikea, Mitsubishi, Pfizer, and Sara Lee. Other recent arrivals include Heineken, for a soccer-themed ad assignment in Europe; Diet Coke, also in Europe; and Harris-Direct, the online brokerage owned by the BMO Financial Group.

"We were looking to get together with an agency that had an approach to the marketplace close to ours and was good at generating ideas from a creative standpoint," said Charles N. Piermarini, president and chief executive at HarrisDirect in Jersey City.

"We're a challenger brand in our space and Strawberry-Frog is a challenger brand in its space," he added. "In a cluttered space, we wanted to make sure we're working with someone with the ability to help set us apart."

However, the online brokerage space is soon to get less cluttered. HarrisDirect and the E*Trade Financial Group surprised Wall Street yesterday with a deal for E*Trade to acquire HarrisDirect for $700 million. E*Trade has its own agency, BBDO Worldwide in New York, part of the Omnicom Group, and the HarrisDirect brand name is likely to "go under the E*Trade umbrella" at some point after the acquisition is completed, said Pam Erickson, a spokeswoman for E*Trade in Boston.

Asked for a comment yesterday about the deal, Mr. Goodson replied that it was "a big surprise."

"One reason we built StrawberryFrog to be agile is that the world is the way it is," Mr. Goodson said. Although "you can't predict the future," he added, the agency was founded on a "flexible model that can grow and morph and shrink according to market conditions."

Meanwhile, Mr. Goodson said he remained optimistic about the agency's chances in several big reviews. Trade publications have reported that StrawberryFrog is a finalist for worldwide accounts from the Credit Suisse Group and the Heineken brand.

Source: Elliott. S. (2005, August 9). A mainstream brand tiptoes toward the quirky. *New York Times*, p. C7.

standards. The status associated with professional work should not be ignored. Sloppy, incomplete work or a lack of attention to detail cannot be accepted in promotion. Only people who are willing to work with high professional standards should consider careers in this field.

Many individuals, from merchandising or design students to member of charitable organizations, may have had opportunities to participate in a variety of fashion shows. A well-planned and well-organized fashion show is a fun and rewarding experience, but fashion show planners who leave everything to the last minute cause only stress and frustration among all of the participants. The same thing is true for other promotion activities. It is a pleasure to work in an atmosphere of quality and professionalism, but it is frustrating to work with people who do not take such activities seriously.

Promotional work almost always requires participation from a variety of people, making professionalism a necessity. In addition, teamwork is a requirement. From the individuals involved in establishing the objectives, plans, and budgets to the personnel concerned with creative ideas and implementation, each person has strengths necessary to contribute to an effective promotional campaign. A promotion team is only as good as its weakest link. If details are overlooked and contingencies not considered, the professionalism of the strongest team members will be forgotten.

Successful people in the promotion industry have many similar personal and professional characteristics. Such people are good planners with the ability to follow through in a prompt and timely manner. They do not leave details until the last minute, and they consider contingencies as a normal function of their jobs. What if there is a big snowstorm in New York and the celebrity commentator is stranded at the airport unable to arrive at the store in Chicago for a personal appearance? The promotion professional prepares for the unexpected and finds a substitute. A positive attitude and sense of humor are helpful when the unforeseen occurs.

Creativity is another attribute of successful promotion professionals. An artistic eye and a flair for the unusual are beneficial. Customers are inspired to make a purchase by an artistic visual merchandise presentation or an inventive advertisement. Successful promotion personnel take the initiative to plan and organize the project in an enterprising manner, bringing all of the elements together.

Successful promotion personnel are able to work under pressure with long or erratic hours to meet very short or unanticipated deadlines. If a client's competition offers a significant price break, how will the client want to respond? It may be necessary to develop a complete new advertisement or commercial to be broadcast within 24 to 48 hours.

Despite being a challenging, competitive, and stressful career, the appeal of working in such a dynamic part of the business world pulls many individuals into careers in the promotion industry.

A variety of professional organizations assist in offering educational opportunities through training, workshops, or seminars. These organizations often provide networking opportunities for professionals and encouragement to students preparing to enter the professions. Those organizations may be oriented to the academic or the professional world. Some professional groups require entrance examinations. To participate in other groups, potential members need sponsorship from an active member. Next, we look at a few of the various organizations in which members can obtain professional or academic contacts.

Professional Organizations

The **Fashion Group International** (**FGI**) is a global nonprofit professional organization with more than 6,000 members in the fashion industry and related fields. FGI has the primary goal of advancing professionalism in the field of fashion and related lifestyle industries. This organization provides a variety of networking and educational opportunities through regional chapters. Fashion executives gain membership status only after being sponsored by a current member. Through the Fashion Group Foundation (FGF), members promote educational programs devoted to fashion and related businesses by creating and awarding scholarships, establishing internship programs, and providing career counseling services, sponsorship of seminars, and other educational activities. This group also supports public service activities, such as career days with design or merchandising competitions for students held by various regional groups, including Dallas, Denver, and New York.

In the closely related field of interior design, the most well-known professional organization is the **American Society of Interior Designers** (**ASID**). With more than 30,000 professionals, students, and manufacturers as members, the organization provides a common identity forum for those who work in interior-design-related fields. The mission of the association is to promote design excellence through professional education, market expansion, information sharing, and creation of a favorable environment for the practice of interior design. Professional members must pass the National Council for Interior Design Qualifications (NCIDQ) exam created by members. Students may join collegiate chapters.

The **Association for Women in Communications** (**AWC**) began as a sorority of seven female journalism students at the University of Washington. It has evolved into an organization with professional and student chapters, representing the following disciplines: print and broadcast journalism, television and radio production, film advertising, public relations, marketing, graphic design, multimedia design, and photography (Fig. 3.9). The related disciplines continue to expand following newer media trends. Newsletters, a quarterly magazine called *Matrix*, and professional conferences assist members in making international contacts and keeping up-to-date with the constantly changing communications industry.

Several organizations provide professional membership to the graphic design and visual communications industries. Many of these originations also offer student participation and design competitions for students and/or professional members. One such group is the **American Institute of Graphic Arts** (**AIGA**).

FIGURE 3.9 Homepage from the Association for Women in Communications.

Academic Organizations

Many of the goals and benefits of academic organizations are similar to those of the professional groups previously identified. Networking and improving professionalism for the industry are the primary concerns. Additionally, academic organizations provide members, who are normally teachers and professors, the opportunity to share academic research.

The **International Textile and Apparel Association (ITAA)** is an organization of professors of textiles, apparel, merchandising, costume history, cultural aspects of apparel, fashion and textile design, and related disciplines. The group sponsors an annual conference at which members of the organization share information regarding the future of the organization and its disciplines, technology, leadership, networking, teaching, research, and service ideas. The group distributes newsletters, research journals, and conference proceedings each year.

The **American Collegiate Retailing Association (ACRA)** consists of faculty and administrators at four-year baccalaureate and graduate degree-granting accredited colleges or universities. Professors of merchandising and marketing who are interested in furthering educational opportunities in the field of retailing make up the membership. The group sponsors an annual spring conference at which members present current research, network, and visit sites of interest to retailing educators. Each January ACRA members are invited to participate in the **National Retail Federation (NRF)** Annual Convention and Expo, held in New York City (Fig. 3.10). ACRA holds a business meeting and research presentations during the NRF convention that features internationally

FIGURE 3.10 Homepage for
the National Retail Federation.

FIGURE 3.10 Homepage for the National Retail Federation.

known retailing experts making presentations. The expo also provides industry suppliers an opportunity to present their latest products and innovations

ACRA is closely related to other academic and professional resources and organizations such as the **European Association of Education and Research in Commercial Distribution (EAERCD),** the **Academy of Marketing Science (AMS),** the **Canadian and European Institutes of Retailing and Services Studies (CEIRSS)**, and the **American Marketing Association (AMA).** Many of the academic and professional organizations have developed Internet websites.

───o AWARDS

One way organizations and associations can provide feedback and recognition for the professionalism, creativity, and hard work associated with developing effective promotional campaigns is through the awards process. A variety of industry trade associations and specialized services establish criteria for acknowledging and honoring outstanding promotional performance. These awards are presented on an international, national, regional, or local level. The awards discussed here give only a sampling of the various tributes paid to promotion executives and their creative messages. They in no way comprise a complete list of all the awards associated with the promotional industry.

The most familiar international prizes given for excellence in the advertising industry are the Clio Awards. Established in 1959, the Clio Awards have formally recognized accomplishment in advertising and design. With permanent representation in more than 36 countries, this truly is international recognition. Clios recognize outstanding performance in print advertising, package design, radio, television/cinema, hall of fame, integrated media, and the World Wide Web categories. Clio Award winners are profiled in a showcase reel, containing annual award-winning commercials.

In 1968, the New York chapter of the American Marketing Association started presenting EFFIE Awards, national awards to honor effective advertising. The EFFIEs are based upon creative achievement of advertising campaigns that meet and exceed the advertiser's objectives. Because these awards focus on advertising campaigns that succeeded in reaching their sponsor's objectives, the receipt of an EFFIE represents confirmation of advertising effectiveness. Award winners in more than 40 categories are selected by professionals from advertising management, research, media, and other creative fields. The awards have expanded into nine European and Latin American countries with plans to extend to other international markets. "The Dove Campaign for Real Beauty," created by Ogilvy & Mather, won the 2006 grand EFFIE award recognizing the most effective marketing communications campaign (Fig. 3.11).

The institute of store planners and *VM+SD* magazine sponsor an annual International Store Interior Design Competition. With 18 categories, such as traditional department store, shop within an existing hardlines store, jewelry store, or manufacturer showroom, designers or design teams working on retail projects can compete for this award. Winners are featured in a *VM+SD* magazine article and honored for their store design projects.

The fields of visual merchandising and identity are also supported by the Planning and Visual Education Partnership (PAVE), a nonprofit alliance consisting of the National Association of Display Industries (NADI), the Society of Visual Merchandisers (SVM), the Institute of Store Planners (ISP), and *VM + SD* magazine. PAVE sponsors an annual student design competition in addition to other activities to educate and motivate retail management, visual merchandisers, store planners, architects, specifiers, manufacturers, and students. By encouraging interaction among the various constituencies, PAVE sponsors seminars and fund-raisers with proceeds targeted to financial aid and student internships. The design competition, open to students enrolled in two-year or four-year academic programs, awards cash prizes to winners of first, second, or third place in each category.

FIGURE 3.11 The 2006 grand EFFIE award "Dove Campaign for Real Beauty."

summary

- Clients, promotion department or agency employees, media representatives, and suppliers are the participants involved in promotion. Clients, persons, or organizations seeking recognition for their products or services create in-house promotion departments or hire outside agencies to assist in achieving promotional goals.

- The tasks necessary for successful promotion are administration, planning, budgeting, coordination, and creation. Specialists or generalists with an overview of the client's needs may accomplish these tasks.
- Retail stores are organized in a manner first established by Paul Mazur. Each store must be able to accomplish the essential jobs of merchandising, operations, financial control, and promotion.
- The promotion division may also be called the advertising, marketing, or public relations division, depending upon the retail firm. In addition to the responsibility for promotion, this division is in charge of advertising, fashion image, public relations, special events, and visual merchandising.
- A full-service advertising agency is organized around five basic functions: management and finance, creative services, media, research, and account management.
- Firms offering specialized services may be used to meet the specific needs of the client. These firms include creative boutiques, direct marketing agencies, fashion show production agencies, market research companies, media buying services, public relations firms, and sales promotion agencies.
- Evaluating an agency's performance should involve a regular and formal process. If expectations have not been met, the client and agency relationship may be dissolved by either group.
- An advertising agency seeks new clients by referrals, solicitations, presentations, public relations, or maintaining a positive image and reputation.
- Work of the highest professional quality is expected in this highly competitive field. Individuals and companies can benefit from participating in professional organizations related to their specialties. Awards and competitions allow professionals to demonstrate their abilities and receive recognition from others.

key terms

account management division
administration
advertising agencies
advertising department
branch operations division
budgeting
clients
coordination
creation
creative boutique
creative services division
design division
direct marketing agencies
fashion department
fashion show production
   agencies

financial control division
full-service agency
factor
human resources division
information technology
   division
management and finance
   division
market research
   companies
media buying services
media division
media organizations
media representatives
merchandising division
operations division

organizational chart
planning
professional
professionalism
production division
promotion division
public relations
   department
public relations firm
research division
sales division
sales promotion agencies
suppliers
traffic department
visual merchandising
   department

key organizations

Academy of Marketing Science (AMS)
American Collegiate Retailing Association (ACRA)
American Institute of Graphic Arts (AIGA)
American Marketing Association (AMA)
American Society of Interior Designers (ASID)
Association for Women in Communications (AWC)

Canadian & European Institutes of Retailing and Services Studies (CEIRSS)
European Associations of Education and Research in Commercial Distribution (EAERCD)
Fashion Group International (FGI)
International Textile and Apparel Association (ITAA)
National Retail Federation (NRF)

QUESTIONS FOR DISCUSSION

1. What are the fundamental tasks of promotion personnel and the personal characteristics needed for success?
2. How is a retail store typically organized?
3. How does a promotion division function within a retail environment?
4. Why would a company seek an outside advertising agency to handle its promotional activities?
5. How is a full-service advertising agency typically organized?
6. What are specialized agencies, and when are they used?
7. Why does a client fire or leave an agency or specialized service?
8. Why is professionalism important in creating promotions?

ADDITIONAL RESOURCES

Belch G. E., & Belch, M. A. (2007). *Advertising and promotion* (7th ed). New York: McGraw-Hill/Irwin.
Keiser, S. J., & Garner, M. B. (2003). *Beyond design*. New York: Fairchild Publications.

ANNUAL PUBLICATIONS

Agency Report. (Published annually). *Advertising Age*. New York: Crain Communications Inc.

REFERENCES

Conti, S. (2006, June 20). Asprey appoints creative director. *Women's Wear Daily*, p. 2.
Karimzadeh, M. (2006, June 19). Calvin Klein's new-look advertising for fall. *Women's Wear Daily*, p.14.
Mazur, P. (1927). *Principles of organization applied to modern retailing*. New York: Harper & Brothers.

FIGURE 4.1 Fashion Week at
Bryant Park.

CHAPTER 4

Promotional Aspects of Fashion Forecasting

New York's fashion shows have long been the province of an exclusive clique of magazine editors, retail buyers, and celebrities who preview designer collections twice a year. But lately, a more buttoned-down set is infiltrating the tents at Manhattan's Bryant Park: Wall Street suits.

"With fashion being such an important driver of [retail] sales these days, fashion matters more than people realize," says Deborah Weinswig, a managing director at Smith Barney who follows the retail industry.

The shows not only influence retailers' buying decisions but can affect the in-house apparel collections they produce themselves. At J.C. Penney Co., for instance, Ms. Weinswig notes that 40 percent of sales come from its own labels. So by attending the shows, she can evaluate how well retailers tap into trends, and turn out products based on them. "If there's a lot of strong fashion out there, they might be able to get the new looks into the stores before the designers do," says Ms. Weinswig. So far, she's encouraged by a spate of very wearable clothes, such as flowing, crushed-velour "fairy tale" tops and classic bottoms that can be translated into mainstream clothing for department stores.

Source: O'Connell, V. (2005, February 8). Style & substance: Wall street's catwalk fancy; bankers hit fashion shows for intelligence, intrigue; runway as 'due diligence'. *Wall Street Journal*, p. B1.

> **After you have read this chapter you should be able to:**
>
> Define various types of forecasting and identify the personnel involved in this activity.
>
> Correlate the business functions of forecasting and promotion.
>
> Identify trend resources in the retail markets.
>
> Discuss theme development in promotion planning.

When financial advisors like Deborah Weinswig act as fashion forecasters they sometimes become de facto players on the promotional team. Weinswig's excitement in spotting a trend of wearable clothes popular with J.C. Penney customers and her prediction that Penney's in-house lines could beat the designers to the racks bodes well for sales at the department store and for the garment's manufacturers. Of course, financial advisors aren't always so enthusiastic; sometimes fashion forecasters work against promotions. Understanding who makes fashion forecasts, how they make them, and what they do with their predictions is essential to a successful promotional strategy.

This chapter begins by introducing fashion forecasting and those involved in the business of forecasting. Next, we discuss the mutual dependence between forecasting and promotion. Although promotion specialists rely on media outlets to communicate trend messages, these same professionals depend on media outlets as sources for identifying and forecasting future trends. The next section of this chapter examines forecasting resources available to raw materials producers, designers and manufacturers, and retailers. In the final section of this chapter, we discuss theme development. Themes based on forecasts are important elements of promotion campaigns. A discussion about conducting a forecast as an oral and a visual presentation concludes the chapter.

——○ THE ROLE OF FORECASTING

Forecasting is the activity of anticipating what will happen next. A **trend** is the general direction in which something is moving. Generating forecasts based on trend analysis has become a necessary management function in many industries. Using all available resources, a forecaster predicts the future. A stock analyst will forecast the direction of the stock market. A television meteorologist will predict the weather. Although predictions are made, forecasters must be ready to change course if the unexpected occurs.

Fashion forecasting specifically looks at fashion trends, and fashion forecasters attempt to predict what consumers will want to wear during the upcoming season. Will consumers want a classic look, a retro style, or something that is new, innovative, or unique? While it may seem like an impossible task, fashion forecasters use various social and behavioral sciences techniques to anticipate the direction and movement of fashion.

A **fashion trend** is the visible direction in which fashion is moving. It may be a color, a fabric, or a style characteristic apparent for the coming season. A major trend is based on well-researched market information, has high sales volume potential, and test markets with positive results against direct competition. Analyzing fashion forecasts is similar to analyzing the weather or the stock market. A fashion director and buyer will decide on the general trends of a season to meet the expected needs of the store's target customer.

In Chapter 2, we discussed the well-defined fashion cycle of a trend. A trend is given birth when a small group of leading-edge people get wind of the idea and try it. As the trend grows, it is discovered by more people. Articles are written about the trend and it is shown on broadcast spots. Key items emerge during this stage of the fashion cycle. A **key item** is a best-selling trend with strong customer demands, available at several different price points, and produced by many different manufacturers.

As the trend reaches maturity, it is seen at chain stores in malls; it declines to the racks at deep-discount outlets; and it dies when it is available at flea markets. A very short-lived trend is considered a **fad.** A fashion fad has quick acceptance and departure within the fashion cycle. A trend that endures over a long period of time, undergoing only minor changes as it progresses through the fashion cycle, is called a **classic.** But where do trends come from?

Linda Allard, designer for the Ellen Tracy lines, was once asked in an interview if all designers got together and decided what the trends were going to be. It was true, as the questioner implied, sometimes there appeared to be a conspiracy when every designer showed the same color, style, and silhouette for a season. Trends appear to be similar because the sources for inspiration are similar. Trends emerge from:

- **Society.** A trend can come from high up, the studios of top designers, or way down, what kids are wearing on the street.
- **Culture.** It can be global in its implications, or extremely individual, sparked by a rock star's wardrobe.
- **Designers.** Trends can come from the lifestyles of the designers themselves. The New York or Paris fashion scene is a tight-knit community that shares a wealth of common experiences. Designers go to the same museum exhibits, movies, and restaurants, and are going to be influenced by the same images.
- **Raw materials vendors.** Fabric fairs play a vital role, although they're not that well known outside the industry. Held regularly in various countries, the fairs are where designers and manufacturers go to see the latest fabrics.

- **Publicity.** Headlines are almost as important as hemlines when it comes to style decisions.
- **Consumers.** The biggest motive in the creation of any trend is cash. New styles mean new reasons to make a purchase. Trends are the lifeblood of the fashion business. They create consumer excitement and encourage customers to visit stores and buy new merchandise.

Consumer behavior is one of the most meaningful factors used to project trends. What better place to learn about consumers than from message sponsors and media who have an acute awareness of consumer behavior and can provide us with insight about society? Through research, promotion executives know what people are buying and what influences the purchase, where and how people are spending their time, what people are thinking and how society reacts, and what impact the government and the economy have on the consumer.

The current marketplace is driven by consumers. Trends appear when consumers take action in the marketplace as a reaction to work, home, or society. Trend identification is based on professional analysis of consumers, the marketplace, the economy, and past experiences. Tracking trends to determine what will come next is the only way for many firms to stay ahead of the competition.

Since forecasts are predictions about the future based on research and best guesses, past statistics are helpful, but will not guarantee the future. Forecasters know a range of possibilities that may occur to confirm or oppose a projection. They select the best guess among many plausible alternatives. As a result, business leaders often plan for a future that never arrives, while a different future passes them by (Mahaffie, 1995). History is filled with forecasts that did not work out in the way the predictor intended. In 1876, Western Union predicted that the telephone would have too many shortcomings to be seriously considered a means of communication. Thomas Watson, chairman of IBM in 1943, predicted that there would be a world market for maybe five computers (Krantz & Cole, 1996).

The most common error in forecasting is overestimating the time it will take for forecasts to be implemented into society. Also, forecasters underestimate the wider implications, and secondary effects that any forecast has on people and situations. John Mahaffie (1995), an associate with Coates & Jarratt, Inc., a Washington, D.C., research firm specializing in the study of the future, offers eight reasons why forecasts fail:

- **Failure to examine assumptions.** On what does the forecast rest? Are there specific social or technological developments that will be required for the forecast to come true? Does the forecast assume things that seem unlikely, given your view of human nature or economic realities?
- **Limited expertise.** Some enthusiasts overshoot their expertise when making a forecast.
- **Lack of imagination.** Other forecasters have the opposite problem. They fail to explore more interesting possibilities for the future out of conservatism or timidness of thought. These tendencies misguide a forecast just as easily as overenthusiasm.
- **Neglect of constraints.** Forecasters are obliged to make predictions that are within the realm of possibility. This failure is summed up in the idea that "people just are not going to go for that."
- **Excessive optimism.** An excessively optimistic forecaster does not weigh the "downside risk." If a forecast does not consider the offsetting or limiting factors in a given potential future, it is likely to be flawed.
- **Reliance on mechanical extrapolation.** Extrapolation means to estimate by extending known information. This works for identifiable limiting factors such as population

growth or market penetration. However, forecasters who use it for unknown factors miss the acceleration of the forecast.

- **Premature closure.** When developing forecasts, some researchers finish their work before all factors are considered. As a result, the more creative and far-reaching possibilities are never explored. Fear may be the reason for early closure and other narrowness of thinking.
- **Overspecification.** The danger in making a concrete forecast, such as an exact statistic or an exact fashion trend for a future year, is that it pushes the science of forecasting beyond its capabilities. It is not possible to have control over all variables that drive change, so no one can be utterly specific about most developments. The real value in forecasting is in showing the directions and characteristics of change.

For a forecast to be useful, Mahaffie (1995) suggests considering the following elements:

- **A clear statement of purpose.** Why was the forecast made? The purpose should give a clear sense of how the forecast is meant to be taken. Is the forecast a mind-stretching exercise or is it highly probable?
- **Clear assumptions.** The technological and social assumptions on which the forecast depends should make it possible for users to evaluate the forecast and decide if they agree or disagree. Without clear assumptions, the users can only take the analyst's word that the forecast is plausible.
- **A time horizon.** Users cannot effectively interpret a forecast if they do not know when the developments it describes are supposed to happen. If no time frame exists, at least explain why.
- **Attention to discontinuities.** Discontinuities are breaks or gaps. Things that could speed up, slow down, or break the forecast should be discussed.
- **Adequate accounting for social and technological forces.** Social forces in technological forecasts, and technological forces in social forecasts, must be accounted for to ensure the full context in which developments will happen.

Any forecast that fails to cover these elements is suspicious, or at least flawed in its presentation. Users who demand forecasting to be a predictive science will be disappointed, but those who use forecasting as a tool to expand their thinking about change will be rewarded (Mahaffie, 1995). But who are these individuals willing to take risks and predict the future?

Forecasting Personnel

There are professional forecasters, and there are professionals who forecast as a responsibility of their job. As it is used in this chapter, a **forecaster** is a nonspecific title given to any individual within an organization who is responsible for trend identification and image. In this section, we first discuss **futurists**, who make long-range forecasts for many industries. Then, we turn our attention to professionals in the fashion and promotion fields. These professionals, called **fashion forecasters**, work for fashion forecasting services or the forecasting division within retail, manufacturing, or advertising firms.

Many other fashion and promotion professionals forecast as a routine part of their job. We discuss these individuals at the conclusion of this section. Job titles include but are not limited to the following: designer, fashion director, buyer, assistant buyer, creative director, fashion coordinator, fashion merchandiser, stylist, store manager, and owner.

Promotion specialists within promotion, advertising, and public relations departments who are involved with brand positioning and merchandise selection are also considered fashion forecasters.

Futurists

Futurists are self-proclaimed, forward-looking individuals who answer such questions as: Who will fight the next war in the Middle East? Where will the best jobs be next year? What will be the hot consumer-electronics products of the year 2010? Because the work futurists do is often categorized as economic forecasting or strategic analysis, profitability statistics are vague. However, it has become a very sophisticated business in high demand by such corporate giants as Coca-Cola, Pepsi, Monsanto, Avon, Rockport Shoes, General Mills, and Saatchi & Saatchi, among others.

Futurists have the ability to spot trends and translate them into real opportunities. They include successful people like Faith Popcorn of BrainReserve; Edie Weiner and Arnold Brown of Weiner, Edrich and Brown; and Vickie Abrahamson and Mary Meehan, cofounders of Iconoculture. These professionals, in addition to running successful consulting agencies, are popular media personalities and authors of best-selling books. Businesses hire futurists to help determine what new products and services consumers will buy.

Media outlets provide a major resource for the trend analysis conducted by futurists. Every month Weiner and Brown read dozens of publications looking for new and offbeat ideas. The employees of Iconoculture gather information from separate sources and compare notes for consensus (Tillotson, 1998). Popcorn and her staff check hundreds of magazines, books, and newspapers for research to pinpoint trends. These professional forecasters do not start trends; they communicate the trends they see in consumer behavior back to clients. Each identified trend provides an opportunity for a forward-thinking promotion executive to get ahead in the marketplace by providing something new and interesting to the consumer.

Fashion Forecasters

Professional fashion forecasters work for independent fashion forecasting services or forecast divisions within retail or manufacturing firms or advertising agencies. Forecasting services contract with clients to provide trend analysis information. Clients either subscribe to or hire a consulting service from the forecasting company. A forecasting division within a retail or manufacturing firm will provide the same services for its parent firm. Forecasting services operate at all levels of the fashion industry, assisting raw material producers, designers and manufacturers, and retailers. They include color and fiber associations, and independent firms that specialize in apparel categories or home furnishings. Cotton Incorporated, the Tobé Report, Doneger Group, and Promostyl are just a few examples of forecasting services. A listing of forecasting and reporting services is shown in Table 4.1.

The Tobé Report, published by Tobé Associates Incorporated, is one of the oldest forecast services, established in 1927. It publishes a weekly report containing illustrations, photographs, and editorials about merchandise trends for apparel and accessory markets. Fashion forecasters, including Tobé Associates, do not include advertising in their reports. This allows fashion forecasters to present a totally unbiased source of fashion information.

Many fashion forecasters work in international fashion centers to identify global trends. For example, Promostyl, a French-based forecasting service, has offices in Paris,

TABLE 4.1   *International Fashion and Color Forecasting Firms*

Firms	Headquarters	Web address
Carlin International	Paris	www.carlin-groupe.com/home_uk.html
Color Association of the United States	New York	www.colorassociation.com
Committee for Color & Trends	New York	www.color-trends.com/index.html
Cool Hunt	Los Angeles	www.coolhunt.net
Cotton Incorporated	New York	www.cottoninc.com
Doneger Group	New York	www.doneger.com
Fashion Forecast Services	Collingwood (Australia)	www.fashionforecastservices.com.au/
Fashion Snoops	New York	www.fashionsnoops.com
Fashikon	New York	www.fashikon.com
Here & There	New York	www.hereandthere.net
Next Trim	Pacific Palisades (CA)	www.nexttrim.com
NPD Fashionworld	Port Washington (NY)	www.npdfashionworld.com
Peclers Paris	Paris	www.peclersparis.com
Promostyl	Paris	www.promostyl.com
Snap Fashun	Los Angeles	www.snapfashun.com
Stylesight	New York	www.stylesight.com
Tobé Report	New York	www.tobereport.com
Trendzine	London	www.fashioninformation.com
Worth Global Style Network	London	www.wgsn.com
Zandl Group	New York	www.zandlgroup.com

London, New York, and Tokyo. Its forecasters attend trade shows, couture openings, and fabric fairs. They visit with new and established designers to learn where their inspiration comes from. Foreign publications are read and broadcasts are viewed for trend insights. Fashion forecasters watch consumers on the street to find out what merchandise and materials are selling fast, what merchandise boutiques cannot keep in stock, and what hot items from last season are out of fashion in the current season.

Fashion forecasters disseminate information about fashion trends through the use of fashion trend portfolios. A **fashion trend portfolio** is a series of visual boards, slides, videos, or kits, projecting major trends in silhouettes, fabrics, colors, patterns, accessory treatments, catchphrases, and theme ideas. Additionally, fashion trend portfolios may include color cards or swatches, fabric swatches, yarn samples, and sketches or photographs of the fashion look. Texture, print, pattern combinations, and other aspects of the fashion image are also included in the fashion trend portfolio. Figure 4.2 are photographs showing a fashion trend portfolio from Doneger Group. Preparing the elements of a fashion trend portfolio are discussed later in this chapter.

Fashion forecasters are responsible for discovering new trends and interpreting specific characteristics of the trend that will be profitable for the firm or client. A clear understanding of the target customer and brand position of the firm or client is critical to trend interpretation. Although the same trend may be identified, it will be interpreted quite differently for a specialty boutique versus a mass merchandiser. Typical products and services offered by fashion forecasting companies are listed in Figure 4.3.

FIGURE 4.2 Fashion trend portfolios from the Doneger Group.

Forecasters

Fashion and promotion professionals forecast as a routine part of their job within many advertising, designer, and retail firms. These experts within the organization determine the look of the firm. They include personnel from the fashion, promotion, advertising, or public relations departments, and divisional merchandise managers and buyers. Anyone involved in the brand positioning of a firm, including trend identification, merchandise selection, or image, is a forecaster.

Products and Services Offered by Fashion Forecasting Companies

- Archive Information from Previous Seasons
- Brand and Product Development
- Buzz from the Media and Entertainment World
- Color Trends and Forecasts
- Competitive Market Analysis
- Consulting Services
- Design Elements (Graphic and Print Trends)
- Design Tools (Sketches, Specs, Computer Programs)
- Fabrications (Fibers and Fabrics)
- Global Trend Research
- Key Items
- Newsletters
- Newspaper Clipping Services
- Promotional Strategies
- Retail Reports
- Retail Strategy
- Runway Reports
- Street Scene Reports
- Store and Merchandise Photographs
- Trade Show Analysis

Forecasters travel to domestic and international fashion centers to visit trade shows, manufacturers, and designers. They keep up-to-date by reading fashion publications and discussing potential trends with fashion editors. They subscribe to fashion forecasting services and watch their own customers to determine what is likely to be the next best seller for their store. Forecasters also analyze store sales. Tracking the success of a specific style, color, or silhouette will give management an idea of what might potentially sell in the future. Electronic tracking is an easily accessible tool to statistically chart hot sellers. In addition to a store's own sales, the competition's sales may be a reference in forecasting future trends.

──○ FORECASTING AND PROMOTION

Fashion forecasting and promotion are cyclical in nature. Fashion forecasters present upcoming trends to consumers through promotion channels. They review these same communication channels as resources to identify the next trend. Promotion is integral to this cycle.

Promotion as a Source

Promotion is the major communication tool used to inform consumers of the latest trends, as shown in Table 4.2. If you doubt this statement, compare the September issue of any fashion magazine with any other monthly issue of the same publication. What do you see? A very large fashion handbook illustrating fall trends in clothing, accessories, makeup, entertainment, food, and home fashions. Take a more in-depth look. The September issue will have more sponsors and more pages dedicated to advertising space than the other issues. Fashion forecasters, who have planned for this selling season

TABLE 4.2   *Top Media Influencing Women's Apparel Purchases*

Rank	Medium	Percentage
1	Newspaper Inserts	44.4
2	Word of Mouth	39.9
3	Direct Mail	34.0
4	Magazines	33.3
5	In-Store Promotions	33.1
6	Coupons	30.6
7	TV/ Broadcast	29.8
8	Newspapers	26.6
9	E-mail Advertising	22.0
10	Internal Advertising	17.2

Adapted from: Power of persuasion. (2006, January 19). *Women's Wear Daily,* p. 12.

months and years in advance, are now dependent on promotion strategies to accurately communicate the season's trends to the consumer. All elements of the promotion mix are used to communicate trend messages to consumers.

Promotion as a Resource

Fashion forecasters are also dependent on promotion as a major resource to discover new and upcoming trends for future seasons. Editors look at the competition to see what they identified as the hottest trend of the moment. Publications outside of fashion are reviewed to identify cultural trends that cross product categories. Electronic media, covering the entire spectrum of attitudes and lifestyles, are constantly monitored for the discovery of the next new look in apparel, body adornment, body modification, and numerous other characteristics that define current culture.

Reading fashion publications is essential for anyone involved in forecasting. As one of the most readily accessible resources, they provide insight to the creative directions of fashion leaders. Creative fashion presentations, trade publications, newspapers, business magazines, foreign publications, consumer fashion publications, CD-ROMs, Internet sites, and other media provide valuable news about fabrics, styles, silhouettes, colors, and fads. Consumer publications interpret the fashion scene based on their readership. *Seventeen* will interpret a style to attract Generation Y. The same trend may be presented on the cover of *Vogue* for a more sophisticated market. *Modern Maturity* may also highlight the trend, showing fashionable baby boomers wearing it.

There are numerous online sites that provide up-to-the minute fashion news to assist forecasters in discovering trends. Figure 4.4 is an example of the Fashion Group's international trend reports and fashion forecasts.

But how are trends introduced into the communication channel? In the next section we discuss the fashion industry market levels and explain the forecasting process from producer to consumer.

FIGURE 4.4 Forecast information is available through the Fashion Group International website.

The Trend Report
Fall/Winter 2005/06

NEW YORK London MILAN *Paris*

by Marylou Luther

Fall/Winter 2005 was a tipping point season, especially in Paris. Big voluminous clothes teetertottered with snug, narrow clothes. Shape and structure replaced bling and cling. Girly tipped over into girly-man. And something the French call exhausted elegance emerged as fashion's latest romantic involvement, replacing the sex-in-the-city culture of recent seasons.

The re-emergence of black was the first big tipoff that something was up, that something different was taking place, or, perhaps more accurately, that something was *about* to happen. Just as black helped to create the sober mood of the season, its dominance totally wiped out ethnic, boho and fashion by travel destination.

YSL Rive Gauche

Black is somber, yes. It also makes women look slimmer. It hides dirt and grime. And thanks to Mary-Kate and Ashley Olsen, who've made washing-and-wearing even the most expensive clothes a new fashion rite, black will stay black with a little help from Woolite's Dark Laundry.

Most of all, black is the color of chic. Think Duchess of Windsor, Audrey Hepburn. For fall, black takes on distinctive new dimensions through surface interest. Prada's black-on-black crochet embroideries and passementerie braids, Donna Karan's draping, twisting, shirring, ruching, whorling, Alberta Ferretti's embroideries, Sonia Rykiel's velvet face profiles on black wool, and Olivier Theyskens' bias ruffles tufted with mohair for Rochas all attest to a truly new dark victory over the blandness of black.

Alexander McQueen

While the fashion world debates whether or not it is really chic to be chic again, designers like Miuccia Prada, Nicolas Ghesquiere of Balenciaga, Theyskens of Rochas, Valentino, Donatella Versace, Giorgio Armani, Karl Lagerfeld for Lagerfeld Gallery, Rykiel, Ralph Rucci, Ralph Lauren, Marc Jacobs, Oscar de la Renta, Carolina Herrera, Narciso Rodriguez and Proenza Schouler have already made up their minds. Their precise tailoring, their structure, their carved silhouettes all invoke a new strict constructionist movement piqued by chic. While some of the fit-and-flare suits are obvious lookbacks at The New Look of 1947 and some pencil-skirted numbers recall Jacques Fath, they manage to look fresh and appealing because they are not literal reincarnations. Even the Ralph Lauren and Rochas designs that evoke the Edwardian era and La Belle Epoque appear believably of-the-moment.

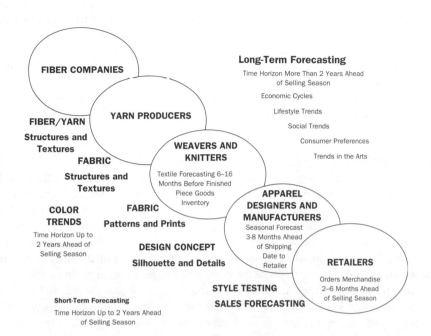

FIGURE 4.5 Short- or long-term forecasts are used by various members of the product distribution channel.

FORECASTING FROM PRODUCER TO CONSUMER

Fashion research takes place at all levels of the distribution channel. The distribution channel is the path through which goods are dispersed from raw material producers to retailers. Fiber companies, mills, converters, and yarn producers use research to develop new fibers, finishes, and construction methods. They research the use and care of products, along with color and design, in order to meet the needs of consumers. Designers research historical influences and important people, places, and events to determine future fashion direction. Apparel manufacturers use research to determine worldwide trends, fabrics and textures, colors, silhouettes and design details, and new products. Retailers use research to determine what products are selling and where buyers can source the goods; customer needs and wants; and elements of store operations, design, and security.

Each market in the distribution channel is responsible for forecasting trends to the next level. Adequate time must be allowed at each level to produce and promote goods. Fashion forecasts are considered to be short-term or long-term, depending on the participant's stage in the distribution channel. For example, fiber manufacturers in the primary market conduct long-term fashion forecasts about one to two years before merchandise arrives in a retail store, whereas retail buyers conduct short-term forecasts, normally two to six months prior to the arrival of products in the store. Evelyn Brannon, author of *Fashion Forecasting*, gives us a continuum of the short- and long-term forecasting done by apparel and textile channel members, as shown in Figure 4.5.

Primary Market Forecasts

Primary market producers are the earliest market to project upcoming trends. The **primary market** is composed of fiber companies, yarn producers, and weavers and knitters who sell to the secondary market, manufacturers and designers. They work six to 16 months in advance of the season to project color forecasts, fiber selection, and fabrication processes. Projections by primary market producers are unveiled to the secondary market manufacturers approximately six to eight months in advance of the selling season. Projections made by primary market producers are not seen by the retail market, until buyers make selections at market, approximately two to six months in advance of the selling season. The general public is not made aware of the apparent trend until goods are available for sale in stores or catalogs.

Color

Fashion projections in the primary market begin with color, the first element that catches the eye of the consumer. Color forecasts are made the farthest in advance of the intended selling season, up to two years ahead of the selling season. Color forecasts are projected using color stories. A **color story** is a collection of fashion, staple, warm, cool, neutral, and dark colors, coordinated for the upcoming season, and different from the last season. A color story is used to introduce accurate values and intensities of color. For example, in one season, the neutral off-white may be darkened slightly and called natural, jute, sand, or stone. In another season, to make the color story different from the past season, off-white may have yellow added to it, and it becomes ivory, light sage, or cream. In one season, green may be a staple color, such as hunter, forest, or kelly, and in the next season it is a fashion color such as military, moss, sage, or pistachio. Fire engine red may imply a warm red for one season, followed by berry, a cool red the following year. Color as an element of design is discussed in Chapter 9.

Color forecasters develop descriptive names for the color story based on consumer trends. The descriptive names become tools to assist promotion staffs in creating the correct message to send to the consumer. In a season when environmental trends are influencing consumers, colors may be expressed as vegetable names, such as tomato, eggplant, and zucchini. In another season, green, purple, and red may be called emerald, amethyst, and garnet, reflecting a strong economy and the willingness of consumers to spend money on luxurious jewels. Descriptive words are used to highlight the warmth or coolness, brilliance, or dullness of a color. Even black, which has less variation than other hues, may be described as midnight in promotion materials and catalogs. The color story is also used to illustrate how the color might be used in fabrication. Hunter green may be represented in heavy flannel or wool fabrics, while moss green may be used to describe sheer, chiffon fabrics.

Color forecasting services distribute color forecasts to fiber, fabric, and apparel producer members. Internationally known color forecasting services include Intercolor and the International Color Authority (ICA). Representatives from the fashion industry make up each of these organizations, meeting twice a year to determine specific color palettes for targeted retail seasons two years into the future. Intercolor representatives analyze the color cycle, looking at the natural evolution of color preferences. The International Color Authority establishes color predictions for fiber, fabric, and yarn producers and sends selected color palettes to members approximately six months after the meeting.

The Color Association of the United States (CAUS) is the chief domestic organization responsible for determining color forecasts for the apparel and home fashions industry. The Color Association is a nonprofit organization made up of industry executive volunteers who evaluate everything from politics to societal issues to the economy to culture and the arts to determine the color climate of the country. Members pay dues to receive annual color forecasts represented by swatch cards that forecast colors for the coming 18 to 24 months. Over 700 companies are members of the organization, encompassing automobiles, home appliances, sporting goods, fashion products, and many other industries. CAUS archives contain individual forecasts and decade volumes dating back to 1915.

Pantone is a leading developer and marketer of products for the accurate communication of color in a variety of industries, including textiles. Pantone develops color communication tools, such as color swatch books, which can be used by professionals to standardize colors across vendors to insure accurate color matching of textiles, buttons, trim, zippers, and other component parts of fashion goods. The Munsell Color System is also a color forecasting resource.

Fibers

Fashion projections in the primary market continue with fibers. Fiber forecasts are made 12 to 24 months in advance of the retail selling season. Primary market producers rely on fiber manufacturers, fiber trade associations, industry fairs, and trade shows for fiber forecasts. Fibers are categorized into natural and synthetic fibers. Synthetic fibers are generally produced by giant chemical companies, such as Du Pont. Synthetic fiber producers have always heavily promoted their products to the fashion industry and consumers. Promotion includes instruction in how to process synthetic fibers, creation of demand for synthetic textiles among garment and home furnishings manufacturers, and discussion of the benefits of synthetic fibers to the general public.

Both synthetic and natural fiber companies must be able to respond rapidly to consumer preferences for texture, color, weight, luster, care requirements, and other characteristics created at the raw material stage of production. The growth of the synthetic market has forced natural fiber producers to promote their products aggressively within the fashion industry.

Natural fiber trade associations are the promotion outlet used to forecast fiber trends to the fashion industry and consumers. Almost every natural fiber has a trade association made up of ranchers, fiber processors, and business and marketing professionals. Two strong trade associations include Cotton Incorporated and the American Wool Council. Each season, the American Wool Council produces a yarn library through its trend forecast service called the Wool Room. New fabrics are as important to apparel designers as the fibers they are made from.

Fabrics

Fabric manufacturers are a large segment of the primary market. As early as two years prior to a market season, textile producers create color stories and sketches of the important fashion trends. They suggest fabrics that will best interpret the projected season's fashion directions. For example, a seasonal trend may be chenille and other fabrics made from nubby, loopy yarns. Nubby, loopy yarns are most likely produced with staple length fibers. Fiber producers and knit fabric producers must forecast trends cooperatively to ensure the correct fiber length is produced for the projected fabric.

Textile collections are a source of inspiration for designers. They review past textiles to project future trends in fabrics. One such collection is at the museum of the Fashion Institute of Technology. The collection consists of 1,300 sample books and over 250,000 indexed swatches and larger textiles, dating back to the 19th century. To protect the swatches from wear and tear, the museum has put the collection on a series of CD-ROMs. The images have been arranged by themes and cross-referenced so that one piece can be placed into as many categories as are appropriate. The images can also be downloaded into design software for use by textile designers in creating new patterns.

FIGURE 4.6 Designers at a trade fair.

Fabric manufacturers show the latest trends in textiles at trade fairs such as the International Fashion Fabric Exhibition (IFFE). The IFFE, held in New York City, allows textile, trimming, and computer-aided design/computer-aided manufacturing (CAD/CAM) manufacturers, and fashion services to introduce the trends they have been creating over the previous 12 months. Apparel manufacturers, the secondary market, purchase the goods to create the next season's fashion line. Figure 4.6 shows designers reviewing fabric samples at a trade fair.

Secondary Market Forecasts

The **secondary market** refers to manufacturers and designers, the distribution channel member between the primary market (raw material producers) and the retail market. Manufacturers are responsible for creating fashions using the forecasted colors and fabrics delivered by the primary market. Manufacturers produce items six to 12 months in advance of the selling season. They present the designed goods to retail buyers four to six months in advance of expected delivery. Manufacturers present a line that balances new trendy items with basic styles from previous seasons.

Fashion merchandise includes aesthetically appealing products that change frequently and are generally considered nonnecessities. Although fashion merchandise is frequently associated with women's apparel and accessories, it includes much more. Fashion is present in such products as men's, women's, and children's apparel and accessories; cosmetics; and home fashions. Food; entertainment; durable goods such as home appliances, electronic equipment, and automobiles; and virtually every other aspect of our global culture also have fashion appeals. Fashion merchandise presents unique problems for manufacturers and retailers because consumer demand for these products is constantly changing. The perception that fashion goods are not necessary creates additional problems for firms promoting fashion.

Basic merchandise is at the opposite end of the product spectrum. Basic merchandise includes functional goods that change infrequently and are generally considered necessities. Apparel basics, such as white T-shirts or nude panty hose, are purchased as replacements when the old product wears out, in contrast to fashion purchases, for which the desire for novelty or change takes priority. Basic products also present promotional challenges for the manufacturer or retailer. Have you ever heard a consumer say, "What a great-looking white T-shirt. I think I'll buy it"?

The collection must be worthy of promotion by the retailers who are going to invest in the look. There is a fine line for manufacturers between *playing it safe,* offering merchandise that is only slightly updated from the previous season and therefore less attractive in promotions, and *going out on a limb,* offering merchandise that is so trendy it allows for exciting promotions but is likely to attract only a few consumers.

Haute Couture

Fashion forecast resources at the secondary market level include haute couture, ready-to-wear, and trade shows. While French haute couture creators have been the traditional innovators and inspirational leaders of fashion, ready-to-wear designers and manufacturers have taken on greater significance as fashion leaders in recent years.

The haute couture was created in 1868 and administered by the Chambre Syndicale de la Haute Couture (Fédération Française de la Couture, n.d.). The designation **haute couture** is an appellation, a legally protected brand name granted to a fashion house by the French Ministry of Industry. *Haute couture,* which is French for "high sewing" or "high dressmaking," results in made-to-measure clothing created for a specific customer. The unique garments are made from high-quality, expensive fabric and sewn with tremendous attention to detail and finish, often using time-consuming, hand-executed construction methods. Each January and July the haute couture houses present fashion extravaganzas in Paris. In January, the creations are for garments to be worn during the following spring and summer, whereas the July shows present fashions for the following fall and winter. Couturiers, the designers of haute couture, have decreased to fewer than a dozen. Today's most prominent couture houses are Chanel, Christian Dior, Jean Paul Gaultier, Givenchy, Valentino, and Christian Lacroix.

Garments and show productions for the haute couture are the most abstract, directional, and innovative of all the fashion presentations. John Galliano, couturier for Dior, has dressed his couture models as historical figures from Marie Antoinette to 20th-century icons such as Marlene Dietrich, even as street people. Under the leadership of Karl Lagerfeld, design director for the House of Chanel, artistry and intrigue are the key words. For one of his couture shows, held at the Grand Palais in Paris, models entered the huge auditorium wearing garments made mostly from black and white, with ruffles and bows. Each model walked into the space and mysteriously disappeared behind a door in a tall white column that was at the center of a circular stage. As the show came to a conclusion, the exterior of the column was raised, and the audience could see each model was standing on a step of an enormous spiral staircase (Fig. 4.7). As expected, the following season's color palette was dominated by black and white, with many skirts and tops featuring large and small ruffles.

Most of the couturiers also produce ready-to-wear lines in addition to their high-fashion collections. With increasing interest and growth in the ready-to-wear lines, the Fédération Française de la Couture, du Prêt-à-Porter des Couturiers et des Créateurs de

FIGURE 4.7 Karl Lagerfeld treats the haute couture audience to a spectacular show at the Grand Palais in Paris.

Mode was created to oversee the activities of the haute couture, prêt-à-porter, and la mode masculine in 1973 (Fédération Française de la Couture, n.d.).

Ready-to-Wear

The ready-to-wear fashion shows are also presented twice each year in each of the major international fashion cities. The circuit starts with Mercedes-Benz Fashion Week in New York in September for spring trends and in February for fall looks. Mercedes-Benz, the creators of automobiles with high style, design, and craftsmanship, is the primary sponsor of New York Fashion Week, which was first produced by 7th on Sixth, the group formed by the Council of Fashion Designers of America (CFDA) to organize, centralize, and modernize the American Collections. Therefore, most of the major American ready-to-wear designers and manufacturers show their collections at one coordinated market. 7th on Sixth became part of IMG Fashion, a division of international sports and lifestyle event and management giant IMG, and manages New York Fashion Week and Los Angeles Fashion Week, in addition to other fashion presentations worldwide (7th on Sixth, 2006).

London is the next significant international city to host its fashion presentations. London Fashion Week features British designers, such as FrostFrench, Jasper Conran, Jean Muir, and Nicole Farhi, in addition to other designers with wide-ranging origins, including Turkey, India, and Russia. The originality of London designers is unparalleled with a creative influence reaching far and wide.

After London, the fashion collections are presented in Milan, Italy. This Italian city offers a businesslike environment for its fashion trend presentations. Milan Fashion Week is owned and produced by Camera Nazionale della Moda Italiana (CNMI). The CNMI has produced well over 100 shows during 15 years and showcased a wide variety of designers, including Roberto Cavalli, Max Mara, Missoni, Dolce & Gabbana, and many more. Milano Moda Donna for women's wear and Milano Moda Uomo for men's wear are the two major activities coordinated by CNMI. Top models, journalists, designers, and fashion photographers are attracted to this stimulating event.

Paris is the next stop for ready-to-wear trend shows. The semiannual fashion circuit used to start in Paris and end in New York, but the schedules were revised several years ago. The French Prêt-à-Porter, which means "ready-to-wear" in English, features many more collections than the haute couture shows (Fig. 4.8). Many design houses that originated as couture houses, such as Nina Ricci, Yves Saint Laurent, Balmain, and Lanvin, show exclusively during the Prêt-à-Porter. Other international designers and design houses, such as Dutch designers Viktor & Rolf, British creators Vivienne Westwood and Stella McCartney, Japanese designer Yohji Yamamoto, and American innovator Marc Jacobs for Louis Vuitton, have all presented their collections in Paris.

While there are countless other international ready-to-wear shows, presentations in these four prominent fashion cities—New York, London, Milan, and Paris—command the most interest and set the most significant trends for other shows to follow. International shows that are growing in significance as we write this chapter include Berlin Fashion Week in Germany, Istanbul Textile and Apparel Exporter's Associates in Turkey, Salón Internacional de Moda de Madrid (SIMM) in Spain, Australian Fashion Week in Sydney, Hong Kong Fashion Week, Japan Fashion Week, FashionNorth Show in Canada, São Paulo Fashion Week in Brazil, and Copenhagen International Fashion Fair in Denmark. Next, we will look at American trade shows and their role in fashion trend forecasting.

FIGURE 4.8 Advertisement of Paris Prêt-à-Porter trade show.

American Trade Shows

Seventh Avenue in New York City is the center of the fashion industry for domestic manufacturers. Markets are generally categorized by the price points of goods sold: budget, moderate, better, bridge, and designer. Forecasters cover the New York market along with regional and international markets. Major trade shows occur semiannually in New York—presenting trends to specialty store buyers from around the country. Some of these shows include Nouveau Collective, a ready-to-wear and lifestyle show; the Train, featuring ready-to-wear designers from around the world, organized by the Fédération Française du Prêt-à-Porter; Fashion Coterie, juried women's apparel and accessories produced by ENK International; and Moda Manhattan, showing women's ready-to-wear and produced by Business Journals Incorporated.

In recent years Las Vegas has emerged as a trade show magnet. MAGIC, which has been held in Las Vegas since 1989, is one of the popular American trade shows (Advanstar Communications, 2005). MAGIC originated in California in 1933 as an association of Los Angeles area menswear manufacturers known as "Men's Wear Manufacturers of Los Angeles" (2005). In 1948 the organization voted to change its name to Men's Apparel Guild in California (MAGIC) and to form a corporation, since the membership has

BOX 4.1

Clothes Call: Fashion Innovators Are First to Interpret Apparel Trends

Fitness expert Rupa Mehta is used to changing and improving her clients' bodies, so it came as a surprise when she started seeing a transformation of sorts in herself. "When I opened my studio, I was amazed at how well dressed everyone was, even to work out. I found that I started dressing cuter, just to keep up," she tells. The twenty-seven-year-old founder and owner of Nalini Method counts models, dancers, top executives, and power brokers among her clientele. "They were all up on the latest styles and are very hip and young in their approaches to dressing," she shares. "It's so interesting to see what they are wearing."

Mehta's typical client could easily be considered a Fashion Innovator. As defined by the Cotton Incorporated *Lifestyle Monitor* ™, the Innovator is on the cutting edge of fashion, often gets asked for advice on clothing, shops for apparel more often than the average consumer, spends more on her wardrobe than other women and is very savvy about what she buys.

"The Fashion Innovator is definitely more interested in clothing than the average consumer," advises Melissa Bastos, Manager of Marketing Research for Cotton Incorporated. "She is influenced by celebrities and fashion magazines and she has a good command of current culture and social happenings. The Innovator is the first to interpret a trend to her taste level and she serves as a fashion ambassador for her peers."

Bastos points to data from the *Monitor* to support her statements. Nearly 80% of Fashion Innovators claim to like or love shopping, compared to slightly more than half of female respondents in the general population making the same claim. The Fashion Innovator puts her money where her passion is; she told the *Monitor* that she spent $129.73 on clothing in the past month versus the average female respondent's $74.60.

Neda Jones and Michelle Siegel, founders of www.nedandshell.com, a website showcasing the latest creations from emerging designers and offering a carefully edited viewpoint on current styles, can certainly be considered Fashion Innovators. According to these former college roommates-turned-entrepreneurs, fashion can translate itself as a form of personal empowerment and express one's true individuality and may explain the motivations for many Fashion Innovators. "To say someone is 'in fashion' implies that they are wearing the latest, but true style mavens have been leaving fashion up to the designers and focusing on fine-tuning their personal style," says Jones. "While I think many social and psychological nuances are at play here, I believe that confidence and the willingness to risk are key factors," adds Siegel. "The issue here is no different from the rest of life. Some just fall in line and take whatever is given to them, others demand to live life on their terms and recognize that how they represent themselves to the world is not just a case of vanity but of self respect."

Alle Fister, founder of the fashion and lifestyle public relations agency Bollare, is a Fashion Innovator in her own right, as evidenced by her numerous appearances on VH1, MTV and SoapNet. Fister echoes the lead-or-follow sentiment. "A lot of fashion-forward thinkers tend to be creatively driven; they don't want to embrace the latest trend, they want to create it; or at the very least, add their own spin to it! I love this mentality! I would so like to differentiate from fashion-forward and trendy," she shares. "A fashion-forward woman does not necessarily embrace every flash-in-the-pan trend. She edits these trends to select only those that fit her personal style, that flatter her figure and allow her to add her own unique twist."

Bastos, the researcher, agrees. "The Fashion Innovator may keep an eye on trends, but she knows what works for her. She values quality and is well-educated on fabrics." According to the *Monitor*, 61% of female fashion innovators (compared to 53% of total women) prefer quality over a bargain, suggesting that the Innovator places a premium on well-made clothing. Ditto her take on fabrics. According to the *Monitor*, two-thirds of Innovators were willing to pay more for natural fibers, like cotton, versus the little more than half of female respondents from the general population making the same claim.

Additional data from the *Monitor* also suggests that the Fashion Innovator is committed to her craft. On average, she spent 108.44 minutes in a typical month shopping for apparel, just slightly higher than the average female respondent's 100.6 minutes. However, factoring in the average 3.35 times a month that the Innovator shops, versus the 2.31 times cited by the general female respondent, indicates that the Innovator is keen to keep current with the evolution of her personal style.

The Fashion Innovator is also efficient at planning her wardrobe for the day, as Mehta, the studio owner, observes. "My typical client can throw a jean jacket over what she has worn to the gym and be all set to meet someone for lunch right after class—she has her look that perfected."

As Mehta's experience attests, Innovators know how to flex their fashion muscle.

Source: Cotton Incorporated Lifestyle Monitor (2006, August 3). Clothes call: Fashion innovators are first to interpret apparel trends. *Women's Wear Daily*, p. 2.

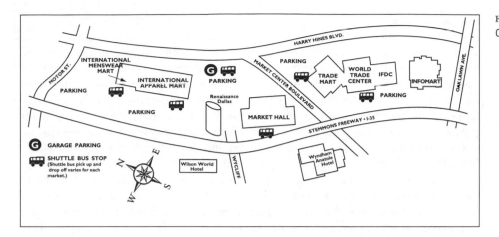

FIGURE 4.9 The Dallas Market Center Campus Map.

grown to include manufacturers outside Los Angeles (2005). MAGIC expanded to include women's apparel with the introduction of WWDMAGIC, a joint venture with *Women's Wear Daily* in 1995. MAGIC also purchased Children's Trade Expo and launched MAGIC Kids in 1997 (2005).

In addition to the men's, women's, children's, and sourcing trade shows that are held each February and August at the Las Vegas Convention Center, MAGIC attendees are able to attend a variety of seminars and special events. Past seminars have included fashion forecasts presented by such prominent fashion, color, and trend forecasters as David Wolfe from Doneger Group. These seminars and events help educate the retail buyers about industry trends in addition to methods to improve their businesses. Box 4.1 details the role of fashion innovators in interpreting fashion trends.

Regional markets offer market weeks and information sources for upcoming trends. New York is still the center of attention for designer and bridge merchandise but regional marts, including Dallas (Fig. 4.9), have become the focus for swimwear, dresses, and accessories bought outside of New York. Each regional market has its own specific influences, which are represented through its merchandise lines. Regional marts include San Francisco, Los Angeles, Atlanta, Dallas, Las Vegas, and Chicago, among others, which feature smaller, more specific shows in a location more convenient and economical for smaller retailers.

Chicago's Merchandise Mart hosts StyleMax, the city's largest apparel market, and Chicago Is . . . Red Hot, a fashion show featuring more than 30 Chicago area apparel and accessory designers sponsored by the Apparel Industry Board, in addition to the National Bridal Market. Diverse seminars, awards ceremonies, and fashion shows are scheduled to entertain and educate participants during the various Chicago Merchandise Mart trade shows.

In Los Angeles, the California Market Center (CMC) produces five fashion weeks, four major gift and home decor markets, and two textile shows, in addition to a range of temporary exhibits, market days, educational events, and seminars throughout the year. The latest fashion events to influence trends and fashion forecasting in Los Angeles is Mercedes-Benz Fashion Week at Smashbox Studios, which is affiliated with IMG, the producers of Fashion Week in New York. Los Angeles's top designers are showcased, including Richard Tyler, Magda Berliner, Trina Turk, Louis Verdad, Cynthia Vincent, Petro Zillia, and Michelle Mason, among others. The event attracts local and national press, buyers, and celebrities and is quickly becoming an incubator for cutting-edge talent.

Precollections

In recent years, precollection presentations have become increasingly important, especially for luxury goods. **Precollections** are previews, which are presented to key retail buyers, fashion editors, and some private customers three months ahead of the official start of each season. Most buyers are not able to wait until the merchandise is shown during the formal runway shows in September/October for spring or February/March for fall, if they want new merchandise in the stores before the shopping season begins for fashion innovators. Customers who purchase expensive, innovative brands—where a jacket can cost $3,500 or a gown requiring around 200 hours to sew sells for nearly $100,000—are interested in having unique clothes earlier than anyone else.

Hypothetically, a precollection for spring merchandise could include 100 or more garments. Showroom models reveal the collection to buyers from stores like Neiman Marcus and Barneys, who place orders, and to magazine editors, who fight over who gets to photograph which gowns first, at the Atelier in Paris. The viewing, lasting 10 days, takes place during July. Designs are modified, added, or subtracted from the precollection as influential retailers and customers select their favorites. By the time these garments are shown as theatrical performances to the press and public during the international fashion show collections held in Paris during October, most of the garments will have already been sold to the top stores and top clients.

Some designers sell new collections directly to consumers. For example, Calvin Klein has allowed private customers to purchase fall merchandise in May. Normally, these goods would be in retail stores in July.

Resort lines are more important than in the past. Resort no longer means simply presenting winter vacation clothes to magazine editors and customers in cloistered studio showings. These lines are created with as much excitement as a spring or fall collection, becoming precollections and forecasting trends for the upcoming spring and summer. The houses of Dior and Chanel, in addition to such American designers as Vera Wang and Carolina Herrera, are presenting elaborate resort collections at staged events to grab attention. With this in mind, Vera Wang presented 28 edited looks from her latest collection of nearly 300 resort pieces during a hot, muggy summer day in Manhattan (Talley, 2006). The collection, based around a subtle, smoky palette of grays, blues, whites, and khaki, forecasts the trends she plans to present for the following spring, summer, and beyond.

Next, we look at forecasting at the retail market level. Retailers have ever increasing interest in knowing the fashion trends as early as possible and presenting them to their consumers.

Retail Market Forecasts

The **retail market** is responsible for communicating trends, developed previously by primary and secondary producers, to consumers. Based on information about their customers, retailers forecast what best-selling items will be in their stores in the upcoming season. Each retailer will interpret trends in a slightly different way to match the brands position of its organization. Box 4.2 profiles a merchandising executive who analyzes the dress market. Buyers for retail stores view fashions four to six months in advance of the expected delivery and make their forecasts. Buyers whose primary customers are fashion innovators will expect very early delivery of goods prior to the start of the selling season. They will make their forecasts based on expected sales. Buyers purchasing goods for the fashion majority will purchase items closer to the selling season and make forecasts based on tested trends from the fashion innovators.

○ BOX 4.2

A Day in the Market with Roseanne

Roseanne Cumella, senior vice president of merchandising at Doneger Group, has her eyes on what's selling at the Donna Morgan showroom in Manhattan, 530 Seventh Avenue, a better-priced dress division of Maggie London.

She tugs at a red printed day dress, priced $128 at retail, and asserts, "What's the message here? It's high-waisted. It's matte jersey, and it's got a patent leather belt. It's hot at retail."

The dress had a 21 percent sell-through at Lord & Taylor the week before, selling 100-plus units of the 450 ordered, and Lord & Taylor is picking 550 more in the same pattern in a different color.

Then she moves to a Biba-inspired ponte knit jumper, a new body for Donna Morgan based on the strength of a long-sleeved ponte that's sold well before. "This is one of the best jumpers in the market, bar none," she says.

Donna Morgan is a core supplier for many department stores, and Cumella is liking much of what she sees. A lot of it is in the details: twin printed borders, eyelet patterns, belts both skinny and wide, oversize prints, and "bra-friendly" straps, at least an inch wide to conceal the undergarment strap. But how long will it stay fresh? Cumella needs to assess how day dresses will evolve, whether in matte jersey, silk or cotton, and with what details.

So she moves to the design room, where patterns and samples are being made and the walls and tables are covered with swatches, sketches, and color stories by monthly deliveries. It's an indication of where some of the market is going and where Doneger provides input. "If they're missing something or too duplicated from what everyone else is doing, we'll call it out," Cumella says.

Next stop in the market is Maggie London, where matte jerseys and sheers are being reordered, and judging from a look into the design room, the label is getting very aggressive in sheer silks, both printed and solids, and crepe de chine.

Then, on a late October Monday, it's on to the Jones New York and Nine West dress divisions of Jones Apparel Group. At Jones New York, it's a more corporate environment, with groupings of day dresses in cotton, silk sheers, and matte jersey organized to make it easy for buyers to shop and merchandise in their stores. Cumella singles out a sleeveless, long poplin dress, priced $140 at retail, with stitch-down pleats and a braided leather belt. "It's flattering to the hip, slimming. It flairs out just enough. These are details that set it apart." It's a new version of a . . . best seller, for April delivery. Not far away is a "desk-to-dinner" cocktail dressing group, but Cumella's day in the market is focused on day dresses.

You can bet several of the items identified by vendors as best sellers, or that catch the eye of Cumella, wind up in the Doneger showroom. They are there for out-of-town store buyers to see when they're in for market week, to either buy directly from the vendor or illustrate the looks Doneger Group predicts will have a positive impact on business and how important certain resources are in a trend for a specific delivery. It's the data on what's selling at full price or promotional prices, what's not selling at any price, and information on emerging and waning trends that is the lifeblood for retailers and what Cumella and her team ascertain from their showroom visits. In effect, Cumella and her team do "a first edit" for retail clients. Cumella supervises a team of 25, including market analysts and assistants. She has two divisions reporting to her, one for coats and suits, another for accessories and intimate apparel. Cumella handles dresses herself. The team visits the market daily.

"The dress business moves fast, but some stores only come into market four times a year," said Barbara Kennedy, president of Jones Apparel dress group. "You have to have someone in the market often to preview the lines. Roseanne also gives us feedback on what looks good and what doesn't look good and can pull stores and manufacturers together. There's nobody really left that does what Roseanne and the Doneger Group do."

Walking between showrooms, Cumella discusses the bigger picture. She says day dresses at better prices have been moving at retail for the past year but were moribund for nine years before. "The challenge will be the third quarter . . . and after," Cumella suggests. Deliveries for March 30, April 30, and May 30, Cumella says, are "happy deliveries," meaning there're plenty of day dresses getting shipped. "Second quarter is a very strong dress period in the dress cycle." Historically, there has been a significant shift in Aug. 30 and Sept. 30 deliveries to social occasion dresses, however, this year, "We're seeing a nicer balance," Cumella says.

Cumella has been shopping the market since 1969, starting her career in the training program at J.C. Penney, where she became a coat buyer. Subsequently, she worked at Associated Dry Goods as a divisional vice president of dresses, coats, and suits and joined Doneger in 1986 when ADG was absorbed by May Department Stores, which is now owned by Federated Department Stores.

"I still get excited about the business," said Cumella. "It's so different all the time. There's such an energy to it. And we have to look at the market from so many different retail eyes and strategies. I get excited that the information we gather can be customized to our clients."

"Our job is not only to accumulate information, analyze it and dissect it, it's separating the fact from the fiction," Cumella says. "A better buyer gets 60 to 70 calls a week from vendors on how hot their lines are and why they need to shop them. Some of that is fabrication, if you know what I mean. It's our job to validate the information."

Source: Moin, D (2006, November 6). A day in the market with Roseanne. *Women's Wear Daily,* p. 191.

Retailers make their forecasts based on merchandise previewed at market weeks, and buying trips to designer showrooms. They also base forecasts on advice from resident buying offices.

Buying Trips

Buyers return from buying trips so filled to the brim with potential new trends, they must sift through to determine what is right for their organization. After reviewing notes, slides, videos, and other materials, buyers identify trends—key items and fads—that they will invest in for the coming season. Buyers have the opportunity to support or weaken a fashion look through their power to place orders. They may place small or large orders, or no orders at all, if they determine the look will not work for their store's retail position. After reviewing all possible sources, the anticipated forecast is presented to top management and marketing and promotion departments of the organization so they may begin to design themes and other creative elements that must accompany the merchandise within the store.

──○ FASHION THEME DEVELOPMENT

To test their projected forecasts, retailers bring merchandise into their stores two or three months ahead of the anticipated season. Fall merchandise will appear in stores in June and July; spring merchandise will appear in stores in January. Retailers use themes to communicate messages about the new merchandise to consumers. A **theme** is the reoccurring idea that is seen in color, silhouette, fabric, and other design components. The theme may be based on style, economics, history, politics, weather, science, humor, or some other aspect of society. Manufacturers also use themes to create a feeling about merchandise presented to buyers. When organizing a line, designers coordinate groups of styles so that the styles reflect a theme.

Each season, themes are prevalent in all merchandise categories: women's, men's, and children's apparel, soft goods, and home furnishings. These themes are promotional tools used to create moods and prepare consumers for what they will see in the marketplace.

Retailers and manufacturers have the opportunity to position their brand as different from their competitors by developing promotional themes. Themes help the firm create a look and image that can be carried through advertising, signage, visual merchandising, fashion shows, and other special events, helping to build brand reputation. In developing a theme, many retailers piggyback themes created by manufacturers or designers. Designer fabric and color stories present themes that are easy for a retailer to adapt in presenting their own merchandise. Shared themes may be part of a co-marketing effort by producers and retailers to increase the brand awareness of a product.

Themes should be creative and imaginative to strengthen advertising messages and

TABLE 4.3   *12-Month Color Themes*

Timing	Theme Name	Colors Presented
January	*Dawn*	Next-to-nothing nudes
February	*Daybreak*	Pale tints
March/April	*Daylight*	Whitening tones
May/June	*Sunup*	Clear brights
July	*High Noon*	Neon brights
August/September	*Dusk*	Spice tones
October/November	*Deep Darks*	Deep darks
December	*Twilight*	Rich hues

promotions. Themes should influence consumers to buy. Ideas for themes should be current and timely. *The Colors of Summer* leads into such themes as *In the Pink, Country Road Red, Summertime Blues,* or *Naturally Neutral.*

In a retail environment, themes may be created for a single department or as a storewide event. In a manufactured line, themes may be specific to merchandise categories such as women's or men's, or designed around a fabric and carried across all categories, such as the use of gray flannel. A theme may be short, lasting several weeks, or longer, lasting through an entire season or a year, depending on the promotion strategy of the retailer. Table 4.3 is an example of a color theme moving from neutral winter colors to bright summer colors to darker fall colors. The theme is presented over 12 months, but updated every two months to look new to the customer. Retail and/or manufacturing themes may be categorized in any of the following ways:

- **Storewide theme.** A storewide fashion theme involves a broad focus to be used throughout the entire store, including all apparel and home furnishings departments. For example, a *Sophisticated Safari* theme may be featured in apparel departments for men, women, and children, incorporating khaki safari jackets with trousers, skirts, or shorts. The accessory department may add safari hats, knapsacks, totebags, and sunglasses. The home store would contribute wicker picnic baskets, travel coolers, and linens. The furniture department would be decorated with wicker, earth tone sheets, mosquito netting, and plants. Virtually every department may contribute some article to the extensive theme.
- **Color theme.** Trends relating to color offer endless suggestions for themes. March brings to mind green for Saint Patrick's Day and the start of spring. Pastel colors frequently replace the darker colors of winter so retailers present a pastel color story around the Easter holiday. Fashion statements such as astro-brights or vegetable colors may be trend features. The theme may apply to ready-to-wear, cosmetics, accessories only, or may be extended over all product categories. For example *Holiday Jewels* may show bright ruby red, emerald green, and sapphire blue in the ready-to-wear, intimate apparel, and costume jewelry departments.
- **Fabric theme.** A fabric theme is based upon the popular fabric of a given season. A fabric theme may be created in one specific department or by a specific designer. Juniors might feature *Work Out,* with stretch fabrics that cling to the body. Men's apparel might stress *The Naturals,* with natural fibers of cotton or linen in neutral shades. Cashmere sweaters may be the item of choice in *Sweater Weather.*

- **Lifestyle theme.** Meeting the needs of a particular focus group of consumers involves a lifestyle theme. The trend for physical fitness has led to seminars with sports figures and trend shops with leotards, tights, and workout equipment located in one spot. Another popular lifestyle theme shows working women what to wear for business activities. *Women Incorporated* may feature seminars on money matters or balancing home and work needs, as well as on appropriate fashions for work.
- **Special occasions.** The special occasion theme emphasizes clothing and other items related to unusual or traditional events. One of the most popular special event occasion themes combines all of the elements required for a wedding. From selection of the bridal gown to the caterer, this event requires more planning than the average consumer is used to arranging. The photographer, music, attendant and parent apparel, household items, and more are all under consideration. *An Affair to Remember* bridal event brings together all of the components necessary to plan a wedding and start a new life as a couple. Other popular special occasions include baby showers, back-to-school, and holidays.

The fashion story presentation, including a theme, should be reflected throughout the entire promotion mix. The forecasting checklist (Fig 4.10) includes trend resources, trend elements, and how the trend is presented through the various promotion mix components. As a primary element of the promotion mix, advertising should document the latest trend in print media, including newspaper, magazine, and direct-response campaigns. A store with in-store video-wall capabilities should highlight the trend through broadcast video clips aimed at a specific market segment. Themes for seasonal events and fashion shows should indicate the trend using lighting, music, and props that accent the trend on the runway. Sales personnel should be thoroughly knowledgeable about the trend and illustrate appropriate trend influences to prospective customers. Packaging and gift-with-purchase displays should feature the trend. Publicity for the vendor should always have the trend depicted formally or informally to the media and consumers. Visual merchandising displays throughout a store should have the trend featured prominently to every customer who walks into the department.

○ THE FASHION TREND PRESENTATION

Once inquiries about the upcoming season are finished, the fashion forecaster pulls together the results and presents the forecast to a live audience as part of a multimedia presentation with supporting documents, or the forecast is presented via electronic delivery. The audience consists of industry professionals at a trade show, at an industry event, or at the forecaster's marketing office. For example, Cotton Incorporated maintains a fabric library and research facility in its New York marketing headquarters. Another international forecasting resource is Doneger Group, a leading source of global market trends and merchandising strategies to the retail and fashion industry. Retailers, manufacturers, designers, trade journalists, and other apparel industry professionals, such as product development teams, merchandisers, and marketers, are the typical audience for fashion forecast presentations.

In addition to scouting for trends, industry professionals are looking for new resources for the most current fabric, color, trims, and findings. Large retail firms, manufacturing companies, and top designers most likely subscribe to several different forecasting services as well as have team members scout for consistent trend information.

The audience anxiously awaits the start of the presentation seminar that will highlight

FIGURE 4.10 Forecast Checklist.

Forecast Checklist

Resources to Investigate for Trend Ideas
- ❏ Primary market (color, fibers, fabrics)
- ❏ Secondary market (global and domestic markets)
- ❏ Retail market (buying trips and resident buying offices)
- ❏ Previous sales figures
- ❏ Competition
- ❏ Market research about consumers (demographic, psychographic, behavioristic)
- ❏ Fashion publications
- ❏ Forecast services
- ❏ Influences from society, media, arts, music, the Internet
- ❏ Other industries
- ❏ Observations of others
- ❏ Your intuition

Elements of a Trend
- ❏ Influence
- ❏ Silhouette
- ❏ Fabrication
- ❏ Pattern or texture
- ❏ Color story
- ❏ Descriptive color names
- ❏ Details or trim
- ❏ Promotional theme

Trend Presentation through the Promotional Mix
- ❏ Advertising
- ❏ Direct marketing and interactive media
- ❏ Sales promotion
- ❏ Public relations
- ❏ Personal sales
- ❏ Special events
- ❏ Fashion shows
- ❏ Visual merchandising

what direction fashion will take. Which new colors, fabrics, silhouettes, themes, images, and ideas will emerge for the upcoming season? The professionals have gathered, maneuvered to get a good seat, and are ready to experience the exciting production.

Organizing Information

Each specific fashion forecasting service decides what kinds of information it will provide, from color, fabrication, and silhouette trends to what is selling at retail. There are various types of reports that interest clients, from complete audiovisual trend analyses to simple reports on what garments people are wearing in specific international locations or Paris Haute Couture trends. Some of the common types of products and services provided by

FIGURE 4.11 Cotton Incorporated offers trend forecast presentations.

forecasting companies are listed in Figure 4.3. Some services offer more comprehensive information about general categories, such as women's, men's, or children's apparel or home furnishings. Other services, such as the marketing program for Cotton Incorporated, offer very specific and focused data about cotton fabric trends. THE COTTON WORKS Fabric Library showcases international cotton fabrics selected from over 350 mills, knitters, and converters from the United States and abroad (Cotton Incorporated, 2006). Figure 4.11 announces a forecast presentation by Cotton Incorporated.

Materials are organized by the forecasting firm into the category and distribution method desired. A simple runway report may be presented as a print newsletter or posted on a website, exclusively for fashion forecast subscribers or open to anyone. A more complex seasonal trend forecast is more likely developed as a slide show or multimedia production, using PowerPoint or other electronic techniques to produce a video, CD-ROM, or DVD presentation with still photographs, live-action runway videos, presented in addition to a live oral presentation by a member of the forecasting service team. Key information is highlighted in bulleted visuals. Graphic designs are used to draw attention to information and visual images.

After determining the type of report to be given, the information is organized. The sequence for a fashion trend forecast normally starts with a label designed to grab the attention of the audience. Then, various elements are reported. The order may depend upon the emphasis desired by the forecaster. Pantone, the color authority, color systems provider, and supplier of leading technology for the selection and accurate communication of color across a variety of industries, would begin its analysis with names and examples of colors predicted for the next season, whereas Tobé might start with key shapes for garments.

The elements of a forecast most commonly include general discussion, based on research, about the direction in which a trend is moving, color stories, fabrication, prints, patterns, silhouettes, styles, and accessories. Merchandise details should be presented in a planned sequence. For example, start with casual moving to sophisticated or start with one color then use a color story to progress to other colors.

From these elements a creative catchphrase or theme is shaped. If ruffles are part of the fashion shape, the title might become *Frill Ride*. Another leading story, such as the return of cowboy fashions, might be completely contradictory to the ultrafeminine ruffle story. The catchphrase for the cowboy or cowgirl theme might be *Way Haute West* or *Spaghetti Western*, complete with the sound track from the old Clint Eastwood movie. The themes are frequently based on current pop culture or on nostalgic themes derived from retro or vintage elements.

Labeling Trends

Trend reporting starts with discussing appeal of the trend via labeling. The label for the trend, according to Brannon, may refer to:

- A look—retro, minimalist, Japanese influence.
- The mood or spirit—youthful, sophisticated, playful.
- A lifestyle message—a family household, extreme sports vacation.
- A tie-in with a celebrity—Jessica Simpson, Heidi Klum.
- A target market—urban youthful, working women, early retirees.
- A brand image or designer's name—Quicksilver, Ralph Lauren.
- A concept—career casual, investment dressing, mix-and-match.
- The source of inspiration, whether historical or ethnic—la Belle Époque, Moroccan.
- A pop culture influence such as a hit movie or TV series—*Miami Vice, Pirates of the Caribbean.*

Reporting Trends

Once the label is established, the basic elements of color, fabrications, silhouette, design details and features, subtleties of fit proportion, and overall coordination are discussed in association to the label. Here the gender (women's and men's), size category (juniors, misses, plus-sizes, petites), price range (designer, bridge, better, moderate, or budget), and season (Fall/Winter, Spring/Summer, Resort) are revealed.

The trends reporter provides a trend map detailing the stage of trend development and probable scope of each trend. The **trend map** identifies which trends are on the rise, continuing to grow, or reaching maturity as well as the strength of the trend. This stage of information parallels the fashion cycle, which was introduced in Chapter 2. This information helps merchandising executives decide whether to continue purchasing the trend or start marking down goods to make room for the next big look. Major trends are strong and more likely to be attractive to large groups of consumers, whereas minor trends are more targeted to small concentrated audiences, known as niches.

Next, we will look at the various tools needed to present the forecast. These tools are necessary to create the visual, written, and oral elements of the presentation.

──o Fashion Forecast Presentation Tools

The traditional method of making the fashion forecast presentation is at a meeting where the forecaster speaks directly to the audience. Since we are such a visual society, many types of visual components, such as trend storyboards, slides, videotapes, sample garments, fabric swatches, and color cards, are used to emphasize the look and feel of the trend. A printed fashion report is also provided to the members of audience, so that they will be able to refer to the content of the presentation. Next, we will look at the various tools used to make the fashion forecast presentation exciting and professional. And we will look at the alternative presentation tools that have emerged since computers and the Internet have revolutionized the fashion and broadcast worlds.

Visual Elements

Traditionally, **trend storyboards** are used to fuse visual and verbal elements into a vibrant yet clear representation of the spirit, mood, and theme of the report. Storyboards emphasize the look and call attention to the trend. These visual statements are built on such materials as foamcore, illustration board, or bulletin boards. Illustrations, fabrics, and color cards should attach easily to the board materials. Boards *neatly* cut to 20" × 30" are an ideal size for a presentation to a small audience of between 30 and 60 people. Larger formats or illustrations projected onto a movie-style screen are more appropriate for large audiences in an auditorium. Storyboards complement information presented in the fashion report.

The board designer should experiment with board layout, deciding whether to have a horizontal (landscape) or vertical (portrait) orientation (Fig. 4.12). Once the decision is made, maintaining the same orientation consistently throughout all of the boards is more professional. It is also a good idea to maintain a consistent background color for the boards. Figure 4.12 shows trend board layouts.

The designer also picks the typeface for the verbal components. By using a creative yet readable typeface or font, the theme is made more evident. It is a good idea to experiment with upper- and lowercase letters, in addition to effects such as bold, italics, or other techniques. Computer-generated typefaces should be used to avoid an amateurish look that comes from poorly hand-lettered boards.

Other visual elements of trend boards include graphics and borders. Graphics can include logos for the trend. Borders keep the eye focused upon the materials composed on the storyboards.

Additional visual elements, including color cards, fabric samples, silhouettes illustrated through line drawings or as photographs, audio/visual examples using theme music or clips from runway shows, support the presentation. Figure 4.13 shows color trends from the pantone color report (2007). If prototype or sample garments can be located, they stress the theme. Next, we look at the written materials supporting the visual components.

FIGure 4.12 Trend boards may be presented vertically or horizontally to direct the viewer's eye to the content.

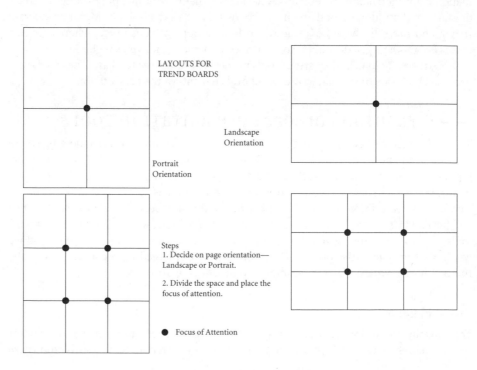

LAYOUTS FOR
TREND BOARDS

Landscape
Orientation

Portrait
Orientation

Steps
1. Decide on page orientation—
Landscape or Portrait.

2. Divide the space and place the
focus of attention.

● Focus of Attention

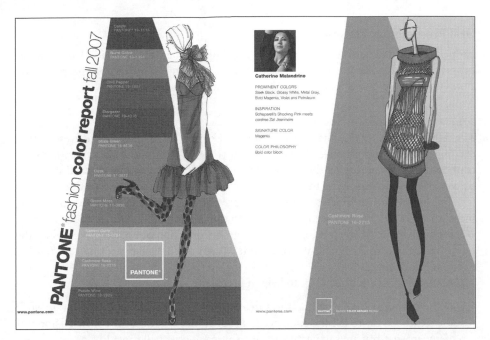

FIGURE 4.13 Pantone color trend forecast.

Written Materials

A **fashion report** is a business document that supports the oral presentation and story-boards, or it may be created for independent presentation on a website. The fashion report is similar to the situation analysis, discussed in Chapter 5, or creative strategy, discussed in Chapter 8. Include a title page and executive summary, discussed as part of a promotion plan in Chapter 5. A table of contents should be included to let the reader know what information the report includes. Standard business reports formatting, with page numbers, headings, and subheadings, make the document more useful. If your budget allows, you can be creative, using color printing and including various images to support your trend.

A complete trend forecast is presented in the fashion report using fashion language to reflect:

- Influences discovered through research
- Overall theme and creative catchphrases
- Specific merchandise
- Silhouettes
- Fabrication (fibers and fabrics)
- Colors and patterns (using color names)
- Accessories

In preparation to the oral presentation, a complete script or notes can be prepared and placed on note cards, printed in large letters. Other speakers prefer to place their script in a notebook, so that pages will not get out of order. Next, we consider the techniques that will assist us in making professional oral presentations.

Oral Presentation Techniques

Fashion forecasters must have public speaking skills. Proper tone of voice, lack of inappropriate gestures, confidence, and fashion authority are essentials for the presenter. These characteristics can make or break a presentation.

Oral Presentation

The fashion forecaster must have great public speaking abilities, making the presentation exciting as well as informative. The speaker must be a performer, communicating with confidence and authority. Yet the speaker should also be enjoyable and entertaining. The communicator should engage the audience immediately with a strong introduction.

In order for an audience to remember a presentation, they must be told something three times. While this may seem repetitious to the presenter, it is helpful to the listener. Tell the audience what you are going to say in an introduction or preview, expand on the points in the body of the presentation, and tell them briefly what you told them in the summary or closing.

Here are some additional tips to help in preparing an oral presentation.

- You should normally determine the three main points you wish to convey to your audience. If you try to tell the audience too much, they will become confused and not remember what you are saying. Since the fashion forecast will most likely cover color, fabrics, and silhouettes in addition to supporting accessory and merchandise category development information, you will need to clearly point out these important topics.
- Develop a script, speaking outline, or notes binder. You should speak slowly, but should not read your report. Notes should be in a large font size, to make it easier to follow. Draw attention to important points by marking them with a contrasting underline or highlight marker. Numbers and difficult-to-pronounce words should be written out with the phonetic spelling. (How many times have you heard Givenchy or Karan mispronounced?)
- Rehearse. You should practice projecting your voice clearly, whether using a projection system or speaking directly to members of the audience. Your voice should be loud enough to be heard.
- Know the amount of time the presentation should and actually does take and keep within the designated time limit.
- Make eye contact with the audience. Plan places in your presentation to pause and look at the audience to gain rapport and to assess audience reaction.
- Practice, practice, practice!
- Comment on information as you present your visual aids, which should be of professional quality and easy for the entire audience to see.
- Proofread visuals and script.
- Dress in a professionally accepted manner.

Equipment Management

In addition to planning the content and rehearsing, plan for contingencies and the possibility of equipment failure. Most people who make many oral presentations know that equipment problems are an unpleasant expectation. Anything that can go wrong frequently does. A projector can jam or fail to focus, a PowerPoint presentation on a CD-ROM may not be compatible to the auditorium computer, a VCR stops playing, or a DVD simply will not work. What can the fashion forecaster do?

First, you should investigate the size of the room, types of equipment available, and ask if technical assistance will be available during the presentation. If there are any doubts about the equipment, bring your own. Today overhead projectors, laptop computers, and data projectors are made to travel or are available through rental services. It would also be advisable to carry samples of actual storyboards in case visual projection equipment does not work and technical assistance cannot get the job done. Backup computer disks or jump drives are a big help when the CD-ROM or DVD does not work. The authors of this book even had to borrow a laptop from a Korean colleague to make a presentation at an international meeting. Can you imagine making PowerPoint work with a computer configured in a foreign language?

Plan on distributing printed copies of the report with key points identified. Not only will the audience appreciate a physical document, it will provide space for their personal notes and thoughts. Backup strategies and contingencies can save the day. If you do not want people to read during your oral presentation, distribute handouts at the conclusion of the presentation.

Alternative Methods of Communication

Trend boards and graphics can be completely computer generated in today's rapidly changing communication world. Graphic designs can be created digitally. Photographs are routinely captured as digital images and easily transferred into presentations. Images are manipulated through cropping, resizing, changing color, and altering focus to create a variety of special effects. Text, in various colors, fonts, or sizes, can be added to visual images and animation effects to create dramatic impact.

While these new methods of communication make the presentations very exciting, they are not without problems. Fashion Group International's semiannual international trend forecast changed from a traditional slide show to a DVD format. Some regional groups had difficulty finding the appropriate equipment to show the program. Renting a DVD projection system is more expensive than using the slide projectors. As we mentioned before, equipment is more prone to failure or have problems with compatibility than through a face-to-face presentation.

Multimedia presentations are becoming more and more commonplace, and even expected with today's rapidly expanding global communication. Fashion forecasts are likely to arrive on a CD-ROM, DVD, or through a website. These methods also allow the audience to interact with the fashion forecaster via participation in electronic chat rooms or by providing feedback through e-mail. It is truly a new wave of communication.

Trends do not appear out of thin air. As we have seen in this chapter, they are changes brought on by consumer preferences and behavior. The development of a trend forecast is based on knowledge of consumers, brand positioning, and industry resources. A fashion forecast for the primary, secondary, or tertiary levels reflects up-to-the-minute fashion trends grounded in research. Using forecast research techniques, the fashion forecaster identifies information about fashion trends directed at the firm's selected target market. Data is collected on the important fabrics, colors, textures, and patterns and combined with information on the latest silhouettes and accessories. Societal and cultural concerns of the season are blended into the forecast, and together with the promotion team, forecasters determine the company's fashion story, which leads to the promotion strategy for the coming season.

summary

- Forecasting is the activity of anticipating what will happen next.
- A fashion trend may be a color, a fabric, or a style characteristic apparent for the coming season.
- A major trend is based on well-researched market information, has high sales volume potential, and test markets with positive results against direct competition.
- Trends emerge from society, culture, designers, raw material vendors, publicity, and consumers.
- There are professional futurists and fashion forecasters, and professionals who forecast as a responsibility of their job.
- Fashion forecasters work for fashion forecasting services or forecasting divisions within retail, manufacturing, or advertising firms.
- Forecasters present upcoming trends to consumers through promotion channels and review these same communication channels as resources to identify the next trend.
- The forecaster must have a complete knowledge of the primary, secondary, and retail markets.
- Each market in the distribution channel is responsible for forecasting trends to the next level.
- Central to the promotional strategy is the theme.
- Forecasters use every source available to research and predict trends.
- Forecasting services are available to clients wishing to buy commercially produced information on trend projections.
- Trends should be reflected throughout the entire promotional mix.
- Trend presentations incorporate oral, written, and visual components.

key terms

basic merchandise	fashion trend	primary market
classic	fashion trend portfolio	retail market
color story	forecaster	secondary market
fad	forecasting	theme
fashion forecaster	futurists	trend
fashion forecasting	haute couture	trend map
fashion merchandise	key item	trend storyboards
fashion report	precollections	

Questions for Discussion

1. What are the similarities and differences between futurists, fashion forecasters, and forecasters?
2. How is forecasting influenced by promotion?
3. How is promotion influenced by forecasting?
4. What distribution channels do consumers rely on for fashion forecast information?
5. What is the importance of a theme to the promotion strategy of a manufacturer? A retailer?

Additional Resources

Brannon, E. L. (2005). *Fashion forecasting* (2nd ed.). New York: Fairchild Books.
Guérin, P. (2005). *Creative fashion presentations* (2nd ed.). New York: Fairchild Books.
Weiner, E., & Brown, A. (2005). *FutureThink: How to think clearly in a time of change.* Upper Saddle River, NJ: Prentice-Hall.

References

7th on Sixth. (2006). *About 7th on Sixth and IMG Fashion.* Retrieved May 27, 2006, from http://www.olympusfashionweek.com/fall2006/img_fashion/

Advanstar Communications. (2005). *Corporate Information: MAGIConline the business of fashion.* Retrieved May 27, 2006, from http://show.magiconline.com/magic/v42/index.cvn?id=10056

Brannon, E.L. (2005). *Fashion forecasting* (2nd ed.). New York: Fairchild Books.

Cotton Incorporated. (2006). *Product trend analysis.* Retrieved May 30, 2006, from http://www.cottoninc.com/Fashion/

Fédération Françoise de la Couture (n.d.). *Federation activities.* Retrieved May 25, 2006, from http://www.modeaparis.com/va/toutsavoir/index.html

Krantz, M., & Cole, P.(1996). Cashing in on tomorrow. *Time,* 148(4), 52. Retrieved June 13, 2006, from the Academic Search Premier database.

Mahaffie, J. (1955, March 1). Why forecasts fail. *American Demographics,* 17 (3), 34.

Talley, A. L., (2006, August). Seasons in the sun. *Vogue,* 86–94.

FIGURE 5.1 Designer
Ralph Lauren.

CHAPTER 5

Promotion Planning

The Polo Ralph Lauren Corporation unveiled the formation of Global Brand Concepts, a group that will focus on developing lifestyle brands in exclusive partnerships with department and specialty stores. The collections could range from women's and children's wear to accessories and home furnishings. But make no mistake: They will not carry a Polo label, nor will they in any way be marketed to suggest Ralph Lauren is behind them.

Observing the retail scene overall, Lauren said, "There are a lot of things that need to be addressed. The large stores . . . sometimes don't see what they need or they want a new brand that says something about their company and gives them an identity, the way you need a face that says, 'Who am I, what do I stand for and what separates me from this other guy across the street?' We are big enough and have a team that is strong enough to develop individuality for these stores."

"If you look at our company, you see Ralph Lauren, Polo, Purple Label, Black Label, Lauren and children's," the designer said. "These are all concepts that grew out of a tie. It's all done under these offices. And there's Rugby retail and Ralph Lauren retail. There will be Lauren retail. They are all different concepts with a soul that has to do with Ralph Lauren.

"This is a place that is designed on every level, and we develop our advertising," he added. "It is like a school here. We do our own branding, our own planning as to how we're going to advertise. That kind of flexibility, that sort of dimension, says, 'What can we do that would be interesting?' "

Hypothetically, a chain like Penney's could contact Lauren about developing a new lifestyle collection. Global Brand Concepts would then enter a contract agreement with Penney's, and Lauren and his team would develop the brand from scratch, a process that would include concept, design, sourcing the fabrics, and contracting out production. Then the group would work on brand-building through advertising and marketing, all of which the retailer would finance.

Source: Karimzadeh, M. (2007, January 8). Ralph to the rescue: Lifestyle
guru creates private brand division. *Women's Wear Daily*, p. 1.

> **After you have read this chapter, should be able to:**
>
> Discuss reasons why planning is essential to the success of promotional activities.
>
> Define the meaning and use of mission statements.
>
> Identify components of a promotion plan.
>
> Compare the diverse categories of promotion calendars and know when to use them.

P OLO DOESN'T NEED A pony to score a goal. Polo Ralph Lauren's brands like Purple Label, Black Label, and Rugby are all seasoned champions brandishing their own popular identities. Lauren has a winning game plan, so why wouldn't it take its well-planned and proven promotional strategy on the road?

Successful promotional endeavors result from activities that are well planned and well implemented. Working out the infinite details, from defining goals and objectives to developing strategies and tactics to achieve results of promotion, and selecting the appropriate management team to carry out various responsibilities, are all part of the planning process. Giant textile producers, leading apparel designers, manufacturers, corporate retail conglomerates, and advertising superagencies all have developed highly sophisticated procedures for promotional planning. Within large firms, formalized and structured planning is essential. Only a few small businesses participate in promotion planning, but all firms would benefit from this process.

This chapter provides a map for promotion planning. We begin with a discussion about strategic planning and goals, objectives, strategies, and tactics. Three building blocks of strategic planning are discussed next: business planning, market planning, and promotion planning. The promotion plan is discussed in detail, including its component parts: situation analysis, communication process, budget, promotion mix elements, execution, and evaluation. This chapter concludes with a look at promotion calendars.

———o STRATEGIC PLANNING

Promotion planning involves the development of strategies and tactics for accomplishing all of the activities necessary to carry out promotional projects. The first step is to develop a strategic plan. **Strategic planning** is the process of determining goals, setting objectives, and implementing strategies and tactics to realize the goals. The strategic plan is often a **long-term plan**, covering more than two years into the future. Simply put, strategic planning is determining what you want to accomplish (objectives), how to accomplish it (strategies), and how to implement it (tactics). Important components of strategic planning include thinking about diverse alternatives, weighing the strengths and weaknesses of each approach, and identifying the best approach in light of current and future market conditions.

Goals are the end results that a business wants to achieve. Goals are broad statements that define what a firm expects to achieve, generally long term. According to its website, the goal of American Eagle Outfitters is to be a leading retailer designing, marketing, and selling its own brand of laid-back, current clothing targeting 15- to 25-year-olds, providing high-quality merchandise at affordable prices (2005).

Goals are realized through objectives, strategies, and tactics. **Objectives** are outcomes desired by the firm over a short time frame. They are considered a **short-term plan,** created for a period of six months to one year. Using this definition, the terms *goals* and *objectives* are *not* interchangeable. Shimp (2007) states three essential reasons objectives should be established prior to strategy and tactic implementation.

1. Setting objectives provides formalized management consensus. The exercise causes everyone from top management to marketing personnel and promotion personnel to agree on the strategy during the planning phase before implementation.
2. Setting objectives guides budget, message, media, promotion choices, and other aspects of strategy.
3. Objectives provide standards by which results can be measured.

Good objectives are written in clear and precise terms. Minimally, objectives should specify *who*—the target market, *what*—the purpose to be accomplished (i.e., create awareness, increase purchase intention), and *when*—the time frame in which it will be accomplished. Additionally, objectives should be quantifiable and measurable, specifically stating the amount of change expected. Examples of objectives are provided throughout this chapter.

Strategies are the plans, methods, or designs by which to accomplish an objective. According to Mintzberg and Waters (1983), strategy has four dimensions: (1) *strategy is a plan*, a set of guidelines intended to influence behavior in the future; (2) *strategy is a*

FIGURE 5.2 Models taking the runway at the Champion fashion show to launch its O2Cool apparel line.

position, the means to define or at least to identify an organization in an environment; (3) *strategy is a perception*, organizational strategy is how the members of an organization view their world, and (4) *strategy is a pattern*, synonymous with consistency, what actually happens in the organization.

Tactics are the specific ways in which a promotion strategy is executed. Specific promotion strategies and tactics are described throughout this text for each promotion mix element.

The following example from apparel manufacturer Champion is used to show the difference between goals, objectives, strategies, and tactics. According to its corporate website, Champion's goal for over 20 years has been to give active women exactly what they want—athletic clothing that is supportive, stylish, and comfortable (2006). To realize this goal, Champion launched a new line for fitness enthusiasts who appreciate performance benefits (Monget, 2006).

A company objective was *to create excitement among 18- to 49-year-olds for its new women's performance athleticwear line, O2Cool*. Many strategies could have been used to accomplish this objective. Hypothetically, the company could have developed an advertising campaign (strategy) to run in national magazines and on cable television (tactics). Or the company could have developed a public relations campaign (strategy) using celebrity spokespersons to endorse the line at select retailers (tactics).

In reality, the company used a fashion show strategy (Fig. 5.2). Tactics included producing four fashion shows for Disney's Minnie Marathon Weekend using models from the Orlando Magic Dancers, and sponsored by Lady Foot Locker (Monget, 2006).

Planning takes place at many levels within an organization. In the following section we will discuss the various levels and show the interdependency of planning at each level.

——o BUSINESS PLANNING

Strategic planning is a three-tiered process beginning at the corporate level, moving to the functional level, and finishing at the area-specific level (Fig. 5.3). Planning begins at the corporate level with development of a mission statement and business plan.

BOX 5.1
Grayson Produces Brand Audit System

As the number of product launches escalates, so do the chances for failure, prompting longtime industry consultant Suzanne Grayson to come up with a numerical system that she said will score a product's potential for success.

Called Brand Audit, it's a system designed either to gauge a new product's chance, or to measure the potential for revitalization of an existing brand by sizing up its strengths and weaknesses versus the competition.

The system focuses on five areas of the marketing mix: product, positioning, consumer appeal, competition, and marketing potential. In addition, there are 29 subcategories of measurement, with numerical scores providing a weighted analysis. On a scale of 100, a score of 80 or more "indicates strong potential for success," Grayson said. "Less than that demonstrates serious need for improvement and [shows] exactly where those improvements should be made."

Grayson, president of Grayson Associates, based in San Juan Capistrano, California, and New York, said that in her consulting experience, companies often rely on "narrowcast thinking" when it comes to new product launches. Products often are based on technology, are conceived out of competitive pressure, or come about simply to mark an anniversary of a previous launch.

"Rarely is a new product concept put through the paces of the marketing mix to determine its true potential," she stated. "And certainly, there is no disciplined methodology for evaluating a variety of new product ideas to assay which ones will have the best long-range potential. In addition, sagging products or brands may be put through the same system to uncover strategic weaknesses, or sometimes hidden strengths, to provide the basis for stimulating growth."

Source: Born, P. (2006, July 21). Grayson produces brand audit system. *Women's Wear Daily*, p. 4.

FIGURE 5.3 Strategic planning model.

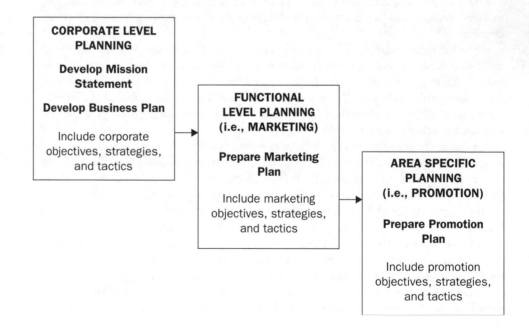

Mission Statement

An organization's mission defines the purpose of the firm and what it wants to accomplish. Most large corporations formalize this explanation into a **mission statement.** The mission statement usually covers a discussion of the company's products, services, and target consumers. This guiding force for the company is frequently presented in corporate literature such as annual reports, newsletters, and corporate websites. Often a significant aspect of the firm's plans and actions, the mission statement is frequently displayed in the retail store or manufacturer's offices.

The mission of the Neiman Marcus Group, a distinguished retailer offering upscale assortments of apparel, accessories, jewelry, beauty, and decorative home products to the affluent consumer, is defined in Figure 5.4.

Professional organizations also define their purpose by writing a mission statement. The organization uses this information as a focus for its meetings, publications, and interaction with professionals. The mission statement for the Fashion Group International is provided in Figure 5.5.

Additionally, organizations may also develop vision statements. A **vision statement** is a positive and inspiring statement that draws upon the mission statement to address where the company wants to be in the future. These statements are generally long range in nature, covering 10–20 years. For example, DuPont defines its vision as follows:

Our vision is to be the world's most dynamic science company, creating sustainable solutions essential to a better, safer, and healthier life for people everywhere (2006).

Business Plan

A **business plan** defines the broadest decisions of an organization. According to the United States Small Business Administration, a business plan precisely defines a business, identifies the goals, and serves as the firm's resume (n.d.). The plan is intended to help a firm allocate resources, handle unforeseen complications, make good business decisions, and inform all necessary stakeholders about the firm's operations and goals. The development of a business plan is beyond the scope of this text.

──o Market Planning

Once planning has taken place at the corporate level, it moves to the functional levels of the organization. We have used marketing, introduced in Chapter 1, to represent a functional level.

Marketing Plan

A **marketing plan,** also known as a **strategic marketing plan** is a document that describes the overall marketing strategy developed for a company, line, product, or brand. Box 5.1 details a system for evaluating a brand's potential. The marketing plan is consistent with the company mission statement and reflects management goals for the marketing mix (product, price, place, and promotion/communication). It is used to set goals and objectives for a specified period of time and should be reviewed and revised on a yearly basis. These plans range from simple to complex in nature. Most include five basic elements:

FIGURE 5.4 Neiman Marcus's mission statement.

MISSION STATEMENT

Our mission is to be the leading specialty retailer of fine merchandise to discerning, fashion-conscious consumers from around the world. We will strive to exceed customer expectations for service, quality and value as we build upon our long-standing tradition of excellence.

As we pursue this mission, we are guided by the following important values. We will maintain an uncompromising commitment to quality and the highest levels of customer service in all of our businesses and endeavors. We will adhere to the highest levels of integrity and ethical standards in dealing with all constituencies, including customers, suppliers and employees. We will aspire to achieve a leadership position in every one of our operating businesses. Our management decisions will emphasize long-term benefits to the value of our businesses, not short-term gains. We will employ capable, motivated people; follow sound management practices; utilize new technology efficiently; and reinvest earnings and additional capital as required to grow our businesses and maintain the corporation's financial health. We will strive to maximize the potential of all employees and maintain a professionally challenging work environment. We will be socially and environmentally responsible and support worthwhile causes, especially in those communities in which we operate.

Design: Sequel Studio, New York

1. Detailed **market situation analysis,** which assesses external and internal environments that affect marketing operations. It is a factual document thoroughly reviewing the company's capabilities. All relevant facts about the company are presented, including: history, growth, products and services, sales volume, market share, competitive status, markets served, distribution system, past promotional programs, and results of marketing research studies.

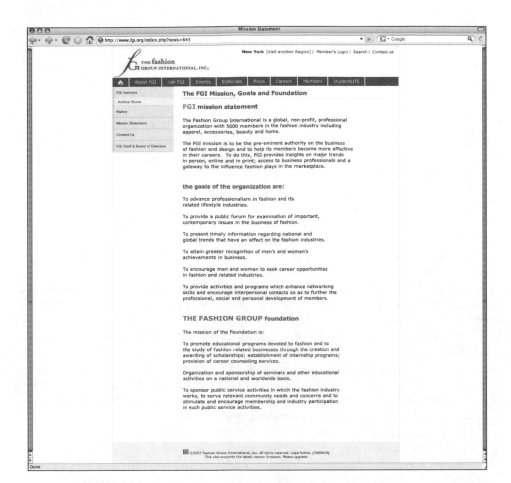

FIGURE 5.5 Fashion Group International's mission statement, organization goals, and the mission statement for the FGI Foundation.

2. Specific **marketing objectives,** which are statements that specify what is to be accomplished by the marketing program. Marketing objectives are expressed as measurable outcomes, typically based upon factors such as sales volume, profits, return on investment, or market share. A retailer may set a marketing objective of *increasing sales by 12 percent over last year's sales during the last quarter of the fiscal year*. This is an example of a broad yet measurable objective.
3. Marketing strategy and program. **Marketing strategies** describe how the company plans to meet the marketing objectives and involve three steps: (i) define the particular target market, (ii) determine the strategic position for each target market, and (iii) develop an appropriate marketing mix (price, product, place, and promotion/communication) for each specific target market.
4. Implementation plan to determine specific tasks to be performed and responsibilities.
5. Process for monitoring and evaluating performance including a feedback mechanism to make necessary changes to the overall marketing strategy or tactics.

While an in-depth discussion of the marketing plan is beyond the scope of this text, a detailed marketing plan outline is provided on page 153 to show readers the complexity of this document and its relationship to promotion planning.

───o PROMOTION PLANNING

Promotion planning is the development of objectives, strategies, and tactics to communicate to consumers about a company, line, product, or brand. The promotional plan evolves from the organization's marketing strategy, which in turn has evolved from the company's corporate business plan and mission statements. The development of a promotion plan is similar to the development of a marketing plan but with the focus narrowed to the promotion element of the marketing mix. This area specific planning takes place simultaneously to, or immediately following, functional planning. Many organizations believe the development of the promotion plan and marketing plan go hand-in-hand. They view each as a building block for the other. During the planning phase, planners review each promotion mix element for consideration in the overall promotion plan.

The promotion plan is typically created for a period of six months to one year. Most retailers use a six-month merchandise plan as a basis for planning. These firms are accustomed to planning sales, stock, markdowns, and purchases for the two six-month periods that constitute the fall season, from August to January, and the spring season, from February to July. It follows that the promotion plan will fall in line with the sales and stock plans. Retail firms normally prepare these merchandise plans approximately 90 days before the start of the season.

Promotion planning may take place at various departmental levels within the firm. The first step, therefore, is the selection of the proper organizational level at which planning will be focused. Promotional planning may be the responsibility of upper management: the CEO, president, and/or vice president in charge of promotion. The corporate management team then translates the goals and objectives to the lower levels of management and operation. This represents **top-down planning**.

Promotional planning may alternatively be the responsibility of individual managers who implement the promotional strategy. The advertising, public relations, merchandising, and marketing managers may be charged with submitting promotion plans to upper management. This flow of information represents **bottom-up planning**.

Should planning and communication occur in an upward or a downward course? In reality, information flows in both directions. Various interactions between top management and middle managers are necessary for the planning process to be successful. A further discussion of top-down and bottom-up management approaches may be found in Chapter 6.

As with the marketing plan, a promotion plan can be a straightforward or multifaceted planning document depending on the needs of the firm. A detailed advertising plan outline is provided on page 158 show the complexity of this document and its relationship to the marketing plan.

Promotion Plan

A **promotion plan** is a document that describes the overall communication strategy developed for a company, line, product, or brand. The basic elements of a promotion plan are shown in Figure 5.6. They include:

- Executive summary
- Promotion situation analysis
- Communication process recommendations
- Budget determination
- Promotion mix recommendations

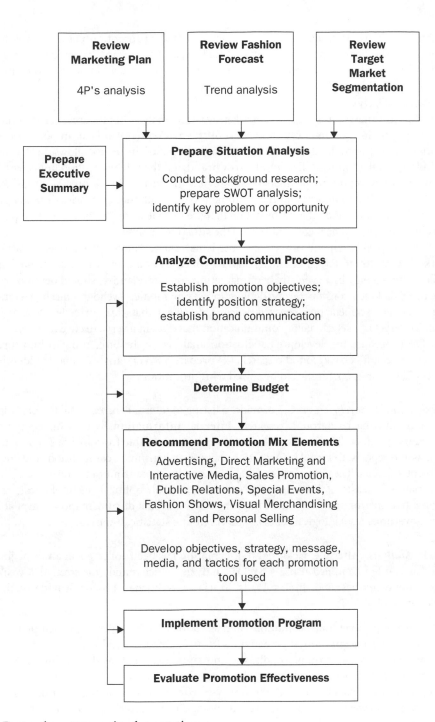

FIGUre 5.6 Promotion planning model.

- Promotion program implementation
- Promotion program evaluation

Executive Summary

The **executive summary** is a brief summary (generally not longer than two pages) of the key elements of the promotion plan or other document such as a fashion forecast or situation analysis. Although it is the first element of the promotion plan, it is written last—after all other components are finalized. The executive summary provides management with a rundown of the promotion plan in an easy-to-read and understand format.

Situation Analysis

The **situation analysis** is similar to a market situation analysis but focuses on issues relevant to promotion/communication. Review of the marketing plan is an important preliminary step prior to development of the promotion plan. The review allows the planner to understand the company, line, product, or brand and the role promotion holds within the firm. Just as important, planners should review the current trend forecast for fashion goods. It is critical to understand the prominent colors, silhouettes, fabrics or materials, design details, looks, and other information that are to be featured in the promotion plan. This information will be incorporated into the situation analysis.

An accurate description of the consumer is necessary. Planners need to assess which market segment(s) to target. Characteristics by which a population can be segmented are endless, limited only by the creativity of marketing analysts. Planners should develop specific profiles of their consumer using demographic, geographic, psychographic, behavioral, and/or benefit segmentation characteristics. A business that can correctly identify its intended target market can tailor communication messages in a very effective manner.

The procedure for developing a situation analysis can be broken down into three phases: (1) conduct background research, (2) prepare a SWOT analysis, and (3) identify key problems or opportunities to be solved with promotion.

Background Research. Figure 5.7 provides a listing of internal and external factors helpful in conducting background research. **Internal information** focuses on company, brand, and product data. Much of this information is available from in-house company records and reports. **External information** focuses on consumer, competition, and environmental factors. These materials and facts generally come from outside sources. This information consists of knowledge of economic, social, political, technological, and competitive environments in which the firm operates. This documentation is available from government, sociological reports, and economic statistical sources.

SWOT Analysis. After the background information has been collected, analysis begins. Analysis is often compiled using a **SWOT analysis**, which stands for strengths, weaknesses, opportunities, and threats. Wells, Moriarty, & Burnett (2006) provide further explanation of SWOT:

- Strengths—positive traits, conditions, and situations, such as growth, which planners can use as leverage in promotion activities for the company, product, or brand.
- Weaknesses—negative traits, conditions, and situations, such as diminishing market share, which planners can address with promotion activities.
- Opportunities—area in which the company can develop an advantage over its competition (often a weakness of another company) and use as leverage in promotion.
- Threats—trend or development in the environment that will erode the business unless the company takes action, such as competition. Planners need to address the threat if it is a critical factor to the success of the company, product, or brand.

Key Problem or Opportunity. By preparing a SWOT analysis, planners are made aware of promotion problems to be solved or key opportunities for promotion previously

---

Promotion Situation Analysis Internal and External Factors

Internal Factors

Assess promotion capabilities
Organization of promotion department
Ability to develop and execute promotional programs
Role and functions of promotion agencies and providers

Review previous promotion programs and results
Previous promotion objectives
Previous promotion budgets
Previous promotion mix strategies and tactics
Previous results

Assess implications for promotion based on brand image

Assess strengths and weaknesses of product/service
What are the strengths and weaknesses of product or service?
What are the key benefits?
Does it have any unique selling points?
Assess packaging, labeling, and brand image
How does our product/service compare with competition?

External Factors

Customer analysis
Who buys our product or service? How is the buying decision made?
Who makes the buying decision? Who influences the buying decision?
What does the customer buy? What needs must be satisfied?
When, where do they buy the product or service?
What are customer's attitudes toward our product/service?
What demographic, psychographic, lifestyle, or other factors influence the purchase decision?

Competitive analysis
Who are our direct and indirect competitors?
What key benefits are used by our competitors?
What is our position relative to the competition?
How big are our competitors' promotion budgets?
What message and media strategies are competitors using?

Environmental Analysis
Are there any current trends or developments that might affect the promotional program?

FIGURE 5.7 Internal and external factors to review when developing a situation analysis.

---

overlooked. The **key fact(s)** will be the focus in the creative strategy, which is discussed in Chapter 8. Two essential criteria for the development of key facts are (1) the problem or opportunity must be identified from the consumer's point of view, and (2) the problem or opportunity must be solved with promotion.

Promotion can solve communication-related problems such as knowledge, perception, attitude, image, or other message-related problems. Promotion cannot solve problems related to price, distribution, availability, quality, and so forth. For example, a retailer has recently seen a sudden increase in returns for a new style of jeans. Customers returning the jeans indicate they are fitting too low on the waist. Decision makers must evaluate whether the fit problem is a marketing problem or a promotion problem. If the jeans do not fit because the size measurements are not to specification, this is a *marketing problem* (dealing with the product). It must be solved at the manufacturing level and cannot be solved with promotion. However, if the jeans are correctly manufactured to size, but new fit guidelines have not been adequately communicated to customers, this is a *promotion problem* and can be solved with a promotion campaign.

Communication Process

From analysis of the promotion situation, planners can now develop processes necessary to communicate with consumers. Box 5.2 profiles how Internet sites can use technology to customize deals for consumers. What strengths and opportunities can be leveraged with communication? What weaknesses and threats need to be addressed with communication? During this stage, planners examine how they can effectively use promotion to communicate with their consumers. The process includes establishing promotion objectives identifying the product or brand positioning strategy, and establishing brand communication.

Promotion Objectives.   Promotion planners believe the objective of advertising and other promotional activities is to communicate with the target audience about a company, product, or brand. **Promotion objectives** are statements that specify what is to be accomplished by the promotion program. Setting objectives requires reviewing the target market and understanding the degree of experience they have with the company, product, or brand. Communication-based objectives are focused on four factors:

1. **Target audience.** The market segments the firm wants to attract, considering such factors as demographics and psychographics.
2. **Product.** The main features, advantages, benefits, uses, and applications of one or more of the company's wares.
3. **Brands.** The company's and competitors' brands.
4. **Behavioral responses.** The responses sought from trial, repurchase, brand switching, or increased usage.

The goal of communication is to persuade the target audience to take action, generally to buy a product. However, before a promotion specialist can convince a customer to take action they must inform, persuade, or remind the consumer about the company, product, or brand. **Communication objectives** take the form of a specific communication effect such as creating awareness or developing favorable attitudes toward a product. This differs from the marketing-directed objectives based on sales, volume, or market share as we discussed earlier in this chapter.

A traditional hierarchical model for promotion objectives is illustrated in Figure 5.8. Consumers generally pass through a progression of stages beginning with lowest level objectives—making consumers aware—to highest level objectives—creating loyal customers. The steps in the promotion pyramid are:

1. To inform or make target consumers aware of available products and services.
2. To arouse interest within the target consumer group.
3. To persuade the target groups to take some form of action.
4. To encourage purchase of the product or service offered by target consumers.
5. To gain loyalty of the consumer group due to the success of the first four steps.

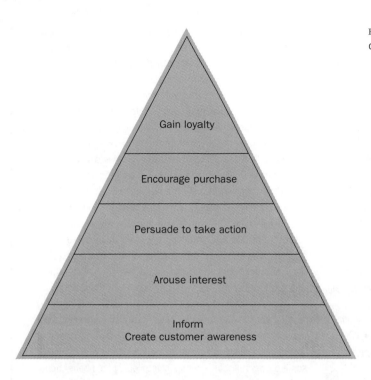

FIGURE 5.8 Promotion objective pyramid.

Gain loyalty

Encourage purchase

Persuade to take action

Arouse interest

Inform
Create customer awareness

○ BOX 5.2

Online Retailers Are Watching You: Sites Take Shopper-Tracking to New Level to Customize Deals in Holiday Season

This holiday shopping season, the price you pay online may depend on your gender and where you live. It may also hinge on what time of day you shop, the speed of your Internet connection, if you are an AOL user, or perhaps even your Google browsing habits.

It means a woman with a high-speed Internet connection in the South may get a flat-rate shipping offer from a retailer like Overstock.com, while a male counterpart in the West may see a promotion for live customer service instead. Some who logged on to Ice.com through AOL may be teased with a first-time buyer discount while someone who accessed the site directly would be left perkless. And someone using the word "cheap" while searching for gift baskets using Google may be surprised with a free shipping deal at a gourmet-food retailer like DelightfulDeliveries.com.

Browser beware: While they are loath to reveal which attributes affect which promotions—both in response to concerns about privacy and intense competition among online retailers—Internet merchants are picking up on a shopper's digital trail and mining the wealth of information they collect about shoppers to tailor their promotional offers with ever-greater precision.

The new targeting strategies are part of retailers' efforts to boost sales by better matching deals with customers most likely to respond as this season's shopping race begins. Since the start of November, Internet retail sales this season are up 23%, according to comScore Networks Inc., thanks to aggressive marketing and shoppers' growing ease with buying more, and more expensive, items online.

As more shoppers migrate online, retailers are finding new ways to track them. Unlike shoppers who head to the mall, online shoppers' intentions and tastes are stored and saved. That presents online retailers from mom-and-pop shops to industry leaders like Amazon.com Inc. with a vast amount of data to tap to better hone offers and display merchandise. This type of customizing earlier centered mostly on product recommendations, with sites displaying items that other shoppers who have purchased that particular item also have bought. But technology now is taking that to a new level, allowing similar customization without the shopper even logging in.

While sophisticated promotional targeting has been possible for years, it is becoming more widely available, with some analysts estimating that up to half of online retailers are using it. With new e-commerce platforms, companies are turning to it to stay competitive. Retailers say the promotions are more based on science than psychology; they choose which offers to target to whom based on real-time testing of what is most effective. The offers that generate the most sales stick.

"We don't want to show parkas on the homepage when someone comes in from Florida," says Patrick Byrne, chief executive of Overstock.com, which tests making various offers, like 5% discounts versus $5 off, to different customer segments based on factors like the type of Internet connection they use.

Overstock.com Inc. has begun displaying one of several thousand promotions—from free shipping offers to discounted merchandise—to different visitors based on some 40 attributes tied to the shopper's session. These include the time of day, determined by the time zone indicated by a computer's Internet address, as well as the shopper's presumed gender. (The company says it can typically determine a shopper's gender after about five to 10 clicks.)

Using a similar method, merchants like eBay Inc. are displaying different homepages to shoppers based on their previous viewing habits while others are targeting by geography. Ice.com, for instance, is displaying specific homepages for cities such as Seattle, Chicago and Los Angeles, and is also experimenting with testing varying offers such as free versus discounted shipping in different parts of the country. Internet fashion retailer Yoox Corp. has begun reducing prices in select regions and for the holidays has created a special, password-protected area of Yoox.com for frequent customers to give them an early look at discounts.

Meanwhile, companies are examining keywords used on search engines such as Yahoo or Google to guess what offers are likely to be popular. Delightful Deliveries Inc., a gift and gourmet retailer, presents different customers with offers based on what search term they used to arrive at the site. Someone who arrived at the site by using Google to search for "gift basket" may be offered a 5% discount, for example, while someone who clicked through after searching for "Christmas cookies" may see a free-shipping deal instead.

Tabitha Eller, 19 years old, of New London, Conn., says she is faced with a different promotion almost every time she goes to shop on Web sites like UrbanOutfitters.com or Anthropologie.com. "It's a challenge because I know it will only be a 'special' for a few days," she says. Ms. Eller says she used to

find it "creepy" that sites would show items she has previously viewed, but now finds it helpful. Others say the constant price variation is irksome. Millie Ritz, 43, of Youngstown, Ohio, last week purchased a "DreamLife" TV game for her nine-year-old daughter and "Guitar Hero 2" video game for her son, both from Amazon.com. After paying around $30 for the TV game and $64 for the videogame package, she returned to the site last weekend to buy the same two items for relatives. The prices were up to $38 and $80, respectively, and she is holding off. "I might as well wait and see if they fall again," says Ms. Ritz.

Offers targeted at first-time buyers may also mean that repeat customers may end up paying more. Ice.com offers discounts sometimes targeted to first-time shoppers coming from a specific site like AOL. The company looks at so-called cookies—data that are transferred between a Web browser and a server when a user visits a site—to determine whether they previously visited the site.

Online merchants insist the data are only used internally and are not shared with other sites. They also say much of the information remains anonymous and is not necessarily pegged to an individual shopper. But the new practices are alarming some privacy advocates, who say retailers should better notify their customers that their actions are being tracked. "The public is totally unaware," says Jeffrey Chester, executive director of the Center for Digital Democracy, a privacy watchdog based in Washington, D.C., that is calling upon the Federal Trade Commission to investigate online-marketing practices.

Retailers that are reluctant to target individual customers are using Web data to tweak their site-wide promotions based on factors like peak traffic times. Outdoor retailer Sierra Trading Post Inc. will refresh promotions like site-wide sales or discounts on skis and snowshoes during peak traffic periods, says Doug Williams, director of e-commerce for the company, which tend to be earlier in the week.

But a growing number of retailers now believe there is a place for tactful and targeted offers on the shopping sites. Kiyonna Clothing Inc., an online fashion site for plus-size women, shows different customers different offers based on real-time information about their sessions. For customers who appear to be on the fence about a purchase (i.e., they have gone back and forth between the checkout page) the site often generates a free shipping offer valid only if the shopper completes the sale that day.

Source: Vascellaro, J. E. (2006, November 28). Online retailers are watching you: Sites take shopper-tracking to new level to customize deals in holiday season. *Wall Street Journal*, p.D1.

Consumer Stage	Sample Objective
Developing awareness	*To create a 90 percent awareness of Sally Hansen ColorFast One Coat Fast-Dry Enamel among 18- to 24-year-old females during the first 6 weeks of the campaign.*
Becoming interested	*To communicate the distinctive benefits of Sally Hansen ColorFast One Coat Fast-Dry Enamel—that it provides a silicone protection and shine that dries in just 90 seconds, salon-style, in cutting edge colors, using 1 coat—to 75 percent of the target audience to interest them in the brand.*
Desiring to take action	*To create positive feelings toward Sally Hansen ColorFast One Coat Fast-Dry Enamel among 50 percent of the target audience and a preference for the brand among 25 percent.*
Proceeding to take action	*To use sampling to elicit experimentation with Sally Hansen ColorFast One Coat Fast-Dry Enamel among 15 percent of the 18- to 24-year-old females during the first 2 months of the product launch.*
Making repeat purchases	*To use cents-off coupons to elicit replenishment purchase of Sally Hansen ColorFast One Coat Fast-Dry Enamel among 10 percent of the 18- to 24-year-old females during the first 3 months of the product launch.*
Becoming brand loyal	*To develop and maintain regular customers of Sally Hansen ColorFast One Coat Fast-Dry Enamel among 5 percent of the 18- to 24-year-old females.*

FIGURE 5.9 Promotion objective examples for Sally Hansen ColorFast One Coat Fast-Dry Enamel.

Additional promotion objectives used in the merchandising environment include:

- To introduce new products.
- To inform about merchandise assortment.
- To establish fashion authority.
- To present special merchandise, prices, or themes.
- To attract new customers.
- To inform about public and community service.
- To provide education.
- To reach persons who influence the purchaser.
- To identify and differentiate brands.
- To build traffic.

Figure 5.9 is an example of promotion objectives for marketing Sally Hansen ColorFast One Coat Fast-Dry Enamel to 18- to 24-year-old women. The well-written objectives are expressed in clear and precise terms. These objectives specify *who, what,* and *when* about the objectives. Additionally, these objectives are quantifiable and measurable, stating the amount of change expected. The objectives address the successive stages that consumers pass through in developing brand loyalty. The first level is developing awareness in the desired target market. The next objective is to communicate benefits and features to arouse interest. Once promotion has brought the consumer from awareness of the new product to knowledge of its benefits, the objective of the next level is to create the desire to take action based upon a positive feeling toward the product. The point now is to turn a certain percentage of the target market toward purchase. This action stage is near the top of the hierarchy. Manufacturers may use sampling or coupons to stimulate action. Consumers will be influenced by the communication message as well as the potential savings with a trial sample or a cents-off coupon. The ultimate communication objective is to turn experimenters into loyal customers. It is hoped

TABLE 5.1   *The Right Tools for the Job—an Objective-by-Tool Matrix*

Objective	Advertising	In-store Promotion	Branded Promotion	Price-off Promotion	Direct Response	Mailers	Events	Exhibitions	Public Relations
Create awareness	yes	yes	yes	yes	yes	yes	yes	yes	yes
Create trial endorsement	yes	yes	yes	yes	yes	yes	yes	yes	yes
Current users	yes	no	no	no	no	yes	no	no	yes
Expand users	yes	yes	yes	yes	yes	yes	yes	yes	yes
Expand usage/users	yes	no	no	no	no	yes	no	no	no
Retain customer base	yes	no	no	no	no	yes	no	no	no
Create perceptions	yes	no	no	no	no	yes	yes	yes	yes
Change attitudes	yes	yes	no	no	no	no	yes	yes	yes

Adapted from: Interactive Financial Mall/Ad focus/Top Tables [On-line]. Available: http://www.fm.co.za/adfocus/tables/tools.htm

that once they use the product, consumers will continue to use it and will repurchase it. The final objective during the product launch is to retain a modest percentage of the target market as brand-loyal consumers.

The top executives of a firm must determine how specific communication objectives will be carried out by which promotion mix activities. Promotion personnel in South Africa have studied this concern and have provided a tool for analyzing which promotion mix tools work best for various communication objectives. Table 5.1 features this objective-by-tool matrix.

Position Strategy. A broad study of the competition was identified in the promotion situation analysis. Planners use this assessment to evaluate the competition and decide their product or brand's point of differentiation or position in comparison to the competition.

Positioning refers to how consumers view and compare competitive products or brands. Positioning is used to cause consumers to perceive a particular company's product, brand, or store image as completely different from other competing brands or products. When developing a promotion strategy, positioning defines the perception consumers will have of the product or brand. Six questions should be asked when developing a position strategy:

1. Do we already *have* a position within the mind of the consumer? If so, what is it?
2. What position do we *want* to have in the mind of the consumer?
3. What companies must be surpassed to establish this position?
4. Do we have an adequate budget to gain and/or hold this position?
5. Do we have the staying power to stick with one consistent positioning strategy?
6. Does our creative approach fit with the positioning strategy? (Belch & Belch, 2007).

For most products, multiple choices exist, causing the consumer to decide between alternatives. Therefore, promotion specialists concentrate on designing positioning strategies that focus on specific benefits the consumer will gain by purchasing their firm's product. Benefits are features that fulfill needs such as quality, service, or value. Sea and Ski has positioned its sunblock as the best, providing consumers with benefits such as oil-free, non-greasy, allergy-tested, and never animal tested, to appeal to a wide range of consumers (Fig. 5.10).

Promotion planners also create positioning strategies that focus on the competition, comparing benefits of their product to their rival's product. Additional positioning strategies include the following:

- Product attributes—positioning based on particular product features important to consumers.
- Price/quality—positioning based on cost to consumer or superiority of product.
- Use or application—positioning based on how product is used.
- Product users—positioning based on group who uses the product.
- Product competitor—positioning based on the strength of the competitors' position.
- Cultural symbol—using the creation or use of a recognized symbol or icon (Arens, 2006).

Having explored the alternative strategies available, planners must decide which strategy is best for their purposes. The development of the positioning strategy is done by (1) identifying all relevant competitors both inside and outside of the product category, (2) identifying how the competition is perceived by consumers, and (3) evaluating the perceived needs of the consumer and selecting a desired position to meet those needs.

FIGURE 5.10 Sea and ski advertisement showing a benefits positioning strategy.

There are three approaches a marketer can take to position merchandise to one or many target groups: undifferentiated marketing; differentiated marketing; or concentrated marketing. An undifferentiated strategy is the most cost-saving approach to promote merchandise, but it is also the most risk-oriented strategy. In an **undifferentiated strategy,** the same positioning strategy is offered to the entire population without regard to market segments. This strategy is successful when a company has one product without variations that they choose to market. The risk is apparent if consumers are not persuaded to buy the product and an alternative strategy has not been developed. For this reason, undifferentiated marketing is used less frequently than the other two marketing methods.

Companies may choose a **modified undifferentiated strategy** by selecting the largest target market within a population and positioning to that segment only. However, most competitors are also communicating with the largest target market, so one segment is overtargeted while all other segments are ignored.

In a **differentiated strategy,** a company will provide a different positioning strategy to each market segment they wish to attract. Planners hope that sales will be increased through advertisements tailored to specific groups based on distinctive needs. This is a costly method and efforts should ensure competing messages are not being presented to the consumer.

Concentrated strategy is used by account executives who want to position to one segment of the population regardless of other segments. The targeted segment may not be the largest segment, but it will have greatest potential for success because of some other factor, such as ethnicity or age. In-language advertisements are examples of a concentrated approach.

Consumers constantly change, along with their tastes and preferences. Competitors also change, repositioning themselves within the market, introducing new products, and eliminating poor performers. A firm must continually monitor the perception consumers have toward the positioning strategy to obtain desired promotion results.

Brand Communication. Brand image or personality is a fundamental point of differentiation. Any name, trademark, logo, or visual symbol that identifies a product or group of a specific firm is a **brand.** The development of powerful, unforgettable brand personalities is aided by promotion. Many terms can be used to explain how promotion planners think about brands. Wells, Moriarty, and Burnett (2006) offer six aspects of a brand, all driven by communication:

1. Brand identity—how consumers perceive the brand. Brands must be distinctive, recognizable, and memorable, made so through identification markers such as the name or logo.

FIGURE 5.11 Global product ad for Clinique moisture control in *Elle*, Spanish edition.

2. Brand position—how consumers understand the brand. Requires consumers to learn about the brand and what it stands for compared to the competition.
3. Brand personality—how consumers feel about the brand. Brands take on familiar human characteristics, such as trustworthiness or snobbery.
4. Brand image—how consumers connect with the brand. The mental impression, associations, or symbolism consumers construct to create meaning for that brand, such as connection with lifestyle, or types of people who also use the product.
5. Brand promise—what consumers believe about the brand. Brand promise sets an expectation level with the consumer. They know what they *expect,* and they *expect* to get it.
6. Brand loyalty—how consumers act toward a brand. Over time consumers develop relationships with brands resulting in brand loyalty, purchasing the product regularly in the face of competition.

When planning promotions it is also important to identify the type of brand that will be promoted so objectives can be applied to the correct distribution channel. Brands are classified as global, mega niche, national, or regional. Products also exist as unbranded merchandise.

Global brands (Fig. 5.11) are brands broadly distributed worldwide. Such brands as Lancôme, Levi's, Hermès, and Gucci have gained international or global brand status. Due to international popularity, global brands may be confused with national brands. **National brands** are available throughout the United

States and include Bobbi Brown, Banana Republic, and Nine West among many others. **Regional brands** are distributed in one region in the United States.

Private label brands create an image of exclusivity through merchandise manufactured for a specific retailer. Corporations such as The Limited, which owns Express, Express Men, and Victoria's Secret, among others, have products manufactured by their own production division called Mast Industries. Nordstrom features collections known by the brand names Nordstrom, Brass Plum, Classiques, and Preview Basics. The store uses its name to create brand identity, which helps to ensure brand loyalty.

Unbranded merchandise (generic) is especially popular in food and beauty retailing. The primary benefit of unbranded products is the budget price point. Pharmaceutical and beauty industries promote generic products as an economical alternative to brand names.

Understanding the brand is critical to understanding how promotion can create an identity for the company, line, or product by emphasizing a symbolic association with certain values, lifestyles, or an ideal.

Budget

The budget is planned after the communication process has been finalized. Planners should determine what the promotion plan will cost and how the money will be allocated. The most common method used to allocate promotion budgets is percentage of sales. Methods for preparing a promotion budget are the focus of Chapter 6.

Promotion Mix Elements

Decisions concerning the role of each promotion mix element are the focus of the next step in the planning process. Particularly in an IMC environment where one simple, unified communication message is the preferred outcome, it is important that the advantages and limitations of all promotion mix elements be considered. Planners should be cognizant of which promotion mix tool works best for various communication objectives. Chapters 8 through 16 focus on the promotion mix elements. Each chapter will discuss the objectives, strategies, tactics, and execution for that particular promotion mix element.

Implementation

Execution is the implementation of the promotional project or activity after planning has been completed. Once the objectives and strategies for each promotion mix tool have been established, steps to implement them must take place. Smaller companies may use existing staff to develop advertising or plan events. Larger companies turn to the in-house promotion division or hire outside agencies to execute the plan as we discussed in Chapter 3. Agencies and clients must work very closely to assure the plan is followed and the objectives are realized. Execution of the various promotion mix elements is discussed in the following chapters.

Evaluation

Promoting merchandise and services in a global environment is a billion-dollar business. In order to justify these allocations, promotion personnel need to have information about various promotion mix activities and be able to evaluate their effectiveness. From the smallest print ad placed in a local newspaper to the global launch of a designer fragrance, the sponsor needs to know what was effective and what was not.

In the absence of evaluation, the sponsor can only guess at the impact of his or her promotional package. Almost everyone agrees that once a project or activity is performed, some evaluation needs to take place. **Evaluation,** the process of judging the worth or value of any activity, helps to determine how effective the communication program is by measuring against some standards.

Success or failure of each promotional project should be measured and evaluated as the starting point for planning for another project or time period. This evaluation serves as a basis for new activities. Research allows the promotional manager to evaluate specific program components and provides input into the next period's situation analysis.

Because billions of dollars are spent on promotion activities each year, avoiding costly mistakes is a very compelling reason to measure promotional effectiveness. Sponsors of promotion programs want to know if their communication packages are achieving objectives. If the objectives are not being met, the manager wants to know so he or she can redirect promotional efforts.

Opportunity from a marketing perspective is viewed as an area into which the company could move to enjoy a competitive advantage. Thus, **opportunity loss** is a missed possibility or a penalty associated with poor communications. There can be losses from ineffective expenditures in addition to potential benefits that are not met. Consequently, evaluating effectiveness of promotion activities may provide an opportunity to make money in addition to saving money.

Measuring promotional effectiveness assists managers in evaluating alternative strategies and making decisions. Typically, promotional executives must make many decisions in developing promotional strategies. They must decide between various creative approaches to determine which message is more effective. Should the cosmetic manufacturer use an emotional or an informational approach? Companies must also decide which media to use for communication placement. Should the furniture retailer place newspaper or television advertisements? Or the decision-maker might need to decide which of the promotion mix components to implement. Should the manufacturer create magazine advertisements or sponsor a special event? Research techniques and pretesting methods can assist the promotion manager in choosing the most effective creative approach, media, or promotion mix element.

Clients are demanding accountability for the expenses allocated for promotional activities. Has the creative department been too creative, losing site of the promotional objectives? Have the media planners appropriately evaluated the best media alternatives? Conducting research helps companies develop more effective and efficient communications. Appropriate measurements will increase the efficiency of promotional efforts in general.

Why Evaluation May Not Happen. Companies and individuals give many reasons why they do not evaluate promotional effectiveness. Many of these reasons are simply excuses as to why a job was not fully executed. Just as we learned in the communication model in Chapter 1, communication is not finished until feedback occurs.

Perhaps the most reported reason for not completing the measurement process is cost. Development of good evaluation techniques and appropriate research methodologies takes resources in cost and time. When time is critical, some managers believe it is better to spend more money on more media placement, more elaborate production, expensive artwork, or bigger celebrity spokespersons rather than on research.

It is true that hiring skilled researchers is expensive. Nevertheless, the risks of creating an ineffective message or of placing it in inappropriate media, or both, may cause a brand to fail to live up to its potential. Spending more money on media placement will not help if the message is poor.

Here is a case in point. A manufacturer of skin care items decided to launch a new moisturizer for people with sensitive skin. As the product went into test markets, sales did not meet expectations. The manufacturer decided to purchase additional advertising space in the regional newspapers and magazines rather than spend money analyzing the advertising. Sales did not improve and the manufacturer abandoned the product. Further analysis showed the problem was in the message, which did not communicate the benefits of the product. Research could have detected the message problem and perhaps saved the brand.

Many managers cite a lack of time as the reason for ignoring the issues of measurement and evaluation. Promotion professions are highly stressful and competitive by nature. Everyone seems to be diligently working on tight deadlines. Copy is sent to the printer in just enough time to get the job done. Managers believe that everyone has so much to do that they just cannot get around to testing.

Proper planning and time-management skills can be implemented to help overcome the rushed feelings associated with this profession. Although the highly charged atmosphere will never be completely eliminated, timeliness is critical. Getting the wrong message out or placing the message in the wrong media is of little value and may actually be a waste of time and money. When faced with a decision about whether to immediately implement an advertising program or to test it first, managers must make some important decisions. Even some testing can help to avoid costly mistakes or improve effectiveness. Proper planning and scheduling will build in some time for testing.

It is difficult to design tests to evaluate exactly what we want to know. Not only is it difficult to isolate the effects of advertising from other variables, but we may also develop research problems relating to validity and reliability or both. **Validity** refers to the testing procedure being free from both random and systematic error. Validity is concerned with bias and deals with the question *Are we measuring what we think we are measuring?* Research bias involves creating an influence or prejudice within the design of the research. **Reliability** means that the procedure is free from random error, and the measure is consistent and accurate. Thus, a reliable test would provide consistent results every time an ad is tested, while a valid test would provide predictive power to the performance of the ad in the market every time it is tested.

Although it is not always possible to determine the exact amount of sales attributed to the influence of promotional elements, research can provide some useful information. This information can be used to *fine-tune* promotion activities in order to help the sponsor improve its chances for meeting objectives.

Conflicting views about promotion objectives may occur within different industries, through products at differing stages of the product life cycle, or even with various people within the sponsoring organization. Top management may wish to know how promotion affects the overall image of the corporation, while the sales manager wants to know how sales were affected by promotion activities, and the creative director wants to know how well consumers recall or recognize the promotion. Lack of agreement by the constituencies often results in a failure to complete any type of evaluation.

With proper design of evaluation instruments, many or all of the questions identified above might be measured. Promotion elements are developed after objectives are established. By focusing on what objectives are to be met, the evaluation process can look at the results in relationship to objectives.

How do we measure creativity? How does a creative message contribute to the communications package? It is difficult to explain what creativity is, let alone determine how to measure its contribution to promotional effectiveness. A natural barrier exists between personnel involved in the creative processes and personnel involved in the sales management operations. Members of the creative team seek an environment where the creative process is not encumbered by measuring promotional effectiveness, feeling that applying these measures stifles creativity. Those involved in the creative side typically take the attitude that the more creative the promotion, the more successful it will be.

Personnel from both the creative and management staffs need to recognize the importance of working together for the success of the brand or product. Ultimately it is the responsibility of the product manager to know how well a promotion program or a specific ad will perform in the market.

Redirection of Promotional Efforts. Evaluation of the individual promotion activities in comparison to the overall communication goals is essential information for the redirection of promotional efforts. What part of the promotional campaign worked? What elements were not beneficial? Should more resources be placed in the sales force or made available for media placement? These are just some of the questions that should be asked prior to developing the promotion plan for the next season.

The planning phase, when goals and objectives are established, is essential. Promotion managers are offered many different choices as to how to spend the promotion budget. In a retail store the fashion show director, advertising manager, visual merchandising director, special events coordinator, and sales manager are all in competition to receive money and resources to implement their programs. Despite an overall goal to improve the fashion leadership and public awareness, the vice president of promotion will have to assess the merits of each project. That might mean that a celebrity designer trunk show would be funded rather than buying more advertising in the local newspaper. Budgets limit the choices, and the executive must direct the reallocation of funds and activities to best meet the promotion objectives.

──o PROMOTION CALENDARS

After decisions are made about which promotional activities will take place, promotion calendars are developed to keep everyone organized. Manufacturers, retailers, and advertising agencies rely on several promotion calendars to assist in achieving their promotional goals. Scheduling annual promotional events, based upon previous timetables, assists professionals in planning the next year's events and activities. Consumers have relatively consistent buying patterns. Back-to-school shopping peaks in August and September, while home fashions sales normally occur in July or August. Coat sales can be anticipated in October and clearance sales take place in January and July.

Calendars are prepared for various market levels and specific promotion mix activities. The most common planning calendars are the trade, retail, and individual promotion mix calendars.

Trade Calendar

The monthly guide to events occurring at the manufacturing level is the **trade calendar**. It is the listing of the major market weeks and generally precedes the retail calendar by two to six months. Merchandise presented and sold during a market week requires time to manufacture and import, and the paperwork must be processed far in advance of the shipment of the merchandise to the retail store. Merchandise arrival is timed so that it is available at the highest peak of consumer demand. It is the basis for the development of the promotional activities at the trade level.

The trade calendar is used by the buying staff, members of the fashion or marketing departments, and upper management of a retail store. Buyers plan trips to coincide with markets for the products they purchase. The divisional merchandise manager (DMM) or general merchandise manager (GMM) may accompany buyers from their divisions and work with several different buyers. Members of the fashion office may be assigned to specific divisions, or the fashion director may attend numerous markets, especially those that are most essential to the image of the firm.

The fashion director may visit the international designer shows in Milan, Paris, and London in addition to the New York shows. The fashion director may travel for several weeks each year.

Many professionals in the fashion industry are also familiar with *The Fashion Calendar.* This weekly calendar, published by Ruth Finley for more than 40 years, serves as a guide to market activities, focusing on the New York market center but also listing events in other cities across the United States and around the world. Retailers, manufacturers, and the press are apprised of dates and related information for key fashion events. This information helps to avoid potential scheduling conflicts.

The trade calendar is also used by manufacturers to schedule fashion shows and showroom activities. The New York fashion industry pulled together under the auspices of the Council of Fashion Designers of America to produce 7th on Sixth, a week of fashion shows created to present new seasonal lines of merchandise two times each year. Many of the famous designers as well as up-and-coming designers come together to present fashion shows, now coordinated by IMG, in tents at Bryant Park. Members of the media and retail community are able to maximize the number of shows they can attend in a short period of time. A sample trade calendar showing the schedule for Mercedes-Benz Fashion Week is provided in Figure 5.12. Like *The Fashion Calendar*, retailers, manufacturers, and the media use the information provided by the trade calendar to avoid potential scheduling conflicts.

Retail Calendar

The retail calendar, also known as the consumer calendar, indicates what merchandise is currently available in the retail store. It identifies what the consumer's fashion needs are throughout the year and is the basis for the creation of all of the promotion mix calendars at the retail level (Fig. 5.13). Themes, activities, and events are all built from the basic elements of the retail calendar.

The retail calendar is planned to have broad classifications of merchandise in the store when consumers want them. For example, October traditionally marks the transition from fall into holiday, so a holiday dress may be purchased in October for the Thanksgiving and Christmas season. A new bathing suit may be purchased in February or March to anticipate the upcoming season or spring break. Although these broad classifications, such as dresses or bathing suits, are normally available during the retail calendar season, theme and promotion mix calendars are developed with the season's specific fashion trends in mind.

The retail and trade calendars have the most consistent schedules from year to year. These calendars represent the continuous flow of new merchandise from the designer and manufacturer to the retail store. Merchandise is presented as a broad classification, like active sportswear. After the lines are reviewed, creative fashion themes are interpreted about the seasonal styles, colors, fabrics, and accessories. Based on these trends, the fashion

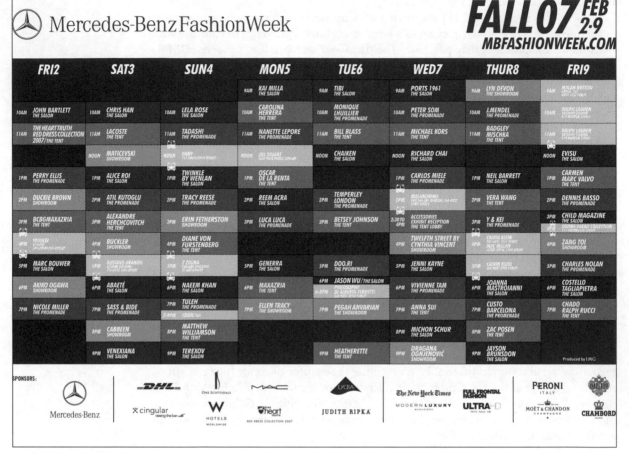

FIGURE 5.12 An example of a trade calendar.

forecasters predict the themes, such as *Olympic Gold,* and the various promotional mix calendars are generated to serve as a guideline for the season's promotional activities.

Promotional Mix Calendars

Based upon the fashion trends of the season, in combination with activities at trade and retail levels, various promotional projects or events are planned. For each of the promotional areas in which the firm is involved, a separate calendar of events is proposed. These promotional mix elements may involve anything from advertising to special events. A retail firm may develop a fashion theme calendar as the basis for the advertising, special events, and visual merchandising calendars. A firm may utilize a single promotion mix calendar or develop an individual calendar for each element.

Fashion Theme Calendar

The fashion theme calendar is a guide that indicates fashion trends and creative interpretations of basic categories. The retail and trade calendars are quite static, listing the general categories of merchandise as they are presented at the trade and retail levels. These

January
Spring Color Story
Resort and Cruisewear
Early Spring Bridal Fashions

February
Spring Color Impact
Spring Dresses
Spring Suits
Spring Knitwear
Spring Shoes

March
Spring Accessories
Spring Coats
Spring Intimate Apparel
Spring Active Sportswear

April
Prom and Graduation Dresses
Swimwear Highlight Shop Opening

May
Summer Color Story
Summer Vacation Clothes
Summer Vacation Highlight Shop

June
Hot Weather Clothes
Transitional Cotton Clothing
Summer Shoes

July
Early Fall Sportswear Registration
Fall Bridal Fashions
Fall Shoes
Early Fall Sweaters and Knitwear

August
Fall Color Story
General Fall Sportswear Impact
Fall Leathers and Suede
Back-to-School Highlight Shop

September
Fall Dresses
Fall Suits
Fall Accessories
Evening Clothes Registration

October
Boots
Evening Clothes Impact
Holiday Fashions
Skiwear Highlight Shop Opening

November
Last Minute Gift Center Highlight Shop Opening

December
Holiday and Christmas Saturation

FIGURE 5.13 An example of a retail calendar.

calendars simply list merchandise by classification such as "Men's Suits," "Junior Sportswear," or "Table Top," and do not take into consideration the more creative elements of the season. Fashion trends reflect these creative interpretations of the basic categories. In a fashion theme calendar, the "Men's Suits" category becomes *Moving to the Top,* while the "Junior Sportswear" classification reinforces the seasonal fashion trend called *Country Comfort Denims.*

Advertising Calendar

The **advertising calendar** for a retail firm identifies when, where, and what items will be advertised. This calendar is used by the promotion department to prepare ads or to send merchandise samples and product information to the advertising agency to create ads.

Store personnel also use advertising calendars. The dates and products on the advertising calendar are essential information for sales associates, who need to know what products will be featured so they can prepare displays of merchandise on the sales floor and gain product knowledge prior to customers arriving in the department. As customers arrive in the store, the merchandise should be featured prominently in a high-traffic area. If

VISUAL MERCHANDISING CALENDAR

MONTH: <u>March</u>

DATES:	March 1–14	March 15–29
PROMOTION THEMES:	<u>Wearin' the Green</u>	<u>Softly Pastel</u>

DISPLAY AREAS	MERCHANDISE TO BE FEATURED	
Main Street Windows	Donna Karan: Spring Designer Fashions	Gucci: Pastel Plaids
Junior Merchandise Windows	Quicksilver: Spring Green Dresses	Tommy Girl: Soft pink, blue, and yellow separates
Men's Windows	Ralph Lauren: Green Blazers	Private Label: Pastel Polo Shirts
Internal/Aisle Presentations	Merchandise focus on: Spring Green	Merchandise focus on: Soft pink, blue, and yellow colors

FIGURE 5.14 An example of a visual merchandising calendar.

merchandise has been delayed, the advertisement should be pulled. But if the ad could not be stopped, sales associates need to have information to properly handle customer inquiries.

Fashion Show Calendar

Locations, themes, dates, and times for the planned fashion shows are included on the **fashion show calendar.** This tool is used primarily by the fashion and sales staffs to plan and perform the various steps in fashion show production. The fashion show calendar may be used as an organizational tool for delegating and following through with responsibilities.

Special Events Calendar

Guest appearances, product demonstrations, vendor promotions, and other special activities are coordinated by using the **special events calendar.** The promotion department or fashion office may maintain this calendar. Plans as far as one year in advance are not uncommon for retailers such as Macy's. As soon as the Macy's Thanksgiving Day parade is presented, event planning for the following year is started. Coordination with the various departments is necessary in order to pull together seamless special events.

Visual Merchandising Calendar

The **visual merchandising calendar** (Fig. 5.14) is developed to organize visual presentations for the business. Visual presentations may be planned at the manufacturing or retail level. Manufacturers will put together displays in the showrooms prior to the start of a market week. Retail stores present merchandise as window displays, internal displays, or special theme shops.

Visual merchandising in the retail environment is frequently based upon the fashion theme calendar. Fashion window displays feature the fashion trends identified in the fashion theme calendar. The visual merchandising staff will take the major fashion themes and plan window treatments or interior displays to reflect these statements for approximately two-week time periods.

If a storewide theme is developed, the internal displays will be set to match the overall theme. The theme *Summertime Blues* could be featured in every department from denims in the apparel departments to blue plates, plastic beverage glasses, and picnic supplies in the home furnishings areas. With a storewide theme the trend can be shown in all areas. If a narrowly focused fashion trend is emphasized in the designer apparel section, perhaps color or fabric could be used to tie in other departments.

Appendix A: Marketing Plan Outline

Date:

Company Name:

Brand or Service:

  I. Executive summary
    A. Situation analysis summary
    B. Marketing objectives summary
    C. Marketing strategies summary
    D. Budget summary
 II. Situation analysis
    A. Industry
       1. Definition of industry and company business
       2. History of industry
          a. Technological advances
          b. Trends
       3. Growth patterns within industry
          a. Demand
          b. Consumption
          c. Growth potential
       4. Characteristics of industry
          a. Distribution patterns and traditional channels
          b. Regulation and control within industry
          c. Typical promotional activity
          d. Geographical characteristics
          e. Profit patterns
    B. Company
       1. Brief history
       2. Scope of business
       3. Current size, growth, profitability
       4. Reputation
       5. Competence in various areas
          a. Strengths
          b. Weaknesses
    C. Product/service
       1. Product story
          a. Development and history
          b. Stage of product life cycle
          c. Quality factors

      d. Design considerations
      e. Goods classification
         i. Consumer or industrial good
         ii. Durable or nondurable good or service
         iii. Convenience, shopping, or specialty good
         iv. Package good, hard good, soft good, service
      f. Packaging
      g. Price structure
      h. Uses
         i. Primary
         ii. Secondary
         iii. Potential
      i. Image and reputation
      j. Product/service strengths
      k. Product/service weaknesses
   2. Product sales features
      a. Differentiating factors
         i. Perceptible, imperceptible, or induced
         ii. Exclusive or nonexclusive
      b. Position in mind of customer
      c. Advantages and disadvantages (customer perception)
   3. Product research and development
      a. Technological breakthroughs
      b. Improvements planned
      c. Technical or service problems
   4. Sales history
      a. Sales and cost of sales
         i. By product/service
         ii. By model
         iii. By territory
         iv. By market
      b. Profit history for same factors
   5. Share of market
      a. Industry sales by market
      b. Market share in dollars and units
      c. Market potential and trends
D. Market
   1. Definition and location of market
      a. Identified market segments
         i. Past
         ii. Potential
      b. Market needs, desires
      c. Characteristics of market
         i. Geographic
         ii. Demographic
         iii. Psychographic
         iv. Behavioral
      d. Typical buying patterns
         i. Purchase patterns

   ii. Heavy users/light users

   iii. Frequency of purchase

  e. Buying influences on market

 2. Definition of our customers

  a. Present, past, and future

  b. Characteristics

   i. Shared characteristics with rest of market

   ii. Characteristics unique to our customers

  c. What they like about us or our product

  d. What they don't like

 3. Consumer appeals

  a. Past advertising appeals

   i. What has worked

   ii. What has not worked and why

  b. Possible future appeals

 4. Results of research studies about market and customers

E. Competition

 1. Identification of competition

  a. Primary competitors

  b. Secondary competitors

  c. Product/service descriptions

  d. Growth and size of competition

  e. Share of market held by competitors

 2. Strengths of competition

  a. Product quality

  b. Sales features

  c. Price, distribution, promotion

 3. Weaknesses of competition (use same factors)

 4. Marketing activities of competition

  a. Product positioning

  b. Pricing strategies

  c. Distribution

  d. Sales force

  e. Promotion

  f. Estimated budgets

F. Distribution strategies

 1. Type of distribution network used

  a. History of development

  b. Trends

 2. Evaluation of how distribution is accomplished

 3. Description and evaluation with channel members

 4. Promotional relationship with channel members

  a. Trade advertising and allowances

  b. Co-op advertising

  c. Use of promotion by dealer or intermediary

  d. Point-of-purchase displays, literature

  e. Dealer incentive programs

 5. Strengths/weaknesses of distribution systems

 6. Opportunities/threats related to distribution

G. Pricing policies
  1. Price history
    a. Trends
    b. Affordability
    c. Competition
  2. Price objectives and strategies in past
    a. Management attitudes
    b. Buyer attitudes
    c. Channel attitudes
  3. Opportunities/threats related to pricing
H. Communication (promotion) strategies
  1. Past promotion policy
    a. Personal versus nonpersonal selling
        i. Use of sales force
       ii. Use of advertising, public relations, sales promotion
    b. Successes and failures of past policy
  2. Sales force
    a. Size
    b. Scope
    c. Ability/training
    d. Cost per sale
  3. Advertising programs
    a. Successes and failures
    b. Strategies, themes, campaigns, media employed
    c. Appeals, positioning, and so on
    d. Expenditures
        i. Past budgets
       ii. Methods of allocation
      iii. Competitor budgets
       iv. Trends
    e. Opportunities/threats related to communication (promotion)
I. Environmental factors
  1. Economy
    a. Current economic status
    b. Business outlook and economic forecasts
  2. Political situation
  3. Societal concerns
  4. Technological influences
J. Corporate objectives and strategies
  1. Profitability
    a. Sales revenue
    b. Cost reductions
  2. Return on investment
  3. Stock price
  4. Shareholder equity
  5. Community image
  6. New product development
  7. Technological leadership

      8. Mergers and/or acquisitions

      9. Overall corporate mission

   K. Potential marketing problems

   L. Potential marketing opportunities

III. Marketing objectives

   A. Market need objectives

      1. Market need-satisfying objectives

      2. Community need-satisfying objectives

      3. Corporate need-satisfying objectives

   B. Sales target objectives

      1. Sales volume

         a. Dollars

         b. Units

         c. Territories

         d. Markets

      2. Share of Market

      3. Distribution expansion

IV. Marketing strategy

   A. General marketing strategy

      1. Positioning strategy

      2. Product differentiation strategy

      3. Price/quality differentiation strategy

   B. Specific market strategies

      1. Target market A

         a. Product

         b. Price

         c. Distribution

         d. Communication (promotion)

            i. Personal selling

           ii. Advertising

          iii. Direct marketing

          iv. Sales promotion

           v. Public relations

      2. Target market B (use same factors)

V. Action programs (tactics)

   A. Product plans

   B. Pricing plans

   C. Distribution plans

   D. Communication (promotion) plans

      1. Sales plan

      2. Advertising plan

      3. Direct marketing and interactive media plan

      4. Sales promotion plan

      5. Public relations plan

VI. Measurement, review and control

   A. Organizational structure

   B. Methodology for review and evaluation

VII. Marketing budget
    A. Method of allocation
    B. Marketing costs by division
        1. New product research
        2. Marketing research
        3. Sales expenses
        4. Advertising, direct marketing and interactive media, sales promotion, public relations
VIII. Appendices
    A. Sales reports
    B. Reports of market research studies
    C. Reprints of journal or magazine articles
    D. Other supporting documents

Adapted from: Arens, W. F. (2006). *Contemporary advertising* (10th ed.). New York; McGraw-Hill/Irwin.

Appendix B: Advertising Plan Outline

Date:

Company Name:

Brand or Service:

I. Executive summary
    A. Summary of information presented in marketing plan
    B. Advertising objectives summary
    C. Advertising strategy summary
    D. Budget summary
II. Situation analysis
    A. Company or product's current marketing situation
        1. Business or industry information
        2. Description of company, product, or service
            a. Stage of product life cycle
            b. Goods classification
            c. Competitive or market positioning
        3. General description of market(s) served
        4. Sales history and share of market
        5. Description of consumer purchase process
        6. Methods of distribution
        7. Pricing strategies employed
        8. Implications of any marketing research
        9. Communications (promotion) history
    B. Target market description
        1. Market segments identified
        2. Primary market
        3. Secondary markets
        4. Market characteristics
            a. Geographic
            b. Demographic

       c. Psychographic

       d. Behavioral

   C. Marketing objectives

      1. Need-satisfying objectives

      2. Long- and short-term sales target objectives

   D. Marketing mix for each target market-summarized from plan

      1. Product

      2. Price

      3. Distribution

      4. Communication (promotion)

   E. Intended role of advertising in the communications mix

   F. Miscellaneous information not included above

III. Advertising objectives

   A. Primary or selective demand

   B. Direct action or indirect action

   C. Objectives stated in terms of:

      1. Advertising pyramid

      2. Purchase behavior

      3. Other

   D. Quantified expression of objectives

      1. Specific quantities or percentages

      2. Length of time for achievement of objectives

      3. Other possible measurements

         a. Inquiries

         b. Increased order size

         c. Morale building

         d. Other

IV. Advertising (creative) strategy

   A. Product concept—how the advertising will present the product in terms of:

      1. Product or market positioning

      2. Product differentiation

      3. Life cycle

      4. Classification, packaging, branding

      5. Involvement

   B. Target audience—the specific people the advertising will address

      1. Detailed description of target audiences

         a. Relationship of target audience to target market

         b. Prospective buying influences

         c. Benefits sought/advertising appeals

         d. Demographics

         e. Psychographics

         f. Behavioristics

      2. Prioritization of target audiences

         a. Primary

         b. Secondary

         c. Supplementary

   C. Communications media

      1. Definition of media objectives

         a. Reach

      b. Frequency
      c. Gross rating points
      d. Continuity/flighting/pulsing
   2. Determination of which media reach the target audience best
      a. Traditional mass media
         i. Radio
         ii. Television
         iii. Newspapers
         iv. Magazines
         v. Outdoor
      b. Other media
         i. Direct mail
         ii. Interactive/digital media
         iii. Publicity
      c. Supplemental media
         i. Trade shows
         ii. Sales promotion devices
         iii. Other media
   3. Availability of media relative to purchase patterns
   4. Potential for communication effectiveness
   5. Cost considerations
      a. Size/mechanical considerations of message units
      b. Cost efficiency of media plan against target audiences
      c. Production costs
   6. Relevance to other elements of creative mix
   7. Scope of media plan
   8. Exposure/attention/motivation values of intended
      media vehicles
D. Advertising message
   1. Copy elements
      a. Advertising appeals
      b. Copy platform
      c. Key consumer benefits
      d. Benefit supports or reinforcements
      e. Product personality or image
   2. Art elements
      a. Visual appeals
         i. In ads and commercials
         ii. In packaging
         iii. In point-of-purchase and sales materials
      b. Art platform
         i. Layout
         ii. Design
         iii. Illustration style
   3. Production elements
      a. Mechanical considerations in producing ads
         i. Color
         ii. Size
         iii. Style

      b. Production values sought
         i. Typography
        ii. Printing
       iii. Color reproduction
       iv. Photography/illustration
        v. Paper
       vi. Electronic effects
      vii. Animation
     viii. Film or videotape
      ix. Sound effects
       x. Music

V. Advertising Budget
    A. Impact of marketing situation on method of allocation
      1. New or old product
        a. Media
        b. Budgeting
        c. Scheduling
      2. Methodology
        a. Central location tests
        b. Sales experiments
        c. Physiological testing
        d. Aided recall tests
        e. Unaided recall tests
        f. Attitude tests
        g. Inquiry tests
        h. Sales tests
        i. Other
      3. Cost of testing

        Adapted from: Arens, W. F. (2006). *Contemporary advertising* (l0th ed.). New York: McGraw-Hill/Irwin.

summary

- Strategic planning is the process of determining what you want to accomplish (objectives), how to accomplish it (strategies), and how to implement it (tactics).
- Strategic planning is a three-tiered process beginning at the corporate level (business plan), moving to the functional level (marketing plan), and finishing at the area-specific level (promotion plan).
- Business planning includes development of a mission statement and the business plan. The mission statement covers a discussion of the company's products, services, and target consumers. The business plan defines the broadest decisions of an organization.
- A marketing plan describes the overall marketing strategy developed for a company, line, product, or brand and contains five elements: market situation analysis, marketing objectives, marketing strategy, implementation plan, process for monitoring and evaluating performance.
- The promotion plan describes the overall communication strategy developed for a company, line, product, or brand and contains the following components: promotion

situation analysis, communication process, budget, promotion mix elements, implementation, and evaluation.
• The promotion situation analysis is developed by conducting background research from internal and external sources, reporting the research in a SWOT (strengths, weaknesses, threats, opportunities) analysis, and determining the key problem or opportunity promotion can solve.
• The promotion pyramid is useful in developing promotion or communication objectives. The five steps include to inform, to arouse interest, to persuade, to encourage purchase, and to gain loyalty.
• Positioning is used to cause consumers to perceive a particular company's product, brand, or store image as completely different from other competing brands or products.
• Common positioning strategies include product attributes, price/quality, use or application, product users, product competitor, and cultural symbols.
• Brand communication is a fundamental point of product differentiation. Six aspects of a brand include: brand identify, brand position, brand personality, brand image, brand promise, and brand loyalty.
• Evaluation is necessary to determine how effective the communication program is by measuring it against the results of the program objectives.
• Reasons why evaluation does not take place include: cost, time, research design problems, disagreements about what to test, and opposition to testing creativity.
• Calendars are tools used by promotion executives to keep track of various activities at the retail and trade market levels.

Key Terms

advertising calendar
bias
bottom-up planning
brand
business plan
communication objective
concentrated strategy
differentiated strategy
evaluation
execution
executive summary
external information
fashion show calendar
fashion theme calendar
global brands
goals
internal information
key fact

long-term plan
market situation analysis
marketing objectives
marketing plan
marketing strategies
mission statement
modified undifferentiated
   strategy
national brands
objectives
opportunity
opportunity loss
positioning
private label brands
promotion calendars
promotion objectives
promotion plan
promotion planning

regional brands
reliability
retail calendar
short-term plan
situation analysis
special events calendar
strategic marketing plan
strategic planning
strategies
SWOT analysis
tactics
top-down planning
trade calendar
undifferentiated strategy
validity
vision statement
visual merchandising
   calendar

Questions for Discussion

1. Why is it important to plan promotion?
2. What are the differences between strategic planning, business planning, market planning, and promotion planning?
3. What is a mission statement and how is it used to direct an organization's promotion activities?
4. What are the differences between goals, objectives, strategies, and tactics?
5. What are the steps in promotion planning?
6. How are calendars used in promotional planning?

ADDITIONAL RESOURCES

Arens, W. F. (2006). *Contemporary advertising* (10th ed.). New York: McGraw-Hill/Irwin.

Belch, G. E., & Belch, M. A. (2007). *Advertising and promotion* (7th ed.). New York: McGraw-Hill/Irwin.

Shimp, T. A. (2007). *Advertising, promotion and other aspects of integrated marketing communications (7th ed.).* Mason, OH: Thomson South-Western.

Wells, W., Moriarty, S., & Burnett, J. (2006). *Advertising principles and practice* (7th ed.). Upper Saddle River, NJ: Pearson Prentice Hall.

REFERENCES

American Eagle Outfitters. (2005). *Corporate profile.* Retrieved May 20, 2006, from http://phx.corporate-ir.net/phoenix.zhtml?c=81256&p=irol-homeprofile

Arens, W. F. (2006). *Contemporary advertising* (10th ed.). New York: McGraw-Hill/Irwin.

Belch, G. E., & Belch, M. A. (2007). *Advertising and promotion* (7th ed.). New York: McGraw-Hill/Irwin.

ChampionUSA. (2006). *About Champion.* Retrieved May 27, 2006, from http://www.championusa.com/womens/about.asp

DuPont. (2006). *Vision statement.* Retrieved May 24, 2006, from http ://www2. dupont. com/Our_Company/en_US/glance/vision/

Mintzberg, H., & Waters, J. A. (1983). The mind of the strategist(s). In S. Srivastra (Ed).), *The executive mind: New insights on managerial thought and action* (pp. 58–83). San Francisco: Jossey-Bass.

Monget, K. (2006, May 18). Champion launches an O2Cool line. *Women's Wear Daily,* p. 10.

Shimp, T. A. (2007). *Advertising, promotion and other aspects of integrated marketing communications* (7th ed.). Mason, OH: Thomson South-Western.

United States Small Business Administration, (n.d.). *Business plan basics.* Retrieved May 20, 2006, from ittp://www.sba.gov/starting_business/planning/basic.html

Wells, W., Moriarty, S., & Burnett, J. (2006). *Advertising principles and practice* (7th ed.).Upper Saddle River, NJ: Pearson Prentice Hall.

FIGURE 6.1 Proctor & Gamble products.

CHAPTER 6

Promotion Budgets

Proctor & Gamble Co., the consumer-goods giant and marketing icon, is sharply cutting how much it commits in advance to buying television commercials next season, according the people familiar with the situation.

The move by P&G, the maker of well-known brand items such as Tide, Crest and Pampers, is the latest sign of rapid changes in how companies reach consumers and TV networks and cable channels draw revenue. In recent years, many big companies have expressed doubts about the effectiveness of traditional TV advertising. Digital video recorders such as those made by TiVo Inc., which make it easier to TV viewers to skip commercials, are growing in popularity, while leisure activities like the Internet and video games are competing for consumers' time.

But big-spending P&G, with roots in the medium's earliest days, exerts wide influence on how other companies make their marketing and advertising decisions. The Cincinnati-based company is the number one U.S. advertiser, spending roughly $2.5 billion on TV—more than 80 percent of its estimated $3 billion ad budget.

While cutting back spending on TV commercials, P&G is looking to shift money into several different forms of TV marketing. Among them is increased activity in the fast-growing area of product placement—use of its products on TV shows—said people familiar with the situation.

By holding back on upfront commitments, P&G could be planning to spend more later in the season. Networks usually reserve about 20 percent of their ad inventory to sell closer to the time that TV shows air, in what is known as the "scatter" market. In recent years, prices in the scatter market have been lower than the upfront market.

Source: Flint, J. & Steinberg, B. (2005, June 13). Ad icon P&G cuts commitment to TV commercials; Top U.S. advertiser explores new ways to reach viewers; a product-placement surge. *Wall Street Journal*, p. A1.

> **After you have read this chapter, you should be able to:**
>
> Explain the significance of the budgeting process.
>
> Implement various methods of budgetary planning.
>
> Plan various methods of allocating budget to promotional activities.
>
> Discuss how channel members share budget expenses.
>
> Differentiate how agencies are compensated for their work.

Proctor & Gamble knows the more things change, the more they stay the same. With $2.5 billion in television advertising on the line, the consumer goods giant knows that innovations like TiVo and the Internet increasingly threaten returns on traditional broadcast advertising. But as a veteran from the olden days of television, P&G can trust that its creative teams will plan and budget effectively to develop promotion strategies to make the 21st century a golden age for TV advertising.

Determining how much to spend on promotion is one of the most confusing and difficult tasks associated with merchandising management. Whether the firm is a small business with limited allocations for promotion or a large company with global concerns and billion-dollar budgets, personnel involved in planning must not ignore the importance of the budget.

As we discussed in Chapter 5, the budgeting process is based upon the plans that define the organization's mission, goals, and objectives. With the mission of the firm in mind, financial specialists establish overall budgets for its operations. Then, in consultation with promotion specialists, they allocate budgets for promotion activities.

Business professionals with an accounting background and the Internal Revenue Service view promotion costs as current business expenses, which are similar to travel or any other short-term expense. As a result of this, financial executives may handle promotion budget allocations as items that can be trimmed or eliminated as sales decline. Although this type of action is understandable, it does not take into consideration the long-term investment benefits of promotional activities.

The financial executive may understand that a new building or warehouse is a contribution to the future, but fail to recognize that promotion can also be an investment in that future. Advertising, one of the promotion mix elements, is used to encourage immediate action and sales, but it can also be more fully developed for a cumulative long-term effect. Building consumer confidence and brand preference, as well as promoting goodwill, are examples of how advertising can be used for long-term impact. Since advertising enhances the reputation and perceived value of a brand, consumers will trust the company and its product. Thus, they are likely to become repeat customers. Although advertising may be considered a current expense for accounting purposes, it is also a long-term investment.

This chapter focuses on how an organization develops the budget and allocation for each promotion mix activity. We start by looking at the theoretical background of sales response methods. Next, various approaches to budget allocation are discussed. Methods of allocating the budget to different promotion mix elements are also considered. Since payments to outside agencies are budget items for many manufacturers and retailers who use such services, compensation procedures for advertising agencies are also introduced. Techniques for extending the budget through cooperative ventures are explained.

───○ ADVERTISING TO SALES RESPONSE MODELS

Before viewing the various pragmatic approaches to budgeting, it is helpful to understand something about how economists and advertising researchers view optimal expenditure. Researchers have developed the concept of marginal economic returns, which means that an organization will continue to invest in any business activity as long as the return on investment is greater than the cost. Related to promotion, the business will continue to invest in promotion as long as the return for that investment is greater than the cost to produce the promotion tactics.

Simple in concept, the allocation and evaluation process related to the concept can be quite difficult. Ultimately, two questions must be answered: (1) *To what promotion tactic should funds be allocated?* (2) *What is the return and how do we measure it?* One approach to answering these questions is to look at the advertising to sales model illustrated in Figure 6.2. Although this model was developed for advertising, it can also serve as a guide for promotion budgets. This model is also the basis for the percentage of sales budgeting method discussed later in this chapter.

The model indicates that advertising is effective between two points, the threshold point and the maximum sales point. Below the threshold a certain number of sales will occur without any advertising; above the maximum sales point, sales will not rise regardless of the money spent on promotion. Between the two points promotion can have the most effect on sales, the sales response to advertising. The shape of the sales response will change based on where the product is in the fashion cycle, consumers' response to

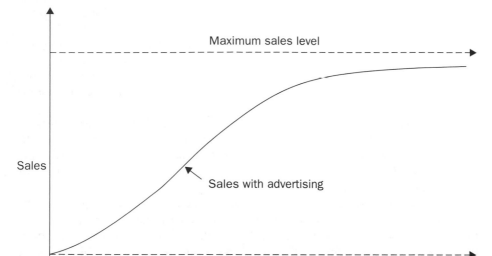

FIGUre 6.2 Advertising to sales model.

advertising, competition, and many other factors. Two theoretical models explain the relationship between sales response and advertising: the diminishing returns curve and the S-shaped curve. Although these models were developed with advertising in mind, they may also serve as a guide for most promotion mix budgets.

In the **diminishing returns curve**, visually represented in Figure 6.3 by a concave-downward shape, sales are stimulated by the dollars spent on advertising. The more a firm spends on advertising, the more it will sell-up to a certain point. Then, the benefits of additional advertising expenses diminish. As the amount of advertising increases, its incremental value decreases. This is because consumers with the greatest potential to purchase are more likely to act after initial exposure, while those who are less likely to purchase are not likely to change even with more exposure to advertising. The key is for promotion executives to determine at what stage this decrease occurs. This is not easy to do, because additional variables such as competitive products or price fluctuations can

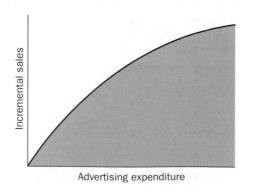
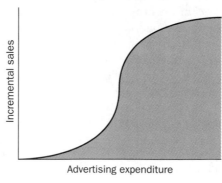

FIGUre 6.3 Advertising to sales models: Diminishing returns curve (left) and S-shaped curve (right).

also influence sales. Budgeting under this model implies that fewer advertising dollars may be all that is necessary to achieve success.

The **S-shaped curve** (Fig. 6.3) also depends upon a relationship of sales to advertising expenditures. Advertising managers who subscribe to the S-shaped curve model believe that initial outlays of the advertising budget have little or no impact on consumers in the early stages of sales. This is indicated by the relatively flat sales curve at the beginning of the campaign. After a certain level of promotional expenditures, advertising efforts begin to have an impact on consumers. Thus, as additional money is spent on promotion, sales will increase. This incremental gain continues only to a point, then the law of diminishing returns takes effect, suggesting that additional expenditures will have little or no impact on sales. In this case, there is no reason to spend any additional dollars on promotion or advertising.

To management, these models might suggest spending on advertising until it stops working. However, practitioners recognize that these models have weaknesses. For one thing, there are other factors that affect sales besides the amount of money spent on advertising, including better personal selling techniques, attractive stores, seasonal changes, or better-displayed merchandise. For another, it is unclear how advertising affects profit for a specific product, especially when a firm is likely to have several different products contributing to profits.

Even though these models may not provide tools for directly implementing the promotion budget, we can use them as a theoretical guide for our appropriations.

———o METHODS OF BUDGET ALLOCATION

In actual practice, theoretical models are rarely used to determine the promotion budget. We now turn our attention to evaluating some of the methods currently being used. There are many different approaches to budgeting. Large companies may use several distinct and scientific techniques, while some small businesses may use simple judgmental techniques or no budget planning at all. Regardless of the size or complexity of the organization, budgeting helps to indicate how, when, and where the firm intends to emphasize its promotional activities. Budgeting also provides a benchmark for evaluating effectiveness. Budget approaches may be considered top-down, bottom-up, or a combination of both. First we look at the **top-down approaches**.

Top-Down Approaches

In approaches designated as top-down, the senior executives establish the budget amount for the entire retail corporation or manufacturing concern at the highest management level of the firm. The money is then allocated to the various departments or divisions. Top-down budget approaches are dependent upon the experience and knowledge of the top management. These techniques are also referred to as judgmental methods since they are contingent upon administrative opinion. The top-down methods include all-one-can-afford, arbitrary allocation, competitive parity, percentage of sales, and return on investment.

All-One-Can-Afford

The philosophy behind the **all-one-can-afford** method, also known as the affordable procedure, is the belief that the portion of the operational budget allocated to promotional activities is the amount the firm can financially manage to spend. Actual tasks, specific projects, or methods of measuring promotional effectiveness are rarely taken into consideration with this simplistic type of planning. All-one-can-afford budgets are often overestimated or underestimated. Overspending or underspending can easily take place in this type of planning, because guidelines for evaluating the impact of various promotional activities have not been established.

In the fashion business, new designers frequently fall into the trap of believing so strongly in the creative process that they assume their designs will sell themselves. They allocate most of their budget to product development. After creating the line there is little or no money left to promote and sell the line. Such start-up companies, with limited financial backing, often think, *We can't be hurt if we know what we can afford and do not exceed it.* While this might be true from an accounting perspective, it does not reflect the significance of a communication and marketing viewpoint. Considering the S-shaped sales response model, this method might not allocate enough money to get the product off the ground. In other circumstances, sales might experience a slowdown in a tough market; this method would likely lead to promotional budget cuts at a time when budgets should be increased.

All-one-can-afford techniques are frequently used in combination with other budgeting strategies. This strategy is often employed for new products where historical information and perspective are unknown.

Arbitrary Allocation

Although arbitrary allocation is one of the weakest methods of budgeting, it is commonly used in the merchandising environment. **Arbitrary allocation** simply means that the budget is determined by management solely on the basis of executive judgment. In this method, the budget is created by management's belief in spending what is necessary. The goals and objectives of promotion are not taken into consideration. These feelings of intuition provide an environment for controlling managers to maintain their power. It is the least reliable or scientific of all budget approaches.

There is no good explanation why arbitrary allocation continues to be used except that it is cheap. It is not a highly recommended method. Our intent is to make people aware of its weaknesses and suggest more professional approaches.

Competitive Parity

Competitive parity is the first of the top-down methods to rely on objective data. **Competitive parity** takes into consideration the amount of money that a competitor spends on promotion and uses this information as a guide to promotion spending.

Although it might seem like corporate espionage, information about the competitors' spending habits is readily available. Data can be found in consumer publications, trade association newsletters, government agency publications, and the Internet. Merchandising firms can fairly accurately estimate the amount that a competitor spends by tracking promotional activities through a **clipping service**. This type of service cuts out competitors' advertisements from local and national print media. Since advertising rates are published information, the advertiser can determine the competitor's media budget and other expenses. Some retail stores assign this research task to executive trainees or assistant buyers.

Competitive parity offers several advantages. First of all, the competition is one of the major environmental factors influencing sales. In addition, competitors' use of promotion expenses is a guide to setting a merchandising firm's promotion expenses. Also, competitive relationships can be stabilized, minimizing aggressive market rivalry. Finally, unnecessary promotional expenditures are reduced.

Despite being a more scientific approach, competitive parity has its limitations. For one thing, this technique fails to recognize the specific goals and objectives of the promotional plan. As such, it would not be desirable in a firm committed to an integrated marketing communications (IMC) environment. It also does not fully appreciate the contributions of the creative process and allocation to alternative media choices. In addition, it does not consider failure of previous or competitors' promotional activities. It also assumes that firms with similar expenses will have equally effective programs.

The primary limitation of competitive parity, however, is the focus on the past. The ability to match competitors' expenditures is limited by the information available. Short of illegally placing a spy on a competitor's staff, it will be impossible for the merchandising firm to know what that competitor will do next. Competitors could take a more assertive stance or decrease their promotional expenses.

Executives and decision-makers must always be aware of what the competition is doing, but they should not just emulate them in setting goals and developing strategies. For this reason, it is unrealistic to use competitive parity as the only approach to promotional budgeting. Competitive parity is more frequently used in combination with another method, such as percentage of sales.

Percentage of Sales

One of the most common methods of promotional budgeting in the merchandising environment is **percentage of sales**. In this approach, the promotion budget is based upon a specific percentage of anticipated sales. Historical information about promotional spending is combined with sales forecasts to set the dollar amount for promotion expenses. This is a simple data-based application that requires the calculation of the amount of money spent on various promotional activities as a percentage of revenues. Even if an organization does not have its own historical data, the company can use industry standards, such as advertising-to-sales ratios developed annually by Schonfeld & Associates (Table 6.1).

The percentage of sales method is widely used in the merchandising environment and is easily defended. First of all, it is simple to calculate. Managers use sales figures as the basis for establishing fundamental financial goals, such as gross margin and profit. It is second nature for management to think of promotional expenses as a ratio to sales in this manner. Many managers feel that this method is financially secure since promotional budgets are linked to sales revenues. The risks associated with promotional activities are minimized since that function is associated with revenues. Finally, budgets are relatively stable. Whether looking at past records or forecasting for the future, the budget will not vary drastically.

Despite the many advantages and consistency of the percentage of sales approach, it does have weaknesses. The very core of this concept is anticipated sales. This is somewhat like the tail wagging the dog. Letting sales levels determine the advertising appropriation reverses the cause-and-effect relationship between advertising and sales. It requires one to think of promotion expenditures as an expense of making sales instead of an investment, whereas sales are actually generated through the use of promotion activities. Firms that consider promotion as an investment are limited by this budget method.

Stability is another problem with the percentage of sales approach. Although stability is desired through a consistent percentage devoted to promotional activities, it is a limiting factor. It does not take into consideration changes in the market, nor does it allow for innovation by competitors or introduction of new products or novel retailing formats. Aggressive firms may wish to allocate more funds to introduce these new products

TABLE 6.1   *Advertising-to-Sales Ratios for Selected Industries*

Industry	SIC No.	Ad $ as Percent of Sales
Apparel and other finished products	2300	4.8
Apparel and accessory stores	5600	3.7
Catalog, mail order houses	5961	3.6
Department stores	5311	4.4
Dolls and stuffed toys	3942	10.9
Drug and proprietary stores	5912	0.8
Family clothing stores	5651	2.2
Footwear, except rubber	3140	4.3
Furniture stores	5712	7.2
Hobby, toy and game shops	5945	4
Home furniture and equipment stores	5700	3.4
Jewelry stores	5944	4.9
Knit outerwear mills	2253	3.3
Men, youth, boys furnishings, work clothing	2320	4
Miscellaneous nondurable goods-wholesale	5190	1.9
Miscellaneous shopping goods-stores	5940	4
Miscellaneous retail	5900	0.7
Perfume, cosmetic, toilet preparations	2844	7.9
Radio, TV, consumer electric stores	5731	3
Rubber and plastics footwear	3021	9.4
Shoe stores	5661	2.4
Soap, detergent, toilet preparations	2840	10
Sporting and athletic goods	3949	5.9
Variety stores	5331	0.9
Watches, clocks and parts	3873	9.8
Women's, misses', children's, infants' undergarments	2340	4.6
Women's clothing stores	5621	3.7
Women's, misses', junior's outerwear	2330	2.6
Wood household furniture, except upholstered	2551	30.4

Note: SIC is the Standardized Industry Code.

Adapted from: Schonfeld & Associates. (2005). *Advertising Ratios & Budgets* (29th ed.). Libertyville, IL. Copyright © June 2005, Schonfeld & Associates, Inc.

or formats. Since new products do not have a past sales record, it may be difficult to forecast accurately the sales on which the advertising will be based. A start-up business cannot rely on historical records to develop its strategy using a percentage of sales budget analysis, whereas a firm with long-term accounting journals could more accurately utilize this method.

If promotion budgets are based solely on sales, they are contingent upon sales. When an economic downturn takes place, promotion budgets will most likely be cut. In such times, it may actually be beneficial to maintain or increase promotion expenditures to assure visibility and protect a strong image. As the economy strengthens, the firm is still in the mind of consumers who now have the purchasing power. Box 6.1 looks at how specialty retailers establish their advertising budgets.

Although percentage of sales budgeting has both strengths and weaknesses, it remains one of the most popular techniques since it is so easy to use. For the greatest effectiveness it should be used in combination with other methods.

Return-on-Investment

In the **return-on-investment** (ROI) budget approach, advertising and promotion are considered investments. The key word here is *investment*. The assumption is that the investment—expenditures on promotion—will lead to some type of long-term return.

This method appeals to financial officers and accountants, who like to have a measurable objective. The expense of promotion is justified by the results of the actions. How to assess the impact of promotional activities is not considered. This method will be limited, as long as sales are the primary basis for evaluation. How to measure success and what the actual return is will remain the primary limitations of this method.

Despite the limitations of top-down budget planning, the various top-down approaches continue to be widely used in the industry. Percentage of sales prevails as the most accepted top-down budgeting method. Alternative budget approaches begin at the lowest management levels, with managers who have the responsibility of putting the plan into action. Next, we look at the bottom-up budget techniques.

Bottom-up Approaches

Bottom-up approaches, also called buildup approaches, consider a firm's goals and objectives and assign a portion of the budget to meet those objectives. Rather than viewing the process as a judgmental method, planners link appropriations to objectives and the strategies to accomplish them. This takes into consideration not only financial plans but communications objectives as well. The idea is to budget in such a way that the promotion mix strategies can be activated to accomplish the expressed objectives. These types of budget approaches work well in an IMC environment, because the budget allocations are associated with the firm's goals and objectives. The bottom-up approaches include objective and task method, payout planning, and quantitative models.

Objective and Task

The **objective and task** method requires that planning and budgeting go hand in hand. This is a bottom-up approach that takes the planning objectives as a significant reason for the budget. The objective and task method consists of three steps: (1) stating the promotion and communication objectives to be achieved, (2) developing the strategies and tactics necessary to accomplish them, and (3) estimating the costs associated with implementing these activities and reaching these objectives. The budget is an aggregate of the costs identified with the performance of the promotional activities.

On an intuitive level, the objective and task approach has the most validity of all of the methods described so far. It takes into consideration all of the specific objectives and develops strategies to achieve them; however, it assumes that the planners know how much it will cost to meet those goals. Herein lies the problem. Is the objective worth attaining? What is the best way to increase brand awareness by 30 percent? Should newspapers be used exclusively or should other media be utilized? Is it possible to determine the best promotion mix? Many alternatives and variable strategies to achieve objectives

BOX 6.1

Establishing an Advertising Budget

Advertising doesn't cost," the old saying goes. "It pays." The short-term dollar-for-dollar return on money spent for advertising may not be apparent, but in the long term, the money you invest in promoting your shop should be rewarded with increased sales.

Most specialty shops need to advertise in order to attract new customers and encourage existing customers to return. Good advertising increases awareness of your products and enhances your store's image. It should help differentiate your shop from the competition, especially the discount stores and category killers that advertise nothing but low prices. Use your advertising to let the public know about your style, service, selection, and knowledgeable staff.

There is no limit to the many different forms that advertising can take, from a Yellow Pages ad to a banner towed by an airplane. Signage, window displays, shopping bags, brochures, and public television underwriting can all be considered part of your advertising program. Think of advertising as a challenge to your creativity and imagination. How many different ways can you find to express the appeal of your store and your merchandise to the buying public? What is the image of your store that you want all your advertising to project?

Pace Your Spending

Most traditional forms of advertising are fairly expensive, so you must spend your advertising dollars wisely, especially at first. Experience, based on the types of advertising that produce the best results for your store, will help guide your future decisions.

An advertising budget normally ranges from 3 to 5 percent of total sales, but can be as high as 10 percent. Retailing marketing consultant Jeffrey L. Greene suggests that four factors be considered in setting the budget: (1) traffic, (2) marketplace awareness, (3) competition, and (4) price sensitivity. If you have high traffic, are well known in your market, have few competitors, and place little emphasis on price, you will not need to spend much on advertising.

A new store needs to advertise more aggressively than one that is well established. Some sources recommend doubling your advertising budget for the first year you are in business. Of course, unless you are opening a franchise or branch store, you will have little way of predicting what this first year's sales will be. Doubling an advertising budget based on a hypothetical sales figure can be dangerous. A leather goods store on our street spent $10,000 on television advertising soon after opening, producing only $12,000 in sales. Had sales been $100,000, this might have been a wise investment. As it turned out, the store went out of business within a year. Check with other stores your size to get an idea of their advertising budget and the types of advertising that works best for them.

If your business is seasonal, budget more of your advertising money for the months when you are busiest. It is always tempting to run big ads to bring in business during slow times and try to increase sales of slow items by advertising them. But as a rule, you should use your advertising to sell what is selling when it is selling.

Allocating Your Advertising Money

There are countless ways to spend the dollars you have allocated to advertising. If you have never done any advertising before, you may be surprised at how little you get for your money. An ad you barely glance at as you read your morning paper may have cost hundreds of dollars. It pays to give careful consideration to getting the most mileage from your advertising money.

Advertising can help make new customers aware of your store, including where it is located, what it sells, and the services it offers. This is image advertising, and it is useful for building prestige and trust among existing customers as well as reaching new ones. A motto, or tagline, used in conjunction with your store name and logo can help create a memorable impression in this type of ad. Try to define your store in a few well-chosen words. If you use radio or television, your tagline can be part of a jingle to help listeners remember it.

A second type of advertising is product promotion, which highlights individual items. Many products, especially national brands, do their own product advertising. Suppliers with an advertising program sometimes allow a store name to appear in their product ads or underwrite store advertising featuring their products by providing an advertising allowance.

The third type is special event or sale advertising, encouraging customers to come in during a specific time. There has been such a proliferation of this kind of advertising from department stores and discounters that consumers have become a bit jaded. Specialty stores must offer an unusual twist to get today's shoppers excited.

Adapted from: Schroeder, C. L. (1997, October). Establishing an advertising budget. *WWD Specialty Stores: A Special Report*, p. 31.

exist, and yet the objective and task budget method depends upon executives to know which strategies and tactics will be able to meet the planned objectives.

Difficulties associated with the objective and task method can be overcome by recording the actual practices that take place. Realistic goals can be set after completing research, estimating costs, and aggregating the expenses to determine a suitable appropriation. This can be measured more accurately by an accumulation of data over time. Collecting and evaluating performance data will make this type of budget planning more realistic. Recorded historical data should provide invaluable information for future appropriations. Although objective and task is a superior method for budgeting, the difficulties associated with setting up this type of budget remain an obstacle to frequent application.

Payout Planning

Payout planning (Fig. 6.4) is a budgeting strategy used for the introduction of new products. The underlying assumption is that a new product requires up to 1.5 to 2 times as much promotion expenditure as an existing product. A budget is determined by looking at the planned revenues for a three- to five-year period. An expected rate of return is set and serves as a basis for creating the payout plan. Planners assume that the product will lose money during the first year, almost break even during the second year, and show profits by the third year. Advertising and promotion rates are the highest in the first year and decrease during the second and third years.

Payout planning is useful for new product budgeting. It may be used successfully in combination with another planning strategy, such as objective and task. The planners probably have some time frame in mind by which a new product must show a profit before the product is deemed unsuccessful and is abandoned.

Quantitative Models

With the development of computer simulations and economic forecasting models, **quantitative models** have been introduced into the promotional budgeting process. Techniques involving multiple regression analysis are used to analyze the relationship of

FIGURE 6.4 Sample payout plan.

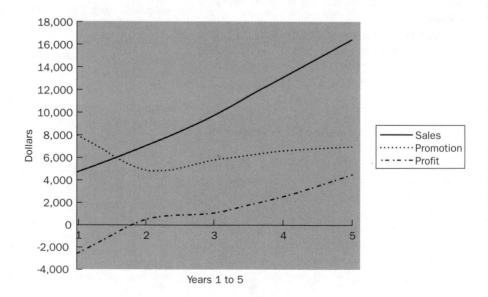

Years 1 to 5

variables to the relative contributions of promotional activities. More recently, computer simulations have been developed to relate awareness levels, purchase frequency, sales, and profitability to alternate television media schedules and other media placement.

Acceptance of computer simulations and economic forecasting models is limited in industry practice. For the most part, these techniques are time consuming and costly. Determining the relevant variables and validating their appropriateness have not provided enough evidence to confirm their effectiveness as predictors. Quantitative models have not reached their potential. As there is considerable interest in this approach, however, better models will probably be created in the future.

How Firms Choose Budget Approaches

How do firms decide which technique to use if each of the methods discussed has limitations? The top-down budgeting methods previously discussed are limited because they are judgmental and often lead to budget appropriations that are not linked to objectives and strategies. Tradition and top executives' desire for control are probably why top-down methods continue to be used.

Bottom-up budget methods take into consideration promotional objectives and expenses related to accomplishing them, but they too are limited. Problems associated with determining which tasks will be required and the costs associated with each are among the flaws associated with bottom-up methods.

By understanding the flaws of various methods, decision-makers can choose the best methods to use for their individual situation. Manufacturers, designers, and retailers select procedures to appropriate budgets for their promotional efforts based upon historical information and experimentation with newer techniques. Box 6.2 addresses the problems of choosing and using a budget approach.

○ BOX 6.2

Does Budgeting Have to Be So Troublesome?

Many medium to large organizations are using budget plans that are incomplete and rarely accurate. Some diverse organizations have even gone so far as to discard budgeting as unworkable on all but an operational unit level, sacrificing a significant measure of managerial control. Why?

Budgeting Lies at the Heart of Business Management
"Budgetary planning and control is the most visible use of accounting information in the management control process. By setting standards of performance, and providing feedback by means of variance reports, the accountant supplies much of the fundamental information required for overall planning and control," say Emmanuel, Otley, and Merchant in their book *Accounting for Management Control*. Historically, a budget is simply a forecast of expenditures and revenues for a specific period of time. However, as the structure of businesses has become more complicated, the function, scope, and manage-

ment of the budget have become accordingly more complex. Departing from its original function as a purely financial document, the business budget is now generally used as a tool to formulate intelligent decisions on the management and growth of a business venture, enabling businesses to set priorities and monitor progress toward both financial and nonfinancial goals.

Effective enterprise-wide budgeting is difficult. The problems encountered in what one industry analyst, the Gartner Group, has called this "painful annual ritual" are considerable: It is not uncommon for line managers and their staff to spend weeks preparing their budget submissions and for central budget managers or management accountants to spend at least as long consolidating, revising, and redistributing budget plans. In a 1995 benchmark exercise, Price Waterhouse reported that budgeting costs large multinational enterprises a median of $63,000 for every $100 million of base revenue within finance departments alone. Factoring in the considerable effort spent by multiple budgeting units would increase this cost many times over.

Most budget processes are inefficient as well as costly. The Price Waterhouse benchmark also found that budget preparation took an average of 110 days from start to finish, and reported that profit forecasts varied from actual results by a median of 10 percent.

Budgeting is troublesome because by its nature it is comprehensive and collaborative—according to the European economist Beatrice Loom-Din, "The budget is the sole corporate task that goes in depth and detail through the entire organization."

This article is intended to examine the problems encountered in preparing enterprise-wide budgets, and to show how software is key in improving the process and its results.

Budgeting Process

No single budgeting method prevails in large organizations. Techniques range from traditional methods focused on cost-center accounting, through project and fund budgeting, to activity-based budgeting (ABB), which is increasingly popular within service enterprises. The starting point for budget creation can be a strategic summary level (top-down budgeting) or come from a detailed operational level (bottom-up or zero-based budgeting). In practice most organizations use a combination of techniques, sometimes known as a "counter current" process. However, despite the range of techniques, most budgeting processes and planning requirements are the same for all companies. Budgeting, by its nature, tends to be:

· Hierarchical—with multitiered checkpoints and control levels
· Iterative—with multiple versions and layered consolidations
· Nomadic—with the sporadic involvement of many people, some in remote locations
· Periodic—typically a once-a-year process with multiple re-forecasts
· Mutable—changing business conditions prolong the process

Budgeting Problems

In itself budgeting remains a conceptually simple exercise, whatever the size of the organization involved or the approach taken; it is the logistics of the process, the arrival at credible figures, that represents the source of difficulty. Again according to Emmanuel, Otley, and Merchant, "the two major problems in the accounting information itself relate to data collection and information disaggregation." This has serious implications because "it is possible that the lack of use of accounting information is as serious a problem as its misuse, particularly at the middle-management level. Line managers will ignore formally produced accounting information when they perceive it to be of little relevance to their tasks." The enterprise-wide budgeting process is difficult to manage, as it is:

· Detailed—requiring a large volume of data for accuracy
· Distant—often perceived as a finance "dictatorship" with little local relevance
· Dependent—relying on the information technology (IT) department and supporting technology
· Unpredictable—the number of cycles needed to agree on a budget is unknown and erratic and may lead to significant deadline overruns

Budgeting Process Problems

In 1996 Hyperion Software undertook some research into large organizations' budgeting processes. Outlined below are five of the seven problem factors identified as the most commonly encountered in the process:

· **Lack of support from line managers**—"All I know is I've got to put numbers in this spreadsheet for Head Office. It doesn't reflect the way we do business here. . . ." *Implication:* Line managers feel disenfranchised, budget figures are produced grudgingly, and budget accuracy suffers as a result.
· **Lack of corporate control**—"I have no idea where my managers get the numbers from." *Implication:* The underlying detail used in the development of operational budgets is never collected or is lost during consolidation. As a result corporate finance has little understanding of how line managers have arrived at their budget submissions.
· **No communication of assumptions**—"Where do the figures come from? I think it's largely 'finger in the air' stuff." *Implication:* The top-level budget model does not tie back to the department managers' detail. Corporate finance spends countless hours trying to reconcile the two frameworks and "forcing" one to match the other. The resulting "plug" creates uncertainty in the plan or forecast and a lack of ownership of the goals by the organization.
· **Poor use of managers' expertise**—"I'm convinced our managers spend the entire budgeting period worrying about the budget, not the business." *Implication:* Managers manage the budget and not the business. As a result corporate finance, aware of this outcome, is reluctant to involve line managers in reforecasts during the lifetime of the budget. Consequently these forecasts do not reflect managers' knowledge of changing business conditions and so may not improve ongoing budget accuracy as intended.

· **It takes too much time**—"How long is our budget cycle? Forever!" *Implication:* The law of diminishing returns sets in. The never-ending, attritional nature of budgeting can seriously undermine support for, and the subsequent effectiveness and accuracy of, the budgets produced.

Defining a Process Solution

Daniel Vasella, Novartis's chief executive, recently described management as a "top-down, bottom-up, top-down process," supporting the view that business needs to take account of the views and expertise of operational staff to succeed in meeting its strategic goals. Likewise, line manager support is key to the success of enterprise-wide budgeting, and organizations should strive to establish a budget-friendly culture in which line managers have:

· Ownership of their part of the budget
· Involvement throughout the process
· Belief that budgeting is meaningful and adds value to their operation
· Clear "downward" communication of strategy, targets, and changes
· Understanding of a sensible budget process that is logical and cohesive

Comfort—the process should ideally be efficient, automated, and user-friendly. Organizations must also consider how they approach budgeting as an exercise in itself. According to the Hackett Group (Hudson, Ohio), a pioneer of innovative thinking in the financial function, improvements will occur by:

· Reducing the time allowed to build a budget. People will use up as much time as they are given, and they will continue to "finesse numbers."
· Reducing the number of iterations until the budget is finalized. The precision improvement in each cycle rarely justifies the extra effort.
· Reducing the "time boundaries" of the budget. Rolling forecasts, by quarter, will be much more accurate than a budget that "looks" 15 to 18 months into the future.

Budgeting System Problems

The procedural problems encountered in budgeting are often exacerbated by the technology used by organizations. The research carried out in 1996 by Hyperion Software found that two of the seven most common problems encountered in budgeting are directly related to the software used by organizations to manage the process:

· Dependence on complex spreadsheets—"My financial analysts are becoming spreadsheet macro programmers." *Implication:* Over time, budget spreadsheet formulas and macros become more and more complex and difficult to understand and maintain. It is a constant battle to force the spreadsheet system to conform to business and user needs. It is usually the case that only one person understands how the spreadsheet budgeting application works, leaving organizations' budget creation processes vulnerable.

Spreadsheets are fully integrated into most organizational cultures—almost all managers use them. Erroneously, spreadsheets are perceived as having low maintenance and little or no development costs. As a result, most organizations rely on spreadsheet software to support their budgeting process. According to IDC, Visicalc, the Lotus 1-2-3 predecessor, became the original "PC killer application" in large part because of its ability to participate in the budget process. This brings a number of problems—spreadsheets were not designed to support process-driven functions like budgeting. Spreadsheets are personal productivity tools, not enterprise-wide "groupware" facilitators. Their use may, in fact, hinder rather than help in the management of enterprise-wide budgeting, as they become part of the problem rather than the solution.

· Inaccuracies—"It's a nightmare. We are constantly checking and rechecking the figures due to poor spreadsheet version control and multiple rekeying of data." *Implication:* Organizations are forced to undertake iterations of the budgeting round to correct data rather than to improve the long-term quality of the management information offered by the budget.

Problems Encountered Budgeting with Spreadsheets

· Little centralized control
· Poor data integrity
· Inflexible reporting
· Unmanageable consolidation mechanics
· Slow turnarounds
· IT department dependence
· Inability to react to and reflect change
· Lack of integration with other systems
· Lack of dynamic financial statements
· Rigid templates for each user involved
· Lack of security at the account level
· Lack of support for multiple line items in an account
· Little facility to view data across different dimensions

These problems are not limited to spreadsheets alone. Any software not specifically designed to support iterative, inclusive, enterprise-wide processes will struggle to meet the requirements of budgeting. In its 1996 report on Budget Management Software, IDC excluded all spreadsheets, proprietary general ledger-based systems, and other online analytical processing (OLAP) tools from evaluation altogether.

Inadequate and inflexible budgeting software has other implications. For example, it can limit an organization's ability to adopt other budgeting methods, such as ABB or fund budgeting.

Defining a Software Solution

The "ideal" budgeting software should offer:

· Flexible analysis, including line item detail, ongoing adjustments, what-if analysis, on-the-fly dimensional analysis, and the ability to satisfy unique budget requirements.
· Powerful automation, to support quick turnaround, consolidation, and distribution of budgetary information. Comprehensive reporting, both during the budget process and for ongoing updates.
· Secure control to give corporate finance centralized maintenance power and enable multitiered review points and budget version management.
· System integration, for data transfer from disparate supporting systems and to promote data integrity by removing the need for rekeying.

· User friendliness, so that all users, both finance and operational, no matter how infrequent their involvement, can produce good budget submissions easily. Enterprise-wide support that understands and supports the nature and process of budget preparation.

Conclusion

The majority of the problems encountered with budgeting arise from managing the process itself. Dedicated budget management software can alleviate many of these issues and help to establish a climate in which budgeting can move from being little more than "a big guesstimation" (R. J. Habig, chief financial officer, PepsiCo) to a much more useful and accurate management tool.

The bottom line, according to the Gartner Group, is that enterprises that do not rethink and retool their budgeting process will annually spend 75 percent more effort than enterprises that do. The choice for large organizations is either to lose many of the undoubted benefits in planning and control offered by budgeting or to apply a software solution to the process and make it less troublesome, less costly, and more effective.

Adapted from: Henderson, I. (1997, October 2). Does budgeting have to be so troublesome? *Management Accounting (British) 75 (2)*, 26–27. Copyright 1997 the Chartered Institute of Management Accountants (UK).

No matter what method is used to establish the budget for promotion, the next step is to allocate it. The allocation decision distributes the promotion budget to the various elements of the promotional mix.

———o ALLOCATING THE PROMOTION BUDGET

As we introduced in Chapter 5, retailers typically focus their planning on the short term by developing six-month merchandising plans. The two six-month periods, which last from February to July and from August to January, also serve as the scheduling timeline for allocating the promotion budget. Considering prior experience as a starting point, anticipating new trends, the staff allocates specific budgets to advertising, public relations, direct marketing, and interactive media, fashion shows and special events, personal selling, visual merchandising, and any other designated promotion activities.

Primary promotion expenses for manufacturers and designers involve fashion shows, trade exhibits, and national advertising to introduce new designs and product innovations for the next season. Fashion show expenses are substantial at the designer level, providing an excellent opportunity to gain publicity for the new merchandise. Designers have put a high percentage of their promotion budgets into fashion shows that cost several hundred thousand dollars. Considering the high cost of hiring supermodels, trendy hairstylists, makeup artists, stage and set designers, and appropriate technical support staff, it is no wonder this promotional tool is so expensive.

Manufacturers also allocate a portion of the promotion budget to national advertising and cooperative advertising. Manufacturers and designers incur production and media expenses, in a similar manner to retail advertisers.

Manufacturers, designers, and retailers are able to extend their budgets by entering into cooperative arrangements. A discussion about entering into such cooperative arrangements follows later in the chapter.

Advertising

Annually, *Advertising Age* publishes a supplement reporting the 100 leading national advertisers. Domestic advertising totals for 2005 are reported in Table 6.2. Total domestic advertising expenditures in 2005 were just over $271 billion, up 2.8 percent from 2004. Measured expenditures are those categories listed on the table: magazine, Sunday magazine, business publications, and so forth, and account for just over $148 billion or 54.7 percent of the total, a 3.0 percent increase from 2004. Unmeasured spending includes direct mail, sales promotion, co-op spending, couponing, catalogs, farm publications, and special events among other types of promotion spending and accounts for approximately $123 billion dollars or 45.3 percent of the total expenditures.

Looking at the table, the top three media as a percentage of the total include network TV (9.9 percent), local newspaper (9.4 percent), and magazine (8.6 percent). Although

TABLE 6.2   *Domestic Advertising Spending Totals*

Media	2005	2004	Percent Change	Medium as Percent 2005	Medium as Percent 2004
Magazine	$23,218	$21,628	7.3	8.6	8.2
Sunday magazine	1,739	1,529	13.7	0.6	0.6
Business publication	5,038	5,234	−3.7	1.9	2.0
Local magazine	451	360	25.2	0.2	0.1
National newspaper	3,467	3,303	4.9	1.3	1.3
Local newspaper	25,537	25,164	1.5	9.4	9.5
FSI (Free Standing Inserts)	1,442	1,392	3.6	0.5	0.5
Network TV	26,706	26,218	1.9	9.9	9.9
Spot TV	17,115	18,794	−8.9	6.3	7.1
Syndicated TV	4,222	3,931	7.4	1.6	1.5
Cable TV network	16,453	14,818	11.0	6.1	5.6
Network radio	1,010	1,028	−1.7	0.4	0.4
National spot radio	2,604	2,617	−0.5	1.0	1.0
Local radio	7,431	7,453	−0.3	2.7	2.8
Outdoor	3,529	3,213	9.8	1.3	1.2
Internet	8,323	7,343	13.3	3.1	2.8
Measured	**148,286**	**144,025**	**3.0**	**54.7**	**54.6**
Unmeasured	**122,788**	**119,741**	**2.5**	**45.3**	**45.4**
Total U.S.	**271,074**	**263,766**	**2.8**	**100.0**	**100.0**

Note: Dollars reported in millions.

Adapted from: 100 Leading National Advertisers. (2006). *Advertising Age.* New York: Crain Communications, Inc. · Reprinted with permission. Copyright, Crain Communications, Inc., 2006.

TABLE 6.3   *Top 10 Domestic Advertising Spending by Category*

| Rank | | | Measured Media | | U.S. Measured Media Breakout for 2004 | | | | | | |
'05	'04	Category	2005	% Change	Magazine	Newspaper	Outdoor	TV	Cable Nets	Radio	Internet
1	1	Automotive	$20,958.6	−3.4	$2,444.3	$6,293.6	$350.6	$8,409.1	$1,461.3	$1,577.6	$422.1
2	2	Retail	18,629.9	−0.7	1,810.6	6,958.0	359.0	5,289.5	993.7	2,183.8	1.035.4
3	3	Telecom, Internet, ISP	9,895.8	4.0	855.3	2,158.9	219.2	3,359.5	979.8	797.7	1,525.3
4	5	Financial services	8,476.9	8.2	1,294.9	1,831.5	246.2	2,337.2	948.3	787.0	1,031.7
5	4	Medicine & remedies	8,441.9	1.8	2,301.2	221.2	18.4	3,832.1	1,387.9	291.1	390.1
6	6	General services	7,867.9	7.9	974.9	2,136.2	497.8	2,011.9	335.1	1,197.4	714.5
7	7	Food, beverage & candy	7,313.2	3.9	1,950.0	61.2	79.8	3,347.8	1,415.0	350.0	108.8
8	8	Personal care	5,648.0	1.8	2,250.8	24.5	24.6	2,327.9	883.2	57.6	79.4
9	9	Movies, video & music	5,582.5	1.8	423.2	1,140.1	105.3	2,601.5	934.0	262.5	115.8
10	10	Airlines, hotel, car rental	5,545.9	2.8	1,460.2	1,573.5	294.4	808.2	509.7	387.1	512.9
15	14	Apparel	2,727.0	5.1	2,089.4	46.3	34.2	291.0	220.8	18.5	26.8

Note: Dollars reported in millions.
Reprinted with permission from the June 26, 2006 issue of *Advertising Age.* New York: Copyright, Crain Communications, Inc., 2006.

only 3.1 percent of total spending, Internet advertising spending increased 13.3 percent indicating the growing importance of this medium in budgeting decisions.

United States spending by category is also reported annually (Table 6.3). The retail category, which includes discount, department, variety, and specialty retail stores, shopping centers, and catalog showrooms, ranked second behind automotive, spending over $18 billion dollars in measured media in 2005 (100 Leading National Advertisers, 2006). Interestingly, this was a decrease in spending by 0.7 percent from the previous year. Newspaper and television were the dominant media choices for retail advertising spending.

Apparel, ranked 15th, includes ready-to-wear, underclothing and hosiery, jewelry, accessories, and footwear. This category, primarily manufacturers and designers of fashion products, use magazines as the dominant medium for advertising. Figure 6.5 is a magazine advertisement for Jones New York and represents apparel advertising spending.

As illustrated in Table 6.4, the top 10 retail advertisers in the United States spent over $2.4 trillion on advertising in 2005 (Frazier, 2006). Wal-Mart Corporation had the highest market share at 10.3 percent and spent $578 million on measured media advertising.

Retail advertising may also be called local advertising due to the emphasis on a local target market. Although some retailers, such as Sears and J. C. Penney, do advertise nationally, most retailers focus on the local or regional areas. Expenses for retail advertising fall into two categories: production and media placement. Production expenses consist of the costs associated with creating the ad, whereas media placement expenses are the costs of running the ad in a print medium or broadcasting a commercial on an electronic medium.

FIGURE 6.5 Magazine advertisement for Jones New York.

JONES NEW YORK
COLLECTION

TABLE 6.4 *Top 10 Retailers by Share of U.S. Market*

		Market share		Ad Spending in Measured Media	
Rank	Retailer	2005	2004	2005	2004
I	Wal-Mart Corp.	10.3 percent	10.4 percent	$578.7	$598.2
2	Home Depot	3.3	3.3	551.2	592.2
3	Kroger Co.	2.7	2.6	150.9	158.5
4	Target Corp.	2.2	2.1	602.0	527.5
5	Sears Holdings Corp.	2.0	2.3	809.6	965.4
6	Lowe's Cos.	1.8	1.7	423.7	366.6
7	Costco Wholesale Corp.	1.8	1.8	0.9	0.9
8	Koninklijke Ahold	1.7	1.9	24.4	30.8
9	Supervalu	1.8	NA	140.7	173.9
10	Safeway	1.4	1.4	194.2	192.1
Top 10 total market		**28.8**	**27.5**	**3,476.3**	**3,606.0**
Industry total (dollars in billions)		**$2,435.7**	**$2,201.7**	**$18,629.9**	**$18,769.7**

Note: Dollars in million.

Adapted from: Frazier, M (2006, June 25). Retail advertisers: Rush is on to rule in-story video TV ads. *Advertising Age*. Retrieved June 26, 2006, from http://adage.com. Reprinted with permission. Copyright, Crain Communications, Inc., 2006.

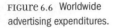

FIGURE 6.6 Worldwide advertising expenditures.

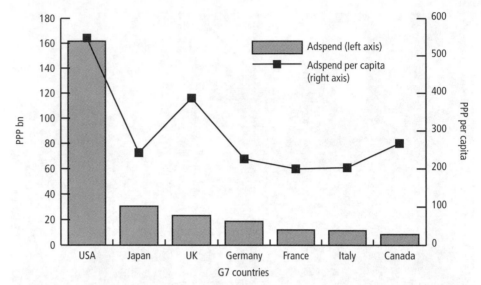

Retail advertising has been criticized for being less sophisticated and more utilitarian than national advertising (Wells, Burnett, & Moriarty, 2006). The short-term emphasis of retail advertising compared to national advertising is among the reasons identified to explain this. Most retail ads are designed to promote merchandise with price as a main feature. These retail ads are run for just a few days. In contrast, a national ad typically features a standardized message that may be used for several months or even years. National advertisers might spend $5,000 or more to produce a newspaper ad and spend an additional $200,000 to run it in 100 large markets. Local retailers simply cannot justify such high production costs for their advertising. A local retailer who places an ad in the local paper might have media costs of only $400, making it unreasonable to spend $5,000 on production.

The United States spends more money on advertising than any other G7 country and spends over five times as much as Japan, the second highest country based on advertising expenditures (Macleod, 2005). Additionally, the United States spends more on advertising on a per capita basis than other countries, 40 percent more than the United Kingdom, the second highest country based on per capita spending (Fig. 6.6). The figures on the chart have been converted to *Purchasing Power Parities*, used as a common currency based on the principle of equalizing purchasing power among nations.

According to Macleod (2005), advertising spending grows each year in countries that have optimistic economic outlooks, such as the United States and the United Kingdom. In other countries where gross domestic product (GDP) has grown at a lower rate and unemployment rates are higher, such as France and Germany, advertising spending is less.

Macleod (2005) also reported on advertising spending according to media type, which varies from country to country (Fig. 6.7). Italy spends more advertising dollars on television than other countries, while Germany spends more on newspaper advertising. France spends the largest portion of its advertising expenditures on magazines.

When preparing budgets, advertising generally has the largest allocation. Even so, other promotion tactics are important and should be considered when distributing promotion dollars.

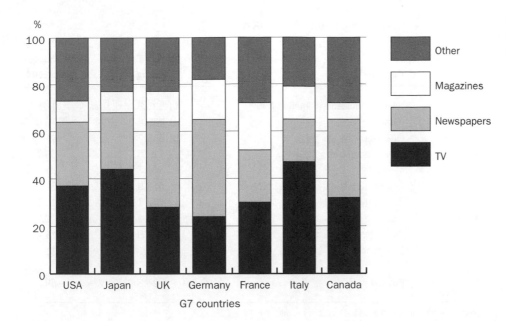

FIGUre 6.7 Worldwide advertising expenditures by media type.

Direct Marketing and Interactive Media

Direct marketing and interactive media activities may be included in the advertising budget or considered as a separate promotion budget allocation, depending upon the firm. Direct marketing is a promotion mix method that attracts interest among retailers and manufacturers, who see the benefits of focusing their promotional attention on their target customers.

Advertising spending by category was reported previously in Table 6.3. Using the same identified categories, Table 6.5 shows United States Internet spending by category. The retail category is again ranked second behind the telecommunications category, spending just over $1 million dollars on Internet spending (of the $18 million in overall advertising spending) (Interactive Marketing and Media, 2006). Similar to the overall decrease in advertising of 0.7 percent, spending by Internet advertising decreased −8.0 percent from the previous year.

Apparel, ranked 21st, spent $26.8 million on Internet advertising, a significant decrease of 59.3 percent from the previous year. While only one year is reported, this might indicate that apparel manufacturers and designers have not found this promotion element to be effective and have adjusted budgets accordingly.

Have you purchased a fashion item online? Storefront retailers, such as the Gap, and direct response retailers like L.L. Bean think you will, if you have not done so already. E-commerce is a rapidly growing promotional strategy for fashion retailers. It is not unusual to see banner advertising on the Internet or website addresses in magazine ads for those and other established retailers. The Gap promotes its website at its retail stores, on Gap shopping bags, and through its print ads. Promotion budgets for these electronic sites were originally derived from the advertising budget. As Internet shopping and website advertising grow in popularity, the promoters of these technologies have separate budgets.

TABLE 6.5   *U.S. Internet Spending Totals by Category*

Rank	Category[a]	2005 Ad Spending	% change from 2004
1	Telecommunications, Internet & ISPs	$1,525.3	16.5
2	Retail	1,035.4	−8.0
3	Financial services	1,031.7	12.7
4	General services	714.5	38.7
5	Media	542.7	35.2
6	Airlines, hotels, car rentals & travel	512.9	23.3
7	Automotive	422.1	15.8
8	Medicine & remedies	390.1	0.5
9	Computers & software	357.8	−11.4
10	Education	254.1	11.1
21	Apparel	26.8	−59.3

[a]These categories are identical to the categories identified in Table 6.3.

Note: Dollars in millions.

Adapted from: Interactive marketing and media (2006). *Advertising Age*. New York: Crain Communications, Inc. Reprinted with permission from the April 16, 2006 supplement to *Advertising Age*. Copyright, Crain Communications, Inc., 2006.

Public Relations and Special Events

Fashion businesses that believe promotion is a critical ingredient to success are using public relations and special events in a much broader role than in the past to more effectively promote products and services to target markets. Adequate budgets must be allocated to complete necessary strategies and tactics associated with public relations and special events. These progressive companies need to allocate budgets to assure these promotion strategies and tactics can be accomplished.

A budget for these activities will be allocated to the fashion director, fashion coordinator, public relations director, or special events coordinator. There has been a trend in department store retailing to combine the activities of the fashion office with the special events and public relations office; as a result these budgets are likely to be merged.

The fashion director, public relations director, or special events coordinator is responsible for scheduling major and minor fashion shows, celebrity appearances, community service projects, or other activities to enhance the public image of the store. This coordinator works very closely with the advertising director and visual merchandising director to bring a coordinated image to the public.

Special events may involve expenses related to physical presentation. This could be anything from a simple table to demonstrate a new cooking appliance to an elaborate setup, with a sound system, and security to launch a celebrity fragrance. Budgeting for public relations and special events needs to take into consideration the expenses required to accomplish the task. If the event is supposed to make money as a charity fund-raiser, the person in charge of planning the budget must consider how revenues will be generated in relationship to the anticipated expenses. The budget takes into consideration planned revenues and expenses as well as actual figures.

Fashion Shows

One of the most crucial elements of planning a fashion show is budget preparation. The budget is the estimate of revenues and expenses necessary to produce the show. The type of show being produced, audience, location, and special features of the show will dictate the projected budget of the show.

The following list is a sample of possible show expenses:

Advertising	Overtime
Alterations	Pressing
Commentator fee	Programs
Deposits	Props
Depreciation of merchandise	Public address system
Dry cleaning	Publicity
Electricians	Rent
Hair and make-up	Stage and runway
Insurance	construction
Lights	Taxes
Meals	Tickets
Model fees	Transportation
Music	Wages

Every show will not have the same elements to consider when developing a budget, but it is well to use some sort of checklist to make sure the budget allows for every expense, planned and unexpected.

Physical facilities should also be considered during the budget process. An out-of-store fashion show may require fees to use the property and rental fees for one or more of the following: tables, chairs, runways, stage, lighting, and public address system. Additionally, a caterer may be needed to provide food service and decorations. An in-store show may eliminate the property fee but may still require rented elements and catering to produce the show.

Show personnel require a large proportion of the estimated budget. All but the smallest shows require the expertise of technicians to guarantee the success of a show. Electricians, music, and lighting technicians may be required to assist with the setup and perform safety inspections. Photographers and video production crews may be hired to record the event for the sponsoring organization. Models may require makeup artists and hairstylists at the performance. In addition to a paid modeling staff, dressers, cue people, transportation staff, hosts, and ushers may need to be hired.

Publicity and advertising are necessary elements for a fashion show and must be considered when establishing the budget. The publicity and advertising budget should be reviewed by the sales promotion division of the organization to determine if cooperative promotions may be beneficial. Publicity costs include the production of news releases, press photographs, or media kits. Elements of sales promotion, such as giveaways, coupons, or samples, have costs associated with them. Invitations, tickets, and programs may be produced. Advertising costs include production fees and the cost of airtime or print space needed to promote the event. As part of a public relations effort, the show producer may include hospitality, such as hotel accommodations for celebrity or special guests, transportation, entertainment, and gratuities.

Expenses related to the use of merchandise should also be considered. Merchandise must be cared for to ensure that it is saleable after the show. Models may require garment alterations. After the show, garments may require dry cleaning or removal of alterations to return the merchandise to a saleable condition. When merchandise has been damaged beyond repair, show personnel may have to cover the cost of the item borrowed from the retailer or department.

Other expenses to consider include taxes, which vary from state to state, and liability insurance to cover the audience, show personnel, and merchandise. Additionally, the show coordinator should have an emergency reserve that can be used on a contingency basis to cover any unforeseen problems.

The preceding discussion has centered on fashion show expenses. Many shows are produced as publicity tools with the intent to sell merchandise. Costs of these fashion shows are supposed to be covered by sales generated from the show. Revenues may also be gained to cover some or all of the show expenses. These revenues come from sales or show sponsorship by an organization or corporation.

Personal Selling

Although personal selling is an essential element of the promotion mix, the allocation for it is not normally considered as part of the promotion budget. Personal selling expenses are usually considered as part of the personnel or human resources budget. This is because the human resources department has the responsibility for initial sales training. Regularly scheduled refresher seminars sponsored by the human resources division help sales associates keep up with the latest sales techniques and provide motivation.

Visual Merchandising

The visual merchandising department has expenses related to the physical presentation of merchandise on the sales floor. Props, signs, merchandise fixtures, and mannequins are part of the visual merchandising budget. Besides interpreting the tangible image of the store, this department works closely with advertising and fashion offices to coordinate a creative storewide image with visual tools in the stores. Additional expenses, incurred by the visual merchandising department, are required for the care and upkeep of existing materials.

———o ADVERTISING AGENCY COMPENSATION

As we introduced in Chapter 3, the types of services provided by various advertising agencies differ according to the organization of the agency, actual services provided, and needs of the client. A variety of methods are used to compensate advertising agencies and other service providers. Payments may come in the form of commissions, fees, cost-plus agreements, percentage charges, or incentive-based compensation. These payments should be considered as part of the budget when a retailer, manufacturer, or designer chooses to use an outside agency for promotion services.

Commissions

The once-standard practice for agencies involved in buying media was compensation through a commission. A **commission** is a percentage of money given to an agent who assists in a business transaction. The agency normally receives 15 percent from the media on any advertising time or space purchased for the client.

This type of compensation is easy to figure out. For example, an agency prepares a television advertisement for a client and purchases time for the ad to run. The television station bills the agency $85,000. The agency bills the client $100,000. The $15,000 difference is the payment for the agency, representing the 15 percent commission.

Compensation by commission has received a great deal of criticism in recent years. Concern is centered on how the commission relates to the services provided. If two different agencies require the same amount of effort to prepare an advertisement, the argument can be made that they should be compensated in a similar manner. The first agency is able to place the ad for $100,000, and the second agency places the ad for $1,000,000. The first agency receives a $15,000 commission while the second agency is paid $150,000. Critics argue that agencies are forced to recommend high media expenditures to improve their commissions. Some clients feel that agencies are overly compensated due to high media costs. Additional debate results from the perception that noncommissionable media, such as direct marketing or sales promotion, are ignored by agencies unless the client specifies them.

There are proponents of the commission system, too. They argue that the commission system is easy and fairer to administer than other payment methods. Emphasis and higher costs are placed on accounts demanding more time and effort.

In order to overcome the inequities of the commission system, many agencies and clients have developed alternative methods of compensation. These include fee or contract arrangements, cost-plus agreements, percentage charges, or incentive-based programs.

Fee Arrangements

A fee arrangement, or payment for services based upon a predetermined rate, may take several different forms. The first is a **fixed-fee rate**, also known as a straight fee. In this method, the agency charges a basic monthly rate for all of its services and credits any commissions earned to the client. The client and agency decide upon the exact work to be done and how much the client will pay for those services. This system assumes a long-term relationship between the agency and client.

In some situations, the agency may hire a specialized agency to provide limited services based upon a **contract**, a written agreement identifying the work to be accomplished, deadlines, and payments. This is a fee for specific activities such as management of a special event, production of a fashion show, or design of a direct-response mailer. A contract fee arrangement is established for a short-term project; it may be for one specific job or task.

Another system used by the agency and client is a **fee-commission combination**. In this instance, media commissions are credited against the fee. Payment is adjusted if the commission is less than the agreed-upon fee. The client pays the difference. If the agency is involved in doing work in noncommissionable media, such as sales promotion, a fee is charged.

Fee arrangements require the agency to keep accurate records of the costs of providing services. By assessing these costs for a specified period of time or project, the agency will add the agency's desired profit to the expenses before billing the client. To avoid any problems or disputes, the fee arrangement should specify exactly what services would be performed by the agency.

Cost-plus Agreements

The **cost-plus agreement** requires the client to pay a rate based upon cost of the work plus an agreed-on profit margin, normally a percentage of total costs. This method requires the agency to keep track of the direct and indirect costs for accomplishing the task. Direct costs relate to the salaries of the personnel and the time it takes to produce the assignment. An allocation for indirect costs, such as the agency overhead and administration, needs to be incorporated into the fees.

Many clients prefer a fee-based or cost-plus system because they receive a precise breakdown of where and how their promotion or advertising dollars are being spent. However, many agencies find these systems too complex because they must provide detailed cost accounting. The expenses of doing a project are often difficult to predict when the agency bids for a client's business. Also, agencies are reluctant to let clients view internal expense records.

Percentage Charges

Another method of compensating an agency is by adding a markup of **percentage charges** to costs for work done by outside suppliers. Services such as graphic design, photography, or market research are billed to the agency and the agency marks up that cost to the client in order to cover its administrative expenses.

This system is used when the agency employs freelancers to accomplish required tasks. These suppliers do not allow a commission, so the agency builds in a markup charge between 17.65 and 20 percent. A 17.65 percent markup yields a 15 percent commission. For example, a firm asks a graphic designer to produce an advertising billboard. The designer bills the agency $10,000. With a markup of 17.65 percent, the agency bills its client $11,765. The $1,765 markup is approximately 15 percent of $11,765. These markup charges allow the agency to cover its administrative costs and provide a reasonable profit for the agency's efforts.

Incentive-based Compensation

Since more clients are demanding accountability for their promotional activities, clients have tied payments to performance in some type of **incentive-based compensation**. The fundamental concept is that payment is based upon how well the activities meet a predetermined performance goal. For instance, an **event bonus** is a premium paid above the fixed fee, if the attendance goal for an event is exceeded. In the case of **media savings**, a new agency receives a share of the media savings it achieved over the previous agency. By using a **unit sales incentive,** a client pays the agency a base fee and a bonus for unit sales above the goal or target sales. In these alternative compensation plans, extra performance incentives provide additional motivation for an agency.

──○ EXTENDING THE PROMOTION BUDGET

Manufacturers, retailers, and designers in the merchandising environment have been able to extend the value of the promotional budget by working in a cooperative manner. These activities not only extend the promotional budget, they also have the capability of enhancing the image of all cooperative partners in the marketplace. Popular cooperative strategies include co-marketing, co-branding, cooperative advertising, sponsorship and co-sponsorship, and strategic alliances. In the next sections, we provide a brief introduction to methods by which such cooperative activities may be used to extend the promotional budget.

Co-marketing

Co-marketing is the creation of cooperative efforts by which the manufacturer and retailer join forces to increase the revenue and profits for both parties. It involves a range of marketing activities, not just a prescribed activity. Co-marketing has gained popularity in the promotion of food products to the consumer market and in the promotion of electronic or personal care products to the business-to-business sector.

Traditional marketing was based upon the premise that manufacturers and retailers were not working together. Manufacturers emphasized increasing their sales to the retailer, a trade channel considered more important than the ultimate consumer. The retailer, on the other hand, concentrated on profit, which was realized from the ultimate consumer, and sought less expensive merchandise or discounts from manufacturers to improve the gross margin and obtain a greater bottom line. The product manager for Heinz ketchup, Mark Trumbull, summed up the problem with the traditional marketing approach: "We focused on how much the retailer would buy rather than how much the consumer would buy. And the retailer was more focused on how cheaply he could buy, not on how much product he could move to consumers" (Marx, 1995, p. 2). The concern was that neither the manufacturer nor the retailer was improving sales by working against each other.

Now mass retailers, such as Target, Kmart, and Wal-Mart, are working to find marketing programs that help differentiate their stores from one another. Co-marketing programs have been used to distinguish merchandise presentation. An example of a successful co-marketing program is that of Wal-Mart and L & F Products, makers of such brands as Lysol, Wet Ones, and Ogilvie Perms. L & F Products became the manager for the home permanents section located in the Wal-Mart stores, controlling the visual appearance as well as the distribution, pricing, promotion, and shelf management for its own as well as other products. The goal was to improve the top-line and bottom-line profits for the retailer in addition to expanding the return on investment for both the manufacturer and retailer. As a result of the co-marketing efforts, Wal-Mart was able to achieve double-digit increases in home permanent sales, while Ogilvie improved its market share volume. The market share grew from about 40 percent to 62 to 67 percent share in two years (Marx, 1995).

Co-branding

Another example of cooperative efforts is the development of co-branded credit cards. **Co-branding** marries a card issuer, usually a bank that wants to increase its volume, with a consumer company in search of a market share boost. In cooperation with L.L. Bean, Visa developed a credit card that offers special shipping rates, discounts, and previews for sales events. Many retailers have developed similar co-branding strategies. This type of card is also used to provide frequent flier miles for a variety of airlines including Alaska Airlines, U.S. Airways, and Delta.

Co-branding has gained acceptance from manufacturers and retailers who act as two brands working together to gain equity and profits for both organizations. Although historically, relations between manufacturers and retailers have been based on mutual distrust

NEIMAN MARCUS

CHANEL

FIGURE 6.8 Chanel and Neiman Marcus developed this cooperative advertisement to extend both budgets.

rather than cooperation, practitioners of co-branding have benefited from teamwork.

Cooperative Advertising

In **cooperative advertising** the manufacturer works with the retailer to develop an ad and shares in the cost of running that advertisement. The advertisement may be placed in local or national media. The brand name of the manufacturer is featured prominently in the ad along with the name of the retailer where the merchandise can be found. Primary or secondary producers may use this strategy to tie the image of the national brand to a particular retail store in a market area.

For example, a fragrance producer such as Chanel might agree to cooperatively sponsor an advertisement with retailer Neiman Marcus in *Vogue* magazine (Fig 6.8). The share of the cost may be split 75/25 or any other ratio decided upon prior to running the advertisement. This means that Chanel pays for 75 percent of the cost, while Neiman Marcus pays the other 25 percent. Sharing the expenses has the effect of extending the budget for both the manufacturer and retailer.

Sponsorship

Sponsorship involves advertisers who lend their name to a sporting activity or another type of special event. Budgets can be extended using sponsorships and are discussed in detail with special events.

Strategic Alliance

Strategic alliance is a partnership between a manufacturer and a retailer working in a particular supply chain that leverages the core competencies of each firm. By combining their individual strengths and abilities, partners are able to create a supply-process synergy that results in increased profitability, efficiency, and market share for each firm, which results in greater value for the consumer. When implemented properly, the strategic alliance supply chain between the partners will look like a well-run vertical company.

Partnerships between retailers and manufacturers began during retail consolidation in the 1980s, when retailers demanded that manufacturers perform *value-added* functions such as inventory management and in-store merchandising. By the 1990s, the power had shifted away from the retailer to the consumer, requiring manufacturers and retailers to work together to satisfy the same master. Strategic alliance partners benefit from manufacturers' knowledge about the product and how to display it, and they benefit from retailers' knowledge of how to develop and deliver a unique store personality and shopping experience. Together, they make an efficient and productive team with

Percent of mentions by respondent type

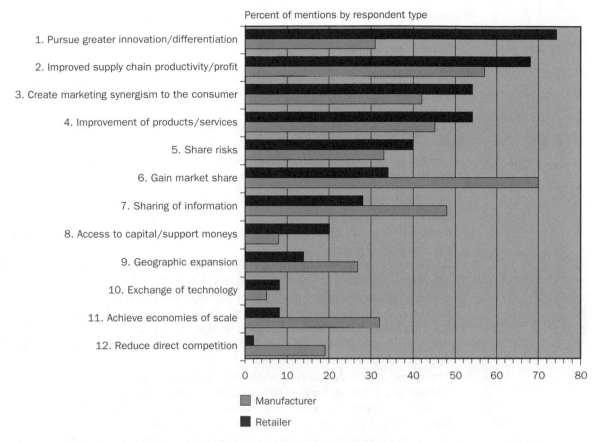

FIGURE 6.9 Primary reasons for entering into strategic alliances.

greater product sell-through, better assortments in stores, and an easier and more pleasant shopping experience.

Among the reasons for entering into strategic alliances listed in Figure 6.9, manufacturers and retailers identify several ways their businesses could improve through shared information and capital. By creating mutual sales and profitability goals, the partners can better meet the needs of consumers by working together. The most practical areas for strategic alliances are: (1) assortment—category management, planning, and development; (2) introduction—product development, product testing, and marketing; (3) replenishment-in-stock and fast turns; and (4) promotion—advertising, direct marketing, sales promotion, and visual merchandising. Although a strategic alliance is not strictly a budget matter, each partner benefits financially from working cooperatively.

Advantages of Cooperative Arrangements

There are several advantages for both the manufacturer and retailer entering into cooperative arrangements.

- **Cooperative arrangements give the manufacturer and retailer extra exposure.** Sharing costs extends advertising expenses.
- **Images of a merchandise manufacturer and retail firm are mutually enhanced.** The label of a fashion designer, such as Calvin Klein, benefits when it is associated with an

upscale retailer like Bergdorf Goodman. Both the designer and retail store profit from strongly linked images created for the product and the store.

- **Retailer and manufacturer benefit from lower advertising rates and better placement in publications.** Because the retailer and manufacturer work together, they are able to run ads more frequently. The more regularly ads run in certain publications, the more prominent their placement and the greater their discount.

Disadvantages of Cooperative Arrangements for Manufacturers

Substantial allocations for cooperative promotional activities are built into the budgets of fashion apparel, accessory, cosmetic, and related manufacturers. Although the advantages are clear, there are also several disadvantages to be considered.

- **Manufacturer identity may be lost in the layout.** Art, photography, copy, and store logo may be featured more prominently than the logo or name of the manufacturer. As a result, the manufacturer's identity may not play as dominant a role as the manufacturer would like it to.
- **Accounting records are a business expense.** Normally after an advertisement runs in a local newspaper, the retail store sends an invoice and tear sheet as proof of the cooperative advertisement. The manufacturer reimburses the store after receiving the invoice. Accounting procedures take time and expense to follow through.
- **Stores are late sending documentation**. Frustrations can easily erupt when the store sends proof of advertising after a lengthy period of time. Prompt attention to detail helps to overcome these frictions.
- **The manufacturer may have limited control over timing, style, identity, message, and content.** If the retailer maintains control over these factors, the manufacturer is at the mercy of the retailer, who chooses when to run the advertisement. The retailer can also decide how much emphasis is placed on the merchandise or brand.
- **The manufacturer has no control over in-store merchandise placement.** The store may choose to run only an advertisement and fail to support the merchandise with in-store display and merchandise presentation.
- **Retailers may take advantage of the manufacturer by considering the advertising allowance as a discount.** Some retailers will ask for a percentage discount for advertising allowance. The manufacturer has very little control over what is advertised and when. A specific contract identifying the merchandise to be advertised and proof of run by a tear sheet will alleviate this problem. The manufacturer controls payment after receipt of documentation.
- **Competition may overstimulate promotional budgets.** The retailer may ask for more than the manufacturer has available for advertising expenses. Fear of losing out to the competition may make the manufacturer spend too much for cooperative advertising.

Disadvantages of Cooperative Arrangement for Retailers

On the surface, retailers may not perceive any problems associated with cooperative arrangements. The following list provides some caution regarding their use.

- **Cooperative advertising money becomes more important that the actual merchandise.** In an attempt to lower advertising costs, buyers are enticed to buy merchandise that does not meet the company's image. The buyer loses sight of the nature of the merchandise, choosing merchandise based on availability of cooperative advertising rather than the merchandise most preferred by the customer.

- **Manufacturer demands may not fit with retailer's style.** The manufacturer places requirements on advertising that may not fit with the type of advertising done by the retailer. The retailer may have a certain approach, such as using only photography as the art in newspaper advertising, whereas the manufacturer may insist upon line drawings. The continuity and identity of the retailer is lost in the transformation.
- **Manufacturer's message must be consistent with the retailer's communication.** The merchandise and sales communication between the two participating firms should be in harmony. The retailer could have a short-term product orientation, while the manufacturer is interested in building a long-term image, resulting in dissatisfaction by either party.
- **Approval for advertising should include the promotion director.** Internal friction could develop between merchandising and promotion personnel, if decisions regarding cooperative advertising ignore the input from the promotion director. Merchants, who desire the benefits of cooperative dollars, could encourage advertising that is inconsistent with promotional strategies established by the promotion division.
- **Cooperative advertising contracts are difficult to execute.** The complexities of the contracts discourage many retailers from participating.

Overcoming Disadvantages to Cooperative Arrangements

Generally the advantages of using cooperative advertising outweigh any of the disadvantages. The best way to overcome any of the limitations is to clearly state the terms of the responsibilities of the retailer and manufacturer in a contract prior to implementation. This contract should consist of terms, including scheduling, location of publication, size of the space, dates to be run, anticipated expenses, and the percentage of contribution by each party. The contract should further identify the type of advertisement. Is it a single-item ad, a part of a departmentalized promotion, or a storewide theme ad? The size and style of the logo or appropriate visual signature should also be stated. A written contract provides a description of the terms that were agreed upon. This should prevent any legal problems.

Because the budget is one of the most important planning documents an organization uses, the time and effort spent on developing a budget are definitely worth it. The budgetary process helps a firm to understand its past practices, current financial position, and opportunities for the future. A number of theoretical and practical methods of preparing a budget have been introduced in this chapter. A well-prepared budget will enable a firm to achieve its general as well as IMC objectives. Although some people think that budgeting is a confusing and boring task, a good budget will assist the organization in achieving its goals.

summary

- The budget is one of the most important planning documents a manufacturer or retailer can develop.
- Budgeting provides an opportunity for the firm to analyze its current position and past practices and set promotion objectives for the future.
- Budgeting forces executives to take into consideration changes in the economy and environment and assess their potential impact on the promotional plan for short- and long-range goals.

- Because budgeting is considered frustrating and confusing, many small businesses ignore the benefits of the budgeting process and simply follow their past practices.
- Researchers have proposed several theoretical models, such as the advertising to sales model, diminishing returns, and the S-curve, that assist budget managers in preparing the plan.
- Whether the budget planners use one of the top-down or bottom-up methods, the firm will benefit from the analysis.
- After the appropriations are made to the promotion division, specific budgets for promotional mix elements are allocated. The firm sets priorities for advertising, direct marketing and interactive media, fashion shows, special events, public relations, and visual merchandising.
- During their budgeting process, retailers and manufacturers should consider agency compensation. Advertising agencies have traditionally been compensated through commissions, but controversy over commissions has led to alternative compensation methods such as fee arrangements, cost-plus agreements, percentage charges, and incentive-based compensation.
- Manufacturers, retailers, and designers can extend the value of their promotional budgets by working in a cooperative manner. Co-marketing, co-branding, cooperative advertising, and sponsorship not only extend the promotional budget, they enhance the image of cooperative partners in the marketplace.

key terms

all-one-can-afford	cooperative advertising	payout planning
arbitrary allocation	cost-plus agreement	percentage charges
bottom-up approaches	diminishing returns curve	percentage of sales
clipping service	event bonus	quantitative models
co-branding	fee-commission combination	return-on-investment
co-marketing	fixed-fee rate	S-shaped curve
commission	incentive-based compensation	strategic alliance
competitive parity	media savings	top-down approaches
contract	objective and task	unit sales incentive

questions for discussion

1. Why is budgeting for promotion so important?
2. Who is responsible for competitive parity promotion budgeting?
3. What method of budgeting is the most common for retailers? How does each method compare with the other techniques? Which techniques might be better than others?
4. How do retailers, designers, and manufacturers extend budgets by sharing promotional expenses?

additional resources

Belch, G. E., & Belch, M. A. (2007). *Advertising and promotion* (7th ed.). New York: McGraw-Hill/Irwin.

annual publications

100 Leading National Advertisers. (Published annually). *Advertising Age.* New York: Crain Communications, Inc.

Schonfeld & Associates. (Published annually). *Advertising ratios & budget.* Libertyville, IL.

References

100 Leading National Advertisers. (2006). *Advertising Age.* New York: Crain Communications, Inc.

Frazier, M. (2006, June 25). Retail advertisers: Rush is on to rule in-story video TV ads. *Advertising Age.* Retrieved June 26, 2006, from http://adage.com

Interactive Marketing and Media (2006). *Advertising Age.* New York: Crain Communications, Inc.

Macleod, C. (2005). Global adspend trends. *International Journal of Advertising,* 24(3), 413–415.

Marx, W. (1995). The power of two. *Management Review,* 84(10), 36. Retrieved June 30, 2006 from the Business Source Premier database.

Wells, W., Moriarty, S., & Burnett, J. (2006). *Advertising principles and practice* (7th ed.). Upper Saddle River, NJ: Pearson Prentice Hall.

FIGURE 7.1 The Life Is Good Festival.

Social Impact and Ethical Concerns

Life Is Good, and Getting Better

   Cynics may scoff at the "spread good vibes" philosophy of Life Is Good, an $80 million apparel company founded by Bert and John Jacobs. With a stick figure named "Jake" as company mascot and the corporate titles chief executive optimist and chief creative optimist, respectively, how serious can these brothers be about forging positive change in their communities? In 2006, the company hosted 15 outdoor family festivals and donated all profits—$725,000—to the Project Joy and Camp Sunshine charities for children in crisis. At a recent event, festival-goers broke the Guinness World Record for carving the most jack-o'-lanterns, bringing heightened awareness to children's causes. Life Is Good will host at least 23 fund-raisers this year, demonstrating that a small company with a fresh idea can make an impact.

Source: Corcoran, C.T. & Power, D. (2007, January 10). Designs on good deeds earn WWD awards. *Women's Wear Daily*, p. 14.

After you have read this chapter you will be able to:

Evaluate the ethical issues and social responsibilities related to promotion.

Discuss self-regulation in advertising and promotion.

Understand some of the laws and government regulations that regulate promotion.

Tapping into the fervor for do-good, feel-good activism found in the hearts, if not always the deeds, of many consumers, Jake the stick figure sells the Life Is Good line. The manufacturer puts its money where Jake's mouth is, donating entire profits from festivals and other initiatives to worthy charities. However, not all companies employ such altruistic spokespersons to promote their products.

   Where does society draw the social or moral line when it comes to selling products? Companies, consumers, governments, lawyers, trade associations, and others struggle daily over the ethical issues raised by advertising campaigns that create word-of-mouth publicity and increased sales but disturb some consumers.

   This text would not be complete without a discussion of the social and ethical concerns that are raised when advertising and promotion are used. However, a thorough discussion of every social or ethical situation, government regulation, and attempt at self-regulation is beyond the scope of this text. The purpose of this chapter is to create reader awareness about possible unethical or unacceptable situations. It is desired that the reader broadly apply the social and ethical standards from one promotion activity to other promotion activities where ethical standards may also apply.

   The chapter begins with a discussion of the ethical and social issues that surface when creating promotion strategies. Then, we discuss self-regulation as a monitor for ethical and social concerns. The chapter concludes with an examination of some of the laws and government regulations affecting advertising and promotion.

──○ ETHICAL ISSUES AND SOCIAL RESPONSIBILITY

We began this book by defining promotion as a comprehensive term for all of the communication activities initiated by the seller to inform, persuade, and remind the consumer about products, services, and/or ideas offered for sale. Through the many different topics related to promotion, and the national and international examples of promotion illustrated in this text, we demonstrate how big in scope promotion activities are. *Promotion is comprehensive.* We send messages to consumers via advertising, direct marketing and interactive media, sales promotion, public relations, personal selling, special events, fashion shows, and visual merchandising. Consumers cannot help but hear or see our communication messages, and they cannot avoid them.

For promotion to be effective, marketers need information about consumers. We demonstrate some of the technological advances that provide promotion planners with that information. Professionals can determine where consumers live, what they buy, where they buy it, how much money they make, and what promotions they react to. They can monitor what consumers watch on television, listen to on the radio, or read in magazines, and how they use the Internet. With increasingly sophisticated marketing tools, some voluntary and some not, sponsors can analyze consumers, and consumers cannot avoid being examined.

Therefore, everyone involved in the field of promotion must be careful not to abuse the influence they have over consumers. Professionals must be responsible to the public and consider the social and ethical ramifications of their messages, before they are sent to consumers. In the next section, we introduce a few of the social and ethical considerations that should be evaluated when planning a promotion, including offensive advertising, plagiarism, and social correctness. This is not an all-inclusive list. The topics are presented in hopes of starting discussions about issues of social responsibility and ethical behavior.

Offensive Advertising

Advertising can offend consumers in several ways, including the product itself, a demonstration of the product in use, or the anxiety associated with a product in the mind of the consumer. Certain products, such as personal hygiene products, hemorrhoid medicines, and other medical products and contraceptives, by nature are offensive to some consumers. Although marketers believe educational information can be derived from advertising items such as condoms, certain segments of the population do not believe in the use of contraceptives and are offended by the advertising of these products to the public.

Some product demonstrations may not appeal to certain consumer audiences because of the personal nature of the product. While consumers are not offended by deodorant advertisements, the product is often demonstrated on the hands, lower arms, or mirrors, away from the actual area of application. Diaper ads do not show a baby being diapered. The diaper is shown either away from the baby or already being worn.

Clothing has always pushed the limit in offending some consumers. For example, up through the early 1960s, fashion magazines did not give advertising or editorial space to underwear or swimsuits because the items were too personal in nature and made consumers uncomfortable. However, society has loosened its stance on the discomfort of personal apparel, and swimsuits and underwear are commonly advertised in print and broadcast media.

An advertisement in the *New York Times* displayed an image from a Calvin Klein campaign introducing boys' and girls' underwear using child models (Fig. 7.2) in 1999.

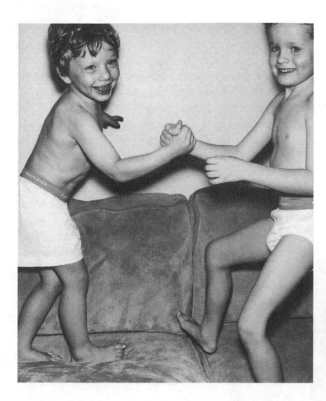 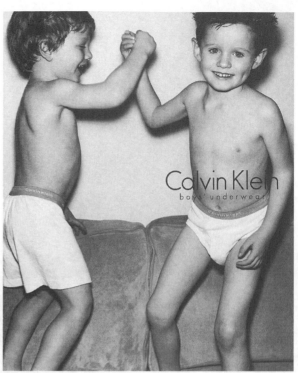

FIGURE 7.2 The Calvin Klein company removed this ad from publication after one run because of controversy.

The integrated marketing campaign included print, broadcast, and transit media advertisements. According to some, the campaign exploited young models in suggestive and tasteless poses hinting at child pornography. The promotion was quickly halted. That was not the first time the firm withdrew an offensive advertising campaign.

Many previous Calvin Klein ads were deemed controversial. In the 1980s, the firm dressed a teenage Brooke Shields in a pair of skintight designer jeans, with the tagline *Nothing comes between me and my Calvins*. The company also graced outdoor and transit ads with male models, including Mark "Marky Mark" Wahlberg, in scanty Calvin Klein underwear. Later, model Kate Moss was associated with the promotion dubbed *heroin chic*, featuring extremely skinny models and young street people, who appeared under the influence of drugs. Although the Calvin Klein Company stood by its work, executive vice president Martin J. Rose commented that the campaign was "quite effective as written" (Elliott, 1995, p. 1). The company moved quickly and ceased the promotion before its scheduled end.

Does Calvin Klein advertising cross the boundaries of acceptability? From the perspective of a marketer—no—the company does what needs to be done to sell products. From the perspective of a consumer—maybe—consumers question the ads but they do go out and buy more product. From the perspective of watchdog groups and the government—yes—that is why the FBI got involved. While no legal action was taken, the ads were investigated. The reputation of the firm caused many to question the boundaries of appropriate advertising.

Consumers can be offended by advertisements that are perceived as too sexual in nature or show nudity. Sexuality and nudity may be perceived as manipulative if they are used solely to get the attention of the consumer with no relation to the product being

FIGURE 7.3 If this ad were used to advertise items other than lingerie, it would not be acceptable in the United States.

promoted. The ad in Figure 7.3 is acceptable because it advertises a line of lingerie. If the same ad, showing an almost nude model, were used to advertise cars or liquor, for example, the ad would not be acceptable to some people. Ads may also be criticized as being demeaning to men and women if the individuals are depicted as sex objects. What is your reaction to the bare-chested male model in Figure 7.4? Is he a sex object or an appropriate model for advertising a belt? Sexuality and nudity are treated differently in countries outside the United States. Some countries are more liberal, while others are more conservative in showing the human form unclothed. In the United States, women's breasts are censored out of most advertisements. In other countries, women's hair, hands, and/or legs and men's facial hair may not be allowed in advertisements. Global promotions should be considerate of the values each country puts on certain areas of the body. Box 7.1 highlights some of the difficulties advertisers face when promoting products in other countries. Products that may not be offensive in the United States are considered offensive in other parts of the world.

Consumers also become offended if an advertisement is perceived as too heavy-handed, implying that they are bad people if they do not use the product or purchase it for their family. In recent years, consumers have criticized computer promotions for making parents believe their child will not succeed at school if they do not have a personal computer at home.

Plagiarism

Plagiarism is the act of using or passing off as one's own an idea, writing, or the creative thought of another. In recent years ethical questions have been raised regarding plagiarism in advertising. In several situations companies have been accused of using ideas without recognizing and crediting the individual who initially pitched the idea. In one example, the creation of an Anheuser-Busch television campaign featuring talking frogs has been questioned. The person bringing the suit claims he pitched the idea to Budweiser but was not recognized by the company for the idea. This case and others like it have ended in court. Marketers should give proper acknowledgment and financial compensation to the creators of promotional ideas.

Trademark and copyright laws protect products and ideas. A **trademark** is a word or symbol that indicates a source of origin and can be protected based on actual use. Trademarks can be symbols, words, smells, colors, names, sounds, or even shapes as long as they are used to distinguish a particular good or service from other goods and services. A trademark owner can prevent others from using the marks if that use is likely to confuse or deceive the public, provided the trademark's owner is using the trademark. This protection is available whether the trademark is registered or not.

A **copyright** is the legal right granted to an author, composer, playwright, publisher, or distributor to exclusive publication, production, sale, or distribution of a literary, musical, dramatic, or artistic work. The federal Copyright Act protects original works of authorship in a tangible medium. Outright copying of the protectable elements of an advertisement or product package is a violation of the copyright laws. However, the Copyright Act protects only the expression of an idea, not the idea itself. If a copycat ad uses similar ideas for an advertisement but produces those ideas in a way that is different from the original ad, the Copyright Act will not protect the owner of the original advertisement from such copying. However, if a copycat ad uses identical portions of the original ad or follows the unique structure, sequence, and organization of the original advertisement, the copycat ad would infringe on the original advertiser's copyright. Copyright protection is available to copyright owners once the work is fixed in a tangible form. As with trademarks, registration is not required in order to have copyright rights to a work.

Counterfeiting

Within the fashion business, a growing problem is the sale of merchandise with counterfeit trademarks. **Trademark counterfeiting** is the development and sale of imitative products bearing deliberately copied trademarks. The growing popularity of American brands around the world has created a market for fake goods with counterfeit trademarks and logos, including symbols and company names. The most popular counterfeit logos include jeans, athletic footwear, baseball hats, and T-shirts with logos of hot brands. The merchandise is promoted as authentic when in reality a counterfeiter has manufactured the merchandise and is misrepresenting the firm in the sale of the goods. In some cases, the consumer is not aware that the goods are counterfeited (Fig 7.5).

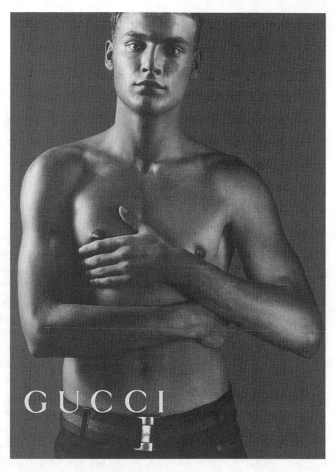

FIGURE 7.4 Gucci used an attention-getting bare-chested male model to advertise a belt.

The International AntiCounterfeiting Coalition (IACC) is a Washington, D. C.-based nonprofit organization devoted to combating product counterfeiting and piracy. The organization reports concerns and fears about counterfeiting in *The Negative Consequences of International Intellectual Property Theft: Economic Harm, Threats to the Public Health and Safety, and Links to Organized Crime and Terrorist Organizations* (2005). The sale of counterfeit and pirated goods adversely impacts national and international economies by decreasing the revenues to the rightful owners or producers, making it harder for them to compete in the marketplace. The World Customs Organization estimates that 7 percent of world trade is in counterfeit goods, worth $512 billion, approximately twice the size of Wal-Mart (Phillips, 2006). This is expected to continue to rapidly grow into the 21st century.

Sales of counterfeit goods also decreases sales tax revenues to governments, resulting in fewer services that can be provided to schools, hospitals, police, road maintenance, and

Culture Shock: A Mixed Message

Bare backs, spaghetti-thin models, and ice-cream cones may be family fare in the West, but in the Middle and Far East, advertisers had better steer clear of such images.

Most of the time, the big international brands are safe sticking to their global advertising strategies. But sometimes, local customs and laws prevent fashion companies from flaunting their racier images. Arab countries are particularly sensitive, especially Kuwait and Saudi Arabia, where nudity is strictly prohibited—not to mention women's faces and flashes of skin in some places. In ads, even a woman's hair, another no-no, must be covered.

Italian companies—often notorious for walking advertising's edge, especially where sex is concerned—adapt their global campaigns to sensitive markets by focusing on accessories or brand image, or by cropping or blacking out potentially offensive images. American firms such as Calvin Klein and Guess often give different ads to the Mideast. Some play up the logo, or for fragrance, the bottle.

Gianfranco Ferré recently had to crop the naked backs of models from the giant photos that cover the walls of a new Ferré Jeans store in Abu Dhabi.

"The photo showed the models with their backs to the camera, wearing Ferré jeans. Now the photo just shows the legs in the jeans," said Patrizia Grassini, the head of advertising at Ittierre, which manufactures its own line, Exte, and jeans and sportswear lines for Gianfranco Ferré, Versace, Dolce & Gabbana, and Romeo Gigli under license.

Grassini said Ittierre is used to censoring its Exte catalogs—blacking out certain pages during printing—for Mideastern markets. In Hong Kong and Taiwan, Ittierre's distributors, who direct the local advertising budget, have refused to use photos that feature models that are too skinny or unhealthy looking.

"In those countries, physical and moral health are closely tied, so no one wants to see skinny models," Grassini said.

Giorgio Armani solves the problem by filling the "mupi" boards that line the roads in Kuwait, Saudi Arabia, and the United Arab Emirates with ads for accessories, a company spokeswoman said.

Like Armani, Gucci creates one global ad campaign and then picks still-life and product shots for markets in the Mideast.

Each season, Diesel, known for its outrageous ads— granny grabbing grandpa's crotch, for example—puts together a "side-order" campaign for the Mideast using the same photographer, models, and location as for the global campaign.

"We focus on the product, and try our best to preserve the image and mood of the global campaign," said Maurizio Marchiore, the head of Diesel's advertising division. "Advertising in the Mideast is always a big problem for us because there are so many restrictions. You can't even show a girl eating an ice-cream cone because it's too suggestive."

But the Mideast isn't the only problem; Diesel had to cancel its spring-summer 1998 campaign in Argentina after human rights groups protested ads for the company's stonewashed jeans.

"The campaign showed models chained to stones and floating in water. What we didn't realize was that it was one way the *desaparecidos* were killed. The day after the protests began, we called a press conference, apologized, and pulled the ads. We're always pushing the limits with our campaigns, and when we push limits, sometimes you have to be ready to take a step backward and admit you are wrong," Marchiore said.

Marchiore said the company received more than 300 letters from angry clerics protesting an ad showing denim-clad nuns saying the rosary in front of a Madonna dressed in jeans. The copy read: "Pure, virginal 100 percent cotton. Our jeans are cut from superior denim . . . The finest denim clothing. This is our mission."

"The letters said the ad was in bad taste," Marchiore said, "and we answered saying Diesel's advertising philosophy is to be provocative and ironic. After the whole episode, one nun wrote back saying she'd bought a pair of our jeans at the store in Covent Garden."

A Benetton spokesman—perhaps the most notorious politically incorrect advertiser—said the company's campaigns were the same throughout the world, and that it took a wait-and-see approach. "We don't censor anything," the spokesman said.

"Every culture reacts differently to certain images. In India, people didn't like the newborn baby with the umbilical cord; in parts of the Mideast, they protested against Israeli and Palestinian kids kissing on the cover of our spring-summer 1998 catalog, called 'Enemies.' In Japan, nudity is OK, but they don't want to see any dead naked bodies," he added.

Sometimes the company offends in ways it could not foresee. "In Turkey, we had some trouble with the campaign that showed the white horse and the black horse mating. It turns out there are opposing parties in Turkey, one with the white horse as its symbol, the other with the black horse."

The British, known for their advertising creativity, have found it occasionally gets them into hot water—at home and abroad. Such companies as The Body Shop, French Connection plc, Levi Strauss, Hennes & Mauritz, and the department store Harvey Nichols have run afoul of the British Advertising Standards Authority.

But controversy has dogged the Brits even when they didn't expect any problem. Levi's, for instance, recently ran a television ad in Britain showing a hamster happily playing on a treadmill then dying when the treadmill breaks. The animal-loving British complained to the standards authority in droves, and the ASA banned the campaign—but not until its scheduled run was over.

Harvey Nichols thought its ad to launch a designer shoe department at its London store was witty and fun—a photograph of a woman in labor wearing a pair of high-heeled, strappy sandals. But 11 people complained and the ASA banned the ads—again, when the campaign had ended.

Julie Bowe, the store's marketing director, couldn't understand why the campaign, created by ad agency Harari Page Moon, caused problems. "Everyone uses sex ad nauseam and no one bats an eyelid," she said. "We chose childbirth and get banned; it's ludicrous." But she admitted the ASA ban had its advantages. The action was reported widely in British newspapers, all of which reproduced the image. "Each time it runs, we get even more publicity," Rowe said.

The Body Shop has created a stir in a number of countries with its poster campaign using Ruby, a size 14 doll. The posters were banned in the Hong Kong subway, for example, where authorities claimed they were too much a distraction. The beauty retailer also raised eyebrows in the U.S. recently with in-store posters showing the naked buttocks of three men.

Anita Roddick, the company's founder and chairman, said European consumers thought the posters were funny and witty, "but women in New Hampshire fainted." The Body Shop recently did an article in its magazine, *The Naked Body*, about six of its posters and the uproar they caused.

One poster showed a man in tiny briefs with a bottle of self-tan lotion stuffed into them and the tagline "Fake It." The poster had to be withdrawn from eight American stores after complaints that the model's pose was immoral. Another showed a mother cuddling her baby and had the headline Mama Toto—which, unfortunately, means something extremely obscene in parts of Mexico.

Of course, some companies want to create controversy. Clothing retailer French Connection has caused double-takes

worldwide for the last several seasons with its FCUK ads. The campaign prompted a string of complaints to the ASA, but French Connection has done little to alter the ads. The tagline has become so successful that it has used it as a logo on its clothing. "It isn't advertising unless it stops you," said Andrea Hyde, the company's global marketing director.

"You have two seconds to capture the audience. Unless you grab their attention, they'll move on to something else." The campaign is global, Hyde said, but French Connection does adapt for the Mideast and Asia.

"We might change the image or the tagline in those areas, but not in the major markets of the U.S., U.K., and continental Europe," Hyde said. But the company is adapting its message slightly this season, and varying where it displays the ads.

Calvin Klein, known for its sexually charged advertising, has had to adjust beauty and jeans ads for the Mideast. Saudi Arabia, for example, discourages showing human figures in outdoor advertising, said a Calvin Klein spokesman. In print, one can only show the face, but no body skin. In Israel, advertisers can't show women with bare skin. "Therefore, we provide some options when taking the campaign to these markets," he said. This spring, Klein shot a beach scene for the jeans campaign for Saudi Arabia with only the Calvin Klein logo—and without Kate Moss.

For Calvin Klein cosmetics, "our images are definitely global," said Michael D'Arminio, advertising manager. "We poll each of the markets to get a sense of what's going on." The company will fine-tune the ads only if there are legal restrictions in a market. In a country where no skin is allowed, for example, the company sometimes will run an image of a bottle. Some countries, like Malaysia, require local performers do voiceovers.

Yves Saint Laurent periodically has stirred things up, but more with its fragrance ads than those for apparel. Clara Saint, a spokeswoman for YSL, said the company has never changed an apparel ad. Rive Gauche ads that showed nudity might have caused some flap, she said, but that is as far as it went.

"The one thing I remember being a big scandal was when Mr. Saint Laurent posed nude for the launch of his men's fragrance in 1971," she said, referring to the famous shot of the designer done by photographer Jean-Loup Sieff. "There was a big noise about that. But otherwise, we haven't changed anything."

Six years later, YSL decided to launch a fragrance named after an addictive drug—Opium. There are still aftershocks from the furor it caused. "Oh, that wasn't just in the Middle East," said Chrystel Abadie-Truchet, international director of marketing for fragrances at YSL's beauty company. "That was a worldwide furor. Everything, from the name to the advertising to the fragrance to the bottle, was controversial. There were demonstrations in New York where some Chinese protested that we were naming a fragrance after a drug that had killed thousands of Chinese people."

Even today, the name Opium cannot be used in ads in certain Mideast countries. In those markets, the scent is sold in a plain wrapper and called simply "Yves Saint Laurent." YSL's Champagne fragrance is called "Champage." "We try to do as little as possible, such as just changing one letter, so that we can keep the graphic design," said AbadieTruchet. "But we have to respect the laws of the country."

Eurocos, licensee of such fragrance brands as Hugo Boss and Laura Biagiotti, has a single brand approach in the U.S. and Europe. But when religious customs dictate, the company complies, explained Rita Schweighoeser, central sales marketing manager of the Frankfurt-based fine fragrance division of Procter & Gamble.

"Religious symbols and women are the most delicate subjects," said Schweighoeser, "so we develop a version of the campaign oriented to the product or use a landscape as background."

"Dressing of a Man," the company's newest ad for Boss Hugo Boss, shows model Alex Lundqvist getting dressed and then entering a gigantic Hugo Boss bottle. In the Mideast print campaign, Lundqvist is shown fully dressed.

Lancaster toned down its Cool Water Woman ad for the U.S. The northern European version shows a naked woman; in the U.S. she's "more discreet."

"Qualitative research shows that the U.S. and Germany are similar in what works in fragrance, but not in advertising," said Patrick Albalodejo, senior vice president of international marketing at the Lancaster Group.

Adapted from: Culture shock: A mixed message. (1999, February 5). *Women's Wear Daily*, pp. 12, 15.

FIGURE 7.5 Street vendors selling counterfeit merchandise often operate in areas that attract tourists.

so forth. Organized crime and terrorist organizations are attracted to counterfeiting due to the low risk of prosecution and enormous profit potential. Operation Green Quest, a multiagency task force established by the U.S. Treasury Department aimed at identifying, disrupting, and dismantling terrorist financial infrastructure and sources of funding, has specifically recognized counterfeit merchandise schemes as a source of terrorist funding (IACC, 2005). For example, an investigation by the intelligence services of Denmark, the United Kingdom, and the United States discovered fake goods being shipped from Dubai to the United Kingdom through Copenhagen, Denmark. Danish customs, using sophisticated risk management software, examined a container filled with counterfeit shampoos, creams, cologne, and perfume. The sender of the counterfeit goods was discovered to be a member of the terrorist group Al Qaeda (2005).

In addition to concerns about economic losses and connection to terrorist groups or organized crime, counterfeiting also is dangerous to health and safety. Fake drugs have caused countless illnesses and deaths. One report states that approximately 192,000 people died in China in 2001 due to counterfeit pharmaceuticals (IACC, 2005). From fake airplane parts, diet pills, vodka, and cola drinks to faulty counterfeit parts used in nuclear power plants, the IACC reports the dark side of selling fake goods.

Although counterfeiting is a global concern, reflecting products from a wide range of industries, only around 4 percent of all counterfeit products are found in designer and luxury goods (Phillips, 2006). But that sector is growing exponentially as well. A carefully developed brand image is undermined by fake goods. Phony Hermès handbags are reported to Joseph Gioconda, an attorney at the New York law firm Kirkland & Ellis, by customs and reports have shown increases from one bag a month to one a week, to eight each day (2006). Hermès International is concerned that premium counterfeits, such as the knockoff Birkin bag hand-stitched in Italy that sells for $1,000, are becoming more desirable than the real thing.

Another problem arises from the movement toward global manufacturing. With more and more products being manufactured overseas, intellectual property—designs, molds, specifications, and trade secrets—are being entrusted to contractors and subcontractors all over the world. It is difficult to police global supply chains, especially with what is known as third shift, midnight shift, or ghost shift manufacturing. **Third shift manufacturing** involves a producer making unauthorized products, without permission from the brand owner, and selling these goods to an unauthorized distributor. For example, a U. S. company orders 20,000 dresses from an overseas factory. Then, the contractor fills that order in two regularly scheduled day shifts and then makes 10,000 unauthorized extra dresses at night, possibly using inferior materials or even using the same materials. The goods, which may be indistinguishable from the trademark garment, are sold out the back door. Sometimes brand owners cannot tell if the unauthorized product is a counterfeit or a third shift manufactured garment.

This type of activity came to light when Too Inc., which runs the Limited Too chain of girl's clothing stores, discovered that T. J. Maxx was selling 653,000 Limited Too garments at discount (Parloff, Chandler, & Fung, 2006). These goods represented more units than Too Inc. had originally ordered from its suppliers. Lawyers for Too Inc. admitted they were not sure if the merchandise was counterfeit or third shift goods. The legality of third shift goods is confusing, and is handled inconsistently in the courts. While some judges allow sales of third shift goods as genuine, other judges have ruled, as in this case, that they are a form of trademark infringement (2006).

Various brand owners and New York City officials created the Mayor's Office of Midtown Enforcement to expose and eliminate counterfeit goods. Approximately 30 different brand holders pay $3,500 each to fund administrative expenses that support police raids of warehouses in Manhattan's *Counterfeit Alley* (Phillips, 2006). These warehouses store much of the counterfeit goods destined for most of the East Coast. In the biggest initiative, 200,000 plastic bags filled with knockoffs worth $12 million were confiscated, replacing uncoordinated and ineffective raids resulting in the confiscation of one day's stock (2006). This program provides an environment in which brands share intelligence with each other and with law enforcement for maximum impact in protecting a brand image.

Whether the brand is luxury, including Hermès, Prada, or Fendi, or mainstream, such as Limited Too, counterfeit or third shift products undermine the economic well-being of brand names. The Internet auction houses, including eBay, Yahoo Inc., and Overstock.com, recognize that selling fakes is becoming a big problem. A test conducted by eBay discovered that four out of five luxury items were fake, and the authenticity of the fifth item was difficult to determine ("What happens," 2006). In this case eBay refunded part of the selling price, whereas the sellers never refunded anything.

Apparel businesses are educating their international partners, explaining the legal boundaries of trademarks in pamphlets printed in several languages. Fila has encouraged consumers to call an 800 number to report suspicious goods, and the IACC has a website and 800 number for consumers to call for information. Figure 7.6 illustrates the seriousness of the Chanel Company's commitment to its logo. Levi Strauss has created a logo with an embedded hologram to protect the mark from being illegally copied. A hologram is a pattern produced on a photosensitive medium that has been exposed by holography and then photographically developed. The hologram is placed on the Levi's so that counterfeit goods that do not have a hologram can be identified.

Trademark infringement has also appeared in cyberspace. Companies are finding the unauthorized use of trademarked names when they try to set up domain names for Web-based retailing addresses. **Domain names** are unique names assigned on a first-come, first-served basis by a company called InterNIC. Clairol filed a trademark infringement suit against a Texas firm to force the firm to stop using herbalessence.com as a domain name. Clairol owns the Herbal Essence and Herbal Essences trademarks. In earlier suits, both Givenchy and Estée Lauder obtained permanent injunctions barring defendants from using infringing names (Young, 1997).

Counterfeit trademarks are illegal because they pass off fraudulent goods as authentic. Another problem within the fashion business is illegally copied goods. These goods are not passed off as authentic; rather, they look so similar to the original product that the consumer may not be able to tell the difference. The fashion industry uses the term **trade dress** to refer to the features of a product that comprise its overall look or image; this includes packaging, labeling, display, product design, and configuration. The product can range from a sweatshirt to a store. Trade dress differs from knockoffs. **Knockoffs** are products that copy either the shape or the design created by a well-known company, but do not bear that company's name. Attorneys who specialize in trade dress saw a rise in trade dress disputes at the end of the 20th century. Further, it was not just the low-end manufacturers who were trying to make a quick knockoff from a brand name; it was also the top designers.

FIGURE 7.6 Chanel's commitment to its trademark is illustrated by this business-to-business ad placed in a trade publication.

WWD, FRIDAY, JUNE 6, 1997

24

A Note Of Information And Entreaty
To Fashion Editors, Advertisers, Copywriters And
Other Well-intentioned Mis-users Of

Our **CHANEL** Name.

CHANEL
was a designer, an extraordinary woman who made
a timeless contribution to fashion.

CHANEL
is a perfume.

CHANEL
is classic elegance in couture, ready-to-wear,
accessories, watches and fine jewelry.

CHANEL
is our registered trademark for fragrance, cosmetics,
clothing, accessories and other lovely things.

Although our style is justly famous, a jacket is not 'a CHANEL jacket' unless it is ours, and somebody else's cardigans are not 'CHANEL for now'.

And even if we are flattered by such tributes to our fame as 'Chanel-issime, Chanel-ed, Chanels and Chanel-ized', PLEASE DON'T. Our lawyers positively detest them.

We take our trademark seriously.

Merci,

CHANEL, Inc.

Social Correctness

The example at the beginning of this chapter illustrates a social concern that is evident in some advertisements. While it may not be illegal to show young models in provocative poses, is it socially correct? Advertisers should evaluate promotions for social correctness in terms of age, gender, and cultural diversity.

A major criticism of advertising in the past has been the negative portrayal of women. In addition to showing women as sex objects, advertisements often depicted them in menial jobs or exclusively as housewives, leading to inappropriate stereotyping of women. Women and men should be represented accurately at all occupational levels in a variety of roles. Advertisements should not use them in **decorative roles**, roles in which the man or woman is placed in the advertisement with no purpose other than to look attractive. Likewise, people with disabilities (Fig. 7.7) should be represented in integrated promotions that show them actively participating and do not bring attention to their limitations.

In advertisements of the past, it was also considered inappropriate to show pregnant women. Pregnancy was a state that was to be ignored, and pregnant women were discriminated against. Socially correct advertisements should depict men and women in all life stages, including pregnancy (Fig. 7.8).

A third criticism of images of women in past advertisements was that they were always pictured as young and thin. In the early 1980s the fashion and advertising industries were directly accused by the public for increased cases of eating disorders such as bulimia and anorexia. Women of all ages and all sizes (Fig. 7.8) should be represented in advertisements.

Culture is a set of socially acquired behavior patterns of a particular society of people. Culture is a way of life and includes material objects, food, dress, ideas, and values. Society is made up of many different religious and ethnic cultures. Within each culture, different segments exist. Black, Hispanic, Jewish, Asian, and all ethnic and religious groups should be equally represented in advertisements. Successful promotions do not stereotype individuals in a manner unbecoming to their culture. They are inclusive of the culture they are targeting and not disparaging toward other cultures or segments within a culture. In many advertising scenarios, a relationship is often depicted in which one side is powerful and one side is weaker. It is important that when it comes to ethnic stereotypes, both the powerful and the weaker side are represented equally.

While the goal of promotion is to encourage and persuade consumers to purchase goods, services, and/or ideas, the persuading should not be done in a misleading or dishonest fashion. A credible integrated marketing communications plan will include the following social and ethical considerations:

- **Persuasion**. The promotional plan will induce a consumer to take action through reason, not manipulation.
- **Ethics**. A promotional plan will be created using principles of correct conduct based on moral values.
- **Gender**. Men and women will be represented portraying contemporary roles in a nonstereotypical manner.
- **Globalization**. Language, customs, tastes, attitudes, lifestyle, values, and ethical and moral standards of each society will be accurately represented.
- **Children**. A promotional plan will not be directed at or contain material that may exploit children.
- **Cultural diversity**. A promotional plan must accurately reflect the behavior patterns, arts, beliefs, and institutions of all individuals of the country in which it is broadcast or published.

FIGURE 7.7 Nordstrom has been a leader in featuring people with disabilities in advertisements.

Style is not a size... it's an Attitude! MARINA RINALDI

FIGURE 7.8 Models in contemporary advertisements may feature models who are pregnant (left), mature (middle), or any size (right).

There might have been a time when scandal and media disgrace would have ended the career of a celebrity or model. However, several models have survived controversial situations. Model Naomi Campbell has been accused of assault by several of her former employees and apparently lost her temper at her former boyfriend's house. She began screaming so loudly that police apprehended her for disturbing the peace. Despite her reputation for being difficult, she still walks the catwalk and is photographed for numerous advertising campaigns.

Another British model, Kate Moss, was publicly disgraced when a photograph showing her cutting and snorting cocaine at a recording session was published in the London tabloid *Daily Mirror*. The pictures were harsh and realistic, causing many top clients, including Swedish retailer H & M, Burberry, and Chanel, to drop her from lucrative advertising campaigns. Ms. Moss, who had estimated annual earnings of $9 million, did not admit to drug abuse, but offered an apology and went to an Arizona clinic for rehab (Trebay, 2006).

After Ms. Moss checked out of the clinic, her career was revitalized with a cover shot on *W* and *Vanity Fair*, a guest editorship at French *Vogue*, and advertising campaigns with Virgin Mobile, Dior, Roberto Cavalli, CK Jeans, Longchamp, Nikon, and even Burberry. Figure 7.9 shows Kate Moss in the Nikon advertising campaign that was shot during her comeback. According to Anna Marie Bakker, director of communications at Nikon, Ms. Moss was selected for the promotion because Nikon is trying to shed its stale image and appeal to unpredictable young consumers. Ms. Bakker also stated, "Part of the appeal is that she is truly an enduring style icon. But most importantly, she appeals to Nikon as we try to move our product forward because she has an edge" (Trebay, 2006, p. G1).

Historically, bad boys and bad girls have a sort of cool or edge that is not appropriate for the middle class. According to Michael Brody, chairman of the media committee of the American Academy of Child and Adolescent Psychiatry, although edge denotes shame, "If you're selling a camera in a celebrity-obsessed culture, why not use a celebrity and one who was captured at the scene of a crime?" (Trebay, 2006, p. G1). Yet, despite these and other prior controversies, including allegedly promoting anorexia and destroying hotel rooms, Kate Moss did not fall from public grace.

Ethical and social considerations should be reflected throughout an entire promotion, beginning with the public relations image of the company and carried through to every aspect of promotion. Advertising, publicity, direct mail, and interactive media messages should reflect an ethical image to the customer. Events produced and/or sponsored by the company should reflect the ethical code the company stands for. The image presented within a store, including visual merchandise presentations, sales promotions, and the sales personnel hired to sell the merchandise, should have a consistent ethical image.

But how does a firm monitor itself to ensure it is upholding ethical and social standards? Through a set of voluntary and obligatory checks and balances that are discussed in the next section.

——o CHECKS AND BALANCES

Professionals in the promotion industry have the opportunity to monitor their actions and messages through a series of checks and balances. The checks and balances include a code of ethics and self-regulation. Codes of ethics set standards of conduct for individuals and companies. Self-regulation sets standards for industries.

FIGURE 7.9 Kate Moss survived controversy and gained several high-paying contracts after her alleged drug abuse scandal.

Code of Ethics

Laws are the body of rules and principles governing the actions of individuals or organizations and enforced by a political authority. They are in place to guard against false or misleading advertising. **Ethics** are the rules or standards governing the conduct of a person or the members of a profession. They are not mandated by law, but rather are directed by moral values. The conduct of an individual or group of individuals may be within the law but outside the social or ethical parameters of a society.

One tool, used to set standards of behavior by professionals and corporations, is a code of ethics. A **code of ethics** is a procedure of conduct the company intends to follow and expects from its employees, clients, vendors, and/or customers. A code of ethics enhances the credibility of a profession, and of companies or individuals working within the profession. In certain industries those who choose not to establish a code of ethics suffer from a lack of respect by clients, employees, and the general public.

Codes of ethics are established through examination of the practices and procedures of an industry or a company and are put in place to protect individuals and the company. A code of ethics may outline how the business expects to treat customers and employees, a policy on fee structures, how advertising and promotion will be handled, and how the company expects to work within a community. A very simple code of ethics for a promotion consultant may include the following statements:

- *I will represent each client fairly and honestly.*
- *I will provide all agreed-upon services in a timely and cost-efficient manner.*

- *I will establish reasonable and proper fees for services and provide written estimates to each client.*
- *I will use honest and factual information in all promotions.*
- *I will operate in a manner that is a credit to the community.*

Professional organizations can assist in setting standards. Many of these organizations have a code of ethics in place for their members. Figure 7.10 illustrates the principles of professional conduct and ethics the **International Special Events Society (ISES)** expects of its members.

The Public Relations Society of America (PRSA) follows a Public as Relations Member Code of Ethics, which was revised and updated in 2000 (Public Relations Society of America [PRSA]). The code applies to PRSA members and is designed to be a useful guide as members carry out their ethical responsibilities. Figure 7.11 lists the core ethical values of the organization.

Good corporate mission statements should include company priorities for interaction in the social and political community. Some organizations choose to include a code of ethics to accompany the mission statement. Ethics policies often prohibit employees from accepting gifts or other tokens. Some businesses have taken steps to monitor business efforts by asking managers and vendors to sign an integrity pledge. The **integrity pledge** prohibits employees from accepting any gifts, samples, loans, free travel, and entertainment or other benefits.

Self-regulation

An industry that voluntarily monitors itself for ethically and socially correct messages participates in a policy of self-regulation. **Self-regulation** means that an entity voluntarily controls or directs itself according to rules, principles, or laws without outside monitoring. Self-regulation is imposed to assure that advertising will not offend, deceive, or

FIGURE 7.10 The principles of professional conduct and ethics of the International Special Events Society.

Principles of Professional Conduct and Ethics

Each member of ISES shall agree to adhere to the following:

1. Provide to all persons truthful and accurate information with respect to the professional performance of duties.
2. Maintain the highest standards of personal conduct to bring credit to the special events industry.
3. Promote and encourage the highest level of ethics within the profession.
4. Recognize and discharge by responsibility, to uphold all laws and regulations relating to ISES policies and activities.
5. Strive for excellence in all aspects of the industry.
6. Use only legal and ethical means in all industry activities.
7. Protect the public against fraud and unfair practices, and attempt to eliminate from ISES all practices which bring discredit to the profession.
8. Use a written contract clearly stating all charges, services, products, and other essential information.
9. Demonstrate respect for every professional within the industry by clearly stating and consistently performing at or above the standards acceptable to the industry.
10. Make a commitment to increase professional growth and knowledge by attending educational programs recommended, but not limited to, those prescribed by ISES.
11. Contribute knowledge to professional meetings and journals to raise the consciousness of the industry.
12. Maintain the highest standards of safety, sanitation, and any other responsibilities.
13. When providing services or products, maintain in full force adequate or appropriate insurance.
14. Cooperate with professional colleagues, suppliers, and employees to provide the highest quality service.
15. Extend these same professional commitments to all those persons supervised or employed.
16. Subscribe to the ISES Principles of Professional Conduct and Ethics and to abide by the ISES Bylaws.

FIGUre 7.11 The Public Relations Society of America core values for ethical behavior.

Public Relations Society of America Code of Ethics Core Values

ADVOCACY
- We will serve the public interest by acting as responsible advocates for those we represent.
- We will provide a voice to the marketplace of ideas, facts, and viewpoints to aid informed public debate.

HONESTY
- We adhere to the highest standards of accuracy and truth in advancing the interests of those we represent and in communication with the public.

EXPERTISE
- We acquire and responsibly use specialized knowledge and experience.
- We advance the profession through continued professional development, research, and education.
- We build mutual understanding, credibility, and relationships among a wide array of institutions and audiences.

INDEPENDENCE
- We provide objective counsel to those we represent.
- We are accountable for our actions.

LOYALTY
- We are faithful to those we represent, while honoring our obligation to serve the public interest.

FAIRNESS
- We deal fairly with clients, employers, competitors, peers, vendors, the media, and the general public.
- We respect all opinions and support the right of free expression.

---

exploit individual consumers or groups. Self-regulation begins with the firm and the advertising agency as part of the negotiation process between the client and the advertising agency. Firms and agencies set guidelines, policies, and standards that ads must conform to and that the firm and the client must accept. Beyond self-regulation by agency and client, nonprofit organizations within various industries assist with self-regulation of advertising and promotional efforts. Some of these organizations, including the Better Business Bureau, the Direct Marketing Association, and the National Association of Broadcasters, are discussed in the following pages.

Better Business Bureau

The Better Business Bureau (BBB) self-regulates advertising to assure the consumer of a correct and ethical message. The **Better Business Bureau (BBB)** system in the U. S. was founded in 1912 to help solve marketplace problems fairly by using voluntary self-regulation and consumer education (Council of Better Business Bureaus, 2003). The BBB in North America, which operates a range of programs and services to promote ethical business conduct, is the preeminent force for marketplace ethics. These programs include voluntary standards and codes of practice, dispute resolution processes, and information and education programs that impact millions of consumers and businesses each year. The mission of the BBB is to foster public confidence in truthful advertising. It is not an enforcement agency but does seek to protect the consumer against untruthful or misleading advertising through voluntary cooperation and self-regulation. To this purpose, it has established a set of advertising guidelines for companies to use based on broad principles of truth and accuracy. Local BBBs regularly monitor advertising for adherence to these principles, as well as compliance with local, state, and federal regulations relating to advertising. When the BBB finds questionable advertising, the advertiser is contacted and requested to substantiate the claims that are being made and to voluntarily comply with the guidelines. In certain areas, local BBBs have also put in place an appeals process for the advertiser.

The Better Business Bureau's guidelines are directed by three basic principles:

1. The primary responsibility for truthful and nondeceptive advertising rests with the advertiser. Advertisers should be prepared to substantiate any claims or offers made before publication or broadcast and, upon request, present such substantiation promptly to the advertising medium or the Better Business Bureau.
2. Advertisements that are untrue, misleading, deceptive, fraudulent, falsely disparaging of competitors, or insincere offers to sell shall not be used.
3. An advertisement as a whole may be misleading although every sentence separately considered is literally true. Misrepresentation may result not only from direct statements but also by omitting or obscuring a material fact. (Council, 1994).

Beyond the three driving principles, the BBB has specific regulations directed toward particular elements of advertisements. Specific regulations cover topics such as price, the use of the word *free,* sales, credit, testimonials and endorsements, rebates, contests, and other elements of advertising. The subjects that the BBB covers with regard to advertising and promotion are very complete.

While Better Business Bureaus monitor advertising in local markets, the parent organization, the **Council of Better Business Bureaus (CBBB)**, develops advertising codes and standards at a national level. Since 1971, the National Advertising Division (NAD) of the CBBB and the National Advertising Review Board have served as the self-regulation monitoring council for the advertising industry. In 1972, as a division of NAD, the Children's Advertising Review Unit (CARU) was established. CARU promotes responsible advertising to children. CARU has developed seven principles that guide advertising directed at children under age 12. The principles are as follows:

1. Advertisers should always take into account the level of knowledge, sophistication, and maturity of the audience to which the message is primarily directed. Younger children have a limited capacity for evaluating the credibility of information they receive and also lack the ability to understand the nature of the information they provide. Advertisers, therefore, have a special responsibility to protect children from their own susceptibilities.
2. Realizing that children are imaginative and that make-believe play constitutes an important part of the growing-up process, advertisers should exercise care not to exploit unfairly the imaginative quality of children. Advertising should not stimulate unreasonable expectations of product quality or performance either directly or indirectly.
3. Products and content that are inappropriate for children should not be advertised or promoted directly to children.
4. Recognizing that advertising may play an important part in educating the child, advertisers should communicate information in a truthful and accurate manner and in language understandable to young children in full recognition that the child may learn practices from advertising that can affect his or her health and well-being.
5. Advertisers are urged to capitalize on the potential of advertising to influence behavior by developing advertising that, whenever possible, addresses itself to positive and beneficial social behavior, such as friendship, kindness, honesty, justice, generosity, and respect of others.

6. Care should be taken to incorporate minority and other groups in advertisements in order to present positive and prosocial roles and role models whenever possible. Social stereotyping and appeals to prejudice should be avoided.

7. Although many influences affect a child's personal and social development, it remains the prime responsibility of parents to provide guidance for children. Advertisers should contribute to this parent-child relationship in a constructive manner (Children's Advertising Review Unit, 2003).

Although the above principles are directed toward advertising to children under the age of 12, they have implications for advertising to other target populations and should be considered in the integrated marketing communications plan.

In 1997, in response to a request by the Federal Trade Commission, CARU established guidelines for advertising to children over the World Wide Web. The guidelines include asking advertisers to make "reasonable efforts" to get children to ask their parents' permission before purchasing a product or service through the Internet, or before answering any personal questions about themselves or their families (Mifflin, 1997). Additionally, advertisers are urged to disclose why information is being requested and how it will be used.

Direct Marketing Association

The **Direct Marketing Association (DMA)** has established ethical guidelines for direct response broadcast advertising, mail list practices, marketing by telephone, and interactive marketing. The philosophy of the Direct Marketing Association is also one of self-regulation rather than government mandates. According to the DMA, self-regulatory practices are more readily adaptable to new techniques, economic fluctuations, and changing social conditions. Because the guidelines are voluntary rather than mandated, use is widespread and incorporated into the business plan of many companies as sound business practice. The DMA Committee on Ethical Business Practice is charged with reviewing any complaint by an individual in violation of the DMA guidelines and has the authority to take appropriate action.

The Direct Marketing Association has put in place generally accepted principles of conduct for individuals and organizations involved in direct mail and direct marketing. As discussed in Chapter 11, the purposes of direct marketing are to promote, sell, and deliver goods and services directly from manufacturer to consumer using a maintained or purchased list of potential customers. The DMA has recognized that businesses should protect the personal privacy of individuals and through the use of guidelines has provided safeguards for the proper handling of personal data contained in files.

The following principles apply to DMA members' relationships with current and prospective customers, donors, and members—whether consumers or businesses. The principles are the underlying framework for the Guidelines for Ethical Business Practice (2006). A DMA Member:

1. Is committed to its customers' satisfaction.
2. Clearly, honestly, and accurately represents its products, services, terms, and conditions.
3. Delivers its products and services as represented.
4. Communicates in a respectful and courteous manner.
5. Responds to inquiries and complaints in a constructive, timely way.
6. Maintains appropriate security policies and practices to safeguard information.
7. Provides information on its policies about the transfer of personally identifiable information for marketing purposes.

8. Honors requests not to have personally identifiable information transferred for marketing purposes.
9. Honors requests not to receive future solicitations from its organization.
10. Follows the spirit and letter of the law as well as DMA's Guidelines for Ethical Business Practice (2006).

Online and Internet marketing opportunities create special circumstances surrounding an individual's privacy and have become the focus of the DMA to ensure ethical marketing practices on the Internet. Because anyone can access the Internet, it is important to limit the disclosure of personal information to only the party that has permission to receive the information. Depending on the circumstances, information collected about a consumer online may include contact or locator information such as name; postal and e-mail addresses; billing information, including account and credit card numbers; transaction information, such as the date of purchase; and information that might reveal the consumer's preferences or choices, such as the time of day purchases are made or sites visited. Because the Internet is growing in popularity, it is important for ethical standards to be developed for the privacy of the individual disclosing information.

The Direct Marketing Association guidelines recommend that all marketers operating online sites, whether or not they collect personal information, should make available their information practices in a prominent place to consumers. These practices should be easy to find, read, and understand by the consumer. The notice should identify the markets and disclose an e-mail and postal address to which the consumer can direct questions or comments. Marketers sharing personal information collected online should furnish individuals with an opportunity to prohibit the disclosure of that information (Direct Marketing Association, 2006).

National Association of Broadcasters

The **National Association of Broadcasters (NAB)** is the trade association for the radio and television industry. Its priority is to maintain a favorable governmental, legal, and technological climate for the free over-the-air broadcasting industry. The NAB represents radio and television broadcasters before the Federal Communications Commission (FCC) and other federal agencies, courts, and legal and regulatory agencies. The NAB practices self-regulation with codes of standards for both radio and television similar to those in place for print advertising. The NAB has voluntarily set TV parental guidelines to offer parents advance cautionary information so that they can better supervise the TV watching of younger children.

The United States is not the only country to establish self-regulation bodies to monitor advertising messages. The concept of advertising self-regulation has developed since the 1960s. It includes 52 countries, 25 of which have well-established systems in place to clear advertising content and handle complaints from industry and consumers about advertising (Ingrassia, 1995). Canada was one of the first countries to establish a self-regulation body to review advertising, with the **Canadian Advertising Foundation** (CAP) founded in 1967. CAP is parent to the Advertising Standards Council, which administers the Canadian Code of Advertising Standards. Only the United Kingdom (1962), the Netherlands (1964), and Italy (1966) preceded Canada with codes of their own (Ingrassia, 1995).

The Canadian self-regulatory body is an organization of media, advertisers, and agencies. It includes public representatives in various positions in consumer associations who review committee work. The Canadian codes have been developed for various product sectors such as cosmetics, feminine hygiene products, nonalcoholic beverages and food, and children's advertising. CAF has been successful in promoting consensus when there is a dispute on advertising content. In traditional Canadian style, meetings rather than fights are held to resolve problems. Such meetings are private, and the nature and results of them are not disclosed to the press or the public.

Occasionally self-regulation has proven so successful that regulations have been retired. Such was the case with the advertising of feminine hygiene products. Advertising adhered to the regulations, and complaints against the ads decreased, so the CAF retired the specific regulations in 1992 (Ingrassia, 1995).

Mexico and other Latin American countries have also established self-regulation bodies that monitor advertising messages. The **Council for Self-Regulations and Ethical Advertising (CONAR)** was established in Mexico in 1995, modeled after similar bodies already in place in Brazil, Argentina, Chile, Venezuela, and Costa Rica (Bedingfield, 1995). CONAR is intended to solve disputes out of court, through amicable negotiation by a board of nine directors drawn from advertising and the media. According to the head of CONAR, Guther Saupe, it was in Mexico's best interest to self-regulate to avoid establishing more laws. In Brazil, 99 percent of all conflicts have been resolved during the past 20 years in which the self-regulatory board has been in place. Chile has had similar positive results; 90 percent of its conflicts have been resolved without involving the government (Bedingfield, 1995).

Advertisers, advertising agencies, and advertising outlets have recognized that consumer trust and confidence must be maintained. They also realize that if they do not self-regulate, the government will step in and put rigid restrictions in place.

──o GOVERNMENT REGULATION

Although professionals within the advertising and promotion professions strive to monitor messages through self-regulation, it is sometimes necessary for the government to intervene to protect consumers in the marketplace.

In the early part of the 20th century, advertising and packaging techniques were designed to increase sales of products rather than assisting consumers in selection and evaluation of sound products. Consumerism has emerged as a reaction to consumers' dissatisfaction with the marketplace. It is a movement seeking to protect and inform consumers by requiring such practices as honest packaging and advertising, product guarantees, and improved safety standards. Consumerism is the promotion of the consumer's interest and is achieved through a set of activities monitored by government, businesses, and independent organizations designed to protect the rights of consumers.

Consumerism began in 1914 when Congress established the **Federal Trade Commission (FTC)** in response to the need for consumer protection. The FTC at its inception, and through later amendments, has been given authority to monitor deceptive acts and practices concerning the consumer. Many other federal acts have followed, all designed to protect the consumer. They include the Food, Drug, & Cosmetics Act; Wool Products Labeling Act; Fur Products Labeling Act; Flammable Products Act; Cigarette Labeling and Advertising Act; and Fair Packaging and Labeling Act.

As a statement to show how important consumerism was to President John F.

Kennedy, in 1962 he established "rights" for consumers. The four consumer rights include:

1. The right to safety
2. The right to be informed
3. The right to be heard
4. The right to choice

These rights have continued to be protected by Congress and are adhered to in all promotion activities publicizing consumer goods. We will now discuss the specific roles of the FTC and the Federal Communications Commission (FCC). There are other agencies that also monitor advertising of specific products.

Federal Trade Commission

In the United States, the FTC is charged with protecting consumers. The **Federal Trade Commission Act** created the commission, which is responsible for controlling and regulating antitrust and consumer protection laws. According to its mission statement, the FTC works to enhance the smooth operation of the marketplace by eliminating acts or practices that are unfair or deceptive and stopping actions that threaten consumers' opportunities to exercise informed choice (Federal Trade Commission, 1999).

The FTC has specific regulations regarding advertising. FTC policy mandates that advertisers substantiate claims that make objective assertions about the item or service being advertised. Additionally, the advertiser must have a reasonable basis supporting these claims. A firm's failure to possess and rely upon a reasonable basis for objective claims constitutes an unfair and deceptive act practice in violation of the Federal Trade Commission Act.

In addition to monitoring the substantiation of advertising claims, the FTC also regulates the labeling of products through various congressional acts. The **Robinson-Patman Act** authorizes the FTC to prevent specified practices involving discriminatory pricing and product promotion. The act stipulates that any manufacturer providing promotional allowances or services to retailers must offer the allowance on a proportionally equal basis to all retailers.

The **Wool Products Labeling Act** of 1939 governs the labeling of wool and wool-blended textiles. The Act requires that wool products moving in interstate commerce be labeled. It also has a provision that mandates that mail-order promotional materials clearly and conspicuously state whether a wool product was processed or manufactured in the United States or was imported.

The **Textile Fiber Products Identification Act (TFPIA)** of 1960 requires that a tag or label with certain information relating to the fiber content of textile products be attached to the item at the time of sale and delivery to the consumer. The following items must appear on the textile label: fiber content and the percentage by weight of each over 5 percent, the manufacturer's name, country of origin of imported fabrics, and identification of fibers by generic names. TFPIA also mandates disclosure in the labeling, invoicing, and advertising of textile fiber products and includes a provision that mail-order promotional materials clearly and conspicuously indicate whether a textile fiber product was processed or manufactured in the United States or was imported. Fur products are handled separately under the **Fur Products Labeling Act** of 1951. This act requires that invoices and advertising for fur and fur products specify, among other things, the true English name of the animal from which the fur was taken.

Federal Communications Commission

The **Federal Communications Commission** (**FCC**) regulates broadcast communications and has authority over telephone, telegraph, television, radio, private radio, cellular telephone, pagers, cable TV, international communications, and satellite communications. The FCC is an independent U.S. government agency established in 1934 by the Communications Act (2006). It is directly responsible to Congress. The FCC has the authority to license, renew, and/or take away broadcast station licenses and has the authority to monitor advertising on these stations. The FCC may restrict products to be advertised and the content of the advertisement. Profane or obscene language and messages deemed to be in poor taste are not permitted to be broadcast. The FCC also requires television stations to disclose who is paying for infomercials at the beginning or end of the commercial.

In this chapter, we have pointed out that professional promotion specialists must be responsible to the public and consider the social and ethical ramifications of their messages before they are sent to consumers. But we do not want to leave you with the idea that advertising and promotion are harmful. In fact, the opposite is true. Advertising is good for consumers. It conveys important information about benefits, price, quality, and availability. For example, the National Fluid Milk Processor Promotion Board has been successful in informing consumers of the benefits of drinking milk by using celebrities in a milk mustache campaign (Fig. 7.12). Promotion represents the right of consumers to choose goods and services from competing suppliers, and we are privileged to live in a country that allows promotion to exist.

FIGUre 7.12 A socially conscious advertising campaign features Elizabeth Hurley for *Got Milk?*

summary

- Promotion professionals must be responsible to the public and consider the social and ethical ramifications of their messages before they are sent to consumers.
- Several social and ethical considerations that should be evaluated when planning a promotion include offensive advertising, plagiarism, counterfeiting, and social correctness.
- Laws are the body of rules and principles governing the actions of individuals or organizations and are enforced by a political authority.
- Ethics are the rules or standards governing the conduct of a person or the members of a profession and are directed by moral values.
- A code of ethics is the procedure of conduct the company intends to follow and expects from its employees, clients, vendors, and/or customers.
- During the evaluation process, an integrated marketing communications plan should examine ethical considerations related to the following elements: persuasion, ethics, gender, globalization, children, and cultural diversity.

- The advertising industry monitors itself through a policy of voluntary self-regulation.
- The Better Business Bureau (BBB) self-regulates advertising to assure the consumer of the correct and ethical message.
- The Direct Marketing Association (DMA) has established ethical guidelines for direct response broadcast advertising, mailing list practices, marketing by telephone, and interactive marketing.
- The National Association of Broadcasters (NAB) is the trade association for the radio and television industry with the priority to maintain a favorable governmental, legal, and technological climate for the free over-the-air broadcasting industry.
- The Federal Trade Commission (FTC) works to enhance the smooth operation of the marketplace by eliminating acts or practices that are unfair or deceptive and stopping actions that threaten consumers' opportunities to exercise informed choices.
- The FTC investigates infomercials that do not disclose their true advertising nature or make deceptive claims about products.
- The Federal Communications Commission (FCC) regulates broadcast communications.

KEY TERMS

code of ethics	Fur Products Labeling Act	Textile Fiber Products
consumerism	integrity pledge	Identification Act (TFPIA)
copyright	knockoffs	third shift manufacturing
culture	laws	trade dress
decorative roles	plagiarism	trademark
domain ethics names	Robinson-Patman Act	trademark counterfeiting
Federal Trade Commission Act	self-regulation	Wool Products Labeling Act

KEY ORGANIZATIONS

- Better Business Bureau
- Canadian Advertising Foundation
- Council of Better Business Bureaus
- Council for Self-Regulation and Ethical Advertising
- Direct Marketing Association
- Federal Communications Commission
- Federal Trade Commission
- International Special Events Society
- National Association of Broadcasters
- Public Relations Society of America

QUESTIONS FOR DISCUSSION

1. What social and ethical issues should a promotion planner be aware of as he or she develops advertising, direct marketing pieces, and other promotion tools?
2. How do the social and ethical issues raised with advertising and direct marketing affect the other promotional techniques such as sales promotion, publicity and public relations, special events, fashion shows, and visual merchandising?
3. What are the advantages and disadvantages related to self-regulation?
4. What are the benefits and detriments to using infomercials?
5. What are the benefits and detriments associated with electronic retailing?

ADDITIONAL RESOURCES

Sheehan, K. (2004). *Controversies in contemporary advertising.* Thousand Oaks, CA: Sage Publications.
Silvulka, J. (1998). *Soap, sex, and cigarettes: A cultural history of American advertising.* Belmont, CA: Wadsworth Publishing.

References

Bedingfield, J. (1995, September 18). Mexico unleashes watchdog to avoid legal ad disputes. *Advertising Age*, pp. 1–6.

Children's Advertising Review Unit. (2003). *Self-regulatory guidelines for children's advertising* (7th ed.). New York: Author.

Council of Better Business Bureaus, Inc. (1994). *BBB Code of advertising*. Arlington, VA: Author. Retrieved July 21, 2006, from: www.bbb.org

Council of Better Business Bureaus. (2003). *About the Better Business Bureau system*. Arlington, VA: Author.

Direct Marketing Association. (2006). *Direct Marketing Association guidelines for ethical business practice*. New York: Author.

Elliott, S. (1995, August 29). Will Calvin Klein's retreat redraw the lines of taste? *New York Times*, p. D1, D8.

Federal Communications Commission. (2006). *About the FCC*. Washington, DC: Author.

Federal Trade Commission. (1999). *Vision, mission, & goals*. Washington, DC: Author.

Ingrassia, J. (1995, September 18). Canada's ad industry self-regulation aids quality. *Advertising Age*, p. 28.

International AntiCounterfeiting Coalition. (2005). *The negative consequences of international intellectual property theft: Economic harm, threats to the public health and safety, and links to organized crime and terrorist organizations*. Washington, D.C.: Author.

Mifflin, L. (1997, April 21). New guidelines for net ads for children. *New York Times*, p. D5. Retrieved August 13, 2006, from LexisNexis database.

Parloff, R., Chandler, C., & Fung, A. (2006, May). Not exactly counterfeit. *Fortune*, 153, 8. Retrieved July 22, 2006, from Academic Search Premier database.

Phillips, T. (2006, January 2). Fighting bogus goods to protect the brand. *Brandweek*, 47, 1. Retrieved July 22, 2006, from Academic Search Premier database.

Public Relations Society of America. (2000). *PRSA Member Code of Ethics*. New York: Author.

Trebay, G. (2006, April 20). Being bad: The career move. *New York Times*, p. Gl.

Weil, J. & Fallon, J. (1998, September 4). Body *Shop's hemp paraphernalia* seized in France. *Women's Wear Daily*, 5.

What happens when an eBay steal is a fake. (2006, June 29). *Wall Street Journal*, p. D 1, D2. Retrieved July 22, 2006, from Academic Search Premier database.

Young, V. (1997). Web wars, *Women's Wear Daily*, 14.

part two

Promotion Mix

FIGURE 8.1 Clinique's
3-step skin care system.

Advertising and the Creative Process

After you have read this chapter, you should be able to:

Explain what advertisers mean by creativity, the creative process, and creative strategy.

List and describe the primary functions of advertising.

Distinguish among the various methods of classifying advertisements.

Identify the characteristics common to successful advertising.

Clinique's best-selling 3-step skin care regime may be pushing 40, but its marketing is taking a decidedly forward-thinking focus.

The cornerstone of the plan is a $10 million TV campaign developed by Arnold Advertising, which is reinforced with a dedicated Internet microsite, in-store promotion, street teams, marketing on college campuses, and print advertising.

Each aspect is targeted to a slightly different consumer, noted Jim Nevins, worldwide creative director for Clinique. The TV spots, which will run on MTV, VH-1, E! and the CW and Fox networks, are aimed at a consumer in the 18- to 29-year-old-age range. Women in the 30- to 45-year-old group are targeted with the print campaign in fashion, beauty, and lifestyle magazines, and the radio spots are expected to appeal chiefly to consumers from 45 to 60 years old.

"Print is always going to be the baseline, but we have to follow the direction in which the consumer is evolving," said Alicia Sontag, vice president of North American marketing for Clinique. "For instance, our young consumers are spending 26 percent of their time online and 63 percent watching broadcast TV. What we've seen is that there is a stark contrast between campaigns with one media element versus those which are surrounded by animation: the Internet, in-store, radio, TV. If you do that, it's successful. Otherwise, it's not enough to break through the clutter."

The commercial is "very stylized and clean—sort of a play on the game Mousetrap or falling dominoes," said Nevins. "One thing hits another to activate: The water activates the Facial Soap, a bubble travels around the Clarifying Lotion and pops on the cap." The final emphasis is on Dramatically Different Moisturizing Lotion.

The TV spots will invite in consumers for deluxe samples (personalized to their skin types) that contain enough product for at least seven days of use.

"Getting people to try the product is the greatest aim of this campaign," said Jane Lauder, -senior vice president of global marketing for Clinique. "We're trying to connect emotionally with our consumers, not only about our products but about their lives."

Source: Naughton, J. (2007, January 19). Clinique's forward push for its 3-step regime. *Women's Wear Daily*, p. 5.

MIXING UP THE ADVERTISING formula keeps Clinique's skin care regime looking fresh. By applying a generous amount on television, an equally healthy portion in print, and a dab here and there over the Internet and through other promotional techniques, the skin care brand's advertising agency effectively disperses its message through a media-saturated society.

This chapter on advertising begins Part II of the text, which focuses on each promotion mix technique in detail. Because advertising is so important to the total promotion package, we discuss it as the first promotion mix element, and devote three chapters to coverage of the topic. This chapter introduces advertising and the creative process. Within this chapter we will introduce key concepts of advertising that may also be applied to other promotion mix elements. Chapter 9 focuses on print media and Chapter 10 focuses on broadcast media. Other promotion mix elements follow, including: direct marketing and interactive media, sales promotion, public relations, special events, fashion shows, and visual merchandising.

This chapter begins by discussing advertising classifications. We then introduce the topic of creativity and the creative process, developed by James Webb Young in the early 1970s and still relevant in the 21st century. Then we turn our attention to the creative strategy that leads into development of the major selling idea. Advertising appeals and advertising executions follow. The chapter concludes by talking about measuring advertising effectiveness.

Advertising is any nonpersonal message, paid for, placed in the mass media, and controlled by the sponsoring organization. Nonpersonal means the advertising is delivered to the audience through mass media—newspapers, magazines, television, radio, and other media that reach mass consumers simultaneously. Advertising is paid for, which means the sponsor buys space or time in the mass media to promote the message. The advertiser's name, logo, or other identifying mark generally appears in the advertisement to show recognition for buying the space or time.

Advertising is the most widely used promotion mix element. When planning promotions, nearly all businesses allocate budgets to advertising first, and then review other promotion mix elements to complement the advertising campaign. As we illustrated in Chapter 6, Table 6.2, domestic advertising expenditures for 2005 were over $271 billion (100 leading national advertisers, 2006). Additionally, as illustrated in Table 6.4, the top 10 leading advertisers in retailing spent over $2.8 billion in advertising in 2005 (Frazier, 2006).

Advertising is an important element of promotion programs because it is a very cost-effective way to reach large audiences. Domestic advertising expenditures in Table 6.2 were spread over a variety of media including magazines, newspapers, television, radio, outdoor, and Internet, all of which attract large audiences to see or hear the advertising message.

Advertising is valued for its contributions to communication. By providing new information, persuading customers to buy merchandise, reminding customers of product attributes and availability, and introducing product innovations, advertising ultimately builds brand equity. Advertising creates awareness about new products, informs consumers about attributes of specific brands, and educates the public about product features and benefits. Advertising helps to keep the product fresh in the mind of the consumer. When an individual needs a new or replacement product, advertising helps to keep the merchandise in the consumer's memory. Innovating, improving quality, or altering consumer perception are ways a firm adds value to its products. Advertising helps to change consumer perception through innovations and quality improvements. By providing consumers with information about products and brands, advertising influences consumer perceptions about the product or brand.

Advertising is also important in contributing to a firm's overall integrated marketing communications plan. Advertising is often the primary promotion mix element used by the firm to support other promotion mix elements. Advertising may be the technique used to distribute coupons for sales promotion activities, the medium to communicate a firm's website for direct marketing, or the technique used to tell prospective clients about an upcoming trunk show or other special event. Advertising enhances the overall integrated marketing communications effort.

Professional organizations are part of the advertising profession. The **American Advertising Federation (AAF)** is the unifying professional organization that binds the mutual interests of corporate advertisers, agencies, media companies, suppliers, and academia. The AAF has more than 50,000 members who share a commitment to making advertising a positive force in America's economy and culture. As advocates for the rights of advertisers, members of the group educate policy makers, the news media, and the general public about the value that advertising brings to the well-being of the nation.

——○ ADVERTISING CLASSIFICATIONS

There are several ways in which to classify advertising: target audience, geographic area, medium, or purpose. These classifications are not mutually exclusive; an advertisement may be defined by its target audience and geographic location or its geographic location and purpose.

Target Audience

The two common ways to classify advertising by audience include advertising to consumer markets and advertising to business and professional markets. Advertising directed toward the consumer, the ultimate user of the product or brand, is known as **consumer advertising**. Advertising that is directed to the consumer audience may be sponsored by the manufacturer, the retailer, or as a cooperative venture between the manufacturer and retailer. The majority of consumer advertising is placed in the mass media. Additionally, advertising through direct marketing and interactive media is often consumer oriented.

Advertising directed to the business and professional markets is known as **trade advertising**. Trade advertising is focused toward professional journals, trade magazines, business publications, and through direct-response materials in contrast to much of consumer advertising, which is concentrated in consumer-oriented mass communication channels. Because trade advertising is targeted toward professional or trade publications, the ultimate consumer is not usually aware of this type of advertising.

The difference between consumer and trade advertising is demonstrated in Figure 8.2. The consumer-directed ad, Figure 8.2, can be found in many different consumer publications from *Self* to *Time*. It informs the consumer about the quality and uses for the original Swiss Army knife. The trade ad, Figure 8.2, was published in the trade paper *Women's Wear Daily*. This ad let merchants know about concerns related to counterfeit watches and actions taken to protect the brand.

Geographic Location

Advertising can be conducted at the global, national, regional, or local levels. **Global advertising** promotes consumer products or brands on a worldwide basis. With increased globalization of media and merchandise, it is often difficult to determine if an ad is national or global and where an ad or a product originated. Figure 8.3 features U.S. apparel in a French publication. **National advertising** promotes consumer products or brands nationwide. Both types of advertising are used to inform or remind consumers of a company and reinforce the brand image in the mind of the consumer.

Regional advertising promotes products or brands within a limited geographic region. **Local advertising** is developed for an immediate trading area. Both types of

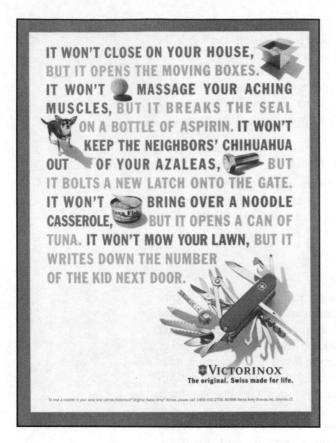

FIGURE 8.2 Consumer (left) and trade (right) advertisements by Swiss Army can be compared.

advertising are used to encourage consumers to shop at a specific store or patronize a specific location. This type of advertising is used to generate immediate traffic and sales by emphasizing price, store hours, merchandise assortment, or patronage motives.

Medium

Advertising can also be classified by medium: print, broadcast, out-of-home, direct-mail, and interactive. The broad term **media** refers to the mass communication organizations whose functions are to (1) provide news, information, or entertainment to an audience of viewers or readers, and (2) furnish advertisers an environment to reach the audience with promotional messages. The singular form of the word, **medium**, is used to describe a particular communication category such as newspapers, magazines, or television. A **media vehicle** is a specific newspaper (i.e., *Kansas City Star*), magazine (i.e., *Elle*), or television show (i.e., *America's Next Top Model)* used to communicate an advertising message. Each vehicle has advantages and disadvantages that will be discussed later.

Referring to Table 6.2, print advertising expenditures included magazines, Sunday magazines, business publications, local magazines, national and local newspapers, and freestanding inserts. Broadcast advertising, also termed electronic advertising, as reported on Table 6.2, includes network and cable television, and national and local radio.

Out-of-home advertising includes outdoor and transit advertising along with Internet advertising. Table 6.2 also illustrates over $3.5 billion was spend on outdoor advertising in 2005 and over $8.3 billion was spent on Internet advertising (100 leading national advertisers, 2006).

Purpose

One additional way that advertising can be classified is by purpose. Advertising purposes include: product advertising, nonproduct (corporate or institutional advertising), commercial advertising, noncommercial (nonprofit) advertising, action advertising, and awareness advertising.

Promotion of specific goods or services is the objective of **product advertising**. The focus with this type of advertising is to urge consumers to take quick action toward purchasing a product. Product advertising is often **action advertising**, which attempts to cause the reader or viewer to take immediate action based on the promotion. In the world of fashion advertising, this sense of urgency is emphasized due to the short-lived nature of some fashion products.

Advertising geared toward building the reputation of the firm, enhancing civic sponsorship and community involvement, and developing long-term relationships between customers and the firm is classified as **institutional advertising, nonproduct, corporate**, or **prestige advertising**. This form of advertising is more closely associated with long-

FIGURE 8.3 With so many firms operating in today's global marketplace, it is not unusual to see ads for American brands in foreign publications or vice versa.

term corporate goals. It focuses on policies, physical facilities, images of the merchandise, or other corporate features. The firm seeks to convince the clientele of the firm's fashion leadership and authority as well as its services. In some instances, institutional advertising may also be considered **awareness advertising,** which attempts to build the image of a product or familiarity with the product's name and package.

Either product or institutional advertising can be considered **commercial advertising**, which is advertising with the purpose of making a profit for the firm. Commercial advertising is directed toward the profit-making sector, while **noncommercial** or **nonprofit advertising** is used by nonprofit organizations. Nonprofit groups such as Goodwill Industries International use advertising to increase donations of used products or cash, promote sales of used goods in their retail stores, or gain volunteer support for their efforts to help disabled and disadvantaged populations.

Effective advertising comes from creative ideas. In the next section we discuss creativity and how it shapes ideas that become the well-known campaigns that influence our buying behavior.

——o CREATIVITY

Creativity is difficult to define, and many individuals look at it from very different perspectives. Some traditional retailing and marketing executives think of the creative members of the staff as the quirky and unconventional people who wear unusual cloth-ing. In other settings, however, the creative staff may dress and act more conservatively, even though they are responsible for innovations and novel approaches to problem solv-ing. In this text, **creativity** is viewed as a quality manifested in individuals that enables them to generate clever or imaginative approaches or new solutions to problems.

Finding a way to create advertising messages that will break through communica-tion clutter in our modern society is becoming more and more difficult. Laurie Tema-Lyn (1997), founder and president of Practical Imagination Enterprises, offers tips for encouraging creativity.

- **Use paradigm-breaking language.** *Why?* It is the word of childhood. *Why is the sky blue?* Similarly, we need to question underlying assumptions about a product, its value, target markets, and so forth. *What if?* It is the phrase of permission, speculation, and imagination. What if we could eat snacks that protect us against colds? *Who?* In an age of narrowly defined target customers, it is remarkable to see who best represents a sea of millions of consumers who are willing to spend money on your product or service.
- **Graze for information.** Scanning information from an array of media beyond your normal professional sources is a way to open a new window to ideas. Website visits, as well as reading issues of nontraditional media, may uncover interesting language and insights about consumer perceptions.
- **Walk on the wild side.** Getting out of the office and exploring new environs recharges your creative batteries.
- **Cross-fertilize.** What can we learn about distribution from the world of ants? How can we connect promotional strategies from the auto industry to advertising jeans? Cre-ative professionals transfer knowledge from fields and industries that are seemingly different.
- **Diversify the team.** It is acceptable to bring together a range of disciplines in the orga-nization. Personnel from research, finance, sales, and customer service to outsiders, who are not afraid to tell the emperor he is not wearing any clothes, bring original ideas to the process.
- **Explore.** Creative firms have developed physical spaces for teams to come together to jam ideas. The Creativity and Innovation Lab began as a division of Polaroid and is now an independent operation. Set up like a grown-up's kindergarten, it is a large room filled with crayons, magazines, toys, and music, free from the distraction of ringing phones. The space symbolically sets the tone that it is safe to explore ideas.

These kinds of activities and ideas promote the flow of creativity, which is necessary to develop and implement advertising and promotion strategy. Next, we look at the creative process.

The Creative Process

James Webb Young, former creative vice president of J. Walter Thompson advertising agency, developed a classic model for approaching the creative process in advertising. Young felt that the process of creativity should be viewed in a manner similar to assem-bly line production. Rather than putting together Ford automobiles, creative personnel are assembling ideas. Young's paradigm of the creative process has five steps.

1. **Immersion.** Collect current and historical information through background research, and then embed yourself in the problem.

2. **Digestion.** Look over and review the information, then attempt to comprehend it.
3. **Incubation.** Put the problem out of your conscious mind and let your subconscious mind do the work.
4. **Illumination.** The Aha moment or birth of a creative idea.
5. **Reality or verification.** Study the idea to see if it will solve the problem. Does it still look good? Then, shape the idea to make it useful and practical.

Immersion

To be immersed by something means to be completely absorbed in it. To immerse yourself into the creative process means to plunge into information about the product, service, or brand you are trying to promote. It is impossible to develop a creative idea without background information about the client and industry, including general trends, conditions, and developments in the client's industry.

As we learned from planning, information can be gathered in numerous ways. First, use the information already gathered for the situation analysis. If this does not provide adequate information, read additional information related to the product, market, or brand. Consider interviewing people. From designers and manufacturing personnel to sales associates and consumers, these people have intimate knowledge about the product and its benefits. They can also point out weaknesses in design, packaging, distribution, or use. Additionally, visit stores or malls where the product is sold. Listen to what people are saying about the product. Listening to what the client has to say can be especially informative, since the client knows the market better than other resources. In certain instances, the promotion specialist can also become more familiar with the product, service, or brand by using it, acquiring first-hand knowledge.

Digestion

After the information has been collected, it is important to digest, or study the information, to systematically learn all you can about the product or brand. Read and review the information you have gathered. Take notes and discuss issues with colleagues. Really get your head around the product or brand that you will be promoting.

Incubation

Incubation may be the most important step in the creative process. During this step you do something else. You put the information away in the back of your mind, to let your subconscious work over the information. Just like looking for your lost keys or cell phone, if you stop looking, you are bound to find the lost item faster because your subconscious mind is able to kick in and help you repeat your steps.

Strong time-management skills allow incubation to work. People working up to the last minute without giving themselves time to think miss out on the opportunity that using your subconscious mind provides, lessening the chance for a really creative idea.

Illumination

The best part of incubation comes at the end, when hopefully the *aha factor* comes into play. You are working on something else, watching a movie, driving, taking a shower, and all of the sudden you know how you are going to solve the problem. Aha, you weren't consciously thinking about the problem and in a flash the solution comes to you, from your subconscious. Now, using your conscious mind, get your idea on paper so you can start developing it into the final solution.

Reality or Verification

During the verification stage, ideas generated during the illumination stage of the creative process are evaluated to see if, in reality, they can work. Inappropriate ideas are rejected, while the remaining ideas are refined and polished into final products. At this stage the creative team is attempting to find the best creative approach prior to producing the actual advertisements. Caution should be taken not to readily abandon a solution just because it doesn't immediately fall into place. On the other hand, one should not waste time on a creative idea that is not suitable for execution. Creative executives walk a fine line when determining whether to keep or dismiss creative ideas.

Young's model is useful for organizing the unorganizable. Developing a creative answer to a marketing question or advertising problem can be an overwhelming task without a starting point. This model gives promotion personnel that starting point.

Global Creativity Index

Richard Florida, an expert on creativity, has developed the Global Creativity Index, which ranks countries' creativity levels on three specific measures: talent—percent of citizens with bachelor's degrees and percent of the workforce employed in creative sectors (including fashion); technology—innovation, patents per capita, and percent of national GDP spent on research and development; and tolerance—openness to self-expression, alternative lifestyles, and social diversity ("Creativity," 2005). The index, presented on a

---

BOX 8.1

Go, Jonny, Go!

Before "cross-media synergies" was the buzz phrase du jour, Acne Jeans creative director Jonny Johansson set out a mandate in 1996—as one of the founders of Acne—to build a company that would produce a mélange of creative endeavors and capitalize on them all.

Outside of its home country of Sweden, Acne Jeans may be best known for its skinny, selvage denim and scenester fashion collections, but Acne, the parent company, is a prolific creative services entity with diversified interests, from fashion to film production to graphic design to advertising.

"Whatever it is that we produce at Acne, we try to bring something unique to the customer, something that is Acne in essence," Johansson says. "Working as a creative collective helps us do this, because, instead of being a one-man band, we are able to benefit from each other's experience and differing backgrounds."

The overlapping, Johansson adds, only buoys Acne's ability to tap into street undercurrents that are primed to become trends.

"To avoid the fashion collections becoming entropic, we feel that it is important to keep our horizons as broad as possible," Johansson says. "Through working with other media such as publishing, architecture, furniture or whatever it may be, the clothing produced becomes one part of a sort of Acne universe."

That universe includes Acne Films, which, since 1997, has produced a series of commercials in collaboration with some of the world's top advertising agencies. An offshoot, Acne Fiction, has begun to embark on TV development and recently produced a 30-minute comedy sketch show that made its debut on Swedish television to strong reviews.

"Our commercial background has given us a different angle to traditional film companies and has worked in our favor," Johansson says. "It means we are not limited to the traditional ways of working that exist within the film industry."

While Johansson may like to think of Acne as a universe, ideas usually emerge from a much smaller space: the coffee machine.

"The mere physical presence of our Acne siblings under the same roof is inspiring in itself. Being surrounded by so many creative people, it is impossible not to be influenced by each other," Johansson says. "We constantly discover new things through each other, and every morning by the coffee machine is kind of like an informal brainstorming session."

Source: Colavita, C. (2007, February 5) Go, Jonny, go! *Women's Wear Daily*. Retrieved May 22, 2007, from http://wwd.com

TABLE 8.1   *Top 10 Most Creative Countries*

Rank	Country	Creativity Index	Description
1	Sweden	80.8	Think IKEA, H&M, Volvo, and Saab. Creative companies roll out products in Sweden that are appealing in design, function, and price.
2	Japan	76.6	Japan, land of innovation and technology, also breeds well-known fashion designers, known for cutting-edge innovations. Issey Myake, Yohji Yamamoto, Comme des Garcons, and Junya Watanabe all hail from Japan and push the envelope every season.
3	Finland	68.4	Finnish residents are known for taking pride in the architectural design of their buildings and structures; 2005 was declared "Design Year Finland," in order to promote the importance and potential that the industry has to boost trade and business.
4	United States	66.6	Although the U.S. is losing much of its creative talent to other countries, the nation still is recognized as part of the top 10. New York alone cranks out a larger gross economic output than all of Russia. It is one of the biggest drivers of the U.S.'s powerhouse economy—fashionable services, products, and ideas have much to do with that.
5	Switzerland	63.7	Beautiful people, land, and products. Companies in Switzerland have created fantastic and timeless lines of watches, including Rolex Tag Heuer, based in Geneva, founded in 1905, and credited with making the wristwatch a popular accessory. To this day, many of its products are still made by hand.
6	Denmark	61.3	Danish design can be compared to Danish lifestyle: laid-back and liberating. Architecture is hugely popular.
7	Iceland	61.2	In Iceland creativity is ingrained in residents at an early age; it has no problem retaining talent.
8	Netherlands	61.1	From creative education comes a creative way of thinking. The Netherlands has numerous design schools.
9	Norway	59.5	Norway has an agency, Innovation Norway, dedicated to the creative development of the country.
10	Germany	57.7	From Volkswagens and Benzes to Karl Lagerfeld and Jil Sander, Germany is well represented in both fashion and design industries. Germany prides itself on quality and functionalism. The fashion scene is more discreet than other countries, focusing on classic and clear styles.

Adapted from: Hall, C. (2005, May 5). Talented nations. *Women's Wear Daily*, p. 13.

scale of 1 to 100, 100 being the most creative, also assesses motivators and people behind the companies and ideas, arguing that economic value comes directly from these motivators. Florida believes that the more creative a nation is, the more potential that nation has for economic growth (Hall, 2005).

Table 8.1 shows the top 10 countries and what they are doing creatively as reported by the *WWDList*. Sweden tops the list with such companies as IKEA and H&M. Box 8.1 profiles a creative Swedish firm. Japan's well-known fashion designers such as Issey Miyake allow this country to be ranked number 2. Although Florida has argued the point that the U.S. is losing much of its creative talent, the nation is still ranked number 4, citing fashionable services, products, and ideas as a strong driving factor (Hall, 2005).

Many advertisements used as examples in this text were selected for their creativity. Creative ads do not just happen. They are a result of systematically planning, researching, and understanding the consumer for which the ad is targeted. Creative advertisements make a relevant connection between the brand and its target audience and present a selling idea in an unexpected manner (Jewler & Drewniany, 2005). A creative ad has two parts: *what* is being said—the creative strategy—and *how* it is being said—the creative execution. In the next section of this chapter we focus on the creative strategy.

──o CREATIVE STRATEGY

After reading a fashion magazine, watching a television broadcast, or visiting a website, consumers easily recognize there are unlimited ways to send and convey advertising messages. Behind each communication is a creative strategy, a plan for determining what the message will say, and a set of creative tactics, how the strategy will be executed.

The creative strategy is the outcome of the promotion plan, which was detailed in Chapter 5. Some information will be repeated in abbreviated form from the situation analysis. The strategy is presented to the creative team in document form, called a **creative strategy, communication brief, creative brief,** or **copy platform**. This document explains consumer insight and summarizes the basic strategy decisions (objectives, target market, positioning, and branding). The document is typically prepared by an account representative or creative manager. Individuals from the advertising agency's strategic planning or research departments, and members of the account team, which includes creative personnel such as copywriters and media planners, may also have input into the creative strategy.

Because the focus of this chapter is advertising, the creative strategy has an advertising focus. Creative strategy documents can be developed for any promotion mix tool to provide guidance for the execution of the promotion. Most creative strategy documents are composed of the following components:

- Executive summary (see Chapter 5).
- Problem. What communication problem or opportunity can advertising solve?
- Target audience. Who do we want to communicate to with the advertising message?
- Brand communication. What do we need to say about our brand?
- Communication objectives. How should the target audience respond to our message?
- Key benefits. What promise are we communicating to the consumer?
- Reasons why. Why should the audience believe our message?
- Tone statement. What is the personality of the advertisements?
- Concept. What is the main selling idea to create an impression of the product or brand?
- Media. Where and when should we say it?

The creative strategy forms the basis for the advertising (direct marketing, sales promotion, and so forth) campaigns. Once the agency has prepared the document, the promotion planners present the creative strategy to the client. The advertising, marketing, or product manager, who represents the client, is typically given the responsibility of approving the creative strategy.

As we stated earlier, creative advertisements make a relevant connection between the brand and its target audience and present a selling idea in an unexpected manner. Next, we look at presenting the selling idea.

──o MAJOR SELLING IDEA

Most advertisements are part of a series of messages coordinated into an **advertising campaign**, which consists of multiple messages presented in a variety of media. These messages focus on a central theme or concept, the **major selling idea**, developed in the creative strategy, which in turn, drives development of the creative executions. The major selling idea is the strongest single thing you can say about your product, service, or brand developed from the key idea, identified during promotion planning. Several approaches to developing the major selling idea include positioning, creating a brand image, developing selling points and buying benefits, or using a unique selling proposition.

Positioning

Positioning was introduced in Chapter 5 and refers to the image consumers have of a brand in relation to competing brands. Positioning is used to cause consumers to perceive a particular company's product, brand, or store image as completely different from other competing brands or products. Advertising can be used to establish that *position* within consumers' minds. Any positioning characteristic can ignite a major selling idea, resulting in a brand occupying a particular place in the mind of the consumer.

Creating a Brand Image

Brand image, as an element of brand communication, was also introduced in Chapter 5. Brand image refers to the connection consumers have with a brand and the meanings they construct about brands.

What makes a consumer choose between Levi's, Calvin Klein, or Arizona Brand Jeans? The creative strategy used to sell these products based on the development of a powerful, unforgettable identity for the brand through **image advertising**. Using image advertising as a main selling idea creates an identity for a product or service by emphasizing a symbolic association with certain values, lifestyles, or an ideal.

Image advertising has been used as the main selling idea for a wide variety of products and services. From soft drinks, automobiles, airlines, and financial services to perfumes, cosmetics, and clothing, image advertising has helped to differentiate brands. Many consumers choose fashion products based on the image of these brands.

Developing Selling Points and Buying Benefits

Selling points are features and characteristics of a fashion product that make it desirable. Selling points include design details, reputation of the manufacturer, color, fabric, comfort, versatility, size, price, or other outstanding features of a product. Recently Land's End featured an advertisement for men's swimming trunks in its catalog. It used highlighted boxes to easily show readers selling points of these shorts, including fast-drying fabric and a rip-grip-closure coin pocket.

Selling points are a list of physical features describing a product. What makes selling points important are the buying benefits associated with each selling point. **Buying benefits** are performance advantages, interpreted by the consumer as a result of the selling point. So, consider the swim trunk advertisement again. What buying benefit may be the result of the selling point *fast-drying fabric*? The wearer doesn't have to bring a change of clothes. What buying benefit is associated with the *rip-grip-closure coin pocket*? Your keys stay safe while water drains from the pocket. Some buying benefits are stated in the catalog copy while other benefits are interpreted by the consumer as they read the advertisement. Determining which selling points and buying benefits are most important to the target audience can lead to the major selling idea.

Unique Selling Proposition

When the advertiser concentrates on a single main claim or benefit, that idea is frequently referred to as the **unique selling proposition** (**USP**). The USP can become the major selling idea. A USP stresses the most important reason for a consumer to prefer this product to all others. Rosser Reeves, former chair of the Ted Bates agency, developed the concept of the USP. In his book *Reality in Advertising,* Reeves (1961) noted three characteristics of USPs:

1. Each advertisement must make a proposition to the consumer. For example, the advertisement must say to each reader, *Buy this product and you will get this benefit.*
2. The proposition must be one that the competition does not or cannot offer. It must have unique characteristics in the brand or claim.
3. The proposition must be strong enough to move mass consumers; that is, pull new consumers to the advertiser's brand.

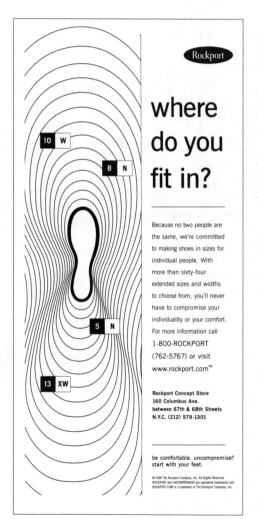

For this appeal to work there must be a truly unique product or service attribute, benefit, or inherent advantage that can be used in the message. The ad featured in Figure 8.4 offers a unique service for people with unusual shoe sizes. With over 64 different shoe sizes, the USP of the Rockport Concept Store is to provide comfortable, attractive shoe styles for each individual. Considerable research about the product and consumer may be necessary, not only to determine the USP, but to document the claim. Some companies have sued competitors for making unsubstantiated uniqueness claims.

The producer must also consider whether or not a USP can be maintained in a highly competitive market. Will competitors be able to match the distinctive brand features, making the USP obsolete? Procter & Gamble invented a combination shampoo and conditioner product as a way of revitalizing its Pert brand. The new product, named Pert Plus, was introduced and its market share grew from 2 to 12 percent. But, despite its initial popularity, it could not sustain its growth when competitors Revlon and Suave quickly launched similar shampoo-conditioner products. The creative strategy tells promotion executives *what* is being said. In the next section we will discuss *how* it is being said—the creative execution.

FIGURE 8.4 Rockport concept shoes has the unique selling proposition of providing comfortable shoes that will fit nearly everyone.

○ ADVERTISING APPEALS

As introduced in Chapter 2, motivations are reasons consumers buy. They are described as the drives within people that stimulate wants and needs. The **advertising appeal** is the approach an advertiser chooses to attract the attention of the consumer and motivate them to take action. Advertisers know that the way the message is presented is an important factor influencing a consumer's response. In advertising, the appeal must be carefully developed with the customer profile in mind, since changing the approach cannot be immediately or directly responsive to consumer feedback. Box 8.2 discusses the impact of Myspace on reaching consumers. From a very broad perspective, appeals can be classified into two categories: informational appeals and emotional appeals.

○ BOX 8.2
MySpace Builds Its Profile

MySpace isn't just for teenagers—its largest audience is adults over 35 years old and 80 percent of the world's top 100 brands are already delivering their messages via the social networking website.

Since News Corp. purchased the site last year for approximately $600 million, it has grown from 17 million unique users to 80 million, said Ross Levinsohn, president of Fox Interactive Media. Even News Corp. owner Rupert Murdoch has a profile—actually, he has one real profile and approximately 70 fake ones, Levinsohn said.

He added that 230,000 new people join MySpace every day, equivalent to the population of Buffalo, N.Y. The average user looks at 650 pages per month and there were 35 billion page views last month, a number that is second only to Yahoo.

MySpace has become a creative outlet for people. "It is built around the principles of friendship," Levinsohn said. "It's about self-expression, discovery, and interaction."

The age group that it is best known for, teenagers, makes up approximately 33 percent of its audience. "We believe that we are nearing market saturation in this market," Levinsohn said. And college students make up about 20 percent of the audience. Levinsohn joked the site is popular with teenagers due to "helicopter parents," or parents who hover over their children.

To state the obvious, it's a website ripe for advertising and brand awareness, and H&M, Victoria's Secret, and the designers behind Heatherette have already jumped on the bandwagon. In less than a year, H&M has added more than 53,000 friends to its MySpace page, which features celebrity photos, weekly sweepstakes (to keep their "friends" coming back), and its clothing catalog.

Victoria's Secret has more than 100,000 friends on its site. Visitors can peruse downloadable content, its online catalog, and soon, the company will introduce an e-commerce function. Heatherette partnered with Macy's to host an "It" girl contest on its MySpace page, which has brought the designer brand 4,000 friends that it can now directly market to. Meanwhile, designer Daniel Barbalho built a profile for his Atlanta-based Esperanza Clothing Co., and soon after, *MTV Spring Break*, *Lucky* magazine, and the publicist of Outkast came calling.

In addition, *Project Runway* has one of the most successful pages of its genre, with more than 72,000 friends. It runs contests and keeps the site current to encourage more page views. Meanwhile, on the profile of *America's Next Top Model*, visitors can view behind-the-scenes video and meet the contestants and judges.

"These are all examples of how a brand can connect," Levinsohn said. "It's not advertising. It's immersive. It's talking with consumers, not at them. It's one of the secrets of social networking and many in the fashion arena are taking advantage."

More than 60,000 fashion and style groups have emerged on MySpace during the past two years and each group has between 10 and 100 people. In the future, Levinsohn said the site will offer original editorial content and a fashion channel will be launched sometime during the next quarter.

Emerging musicians also dominate the site. "We offer the best promotional platform for music on the Internet today," he said. "We have more than three million bands."

Beginning this month, bands can sell music directly to consumers and they can choose the price, which is different from iTunes or Napster. Every major record label has broken artists on MySpace and 10 of the last number one songs were launched with campaigns on the site. On the TV side, MySpace offers Fox television shows in almost high-definition quality.

With its dominance on the Web, Levinsohn said MySpace is focusing on safety. "Our number one objective is to make our site and the Internet as a whole safer," he said. The company is working with government interest groups and has produced a series of spots with celebrities, such as Kiefer Sutherland, for its online safety campaign.

MySpace has pursued an aggressive global strategy, reaching out to countries such as the U.K., France, Germany, and Australia. MySpace is now considering ways to refine the brand. In this vein, the company has partnered with Steven Spielberg and Mark Burnett, the man behind *Survivor*, for a television show on Fox called *On the Lot*. The show will look for the next Steven Spielberg and aspiring filmmakers will be able to submit their films via MySpace.

One of the ways the site makes money is by creating partnerships. . . . MySpace linked with another Fox project, the movie *X-Men: The Last Stand*, to create a profile. Within three weeks, the page received approximately 3 million friends. For businesses interested in advertising on MySpace, Levinsohn emphasized that it's important to understand the site and what it is all about.

"Ads are controlled and they are professionally produced," he said. "We've seen our ad revenue double, quarter to quarter, over the last eight quarters."

So far, the site hasn't changed its ad format and there are no plans to do so in the future. Fox Interactive has 40 sites and 230 people work at MySpace.

Levinsohn admitted that he's not entirely sure what the future holds for MySpace, but added that online businesses will continue to flourish for years to come. "Creative people and risk-takers are going to win," he said.

Source: Wicks, A. (2006, November 15). MySpace builds its profile. *Women's Wear Daily*. (Section II) p. 26.

Informational Appeals

Informational appeals, also considered **rational appeals**, spotlight a consumer's utilitarian, functional, practical need for the product. The advertising problem is solved by factually telling the consumer about a product. The consumer, viewing the ad, logically comes to the conclusion that the product meets their need. Reviewing the hierarchy of needs theory from Chapter 2, consumers who are motivated to meet basic physiological needs or safety needs may be convinced through rational appeals. When developing a major selling idea, selling points and buying benefits, or positioning attributes, are often the basis for informational appeals.

Fashion products provide many rational motives that can be used to develop informational appeals. Convenience, comfort, value, health, or beauty are just a few. Fashion also invokes our senses, which can be used as rational appeals. The sight of beautiful clothes, touch of fabrics, or smells from fragrances all offer utilitarian or functional reasons to buy a new product. Quality, durability, dependability, and performance are also rational motives for buying fashion products and can be used in informational appeals.

Emotional Appeals

Expressive or poignant pleas are the motivation behind emotional appeals. **Emotional appeals** spotlight a consumer's psychological or sociological need for the product. Feelings rather that physical attributes are used to convince the consumer they need the product. Consumers who are motivated to achieve love and belonging or esteem needs may be convinced through emotional appeals. Fashion-oriented products are often promoted with an image that conveys a sense of the product rather than specific information.

Fashion products provide many emotional motives. From a psychology perspective, fashion products provide consumers with feelings of safety and security, love, happiness, joy, nostalgia, and excitement, among other feelings. Fashion products allow consumers to have a sense of pride, accomplishment, self-esteem, pleasure, and comfort, among other states of being. From a sociology perspective, fashion products give consumers a sense of status and respect, involvement, affiliation, acceptance, and approval, among other social-based feelings. When developing a major selling idea, brand image is often the basis for emotional appeals.

Combining Appeals

An advertising executive may choose to combine the two types of appeals because consumer decision making is often both a rational and emotional decision. Advertisements may begin by using rational appeals such as product benefits to draw in the consumer. However, the advertisement may also encourage the consumer to feel or think a certain way about the brand, solidifying the brand image in the mind of the consumer. After the appeal has been determined, the promotion team begins working on the creative execution, which is the topic of the next section.

ADVERTISING EXECUTION

The **creative execution** is the way in which the advertising appeal is presented and turned into an advertising message. There are numerous execution styles. Just as an advertising executive may choose to combine types of advertising appeals, they may also choose to combine execution styles to create the right message for the consumer. We will discuss a few here, including: straight sell, demonstration, testimonial, slice of life, personality symbol, imagery, and dramatization.

Straight Sell

The **straight sell** execution presents information as a straightforward or factual message using an informational appeal. The focus of the message is often selling points or attributes of the product. This is the most basic of all advertising executions. Many print ads use this execution style. The layout features a large picture of the product surrounded by factual copy.

Demonstration

Demonstration advertising execution shows the consumer how to use the product. Infomercials often use this execution style to show viewers displays of equipment, or results from health or beauty products.

Testimonials

The testimonial execution presents information from a user of the product who praises the product based on personal experience. This execution style works well when the target audience has a positive reaction to the person making the testimonial. Celebrity spokespersons are often used in a testimonial execution. Advertising executives hope celebrities will have a positive influence on the target audience to encourage them to use the product. Cosmetic companies have long used celebrity spokespersons, such as Queen Latifah in Figure 8.5, to give testimonials based on personal experience.

Slice of Life

This type of advertising execution is widely used for packaged-goods products. **Slice of life** advertising executions present a problem consumers have in daily life, and then show

FIGURE 8.5 Testimonial advertising execution featuring Queen Latifah as a celebrity spokesperson for Covergirl cosmetics.

FIGURE 8.6 The Target dog is a contemporary personality symbol advertising execution.

FIGURE 8.7 Imagery advertising execution.

how the advertiser's product will solve the problem. To effectively execute a slice of life advertisement, consumers have to believe the problem and the solution are real-life situations. The drama cannot be trite, silly, or phony.

Personality Symbol

Do you remember the Jolly Green Giant or Mr. Clean? If you do, then the personality symbol execution style has been effective. The personality symbol execution style uses a central character or personality symbol to deliver the advertising message. The Target dog (Fig. 8.6) serves as a contemporary personality symbol for fashion marketing.

Imagery

Advertisement executions that are nearly all visual with very little information presented are imagery executions. Imagery advertisements are used when the objective is to associate the brand with pictures, illustrations, or symbols rather than information (Fig. 8.7). Often these advertisements are emotional appeals. Designer clothing and cosmetics use this execution style to distinguish brands when differentiation by product attributes is difficult. Imagery ads are extremely popular for international fashion ads, since they do not need translation. The same Gucci ad can run in a French, Spanish, Japanese, or English language magazine.

Dramatization

This execution style is particularly effective for television. Dramatization focuses on telling a short story about the product or brand. It is similar to slice of life but uses more excitement and suspense to generate interest in the consumer to take action. The drama is meant to pull the viewer into the action and make them *feel* as though they are part of the story. By doing so, they remember the brand or the product.

The development of the creative strategy leads into the development of the creative execution, which leads to development of creative tactics. Creative tactics in print advertising include components such as headline and copy and will be discussed in Chapter 9. Creative tactics in broadcast advertising consist of video and audio components among others and will be discussed in Chapter 10. In the last section of this chapter we focus on evaluation of advertising.

○ measuring advertising effectiveness

John Wanamaker, the founder of Wanamaker's Department Store, once said, "I know half of my advertising is wasted. The trouble is I don't know which half." Are we really able to measure the effectiveness of advertising? John Wanamaker was wrong. Only 37.3 percent of advertising budgets are wasted (Neff, 2006).

A simplistic way to view an advertisement's success is to measure whether the ad met the advertiser's sales objectives. This approach defines success simply as sales revenue generated by the act of publishing or broadcasting an ad. Actually, advertising success should be the function of a fully integrated marketing communications package and measured in that context.

Evaluation Research Methods

Research was introduced in Chapter 2. A variety of scientific and nonscientific research methods have been developed to measure the effectiveness of promotion mix elements.

Marketing researchers have thoroughly studied print and broadcast advertising effectiveness and developed a variety of inquiry methods. As a result of this extensive commitment, a whole industry of advertising measurement companies has emerged. Direct marketing and sales promotion executives also use their methods. Much of the evaluative advertising research is directed toward investigation of media usage and the creative promotional message.

Media Research

Media research is investigation that attempts to determine the size of advertising outlets and their ability to attract the target audience. Specific advertising media are evaluated by a number of targeted media measurement organizations. Several leading companies provide media research data. Many other companies exist that provide media research data to clients.

TNS Media Intelligence, part of London-based TNS Group, provides strategic advertising intelligence to advertising agencies, advertisers, and media properties in the United States (2006). The company combines industry standard resources for competitive monitoring of advertising expenditures, occurrences, creative executions, and broadcast verification data into a single company for more than 22 million brands across 20 media. Data from this service has previously been reported in this text. The United States arm of TNS Media Intelligence was officially formed in 2000 and acquired Competitive Media Reporting (CMR).

Simmons Market Research Bureau (SMRB), a subsidiary company of Experian Marketing Solutions, provides comprehensive information on consumer behavior, including media consumption and product preferences (n.d.). The Simmons database contains detailed usage information available on over 8,000 brands, 400 product categories, and every media genre accessible in the United States.

MediaMark Research, Inc. (MRI), offers demographic, lifestyle, product usage, and exposure to all forms of advertising media collected from a single sample (2006). The company conducts more than 26,000 personal interviews with consumers annually throughout the United States to produce syndicated reports and data for electronic access. The information is provided to magazines, television, radio, Internet, and other media and leading national advertisers and advertising agencies in the United States.

Nielsen Media Research is a provider of television audience measurement and related services in the world (n.d.). The company operates in more than 40 countries and offers television and radio audience measurement, print readership, and customized media research services. Nielsen Media Research also provides competitive advertising intelligence information through its Nielsen Monitor-Plus service in the United States and abroad.

Message Research

Message research is inquiry that is done to evaluate effectiveness of the creative message, from copy to visual impact of the advertisement. Tests that are administered prior to the implementation of the advertising campaign are pretests. Those measures taken after an advertisement has been placed in the media are known as **posttests**.

Pretests occur at a number of different times during the development of the advertisement, from idea generation through rough copy to a final version. Concepts may be reviewed prior to creating a rough ad or storyboard. At this point the ad is little more than an idea or positioning proposal. Rough outlines may be reviewed with headlines, rough copy, and preliminary illustrations or art. A final ad can be critiqued prior to publication or broadcast. A variety of methods can be used to provide analysis. A discussion of many of these techniques follows.

Relatively inexpensive feedback is one of the best advantages of pretesting. Any problems with the concept or message can be detected early in the process. Before huge investments are made in developing final ads or commercials, the concept or artwork can be modified. Potential consumers may evaluate more than one concept to determine which approach is more effective. Pretesting allows advertisers to communicate messages better and to reduce the number of unsuccessful presentations.

Posttesting is also a common evaluation tool used by advertisers and agencies. Posttesting allows the sponsor to measure whether or not the objectives for the advertisement were met. At the same time, posttesting provides input into the next time period's situation analysis. It helps supply essential information about what worked and what did not. Survey research methods are used as posttests a majority of the time.

Focus Groups

Focus groups, introduced in Chapter 2, are assemblies of potential consumers, gathered together with a facilitator who conducts a discussion based upon some predetermined questions. The strength of this type of evaluation is through insights consumers can provide regarding consumer motivations, creative content of advertisements, and their reactions to different types of ads. Some advertisers mistakenly believe that focus groups represent the entire population and unfortunately attempt to draw quantitative conclusions from their research. Another weakness is the halo effect, which refers to some focus group members influencing others. The opinion of a few individuals can dominate the reactions of the group, leading to inaccurate data.

Consumer Jury

Advertising researchers can use consumers in another type of analysis, the consumer jury. Similar to a focus group, a **consumer jury** is selected from target customers, but the 50 to 100 participants are interviewed individually or in small groups. Typically 25 or so questions are developed, focusing on aspects of the company, its products, and sample advertisements. Consumers are asked to evaluate ads by answering such questions as:

- Which of these ads would you most likely read if you saw it in a magazine?
- Which of these headlines would interest you the most in reading the ad further?
- Which layout do you think would be most effective in causing you to buy?
- Which ad do you like best?

Effectiveness of advertising can be evaluated through favorable reactions on a predetermined rating scale. This type of measurement has several advantages: (1) the dimensions of opinions can be isolated, (2) the technique is standardized and can be compared over time, (3) it is reliable and replicable, (4) allowances are made for individual frames of reference, and (5) research problems associated with open-ended questions are reduced. Although consumer juries ease some of the research design problems, they are not without limitations. Some researchers believe the atmosphere of testing introduces bias into the rating system. This could also lead to ratings with questionable validity.

Portfolio Test

The investigation method known as the **portfolio test** involves participants who are exposed to a portfolio of test and control advertisements. **Test ads** are the ads being pretested, being measured for their potential effectiveness. The **control ads** have been evaluated extensively over a period of time and provide a basis for comparing the effectiveness of test ads. Respondents are asked to recall information from the ads; those ads with the highest recall are assumed to be the most effective.

Control ads allow the advertiser to compare the test ad with effectiveness of the control ad. Additionally, the researcher can identify any respondent with scores outside the norm. In other words, if the subject provides responses outside what is expected on the control ads, his or her responses may be eliminated from the analysis of the test ad.

Critics of portfolio tests challenge whether or not recall is the best test to use to measure an advertisement's effectiveness. Factors relating to the ad's creativity and/or presentation may affect recall. Test bias and the simple fact that the respondent is involved in a testing situation may impact the subject's responses.

In an attempt to improve upon the portfolio test, ad agencies or research firms may develop a dummy advertising outlet, which consists of ads and editorial content placed in *dummy* magazines. These magazines are distributed to randomly selected homes within a predetermined geographical region. Participants are told the publisher is interested in their opinions of editorial content and are asked to read the publication as they normally would. Readers are interviewed on their reactions to ads in addition to editorial content. The ads are judged by recall, readership, and interest-generating capabilities.

A more natural environment than that created by the standard portfolio test is the advantage offered by this research technique. Readership takes place in the participant's home, more closely associated with a normal setting. This hopefully provides a more realistic result. However, the testing effect cannot be eliminated and bias may still exist. While this method offers some advantages over the portfolio method, it cannot guarantee an exact measure of the advertising impact.

Readability Test

The **readability test**, which does not require consumer interviews, relies on the forecasting formula developed by Rudolph Flesch (Belch & Belch, 2007). The Flesch formula focuses on the human-interest appeal in the material, the length of sentences, and the familiarity of words. These components are considered and correlated with the educational background of target audiences. Determining the average number of syllables per 100 words assesses readability of copy. Test results are compared to previously established norms for various target audiences. Testing suggests that copy is best understood when sentences are short, words are concrete and well known, and personal references are made.

Although this method overcomes some of the bias associated with consumer input, there are some disadvantages. Copy may become too mechanical and unoriginal. Without consumer input, contributions such as creativity cannot be evaluated. The most beneficial use of this testing method is in combination with another technique for pretesting.

Physiological Profiles

In an attempt to overcome the biases associated with voluntary reactions, some researchers have developed **physiological profile** techniques for measuring the involuntary reactions to ads. Involuntary reactions are responses over which the volunteer has no control. Although these techniques are less commonly used than previously mentioned techniques, involuntary reactions are used to measure physiological responses.

The eye camera tracks eye movements with infrared light sensors as a subject reads an advertisement. The beam allows researchers to determine the exact location where the subject focuses. This reading provides data on which elements of the ad attract attention, how long the viewer focuses on them, and the order in which the components are being viewed.

Thus, eye camera tracking furnishes information that can identify strengths and weaknesses of an ad, helping the designer create an ad in which the eye follows the intended path. If the background distracts the viewer's eye from the brand or product, the designer can adjust the distraction prior to finishing the ad.

Although eye tracking has some interesting attributes, the tests are conducted under highly unnatural laboratory conditions. It is questionable whether or not the results would be the same if the subject were not looking into a large device. As the eye lingers on an element of the ad, the meaning is not clear. Is it a lack of comprehension or interest in an attractive detail? Because it is impossible to read the mind of the viewer, this method could lead to unreliable conclusions.

In addition to the eye tracking techniques, galvanic skin response (GSR), pupil dilation response (PDR), and brain wave measurements are used to measure physiological changes. Galvanic skin response, also known as electrodermal response, measures the skin's resistance to or conductance of a small amount of current passed between two electrodes. Researchers assume that an increase in GSR was an indicator of arousal of interest in the advertisement.

Pupil dilation response measures minute differences in pupil size and appears to be a gauge of the amount of information processed in response to an incoming stimulus. Dilation was associated with action, while constriction involved the body's conservation of energy. Thus, it is assumed that if the pupil dilated, there is strong interest in the ad. High costs and methodology problems have led to a declining interest in this type of testing.

Brain wave research involves taking electroencephalographic (EEG) measures from the skull to determine electrical frequencies in the brain. EEG research measures brain activity as alpha waves and hemispheric lateralization. While this research has appealed to the academic community, it has not gained much support from advertising practitioners.

Test Markets

In order to evaluate the potential for advertising success, some manufacturers introduce products and advertising campaigns in special test market cities prior to national launches. These **test markets** are geographical areas that have been selected as representatives of the target market. If the demographic, socioeconomic, and psychographic profiles of the test market are similar to the desired target population, the advertising and product will be introduced in that region. The test market might be Portland, Oregon; Buffalo, New York; or Columbus, Ohio, if the profile of the city matches the profile of the target market.

The use of test markets has the added benefit of being a realistic presentation of the product or ad in a real setting. Well-designed research can be conducted with a high degree of control. The primary problem associated with test marketing is the high cost and long time necessary to complete the research. Figure 8.8 provides criteria for selecting a target market.

Product test marketing generally takes the following steps:

1. The manufacturer places the product in an unlabeled container and makes it available to consumers through a testing company, such as the Home Testing Institute.
2. The test marketing company distributes the product samples to panel members with a letter describing how to use the product. The correspondence also indicates that the panel member will be given an opportunity to provide opinions about the product in a specified period of time, such as four weeks.
3. The consumer responds to a set of questions.
4. The responses are analyzed.
5. The results are used to redesign the product or develop creative strategy and position the product in relationship to other brands in the market.

Qualities of Effective Advertising

While more difficult to establish criteria for assessing advertising in terms of the composition of the advertisement, there are several identifiable qualities that can improve an

FIGURE 8.8 Checklist for selecting test and control markets.

Checklist for Selecting Test and Control Markets

❑ **Size Characteristics:** Population areas between 100,000 and 300,000 are normally used. The area must be large enough to support a variety of economic activities, but not so large that it is too expensive to conduct the research.

❑ **Population Characteristics:** The area should have a diverse population with characteristics similar to the target population. An ethnically distinct or unique population usually should be avoided; the bias created would limit the objectivity necessary for a test market.

❑ **Distribution Characteristics:** The product should be readily available in a variety of merchandise outlets. The researchers should not inform members of the distribution channel about the test situation in order to avoid their creating some type of special sales promotion causing a bias in the test.

❑ **Competitive Characteristics:** While it is impossible to control what competitors do during a test period, their actions should be monitored to assess any changes that would make the test invalid.

❑ **Media Characteristics:** Media placement must be accessible and available for use. The media in the test market must be comparable in test and control areas.

advertiser's chances for accomplishing its goals. Many of these attributes may be common throughout most effective advertisements. Those considerations customarily associated with successful advertisements are:

- **Consistency with marketing strategy.** A well-coordinated marketing communications strategy should be developed and serve as a plan, integrating advertising into the package. Thus, the advertising is compatible with all of the other elements of a correlated communications program.
- **Obvious intention.** The reader or viewer of an ad should be left with a lasting impression of the product or service being promoted. The main message or idea should be apparent to the audience. The first television advertisements for Infiniti automobiles were so obscure that audiences were not sure what product was being promoted.
- **Evident objective.** Is the advertisement consumer or trade oriented? Is the purpose of the advertisement to produce merchandise sales or to develop an institutional image? What is the advertiser trying to communicate? If the objective of the advertisement is difficult to identify, the ad cannot be very productive.
- **Consistent identity.** By using a consistent visual or audio style throughout various advertisements, the sponsor's ads can immediately be recognized. The layout, graphics, artistic style, copy, typography, sound effects, or video effects contribute to an identifiable image. Consistency gives a positive, easily recognized image to the advertising. With a theme or consistent graphics program, each advertisement benefits from prior ads and builds for the next ads.
- **Good relationships between the visual and verbal elements.** In a print ad the visual elements include the artistic elements, and the verbal element is the copy. Advertising copy can be enhanced by appropriate visual stimulus. In a television commercial the spoken words or music reinforce the video.
- **Targeting the consumer's point of view.** The needs, wants, and values of the consumer take precedence over those characteristics of the advertiser. The consumer purchases products based upon his or her perceptions.
- **Simplicity.** Although repetition and superfluous language have entered the advertising world, today's sophisticated consumers appreciate simple, concise, and direct language and advertising production styles.
- **Creativity secondary to advertising strategy.** Creativity enables the advertiser to bring humor and/or charming themes into the advertisement. But an ad should not be cute for cuteness's sake or humorous for humor's sake. When consumers remember the ad for its creativity and cannot remember the product, it is ineffective.
- **Delivery of what it says it can.** Good advertising never promises more than it can deliver. Consumers learn very quickly when they have been deceived or misled, causing resentment toward the advertiser. These customers will not trust or continue to purchase from such an unethical advertiser.

Figure 8.9 is a checklist for planning effective advertising. Using this examination technique can be helpful in creating ads as well as evaluating and critiquing ads. Students and advertisers may wish to develop their own criteria or add to these.

summary

- Advertising is any nonpersonal information paid for and controlled by the sponsoring organization and can be classified by target audience, geographic area, medium, or purpose.

FIGUre 8.9 Checklist for planning effective advertising.

Checklist for Planning Effective Advertising

❑ **Determine the function of the advertisement.** Is the function to inform, persuade, remind, add value, or assist other company efforts?

❑ **Determine the advertising classification.** Is the advertising directed toward a particular target consumer or trade customer? Is it directed to a particular geographical location? Which advertising medium was used and was it the most effective outlet? For what purpose was the advertising created (product vs. institutional, commercial vs. nonprofit)?

❑ **Identify and evaluate the appeal, approach, and selling points.** Do these conditions meet the wants and needs of the target customer?

❑ **Identify the relationship between the visual and verbal.** Is the ad attractive, using an appropriate combination of art and copy or video and sound? What attention-getting devices are used? Are they appropriate in relationship to each other, the product, and the target customer?

❑ **Determine if there is a unique selling proposition (USP).** What is the primary benefit? How does the product stand out from all of the others?

❑ **Identify how image and continuity are achieved.** How does the advertiser create a consistent identity through the use of a logo, layout, artistic style, or other mechanism? Does the ad build on previous ads and build for the future?

❑ **Determine the nature of the requested response.** What is the consumer being asked to do? Request? Buy? Remember?

❑ **Evaluate whether the selling message is obvious or lost in creativity.** Did the advertiser use a whimsical theme or humor in an appropriate manner to encourage the desired action from the consumer? Or did the advertiser use ingenuity for the sake of ingenuity?

- Manufacturers, designers, and retailers have identified several functions that advertising helps them accomplish, which includes providing information, persuading consumers to try their products or services, reminding consumers about the brands, adding value by improving the image or quality of the product/service, and by assisting the company's overall marketing efforts.

- The targets for advertising energies are private end-users known as consumers or business users identified as trade consumers.

- Advertising may be directed toward any number of different geographical regions from global, national, regional to local.

- Creativity, a quality manifested in individuals that enables them to generate clever or imaginative approaches as solutions to problems, can be nurtured and developed in any individual.

- The creative strategy is the outcome of the promotion plan. The document explains consumer insight and summaries the basic strategy decisions (objectives, target market, positioning, and branding). The document is typically prepared by an account representative or creative manager. The creative strategy forms the basis for advertising campaigns.

- The central theme or concept, the major selling idea, is developed in the creative strategy, which, in turn, drives development of the creative executions. The major selling idea is the strongest single thing you can say about your product, service, or brand developed from the key idea, identified during promotion planning.

- Approaches to developing the major selling idea include positioning, creating a brand image, developing selling points and buying benefits, or using a unique selling proposition.

- The advertising appeal is the approach an advertiser chooses to attract the attention of the consumer and motivate them to take action and can be classified into two categories: informational appeals and emotional appeals.
- The creative execution is the way in which the advertising appeal is presented and turned into an advertising message. Advertising execution styles include: straight sell, demonstration, testimonial, slice of life, personality symbol, imagery, and dramatization.
- Advertising uses research methods to evaluate message effectiveness. Methods include: focus groups, consumer juries, portfolio tests, readability tests, physiological profiles, and test markets.

Key Terms

action advertising	emotional appeal	physiological profile
advertising appeal	global advertising	portfolio test
advertising campaign	image advertising	posttests
awareness advertising	imagery	prestige advertising
buying benefits	informational appeal	pretests
commercial advertising	institutional advertising	product advertising
communication brief	local advertising	rational appeal
consumer advertising	major selling idea	readability test
consumer jury	media	regional advertising
control ads	media research	selling points
copy platform	media vehicle	slice of life
corporate advertising	medium	straight sell
creative brief	message research	test ads
creative execution	national advertising	test market
creative strategy	noncommercial advertising	testimonial
creativity	nonproduct advertising	trade advertising
demonstration	nonprofit advertising	unique selling proposition (USP)
dramatization	personality symbol	

Key Organizations

American Advertising Federation (AAF)

Questions for Discussion

1. Why do manufacturers and retailers advertise?
2. What is creativity? Why is it so difficult to define?
3. Discuss the steps in the creative process.
4. How is advertising evaluated?

Additional Resources

Arens, W. F. (2006). *Contemporary advertising* (10th ed.), New York: McGraw-Hill/Irwin.

Belch, G. E., & Belch, M. A. (2007). *Advertising and promotion* (7th ed.), New York: McGraw-Hill/Irwin.

Briggs, R., & Stuart, G. (2006). *What sticks: Why most advertising fails and how to guarantee yours succeeds.* Chicago, IL: Kaplan Publishing.

Brown, P., & Rice, J. (2001). *Ready-to-wear apparel analysis* (3rd ed.). Upper Saddle River, NJ: Prentice Hall.

Florida, R. (2002). *The rise of the creative class.* New York: Basic Books.

Florida, R. (2005). *The flight of the creative class.* New York: HarperCollins.

Wells, W., Moriarty, S., & Burnett, J. (2006). *Advertising principles and practice* (7th ed.). Upper Saddle River, NJ: Pearson Prentice Hall.

Young, J. W. (2003). *A technique for producing ideas.* New York: McGraw-Hill.

ANNUAL PUBLICATIONS

100 Leading National Advertisers. (published annually). *Advertising Age.* New York: Crain Communications, Inc.

REFERENCES

100 Leading National Advertisers. (2006). *Advertising Age.* New York: Crain Communications, Inc.

Belch, G. E., & Belch, M. A. (2007). *Advertising and promotion* (7th ed.). New York: McGraw-Hill/Irwin.

Creativity: The next economic indicator? (2005, May 5). *Women's Wear Daily,* p. 13.

Hall, C. (2005, May 5). Talented nations. *Women's Wear Daily,* p. 13.

Frazier, M. (2006, June 25). Retail advertisers: Rush is on to rule in-story video TV ads *Advertising Age.* Retrieved June 26, 2006, from http://adage.com

Jewler, A. 1., & Drewniany, B. L. (2005). *Creative strategy in advertising* (8th ed.). Belmont, CA: Thomson Wadsworth.

MediaMark Research, Inc. (2006). Retrieved July 9, 2006, from http://www.mediamark.com/

Neff, 1. (2006). Half of your advertising isn't wasted—just 37.3%. *Advertising Age,* 77(32), Retrieved August 17, 2006, from the Academic Search Premier database.

Nielsen Media Research. (n.d.). *About Nielsen media research.* Retrieved July 9, 2006, from http:// www.nielsen.com/nielsen_media_research.html

Reeves, R. (1961). *Reality in advertising.* New York: Knopf.

Simmons Market Research Bureau. (n.d.). *About Simmons.* Retrieved July 9, 2006, from http:// www.smrb.com/about.html

Tema-Lyn, L. (1997, March 31). All the world's a stage, and the players are marketers. *Marketing News.* Retrieved July 3, 2006, from LexisNexis Academic database.

TNS Media Intelligence. (2006). *The gold standard for competitive advertising information.* Retrieved July 9, 2006, from http://www.tns-mi.com/aboutIndex.htm

FIGURE 9.1 Rihanna and Zac
Posen at Fashion Rocks.

CHAPTER 9
Print Media

It's a familiar story from magazine publishing companies lately: part of staying relevant means staging outsize, razzle-dazzle productions that incorporate television, the Web, and wireless communications—but have relatively little to do with the print product.

But even at a time when magazine companies are constantly competing for attention outside of their glossy publications, Fashion Rocks is an unusually elaborate production.

Mr. Richard D. Beckman, the president of the Condé Nast Media Group, said it was now four times the size it was at its debut in 2004. The concert includes performers like Kanye West, Christina Aguilera, Faith Hill, and Beyoncé.

CBS broadcast the two-hour event, and it later played in some 20 countries. A website contains video, promotions, and commentary on fashion, beauty, and music.

Anna Wintour, editor of *Vogue*, supervised a corresponding one-time glossy publication titled "Fashion Rocks," with Beyoncé and Jamie Foxx on the cover. The magazine, aimed at young men and women, is delivered to subscribers of 17 magazines, including *Vogue*, the *New Yorker*, and *Details*, and stand-alone copies are offered on newsstands.

The program has brought in upward of $45 million in ad revenue and at least 32 major advertisers, 10 of them spending in the seven figures. The top sponsors are the Chevrolet division of General Motors, Cingular, the Citi unit of Citigroup, and L'Oreal Paris, all big Condé Nast advertisers.

One top advertiser, Citi, saw an opportunity to reach a wide range of consumers who are interested in fashion and music "from country to rap," said Mark Ingall, managing director of global strategic media for Citigroup in New York.

"We know from the demographics of the magazine that these are the people we want to reach," Mr. Ingall said.

Luring marketers to spend more ad dollars in print magazines is becoming an increasingly difficult task. For companies like Condé Nast and Hearst, staging elaborate multimedia productions is a way to keep ad dollars coming to magazine publishers—even if it involves selling sponsorship of an event instead of just ad pages in a magazine.

Not that magazines are dead yet, Mr. Ingall of Citigroup said: "In the laws of supply and demand, if people are still willing to pay $3.99 on the newsstand, I'd imagine that there's still some value to them."

Source: Bosman, J. (2006, August 8). Ads in a mere magazine? How last century. *New York Times*, p. C4.

> **After you have read this chapter you should be able to:**
>
> Use the basic terminology related to media and media planning.
>
> Evaluate and select various media to be used prior to advertising.
>
> Differentiate among the categories of print media used by advertisers.
>
> Evaluate the advantages and disadvantages of each print medium.
>
> Explain the print media creative process.

NEW TIMES CALL FOR new measures. When electronic media started biting into magazine sales, Condé Nast kicked up the volume with a rock 'n' roll event that kept its big advertisers excited and reminded its readers what's inside those glossy covers. What rocks? *Fashion* rocks. Promoting your product or service through the print media can rock too, especially with a magazine that's willing to go live to keep their consumers on the same page.

This chapter will focus on media in general and print media specifically. The chapter begins by discussing how media are measured. Media are selected through media planning, which will be discussed next. Then the chapter moves to specific print media, first discussing newspapers followed by magazines. Then, the focus of the chapter moves to creative development for print media.

───○ MEASURING THE MEDIA

Media was introduced in Chapter 8. Advertisers have a wide variety of media and media vehicles from which to choose to place the advertising message. Most advertisers select more than one medium and vehicle for message delivery. Reasons for selecting specific media and media vehicles are based on the objectives of the promotion, attributes of the product or brand, budget, and preferences based on research and the target market, among other reasons. Before we discuss specific media, it is important to understand how to measure media to evaluate which media or media vehicle will provide the best potential for advertising success.

Reach, Coverage, and Penetration

Reach, coverage, and penetration are all related to the audience or potential audience that an advertiser is trying to attract. Although many people use these terms interchangeably, it is important to understand the distinctions.

Reach describes the percentage of target audience, homes, or individuals exposed to an advertiser's message at least once in a period of time, usually four weeks. Thus, reach represents the number of target customers who see or hear the advertiser's message during the designated time period. Advertisers want to know how many people a media vehicle can reach without counting individuals more than once. Reach is normally expressed as a percentage of the total audience of different homes or unduplicated individuals who are exposed to a message.

A variation of reach is a cume, or **cumulative audience**. This refers to the total number of different people who are exposed to a schedule of advertisements. The term cumulative audience implies that additional unduplicated individuals will be added to the reach as the time period progresses. Consideration of unduplicated and duplicated research figures into reach analysis. Unduplicated reach symbolizes potential new exposures, while duplicated reach provides a gauge of frequency.

Coverage refers to the potential audience that might receive the message through a media vehicle. Most advertisers are interested in choosing media that will communicate or "cover" all of the advertiser's active and potential target audience. Coverage is frequently expressed as a percentage of a population group. For instance, the estimated population for a target group is 1.2 million. A magazine declares a readership of 72,000 fitting within that target population—or 6 percent coverage. Coverage relates to potential audience, whereas reach reports the actual audience delivered. Therefore, reach is always smaller than coverage.

Penetration refers to the total number of persons or households that are able to be exposed to a medium by the nature of that medium's geographical circulation or broadcast signal. Television penetration is the percentage of total households that own at least one television set reached within a specific geographical region. Billboard penetration is the percentage of drivers and passengers that are exposed to a billboard within a specific geographical area.

Frequency and Scheduling

Advertisers typically want to have their message in front of consumers at all times, reminding them about the features and benefits of their product. But, it is unrealistic and unaffordable to maintain such a constant pace for promotional communication. Frequency and scheduling are ways advertisers plan the pace of media exposure.

Frequency is defined as the number of times the receiver is exposed to the media vehicle within a specified period of time. Frequency increases the chance that target audience members will be reached. An advertiser running an advertisement in the local newspaper on a weekly basis will reach additional target customers by adding ads to the Sunday magazine supplement. Frequency is closely related to scheduling.

Scheduling involves setting the time for advertisements or commercials to run. The primary objective of scheduling is to time promotional efforts to coincide with the period when the target audience can be attracted. For some products the scheduling is obvious, for others it is not so clear. Three scheduling strategies are used by media planners: continuity, flighting, and pulsing.

Continuity

Continuity refers to a steady placement of advertisements over a designated period of time. This pattern could mean every day, every week, or every month. The fundamental factor is regularity in the pattern so that no gaps or lapses occur. Merchandise ideally suited for this pattern of scheduling are products consumed on a regular basis without regard for seasonality. Skin care items, shampoo, and basic stock items such as white shirts, hosiery, undergarments, towels, and sheets benefit from continuity scheduling.

Flighting

Flighting uses a much less regular schedule, involving periods with moderate to heavy exposure followed by a hiatus or lapse prior to restarting the advertising schedule. Sometimes there are substantial advertising expenditures followed by periods with limited expenses. Seasonal items such as skis, ski apparel, and accessories benefit from a flighting scheduling pattern for promotion. Between October and April, ski-related manufacturers advertise heavily, but they rarely spend any promotional money during the spring and summer.

Pulsing

Pulsing, the third method of scheduling, is a combination of the first two methods. An advertiser using a pulsing strategy maintains a continuity of advertising with a step-up effort at certain times of the year. Fragrance and cosmetic lines use a pulsing strategy. Although fragrance and color cosmetics are advertised regularly, manufacturers increase advertising during holidays such as Christmas and Mother's Day, gift-with-purchase promotions, or at the start of a fall or spring fashion season.

The scheduling strategy used by an advertiser depends upon several factors, such as the media objectives, consumer buying cycles, and budget, among other concerns. Since advertisers have differing objectives and budget limitations, they find themselves deciding between reach and frequency. The advertiser faces trade-offs between having the message seen or heard by more people and having a smaller number of people exposed to the message more often.

In addition to continuity, flighting, and pulsing techniques, the radio industry uses blinking/bunching, bursting, and sliding. A **blinking/bunching** approach schedules advertising activity over a short period, involving one week on, one week off, and so forth. **Bursting** is a pattern in which heavy advertising is concentrated over a short period, placing one week's advertising within a four-day period. **Sliding** occurs when the frequency of advertising is changed over the course of the advertising campaign. Normally an advertiser using a sliding strategy launches the campaign with heavy advertising and decreases the quantity of advertisements as the campaign progresses, with a possible hiatus between schedules.

Ratings, Gross Rating Points, and Share

Ratings, gross rating points, and share are some of the various tools used by media measurement services to provide this additional information to evaluate media choices. Most of these terms originated in the broadcast industry but are used by most media today.

The audience size, an estimate of the total number of homes reached expressed as a percentage of the total population, is known as **ratings** or program ratings. Ratings are established by an independent research service, such as Nielsen Media Research. A rating of 20 equals 20 percent of all people in the market. The program rating is calculated by dividing the number of households (HH) tuned to a particular show by the total number of households in the area. If 10 million households watched a particular television show, the national rating would be 10.6. The calculation follows:

$$\text{Rating} = \frac{\text{HH tuned to show}}{\text{Total U.S. HH}} = \frac{10,000,000}{94,000,000} = 10.6$$

The next example shows how this information can be used by an advertiser to predict reach. Assume there are 94 million homes with television sets in the United States and a TV program has a rating of 25. The advertiser can estimate the potential audience. The calculation is 25 percent of 94 million (0.25 × 94 million), or 23.5 million homes.

Another method of measuring media involves **gross ratings points (GRPs)**, the sum of all ratings delivered by a commercial schedule. This information helps the advertiser and media buyer know how many potential audience members might be exposed to a series of commercials. This measurement combines the program's rating with the average number of times the home is reached during the defined time period (frequency of exposure). The calculation for GRPs is as follows:

$$\text{GRPs} = \text{Reach} \times \text{Frequency}$$

GRPs show the number of listeners or viewers that might be reached by a media schedule, using a duplicated reach estimate. In order to determine unduplicated reach, media specialists look at target ratings points. **Target ratings points (TRPs)** refer to the number of people in the primary target audience the media buy will reach. Unlike GRPs, TRPs does not contain waste coverage.

Just what do these ratings points mean? A purchase of 100 GRPs could reflect several conditions. In one instance, it may mean that 100 percent of the market is exposed to the message once. In other cases, it may mean 50 percent of the market is exposed twice, 25 percent is exposed four times, and so on.

A sample media buy can be described as follows. Revlon purchased 1,800 GRPs during a four-week period to introduce *Stone Edge: Nature's Muted Tones Bring Color Down to Earth,* the latest line of lip, nail, and eye color cosmetics (Fig. 9.2). This purchase consisted of 50 separate magazine advertisements, estimated to reach 96 percent of the target audience an average of 12 times. Prior to the buy, the media planner needed to determine whether or not this would be an effective purchase. Certainly a reach of 96 percent is desirable, but is the frequency level too high or not high enough? Does this level of GRPs impact consumer awareness and make them more likely to purchase the product?

Researchers at Foote, Cone & Belding advertising agency and others have explored these questions. David Berger, vice president and director of research, determined that 2,500 GRPs were likely to lead to an approximate 70 percent probability of high awareness, but 1,000 to 2,500 would yield approximately a 33 percent awareness, and less than 1,000 would impact virtually no awareness (Rothschild, 1987). In this still relevant type of analysis, if an increased awareness level leads to trial, then it would be desirable for Revlon to increase its GRPs.

In terms of media planning, **share** refers to the size of an audience for any given time period. This figure, also originated in the broadcast industry, considers variation in the number of sets in use and the total size of the potential audience, since it only considers the households that have their televisions turned on. It is also expressed in terms of a percentage, as follows:

FIGURE 9.2 Advertisement for Revlon's Stone Edge colors.

$$\text{Share} = \frac{\text{Number of TV households tuned in to a program}}{\text{Number of households using TV at that time}} = 100$$

Next, we turn our attention to media planning and strategy development. Media planning evolves from overall promotion planning. Once the marketing strategy has been developed, the promotion strategy is planned with the appropriate selection of media.

──o MEDIA PLANNING

Media planning is the task of deciding when, where, and how the advertising message will be delivered. The executive designated with the responsibility for developing the media plan is known as a **media planner**. This executive has the responsibility of analyzing the appropriate media location for the message, which requires careful quantitative and qualitative research. The ultimate desire is to attract the target customer with a minimum of waste and a maximum of efficiency.

FIGURE 9.3 Advertisement for Swatch's Irony Metal Collection.

Media Objectives and Strategy

Developing media objectives and strategy is a complex and involved process. As the media planning process takes place, ideas are generated, evaluated, altered, used, or abandoned. This process leads to a media plan. Box 9.1 details the strategy behind advertising luxury products.

Media objectives are the goals to be attained by the media program and accomplished by media strategies. Media objectives are determined by a media situation analysis, a process similar to the situation analysis discussed in Chapter 5. Planning media objectives is a part of the *big picture,* assisting the firm to attain its communication and marketing objectives. The purpose of media objectives is to translate marketing objectives and strategies into goals that media can accomplish. An example of a media objective follows: *Create awareness of Swatch Irony Metal Collection watches* (Fig. 9.3) *in the target market of men and women between the ages of 18 and 32 years through the following strategies:*

- *Utilize magazine print medium to provide coverage of 80 percent of the target market over a six-month period.*
- *Reach 60 percent of the target audience at least three times over the same six-month period.*
- *Concentrate heaviest advertising during fall and winter with lighter emphasis in spring and summer.*

Media strategies are plans of action designed to achieve media objectives. Media strategies translate media goals into general guidelines that will control the planner's selection and use of media. The best alternatives should be selected. Media strategy specifies target audience, defines the media objectives, selects the media categories to be used with specific vehicles, and directs media buying. Broad media and specific media vehicles are recommended. If magazines are to be used, then which ones should be used? If radio or television is recommended, which markets will be used? Additional decisions involve determining media schedules, allocating the media budget, and choosing the appropriate geographical locations for the advertising message.

The media plan formalizes the planning process. The goal of the media plan is to identify and articulate the most worthwhile combination of media and media vehicles that enables the advertiser to communicate the message in the most effective manner to the largest number of potential customers at the lowest cost.

Difficulties in Media Planning

A number of problems make development of media objectives and implementation of a media strategy difficult.

○ BOX 9.1
Show Me the (Luxury) Products

Forget about provocative sexual imagery. Don't even think about waiflike models. People's lust for luxury fashion is best stirred by hot shots of the goods themselves, based on a recent survey.

Despite fashion's longtime use of sexual innuendo and the vogue for marketing that strikes an emotional chord, wealthy adults responded most favorably when luxury goods themselves were portrayed front and center in the print ads of 20 fashion brands. The ads were shown to them in August by the Luxury Institute. "Less is more," said the institute's chief executive officer, Milton Pedraza. "The consumer is looking for the product as hero."

Not that this desire makes a product-centric take a breeze to pull off.

"It's easy to show products in a way that is boring," said Reed Krakoff, president and executive creative director at Coach, whose ads were most favored among those of the 20 brands consumers considered. "A lot of times, people look for a gorgeous image and wonder, does it show enough of the product?" added Krakoff, who leads the development of Coach's ads, created entirely in-house. "We look at [product] as a way to create excitement."

For example, in a bid to stand out in a sea of color fashion ads, Coach chose a black-and-white palette for its spring print campaign featuring a pair of pumps and a handbag—the first time it had used black-and-white photography in its ads in seven years. "We thought, when it's not in color, it's going to catch people's attention, and we were going for a romantic, vintage-y feel," Krakoff recalled.

While many luxury ads have long highlighted the products themselves, people may want more of the same because it's hard to buy into an extravagant fantasy without a strong portrayal of the particulars, observed Raul Martinez, chief executive officer at ad agency AR, whose clients include D&G, Versace, and Calvin Klein. "Whether you're buying a $5,000 bag or a $29.99 bag, you want to see it," Martinez said. "Luxury is a dream, and you want to buy into that world. There's an allure to that."

The tactic apparently has not been used to its greatest effect, however, as the top-ranked advertising (by Coach) scored a 6.58 on a scale from zero to 10, in the Luxury Institute study. The ratings of the affluent crowd's 10 favorite campaigns declined on a gentle slope, bottoming at the 5.24 accorded the ads of the Calvin Klein Collection, ranked 10th by those adults.

Part of the problem, Pedraza said, is that "there is not a great deal of consumer feedback that goes into creating these ads. Many of the companies said they are not doing ad testing."

Affluent adults who were asked what main message they took from a Dolce & Gabbana ad picturing women in suggestive poses amid haystacks made comments ranging from "funky, fresh, fun fashion" to "It comes across as way too much sex among women." The ad was not among the group's top 10 favorites.

For the popular Coach ad, in contrast, there were numerous interpretations of its message, such as "Coach sells (or has or makes) shoes" and more than a dozen references to the portrayal as either classy, classic, elegant, expensive, or fine.

Neither Coach nor Polo Ralph Lauren, whose Polo Jeans G.I.V.E. ads rated as the second favorite among the affluent adults, solicit opinions from consumers about ads while the spots are being developed or after they have been seen.

"Our philosophy here is that we are the consumers, and we use our own gut instincts," said David Lauren, senior vice president of advertising, marketing, and corporate communications at Polo Ralph Lauren, which seeks to address an aspirational sensibility with all of its brands. "Sometimes the product is the hero. Other times, it's a lifestyle shot with no product or with product and a model," Lauren added.

Style and design were the biggest influence on people who purchased luxury fashion goods in April through June, reported 610 of the 1,000 consumers who bought such things, in Unity Marketing's second-quarter Luxury Tracking Study. "So ads [mostly] featuring products are zeroing in on that," noted Unity president Pamela N. Danziger.

While acknowledging it's difficult to measure a print ad's sway over consumers' purchases given the many possible influences, Krakoff said Coach's black-and-white campaign was probably effective since the bag, the brand's priciest ever at $798, "sold out twice." (Previously, Coach's highest-priced bag was $498.)

Celebrities featured in ads—such as Halle Berry's turn in the Versace campaign—did not make people any more or less likely to buy the brand advertised, the Luxury Institute found, but the celebs did heighten people's awareness of them.

Consumers signaled how effective they found the print ads for the 20 luxury fashion brands by considering their relevance, clarity, distinctiveness, and appropriateness for the label being marketed. In the case of seven of their 10 top-rated ads, people considered it equally likely they would buy those brands after seeing the ads. The notable exception was Calvin Klein Collection, which placed as the seventh most-likely brand they would buy, after seeing ads that ranked as only their tenth favorite.

Source: Seckler, V. (2006, October 4). Show me the (Luxury) products. *Women's Wear Daily*, p. 14.

- **Inconsistent terminology.** Many of the terms associated with the media are confusing and may be used incorrectly. Terms such as *reach* and *coverage* may be used synonymously, adding to the confusion.
- **Inconsistent measurement tools.** The methods for evaluating the cost of using a particular medium may be inharmonious with evaluation in other media. Magazines commonly use CPM, while broadcast media refer to cost per ratings point (CPRP), and outdoor media use the number of showings. The cost-effectiveness measure for newspapers is based upon the daily inch rate. How can a media planner compare number of showings to CPM, CPRP, or a daily inch rate?
- **Lack of information.** Even though there is a tremendous amount of information about markets and the media, media planners often require more than is available. Timing of the measurements for television audiences are during sweeps periods: February, May, July, and November. During these times the television networks offer many highly attractive special programs, exciting sporting events, and new episodes of popular shows instead of reruns, trying to obtain the highest audience numbers possible. These measurements are generalized for the following months, but might not take into consideration the popularity of certain programs without competition from special programming that ran during sweeps. Planning decisions are based upon historical data, created during especially strong program periods. Lack of information is also a problem advertisers face during the introduction of the new fall programs. Although the advertiser has an opportunity to preview the new program, it is untested with the consumer market. The advertiser does not have actual audience measurements.
- **Time urgency.** Advertisers are always in a hurry, working under tight deadlines. Print schedules, competition actions, and the general nature of the advertising business places a huge time pressure on promotion executives. Whether the pressure is real (as when a competitor offers a price break) or imagined, media selection without proper planning and analysis cannot lead to the most effective placement of creative strategy or budget.
- **Difficulty measuring effectiveness.** Because there are many problems associated with evaluating the effectiveness of advertising activities in general, we can assume that this difficulty is also associated with measuring the effectiveness of the various media or media vehicles. How can the media planner assess the effectiveness of running an advertisement in *Vogue* versus *Elle*? Because of an inability to quantify the differences, the media planner must guess at the impact of one outlet versus another. To complicate the evaluation process, how does the media planner compare the print ad placed in a magazine to a television commercial?

Media Measurement Services

Independent research companies such as those discussed in Chapter 8 provide unbiased evaluation of consumers and their use of media. The media planner can also use outside results as a source of information. For example, in Chapter 4, Table 4.2, *Women's Wear Daily* provided information about the top media influencing women's apparel purchases. Researchers from the publication found newspaper inserts to be the most influential media for women purchasing apparel ("Power," 2006).

The Lifestyle Monitor, created by Cotton Incorporated, provides another outside source for media planners to use when determining media and media vehicles. The Lifestyle Monitor is a study that uses survey research to investigate the attitudes and behaviors of American consumers. The articles resulting from this research appear every Thursday in *Women's Wear Daily* and are archived at www.cottoninc.com/lsmarticles. Table 9.1 illus-

TABLE 9.1   *Sources of Clothing Ideas: A Decade Makes a Difference*

	1994	**2004**	**+/− pts.**
Already Own and Like	57%	72%	+15
Store Displays	56%	53%	−3
People See Regularly	38%	36%	−2
In Catalogs	37%	38%	+1
Family Members	25%	31%	+6
Commercials & Ads	27%	32%	+5
Fashion Magazines	27%	34%	+7
Salespeople in Stores	19%	17%	−2
Celebrities	10%	17%	+7

Adapted from: Cotton Incorporated. (2005). *Comparison shopping: Today's retail experience evolves over the last decade.* Retrieved July 9, 2006, from http://www.cottoninc.com/lsmarticles/?articleID= 413 &searchTerm=media

trates the results from one such article. Shoppers were asked what sources they use for clothing ideas. The study was longitudinal and compared responses from 1994 to 2004.

The most dramatic change was evident in the source of clothing ideas *already own and like.* Responses increased from 57 percent to 72 percent, an increase of 15 points (Cotton Incorporated, 2005). Media planners might interpret this data to mean consumers are becoming more brand loyal. This may help them decide on a media plan that meets the promotion objective of increasing brand loyalty.

Another valuable statistic that media planners might use is the response indicating that *fashion magazines* have become a more important source of clothing ideas, increasing seven points from 27 percent in 1994 to 34 percent in 2004. Media planners using this data may want to include fashion magazines in the media plan. As part of the media selection process, media planners need to evaluate media costs, the focus of the next section.

Media Costs

The expense associated with the placement of an advertisement in a print or broadcast outlet is known as the **media cost.** The cost of doing any promotion activity is closely tied to the promotion budget, established early in the planning process. Key executives need to have a basic knowledge of media costs, since the costs will most certainly affect the selection of media the sponsoring organization will utilize.

The **media buyer** is the executive in charge of media placement who must deliberate the pros and cons of each medium in relationship to the advertising budget. Each specific medium provides potential advertisers with information about the circulation or size of the medium's audience via its distribution. From circulation information the media buyer assesses the potential customers that can be expected to respond to the advertisement, also known as the maximum rate of response.

Print Media Costs

Print media cost relates to the price paid for space, a full or partial page, in a newspaper or magazine. The costs associated with print media placement vary from the type of medium to the complexity of the visual message to be reproduced.

One method used to make comparisons between media and competitors within a medium is to calculate variations in cost and circulation. One common measurement used in the print media is to evaluate the cost-per-thousand or CPM. This measurement, determined by dividing the medium's audience into the cost for space is the cost of attracting 1,000 readers.

A comparison between two publications will show how a print media buyer would use a CPM analysis to select an appropriate publication for the advertisement. The media buyer for a children's apparel manufacturer wishes to consider two different magazines for placement of a full-page, four-color launch for a line of back-to-school fashions.

Magazine A has a general circulation of 2 million readers with an advertising rate of $25,000 for a full page, four-color ad. The CPM calculation follows:

$$\frac{\$25,000}{2,000 \text{ (circulation in thousands)}} = \$12.50 \text{ CPM}$$

The media buyer needs to have additional information from an alternative choice in order to make a decision. Magazine B provides the following circulation and rate data. This publication has a circulation of 2.5 million readers. Nearly 50 percent of the audience are mothers with school-age children between six and 18 years of age. An advertisement meeting the buyer's specifications costs $29,000. The media buyer considers the CPM for the general readership and mother audience. The two formulas are as follows:

<table>
<tr><th>Magazine B
General audience</th><th>Magazine B
Mothers with school-age children</th></tr>
<tr><td>$\frac{\$29,000}{2,500} = \$11.60$ CPM</td><td>$\frac{\$29,000}{1,250} = \$23.20$ CPM</td></tr>
</table>

In order to have a more complete comparison, the media buyer asks Magazine A for the number of readers who are mothers with children in the target ages. This magazine provides data that out of the 2 million readers, 75 percent meet the additional criteria. The new calculation shows a CPM of $16.67 ($25,000/1,500). Armed with the comparative information, the media buyer has better data to make a decision.

	Magazine A	Magazine B
CPM for general circulation	$12.50	$11.60
CPM for mothers with school-age children	$16.67	$23.20

These statistical facts help the advertiser to make an informed decision. Based upon the data for general circulation, the media buyer might select Magazine B as the better choice because the CPM for the general circulation is less. After further analysis, however, the executive selected Magazine A, because the targeted customer, mothers with school-age children, reading Magazine A make the cost-per-thousand contact lower.

Like magazines, newspapers use the cost-per-thousand as a measurement of cost-effectiveness. The following example shows a comparison between newspapers. If all other factors were equal, the advertiser would find Newspaper B to be more cost-effective than Newspaper A.

	Newspaper A	Newspaper B
Cost-per-page	$23,000	$10,800
Circulation	425,000	380,000
Calculation	23,000/425	10,800/380
CPM	$54.12	$28.42

——o Broadcast Media Costs

Television and radio are the dominant broadcast media and share similarities in costing. Evaluating media costs and analyzing techniques to measure media effectiveness are among the media issues common to television and radio.

Broadcast and Radio Media Costs

Television and radio use cost per ratings point (CPRP) for comparison figures. This measurement, also known as cost per point (CPP), is based upon the following formula:

$$CPRP = \frac{\text{Cost of commercial time}}{\text{Program rating}}$$

Advertising in a local television market can be used as an example. A men's wear specialty retailer wants to run a 30-second ad prior to Father's Day. The retailer has information about the cost of commercial time and the program rating provided by the television station. The results of the analysis indicate that the spot advertisement would be less expensive to reach an individual audience member on Program B, but Program A would provide the larger audience reach.

	Program A	Program B
Cost per 30-second spot ad	$8,000	$2,000
Rating	18th	6th
Reach (total persons)	325,000	138,000
Calculation	8,000/18	2,000/6
CPRP	$444.44	$333.33

Similar to the other media, radio stations generally publish their advertising rates on a **rate card**. The radio industry offers several different rate and package plans. First, the single price cards reflect a single price for each of the dayparts, time periods, and days of the week. This is the simplest and most direct method of pricing advertising.

Some stations offer a second method, grid cards, a multilevel rate card, in which the rates for each time period vary, week to week, depending upon available airtime. In this system, an advertiser wishing to book time on very short notice may pay a higher rate than an advertiser willing to wait a while.

A package plan known as a total audience plan, guaranteed audience plan, or reach plan is a rate given for a combination of time periods. The distribution of announcements to be run in each daypart is determined by the station. This strategy uses a broad combination of dayparts intended to give the advertiser an increased opportunity to reach more potential customers than it might by a schedule limited to breakfast time.

Other scheduling formats, such as run-of-schedule (ROS) or the best-time-available (BTA), are forms of package plans that typically offer lower rates than the total audience package plan. ROS or BTA plans may run at any time between 5:00 A.M. and 1:00 A.M. with no guaranteed distribution by daypart. The positive aspect of lower cost may not be worth it to the advertisers if they cannot be promised ideal timing for their commercials. Each advertiser will have to measure the tradeoffs with this system.

Comparison between media outlets can be very helpful as a decision-making tool. It does make sense to compare one magazine to another, but it is misleading to draw conclusions between media. Television is able to provide sight and sound, while newspapers provide advantages of immediacy and relatively low costs. Other characteristics besides cost-effectiveness must be considered when making media selections. Magazines have a longevity not experienced by TV or newspapers. Additionally, magazines have a pass-along rate, an estimate of how many people read the magazine without buying it. Individuals may see it and read it in a medical office waiting room or share the copy with roommates and family. But there are many other factors besides cost and cost-effectiveness that impact an advertiser's decision to select a particular medium.

Media Selection

As we can recognize, the task of the media buyer is a complicated one. Planning and placement of the media budget is critical to the success of an advertising program. Figure 9.4 can serve as a guide to the selection of media. The questions posed in the Media Selection checklist must be considered prior to making final media decisions.

——o Newspapers

Newspapers are the primary advertising medium used by retailers and the medium with the highest share of advertising expenditures in the United States. In Chapter 6, Table 6.3 indicated that retail as a category spent over $18 trillion on measured media expenditures in 2005 (100 Leading National Advertisers, 2006). Of that measured media, over $6.9 billion, or 37.3 percent, was spent on newspaper advertising. Retailers as a sector spent over one-third of their advertising budget on newspaper advertising, the largest portion of the budget spent on any media.

Table 9.2 shows the top 10 United States newspapers by circulation for weekday and Sunday editions. *USA Today* and the *Wall Street Journal* are the two most read newspapers on a daily basis. Both publications have a daily circulation of over 2 million copies. Interestingly, neither of these publications publishes a Sunday edition. The two most often read Sunday newspapers are the *New York Times* with a Sunday circulation of over 1.6 million copies, followed by the *Los Angeles Times* with Sunday circulation of over 1.2 million copies.

Although newspapers are the primary print medium selected by retailers, manufacturers and designers rarely use local or regional newspapers. Unless they are participating in cooperative advertising with a retailer in the local trading area, most manufacturers and designers have national advertising goals, placing advertisements in widely distributed newspapers with broad circulation.

Newspapers are low in purchase cost, and many U.S. citizens read the local newspaper as a chief source of news and information about their local communities. According

FIGURE 9.4 Media selection checklist.

Media Selection Checklist

☐ **Who is the target customer?** The target customer should be defined in terms of demographics and lifestyle. The customer could be a prospect, regular user, or an inactive customer. The media buyer should take into consideration any primary or secondary research accumulated about the customer or potential customer. Additionally, the geographical location of the consumer must be considered in light of the media options.

☐ **What are the advertising and media objectives?** Is the advertiser interested in selling merchandise or the institution? Is the advertiser interested in creating advance awareness for a new product? Does the advertiser want to emphasize the image of the designer, manufacturer, or retailer?

☐ **What type of message is the advertiser sending?** Is the advertisement for a product or service? Is the emphasis on value, quality, prestige, service, or some other characteristic?

☐ **What are the product's properties?** At what stage of the product life cycle is the merchandise? Is it a new product or an established brand? Is the merchandise in a highly competitive or exclusive environment?

☐ **Is the particular medium suited to the merchandise or producer?** The audience for a particular publication should be interested in the category of merchandise. It seems obvious that Coach leather handbags would receive a more positive response in *Vogue* rather than *Details*.

☐ **Who is the competition and where do they advertise?** Understanding the role of the competition and estimating the expenditures of the competition helps the media buyer justify maintaining a competitive stance.

☐ **How much does it cost to advertise in a particular medium?** How does that relate to the advertising budget? Can the advertiser afford the expenses for creative development and placement?

☐ **Where is the business located?** If the business is in a high-traffic area, perhaps advertising is not as essential as it would be if the advertiser is in an out-of-the-way location.

☐ **What has the advertiser done in the past?** What media placement has been successful versus ineffective in past advertising programs?

to the Newspaper Association of America (2006a), 47 percent (110.5 million) of adults (18 and over) read an average issue of a daily newspaper. Five weekday issues reach 65 percent of adults. Sunday readership is higher; 55 percent of adults (118.8 million) read an average issue of a Sunday newspaper nationwide. Four issues of a Sunday newspaper reach 67 percent of total adults.

Newspaper readership continues to decline. In 1998, average weekday readership for all adults was 58.6 percent (Newspaper Association of America, 2006b). In 2005 readership had dropped to 51.6 percent. While newspapers are read more often on Sunday, readership has also fallen. In 1998, 68.3 percent of adults read a Sunday paper. In 2005 readership dropped to 59.6 percent.

Demographic statistics indicate differences in newspaper readership (Table 9.3). Gender differences are evident in newspaper readership. Men are more likely to read a daily newspaper (49 percent) than women (45 percent). However, on Sunday, women are more likely to read a newspaper (57 percent) as opposed to men (54 percent) (Newspaper Association of America, 2006a). Income plays an important role in segmenting newspaper audiences. Readership increases steadily with higher earnings. Among adults with household incomes of $75,000+, readership is 55 percent on weekdays and 65 percent on Sundays.

Education and occupation correlate with newspaper readership for both weekdays and Sundays. Of adults who graduated from college, 57 percent read a weekday paper

TABLE 9.2   *Top 10 U.S. Newspapers by Circulation: Weekday and Sunday*

Weekday

	City, State	Newspaper Name	Daily Circulation	Avg. Weekday Audience	Circulation as Percent of Audience
1	Washington, D.C.	*USA Today*	2,272,815	6,980,074	32.6%
2	New York, NY	*Wall Street Journal*	2,049,786	5,242,129	39.1%
3	New York, NY	*New York Times*	1,142,464	5,065,303	22.6%
4	Los Angeles, CA	*Los Angeles Times*	851,832	2,274,021	37.5%
5	Washington, D.C.	*Washington Post*	724,242	1,750,865	41.4%
6	New York, NY	*New York Daily News*	708,477	2,832,994	25.0%
7	New York, NY	*New York Post*	673.379	2,142,143	31.4%
8	Chicago, IL	*Chicago Tribune*	579,079	1,638,704	35.3%
9	Houston, TX	*Houston Chronicle*	513,387	1,227,446	41.8%
10	Phoenix, AZ	*Phoenix Republic*	438,722	1,022,560	42.9%

Sunday

	City, State	Newspaper Name	Daily Circulation	Avg. Weekday Audience	Circulation as Percent of Audience
1	New York, NY	*New York Times*	1,683,855	6,921,611	24.3%
2	Los Angeles, CA	*Los Angeles Times*	1,231,318	3,380,249	36.4%
3	Washington, D.C.	*Washington Post*	960,684	2,380,768	40.4%
4	Chicago, IL	*Chicago Tribune*	957,212	2.518.082	38.0%
5	New York, NY	*New York Daily News*	795,153	2,828,879	28.1%
6	Philadelphia, PA	*Philadelphia Inquirer*	705,965	1,806,803	39.1%
7	Denver, CO	*Denver Post/Rocky Mountain News*	704,806	1,332,641	52.9%
8	Houston, TX	*Houston Chronicle*	692,557	1,646,446	42.1%
9	Detroit, MI	*Detroit News— Free Press*	669,315	1,662,549	40.3%
10	Minneapolis-St. Paul, MN	*Star Tribune*	606,698	1,470,513	41.3%

ABC = Audit Bureau of Circulations, Scarborough Research

Adapted from: Newspaper Association of America. (2006, March 31). Top 50+ Newspapers reporting to ABC. Retrieved July 10, 2006, from http://www.naa.org/nadbase/

and 66 percent read a Sunday newspaper (Newspaper Association of America, 2006a). Five daily issues reach 75 percent of adults who graduated college. People in occupations with more job responsibility show stronger readership of newspapers. As an example, 54 percent of adults employed in business or management read a daily newspaper, and 64 percent read a Sunday issue.

Racial and ethnic groups differ in their reading levels. Of the adult population, 49 percent of whites read a daily newspaper, compared to 44 percent of African-Americans, 38 percent of Asians, and 31 percent of adults of Hispanic origin. On Sunday, the reach among racial/ethnic newspaper readers is 58 percent whites, 55 percent African-Americans, 39 percent Asian, and 37 percent Hispanic (Newspaper Association of America, 2006a).

TABLE 9.3   *U.S. Daily and Sunday Newspaper Readership Demographics*

Education

Education Level	% Daily	% Sunday
Bachelor's Degree Plus	57.4	65.9
Some College (No Degree)	45.4	56.1
High School Graduate	46.2	54.4
Did Not Graduate From High School	31.4	37.6

Age

Age	% Daily	% Sunday
18–24	30.2	42.2
25–34	34.4	45.1
35–44	42.6	53.9
45–54	52.0	60.4
55–64	57.6	64.7
65+	64.8	65.7

Race and Ethnicity

Race/Ethnicity	% Daily	% Sunday
White	49.3	58.0
African-American	43.7	54.8
Hispanic	30.9	37.1
Asian	37.7	38.7
Other Race	33.4	38.6

Household Income

Income	% Daily	% Sunday
$75,000 or more	54.6	64.6
$60,000 to $74,999	46.6	58.9
$50,000 to $59,999	47.1	58.0
$40,000 to $49,999	44.6	51.9
$30,000 to $39,999	46.6	52.3
$10,000 to $19,999	41.1	45.3
Under $10,000	30.1	35.4

Job Responsibility

Job Responsibility	% Daily	% Sunday
Management, Business and Financial Operations	53.6	63.5
Professional and Related Occupations	51.6	62.3
Sales and Related Occupations	47.8	57.6
Production Occupation	40.0	45.3

Adapted from: Newspaper Association of America. (2006). *Daily and Sunday newspaper audience.*
Retrieved July 10, 2006, from http://www.naa.org/researchpages/

TABLE 9.4   *Newspaper Section Readership by Gender*

Daily Newspaper Section Adults Read	Adults %	Men %	Women %
Business/Finance	35	40	30
Classified	32	32	33
Comics	30	29	31
Editorial Page	37	36	38
Fashion	16	6	27
Food/Cooking	29	17	42
General News	60	57	63
Home/Furnishings/Gardening	25	16	33
Movie Listing and Reviews	27	22	32
Science and Technology	21	25	16
Sports	36	49	23
Travel	23	20	26
TV/Radio Listings	27	25	29
Average Weekday Audience (000)	103,363	51,582	51,781

Adapted from: Newspaper Association of America. (2005). *Section readership.* Retrieved July 10, 2006, from http://www.naa.org/marketscope/readership2005/

Table 9.4 shows newspaper readership by section. General news is the most read section of the newspaper by both men and women (Newspaper Association of America, 2005). Men are more likely than women to read the business/finance and sports sections of the paper, while women are more likely to read the fashion and home/furnishings/gardening sections of the paper. When planning newspaper advertising, media planners may want to consider paying a slightly higher rate to get an ad in a preferred position.

Newspaper Formats

Newspapers in the United States fall into one of two different formats. A paper is either a **broadsheet**, the large standard size six columns wide, or a **tabloid**, approximately half the size of a broadsheet with five columns. The *New York Times, Wall Street Journal,* and *Los Angeles Times* fit the broadsheet category. Tabloids have been popular in the trade press. *Women's Wear Daily* and *Daily News Record* are published as tabloids. The *Rocky Mountain News* is an example of a daily newspaper that publishes in the tabloid format. Some local papers with a high number of commuters sell tabloid-size newspapers, making it easier for train or bus riders to read during their commute.

Newspaper supplements are targeted special issues covering topics from shopping to wedding planning, home improvements, back-to-school, traditional fashion season change, to photographic displays, entertainment sections, or Sunday news and feature magazines. Newspapers, including the *San Francisco Chronicle* and the *New York Times,* publish a magazine supplement each Sunday. The Sunday magazine published by the *Denver Post* is called *Empire Magazine.* Other papers insert national newspaper magazines, such as *USA Weekend* or *Parade*, into their Sunday papers.

The *New York Times* publishes several special fashion supplements to its Sunday magazine annually. The *New York Times Style* magazine is presented at the beginning of the fall and spring seasons; publication dates are in August and March (Fig. 9.5). The women's fashion supplement has editorial features on trends for the upcoming season and advertising from major retail stores, designers, and manufacturers of apparel. Additional supplements cover the men's design, living, travel, beauty, and holiday markets.

Since supplements are directed to a special-interest group, they may be used to target a specific audience for advertising. The wedding planning supplement is an ideal place for photographers, musicians, rental halls, or bridal stores to advertise. Stores such as Target, Kohls, and Wal-mart provide color inserts to local papers on higher-quality stock than typical newsprint. These inserts enable the advertiser to use color more effectively with high impact for the consumer. These supplements take on some of the advantages of magazines with longer lives and higher-quality printing.

FIGURE 9.5 The *New York Times Style* magazine supplement.

Newspaper Advertising Rates

Each newspaper has a rate schedule that specifies the cost of space in that publication. These costs are directly related to the size, the amount of space the advertisement fills, the circulation, or the number of the newspaper's distribution and readership, and the position of the ad in the newspaper, or the place or location it occupies.

The **standard advertising unit** (**SAU**) is used to measure the space by which advertising is sold. Ads are measured by column width and depth in inches. The greater the number of widths and inches the ad spans, the greater the cost. Under this system all newspapers use column widths of $2\frac{1}{16}$ inches wide, making broadsheet papers six columns wide and tabloid formats five columns wide. The column inch is the unit of measurement, standardized into 57 units or format sizes (Fig. 9.6). The column inch is 1 inch deep and one column wide.

This system of measurement allows a national advertiser to prepare an ad in a particular SAU, and it can be used in any newspaper that accepts SAUs. Since nearly 90 percent of the daily papers in the United States use SAUs, rates quoted on that system permit national advertisers to produce consistent advertisements. The production and purchase processes have been simplified tremendously.

In addition to the considerations of column inch and SAU, newspapers offer other options and considerations to the media planner. Many newspapers offer flatrates, which means they do not offer any special discounts for quantity or regularly scheduled space purchases. Other publications offer open-rate structures, allowing discounts under specific conditions. These conditions usually are granted to advertisers buying frequent or bulk amounts of space, determined by the number of column inches purchased in a year.

FIGURE 9.6 Standard advertising units are used to measure advertising space in newspapers.

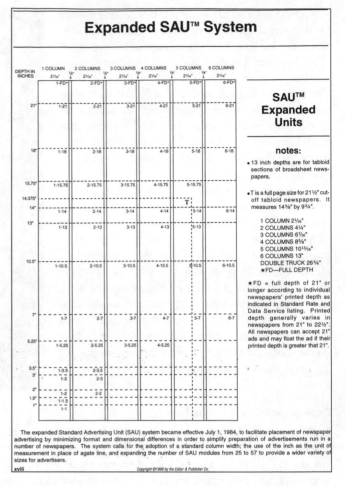

Newspaper advertising rates may vary due to special requests from the advertisers. These requests include such factors as the position where the ad is placed or the use of color. Basic advertising rates established by the newspaper are for the run of paper (ROP), which means that the ad can be placed on any page or section, determined by the newspaper. The advertiser desiring a specific page or news section is required to pay a higher price for this preferred position, which may be the back page of the front section or some other highly demanded position. Color advertising may be available for higher impact. These pages may be limited to certain positions, through preprinted inserts or in the Sunday supplements.

Advertisers may be able to buy newspaper space based upon combination rates whereby a discount is offered when the advertiser agrees to purchase space in several newspapers. Thus, combination rates may apply when the newspaper publisher owns several newspapers.

Types of Newspaper Advertising

The major classifications of newspaper advertising are display, classified, public notices, and preprinted inserts. Different types of ads are used by advertisers to achieve their various goals.

Victoria's Secret Fashion Show. The Internet is an emerging global medium. It is also an essential tool in intergrated marketing communications campaigns. Victoria's Secret first used the Internet to broadcast a live fashion show—the most watched Internet fashion event to date in 1999. Much of the show's success was attributed to the campaign, which combined traditional and nonconventional promotion mix tools to sell Victoria's Secrets image and merchandise to the world. By 2006, the show was more glitzy and glamorous than ever. Its Hollywood debut was complete with a star-studded audience, top models from around the world, a $6.5 milllion bra, and a performance by the king of sexy himself, Justin Timberlake. Costing $600,000 a minute to produce, the 20 minute show was broadcast on CBS on December 5 as the "sexiest night on television."

An advertising executive's dream checklist may once have included a Hollywood star, a big budget, and a much lusted after product. Now, a celebrated director has been added to the mix. Luxury brands are trying to broaden their consumer base and appeal to mass audiences using big-name directors and giving them free creative reign to create a story using their product. For example, Christian Dior used director Rob Marshall for a film starring Monica Bellucci.

The Heart Truth's Red Dress Collection was presented during
Fasion Week on National Wear Red Day, part of a campaign by the
National Institutes of Health to raise awareness of the risk of heart disease for
women. Designers such as Betsey Johnson, Calvin Klein, and Zac Posen and
celebrity models such as Angela Bassett, Lauren Hutton, and Paula Zahn
participated in support of the campaign.

Pretty Polly, well-known U.K. hosiery brand, was successfully reintroduced to the British market after years of declining sales. Helen Atkins, Pretty Polly's marketing director, devised a relaunch that included product and package redesign, point-of-purchase presentations, advertising, public relations, and sales promotion. With a limited budget, the new image was presented on 60-foot billboards placed in high traffic areas and attached to a helicopter flown over parts of London. The traffic stopping signs created newsworthy stories that were featured in the Britsh press and on television.

Intel Bunny People. As a promotion tool, a fashion show may create one of the most spectacular atmospheres to excited consumers. Fashion shows combine lights, music, and models to entertain and electrify audiences about merchandise. Realizing the effect fashion shows can have on an audience, Intel created an advertising campaign that featured models in flashy colored clean room suits carrying processor chips as props down the runway. It is a compliment to this promotion mix tool that a supplier of nonfashion goods would use it in a successful campaign.

It's the new look.

The Pentium® II processor for a whole new style of computing.

Intel's engineers have done it again. Their latest design, the Pentium® II processor, is unlike anything you've ever seen—from its unique package to the amazing effect it has on your multimedia applications. That's because it's been designed with new architectural features, plus Intel MMX™ media enhancement technology. Now, enhancing your favorite photos or making a video phone call on your PC is better than ever. The Pentium II processor. You'll love what it does for your image. ► www.intel.com/home

The Computer Inside.™

Giorgio Armani describes his store on the Avenue Montaigne in Paris as an "experimental boutique." The new flagship features an onyx staircase, backlit floors, a lack of traditional window displays, and clothing and accessories sparingly showcased in onyx wardrobes. The spare merchandising scheme and luxurious decor convey exclusivity and quality to discriminating customers.

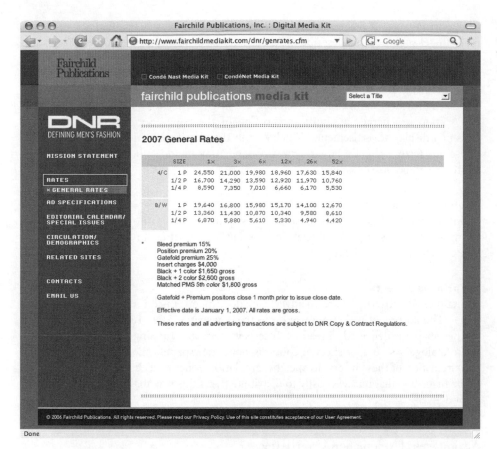

FIGURE 9.7 Rate card and
display specifications for
the trade newspaper
Daily News Record.

Display Advertising

A **display advertisement** includes copy and artistic elements, such as illustrations, photography, headlines, and/or other visual components. Display ads vary in size and appear in all sections of a newspaper except on the front page, the editorial page, and the first page of major sections. Display ads may be black-and-white, or color may be introduced. Although a display ad does not require *pictures,* they normally will contain some type of art through a logo, photograph, or drawing.

Display ads are purchased by amounts specified on rate cards. These documents list the costs for space, production (mechanical and copy) requirements, deadlines, and other publication information such as preferred position and circulation, discussed earlier in the chapter.

Figure 9.7 is a rate card for the trade newspaper *Daily News Record (DNR).* A one-page, four-color advertisement run once in the newspaper costs $24,550 (Fairchild Publications, 2006a). Notice that the cost per advertisement diminishes as the number of runs increases. If you were a media planner for a menswear supplier, and knew your audience read *DNR* on a regular basis, it would be more cost-effective to run the advertisement 26 times per year at a cost of $17,630 for each ad.

Classified Advertising

Classified advertisements differ from display ads because they normally contain only copy. They provide a community marketplace for goods, services, and every type of opportunity, from real estate and used cars to garage sales. Classified ads are organized under subheads that describe the class of goods or services to be offered. For example, people who are looking for a job will look for the subhead labeled *Help Wanted.*

Classified ads are purchased by the number of lines the ad occupies and the number of times it runs. Rates may also depend upon the category where it is placed. Since classified ads provide a significant source of advertising revenue for a newspaper, the classified section is generally a significant portion of the paper. Some papers also accept classified display advertisements, which run in the classified section of the newspaper. These ads feature slightly larger type sizes and may include photos, artistic borders, white space, and possibly color.

Public Notices

Newspapers carry legal notices for a fee. These public notices inform the citizens about changes in business or personal relationships, public government reports, notices by private citizens, and financial reports.

Preprinted Inserts

Sometimes advertisers prepare an advertising document, which is delivered to the newspaper. The document is then inserted into the newspaper as a preprinted insert before the newspaper is delivered to readers. Inserts vary in size, ranging from a postcard to a flyer, catalog, brochure, or sheet of coupons. Some newspapers allow advertisers to limit the circulation of these inserts to specific circulation zones or to home subscribers only. Some firms find that it is less costly to distribute flyers this way than by mail or door-to-door delivery.

Advantages of Newspaper Advertising

Newspaper advertising provides many benefits to the advertiser. Besides the widespread acceptance and readership of the medium, newspapers offer the following advantages:

- **Immediacy.** Daily newspapers have relatively short lead times for the insertion of an advertisement. This short time period allows for quick response to product or service announcements, fast testing of consumer interest, or rapid switching of advertising needs to meet the current conditions in the community. Marketing tie-ins can be immediately covered with extensive, next-day editorial coverage of such activities as sporting events, political ceremonies, or special events such as presentation of the Oscars or other award ceremonies.
- **Local emphasis.** Many newspapers focus on a city or town rather than a state or large geographical region. City newspapers offer benefits to small retailers wishing to place the core of their advertising close to their local target market.
- **Flexible production.** Production of the ad can be adjusted to the budget of the advertiser. Newspapers offer a wide range of sizes from as large as two full pages to something as small as a business card. The advertisement may be developed with a lot of copy or limited copy. It may be created with drawings or photography. Preferred position has the highest visibility, either in the first few pages of the general news section or in the Lifestyle, Fashion, or Art sections where fashion-related news appears. Customers may learn to associate advertising from a particular retailer with a specific position. A top department store may always place a full-page ad on the back page of

the first section of the paper. Thus, the budget of the advertiser is met with position, size, and style variables taken into consideration.

- **Short closing times.** Deadlines for submitting advertising material for publication are known as closing times. Daily newspapers rarely have closing times that exceed 24 hours. This allows the advertiser to make changes in copy or art right up to the last minute, an advantage when the product has not arrived from the manufacturer in time for the advertisement. Closing times for Sunday papers are frequently longer, ranging from four to six weeks for Sunday supplements.
- **Geographical target market flexibility.** Newspapers published in large metropolitan areas have recognized the need for targeted coverage. As a result, many newspapers offer **zone editions,** providing news and advertising focused to an area within the city. For example, the *Chicago Tribune* has offered several zone editions and supplements to specific neighborhoods and suburban areas. The city zone is the area defined by the corporate limits of a community, while a retail trading zone includes a geographical area around a central city.
- **Credibility.** Newspapers are believed to be a source of credible information. Although research may not be able to prove the veracity of the printed word, it is recognized as a believable resource. This attribute has been known to carry over to the products and services advertised within the newspaper's content.
- **Reseller support.** Dealer and local distributors work together with newspapers as the most frequently used medium for reseller support. Cooperative advertisements with shared costs, identification and promotion of a local dealer for a national product, promotion of quick action through coupons, and other means to join dealer support are all methods used for reseller support.
- **Color reproduction.** Since standard color printing in the run of paper has become more common, advertising has benefited. Approximately 90 percent of all newspapers offer black-and-white plus one ROP color: nearly 70 percent offer black-and-white plus three ROP colors. This allows for more realistic color reproductions, despite the porosity of newspaper stock, called newsprint. Newsprint is an off-white pulpy stock made from inexpensive paper. Newsprint comes in various qualities, light to heavy and smooth to rough. Truly accurate reproduction is not technologically possible using newsprint, and the cost of running a full-page ad in full color (black plus three colors) runs roughly 30 percent higher than for a black-and-white ad. Many advertisers desiring color sophistication revert to supplemental inserts.

Disadvantages of Newspaper Advertising

Every advertising medium has limitations. The following list provides some of the disadvantages of advertising in newspapers.

- **Short shelf life.** Newspapers are typically read and tossed into the recycle bin; they are not retained for very long. Since the exposure is limited to a short period of time, advertisers have little opportunity for repeated exposure for their ads. Magazines are the print medium to use to overcome this obstacle.
- **Reproduction problems.** Printing techniques prevent high-quality reproduction and printing errors do occur. Due to the quick turnaround, detailed preparation and care in production are not as strong as in other media.
- **Clutter.** Each ad competes with editorial content in addition to competing with other ads on the same page.

- **Small shared audience.** Sharing issues of a publication are referred to as the pass-along audience. The pass-along audience of newspapers is much smaller than through other media such as magazines.
- **High costs of reaching a national audience.** Reaching a national audience by newspapers is more costly in comparison with national media such as network television or magazines. National newspaper coverage costs more than other nationally produced media does. Box 9.2 discusses how some major newspapers are addressing their ad rates.
- **Inability to show products true-to-life.** All print advertising is limited by the ability to show the product in three dimensions, and the product cannot be seen in action with the advantages of sound and motion.

──o Magazines

Although newspapers remain the primary resource used by retailers for print advertising, manufacturers and designers prefer to use magazines. There are many characteristics that make magazines the natural choice for firms desiring a national or international audience. Customers familiar with national or global brands are likely to translate that increased awareness into sales for prestige-oriented products. Despite increased postage rates, magazines show continued strength and vitality in the international marketplace, with many new magazines introduced each year. According to the Magazine Publishers of America (2006a), 84 percent of adults age 18 and over read magazines. The average reader spends 44 minutes reading each issue of a magazine. Table 9.5 shows the top 10 consumer magazines and fashion-related titles by circulation. Note the top two titles are published by AARP (Formerly known as American Association of Retired Persons) and are targeted to the baby boomer and the traditionalist with circulation rates of over 22 million subscriptions (Magazine Publishers of America, 2006c). The top fashion-related title, *Seventeen,* ranks 37, and has a circulation of just over 1.6 million subscriptions and is targeted to Generation Y.

Over the last decade, the number of total magazine titles in the marketplace has increased while the number of consumer magazines has decreased. In 1997, 18,047 titles were available, and of those, 7,712 were consumer-only titles (Magazine Publishers of America, 2006a). In 2005 the total number of titles had increased to 18,227 titles, but the consumer titles had decreased to 6,325 titles. Using broad statistics, men's publications numbered 134 titles in 1999 and only 61 titles in 2006, over a 50 percent decrease in the number of titles available (Magazine Publishers of America, 2006b). Women's titles too have declined in number. In 1999 there were 419 titles directed at women; in 2005 the number had dropped to 276.

According to the Magazine Publishers of America (2006a), demographic changes are redefining the magazine market. Teenage readers are reading at a rate of 81 percent, similar to the adult population. Eighty-three percent of African-American adults read magazines, and they read on average 12.8 issues per month, compared to 9.6 issues (per month) for all U.S. adults. This population is also younger; 73 percent of African-American adults who read magazines are between the ages of 18 to 49 compared to 63 percent of the U.S. adult population.

There were over 113 Asian-American titles published in the United States in 2005 (Magazine Publishers of America, 2006a). Asian-American magazine readers are younger, more affluent, and better educated than magazine readers overall. Nearly 74 percent of adult Hispanics read magazines; approximately 8.2 issues per month, similar to the U.S. average. In 2005 as compared to 2004, the total paid circulation for Audit

TaBLe 9.5   *Top 10 Total Magazine Circulation*

	Publication Name	2005 Subscriptions	2005 Single Copy	2005 Total Paid	% Change From 2004 To 2005
1	AARP the Magazine	22,673,663	1,992	22,675,655	0.0%
2	AARP Bulletin	22,075,011	0	22,075,011	−0.1%
3	Reader's Digest	9,658,765	453,008	10,111,773	−0.4%
4	TV Guide	7,881,625	329,956	8,211,581	−8.9%
5	Better Homes and Gardens	7,407,332	213,600	7,620,932	−0.1%
6	National Geographic	5,237,108	166,826	5,403,934	−1.2%
7	Time	3,887,480	151,028	4,038,508	0.1%
8	Good Housekeeping	3,864,089	770,674	4,634,763	0.1%
9	Ladies' Home Journal	3,832,710	289,750	4,122,460	0.2%
10	AAA Westways	3,676,058	0	3,676,058	1.4%
	Top Fashion-Related Titles				
37	Seventeen	1,679,425	355,037	2,034,462	−4.5%
45	Glamour	1,462,523	909,463	2,371,986	−0.3%
60	Teen Vogue	1,177,486	233,123	1,410,609	141.7%
71	Cosmo Girl!	972,657	410,811	1,383,468	0.8%
76	Cosmopolitan	939,558	2,030,394	2,969,952	−0.6%
77	InStyle	934,989	848,247	1,783,235	1.6%
80	FHM (For Him Magazine)	906,033	371,478	1,277,511	4.7%
92	Vogue	819,001	441,315	1,260,316	−0.7%
93	Lucky	808,501	257,907	1,066,408	6.3%
101	Allure	757,722	302,377	1,060,099	3.5%

ABC = Audit Bureau of Circulations, Scarborough Research

Adapted from: Magazine Publishers of America. (2006). *Total average circulation for ABC magazines.* Retrieved July 11, 2006, from http://www.magazine.org/content/Files/AllcircABC05.xls

Bureau of Circulations–measured Hispanic-directed magazine titles grew by 11.6 percent. This is a growing, lucrative market for magazine advertisers.

Magazines may be published on a weekly, monthly, bimonthly, or quarterly basis. Purchase price and perceived strength of the advertising are related to the frequency of publication. The amount of time an advertiser has to prepare and submit layouts to the publication will also vary with the amount of time between publications.

Fashion magazines consist of editorial content and advertising. **Editorial content** involves the feature stories and fashion spreads controlled by the magazine editors, writers, and photographers. Editorial credit is given to manufacturers and retailers within fashion articles. Advertising includes the pages and partial pages paid for by the companies wanting to promote their products and services. A healthy balance exists between advertising and editorial pages. Most magazines contain both editorial

TABLE 9.6   *Top 10 Magazine Subject Areas by Number of Editorial Pages*

	Type of Editorial	Editorial Pages	Percent
1	Entertainment/Celebrity	28,251.7	16.7%
2	Wearing Apparel/Accessories	22,697.5	13.4%
3	Home Furnishings/Management	13,257.8	7.8%
4	Travel/Transportation	11,660.7	6.9%
5	Food & Nutrition	11,385.1	6.7%
6	Business & Industry	11,031.9	6.5%
7	Culture	10,371.3	6.1%
8	Health/Medical Science	8,577.6	5.1%
9	Beauty & Grooming	8,273.2	4.9%
10	Sports/Recreation/Hobby	7,066.6	4.2%

Adapted from: American Society of Magazine Editors. (2006a). *Editorial pages by subject.* Retrieved July 11, 2006, from *http://www.magazine.org*

and advertising content. The editorial content keeps the readers interested, while the advertising revenue enables magazines to keep subscription and newsstand costs affordable for average consumers. In 2005, the ratio for consumer magazines was 47.2 percent advertising and 52.8 percent editorial (American Society of Magazine Editors, 2006b).

According to the American Society of Magazine Editors (2006b), Entertainment/Celebrity (16.7 percent), Wearing Apparel/Accessories (13.4 percent), and Home Furnishings/Management (7.8 percent) are the top three subject areas for editorial content (Table 9.6). This speaks well for the fashion industry, as all three categories are very important media for fashion-related products and services.

Fashion magazines are distributed by two different methods: through subscription or over the counter at a variety of retail outlets. The specific magazine can provide the potential advertiser statistics about the primary method of sales. Magazines with a higher percentage of subscriptions can provide a more consistent target audience with well-defined demographic information.

Consumer and Trade Magazines

Magazines may be classified as either consumer or trade oriented. Trade publications direct the flow of information between businesses. Examples of trade magazines are *Stores*, the publication of the National Retail Federation, and *Visual Merchandising and Store Design* (*VM + SD*), published by ST Publications, Inc., representing the display and store planning industries.

In contrast, consumer publications are directed to ultimate consumers. These publications are classified as general interest, news, fashion, sports, or any other special interest. Examples of news publications include *Newsweek, Time,* and *U.S. News and World Report.* Besides general news topics, these publications regularly contain articles relating to the fashion industry, making them resources for apparel, home fashions, or cosmetic advertisements.

─────○ BOX 9.2

Newspapers' Future: Think Like a Magazine

While it's no news circulation is slipping at major metropolitan newspapers such as the *New York Times*, the *Wall Street Journal*, and the *Los Angeles Times*, observers are asking why these publications are continuing to raise ad rates as some subscribers head for the door.

But the *L.A. Times* has a bone to pick with those who wonder whether it is still a viable avenue in which to advertise and obtain news. Looking ahead, a spokeswoman indicated the paper will start thinking more like a magazine when it comes to readers and focus on growing its individual paid circulation. The Audit Bureau of Circulations Fas-Fax report showed that for the six months ended in September, the West Coast paper fell 8 percent in daily circulation, but the spokeswoman countered that ABC's number included "other paid circulation," such as copies delivered to hotel rooms. Incidentally, ABC's statistics also showed that the *L.A. Times* individual paid circulation is up. "Individually paid copies deliver a more engaged reader to advertisers and therefore a more favorable return on investment," she said—in other words, newsstand.

And that's not the only magazine trait the *Times* will start exhibiting. Looking forward, the newspaper will offer more options for advertisers, including front-section strips in several sections, innovative ad units, and multimedia packages. On the edit side, the *Times* is ramping up its fashion and lifestyle coverage. Late last year, Elizabeth Snead, who has covered fashion for *USA Today* and E! Online's *Fashion Police*, joined its online awards website, *The Envelope*, for its "Styles & Scenes" coverage. The paper also recently unveiled a redesign of its Sunday Calendar. The two-part section was renamed "Movies-TV-Style" and "Arts & Music."

"The intensified editorial ranges from society events and fashion trends to pop culture and Web discoveries and the rich arts scene," said a spokeswoman.

But fashion advertisers may really start to take notice once the paper introduces a new weekly fashion and lifestyle section, for print and online. Sources close to the *L.A. Times* confirmed plans are under way, but no timetable has been set.

Meanwhile, the *Wall Street Journal* has also expanded its style coverage. Journal publisher L. Gordon Crovitz previously told *WWD* that female *Journal* readers purchase "more women's fashion items than do all the readers of the women's magazines—combined."

As the *L.A. Times* and the *Journal* continue to chase those stylish ad dollars, some advertisers are seeking ad rate cuts, especially since newspapers are cutting deals like never before.

"I suspect that many, but not all, newspaper publishers are running scared," said Gene Willhoft, president of Absolute Media. Still, Willhoft said, there is a major hurdle for advertisers who seek lower ad rates. The *L.A. Times* and *New York Times* "are very important papers in their respective DMAs [designated market area] and are tough to buy around if the target is an upscale, educated audience," he said. "Advertisers must be prepared to walk away or the negotiations may not be successful."

George Janson, managing partner and director of print at mediaedge:cia, said he is open to negotiating rates but isn't happy about the fact that even though newspaper circulation drops every year, ad rates still rise (the *L.A. Times*, *New York Times*, and the *Journal* are all planning increases for 2007). Janson works with clients including Chanel and Xerox.

Regarding its ad rate increase, a *New York Times* spokeswoman contended the paper "remains one of the best places to reach an influential, educated, high-quality audience. Advertisers continue to value that reach and are willing to pay a premium for it."

One executive who agrees with that philosophy is Ruediger Albers, president of jewelry firm Wempe. He advertises in the *New York Times* and the *Wall Street Journal* and partially attributes Wempe's success to his regular exposure in both papers. "What's the alternative to reaching one million people that have the spending power of *New York Times* readers?" he asked.

As for the *Journal*, Albers is partial to its value-added opportunities, such as being invited to an event where he can mingle with other advertisers and consumers. At one event, a chance meeting with S. Epatha Merkerson led to the actress wearing (and being photographed in) Wempe jewelry at major award shows. Albers is considering increasing his schedules in both papers, but negotiations aren't finalized. Presumably rates and placement remain an issue.

Amid weakening ad trends, the Internet seems to offer more hope. The New York Times Co. recently reported that its Internet revenue might increase 30 percent next year, and a source said the *L.A. Times* "is in the same ballpark, if not slightly ahead of the *New York Times* projection." A spokeswoman said Dow Jones Online isn't reporting forecasts for 2007, but this year online revenues were up 20 percent.

Ad-tracking firm TNS Media Intelligence projects advertising budgets to stall next year, but the silver lining will be growth in online media (including search), which is coincidentally expected to grow up to 30 percent. Sarah Baehr, vice president of media at Avenue A | Razorfish, said the company predicts that online will outpace other media growth for three main reasons: The share of online media is still disproportionately small compared with offline media, several marketers haven't maximized their fullest potential online, and the accountability and tractability of online (compared to other media) are compelling.

While speaking at a *New Yorker* breakfast, Sir Martin Sorrell, group chief executive at WPP Group, said people spend approximately 20 percent of their time online, but advertising online budgets are still in the single digits. He cited News

Corp. owner Rupert Murdoch as an excellent example of utilizing the Internet (MySpace, for one) and said most established agencies aren't moving fast enough to gain a foothold in this arena. Sir Martin contended the delay is partially due to the fact that top executives at agencies are nearing retirement and want to coast in their jobs and leave the Internet issue to their future replacements.

Source: Wicks, A. (2006, December 15). Newspapers' future: think like a magazine. *Women's Wear Daily*, p. 10.

FIGURE 9.8 Fashion publications for Hispanic women include *Latina*, a bilingual magazine (left); the Spanish-language edition of *Cosmopolitan* (middle); and (c) *Vanidades*, a Spanish-language magazine (right).

Media planners wanting to attract a fashion- or home-fashion-oriented audience may select a fashion or home furnishings magazine in which to target advertisements. Fashion magazines may be further targeted to a specific target audience. *Glamour* is focused toward college students and women entering careers. *Vogue, Harper's Bazaar,* and *Elle* strive to attract a slightly older and sophisticated target market, while *Seventeen* and *Teen Vogue* appeal to the teenage market. The audience for *Latina*, the Spanish edition of *Cosmopolitan* and *Vanidades* is Hispanic women (Fig 9.8). *Elle Decor, Metropolitan Home,* and *House and Garden* are known as shelter magazines because they target consumers interested in residential interior design and gardening.

International Magazines

Magazine distribution has been influenced by the trend toward globalization. The Greek fashion magazines shown in Figure 9.9 incorporate English and French words and phrases into the editorial and advertising copy.

Vogue, one of the leading fashion magazines, originated in the United States during the 19th century. The popularity of the publication led to the establishment of ten international editions. British and French editions can be found throughout newsstands in the United

FIGURE 9.9 Greek fashion magazines.

States. There are also editions of *Vogue* in such Asian markets as Taiwan, Korea, and Japan.

Elle started in France after World War II and has also expanded into many other countries. Editorial staff and content are determined by the publication within a particular country and are not likely to be exactly the same throughout the world.

The three leading Spanish-language fashion magazines are *Cosmopolitan, Vanidades,* and *Harper's Bazaar.* International designers and top international fashion models are featured in these publications, emphasizing the topics Latin American women are interested in—particularly fashion, beauty, the arts, men, careers, family, and celebrities. The ads from international companies, including Lancôme, Chanel, and Estée Lauder, are similar to U.S. versions. All three publications are divisions of *Editorial Televisa,* the largest publisher of Spanish-language magazines in the world and leader in Latin America. Growth potential for the Hispanic market has spurred the growth of these publications.

Italian Vogue, Marie Claire, and *Elle* are considered to be the big three fashion magazines in Italy. In addition to these monthly fashion glossies, there are countless other weekly and monthly publications in Italy. The launch of *Io Donna* and *D Donna della Repubblica,* fashion magazines distributed once a week with daily newspapers, sparked major changes in the weekly fashion publications in Italy. A fresh and more dynamic approach to fashion presentation led to updates in the more traditional *Grazia, Anna,* and *Arnica.* Updated versions of the weeklies are easy to read and provide editorial content on how to wear the latest trendy as well as practical fashions.

In the 1990s French fashion publications struggled, and many of the top magazines, including French *Glamour, Maison & Jardin,* and *Vogue Hommes,* closed. Attracting advertisers who had shifted their dollars into other media such as outdoor advertising was difficult for French magazines. To combat the problem, *Jalouse, DS,* and *Ezmina* were launched, priced much less than French *Vogue,* the most expensive fashion magazine in France. Editorial content mixes social issues with fashion, travel, and beauty articles.

FIGURE 9.10 Rate card for consumer magazine *Jane*.

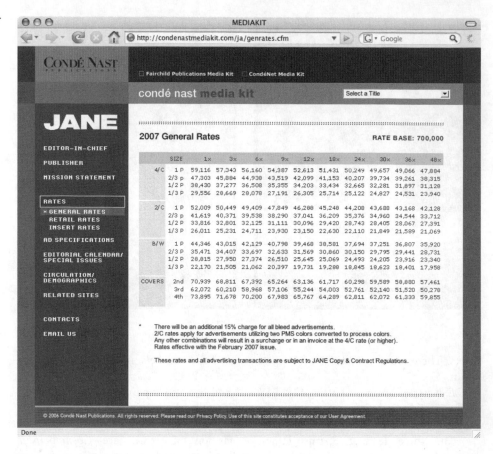

Fashion magazines are available almost anywhere in the world. Most of the top international publications have jumped into markets beyond those listed above, including Russia, Japan, Brazil, and other countries.

Magazine Media Rates

Magazines provide potential advertisers with advertising rate cards (Fig. 9.10) providing information about the cost of black-and-white or color ads. Discounts may be given if an advertiser purchases ads in continuous issues. Certain positions in the magazine command higher price. The preferred position for advertising includes the back cover, inside the back cover, and inside the front cover. Placement of advertising at various locations within the magazine can have a strong impact on the consumer's recall of the advertisement (Fig. 9.11). Strong recall position implies preferred position and associated higher costs. Based on a control advertisement, full page, four color ranked at 100 on a scale of 1 to 100, 100 equating full recall; multipage units had the highest recall, followed by the inside front cover (Magazine Publishers of America, 2006a).

Specialized features also add to the cost of magazine advertising. Specialized features include bleed pages, cover positions, insert, gatefolds, and special sizes.

Bleed pages are a technical feature that allows the dark or colored background to extend to the edge of the page. It is said to *bleed* off the page. Although many magazines

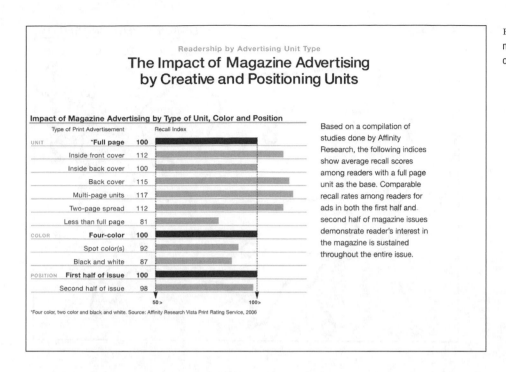

The Impact of Magazine Advertising by Creative and Positioning Units

Readership by Advertising Unit Type

Impact of Magazine Advertising by Type of Unit, Color and Position

Type of Print Advertisement		Recall Index
UNIT	*Full page	100
	Inside front cover	112
	Inside back cover	100
	Back cover	115
	Multi-page units	117
	Two-page spread	112
	Less than full page	81
COLOR	Four-color	100
	Spot color(s)	92
	Black and white	87
POSITION	First half of issue	100
	Second half of issue	98

50 >   100 >

*Four color, two color and black and white. Source: Affinity Research Vista Print Rating Service, 2006

Based on a compilation of studies done by Affinity Research, the following indices show average recall scores among readers with a full page unit as the base. Comparable recall rates among readers for ads in both the first half and second half of magazine issues demonstrate reader's interest in the magazine is sustained throughout the entire issue.

FIGURE 9.11 Impact of magazine advertising by type of unit, color, and position.

offer this option, it costs the advertiser 10 to 15 percent more to print these types of pages. Bleeds offer greater flexibility for advertising expression, with a slightly larger printing area, and a more dramatic effect.

Cover position offers a more desirable position for an advertising message. Publishers are willing to sell the first page inside the magazine (second cover), the inside back cover (third cover), and the back cover (fourth cover) for a premium. The highest price is for the back cover, considered to be a prime location for advertising.

Rather than buying a standard advertising page, an advertiser may purchase an **insert**, which is an ad printed on high-quality paper stock. This type of ad adds weight and drama to the message. The advertiser has an insert printed separately and sent to the magazine for insertion at a special price. Another option is a multiple-page insert, devoted to one brand or manufacturer. Despite high costs, these multiple-page inserts offer a particularly strong focus for the advertiser.

A **gatefold** is a special kind of insert, created by extra-long paper. The sides are folded into the center to match the size of the other pages. When the reader opens the magazine, the folded page swings out like a gate to present an oversize ad. Gatefolds are dramatic methods of magazine advertising that are sold at a substantial premium. Not all magazines provide gatefolds.

Advantages of Magazine Advertising

Magazines offer advertisers a number of strengths and benefits. These advantages include:

- **Selective audience.** Magazines provide detailed analysis of the readership of its audience to potential advertisers. Demographic as well as lifestyle information is available in addition to statistics on the size of the magazine's circulation. The advertiser can

FIGURE 9.12 Split-run regions for *Glamour* magazine.

know the percentage sold to subscribers versus over-the-counter sales, which will indicate the regularity of the audience.

- **Geographical editions.** Magazines have traditionally reached a broad market with general-interest publications. As magazines have focused toward more specific topics and target audiences, they have started to narrow even more to meet the regional demands for readers and advertisers. **Split-run advertising** allows an advertiser to elect to advertise in one or more geographical editions depending upon the advertiser's needs. Small premiums may be charged for regional advertising, but advertisers feel that it is worthwhile to increase the efficiency of reaching the target audience. Figure 9.12 shows the geographical split-run regions for *Glamour*.

- **High-quality reproduction.** In comparison to newspapers, magazines use higher-quality stock and reproduction techniques. Magazine printing technology can provide more true-to-life illustrative reproduction.

- **Long life and pass-along audience.** Magazine reproduction quality is so good that many readers may wish to keep magazines for a long period of time. The life of a magazine may last several months to several years. In addition to the individual that purchased the copy, research indicates that three to four other adults will read the publication. Each reader takes more than three days to read a magazine, spending 60 to 90 minutes. This long life and multiple readership provide more opportunities for the reader to view advertisements.

- **Controlled circulation and receptivity in some business magazines.** The audiences for trade and business publications purchase these magazines because they want to keep up-to-date with current trends within the industry. Editorial content has a high degree of credibility. Advertisers benefit from this attitude, making their advertisements have more perceived believability.

Disadvantages of Magazine Advertising

Despite their many strengths, magazines also have several limitations. These disadvantages are as follows:

- **Inability to show products true-to-life.** As with all print advertising, magazine advertising is limited to a two-dimensional image. Motion and sound cannot help the audience interpret the product or service. Improved product sampling techniques have helped cosmetic advertisers with this problem by providing fragrance tester strips and eye shadow samples. Other products have not been able to overcome this limitation.
- **Expensive**. Full-color advertising in national magazines is expensive, as indicated by rate cards.
- **Long lead time.** In comparison to newspapers, magazines have a substantial lead time. The lead time varies with the publication schedule. Weekly magazines have shorter lead times than monthly publications.
- **Editorial and advertising conflicts.** Magazine editors have been criticized for writing articles featuring producers, designers, or retailers who are heavy advertisers in the magazine. Thus, the selection for editorial credit and articles can be perceived as biased toward firms that buy advertising on a regular basis.

─────○ CREATIVE DEVELOPMENT FOR PRINT MEDIA

Print advertisements are prepared for publication in newspapers, magazines, and direct marketing materials such as catalogs, billing inserts, and the like. Advertisements consist of three elements: copy, art, and space. Every print ad starts with space, the blank canvas on which the verbal component is created by copy, and the visual component is built through artwork (Fig. 9.13). The shape of the space is determined by the size of the pages of newspapers and magazines.

One of the first questions to be answered in the development of a print ad is: What are the dimensions of the ad? The amount of space an advertiser purchases from a publisher is an important consideration. How big is the space? Where will it be located on the page or within the publication? How will it be noticed?

The space of an advertisement that is not occupied with artwork or copy is referred to as **white space**. These *unused* areas of the ad are created by the placement of the copy and artistic components. Such variations can be used to stimulate eye movement, attract attention to the copy, and provide distinctiveness in the style of the ad. Next, we look at the various components of copy and art that contribute to the finished print ad.

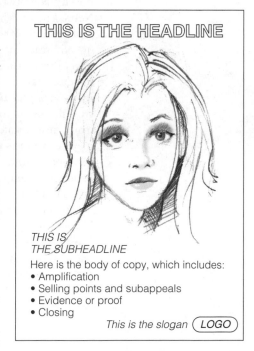

THIS IS THE HEADLINE

THIS IS THE SUBHEADLINE
Here is the body of copy, which includes:
- Amplification
- Selling points and subappeals
- Evidence or proof
- Closing

This is the slogan (LOGO)

FIGURE 9.13 Components of a print advertisement.

Copy

The verbal component of a print advertisement is called the **copy.** Copy consists of all words used to articulate the advertiser's message. In print advertising this is all of the reading material in the ad, consisting of the headline, subheadlines, body copy, and advertiser's slogan. Each of these segments contributes to clarifying what the advertiser wants the customer to know.

Headline

In print ads, the **headline** is the boldest statement. The headline is written taking into consideration what would have to be said if only one or two lines of space were available for the message. The copywriter puts forth the main theme in a few words.

Headlines should be written to attract attention and work with the visual elements to generate consumer interest. Many copywriters feel the most effective headlines emphasize the primary selling point or main appeal of the merchandise, giving the consumer a reason to respond to the ad. It is also common to include the name of the brand, manufacturer, or retailer in the headline.

Headline information can be used for several purposes. Here are seven of the most common types of headlines.

- **Advice.** This headline offers advice to the consumer, for example: *You owe it to yourself to try Nail Strength.* It is normally followed by a subheadline that offers some type of claim or promise, such as: *You will have stronger, prettier nails in just 2 weeks.* A properly developed advice headline appeals to self-interest or self-improvement, helping the consumer to solve a problem or improve health.
- **Command.** The command headline uses the hard-sell approach. The consumer is told to act before the offer is over, as in: *Use this coupon on November 25th or 26th to save 15% off the regular price.*
- **Curiosity.** The curiosity headline is considered to be the most provocative approach, attempting to arouse interest in the unusual. Frequently it is presented in the form of a question. *Where do you want to go today?* has been the stimulant for Microsoft Internet Explorer. The audience members can decide for themselves just what Internet categories interest them. The risk in a curiosity headline is that it is often used strictly for novelty. Novelty without meaning is useless as an advertising tool.
- **News.** The news headline is the most straightforward technique, playing a role similar to a headline for a news story. The news headline should be direct and timely, frequently featuring a brand name. For example, *97% of Prizm Owners Would Recommend Prizm to a Friend.*
- **Product claim.** The product claim headline is similar to the advice headline, as in: *It works with your skin, not just on it.* Although many product claim headlines are successful, this approach has been weakened by advertisements that make unrealistic or irresponsible statements. Unrealistic statements for weight-loss products have made many consumers wary. If this approach is taken, the advertiser should take care to supply supporting documentation in the body copy.
- **Product or company name.** The name of the brand may be so significant that it is used as the headline for the advertisement. This approach may be effective when the product is so timely that merely mentioning it will be sufficient to arouse interest. *Lord & Taylor: The Signature of American Style* is an example.
- **Prospect selection.** Products that have a specific target audience may use the prospect selection headline, in which the target customer is mentioned. Because very few products are of interest to everyone, this headline helps to direct the ad to consumers who are interested in or need the product. A headline that starts, *For women with sensitive skin . . .* or *Parents with toddlers . . .* attracts those audience members fitting into specific categories.

Subheadline

Subheadlines are secondary statements that are used when the primary headline needs further clarification or there is a secondary appeal or selling point. Although subheadlines

Copywriter Background Information Checklist

☐ **Target audience:** Who is the target customer? An accurate demographic and psychographic profile of the customer should be available.

☐ **Positioning of the product or service**: What are the key appeals or selling points of the product or service in terms of quality, value, price, and so forth? What is the target customer's point of view of these factors?

☐ **Position of the competition:** What are the selling points of the competition and how can the copywriter point out differences?

☐ **Objectives:** What are the advertising objectives and creative strategy? Is this a single ad or will it be a part of a series? Is the emphasis on product or image? Is it part of a campaign? Are the goals long or short term?

☐ **Copy platform:** What is the basic foundation of the creative strategy? The copy platform should include a discussion of the appeals and approaches in order to develop catchphrases or ideas to be included in the advertising.

☐ **Media style:** Which medium will be used? What is the editorial style of the publication or programming? This enables the copywriter to tailor the message to the medium being used. The medium's editorial content or programming style sets the tone for the copy.

☐ **Response desired:** What is the reader or viewer expected to do? The feelings and preferences of the consumers should be taken into consideration as the copy is developed.

are not always used, they can be helpful in providing backup to the main headline. Product claim, advice, or curiosity headlines might need a follow-up. For example, the curiosity headline *How do you top a luscious cheesecake yogurt?* is followed by the subheadline: *Discover all the ways Dannon tops yogurt.* The subheadline is the connection between the headline and artwork in this ad.

Body Copy

Body copy is additional copy created to support and reinforce the headline. By attempting to stimulate desire in a product or response to ideas, body copy adds selling points, offers evidence or proof of claims, provides subappeals to the main appeal, or asks the consumer to take action.

Copywriters are increasingly faced with knowledgeable consumers who demand more factual information. Information that will assist the copywriter in preparing the written portion of the ad is found in Figure 9.14. Statistical documentation and research that supports the claims featured in the headlines are ways copywriters can include hard information on the product and its benefits throughout the message.

It may be helpful to classify the different approaches that can be used in developing body copy.

- **Direct-selling news copy.** This method presents the message in a straightforward, factual manner. Using the newspaper story as a guideline, news copy is written as an article with informative content. Details about new products are frequently presented in this manner.
- **Implied suggestion.** In contrast to the direct-selling news copy approach, implied suggestion provides an opportunity for the reader to draw his or her own conclusions from the points presented. The copywriter tries to make the details so obvious that the reader will draw a favorable conclusion about the product or service.

- **Narrative description.** A human experience with some type of problem and a solution involving the product or service is created by the copywriter of a narrative description. Hopefully, the reader will see a connection between his or her problem and the favorable use of the advertiser's product. A variation of narrative description is the story-form, in which human experience using the product is also told in a straightforward description. This may involve an analogy between the story and the product benefits.
- **Monologue and dialogue.** The presentation by an individual about the benefits of merchandise or services from a personal point of view is a monologue. If the story is told by two or more people it is a dialogue. This format is often presented as a testimonial message. A testimonial suggests the reader can emulate or imitate the person giving the statement. By following the exemplary behavior of the authority, the reader can achieve the same benefits or results.
- **Humor.** Product value can be enhanced by utilizing a humorous situation. Although some critics believe that humor does not sell, humor has been used to successfully entertain and provide information about products and services. A television commercial, such as the one in which men shopping with their wives are sucked into the display window of a Radio Shack store, may cause consumers to remember the product as a result of the humorous scenario.
- **Comic strip or continuity**. Fictional or cartoon characters have gained popularity as product or service spokespersons. Snoopy has become a spokesperson for financial services, while Bugs Bunny and Daffy Duck have been used in VISA commercials.

Slogan

Slogans are repeated selling points or appeals that are primarily associated with the product, brand, or company. Slogans are words creatively combined to embody the company or product image. Generally slogans are short and to the point and feature the name of the company or brand. Through repetition, a slogan becomes familiar, provoking prompt consumer recall of the advertiser's message.

Slogans may be developed for specific products or institutions. Successful slogans may remain popular for many years. The slogan *Macy's Way to Shop* is an example of a product slogan that has been popular for a long time. Slogans may be so powerful that they become part of popular culture. *Just Do It* has become a slogan for more than just the Nike corporation.

Legal protection for slogans was awarded under the Lanham Act of 1947. If a business registers its slogan and certain additional conditions are met, legal protection is guaranteed.

Art and Design

Advertising depends heavily upon the use of visual arts to produce aesthetically pleasing and creative advertisements. Design elements consist of the core components of design—color, shape, texture, and line—and design principles are standards for visually organizing all design elements into a unified composition. The design principles are balance, contrast, emphasis, proportion, rhythm, and harmony.

In order to create aesthetically pleasing advertisements, visual displays, or other promotional materials, a basic understanding of artistic components is necessary. These components are known as the principles and elements of design. The term **art** refers to a system of skills, used in a creative manner, to make things of beauty. The fashion industry heavily depends upon the use of visual arts, including design elements and principles, to produce aesthetically pleasing and creative visuals. These elements and principles apply to clothing, accessories, and home fashions as well as advertising and other promotion mix elements from sales promotion and direct marketing to visual merchandising. Knowledge and the ability to apply the design elements and principles of design are necessary to coordinate all components of a line presentation or a successful advertisement.

Design Elements

Design elements consist of the core components of design: color, shape, texture, and line. These elements are necessary for the clothing design or the promotion element to come alive and spark the interest of the customer. Color, shape, texture, and line are significant visual building blocks.

Color. **Color** is the property of reflecting light of a visible wavelength resulting in a visible color spectrum. Color is the first design element a viewer of an advertisement, product, or display will notice. For many customers, color is a more significant factor in attracting their attention than any other design component. Individuals working with color must have a basic understanding of terminology. Hue, value, and intensity are terms commonly used to describe color.

The names of colors visible to the human eye are known as **hues.** On the spectrum these colors are positioned according to the wavelength of their light rays: red, orange, yellow, green, blue, and violet. The rays of red have the longest wavelength, those of violet the shortest. **Value** refers to the lightness or darkness of a color. White added to a hue to achieve a light variation of that hue is called a **tint.** The addition of gray to a hue creates a **tone.** The addition of black to a hue creates a **shade.** Pink is an example of a tint of red, while burgundy is a shade of red. **Intensity** is the purity, brightness, or saturation of a color, ranging from bright to dull.

Hues are often presented visually on a **color wheel,** a chart that organizes color relationships according to hue, value, and intensity of color. There are a variety of color wheels in existence, but the traditional one used in the fashion industry is the pigment wheel (Fig. 9.15). Colors placed on the traditional color wheel consist of primary, secondary, and tertiary colors.

The hues of red, yellow, and blue are known as the **primary colors.** Under this system, two primary colors are combined to form **secondary colors.** For example, red and yellow are combined to make orange. Thus, the secondary colors include orange, green, and violet. Combining a primary and secondary color creates a **tertiary color.** For example, red and orange combine to make red-orange and so forth. These hues with the addition of black and white provide designers with limitless color selections. **Complementary colors** are defined as colors positioned on opposite sides of the color wheel. Orange and blue are complements.

Color selection often involves other considerations beyond basic color knowledge. The emotional response to color may influence mood or feelings. Although a color cannot feel hot or cold, it can create feelings of warmth or coolness. **Warm colors** (red, orange, or yellow) project sensations of warmth. Blue, green, and violet are the **cool colors** projecting calm or cool moods.

Much research has been done on the psychology of color. The fashion designer or advertiser should take into consideration any positive and negative connotations regarding color. In some cultures, black is a color associated with sophistication, whereas in

FIGURE 9.15 Color wheel.

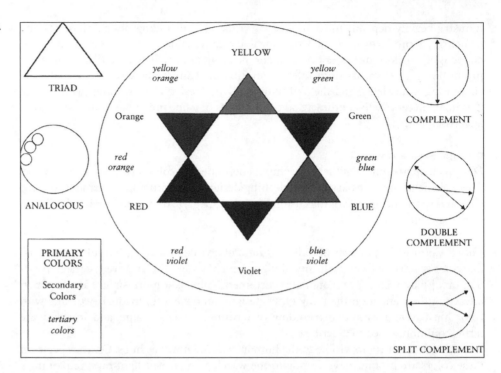

others it has connotations of mystery and death. On one hand, black can be considered the height of fashionable elegance, but it can also be extremely dark and depressing, depending upon the viewer's mood. Some colors can be used to make the viewer upbeat, full of good feelings, and in a mood to buy. Other colors will make the viewer aloof, detached, and unresponsive.

Color images also differ between countries and cultures. Two different advertisers used green hats to promote products in Hong Kong; one firm was advertising beer while the other promoted cleaning supplies. Asian consumers avoided purchasing both products. What the foreign advertisers failed to understand was that a green hat symbolized a fool in China. These types of color associations make it difficult if not impossible to reach an individual consumer.

Shape. **Shape** refers to the physical form of the end product. Shape takes on many aspects, from the silhouette of the garment or product to the size and shape of a print advertisement or direct mail piece. The advertisement may be two-dimensional or three-dimensional. A newspaper or magazine advertisement is presented in a flat two-dimensional format. Three-dimensional shapes have the appearance of depth and thickness. Pop-up advertisements, fashion shows, special events, and visual merchandise presentations are examples of promotion using a three-dimensional format.

Texture. **Texture** describes the uniformity or variation of the surface of an object. A smooth and shiny surface will reflect light and appear lighter. A rough, napped, or nubby texture absorbs light and will appear darker. Texture can be actual—the surface we are able to touch—or implied, something we see as visual design representation in an advertisement. In a manner similar to color, texture provides psychologically suggestive symbols to the viewer. Smooth silks and satins suggest femininity and sensuousness. Velvet is a napped fabric hinting at an elegant and sophisticated mood. Corduroy, another napped texture, sets a mood for a more outdoorsy, rugged, and casual tone.

Line. **Line** directs the eye through the garment or advertisement. Lines can be vertical, horizontal, diagonal, or curved. Used effectively, lines can pull the viewer through the entire presentation. Lines can also set a mood and create an atmosphere. Vertical lines add height and stability. Straight lines are considered to be masculine, sending the message of strength and dignity to the viewer. Men's fashions and women's classic apparel are suited to this quality.

Low and wide lines are used to create a tranquil mood through the use of horizontal lines. Objects in an advertisement dominated by horizontal lines appear wider, with an easy or restful feeling. Loungewear and sleepwear are perfectly set in the horizontal mode.

Movement and action are suggested by the use of diagonal lines. The merchandise featured in diagonal formats should be as expressive and dynamic as the background. Children's active apparel, sportswear and activewear are commonly portrayed in this spirited format.

The arc, circle, and sphere are examples of curved lines. This type of line represents grace, softness, and femininity. Curved lines can break up and ease the tension produced by too many straight lines. Curved lines serve as an ideal support for feminine apparel.

Design Principles

The **design principles** are standards for visually organizing all design elements into a unified composition. This organization of the different elements will achieve an integrated, tasteful end product. The design principles considered here are balance, contrast, emphasis, proportion, rhythm, and harmony.

Balance. The sense of equilibrium achieved through the distribution of visual weight in a design is **balance.** When a garment or an ad is balanced, it has provided a feeling of stability. In a classic definition, balance occurs when the parts of the design have equal weight. This is measured by placing an imaginary line through the middle of the design. Balance results when both sides of the design have equal visual weight. Two types of balance, symmetrical and asymmetrical, are commonly used in advertisements and merchandise displays.

Symmetrical balance is also called **formal balance.** In this type of balance, identical articles or similar size objects are placed on either side of an imaginary line in the center of the design space. In this case physical weight is similar to visual weight in producing a sense of equilibrium. Although the products may not be exactly the same, the visual image appears equal and provides a mirror image from one side to another. Formal balance is commonly used for luxury and prestige products.

In **asymmetrical** or **informal balance,** the two sides of the design appear of equal weight, although they are not replicas of each other. Visual balance is achieved using dissimilar items. For example, a photograph of a model is placed on one side of the space, balanced with copy and the store's logo on the other side. Although the right and left sides are no longer mirror images, the visual weights are equal.

Informal balance is considered to be much more interesting than formal balance, because it is more dynamic and active. A sense of action is created in this type of balance. Informal balance is more stimulating. It can be used by a wide assortment of product categories to urge the consumer to make a purchase decision more rapidly.

Contrast. Objects with differences are placed in the same presentation to point out their dissimilarity. This is the design principle known as **contrast**. A difference in texture, color, line, or shape is a way of drawing attention to the object featured. For example, a diamond ring with a smooth and highly reflective surface is set apart from the absorbing background of black velvet. A bright pink suit is the highlight when placed with a series of models wearing gray flannel. Another example is the reverse ad, using white letters against a dark background. This difference in color or texture will heighten the item being featured.

Emphasis.   The principle of visual organization where certain features of a composition assume more importance than others is **emphasis**. In garment design, advertising, and visual merchandise presentation, emphasis is the point where the eye is first drawn into the design. From this initial contact, or focal point, the eye will move through and read the exhibit. The focal point may be created by many means. Size is a noticeable method of creating emphasis, because the eye is attracted to the largest item in a design. Another common method is through the use of contrast, an interruption to the general feeling of a design, such as a color or texture that stands out from the rest of the presentation.

The placement of the focal point is an important consideration. This should be either in the optical center or in the upper left corner of the design space as it is viewed from the front. Optical center is halfway from the left and right, but slightly above the lower half. This enables the viewer to scan all sides of the advertisement. The upper left corner is the location where English-speaking readers start a page. Readers skim the advertisement like the page of a book. The upper right corner can also be used as the point of emphasis, but this is a slightly less comfortable way to read an advertisement.

Proportion.   The principle of visual organization known as **proportion** refers to the ratio of one feature of the design to any other feature. In an advertisement, this involves the relative size relationship of the various elements of artwork and copy to the total space, thus it is the agreement of physical elements to white space.

Rhythm.   **Rhythm** is the design principle that leads the viewer's eye through the design via recurrent motifs. Also known as movement, rhythm should lead the eye from the focal point to the secondary objects and the remainder of the design through repetition of elements that are the same or only slightly modified. This principle of design makes the viewer read the material in the sequence desired.

Harmony.   **Harmony** is also referred to as **unity** and is the chief goal of fashion design or visual composition. It relates the various elements of the design so they look as though they belong together in a coordinated and pleasant visual effect. Balance, proportion, emphasis, contrast, and rhythm combine with the design elements to produce a commercial success.

Fashion designers, graphic designers, artists, visual merchandisers, and many other professionals involved in the creative process use the principles and elements of design to create aesthetically pleasing designs. In addition to print and broadcast advertisements, designers create merchandise displays, point-of-purchase presentations, stage sets for fashion shows, and floor plans for special events and many other activities using these principles and elements of design.

Organization of the different design elements and principles is used to achieve an integrated, tasteful end product. Effective visual messages combine creative strategy with design and copy to complete the process. Several ideas are worked up into preliminary ideas and tested in the first steps of advertisement development. As ideas become solidified into a prospective ad, final presentations are shown to the client for approval. Next, we look at the visual components of the print ad.

FIGURE 9.16 Thumbnails and a rough.

Layout

Layout is the arrangement of the physical elements of art, copy, and white space within the boundaries of the print advertisement. The layout becomes the blueprint where the elements of art and copy are placed. Layout assists art and copy to complete the selling job more effectively. Planning steps in developing the layout include the design of thumbnail sketches, roughs, and the comprehensive.

Thumbnails are preliminary unpolished designs produced in a small size so several versions can be tried. A variety of alternatives are evaluated and a few of the designs are chosen to be worked up. **Roughs** are workups of the chosen thumbnails, rendered in actual size to represent where the art, headlines, copy, and logo will be placed. Figure 9.16 shows a series of thumbnails and a rough.

After the rough is approved, the layout artist does a comprehensive layout. The comprehensive will give a realistic impression of the final ad. Testing, evaluation, and revision may be done throughout this entire process.

Typography

Typography involves the selection and setting of a **typeface,** the style of type, to be used in headlines, subheadlines, body copy, or logos. One of the most important considerations in selecting a typeface is its readability. The type style, boldness, size, length of line, and spacing between letters, words, and paragraphs are all factors that need to be taken into consideration as the typeface is selected.

There are five common groups of type styles used today. These include Roman, Gothic, square serif, cursive or script, or ornamental. Roman is a popular type style with good readability, distinguished by serifs, extra small lines or tails. Serifs finish the ends of the bold strokes of letters in various designs or sizes. Gothic, a sans serif style, is also referred to as block or contemporary. The style is characterized by bold and clean strokes without serifs. Although it is not as readable as roman, Gothic is the second most popular style due to its modern appearance. Square serif styles are a combination of sans serif and Roman styles, resulting in even letter strokes. Cursive or script type most closely resembles handwriting. Letters connect and offer a more feminine feeling, but these styles are not as readable as other typefaces. Cursive type can be successfully used in headlines, announcements, or invitations. Ornamental type covers a wide variety of novel styles. It can offer special effects, but generally is not very easy to read.

In addition to considering the typeface style, the designer also needs to consider which elements within a type family will best assist in the overall design. Each typeface has variations in proportion, weight, or slant of the letters. The type may be light, medium, bold, extra bold, condensed, extended, or italic. These variations enable the typographer to provide contrast or emphasis without changing the type family. A **font** refers to a complete range of capitals, small capitals, lowercase letters, numerals, and punctuation marks for a particular typeface and size.

Type size is measured in points. There are 72 points to an inch, so one point is equal to $\frac{1}{72}$ of an inch. Typically text material is printed as a measurement of 8 or 10 points. Larger sizes are necessary for headlines, subheadlines, and logos. Figure 9.17 shows different typefaces and styles.

Logo

Logos are graphic symbols or distinctive typefaces that represent a company's name, mark, or emblem. Graphic symbols may be incorporated with the typographic signature to complete the logo. Bloomingdales, Macy's, and Dillard's are department stores that use specialized lettering as their signature in ads. Lord and Taylor includes a single red rose with its distinctive script signature. A graphic symbol such as the NBC peacock or the CBS eye is shown often enough for the viewer to associate the visual image with a particular company. The swoosh created by Nike is so memorable that an ad with the symbol does not even require a headline. Logos are first associated with print media. But logos can also be developed or adapted for electronic media. In the broadcast field, a logo can be created by a musical song or jingle, and visual images can be animated.

Photography

Photography is a process for visual reproduction of a pictorial image. The process was originally created by reproducing images on a light-sensitive material. Modern technology has taken that process from one requiring film to one that goes directly to a digital image. Photographs present the most realistic image of products but have limitations in the reproduction process.

Photographs cannot be reproduced in newspapers without using a halftone process. The halftone process converts photographic images using screens, which break up continuous tones into dots. Solid areas are dots in close proximity, while lighter shades are made up of dots that are farther apart. Blacks are not truly black, nor are whites absolutely white. The human eye sees the dots as black, white, and shades of gray. That is why a photograph reproduced in a newspaper is not as sharp and clear as the original.

FIGURE 9.17 Typefaces and styles in several sizes.

There are several advantages of using photography in print ads. First, photography shows the actual product, not an artistic interpretation. This results in the most realistic representation of the merchandise. Photography can also be used to create dramatic moods and provide true-to-life impact. Photography is a mainstay in advertising apparel and fashion-related goods, especially popular in magazines and other publications where the reproduction justifies the expense associated with photography.

The disadvantages of photography prevent some advertisers from selecting this illustration form. The cost of a photo shoot includes many people above and beyond the photographer and his or her photo assistants. Models must be hired, and photo stylists provide behind-the-scenes production assistance. Stylists generally work as freelancers, helping with everything from making location arrangements and furnishing props to hiring models and hair and makeup personnel. In addition to the costs, photographs do not reproduce in newspapers as well as line drawings. The halftone process limits the details that can be seen in newspaper reproductions.

Illustration

Artistic illustrations for print ads can be created by line drawings or halftone illustrations. Illustrations are visual matter used to clarify or decorate the text in an ad. **Line drawings** are made using lines to represent the pictorial image, whereas **halftone illustrations** use shades or tones created by watercolor, chalk, pencil, markers, or other art medium to illustrate the image with tonal qualities.

Line drawings reproduce better than halftone illustrations or photography in

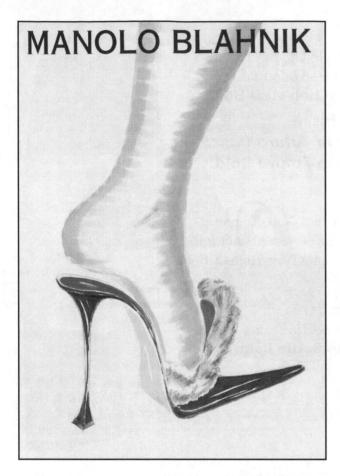

MANOLO BLAHNIK

FIGURE 9.18 Pictorial illustration.

newspapers. Greater detail is possible with line drawings since the halftone screens are not used. Because halftone illustrations and photography can be used to create dramatic moods and image development, they are more likely to be used in magazine ads. Although each of the methods of presenting images is used in various media, the strengths and weaknesses of each illustration style direct their use.

Illustrations can also be categorized as either pictorial or symbolic. Pictorial illustrations are descriptive, portraying merchandise in a true-to-life manner (Fig. 9.18). Customers can see how a product looks and may be used. A pictorial illustration is generally accompanied by direct and clear copy, persuading customers to make up their minds to purchase merchandise by seeing and reading the advertisement. Pictorial advertisements are best used for merchandise with immediate sales impact.

In contrast, symbolic illustration (Fig. 9.19) is more decorative and fundamentally impressionistic. It seeks to create an atmosphere, mood, or image. As such, symbolic illustration suggests the nature of the merchandise but leaves the details to the viewer's imagination.

Paste-up

After all the decisions regarding layout, copy, use of logos, and style of artwork are made and the roughs have been tested, the ad is put into final format. This format is called a **paste-up** or **mechanical.** The paste-up shows the format of the art, copy, and logo in its presentation layout. In addition, the copy has been converted into the desired typeface. The final paste-up should be **camera ready,** meaning that it is ready to go to the printer. No additional changes are made to camera-ready paste-ups.

How the artwork will be used determines what happens next. If the ad is a black-and-white ad in a newspaper, the camera-ready art may be taken to the newspaper office as a paste-up or sent as an electronic file from a computer. A variety of methods are used depending upon the technology used by the designer and publication site. Color printing can be delivered as a mechanical or electronic image.

──o VISUAL FORMATS FOR PRINT ADVERTISEMENTS

Art directors and graphic designers may be able to use visual formats that can be classified according to features or other techniques of presentation. The following list illustrates common visual formats that are used for print ads.

• **Single product.** This powerful presentation of the product is shown without background or setting. This simple visual form emphasizes the intrinsic characteristics that command attention. Distinctive items such as fine jewelry or designer apparel and similar products can attract attention without the use of a background that may detract from the product.

- **Product in a setting.** In order to give the target customer an idea of how the product can be used, the advertiser places the product in a background. This setting may imply using the product in a pleasant or satisfying environment. Sporting equipment or apparel, such as skis with outdoor clothing, is placed on models using the merchandise in a realistic winter scene.
- **Product in use.** This widely used visualization places the product in service by individuals representing the desired consumer. The reader is stimulated by identifying with the product user and identifies him- or herself as the recipient of its benefits.
- **Product benefits.** Positive results derived from product use are depicted. Hopefully, consumers will see themselves as the ones who will benefit from product use.
- **Need dramatization.** The potential customer may realize that he or she has a need for a product illustrated in a dramatic manner. Customers may not even be aware that they could benefit from the use of the product. Typically baking soda is used as an ingredient for food. Need dramatization gave potential consumers the idea of using baking soda as a refrigerator deodorizer.

FIGURE 9.19 Symbolic illustration.

- **Product use explanation.** By explaining how the product is used, consumers without knowledge of its use may be more likely to try it. If the consumer has used the product incorrectly in the past, getting poor results, proper explanation of use can help to overcome objections to trying it again. Furthermore, consumers may have a limited view of how the product should be used and the advertiser shows alternative methods of using it.
- **Product details.** A frequently used advertising theme centers on an improvement of some product detail. The detail may be enlarged or a cross-section profiled to call attention to that detail.
- **Dramatization of evidence.** In order to support claims made by the advertiser, effective illustrations can be created to support claims with supplementary evidence.
- **Comparison.** This technique shows a comparison between a competitor's brand and the advertiser's brand, or before and after pictures are compared to make clear *how* the product can improve appearance or performance.
- **Headline dramatization.** An illustration can effectively strengthen a headline by communicating what the headline states in words through a visual presentation.
- **Symbolism.** Advertisers can use a symbol to associate the product or service with some basic concept. Using a visual symbol such as an eagle represents strength and patriotism.

Every print advertisement starts as a blank space and is shaped into a creative message through artwork and copy. The artwork and copy in one print advertisement may be minimal, using few words and images, while a contrasting advertisement may be very busy with multiple images and detailed copy. Both creative messages are effective in attracting the attention of the consumer because the creators have balanced the visual and verbal components of the advertisement into meaningful communications.

summary

- Advertising media are the places where advertising messages are placed. These range from print to broadcast or electronic sources. Traditional advertising media include newspapers, magazines, radio, and television. Innovative technologies are providing alternative places to advertise.
- Newspapers have been one of the most significant print media used by retailers for advertising. With high readership and low costs, newspapers are ideal for product advertising.
- Magazines are another popular print medium, primarily used by fashion manufacturers and designers. Magazines offer a variety of formats suited to targeting specific markets.
- Print media use the copy platform as a guideline to design art and copy into an advertising layout.
- Copy, the verbal component of a print advertisement, consists of all of the words used to articulate the advertiser's message. In print advertising this is all of the reading material in the ad, consisting of the headline, subheadlines, body copy, and advertiser's slogan.
- The visual arts, including design elements, color, shape, texture, and line—and design principles—balance, contrast, emphasis, proportion, rhythm, and harmony—are used to produce aesthetically pleasing and creative advertisements.
- Advertising media are being modified due to influences from the changing roles of media planners and buyers, and to the challenges posed by emerging technologies.

key terms

art	gatefold	reach
asymmetrical balance	gross ratings points	rhythm
balance	halftone illustration	rough
bleed pages	harmony	scheduling
blinking/bunching	headline	secondary colors
broadsheet	hue	shade
bursting	informal balance	shape
camera ready	insert	share
classified advertisement	intensity	sliding
color	layout	slogan
color wheel	line	split-run advertising
complementary colors	line drawing	standard advertising unit (SAU)
continuity	logo	subheadline
contrast	mechanical	symmetrical balance
cool colors	media buyer	tabloid
copy	media cost	target rating points
cover position	media objectives	tertiary colors
coverage	media planner	texture
cumulative audience	media planning	thumbnail
design elements	media vehicle	tint
design principles	paste-up	tone
display advertisement	penetration	typeface
editorial content	photography	typography
emphasis	primary colors	unity
flighting	proportion	value
font	pulsing	warm colors
formal balance	rate card	white space
frequency	ratings	zone editions

QUESTIONS FOR DISCUSSION

1. Who is responsible for evaluating and selecting media outlets? Why is that job so important?
2. How should advertisers select appropriate media for their advertising message?
3. Newspaper advertising has been a significant media outlet for retail advertisers in the past. Is retail newspaper advertising still justified?
4. What are some of the future trends in advertising media anticipated at this time?
5. How important are the arts to creative advertising?

ADDITIONAL RESOURCES

Belch, G. E., & Belch, M. A. (2007). *Advertising and promotion* (7th ed.). New York: McGraw-Hill/Irwin.
Brannon, E. L. (2005). *Fashion forecasting* (2nd ed.). New York: Fairchild Publications.
Marsh, C., Guth, D. W., & Short, B. P. (2005). *Strategic writing.* Boston: Pearson Education.

ANNUAL PUBLICATIONS

100 Leading National Advertisers. (Published annually). *Advertising Age.* New York: Crain Communications, Inc.
Newspaper Association of America. (Published annually). *Daily and Sunday newspaper audience.* Vienna, VA: Author.
Magazine Publishers of America. (Published annually). *Magazine handbook: A comprehensive guide.* New York: Author.

REFERENCES

100 Leading National Advertisers. (2006). *Advertising Age.* New York: Crain Communications, Inc.
American Society of Magazine Editors. (2006a). *Editorial pages by subject.* Retrieved July 11, 2006, from http://www.magazine.org/editorial/editorial_trends_and_magazine_handbook/15538.cfm
American Society of Magazine Editors. (2006b). *Historical advertising/editorial ratios.* Retrieved July 11, 2006, from http://www.magazine.org/editorial/editorial_trends_and_magazine_handbook/15539.cfm
Cotton Incorporated. (2005). *Comparison shopping: Today's retail experience evolves over the last decade.* Retrieved July 9, 2006, from http://www.cottoninc.com/lsmarticles/?articleID=413&searchTerm=media
Fairchild Publications, Inc. (2006a). *Daily News Record 2006 general rates.* Retrieved July 11, 2006, from http://www.fairchildmediakit.com/dnr/genrates.cfm
Fairchild Publications, Inc. (2006b). *Jane 2006 general rates.* Retrieved July 11, 2006, from http://www.condenastmediakitxom/ja/genrates.cfm
Magazine Publishers of America. (2006a). *Magazine handbook: A comprehensive guide 2006/07.* Retrieved July 11, 2006, from http://www.magazine.org/content/Files/MPAHandbook06.pdf
Magazine Publishers of America. (2006b). *Number of magazines per category 1999–2005.* Retrieved July 11, 2006, from http://www.magazine.org/editorial/editorial_trends_and_magazine_handbook/1145.cfm
Magazine Publishers of America. (2006c). *Total average circulation for ABC magazines.* Retrieved July 11, 2006, from http://www.magazine.org/content/Files/AllcircABC05.xls
Newspaper Association of America. (2005). *Section readership.* Retrieved July 10, 2006, from http://www.naa.org/marketscope/readership2005/
Newspaper Association of America. (2006a). *Daily and Sunday newspaper audience.* Retrieved July 10, 2006, from http://www.naa.org/marketscope/DSN/index.html
Newspaper Association of America. (2006b). *Readership statistics.* Retrieved July 10, 2006, from http://www.naa.org/readershippages/research-and-readership/readership-statistics.aspx
Power of Persuasion. (2006, January 19). *Women's Wear Daily,* p. 12
Rothschild, M. L. (1987). *Marketing communications.* Lexington, MA: D.C. Heath

FIGURE 10.1 Nielsen students.

CHAPTER 10

Broadcast Media

For decades, Nielsen Media Research has affixed the same value to every college student watching television while away at school: zero. As a result, industry executives have complained for years that shows appealing to a younger audience have been underrated.

But, starting today, college students count.

"It's going to validate what advertisers have always assumed, which is that college students are watching our programming," said Jeff Lucas, a senior vice president at Comedy Central. Mr. Lucas said that the network's own research shows that *South Park*, *The Daily Show with Jon Stewart*, and *The Colbert Report* have a large college audience.

It's too early to know how much more advertisers will pay for shows with larger audiences because of the college ratings. Network executives, of course, said they expect to be paid for the higher ratings. If advertisers decide to spend more on shows that demonstrate high college viewership, TV networks may decide to dedicate more of their scheduled programming to college tastes.

The college ratings are the first of two major changes in the way viewing habits are rated. In May, Nielsen will start releasing figures on the number of people who actually watch commercials, separating them from viewers who walk away or switch channels when the ads come on. The potential impact of ad ratings on network revenue has not been calculated.

Source: Story, L. (2007, January 29). At last, television ratings go to college. The *New York Times* (Section C) p. 1.

After you have read this chapter, you should be able to:

Discuss the different television and radio formats.

Evaluate the strengths and weaknesses of each broadcast medium for advertising.

Explain how broadcast media are measured.

List the broadcast media measurement services.

Explain how broadcast commercials are produced.

Do COLLEGE STUDENTS WANT to watch Jon Stewart, Stephen Colbert, and their Comedy Central cohorts 24 hours a day? With viewers increasingly tuning out traditional advertisements, will consumers accept product placement in lieu of TV or radio commercials? Nielsen's ratings present as many challenges as they provide solutions for the promotion of goods and services through broadcast media.

The purpose of this chapter is to analyze broadcast media. First, we discuss television, from the different television formats and advertising categories to how television influences fashion trends and brand globalization. Advantages and disadvantages of using this medium are explored. In addition to television, radio offers opportunities for fashion advertisers. Radio formats, programs, and sponsorship are introduced prior to analyzing the advantages and disadvantages of using radio for advertising. Creative production of television and radio commercials concludes this chapter.

○ TELEVISION

Could you live without television? Television has a significant role in our everyday lives; it is the primary source of news, information, and entertainment for many people. **Television** is the broadcast medium in which sight is combined with sound and motion to produce the most realistic reproduction of life. It is this combination of visual images with sound that attracts and holds the attention of the viewer.

Television viewing has changed significantly in the past 50 years. Television sets were a new commodity to many households in the 1950s. Households of that era watched an average of 4.5 to 5 hours per day. This average has continued to increase each decade. In the 21st century, 24-hour programming on numerous network and cable channels has increased household television watching to over 8 hours per day (Television Bureau of Advertising, 2005a). Women watch more television than men, averaging just over 5 hours per day. Men watch approximately 4.5 per day, while children and teens watch the least television, slightly more than 3 hours per day (Television Bureau of Advertising, 2005b).

Television has several formats that must be considered when analyzing the medium as a potential resource of advertising. Television programming consists of networks, local stations, syndication, and cable. Table 6.2 in Chapter 6, shows the greatest amount of measured advertising (9.9 percent) was spent on network television, over 36.7 trillion (100 Leading National Advertisers, 2006). Together network, spot, syndicated, and cable television totaled in excess of $64 trillion, or 23.9 percent of the total domestic advertising expenditures.

Network Television

A network is formed when two or more television stations broadcast the same program, which originates from one source. Network television is an alliance between regional television stations, called **affiliates,** and one of the national television companies. A national television company normally provides entertainment, news, and sports programs of national interest. Although it is assumed that affiliates will broadcast all of the programs offered nationally, it is up to the affiliate to decide which network programs to show and what local programming should be offered.

For decades network television consisted of three major networks. These national networks, known by their initials, include NBC (National Broadcasting Company), ABC (American Broadcasting Company), and CBS (CBS officially changed to this designation from Columbia Broadcasting System in 1974). NBC, ABC, and CBS each own 15 regional stations and have approximately 150 affiliates.

Figure 10.2 shows the television reach of the top six broadcast affiliates. NBC, CBS, and ABC all have a reach of 75 percent or more. Fox Broadcasting Company is the fourth major network with a reach of nearly 70 percent (Media Information Center, 2005c). Fox uses a group of affiliated independent stations to broadcast programming. Figure 10.2 identifies two additional networks, WB and UPN. These two networks merged in 2006 to become one network. The network is a joint venture between Warner Bros. Entertainment and CBS, known as the CW network ("C" for CBS and "W" for Warner Bros.).

The CW has affiliates from both Warner Bros. Entertainment and CBS broadcasting programming. Both networks previously targeted women aged 18–34. Forming one network from two direct competitors has allowed for stronger offerings of higher-rated shows that command bigger ad rates and higher payments from former WB and UPN affiliates (Levin & Lieberman, 2006).

National advertisers may purchase time from any of the networks, enabling their message to be broadcast across the nation through local affiliates. Network advertising represents a mass medium since the commercial is shown simultaneously throughout the country. The affiliates, who pay a fee to the networks for their programs, receive a percentage, usually 12 to 25 percent, of the revenues paid to the network by national advertisers.

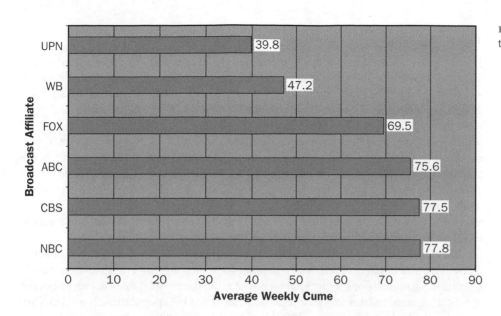

FIGURE 10.2 Broadcast television reach.

Television sponsorship is an arrangement whereby the advertiser takes full responsibility for the production of the program and provides the accompanying commercials. As a sponsor, the advertiser generally has input into the program content as well as the advertising that appears during the broadcast. In the early years of television, most programs were created for advertising sponsors. Examples of early sponsored television programs include *Bonanza*, sponsored by Chevrolet, and *Hallmark Hall of Fame*. Sponsorship has a powerful impact, but it is very expensive—too expensive for most advertisers today. Although sponsorship was widespread during TV's infancy, most shows are now produced by the network or by an independent production company.

Sponsorships represent less than 10 percent of network advertising (Wells, Burnett & Moriarty, 2006). The rest of network television advertising is sold as **participations**, in which advertisers pay for commercial time during one or more programs. This time is sold as 15-, 30-, or 60-second commercials.

Public Broadcasting Service (PBS) is the television network with the specific mission to present programs that educate and entertain, inform and inspire—free and accessible to everyone. Programs consist of documentary, art, news, public affairs, and children's presentations. Although many people consider public television to be "commercial free," a ruling by the Federal Communications Commission (FCC) in 1984 liberalized the guidelines (Wells, et al, 2006). PBS stations were allowed to reinterpret the distinction between underwriting and outright sponsorship. Current FCC guidelines allow ads to appear on public television only during the local 2.5-minute program breaks. Each station develops and maintains its own specifications for acceptability. While some PBS stations may choose to run commercials that have been broadcast on network or local programs, other stations will not run any ad that has been shown on commercial television. These stations run "value neutral" ads, featuring messages that include nonpromotional corporate and product logos and slogans. In other words, there is no attempt to "sell" through these "ads." Because public broadcasting reaches affluent, educated households, as well as minority low-end consumers, PBS is an attractive medium for advertisers.

Local Television

Local television stations serve a regional geographical area and may be affiliated with a national network or broadcast independently. If the station is affiliated with a national network, it will most likely run locally produced shows in addition to network shows. For example, WICU-TV is the local affiliate for NBC in Erie, Pennsylvania. Independent channels, such as KTVK-TV—Channel 3 in Phoenix—offer locally produced programs and syndicated shows; these are discussed in the next section of the chapter.

Advertising on local channels is sold as spot announcements. These local spots are sold for a specific amount of time, usually 10, 20, 30, or 60 seconds. Spots may be sold to national, regional, or local advertisers, although local buyers dominate local spot slots. Time for spot advertising is negotiated and purchased directly from local television stations. A station rep is an individual who acts as the sales representative for local stations, enabling national advertisers to buy local spot time.

Nielsen Media Research measures viewing audiences in 210 local markets known as **designated market areas (DMAs).** Measuring local viewing audiences can help advertisers make nationally or locally purchased spot advertisements. Table 10.1 identifies the top 10 designated market areas for television across the U.S. population. New York City is the largest DMA with over 7 million households, representing 6.7 percent of the U.S. population. Across the country, Los Angeles is the second largest television-viewing DMA with over 5.5 million television homes, representing 5 percent of the U.S. population (Nielsen Media Research, 2005a).

Nielsen Media Research measures and reports on television-viewing audiences for two ethnic groups—African-Americans and Hispanic-Americans. Both demographic groups are important to advertisers. The African-American television-viewing audience is the largest minority segment measured by Nielsen Media research. African-American households represent more than 13.2 million television households in the United States. This translates to 12 percent of the total U.S. television households and 13 percent of total persons in television households (Nielsen Media Research, 2005c).

The average African-American home is slightly younger than the total U.S. household; the African-American television household age is 30.2, compared to 37.2 for the total U.S. These television households have 6 percent more youth (represented as nonadults under age 18) as compared to total U.S. households. Additionally gender differences are evident. There are 30 percent more women than men in African-American households, and 7 percent fewer men in African-American television households compared to total U.S. households. These differences reflect different viewing habits in terms of networks watched, shows viewed, and dayparts viewed, among other differences (Nielsen Media Research, 2005c).

The top 10 designated market areas for African-American television households are shown in Table 10.2. New York City is still the largest DMA with over 1.2 million African-American households, representing 17 percent of the total population in that area. However, an advertiser who wants to attract the African-American population may consider Chicago, Washington, D.C., or Atlanta in addition to, or instead of, Los Angeles (Nielsen Media Research, 2005c).

Local area advertising also plays a role in directing television advertising to Hispanic-Americans. Hispanic-American television households represent approximately 10.9 million television households in the United States. Language usage is an important demographic consideration when advertising to Hispanic-American households. A substantial share of

TABLE 10.1 *Top 10 Designated Market Areas (DMA) for Television*

	Designated Market Area (DMA)	TV Homes[a]	% of U.S.
1	New York	7,375,530	6.7
2	Los Angeles	5,536,430	5.0
3	Chicago	3,430,790	3.1
4	Philadelphia	2,925,560	2.7
5	Boston (Manchester)	2,376,310	2.2
6	San Francisco-Oakland-San Jose	2,355,740	2.1
7	Dallas-Ft. Worth	2,336,140	2.1
8	Washington, D.C. (Hagerstown)	2,252,550	2.0
9	Atlanta	2,097,220	1.9
10	Houston	1,938,670	1.8

[a]Estimates used throughout the 2005–2006 television season, which started on September 24, 2005.

Adapted from: Nielsen Media Research. (2005). Top 10 designated market areas. Retrieved July 9, 2006, from http://www.nielsenmedia.com/DMAs.html

TABLE 10.2 *Top 10 Designated Market Areas (DMA) by African-American Population*

	Designated Market Area (DMA)	TV Homes[a]	African-American TV Homes	% of U.S.
1	New York	7,355,710	1,287,960	17.5%
2	Chicago	3,417,330	593,570	17.5%
3	Washington, D.C. (Hagerstown)	2,241,610	593,570	23.5%
4	Atlanta	2,059,450	521,650	25.3%
5	Philadelphia	2,919,410	510,240	17.5%
6	Los Angeles	5,431,140	482,390	8.9%
7	Detroit	1,943,930	391,020	20.1%
8	Houston	1,902,810	320,090	16.8%
9	Dallas-Ft.Worth	2,292,760	309,990	13.5%
10	Miami-Ft. Lauderdale	1,496,810	289,860	19.4%

[a]African-American Television Audience, ratings data based on October-November 2004.

Adapted from: Nielsen Media Research. (2005). TV audience special study: African-American television audience. Retrieved July 13, 2006 from http://www.nielsenmedia.com/E-letters/African-AmericanTVA-final.pdf

television viewing in Hispanic-American homes is of Spanish-language television (Nielsen Media Research, 2005b).

Table 10.3 shows the top 10 local area markets for Hispanic-Americans. Again, variations occur from the total U.S. population, after New York City is considered. Phoenix, Miami, Denver, and Sacramento all have a large percentage of households in which Spanish is the dominant language spoken and influences television viewing.

TABLE 10.3   *Top 10 Local Markets by Hispanic-American Population*

	Designated Market Area (DMA)	TV Homes[a]	% Hispanic	% Spanish Dominant[b]
1	New York	7,355,710	16.4%	51.5%
2	Los Angeles	5,431,140	31.6%	48.4%
3	Chicago	3,417,330	12.7%	46.1%
4	San Francisco	2,359,870	14.1%	41.4%
5	Dallas	2,292,760	17.0%	50.9%
6	Houston	1,902,810	23.9%	48.6%
7	Phoenix	1,596,950	18.4%	45.4%
8	Miami	1,496,610	40.3%	62.8%
9	Denver	1,401,760	13.9%	40.3%
10	Sacramento	1,315,030	16.8%	37.8%

[a]Estimates as on January 1, 2005

[b]Homes in which only Spanish or mostly Spanish is spoken, using all persons 2 + in the home.

Adapted from: Nielsen Media Research. (2005). Nielsen Media Research's Hispanic local markets. Retrieved July 12, 2006, from http://www.nielsenmedia.com/ethnicmeasure/hispanic-american/localmarkets.html

Syndication

Syndicated programs are shows that are sold and distributed to local television stations to fill open hours. Syndicated programs have boomed because of growth in the number of independent television stations and the prime time access rule, which forbids network of affiliates in the 50 major U.S. television markets from broadcasting more than three hours of prime time programming in any one four-hour slot. There are several categories of syndicated programs, including off-network, first-run, and barter syndication.

Off-network programs consist of reruns of network programs, old or current, that are brought by individual stations. FCC regulations require that at least 88 episodes of a network show must exist before it can be syndicated.

First-run syndication refers to shows that are produced specifically for the syndication market. Some shows that are dropped by the networks continue to create new episodes in syndication. These shows continue production in syndication because they have not met the 88-episode rule imposed by the FCC. Popular syndicated shows include talk shows, news, game shows, entertainment news, comedies, reality shows, or dramas. These shows are *sold* to local channels and may or may not be viewed on a national network affiliate.

Under the barter syndication system, both off-network and first-run syndicated programs are offered to local stations for free or at a reduced rate if the station gives the syndicator a portion of its commercial time instead of cash. The syndicator negotiates a price with the station by dealing with cash, barter, or a combination of the two. The cash deal is obvious; the syndicator grants the stations the rights to run the show for a specified period of time for a cash license fee. Syndicators are able to do this because some of the advertising is already presold to national advertisers. Typically half of the advertising is presold, allowing the local stations to sell the other half. Benefits are gained by national advertisers who are able to break into the local markets and by local stations that receive free programming and time to sell local spots.

Cable Television

Early cable television channels were developed to broadcast signals through wires rather than airwaves to geographically isolated regions. Programming for these pioneer channels frequently consisted of reruns of network programs. However, alternative programming with an emphasis on information and entertainment and targeting of specific markets has led to rapid growth of **cable television**. Cable television has evolved into a mass broadcast medium, offering programs for both niche and general markets. Of all households with television sets, 67.5 percent have cable television (Media Information Center, 2005a).

Cable subscribers pay a monthly fee for which they receive an average of 30 or more channels. The local cable system broadcasts local networks, such as CNN, ESPN, CNBC, or MTV and local cable channels. Subscribers may also select premium channels for additional fees. These channels include HBO, Showtime, and the Movie Channel.

Figure 10.3 shows the television reach of the top 12 cable networks. As compared with the network reach (Fig. 10.2), cable reach is much smaller. The top network, Turner Broadcast System, Incorporated (TBS), has a reach of just over 39 percent compared to network affiliates NBC and ABC, both with over 77 percent reach (Media Information Center, 2005c). The cable networks identified in Figure 10.3 indicate a wide variety of viewer preferences from nonsubscription-based movie channels to children's programming, to music, sports, and entertainment. Advertisers who seek a specific target market based on psychographic data may see cable television as a good medium to consider.

Cable channels such as CNN and CNBC also broadcast internationally. The impact of global brands is enhanced with television commercials that are simultaneously broadcast

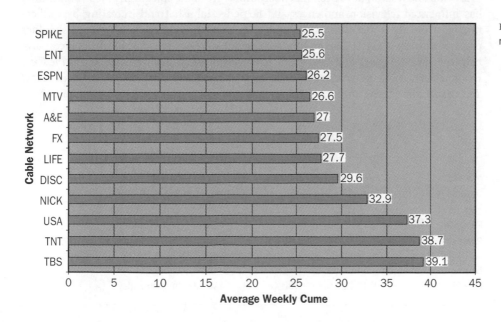

FIGURE 10.3 Cable television reach.

to several countries. This is particularly significant in the European markets, since television commercials for brands ranging from Nike to Johnson's Baby Shampoo are simultaneously broadcast to several countries.

At first cable channels were dependent upon wires. As technology has evolved, network and cable television now can use satellites to broadcast signals. Consumers are able to purchase personal satellite dishes to receive these signals. To protect the cable industry, scramblers have been added to the sites, requiring consumers to purchase contracts similar to monthly cable charges in order to unscramble the signals.

Commercial Scheduling

The cost of buying advertising time on television varies with the time of day, the type of program, and length of the commercial. Since the demographics and size of the audience changes throughout the day, TV time is divided into **dayparts** or time periods. Dayparts may vary from station to station, but the common classifications for a weekday are shown in Table 10.4. **Prime time**, programming that is broadcast between 8 P.M. and 11 P.M., delivers the largest audience and has the highest commercial placement costs.

Advertisers are also interested in who specifically watches the different programs. Individual television stations can provide target audience information for potential advertisers.

Most television commercials are sold in 15-, 30-, or 60-second time periods. For many people, the start of a television commercial provides a signal to grab the remote or bolt to the kitchen for a snack. But a few advertisers are experimenting with snack-proof and zap-proof ads: the 1-second commercial. Decathlon Sports has a 10-second advertisement demonstrating how easy it is to set up one of their tents in 2 seconds (2006). Additional innovative television advertisements are discussed in Box 10.1.

Influences on Fashion

Television and fashion have been inevitably linked from the start of the medium. Fashion has influenced television audiences and helped establish trends, creating best sellers ranging from the Y necklace and Jennifer Aniston's haircut from *Friends* to shoulder pads as worn by Crystal Carrington, a character on *Dynasty*. Fashion influences have helped create storylines and television characters on such programs as *Sex in the City*. Fashion has become the primary topic on such reality-based programs as *America's Next Top Model* and *Project Runway*. Tommy Hilfiger had a short-lived reality show where

TABLE 10.4   *Common Television Dayparts*

Morning	7:00 A.M. to 9:00 A.M.	Monday through Friday
Daytime	9:00 A.M. to 4:30 P.M.	Monday through Friday
Early fringe	4:30 P.M. to 7:30 P.M.	Monday through Friday
Prime time access	7:30 P.M. to 8:00 P.M.	Sunday through Saturday
Prime time	8:00 P.M. to 11:00 P.M. 7:00 P.M. to 11:00 P.M.	Monday through Saturday and Sunday
Late news	11:00 P.M. to 11:30 P.M.	Monday through Friday
Late fringe	11:30 P.M. to 1:00 A.M.	Monday through Friday

BOX 10.1

Testing, Testing

The old, 30-second formula for TV ads is on its way out. But what will replace it?

When it comes to advertising on TV, "spray and pray" is yesterday's news. Now, marketers are frantically trying to find a replacement.

Advertisers know that the old formula—where they place the same 30-second ad on as many channels as possible, and hope the commercial's message will stick in the consumer's mind—makes less and less sense. As a result, the airwaves are filled these days with a dizzying array of commercial stunts— short ads, long ads, commercials thinly disguised as half-hour pieces of entertainment, commercial-free premieres sponsored by a single advertiser, and even several ads from one advertiser aired back to back to back during a single commercial break.

"It's sort of the Wild West out there right now" as marketers try to cope with dramatic changes in the media landscape, says Page Thompson, chief executive of Omnicom Group Inc.'s OMD North America, a media-buying firm.

With so much experimentation going on, there are no clear winners or losers yet among the strategies being tried. Perhaps the only thing that is clear is that the environment is so different that the old ways of doing business aren't good enough anymore.

The conventional ad emerged at a very different time, when most people had a choice of just three big TV networks and a handful of independent TV stations. There was no cable, Internet, or video games to distract them. Then, the ad world believed that so long as viewers watched a couple of big-name shows each week, advertisers could be reasonably sure that the clever slogans and familiar jingles they devised would be heard—and remembered.

Now, however, viewers have dozens—sometimes hundreds—of TV channels to choose from, not to mention websites, DVDs, videogames, video-on-demand programs, and podcasts. At the same time, digital video recorders are making it easier for consumers to shun ads altogether; watching a program recorded on a DVR allows viewers to fast-forward through the commercial breaks.

Just for You

Faced with these challenges, ad executives say the main drawback of the traditional ad campaign is that it is too broadly targeted: TV ads need to be more relevant to a narrower audience if they're to get anyone's attention. "People who are passionate about their favorite shows watch them differently," says Bill Morningstar, executive vice president of national sales for the new CW network, jointly owned by CBS Corp. and Time Warner Inc. They're more attentive and so might be more receptive to carefully targeted ads. "How do we tap into this environment?"

Some advertisers are sharpening their focus by running ads aimed at audiences watching particular programs or channels.

Johnson & Johnson's Neutrogena, for example, recently ran an ad during *Saturday Night Live* aimed only at the people watching that show. The spot showed outtakes from other Neutrogena ads, depicting fresh-faced actresses committing a series of verbal bloopers. "Now you know why we don't do live commercials," said an announcer, who then went on to salute "the people who do live TV the best—*SNL*." A slightly different version of the spot, crafted by Omnicom Group's Rogers & Tarlow, introduced a live season premiere of the sitcom *Will & Grace* last year. At the end of that ad, a Neutrogena logo appeared on the screen and the camera zeroed in on the "o" and then appeared to pass through it to show the beginning of the episode.

Philips Electronics NV used a different approach last year, paying about $2 million to be the sole national sponsor of one episode of *60 Minutes* on CBS. The program typically attracts Philips's target audience: middle-aged, affluent, and well-educated people.

In some cases, advertisers are shifting from just interrupting programs with ads to creating programs outright. The idea: Even in a show that has high viewership among the target audience, many of those viewers might be ignoring the ads. But if the show itself can be crafted to promote a product, you can reach more people.

This is more subtle—and, the advertisers hope, more powerful—than product placement. Consider two shows created by Unilever aimed at what has become one of the hardest audiences for advertisers to reach: men between the ages of 18 and 34. "This is someone who is overmarketed to, highly saturated with messages, skeptical," says David Rubin, director of brand development for Axe, a line of Unilever body-grooming products for men. For this kind of audience, he says, advertisers can't rely on the hard-sell sledgehammer; they need to think of ways to make a deeper connection with the specific customer base.

"More Like Content"

To that end, the shows that Unilever created played up attitudes embodied by Axe. *The Gamekillers*, a one-hour show that was repeated several times on Viacom Inc.'s MTV network, told viewers about different characters that can ruin a guy's attempts to attract a woman. *Exposing the Order of the Serpentine*, a half-hour show that ran several times on Viacom's Spike channel, told of a fictitious brotherhood that has devised rituals to help guys get over the shock of "a questionable hookup" with a woman, says Mr. Rubin. Axe ads ran on both shows, along with commercials from other companies. But for Unilever the ads weren't the main point – the shows were.

More advertisers are likely to explore this avenue, says Kevin Roddy, executive creative director of the New York office of Bartle Bogle Hegarty, Unilever's ad agency, which helped devise the programs. "We need to be much more like content than more like an interruption," he says.

That idea has also led to ads with qualities akin to those of TV programs. The CW network is offering a new ad-sales format known as a "content wrap." During the course of an evening, an advertiser will get to tell a story over three different two-minute commercial breaks, says the network's Mr. Morningstar. The ads could be tailored to suit the network's programming on a given night, he says. So if Wednesday night is full of shows related to fashion, then the wraps would be aimed at audiences who watch those shows.

In a similar vein, Procter & Gamble Co. has been experimenting with a format known as a "showmercial," or a series of ads that tell a story. One of the nation's biggest advertisers, P&G recently aired a series of vignettes about a family of dogs known as "The Poocharellis," who got into situations that required Febreze, an odor-killing air freshener. The vignettes were 90 seconds long and aired on Viacom's Nick at Nite. A previous P&G campaign told of women getting makeovers, with the story being told over the course of an entire movie on the Lifetime cable network, which is owned by Hearst Corp. and Walt Disney Co.

Still, what advertisers really want is the ability to deliver different ads to different viewers or households, through use of cable, satellite, or other technology. Advertisers, conscious that the Web and mobile devices make it possible to target individual customers, want to know why they can't do that on TV, says

Bill Katz, chairman of New York-based Visible World Inc.—one of a number of companies that are hard at work trying to turn that vision into a reality.

Visible World allows advertisers to digitally customize their ads with different messages for specific audiences. A maker of soup might change the last 10 seconds of an ad if a snowstorm hits in a certain region of the country, for example, telling that particular audience how good a warm bowl of chicken noodle might taste right now.

One-to-One?

Invidi Technology Corp., a Princeton, N.J., company, says it is in the final stages of testing a technology that will allow advertisers to deliver specific ads via set-top boxes to individual households. "If you don't have anybody in diapers when you see a diaper commercial, it's a wasted impression," says David Downey, Invidi's chief executive.

Meanwhile, advertisers and TV networks are pursuing any number of other initiatives. Themed ad breaks are one idea being discussed. For instance, one might center on taking a vacation, and feature messages from an airline, a hotel, and a travel service. Other ads could offer a secret code to help viewers win a video game. There's even a new series of ads that is trying to entice viewers to use ad-skipping DVRs to advertisers' advantage: In one example, an ad from Yum Brands Inc.'s KFC included a single frame in which a code word appeared that viewers could use to claim a coupon for a free chicken sandwich. Only viewers who used their DVR or videocassette recorder to slow the ad and watch it frame by frame could see the code.

Getting all this right might take years, but you can expect Madison Avenue to keep on trying, and it should be fun to watch. "There will be acrobatics," says OMD's Mr. Thompson.

Source: Steinberg, B. (2006, July 11). Testing, testing. *Wall Street Journal*, p. R6.

designers weren't "fired." Instead they were "out of style." The Style Network is a cable channel with complete fashion content. Whether it is involved in creating fashion trends, best sellers, and entertaining characters, or providing information, television has an impact on fashion and vice versa.

Television, perhaps more than any other medium, has had an impact on worldwide trends, creating a global village. Worldwide access to commercial television has influenced the growth of global brands. It is not surprising that teenagers in Bangkok are just as aware of such brands as Levi's and Calvin Klein jeans, Timberland boots, and Adidas and Nike footwear as their counterparts in America. One of the most important sources of brand information comes from television commercials broadcast internationally.

Advantages of Television Advertising

Television offers a number of benefits to advertisers. These advantages include:

- **Audience size.** Television reaches a large audience. Networks have a vast amount of research on the size and demographics of the audience and make this information available to advertisers. Both national and local advertisers are able to target specific viewers. Box 10.2 discusses ways the networks are working to expand their appeal to audiences.
- **Versatility and flexibility.** Messages, creative innovation, and technical capabilities are unlimited. Television commercials may use still photography, video, action, or any combination of techniques.
- **Ability to show products true-to-life.** Television brings the combination of sight and sound to the message. Viewers can see a fairly realistic representation of merchandise, increasing the impact of the message and improving the chances for response.

Disadvantages of Television Advertising

Even though television offers advertisers many benefits, it also has some weaknesses, which are illustrated next.

- **Television advertising avoidance.** With the introduction of television remote controls and with so many choices on television, the audience can easily switch channels, mute the sound, or leave the room during commercials. Consumers zip or zap commercials. VCRs have also created an atmosphere where the audience can avoid the advertising message. **Zipping** occurs when consumers fast-forward through commercials during the playback of a previously recorded program. **Zapping** takes place when the consumer uses the remote control to change channels during a commercial. Either way, the consumer avoids watching the commercial.
- **Costly.** Television airtime and the production of TV commercials is very expensive. Hiring competent personnel, from on-air talent to technicians, is costly. Skilled experts are required to complete professional-quality television advertising.
- **Long response time.** Writers, actors, musicians, photographers, and editors require time to produce television commercials. It may take as much as three to four weeks to produce a commercial before it is ready for broadcast. This long response time prevents quick response to meet current market conditions.
- **Limited amount of broadcast time.** Most advertisers want the impact of running commercials during prime time. These spots are frequently purchased by large network advertisers, making cost higher due to high demand.

───o RADIO

Radio is the broadcast medium that allows sound to travel via electrical impulses called signals. Electromagnetic waves with height (amplitude) and width (frequency) transmit these signals. The **radio frequency** is the number of radio waves a transmitter produces in a second. Thus, a radio station assigned a frequency of 107,000 cycles per second (megahertz) can be found at 107 on your radio dial. The FCC assigns these frequencies so radio signals will not interfere with one another.

Radio stations are designated as AM or FM. An AM, or amplitude modulation station, uses ground waves during the day and sky waves during the evening. That is why nighttime listeners of AM radio are able to pick up signals from transmitters beyond the

○ BOX 10.2

TV Is Getting to Look More Like the Movies

The broadcast television networks are asking Madison Avenue to go to the movies.

A major trend becoming evident this week, as the broadcasters present their . . . schedules to agencies and advertisers, is the increasing "cinema-zation," of prime-time network programs. Many new series are seeking to emulate theatrical films, with higher production costs, more complex plot lines, and larger casts filled with more complicated characters.

Among the examples are several new dramas on NBC, including *Friday Night Lights*, based on the movie of the same name; *Day Break*, a new series on ABC that the network describes as a "reimagining of the *Groundhog Day* concept," referring to the 1993 Bill Murray film; and the telenovelas, or limited-run dramas, to appear on the new My Network TV network. Jack Abernethy, chief executive at Fox Television Stations, which is helping to create the new network, praised the telenovelas for what he called their "rich, cinematic look."

Mr. Abernethy and the other network executives are outlining their plans this week during screenings that are called upfront presentations because they offer previews of prime-time programs ahead of the fall season. Their goal is not to win Oscars rather than Emmys, but to woo increasingly fickle viewers, especially those 18 to 34, by serving episodes of TV shows that do not look or seem like TV shows.

"It's not only important, but imperative, to increase engagement with a show," said John Rash, director for broadcast negotiations at Campbell Mithun in Minneapolis, an agency owned by the Interpublic Group of Companies.

"It has been proven to work with *24* and *Lost*," Mr. Rash said, citing the hit dramas on Fox Broadcasting and ABC. Series like those are known for "their multiple characters with multiple motives, which make the characters more appealing," he added.

Another reason for the trend is that TV shows with cinematic qualities can be extended more effectively beyond the TV set, onto websites, iPods, and cell phones. That is significant as the broadcast networks create more content for the digital media, trying to follow consumers and advertisers there.

"The broadcasters are catching up with the audiences, particularly the younger audiences," Mr. Rash said. "Anything that makes network television shows more relevant, more of a cultural phenomenon, is a smart strategy."

At the NBC upfront presentation on Monday, movies were much on the minds of those who spoke. Keith Turner, president for NBC Universal sales and marketing, talked about "our new shows, which have the look and feel of theatricals" as he asked advertisers to consider NBC's "ideas that reach across multiplatforms," from TV and the Internet to iPods and mobile phones. And the actor Jeff Goldblum, introducing his new drama, *Raines*, said, "It has a very kind of film noir feel to it."

At a news conference yesterday, Steve McPherson, president at the ABC Entertainment unit of ABC, referred to one new sitcom, *Big Day*, this way: "If *24* married *Father of the Bride*, this would be the spawn." The series is centered on the wedding day of a young couple.

Mr. McPherson said Dan Jinks and Bruce Cohen, who produced the 1999 film *American Beauty*, were the executive producers of another series, a drama titled *Traveler*. In an ABC news release listing the . . . prime-time schedule, *Traveler* was described as a combination of two movies, *The Fugitive* and *Enemy of the State*.

"There are more places for content to be seen," Mr. McPherson said, referring to ABC initiatives like offering episodes on itunes.com and as streaming video at abc.com. "This is all good news for everybody."

Four series, including *Desperate Housewives* and *Lost*, have been available on abc.com—with commercials—and in the first two weeks have been watched more than two million times as video streams. A survey conducted for ABC showed that 86 percent of viewers "could recall what the advertiser was," said Kevin Brockman, an ABC spokesman. The advertisers include Ford Motor, NBC Universal, part of General Electric, and Toyota Motors Sales USA.

Digital extensions of TV were also featured at the My Network TV upfront presentation yesterday at the Hilton Theater in Times Square. There will be "fresh content produced specifically for our website" (mynetworktv.com), including "more than 3,000 sponsorable program clips," said Bob Cook, president and chief executive officer at Twentieth Television, which is starting My Network TV with Fox Television Stations, both parts of the News Corporation.

My Network TV will team up with a corporate sibling, the MySpace website, for social networking features to help give "young adults that self-expression and recognition they all crave," Mr. Cook said.

daytime range of the station's ground waves. An FM, or frequency modulation station, differs from AM in that the frequency is adjusted rather than amplitude. An FM station signal remains constant from day to night. Because the signal put out by an FM station follows the line of sight, the distance of a signal depends upon the height of the antenna; typically 50 miles is the maximum signal distance.

In addition to AM and FM delivery systems, cable radio was launched in the 1990s. This technology uses cable television receivers to deliver static-free radio programs via wires plugged into the cable subscribers' stereo.

Upon first consideration, it does not make too much sense to advertise such visually oriented products as apparel and home furnishings on the radio. How can advertisers translate such strong visual images into a medium such as radio? According to research conducted by Jack Trout, however, there is much evidence that the mind works by the ear, that thinking is a process of manipulating sounds rather than images (even when pictures and photographs are involved). As a result, you see what you hear, not what the eye tells you it has seen (Trout, 1995). Repeated studies show that the ear works much faster than the eye, making radio an ideal medium for advertisers. Research indicates that over 93 percent of all consumers listen to the radio some part of each day (Arbitron, 2006). With numerous radio formats and so many places to listen—from the home, car, or office to just walking around with personal earphones—radio is available anywhere.

Although retailers rarely use radio as their exclusive advertising medium, radio is a medium that is used in combination with other media to present a communication package. There is an immediacy about radio—the audience feels that it is current and timely—making it a good vehicle for a coordinated advertising program.

Formats

Radio advertising is available on national networks and through local markets. Network radio, similar to television networks, consists of a group of local affiliates connected to one or more of the national radio networks through telephone wires and satellites. The four major radio networks include Westwood One, CBS, ABC, and Unistar. Radio networks also use syndication, a distribution method introduced under the discussion about television.

More than 20 different radio formats have been identified on a national level, from Alternative to Contemporary Hits, Country, and Jazz. Radio formats have been developed to fit every possible interest. Locally operated radio stations may follow these more common models or vary from these national formats. Table 10.5 shows the radio formats and audience ages. This information helps an advertiser select the most appropriate format to reach the target audience.

In a manner similar to television, radio broadcasters use dayparts as time blocks or periods that break up the broadcast day. These radio daypart classifications are divided into five different segments. The most common dayparts for radio are illustrated in Table 10.6.

Drive time or **traffic time** is the period when radio listenership is the highest. This prime time for radio often features news and weather reports and corresponds to the transition from home to work and work to home. Although these hours may shift in one region versus another, drive time usually falls between 6:00 A.M. and 9:00 A.M. in the morning, while the evening drive time is normally between 4.00 P.M. and 7.00 P.M.

Radio stations sell advertising time to national firms as well as regional and local advertisers. Typically radio commercials are sold as 60-second or 30-second announcements, but shorter commercial lengths, such as 10, 15, or 20 seconds, may be available from some

TABLE 10.5   *Radio Formats Listened to by Age*

Format	12–17	18–24	25–34	35–44	45–54	55–64	65+
Contemporary Hits Radio (CHR)	40.3	26.2	14.5	7.7	4.1	1.7	1.0
Urban	18.5	14.2	11.6	10.2	8.8	7.0	3.5
Alternative	7.8	7.8	7.0	5.0	2.8	1.0	0.4
Adult Contemporary	7.6	10.1	14.7	17.2	17.0	15.2	11.8
Hispanic	6.8	14.2	15.4	10.1	6.8	6.1	5.3
Country	6.0	7.7	7.8	8.6	9.3	11.6	9.8
Rock (AOR, Classic Rock)	5.8	9.4	10.0	11.6	9.1	3.0	0.7
Oldies	2.5	3.6	4.1	6.4	11.5	12.3	5.9
News/Talk/ Information	2.2	4.3	11.0	16.1	20.5	28.3	41.9
Religion	1.9	1.4	2.2	3.2	3.1	3.8	3.6
NAC/Smooth Jazz	0.5	0.7	1.5	2.8	4.9	5.5	4.0
Classical	0.2	0.2	0.4	0.6	1.2	2.4	4.5
Adult Standards	0.1	0.1	0.2	0.3	0.7	2.2	7.5
Remaining Formats	0.1	0.0	0.0	0.1	0.1	0.1	0.2

Adapted from: Media Information Center. (2005). *Radio formats listened to by age.* Retrieved July 12, 2006, from http://www.mediainfocenter.org/music/radio_content_measures/format_age.asp

TABLE 10.6   *Common Radio Dayparts*

5:00 A.M. to 10:00 A.M.	Monday through Saturday
10:00 A.M. to 3:00 P.M.	Monday through Saturday
3:00 P.M. to 6:00 P.M.	Monday through Saturday
6:00 P.M. to 1:00 A.M.	Monday through Saturday
5:00 A.M. to 1:00 A.M.	Sunday

stations. Although costs do vary by length, they are not proportionally priced. A 30-second announcement usually costs between 75 and 80 percent of a 60-second announcement.

Programs and Sponsorship

Radio stations present regularly scheduled feature programs such as news, weather, traffic reports, sporting events, or other special-interest programming such as gardening or syndicated music programs. Advertising time may be sold as spots or through **program sponsorship**, which may include an opening mention, a commercial during the program, and a closing credit. Sponsorship is a long-term commitment (13 to 52 weeks) at premium rates. Commercial times and lengths are subject to variation in different markets and from station to station.

Another way a radio advertiser can tap into regularly scheduled programs, without investing in sponsorship, is to buy **adjacencies,** commercials sold at a premium rate, to run just before or after a program. This is another way to secure some of the advantages of advertising during a program without the expense and commitment of sponsorship.

A local retail firm or regional shopping center can tap into a local promotion by using a **remote**, a live broadcast on location. The radio station sends the station's announcers to the store, mall, or other designated location for a promotional event. While broadcasting regular news and music, the announcers promote the retailer or mall and may have merchandise specials or giveaways.

Advantages of Radio Advertising

Some of the advantages radio offers advertisers include the following:

- **Specific audience.** Since each station programs to a very specific audience through one of the focused radio formats, the audience demographics for a radio station are readily available to the advertiser. With the turn of a radio dial, audiences for country, news/talk, hard rock, or adult contemporary can be easily selected.
- **Nearly universal medium.** The average American listens to the radio more than three hours on weekdays and nearly six hours each weekend. Listeners tune in at home, at work, and during leisure activities in addition to listening in their cars, while commuting or shopping.
- **High degree of frequency.** Radio builds top-of-mind awareness with repetition. Repetition builds awareness through affordable frequency.
- **Timing is more immediate.** Although most retail advertising is planned long in advance, there may be occasions when an advertiser needs to bring an advertising message to the audience immediately. An unplanned celebrity personal appearance or weather changes can lead to an unanticipated opportunity. A radio spot can be produced, scheduled, and aired more quickly than through print media or television.
- **Cost-effective.** The relationship between low costs and highly selected audience are documented through research studies. Radio delivers more advertising impressions than any other media for the same budget. In addition to the cost advantages associated with reach and frequency, radio commercials have a much lower production expense than other media. This allows the advertiser to change the message, or develop creative messages to match the format and demographics for each radio station used.
- **Least ignored advertising medium.** Research studies show that while almost 60 percent of television audiences switch channels during advertising, only 28 percent of radio listeners avoid advertising messages.
- **Audience consistency.** People listen to the radio to find out about community events. From traffic reports to school closures, the audience tunes in to find out what is happening daily in their communities. This interest is consistent from day to day and throughout the year. Unlike other media, such as television, with a summer decline of audiences, radio listeners tune in all year long.

Disadvantages of Radio Advertising

The following list identifies some of the weaknesses associated with radio advertising:

- **Inability to deliver a visual image.** Research shows that a visual image is suggested through sound, but it does not provide the subtleties that can be furnished with a visual image. Colors, silhouettes, and other product characteristics cannot be visually represented by sound alone.

- **Lack of listener attention.** Radio is a companion medium; in other words, the listener is involved in more than one activity at one time. Because the radio is *on* during times that the listener is at work or driving, it may serve as background noise to the primary activity. Under those conditions, the listener may be distracted by other actions as the advertising message is run and may tune out the commercial.
- **Nonretrievable format.** While clipping services help print advertisers save copies of advertising messages, radio commercials are typically aired and the tape is lost or forgotten. Archival copies are not generally available.

──o Creating Broadcast Commercials

As we learned in Chapter 3, in a large full-service advertising agency with a complex corporate structure, the head of creative services focuses on creation and execution of the advertisements, while gaining marketing, management, and account services from other divisions. In a smaller firm, the owner may have complete responsibility for every aspect of creative development in addition to running other functional operations.

Coordination between the creative strategists, copywriters, artists, freelance workers, talent, production workers, and copywriters is the responsibility of the creative services director. This director, who sets the tone for the creative strategy of the organization, is responsible for the overall creative and aesthetic quality of advertising production under his or her leadership, and typically supervises verbal and visual personnel in the organization. From idea individuals to visual and verbal experts, a variety of people with unique skills must be pulled together to execute creative advertisements.

Creating Television Commercials

With the advantages of sight, sound, color, and movement, television offers an exceptional method of presenting an advertising message. Television incorporates all of the elements of copy, art, and layout previously discussed in relationship to print advertising along with live-action, and special effects or animation. In print advertising, the relationship between copy and art may be considered the visual interpreting the verbal. However, in television the relationship between art and copy could be viewed as the verbal interpreting the visual.

Creation and production of television commercials demand a complex combination of skills. Acting, art directing, casting actors, directing, designing, graphics, filming, film editing, musical directing, producing, set designing, and writing are just some of the creative expertise needed to produce television commercials. Both radio and television commercials depend upon hiring the right talent, which includes actors, announcers, disk jockeys, celebrities, singers, dancers, and models, to bring the concept alive.

An outside directory may be hired to turn the creative idea into a commercial. Television commercials are beginning to look a lot like movies. Retailers and manufacturers rarely produce television commercials with an in-house staff, relying on advertising agencies and television production specialists to produce ads. With the high costs of maintaining electronic equipment, studios and specialized personnel, retailers, and manufacturers have found hiring outside personnel to be more cost-effective in meeting their needs.

Creative Development

The creative staff pulls together the concept for the television commercial and presents it to the client through the storyboard. **Storyboards** (Fig. 10.4) are graphic presentations, part advertising layout and part script, the written copy (Fig. 10.5) to be read by

FIGURE 10.4 Storyboard for DSW.

DSW Spring 2007 TV Commercial storyboard

DSW. UNLEASH YOUR PASSION FOR SHOES.

performers, that describes television commercials of any length. The storyboard is exhibited as a strip of video visuals, either rough sketches or photographs, similar to a cartoon strip. The storyboard for a television commercial is a layout that is comparable to a print layout or radio script, functioning as a part of the planning procedure.

An audio script includes other visual and verbal components that accompany the storyboard. Figure 10.6 is a television advertisement script form explaining the design for commercials. Visual components include camera direction and descriptions for actors and sets. Verbal elements include the characterization of the voice-overs, sound effects, and music. As the planned commercial is presented to the client, the agency will probably produce an audio tape to simulate the sound that will be incorporated into the final production.

Production Techniques

The three major categories of production techniques used today are live action, animation, and special effects. **Live action** portrays people, animals, and objects as lifelike in everyday situations. It is the most realistic format, but it lacks the distinctiveness created by animation or special effects. **Animation** uses illustrated figures, such as cartoon characters or puppets, and inanimate objects come to life. Popular with children's advertising, animations are created as cartoons, photo animation, stop-motion photography, or computer generated video animation. **Special effects**, such as moving titles, whirling logos, and dissolve images have been developed as a result of computer technologies. **Digital video effects units** are able to

FIGURE 10.5 A excerpt from a television advertisement script.

VIDEO	AUDIO	
1. OPEN WITH CAMERA MOUNTED IN NOSE OF PLANE AS IT WEAVES IN AND OUT OF CLOUDS, SOARS STRAIGHT UP AT SUN, THEN DIVES BACK THROUGH CLOUDS.	SOUND:	MUSIC UP FOR THREE BARS, THEN DOWN AND HOLD UNDER.
	ANNCR:	(VO) FOR THOUSANDS OF YEARS, THE SUNLIGHT . . .
2. PLANE BURSTS THROUGH CLOUDS AND CONTINUES DIVE TOWARD SEA FAR BELOW.		. . . AND THE SEA AND THE MASTERLESS WINDS HAVE MET IN LONELY RENDEZVOUS.
3. SEA SEEMS TO RUSH UP AT PLANE AS DESCENT CONTINUES.		MAN DID NOT DARE VENTURE IN THE ENDLESS STREAM THAT FLOWED FOREVER.
4. DISSOLVE TO SHOT OF OCEAN AS AIRPLANE SKIMS TOPS OF WAVES (WIDE ANGLE LENS).		THE SEA WAS THE END OF EARTH . . . THE BEGINNING OF HEAVEN.
5. CROSS DISSOLVE TO CLOSE SHOT OF RAGING STORM, HUGE WAVES.		BOUNDLESS . . . INFINITE. AWESOME AND TERRIBLE IN ITS MINDLESS FURY.
6. DISSOLVE TO LONELY SEAGULL SILHOUETTED AGAINST SKY.	SOUND: ANNCR:	RAUCOUS CRY OF SEAGULL BUT THEN CAME THE ADVENTURERS AND THE BOLD ONES . . . WHO SAILED FORTH IN FRAIL CRAFT TO DEFY THE UNKNOWN VASTNESS.
7. PAN UP TO HUGE MOON, THEN TO RAYS OF MOON ON WATER.		HARDY MEN WHO STEERED BY THE SUN, MOON, AND STARS.
8. CUT TO MLS FROZEN WATERS IN ARCTIC. LARGE ICEBERG IN FG.		TO THE NORTH . . . A WORLD OF ICE.

manipulate graphics in a number of ways, from fades to wipes, zooms, rotations, and other effects. Music and sound can also be digitally manipulated. Video directions for various television shots are demonstrated in Figure 10.7.

Production Stages

Television commercial production goes through three stages: preproduction, production, and postproduction. Once the client has approved the storyboard and script, the preproduction stage begins. This stage includes all the work done prior to the actual day of filming, such as casting, arranging for locations, estimating costs, finding props and costumes, and other related preparations. A team including a writer, director, producer, art director, and musical director is assembled. A studio is selected through a bid process followed by casting talent. Every aspect of production is planned during the preproduction phase.

Production of a television commercial may take a day or more, depending on the complexity of the commercial and where it is being shot. The production of television commercials has become similar to production of a television show or a movie, incorporating the activities of cinematographers, sound specialists, stage set designers, and talent.

FIGURE 10.6 A television script form.

ADVERTISER

RUN DATE

LENGTH

VIDEO	AUDIO
DESCRIPTION OF WHAT IS SHOWN ON THE SCREEN IS TYPED ON LEFT ⅓ OF PAGE, SINGLE-SPACED IN CAPS.	COPY FOR WHAT IS HEARD IS TYPED ON THE RIGHT ⅔ OF THE PAGE, UPPER AND LOWER CASE, DOUBLE-SPACED. UNDERLINE OR USE CAPS FOR EMPHASIS. ANY SPECIAL INSTRUCTIONS ARE PUT IN CAPS AND IN (PARENTHESES).

1. NUMBER EACH SCENE AND MAKE SURE IT IS LINED UP DIRECTLY ACROSS FROM THE AUDIO THAT GOES WITH IT.

OLD MAN (DISGUSTEDLY): WHAT DO YA MEAN BY THAT?
CHILD (EXCITEDLY): MOM! LOOK, MOM! NO CAVITIES!

2. WHEN USING FILM, SAY IF IT IS SOUND-ON-FILM AND DESIGNATE "SOF." PUT SOF SYMBOL ON AUDIO SIDE ALSO. INDICATE THUS:

INDICATE AFTER TALENT WHETHER TO BE (ON CAMERA) OR (VOICE OVER), WHICH CAN BE ABBREVIATED (VO).
ANNCR: (VO) HERE AT LAST, LADIES, IS . . .
MUSIC SHOULD BE CUED AND UNDERLINED, AS FOLLOWS:

3. ROLL FILM, R27-3, SOF

MUSIC: IN
MUSIC: OUT

4. WHEN USING SLIDES, USE "SLIDE" OR "SL" AND GIVE DESCRIPTION THUS:

MUSIC: IN AND UNDER ON CUE
MUSIC: UP AND HOLD UNTIL END

5. TAKE SLIDE, TWO BOYS ON TEETER-TOTTER, (OR)

SOUND EFFECTS SHOULD BE INDICATED WITH THE WORD "SOUND" OR

6. SLIDE 23D, MALE STUDENT STUDYING INLIBRARY.

"SFX" AND UNDERLINED WITH BROKEN LINE.

7. WHEN LIVE STUDIO, DESCRIBE THE SCENE Here. INDICATE A "TAKE" (DIRECT VIDEO TRANSITION) OR A "DISSOLVE" (A SLOW VIDEO FADE-OUT OF ONE SHOT AND A FADE-IN OF ANOTHER).

SOUND: DOORBELL RING

SFX: DOG BARKING

WHEN SOUND ON THE FILMTRACK (SOF) IS USED, INCLUDE THE FINAL SENTENCE IN THE AUDIO AS A CUE TO THE TALENT.

HELP ALL PEOPLE CONCERNED—DIRECTOR, CAMERAMAN, TALENT, AND CLIENT—UNDERSTAND BOTH THE AUDIO AND VIDEO AND HOW THEY ARE RELATED.

8. SOME TERMS TO USE TO INDICATE SCREEN COMPOSITION.

WS: WIDE SHOT
MS: MEDIUM SHOT or MCU
CU: CLOSE-UP
BCU: BIG CLOSE-UP
ECU: EXTREME CLOSE-UP

Once all of the scenes are recorded, the commercial enters the postproduction phase, in which the film editor, sound mixer, and director actually put the commercial together. Film or videotape is edited into a **rough cut** for review or testing prior to making the final commercial. The rough cut may have scenes substituted, music or sound effects added, or last-minute changes incorporated. After the client approves the final commercial, copies are made for delivery to television stations and networks.

FIGUre 10.7 Video directions for television advertisements.

ECU (extreme close-up). When used to describe a shot of a person, the camera would reveal only the individual's head.

When used to describe a shot of an inanimate object, the camera would fill the screen with the product.

CU (close-up). When used to describe a shot of a person, the camera would reveal the individual's head and shoulders.

When used to describe a shot of an inanimate object, the camera would frame the item so that some blank area around it is visible.

Tight MCU (tight medium close-up). When used to describe a shot of a person, the camera would reveal the individual from head to chest.

When used to describe an inanimate object, the camera would frame the item, as well as additional accessories.

MCU (medium close-up). When used to describe a shot of a person, the camera would frame the individual from head to waist.

When used to describe a shot of an inanimate object, the camera would frame the object, as well as the foreground, background, and accessories on the side of the screen.

Loose MCU. When used to describe a shot of a person, the camera would frame the individual from head to hips or slightly below ¾ length of the jacket. This shot is not used on inanimate objects.

MLS (medium long shot). When used to describe a shot of a person, the camera would frame the individual from head to knees or slightly below hem length. This camera shot should not be used on inanimate objects alone. It may be used when a person is with the object. Example: MLS/Announcer & refrigerator, *not* MLS/Refrigerator.

LS (long shot). When used to describe a shot of a person, the camera would frame the individual from head to toes. Do not use this on inanimate objects alone. It may be used when a person is with the object. Example: LS/Announcer & refrigerator, *not* LS/Refrigerator. In this case, the proper instruction is "COVER" (see definition).

ELS (extreme long shot). When used to describe a shot of a person, the camera would frame the individual from head to toes with plenty of foreground and headroom showing the picture.

Normally this shot would not be used on inanimate objects except in rare cases when a dramatic effect is desirable (as shown in the sketch) or when the item is part of a large set. For example, a refrigerator in a kitchen setup.

Cover. This shot is usually used only on large inanimate objects or when the announcer is part of a large set, such as a kitchen or living room. Generally, a cover shot means the camera frames the item or display so that all portions of it are visible. For example: Cover shot of sofa, cover shot of a mass coffee table display, cover shot of a refrigerator. The term "Cover" is *not* used for small items, such as packages or containers. In these cases the terms CU and MCU should be used.

Most national commercials are still shot on film, because film is extremely flexible and versatile. It can be used for a variety of optical effects. Film prints are less expensive than videotape dubs. In recent years, videotape has gained in popularity, especially for local productions. Video offers a more brilliant picture and better fidelity than film. It looks more realistic and tape quality is more consistent than film stock. The chief advantage of video is its immediate playback function, greatly speeding the editing process.

Creating Radio Commercials

Radio commercials are dependent upon voices, sound effects, and music to communicate the advertiser's message. The advertiser must get the message across in 30 or 60 seconds, which requires as few as 125 words. Intriguing sound effects, ranging from animal sounds to footsteps walking on a wooden floor, must be skillfully blended with music and voices into a successful radio commercial.

Radio advertising is directed to a targeted customer as defined by the demographic information about the audience compiled by the radio station. Thus, the radio commercial needs to be developed with a specific listener in mind.

The radio commercial normally consists of announcements read from scripts with or without the use of special sound effects, singing, or music. Radio personalities, station announcers, disc jockeys, news commentators, the advertiser, or actors read announcements. These people are considered the talent for a radio production. Professional actors can imitate the voices of famous celebrities or create multiple voice dialogues. On-air personnel may read some radio commercial announcements live, while others are taped in advance at a studio and replayed during the scheduled time. Commercials involving sound effects and/or music should be done in advance rather than *live*. Editing can help make these commercials sound more professional.

The copywriter for a radio commercial works with the copy platform to prepare a script. The radio script will include information about any special sound effects or music in addition to the announcement to be read. Figure 10.8 is an example of a radio script.

Narrative Dramatization

The **narrative dramatization** is a form of radio commercial with actors portraying individuals in real-life situations. These sequences may use music or sound effects to give listeners a slice-of-life experience. Although challenging, it is possible for a dramatization to demonstrate the use of products through visualization in sound.

Musical Commercials

Singing and music are vivid attention-getters. A **jingle** is a catchy verse or song with an easy rhythm that is used to create a verbal link to the product. When a jingle is amateurish it can be irritating, but a well-produced musical interpretation has the capability of preparing the audience with a recognition factor. Many popular musical artists have lent their expertise to the creation of jingles, elevating the professionalism of the approach.

Production Stages

In a manner similar to television, radio goes through three stages of production, which include preproduction, production, and postproduction. During the preproduction stage, a radio producer is hired to estimate costs, prepare a budget, select a studio, and find a casting director. Music and talent are coordinated during a rehearsal. Production involves cutting the spot, or actually recording the commercial. Sound recording takes place at a recording studio. The postproduction stage is the finishing phase where sound engineers mix voices, music, and sound effects into the finished commercial. A radio spot is much easier to produce than a television commercial.

Creative development for broadcast media differs from print media through the addition of sound and movement as imaginative variables. Radio creates images with sound, but without a visual element. Television is able to use the benefits associated with sound and movement to enhance the selling opportunity. Computer-based technologies are now able to incorporate video and sound into advertising and promotion, opening up a wide range of creative opportunities.

This chapter has focused on two main broadcast media, television and radio. Both play a significant role in our lives every day, as communication sources that provide news, information, and entertainment. Accompanying the news, information, and entertainment are sponsored messages designed to grab the attention of the listener or viewer. We wake up to these media, listen to or watch these broadcast vehicles throughout the

FIGURE 10.8 A radio advertisement script.

Sample Radio Script

Client:	Favorites to Wear
Product:	Spring Floral Dresses
Agency:	Indelible Ink
Title:	Spring Is Here
Length:	30 seconds

Music:	"FAVORITES TO WEAR" THEME SONG
1ST FEMALE VOICE:	IT FINALLY FEELS LIKE SPRING. HAVE YOU SEEN THE TULIPS BLOOMING IN FRONT OF THE BOOKSTORE DOWNTOWN?
2ND FEMALE VOICE:	YES, AND THESE WARM AND SUNNY DAYS ARE TOO HOT FOR MY WINTER CLOTHES. I'M DREAMING ABOUT SOFT . . . FLOWING . . . COOL DRESSES.
1ST FEMALE VOICE:	I KNOW WHAT WE NEED. "FAVORITES TO WEAR" HAS PUT FLORAL DRESSES IN THEIR WINDOW. LET'S HEAD OVER THERE ON OUR LUNCH BREAK. I'M READY FOR A CHANGE TOO!
ANNOUNCER:	THE NEWEST FLORAL PRINT DRESSES HAVE ARRIVED AT "FAVORITES TO WEAR." COME TO HISTORICAL DOWNTOWN CAMBRIDGE AND SEE ALL OF THE NEW SPRING MERCHANDISE.
MUSIC:	"FAVORITES TO WEAR" THEME SONG

---

day, at work and at home, and use these formats as entertainment during leisure hours. The creation and production of radio and television commercials are highly complex and require expertise in broadcast strategy and creativity.

summary

- Broadcast media, similar to print media, use the copy platform as a guideline to create television and radio commercials.
- Television plays a significant role in the everyday lives of people throughout the world and has contributed to the globalization of everything from fashion to music.
- Television advertising makes product information available to people from many cultures throughout the world.
- Although radio may not seem like an ideal medium for visually oriented products, its availability to specific target groups keeps it a thriving advertising medium.
- Television and radio advertising media costs are determined by the time of day, called dayparts, when the commercial is broadcast.
- Television and radio commercials are written as scripts and through performance are brought to life.
- Television and radio commercials go through three stages, which are preproduction, production, and postproduction.

key terms

adjacencies	designated market areas	narrative dramatization
affiliates	digital video effects units	participations
animation	drive time	prime time
cable television	jingle	program sponsorship
dayparts	live action	radio

radio frequency	special effects	traffic time
remote	storyboard	zapping
rough cut	television	zipping

QUESTIONS FOR DISCUSSION

1. What are the steps in creating a television commercial?
2. What are the steps in creating a radio ad?
3. In what ways is technology challenging and changing broadcast commercials?
4. What are the similar and different characteristics of print media and broadcast media?
5. What does television syndication mean? What is the difference between off-network and first-run syndication?
6. Think of a television commercial that you have seen recently. Was it effective? What made it effective? How long do you think it took to produce? How much do you think it cost to produce and broadcast it?

ADDITIONAL RESOURCES

Belch, G. E., & Belch, M.A. (2007). *Advertising and promotion* (7th ed.). New York: McGraw-Hill/ Irwin.

Marsh, C., Guth, D. W., & Short, B. P.(2005). *Strategic writing*. Boston: Pearson Education.

Wells, W., Moriarty, S., & Burnett, J. (2006). *Advertising principles and practice* (7th ed). Upper Saddle River, NJ: Pearson Prentice Hall.

ANNUAL PUBLICATIONS

100 Leading National Advertisers. (Published annually). *Advertising Age*. New York: Crain Communications, Inc.

REFERENCES

100 Leading National Advertisers (2006). *Advertising Age*. New York: Crain Communications, Inc.

Arbitron. (2006). *Radio today: How America listens to radio*. Retrieved July 12, 2006, from http://www.arbitron.com/downloads/radiotoday/06.pdf

Decathlon's ten-second ad for a two-second tent. (2006, July 14). *Advertising Age*. Retrieved July 18,2006, from http:adage.com/vidt?pId=1

Levin, G., & Lieberman, D. (2006, January 25). 2 weak links join for survival; Network's union helps create new power base. *USA Today,* 1B. Retrieved July 12, 2006, from LexisNexis Academic database.

Media Information Center. (2005a). *Cable & VCR households*. Retrieved July 12, 2006, from http://www.mediainfocenter.org/television/size/cable_vcr.asp

Media Information Center (2005b). *Radio formats listed to by age*. Retrieved July 12, 2006 from http://www.mediainfocenter.org/music/radio_content_measures/format_age.asp

Media Information Center (2005c). *Television reach: Broadcast vs. cable*. Retrieved July12, 2006 from http://www.mediainfocenter.org/television/competitive/broadcast_vs_cable.asp

Nielsen Media Research. (2005a). *210 Designated market areas*. Retrieved July 9, 2006, from http://www.nielsenmedia.com/DMAs.html

Nielsen Media Research. (2005b). *Nielsen Media Rresearch's Hispanic local markets*. Retrieved July 12, 2006 from http://www.nielsenmedia.com/ethnicmeasure/hispanic-american/localmarkets.html

Nielsen Media Research. (2005c). TV audience special study: African-American television audience. Retrieved July 13, 2006, from http://www.nielsenmedia.com/E-letters/African-AmericanTVA-final .pdf

Television Bureau of Advertising (2005a). *Time spent viewing—households*. Retrieved July 12, 2006, from http://www.mediainfocenter.org/television/tv_aud/time_house.asp

Television Bureau of Advertising (2005b). *Time spent viewing—persons*. Retrieved July 12, 2006, from http://www.mediainfocenter.org/television/tv_aud/time_persons.asp

Trout, J. (1995). *The new positioning*. New York: McGraw-Hill.

Wells, W., Moriarty, S., & Burnett, J. (2006). *Advertising principles and practice* (7th ed.). Upper Saddle river, NJ: Pearson Prentice Hall.

FIGURE 11.1 Homepage for JCPenney.

CHAPTER 11
Direct Marketing and Interactive Media

In an effort to compete with rivals such as Macy's and Wal-Mart, J.C. Penney rolled out merchandising and technological innovations aimed at making website navigation fast, easy, and focused in the latter half of the first decade of the 21st century. Penney's is aggressively pursuing a strategy aimed at doubling its annual Internet revenues (Williamson, 2006). The retailer spotlighted trendier lifestyle fashions with bigger thumbnail images and shorter, less obtrusive copy, and breakout "instant outfit" suggestions on almost every Penney's website fashion page (p. 3). Additionally, Penney's shortened the Web address from jcpenney.com to jcp.com and linked the site to stores and catalogs with a branding campaign that guided shoppers to the Internet when they could not find a product. The Internet as interactive media has changed the face of retailing and promotion.

Every day, consumers are asked to sort through an incredible number of direct appeals. Over 11 million pounds of mail with a direct advertising message are delivered to homes in the United States daily. Included within this advertising mail are catalogs, coupon packages, free samples, brochures, solicitation appeals, and other requests for recipient response. Beyond mail, solicitations are sought through television, radio, computer, and outdoor media. These forms of appeal are components of the process known as direct marketing.

Source: Williamson, R. (2006, April 17). Penney's aims for $2B internet revenues. *Women's Wear Daily*, p. 3.

> **After you have read this chapter you should be able to:**
>
> Incorporate direct marketing into a promotion plan.
>
> Contrast the different direct marketing strategies available to promotion specialists.
>
> Examine the components of successful database management.

THIS CHAPTER FOCUSES on direct marketing as a promotion strategy. It begins with a discussion of the role of direct marketing and the advantages and disadvantages of using this strategy. Next, the discussion focuses on database management, which is crucial to the success of direct marketing. Direct marketing media are then discussed, followed by support media. The chapter concludes with dialog about interactive media.

ROLE OF DIRECT MARKETING

Direct marketing is the process by which organizations communicate directly with target customers to generate a response or transaction. Companies that sell directly to the consumer using **direct marketing** strategies are called **direct sellers.** Mary Kay, Avon, Tupperware, Pampered Chef, and others have built strong businesses based on this marketing strategy. Besides direct sellers, many other businesses also use this marketing strategy. Direct marketing uses direct-response media to implement the promotion process. **Direct-response media** tools include direct mail, telemarketing, interactive print and broadcast media, the Internet, and other media.

In Chapter 4, Table 4.2, several of the top media influencing women's apparel purchases were direct-response media. The top media influence—newspaper inserts—was used by women 44.4 percent of the time to influence apparel purchases. Direct mail, ranked number 3, influenced apparel purchases 34.0 percent of the time, and e-mail advertising and Internet advertising both made the top 10 list as media influencing women's apparel purchases ("Power," 2006).

In 2005, the U.S. economy generated $26 trillion in sales (Direct Marketing Association, 2006). Of that, 7 percent was generated through direct marketing advertising expenditures. Total direct marketing advertising expenditures were $161.3 billion and generated $1.85 trillion in sales. Direct mail and telephone direct-response media accounted for the largest proportions of direct marketing advertising dollars. Direct mail including catalog and non-catalog materials accounted for 31 percent ($49.8 billion), and telephone marketing accounted for 29 percent ($47 billion).

Direct marketing is important to the promotion mix. Direct marketers use the tool to reach consumers where they live. Changing consumer attitudes, increasingly sophisticated and personalized techniques, and an improved image have contributed to the overall support and growth of direct marketing as a promotion strategy in an IMC environment.

Direct marketing is a form of advertising. It is a sponsored message delivered through print, broadcast, or interactive media requiring the consumer to respond by return mail, a toll-free number, an interactive link, or a store visit. Direct marketing is also a form of public relations. Although many direct marketing programs are implemented to generate sales, some programs seek to build a company's image, maintain customer satisfaction, or educate the consumer as public relations efforts.

Direct marketing is a form of personal selling (through telemarketing) and sales promotion (through couponing and other tactics) and may be part of other promotion mix strategies as well, aimed at encouraging a consumer to respond directly. Victoria's Secret direct marketing campaigns contain pieces that serve as strong IMC promotion tactics, by combining magazine advertising and sales promotion in a direct marketing appeal. The print advertisements appear in consumer magazines along with a sales promotion coupon to encourage consumers to directly respond by visiting a Victoria's Secret retail location.

Advantages of Direct Marketing

Direct marketing allows businesses to create relationships between the company and its customers. This is a strong advantage of a direct marketing program. Other advantages of direct-response promotions include:

- **Shopping convenience.** Foremost for customers, direct marketing offers increased shopping convenience and service by allowing individuals to shop at home using a catalog, telephone, computer, or other delivery vehicle during leisure time, rather than shopping at a retail establishment.
- **Instant payment by credit card.** Most direct-response promotions offer the consumer the opportunity to pay by credit card, the dominant payment form by a majority of the population. Sellers encourage the use of credit cards as a guarantee that they will be paid. Offered as part of customer incentive programs, credit cards are popular among retailers to encourage brand loyalty.
- **Selective reach and segmentation.** Direct marketing appeals can be addressed to a specific individual or family, zip code area, or other segmented population, rather than a general audience, allowing for selective reach. The advertisement is only sent to those

consumers whom the promoter wishes to contact, eliminating waste. Segmentation capabilities are limitless based on consumer demographics and lifestyle characteristics.

- **Frequency.** Direct marketing offers the opportunity for the sponsor to develop frequency levels. Frequency levels are the number of times a consumer is exposed to an appeal in a specified time. Recent purchasers will have a higher frequency level than consumers who have not made a purchase within the last twelve months. Higher frequency may result in more sales. However, receiving too many exposures, such as duplicate catalogs or repeated broadcasts of infomercials, may turn consumers off.
- **Effectiveness.** Results of each direct marketing transaction can be evaluated for success because each transaction requires action on the part of the customer by return mail, sending in a coupon, making a telephone call, responding over the computer, or some other direct response. In addition, this direct interaction between company and customer allows the company to create a customer database for use in promoting future products or services.

Disadvantages of Direct Marketing

Although direct marketing is popular in the advertising arena, there are disadvantages associated with this promotion mix element. They include:

- **Image.** The image of direct marketing has not always been positive. Many consumers consider direct marketing appeals as uninvited solicitations. Direct-response advertisements received through the mail are referred to as *junk mail,* and often times are discarded without being read. Telephone solicitations have been so unpopular that a national do-not-call registry has been activated in the United States. Early infomercials and cable shopping networks were produced as low-budget productions, adding to consumers' negative opinions of direct-response broadcasts.
- **Accuracy.** Although direct marketing allows the sponsor to target specific audiences, if the database is not up-to-date, accuracy becomes a problem.

In order for any direct marketing campaign to be successful, five components should be carefully considered and executed. They include:

- **List.** The list is properly managed and contains well-researched potential and repeat customers.
- **Offer.** The offer is crafted to match the intended outcome of the promotion to generate immediate sales or build long-term customer relationships.
- **Format.** The format creates urgency in the consumer to respond to the offer.
- **Follow-up.** Requests are acted upon immediately and communication with the customer is constant and meaningful.
- **Analysis.** Evaluation is constant and effective in making marketing decisions.

In part, effective marketing decisions are based on accurate information provided in the database. Database management is the subject of the next section.

——o DATABASE MANAGEMENT

The key to successful direct marketing is target marketing through segmentation. Target marketing is achieved by using a consumer database to identify the specific population of customers to receive the promotion appeal. A **database** is a collection of data arranged for ease and speed of search and retrieval. Within the database, a computerized record of each previous buyer and/or potential prospect is maintained. This record includes the customer's background, purchase patterns, and interests, which serves as a source for future targeted marketing efforts. The database allows a company to identify the individual characteristics of each consumer and serve his or her needs.

Manufacturers and retailers use database management in many areas of the business. Current customers are identified by spending habits and customer loyalty. How often do they purchase, when was the most recent purchase, how much do they spend, and what motivated them to purchase, are all questions that can be answered from the database. The database allows businesses to track patterns of behavior including fashion awareness, food preferences, home fashion preferences, and entertainment choices. By understanding the lifestyle characteristics of an individual, a business can focus on specific products and promotions that are most likely to increase purchases by the consumer.

Firms use database management to research the trading area. A **trading area** is the city, county, state, or region a company services. A trading area for a convenience store may be only a few blocks in the surrounding neighborhood. A trading area for a company such as Levi Strauss or Nike is worldwide. Businesses can plot boundaries of a trading area and identify heavy spenders based on information in the database. Promotion and advertising decisions can then be based on patterns within the trading area.

Effective database management can stimulate repeat purchases and **cross-selling**, the sale of additional products and services to the same customer. Cross-selling merchandise may be from the same company, or associate companies, with products that appeal to the same model customer. For example, telephone sales representatives offer special sales on merchandise available only during the phone call. After ordering from a catalog, consumers are often sent unsolicited issues of other catalogs to influence similar purchases.

But how does database management work? First, information is collected for input into the database. Direct marketing companies have the option of creating their own in-house list or purchasing database lists from list brokers. **In-house lists** are developed, owned, and maintained by the company. Lands' End creates its own in-house lists for specialty catalogs by using direct-response customer information from its general merchandise catalog. Companies who choose not to maintain an in-house list may purchase brokered lists. **Brokered lists** are offered for sale or rent through negotiation of a contract in return for a fee or commission.

Much of the data is voluntarily offered by consumers, often from sales promotion tools such as coupons, warranties, sweepstakes, contests, or other promotions that ask for information. Consumers voluntarily participate in list generation by filling out surveys or response cards, ordering merchandise through direct response, or filling out a credit card application. Data also can be collected from public records, such as the United States Census Bureau, or private companies. One such company is Equifax Direct Marketing Solutions. Its product is Lifestyle Selector (Fig. 11.2), a national database composed of consumers who have voluntarily returned questionnaires (often packaged with consumer product warranties) answering demographic and lifestyle-oriented questions about interests and hobbies. The company offers the list for sale to interested businesses. Additionally, data can be gathered from retailers and vendors who share information about customers to understand buying behavior.

Once the data has been collected, it is compiled, merging different data sets into one. Many firms, including Federated Department Macy's Inc. Stores, Sears, and Fossil

The
Lifestyle Selector®

Description: The Lifestyle Selector is the direct marketing industry's largest and most comprehensive database of self-reported consumer information. More than 500 response segments cover all aspects of how consumers live, what they spend their money on, and what interests they possess. This file is primarily derived from two sources: responses to consumer surveys and from product registration cards filled out voluntarily by consumers after they have completed a product purchase. This high-performance list has played an integral role in the success of thousands of companies' direct marketing campaigns for more than 24 years.

Source: Responses to Equifax surveys; product registration card submissions

	3-Month	24-Month
Gender		
Female	1,518,100	10,695,950
Male	2,055,100	11,288,100
Adult Age		
Adults (18+)	3,411,300	20,715,350
Inquire for specific respondent/spouse age counts		
Children's Age		
Children (0–18)	3,035,250	16,686,300
Inquire for counts by specific age(s)		
Marital Status		
Married	2,476,450	13,631,350
Unmarried	912,750	6,185,800
Divorced/Separated	38,700	547,400
Widowed	28,150	309,300
Household Income		
$15,000 and Under	209,400	1,759,700
$15,000–$19,999	61,700	1,240,900
$20,000–$29,999	342,400	2,421,150
$30,000–$39,999	414,500	2,684,000
$40,000–$49,999	415,750	2,683,650
$50,000–$59,999	326,100	1,783,200
$60,000–$74,999	549,400	3,375,000
$75,000–$99,999	454,550	2,520,700
*$100,000–$149,999	425,400	2,420,300
*$150,000–$174,999	66,700	417,700
*$175,000–$199,999	13,650	61,250
*$200,000–$249,999	15,100	57,600
*$250,000 and Over	24,550	101,300
Telephone Numbers	2,824,600	15,491,400

*Aggregated Financial Data

NOTE: Aggregated Financial Data elements are available for modeling and data enhancement use. Please call for pricing. Aggregated Financial Data elements will be available for straight selection soon.

FIGUre 11.2 Example of segmentation classifications from the Lifestyle Selector.

participate in **data warehousing,** in which all databases (customer, employee, branch, and so forth) within a firm are maintained in one location and accessible to employees at any locale (Berman & Evans, 2007). Data warehousing allows for better analysis and data manipulation because all information is housed in one location. Data warehousing allows **data mining,** in-depth analysis of the information to gain insights about customers, products, and vendors, to occur. Data mining allows firms to tailor promotion efforts, which in turn lead to better performance by the company.

Knowledge gained from data mining and other analysis tools is used to identify model customers based on common characteristics of high-volume users. Model customers are formed into new target markets classified according to interests, income, brand loyalties, and many other segmentation bases. The information is also used for many other purposes. New products can be developed based on needs identified by the model customer. The success rate of specifically targeted advertisements can be analyzed as well as the value of sales promotion tactics. A myriad of opportunities are available for companies that understand how to use the database effectively.

Database management comes full circle when firms match new products with new target markets and implement the strategies identified previously. New products are offered and new promotion techniques are used and data is once again collected into the database, starting the process over again. The database is constantly refined and updated, allowing data mining to recur and new opportunities to be continually discovered.

For companies to remain successful, their ultimate responsibility is to be accountable to their customers. Particularly in direct marketing, when customer decisions are based on reliability and competence, the sponsoring company should pay attention to detail through information management. A good system is built on selectivity, retrieval capabilities, and fast turn-around and response times.

Database management has far-reaching implications for integrated marketing communications. Beyond a direct marketing campaign, data about specific target markets can assist businesses in determining store locations, merchandise selection, store layout and visual displays, personal selling and service opportunities, and potential special events and other sales promotion activities.

──o DIRECT MARKETING MEDIA

Various direct-response media are used to accomplish direct marketing objectives. Each medium offers the consumer an opportunity to purchase directly from the marketer. Direct-response media services are designed to generate a sale or identify a lead.

Direct marketing appeals follow a one- or two-step approach. An appeal that directly obtains an order follows a **one-step approach.** Catalog shopping is an example of a one-step approach. The consumer shops the catalog and responds by making a purchase. The objective of a one-step approach is to make an immediate sale.

An appeal that first identifies and/or qualifies potential buyers and then follows up with a second request to generate a response follows a **two-step approach.** Two-step approaches generate leads. Book, music, and movie clubs use this marketing strategy. Promoters make the offer to readers through magazines, newspapers, or the Internet. When the consumer responds, they are not immediately enrolled; instead, they are first questioned about income, ability to pay, and so forth. If the consumer meets the qualifications, they are then sold a membership. Although used less frequently than one-step approaches, two-step approaches offer the opportunity for repeat sales because customers are predisposed to respond positively to the communication.

Direct Mail

Direct-response advertisements delivered through the mail are **direct mail** pieces. Generally, the pieces are unsolicited. As we pointed out earlier, direct mail is the most heavily used traditional direct marketing media according to the Direct Marketing Association (2006). Over 100 billion pieces were mailed in 2005, an increase of 6 percent from the previous year. However, predictions indicate that higher postage and paper costs, and increased use of digitally transmitted financial statements, may cause direct mail to decrease in the future (Kimmel, 2006). Direct mail includes catalogs, cards, card decks, letters, brochures, pamphlets, flyers, diskettes, CDs, and other sales promotion tools.

Insert media is a type of direct mail and takes on many forms. Some of the most typical types are discussed here. Package inserts are pieces inserted with a previously purchased product. This media carries a high rate of awareness since the package is guaranteed to be opened. Billing statement inserts are pieces inserted with utility or other bills, which imply endorsement from the billing organization. Envelope advertising, similar to billing statement insert media, allows an advertisement to be run on the back of a statement's payment envelope. This puts the ad in the eye of the consumer prior to any of the ads inside.

Co-op mailings combine inserts from a group of noncompetitive advertisers in the same envelope. Mailing volume is usually high and can be sent as a mass mailing for zip code saturation. Newspaper inserts, also called Free Standing Inserts (FSI), are accepted into Sunday papers or weekday coupon sections of the newspaper. An FSI is a cooperative, full-color, multipage flyer offering local, regional, and national products. Take Ones are slots holding a stack of inserts at a heavy-traffic consumer area such as a supermarket. All these forms and others allow for effective direct mail campaigns.

There are several advantages to using direct mail. It covers a wide audience and offers the audience an opportunity to read and reread the message, allowing a more permanent sales appeal. It is ideal for merchandise that is easy to visualize and has well-known characteristics. Direct mail can enhance the image of an organization and showcase products, service commitments, quality guarantees, or other promotional goals. Consumers use printed materials as one way to judge the credibility of an establishment. Although they may dislike the volume of direct mail appeals they receive, it does add to the trustworthiness of the firms sponsoring the pieces.

Direct mail has a relatively low cost per piece produced. Printed pieces are mass produced in high volumes for relatively little expense. Videos, computer discs, and CD-ROMs have higher production costs, but potentially offer a greater return for the sponsoring company.

There are disadvantages associated with direct mail. For one thing, direct mail is a relatively impersonal sales approach, even if the piece is personalized. For another, as opposed to personal selling, there is no opportunity for immediate feedback to the sponsoring company. Additionally, direct mail pieces do not always spark a sense of urgency and excitement in the reader, and the rate of return is often low. Last of all, there is always the possibility that the direct mail piece will be discarded before being read.

Catalogs

The growth of catalog marketing has paralleled the development and expansion of the U.S. Postal Service, which has made catalogs widely available to rural and metropolitan residents. A **catalog** is a published list of items for sale, usually including descriptive information or illustrations (Fig. 11.3). There are over 8,000 titles devoted to every

POTTERY BARN

inspired by the *Sea*

BUY MORE, SAVE MORE
New reduced delivery charges on Outdoor Furniture
plus free shipping on Outdoor Pillows,
see page 141 for more.

FIGURE 11.3 Pottery Barn, a home fashion retailer, supplements its promotion mix strategy with a catalog.

imaginable product line offered by small and large retail and manufacturing firms. Small businesses, in particular, use catalogs as a way to gain national exposure and distribute new products. Catalogs feature men's, women's, and children's apparel, home fashions, electronics, auto accessories, power tools, and recreation equipment, among many other product lines. Consumers like catalogs because they can find unique and specific items not available in their local market area. Additionally, catalogs provide descriptive details to help the consumer visualize the product. Catalogs are one of the most popular direct mail outlets to solicit customer response.

Catalog shopping saves time, is stress free, and is convenient for families and individuals who have less time to shop or cannot shop. Catalog shopping is particularly popular with special-size customers who cannot find their size in a store. Another target market continually tapped for mail-order purchases includes people who have no choice but to purchase from catalogs because they cannot shop elsewhere. These markets include rural residents, elderly people, people with disabilities, or others who have difficulties leaving their home.

Catalogs have multiple advantages, including convenience, availability of hard-to-find merchandise, ability to comparison shop with other catalogs, and easy payment opportunities with credit cards. Return policies are generally easy to implement. New customers have an opportunity to become acquainted with a retailer by reviewing a catalog and current customers can be introduced to the new trends of the season. Increasingly, companies are using catalogs to offer special incentives and sales promotions to their customers. The catalog featured in Figure 11.4 invites customers to *buy now, pay later.*

Catalogs can be an image-building tool as well. Through creative use of design, photography, and copy that provide a strong fashion statement and illustrate a fashion direction, a company can build one-on-one communications with the customer.

There are also disadvantages to catalog shopping. These include inability to touch the products or to try products on for size before placing an order. Also, although companies allow for exchanges or refunds, this may be a time-consuming and costly experience for the purchaser of an unsatisfactory product.

Telemarketing

Telemarketing is sales by telephone. The Direct Marketing Association (2006) reports telemarketing is the second largest traditional direct media strategy behind direct mail in terms of total advertising expenditures. The advantages of telemarketing include a personal approach by the caller, instantaneous feedback, and the opportunity for multiple sales. As with direct mail, a wide audience can be marketed to through this approach. Disadvantages of telemarketing include higher costs than direct mail and difficulty in reaching potential customers.

Prior to 2003, most of the telemarketing calls consumers received were unsolicited, **outbound calls**, initiated by the vendor. In response to increased consumer frustration with unwanted telemarketing calls, Congress passed the National Do-Not-Call Registry, which covers both traditional and wireless telephones. Since 2003, more than 106 million phone numbers have been registered on the national list ("Fear not," 2006). Although marketers predicted the registry would hurt the telemarketing industry, it has not; rather, it has changed the telemarketing business. Telemarketers have shifted their business from cold-calling for prospects to managing existing customer relations. Firms have shifted their sales tactics, using **inbound calling,** initiated by the consumer, and other strategies to keep connected with their customers over the telephone.

Broadcast Media

Although two direct-response broadcast media exist—radio and television—the majority of direct-response broadcast advertising is conducted over the television (Belch & Belch, 2007). Direct-response TV experts predict that in five or 10 years, all TV advertising will be some form of direct-response as

FIGURE 11.4 Incentives offered by catalog vendors encourage consumers to respond directly to the advertisement.

marketers move from measuring how large the audience is to how engaged the audience is, allowing for greater return on investment (Neff, 2006). As reported by Neff, direct-response advertising grew 16.4 percent in 2005 to $3 billion in advertising expenditures. Proctor and Gamble, the top spending brand in conventional advertising, has made direct-response television a major part of its media mix, using the medium to promote Cover Girl and Olay among other brands.

Three types of direct-response television media are currently being used by advertisers: TV spots, infomercials, and homeshopping. Considered short-form programs, direct-response **TV spots** are less than 30 minutes in length. Examples of short-form television content include movie trailers, product promotions, and mini-episodes of television programs.

An **infomercial** is a 30- to 60-minute television commercial that looks like a television program. Early innovators of this medium were primarily unknown companies selling skin care, treatments for baldness, exercise equipment, teeth whitening, and other health-related merchandise. With the success of these firms and growing respectability of the direct-response medium, better-known brands have started to promote their products via this outlet. Bath & Body Works used an infomercial in its first national advertising effort with celebrity Christie Brinkley as spokesperson for its exclusive Patricia Wexler MD Dermatology skin care collection (Prior, 2006). A spokesperson for the company explained, "Infomercials are a viable retail channel for any brand that has a multidimensional, highly differentiated story to tell" (p. 4). According to the company, the infomercial is a necessary first step before pursuing more abbreviated forms of advertising, such as print ads.

In contrast to the traditional 15-, 30- or 60-second television advertisement, the infomercial is more detailed, informative, and imaginative. The format generally consists of a news or talk segment combined with entertainment. The programs run on network, local, or cable stations. The sponsors of infomercials believe audience members will turn on and find the show so persuasive, they will watch the entire program. With excitement generated, they believe viewers will pick up the telephone and order the product. During an infomercial, consumers are asked to respond by calling a toll-free 800- or 900-number to place an order. Some consumers dislike infomercials because of their similarity to regular programming. They look like a reliable (objective) TV report, when in fact, they are a paid advertisement.

Homeshopping is a direct-response medium in which consumers shop via their television set from home. QVC (Quality-Value-Convenience) and the Home Shopping Network (HSN) dominate the industry (see Box 11.1). Homeshopping networks broadcast programs with hosts in a manner similar to a talk show. Hosts converse with designers or celebrities while promoting various items of merchandise. The celebrities and hosts interview shoppers who call into the show to make purchases.

○ Support Media

Print and broadcast media—newspaper, magazine, television, and radio—dominate the advertising arena and are considered primary media. However, there are many other places where advertising is viewed, such as the sides of buses, inside restroom stalls—even the plastic used to cover your dry-cleaning can communicate an advertised message. These less dominant forms of advertising are called support media (also known as **alternative media, nonmeasured media,** or **nontraditional media**). **Support media** is used to reinforce messages sent to target markets through more dominant, traditional media (Belch & Belch, 2007). We will discuss outdoor media and Yellow Pages among other support media.

Outdoor Media

Outdoor media may be among the oldest forms of advertising. During the 17th and 18th centuries, shopkeepers used signs to attract consumers to their stores. Because so many individuals could not read during that era, signs and symbols were used to identify businesses. Perhaps one of the most famous shopkeeper symbols was the red-and-white striped barber pole. Customers could find the place for haircuts and shaves by looking for this symbol. Now outdoor media are used in fashion promotion. As reported in Chapter 1, the Gap plans to use outdoor media to supplement television, radio, and print advertising.

As reported in Table 6.2, Chapter 6, outdoor media accounted for over $3.5 billion in total advertising spending in 2005 (100 Leading National Advertisers, 2006). As support media, outdoor media accounted for 1.3 percent of total advertising expenditures. The top three U.S. advertisers of outdoor media in 2005 included Time Warner ($70.9 million), Anheuser-Busch Company ($58.8 billion), and General Motors Corporation ($48.3 billion). Both Time Warner and General Motors significantly increased their spending on this medium from the previous year. Time Warner increased outdoor media advertising expenditures by 91.2 percent and General Motors increase spending on outdoor media by 49.2 percent (Fact Pack, 2006).

Consumers encounter advertising messages at bus stops and train stations, in addition to signs placed above the seats in subways, buses, or trains. These constitute **transit**

BOX 11.1

Sephora's World Grows: Home Shopping Network Latest Channel for Chain

Sephora's drive to extend its reach is being beamed across the television airwaves with the debut today of a series of one-hour shows on Home Shopping Network.

The French-based beauty retail chain is broadcasting four shows today—at 1 A.M., 9 A.M., 1 P.M., and 4 P.M.—from its Fifth Avenue store near 48th Street in New York. A trio of personalities—Julie Redfern, the Sephora beauty editor, and Dianna Perkovic and Collen Lopez from HSN—will pitch Sephora's top picks for holiday gifts and beauty tips to navigate a season of partying. The initial program will focus on best sellers from nine core brands and its own label.

"Our hosts are there to editorialize," said Betsy Olum, senior vice president of marketing at Sephora. "They are not there to hawk products; they are there to describe trends and show new product."

She described the broadcasts as the preview shows, with a regular schedule starting in February and plans calling for five hours of programming per month from a permanent set that will be built in HSN's headquarters in St. Petersburg, Fla. It will be complete with prominent Sephora signage and fixtures designed to create an in-store ambience.

"We believe there is a huge market out there," Olum said, "with more demand than we can satisfy by building 30 or 40 new stores a year."

While Sephora has steamed ahead with store openings, the retailer also has relentlessly pursued what Sephora president David Suliteanu calls "brand enhancement opportunities." First, the company, which is owned by LVMH Moët Hennessy Louis Vuitton, struck up a partnership in March with Klinger Advanced Aesthetics to tap into the burgeoning consumer demand for spa treatments. Then in late September, J.C. Penney Co. unveiled new and renovated stores containing sizable Sephora store-within-store boutiques. "Penney's gave us the opportunity to reach out to a new clientele who may not have previously shopped us before," Olum said, adding the reduced and edited assortment in the Penney's boutiques "allows them to shop for beauty in a different way. The assortment is smaller and more focused and isn't overwhelming."

And there seemed to be no objections from Penney's to Sephora's latest move. "Anything that Sephora does to raise brand awareness is a benefit to J.C. Penney," said Darcie Brossart, vice president of corporate communications.

The appeal of HSN has become apparent to Sephora. "Whenever any of our brands would go on TV there would be a lift in our store business," Olum said. The appeal of the shopping channel is evident from the statistics Olum ticked off: HSN reaches 89 million households, 75 percent of customers are female, the average age is 25 to 54, and the average household income is $61,000 a year.

Olum underscored the potential and discussed why Sephora decided on HSN, rather than QVC, and alluded to the apparent desire to move the network's programming forward by Mindy Grossman, chief executive officer of the parent IAC/Interactive Corp., headed by Barry Diller.

"First and foremost, HSN did not have a broad beauty offering, so there was an amazing and immediate opportunity for us," Olum stated. "Additionally, with their great demographics and Mindy Grossman at the helm, the partnership promises to be even more exciting."

Today's Sephora preview will feature best sellers from nine of the retailer's core brands, including Make Up For Ever, Cargo, Dior, The Balm, T3 hair dryers, Oscar Blandi, Urban Decay, Lip Fusion, and the Sephora brand of bath and body care and accessories and implements. These brands also are expected to return in the February lineup, which currently is being put together by Nicole Frusci, director of brand marketing for Sephora. Spokesmen, experts, and in-house makeup artists also will make appearances on the shows; for instance, Oscar Blandi was scheduled to appear in the 9 A.M. segment.

Michael Henry, vice president of merchandising for beauty at HSN, noted that Ken Pavés appeared on a show in October selling hair extensions. The show rang up four times the expected sales and the customer age was seven years younger than the average, he said.

Scott Sanborn, senior vice president of marketing, said the emphasis in the Sephora-HSN shows will be "on new discoveries in products and new ideas on how to use products." For instance, Dior is featuring a new mascara and Lip Fusion has a holiday set. Olum said that as in the case of Penney's, Sephora is offering its best picks of its core vendors, not slanting its assortment for TV.

HSN now has core beauty business, with its major brands consisting of Susan Lucci, Lauren Hutton, and Marilyn Miglin.

Henry said he sees opportunity to build up the color cosmetics and hair categories. He said skin care now does about 50 percent of the portfolio, and he would like it to represent only 40 percent. Conversely, makeup now claims 25 percent, and Henry would like it to be 35 percent.

Sanborn said the hookup with Sephora was attractive because the specialty chain's image as "the beauty authority" provides a platform of credibility for the network. But HSN apparently has built up its own following in beauty. Sanborn noted the channel has had no problem selling beauty serums priced over $100 apiece. White noted the market perceptions have changed dramatically since the eighties, when home television shopping was first introduced. The mass-class divide has completely blurred and so have the boundaries between price points.

The HSN executives also expect the Sephora shows to have a ripple effect. Two of the Sephora brands, Lip Fusion and Go Smile, have been scheduled for their own shows in January. The promotional theme running through that month will be "the new you." The HSN approach is highly editorial with tightly edited offerings and live demonstrations that can be very persuasive. Sanborn noted, "What works on TV is being able to show dramatic results, and that can really drive sales."

Henry added, "We are curating the assortment" and picking up marketing materials from the Sephora website. With the explosion in lifestyle retailing, the HSN-Sephora pitch will be: " 'Here are the five things you need to buy,' and that is how we get into the homes." He added, "We really are presenting the product to the customer in more of a problem-solving way than as marketing."

News is also a factor. Sanborn pointed out that Clever Carriage Co. sold out of 11 styles of handbags by showing different looks. It took 40 minutes, well short of the hour that was allotted.

Sephora's Olum sees the opportunity of entering so many households. "This is a destination for them. They flip on the TV and are ready to shop."

White also sees a chance to acquaint his customer with the world of Sephora. "Probably what will happen is that there will be a customer who will be educated about Sephora."

Source: Born, P. (2006, December 13). Sephora's world grows: Home Shopping Network latest channel for chain. *Women's Wear Daily*, p. 1.

media. These messages represent out-of-home direct-response advertising. **Out-of-home media** are advertising displays that reach consumers on the move through placement on bus shelters, bus exteriors, taxi tops, kiosks, street furniture (newsstands and benches), indoor out-of-home (airport or mall), spectaculars, painted walls, and even toilet stalls. Blimps (Fig. 11.5) are a modern out-of-home medium. These media have been gaining in popularity in the United States and international cities that have a large population base.

The Outdoor Advertising Association of America distinguishes on-premises signs from outdoor advertising. Signage used to promote goods or services offered by businesses on the property where the sign is located is considered **on-premises signage.** Store signage with a business logo such as Niketown is on-premises signage. Out-of-home advertising promotes products and services that are not available for sale at the location and are considered to be remote or off-premises signage.

One of the most famous places for off-premises media is Times Square in New York City (Fig. 11.6). Billboards for Tommy Hilfiger, Calvin Klein, Liz Claiborne, Perry Ellis, Banana Republic, Levi's jeans, and the Wonderbra have appeared there. In addition to signs, Times Square is home to a 35-by-27-foot animated screen operated by Panasonic and NBC. The NBC-TV network, through its local affiliate in New York City and other NBC ventures, broadcasts news and public service announcements over this screen as out-of-home media.

London's Piccadilly Circus and central areas of Paris and Los Angeles have also become centers for

FIGURE 11.5 The Tommy Hilfiger blimp—one of many forms of out-of-home media.

FIGURE 11.6 Billboards in Times Square.

apparel advertising billboards. Even Berlin has endorsed fashion-oriented billboards. Famous male models and actors have been used to advertise men's underwear lines for designers such as Calvin Klein. Attractive female models wearing the latest creations from Victoria's Secret have been featured in London. Both the scantily clad men and women caused controversy and were said to be the cause of several traffic accidents.

To maintain growth in the direct marketing out-of-home media, billboard companies use target marketing. The market they are targeting is drivers, particularly drivers with cell phones. These consumers have been labeled direct-response driver-consumers. Nine out of 10 American adults drive, and they typically spend more than an hour a day behind the wheel, according to the Department of Transportation. Two-thirds of all car trips are made alone. If drivers see a billboard or hear a radio commercial that promises to fill an immediate need, he or she might be persuaded to pick up the phone and directly respond to the advertising.

There are several advantages to using outdoor media. For one thing, it can provide broad coverage of local markets. The advertisements selected for these media can be targeted to the selected market within local geographical areas. By specifying a billboard location on a specific bus route, the advertiser has the ability to direct who sees the ad.

The large size of the ads makes outdoor advertising media big, bold, and hard to miss. High-quality images are possible using the industry's latest printing technology. Transit media have a high frequency of exposure and repeat exposure. Research has indicated that more than 60 percent of all adults in the selected market will have seen the message within the first week. By the end of the month, close to 90 percent of the adults will have seen the message. Close to 40 percent of the adults will be able to recall the message content. According to the Outdoor Advertising Association, outdoor advertising costs 80 percent less than television, 60 percent less than newspaper, and 50 percent less than radio advertising.

FIGURE 11.7 Advertisement for Yellow Pages online.

Disadvantages of other direct-response media are common with outdoor media as well. First, there is the attitude of the consumer. The consumer in transit is faced with many distractions, from heavy traffic to scenery, to unpleasant weather. These distractions can cause consumers to be unresponsive to outdoor media. Second, there are creative limitations with outdoor media. A strong first impression to the consumer must be created in a very brief period. The type of copy and artwork are limited to a few words and/or a strong graphic image to capture the interest of the passersby. Third, as with other media, outdoor media may have a negative image. The federal government enacted the Highway Beautification Act, requiring state governments to provide control of outdoor advertising and junkyards on interstate and primary highway systems. Provisions of the act restrict outdoor advertising in commercial areas and attempt to stop the proliferation of signs. Many people want to limit or eliminate billboards from the nation's highways and some states have enacted stronger limitations than the federal laws.

Yellow Pages

As an advertising medium, the term "yellow pages" includes both printed Yellow Pages directories and Internet Yellow Pages. **Yellow Pages** are a volume or section of a telephone directory that lists businesses, services, or products alphabetically according to field. Consumers frequently use Yellow Pages to locate businesses or the services they desire. Advertisers may choose to simply include the name of their business with a phone number or to purchase a display advertisement in color. In addition to the traditional telephone directories, Yellow Pages are showing up on the Internet (Fig 11.7). Box 11.2 discusses the success of this strategy.

There are several advantages to using the Yellow Pages as a direct marketing strategy. They generate inquiries that bring in new customers. Yellow Pages are a strong medium for local and small firms. Many small firms do not have big budgets for promotion and may use the Yellow Pages as their sole promotion tool. Small business owners believe that many customers are brought into their local retail firm though Yellow Page ads more often than from other methods.

As with all direct-response advertising, there are disadvantages with this strategy. Yellow Pages ads have to conform to strict requirements in size and printing capabilities and therefore creativity is limited. Also, not all consumers have access to telephones and directories, and directories are not always available at pay phones. Finally, regulation of Yellow Pages is increasing. For example, since Yellow Pages are alphabetical, some businesses have added A's to their name so that consumers will view their ads first. However, Yellow Pages publishers are limiting the number of A's that can be used in an advertisement so advertisers will be held in check. Aaron's or AAA Travel will still be accepted, but AAAAAAA Publishers will not. Direct-response print media, including Yellow Pages, is the most popular form of direct marketing used by sponsors. However, telemarketing is nearly as popular as a direct-response media.

⊙ BOX 11.2

Let Your Fingers Do the . . . Surfing

Yellow page publishers are searching for ways to stay relevant in a new-media world.

When Jackie Mitchell was launching her doggie day-care business in Tacoma, Wash., two years ago, she spent most of her limited advertising dollars in the local yellow pages. Now her business, Bark Central, is booming—but she says more customers have found her through her website than through the phone directories.

This isn't the usual tale of new media overtaking old media, however. In a new twist, Ms. Mitchell is paying the nation's third-largest publisher of yellow pages, R.H. Donnelley Corp., to both run her website and distribute online ads on search sites like Yahoo Inc.'s.

The yellow pages are finally getting Internet-savvy. After years of fruitlessly trying to sell ads on their own websites—which get relatively few visitors—many of the directories have begun reselling ads to their customers on bigger, high-traffic websites such as Yahoo and Google Inc.

"We're media agnostic," says Simon Greenman, senior vice president of digital strategy, innovation, and products at R.H. Donnelly. "Our strategy is to connect our customers with their customers wherever they may be."

Clicks by the Bundle

Only about 14 percent of U.S. print yellow page advertisers—about 600,000—are currently purchasing online ads from the yellow pages as well, according to estimates from Kelsey Group, a local-advertising research firm in Princeton, N.J. By 2010, the number is forecast to hit 1.2 million advertisers, or about 30 percent.

One reason for this slow growth is the relatively low traffic that the yellow pages attract to their websites. The most popular yellow pages site, Verizon Communications Inc.'s Super-Pages.com, attracted 17 million visitors in April, according to comScore Media Metrix, an Internet measurement firm based in Reston, Va. By comparison, Yahoo attracted 128 million visitors and Google attracted 108 million visitors to their search pages during the same period.

So the publishers of the top directories—including AT&T Inc., BellSouth Corp., Verizon, and Donnelley—decided to offer small businesses a service that would allow the businesses to get their ads seen by consumers using those high-traffic sites.

The service, called click packages, works like this: The yellow pages, on behalf of advertisers, bid on search keywords like "carpet cleaner" in online auctions. The top bidders' ads—typically a few lines of text—then run on the right-hand side of a page with results of a search for the keyword. The advertiser pays a flat monthly fee for a guaranteed number of customer clicks on those ads, which link to the business's website. So the yellow pages will keep bidding for various keywords until the guaranteed number of clicks is reached. And the ads stay up as long as it takes to generate those clicks.

Micha Anderson, president of Chastain Chem-Dry, a carpet-cleaning service in Atlanta, spends $1,625 a month for 750 clicks from BellSouth—meaning BellSouth will keep bidding on keywords until at least 750 people click on Chastain Chem-Dry's ads and land on the business's site each month. BellSouth buys ads on websites including Yahoo.com, InfoSpace Inc.'s InfoSpace.com and Switchboard.com, and Ask.com, which is owned by IAC/InterActiveCorp. BellSouth keeps a percentage of the monthly fee depending on how many clicks are purchased.

Mr. Anderson says he doesn't pay attention to what keywords have been purchased on his behalf. He just knows that the traffic to his website has nearly quadrupled since the program began. "I don't know what exactly are the mechanics of how they drive the traffic for us," he says, "but it's effective."

High Cost of Convenience

Charles Stubbs, chief executive of YellowPages.com, a joint venture between AT&T and BellSouth, says, "Small-business people are busy people and they don't have time to spend two hours a day to manage their online advertising accounts."

There's a price for that convenience, however. Kirsten Mangers, the chief executive of WebVisible, the company that manages the bundle-of-clicks technology for Donnelley and others and trains sales representatives to sell those clicks, says that "if the average cost per click is 50 cents or a dollar, [the customer] may [actually] spend $2 or more for a click," but they are paying for the yellow pages to manage their accounts.

WebVisible, a unit of Atlanta-based SME Global Solutions Inc., buys between 300 and 600 keywords for each business and uses proprietary software to manage the advertising campaigns. Since some clicks cost more than others, WebVisible manages the bidding to allow its clients to offer flat-rate click packages.

Mr. Anderson of Chastain Chem-Dry pays top dollar for his clicks—about $2.17 per click, based on a monthly fee of $1,625 for 750 clicks. The top bid recently for "carpet cleaner" on Yahoo was $1.20 per click, according to information available on Yahoo's website.

Yellow Book USA Inc., the leading independent publisher of yellow pages, says the markup of clicks can inflate costs for small businesses. "In the bundle-of-clicks model, there is an incentive for the middleman to maximize his profit at the expense of the advertisers," says Gordon Henry, chief marketing officer of Yellow Book USA.

Yellow Book says it's in the process of rolling out a product called WebReach, which won't charge a flat fee to advertisers. Instead, advertisers will pay according to the price of the clicks purchased—so barbers will likely pay less per click than mortgage brokers. Mr. Henry adds that WebReach will only purchase ads on the top-tier search engines—Yahoo, Google, Ask.com, Microsoft Corp.'s MSN.com, and Time Warner Inc.'s AOL.com—unlike other yellow pages, which purchase across as many as 30 sites.

Mr. Henry says Yellow Book will still charge an undisclosed management fee for managing the account. "We're taking a small fee to track the advertising, explain it to the advertiser, and take that worry and hassle out of his hands," he says.

Verizon also offers a pay-per-click account that charges according to the price of the click instead of a flat rate.

Building a Site

The click packages aren't the only services the yellow pages are offering. Most also will design and manage a website for small-business advertisers—many of whom don't have an existing Web presence.

BellSouth designed a three-page website for Chastain Chem-Dry, which includes a complete listing of its services, locations, and contact information. It also manages the site.

Donnelley designed and manages the Bark Central website. Ms. Mitchell pays Donnelley $100 per month, which includes a clicks package of 240 guaranteed clicks and the design and management of the site. The Bark Central site includes contact information, a list of services, hours of operation, rates, and requirements like vaccines. Customers also can send an e-mail or make a reservation through the site.

The Direct Route

Some small businesses, however, say they don't need help from the yellow pages to make a connection.

Michael Jimenez of San Rafael, Calif., says sales at his upholstery business have risen 13 percent in the past 18 months. He credits the ad space he buys directly from Google. His ads run alongside some of the search results in Google.

To buy those ads, Mr. Jimenez bids on a bunch of keywords, such as "upholstery," "custom upholstery," and "upholstery shop" on Google. If his bid is among the top in a certain category, his ad will show up alongside the results for a search on that word. He only pays when someone clicks on his ad and lands on his Web page, MichaelsUpholstery.com. Mr. Jimenez says he pays an average of $50 per month for clicks.

The small-business owner says Yahoo approached him about nine months ago with an offer to buy keywords. He now spends $15 a month with Yahoo, which bids on keywords such as "Marin upholstery" on his behalf.

Mr. Jimenez says about 70 percent of the traffic to his website now comes from Google and Yahoo. And business has increased so much that he has been having a hard time keeping up with the volume.

Executives at the yellow page directories say they aren't worried that too many companies will follow in Mr. Jimenez's footsteps. "The vast majority of small businesses have neither the time nor awareness to effectively market their products on the Internet," says Bill Hammack, an industry consultant and former executive at Donnelley.

Mr. Jimenez still pays about $600 a month for several listings in the local yellow pages, which includes the online yellow pages. But he says the online Yellow Pages haven't yielded much traffic.

"The thing that keeps us from pulling from yellow pages," he says, "is that our clientele in Marin County is an older clientele and they still use the yellow pages."

Source: Angwin, J. (2006, July 10). Let your fingers do the . . . surfing. *Wall Street Journal*, p.R5.

Other Support Media

There are other types of support media that you may never have considered. One example is at the movie theater. **On-screen entertainment** is the slide show that is shown before the movie. These presentations are created by the National Cinema Network (NCN) and show ads along with trivia and tidbits about Hollywood to movie-goers. According to the NCN, the potential audience for prefilm ads is close to 90 million a month. Those who benefit most from this advertising are small businesses that occupy space near theaters.

The dry cleaner provides another source of direct-response media. Look World-wide, a Miami-based advertising agency, has coordinated more than 10,000 dry cleaners in the largest metropolitan markets into the International Cleaners Advertising Network. Marketers can place ads on cleaners' plastic bags, paper-covered hangers, and protective paper garment covers, as well as offer samples that come in bags attached to the hangers. Benefits of the network include reaching professional, higher-income consumers, as well as "repeat impressions" as dry cleaning goes from store to home or office.

CBS may have taken support media to a new level with egg-vertising. The network placed laser imprints of its trademark eye insignia, as well as logos for some shows, on 35 million eggs during September and October 2006 (Joachim, 2006). Slogans included *Crack the Case on CSI* and *Scramble to Win on CBS* promoting *The Amazing Race*, among others. CBS spokespersons said that newspaper, magazines, and websites are so crowded that they wanted to try something else.

———o INTERACTIVE MEDIA

Probably the biggest promotion change that occurred between writing the first and second editions of this book is the impact of the Internet and interactive media. The **Internet** is a global data communication system that started in 1969 with the connection of two computers, one at UCLA and the other at Stanford University, by the U.S. Department of Defense as a fail-safe way to connect vital research agencies across the United States (Belch & Belch, 2007). What began with 15 researchers has grown to over a billion users today.

The most significant change to the Internet has been the development of the **World Wide Web (WWW),** which is the business component of the Internet. The web is the portion of the Internet that supports a graphical user interface for navigation with a browser such as Internet explorer (Strauss & Frost, 2001). The place where providers make information available to Internet users is called a **website.** Website addresses have affected direct marketing in a positive way by giving advertisers an efficient way to market their products. Placing an Internet address in an ad enables the reader to acquire additional information about the product or sponsor at a time convenient for the consumer. These addresses appear in print media, broadcast media, sales promotion tools, and many other sources.

Table 11.1 identifies the top 10 retail websites offering apparel and footwear and the highest customer satisfaction scores. Businesses that sell goods directly over the Internet participate in **e-commerce.** It is interesting to note that only two of the 10 retailers are strictly online stores, Amazon.com and Zappos.com (an online shoe store). The other eight retailers participate in multichannel retailing. QVC and HSN are homeshopping networks utilizing broadcast media. L.L. Bean and Chadwick's are catalog retailers. Old Navy customers can shop in-store in addition to the e-commerce website. Nordstrom, J.C. Penney, and Neiman Marcus have in-store, catalog, and e-commerce retail opportunities, which have additional challenges in meeting expectations for online and offline consumers (Hall & Gustke, 2006).

In addition to e-commerce websites, direct marketers advertise directly on the Internet. Referring to Table 6.2, Chapter 6, total advertising spending on the Internet in 2005 was over $8 billion (100 Leading National Advertisers, 2006). Percent change from the previous year may be a more meaningful statistic than dollar amount. Internet advertising spending increased 13.3 percent from the previous year. This was the

TABLE 11.1   *Top 10 Retail Websites Offering
Apparel and Footwear Ranked by
Customer Satisfaction Scores*

	Site	Satisfaction Score
1	Amazon.com	83
2	QVC.com	82
3*	LLBean.com	80
4*	OldNavy.com	80
5*	Chadwicks.com	78
6*	HSN.com	78
7*	Zappos.com	78
8	Nordstrom.com	77
9*	JCPenney.com	76
10*	NeimanMarcus .com	76

*Indicates tied score.

Adapted from: Hall, C., & Gustke, C. (2006, June 29). Getting satisfaction. *Women's Wear Daily*, p. 12.

second largest change reported; only local magazine advertising spending had a higher increase.

The fastest growing form of advertising on the Internet is **paid search,** in which the advertiser only pays when a customer clicks on their ad or link from a search engine page. Table 11.2 shows the breakdown of online advertising spending. Paid search advertising constituted 41.5 percent of all online advertising (Interactive Marketing and Media, 2006). Figure 11.8 illustrates a paid search advertisement. At the top and to the right of the search engine results list are sponsored links, which are paid search advertisements.

The most common form of advertising on the Web is **banner.** These advertisements are sponsored messages that appear on websites by third-party vendors. Banner ads are used to create awareness or brand recognition. Figure 11.9 shows a banner advertisement for Gromwell (a fashion talent agency) on the wwd.com website. Sponsors hope website visitors will click on online advertisements to learn more about products and purchase them.

Sponsorships are another common form of Internet advertising. **Regular sponsorship** occurs when a company pays to sponsor a section of a site. More involved sponsorship is **content sponsorship** in which the sponsor provides advertising dollars in return for name association and provides content (Belch & Belch, 2007).

Pop-up advertisements appear on screen when the Internet is accessed. These ads are generally larger than a banner ad and are used to get your attention. For example, when accessing Style.com a video advertisement for Chanel featuring Karl Lagerfeld appears. **Pop-under advertisements** appear under a web page and only become visible when the user leaves a site.

TABLE 11.2 *Online Advertising Spending*

Format	Projected 2006	As % of Total
Paid search	$6.47	41.5
Rich media	1.79	11.5
Classified	2.73	17.5
Display ads	2.89	18.5
Sponsorships	0.62	4.0
Referrals	0.78	5.0
E-mail	0.16	1.0
Slotting fees	0.16	1.0
Total	**15.60**	**100.0**

Adapted from: Interactive Marketing and Media (2006). *Advertising Age.* New York: Crain Communications, Inc. Reprinted with permission from the April 17, 2006 supplement to *Advertising Age.* Copyright, Crain Communications, Inc., 2006.

Advantages of the Internet

There are many advantages to using the Internet in direct marketing, including:

- **Target marketing.** Direct marketers have the ability to be very selective when using the Web.
- **Message tailoring.** Precise targeting allows for messages that appeal to very specific needs and wants of the target audience.
- **Interactive capabilities.** The Internet allows a user to click through in numerous ways, increasing involvement and satisfaction because it is user driven.
- **Information access.** The amount of information the Internet provides is mind-boggling and it is growing every day. Cost, comparison shopping, product specifications, shipping information, and many other details can be found on the Internet.
- **Creativity.** A company's image can be enhanced by creatively designed websites on the Internet, fostering increased brand awareness and loyalty.
- **Exposure.** Small companies can compete with large corporations on the Internet.
- **Speed.** Speed is everything. Users want to find relevant information and products quickly.

Disadvantages of the Internet

Just as there are advantages to this technology, there are also disadvantages to using the Internet in direct marketing activities:

- **Clutter.** As the number of advertisements on the Internet continues to increase, advertisers need to figure out how to get their message noticed.
- **Annoyance.** High-speed cable and DSL technologies have allowed Internet speeds to continually increase. Even so, a message is lost on slow-loading websites because users are impatient and will go somewhere else.
- **Measurement problems.** Researchers have yet to develop accurate, reliable measurement methods to evaluate Internet effectiveness. While the number of unique users

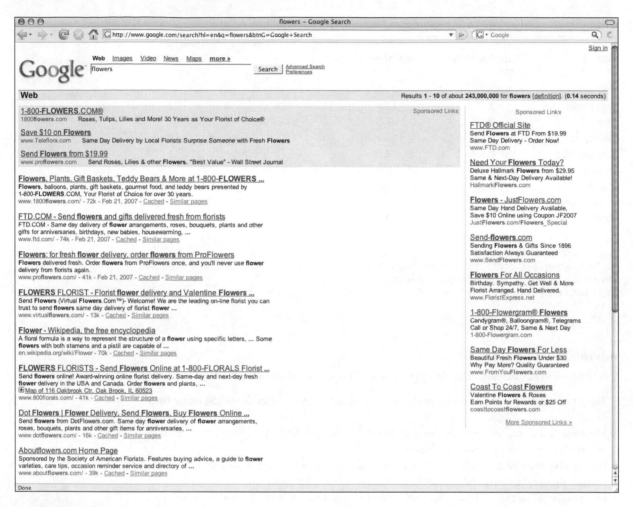

FIGURE 11.8 Google search engine showing sponsored links.

and amount spent can be quantified, other ways to evaluate effectiveness are not yet available.

summary

- Direct marketing is a promotion strategy created by the sponsoring company or organization to inform consumers in a direct manner.
- The key to successful direct marketing is efficient and effective database management.
- Target marketing is achieved by using a consumer database to identify the specific population of customers to receive the promotional appeal.
- A database is a collection of data arranged for ease and speed of search and retrieval.
- Direct-response media include direct mail, telemarketing, broadcast media, support media, and interactive media.
- Direct mail includes catalogs, cards, card decks, letters, brochures, pamphlets, flyers, video tapes, diskettes, and promotional items.

FIGURE 11.9 Banner ad on a website.

- Direct-response print media includes any form of printed material that requests a direct response including direct mail, "take one" brochures at stores, package inserts, sales promotion premiums such as matchbooks, Yellow Pages, newspaper advertising inserts, and direct-response advertising space in newspapers and magazines.
- Telemarketing is the selling of products or services, or fund-raising for an organization or institution, using the telephone to contact prospective customers.
- Direct-response broadcasting includes all direct-response advertising communications conducted through local, national, or cable radio and television channels including home shopping and infomercials.
- Interactive media is the newest direct-response marketing strategy.
- Outdoor media include displays that reach consumers on the move through placement on bus shelters, bus exteriors, taxi tops, kiosks, street furniture (newsstands and benches), indoor out-of-home (airport or mall), spectaculars, painted walls, toilet stalls, and blimps.
- Sponsors are continually developing other direct-response media to promote their message to consumers.
- The biggest impact to direct marketing has been interactive media advancing technologies.

key terms

alternative media	homeshopping	pop-under advertisement
banner advertisements	inbound call	pop-up advertisement
brokered list	in-house list	regular sponsorship
catalog	infomercial	support media
content sponsorship	Internet	telemarketing
cross-selling	nonmeasured media	trading area
data mining	nontraditional media	transit media
data warehousing	on-premises signage	TV spots
database	on-screen entertainment	two-step approach
direct mail	one-step approach	website
direct marketing	outbound call	World Wide Web (WWW)
direct-response media	out-of-home media	Yellow Pages
direct sellers	paid search	

questions for discussion

1. Why is direct marketing effective as a promotion strategy?
2. What challenges are inherent in direct marketing strategies?
3. What are the strengths and weaknesses of various direct-response promotion strategies?
4. What makes a database list effective?
5. What are the pros and cons of maintaining a database list in-house?
6. How can vendors acquire names for a database?

additional resources

Belch, G. E., & Belch, M. A. (2007). *Advertising and promotion* (7th ed.). New York: McGraw-Hill/Irwin.

Meisner, C. (2006). *The complete guide to direct marketing: creating breakthrough programs that really work.* Chicago, IL: Kaplan Publishing.

annual publications

100 Leading National Advertisers (published annually). *Advertising Age.* New York: Crain Communications, Inc.

Interactive Marketing and Media Fact Pack 4th Annual Guide to Advertising Marketing. (2006). *Advertising Age.* New York: Crain Communications, Inc.

references

100 Leading National Advertisers (2006). *Advertising Age.* New York: Crain Communications, Inc.

Belch, G. E., & Belch, M. A. (2007). *Advertising and promotion* (7th ed.). New York: McGraw-Hill/Irwin.

Berman, B., & Evans, J. R. (2007). *Retail management* (10th ed.). Upper Saddle River, NJ: Prentice Hall.

Direct Marketing Association. (2006). U.S. direct marketing today: Economic impact 2005. Retrieved July 14, 2006, from http://www.the-dma.org/researclVeconomicimpact2005ExecSummary.pdf

Fear not your telephone. (2006). *State Legislatures.* Retrieved July 16, 2006, from the Academic Search Premier database.

Hall, C., & Gustke, C. (2006, June 29). Getting satisfaction. *Women's Wear Daily,* p. 12.

Interactive Marketing and Media Fact Pack 4th Annual Guide to Advertising Marketing. (2006). *Advertising Age.* New York: Crain Communications, Inc.

Jaochim, D.S. (2006, July 17). For CBS's fall lineup, check inside your refrigerator. *New York Times.* Retrieved July 17, 2006, from http://www.nytimes.com/

Kimmel, L. (2006). Direct marketing can't get lost in the mail. *Advertising Age, 77(3).* Retrieved July 16, 2006, from the Academic Search Premiere database.

Neff, J. (2006). What P&G learned from Veg-O-Matic. *Advertising Age,* 77(15). Retrieved July 16, 2006, from the Academic Search Premier database.

Power of Persuasion. (2006, January 19). *Women's Wear Daily*, p. 12.

Prior, M. (2006, April 28). Bath & Body Works turns to infomercials. *Women's Wear Daily*, p. 4.

Strauss, J. & Frost, R. (2001). *E-marketing* (2th ed.). Upper Saddle River, NJ: Prentice Hall.

FIGURE 12.1 Holiday doorbusters.

CHAPTER 12

Sales Promotion

An annual ritual of stamina and social theater: the early-morning after-Thanksgiving sale. Flocking to malls and shopping plazas to jockey for holiday bargains has become as much of a tradition as family gatherings and football games.

Known as doorbusters, these sales have become an increasingly crucial part of overall annual sales for retailers. Carefully selected and priced, doorbuster items are meant to give a jump-start to holiday spending; the average shopper intends to spend $738, up 5.1 percent from last year, according to a survey by the National Retail Federation.

While they date back at least a decade, doorbusters [recently] have propelled the day after Thanksgiving into the biggest shopping day of the year, displacing the Saturday before Christmas, according to ShopperTrak. Analysts say that each year these sales become more extravagant, with earlier starts, deeper discounts and longer lines.

Among retailers, doorbuster strategy is a closely guarded secret. Best Buy, Toys "R" Us and Circuit City all declined to talk about how they approach the selection and pricing of doorbuster items.

Stores are also hoping to drive additional sales. Lois Huff, an analyst at Retail Forward, said that retailers were counting on customers not to leave immediately with one item. "It's all about getting the customer hooked," Ms. Huff said.

Source: Warner, M. (2005, November 26). The doorbusters. *The New York Times*, p. C1.

> **After you have read this chapter, you should be able to:**
>
> Discuss the role of sales promotion activities in integrated marketing communications.
>
> Examine the growth of sales promotion.
>
> Describe objectives of consumer-oriented sales promotions.
>
> Explain consumer-oriented sales promotion tactics.
>
> Describe objectives of trade-oriented sales promotions.
>
> Explain trade-oriented sales promotion tactics.

For many consumers, the day-after-Thanksgiving doorbuster has become a holiday unto itself (Fig 12.1). This retail phenomenon offers a veritable harvest of opportunities for sales promotion, from marked-down items and free gift wrapping to the well-kept secrets of Toys "R" Us and the big box next door.

This chapter begins by defining sales promotion and discussing the significance and growth of sales promotion as an integrated marketing communication activity. Next, we evaluate consumer-oriented sales promotion and describe the tactics of consumer-oriented sales promotion. Consumers are not the only target market for sales promotion. Trade-oriented sales promotions are another part of the promotion mix that is discussed, including tactics for trade-oriented sales promotion. The final segment of this chapter concentrates on sales promotion management. The chapter concludes with a discussion about measuring sales promotion effectiveness.

ROLE OF SALES PROMOTION

Sales promotion refers to those activities that provide extra value or incentives to the sales force, distributors, or ultimate consumer. It is a set of paid marketing endeavors,

TABLE 12.1 *Top 10 Sales Promotion Agencies*

Rank	Agency Name	2005 Revenues (US$ mil.)	2-Year Growth
1	Draft*	387.4	15%
2	Digitals*	252.0	22%
3	Wundermanl	225.6	19%
4	Bensussen Deutsch & Associates	145.5	23%
5	George P. Johnson Company	142.6	21%
6	Jack Morton Worldwide*	116.28	5%
7	Arc Worldwide*	114.8	20%
8	GMR Marketing LLC*	111.0	34%
9	Tracylocke*	105.6	21%
10	Momentum Worldwide*	94.77	56%

*Revenue estimated by *PROMO* editors; not verified.

Adapted from: PROMO's 2006 Agency of the Year. (2006, June). PROMO, p. 19.

other than advertising and personal sales, sponsored by the vendor, to encourage buyer action through a direct incentive intended to add extra desirability to a purchase. Table 12.1 features the top 10 sales promotion agencies identified by *PROMO* magazine, the publication targeting marketing professionals involved in sales promotion activities.

As we learned in Chapter 8, appeals are used to provide consumers with a reason to buy a service or product. Once the consumer has a reason to buy the product or service, sales promotion is used to prompt its actual purchase. The **incentive**, something put in place to induce action or motivate effort, is the chief element of the promotion and is used to attract the consumer with a promise of reward. Incentives are used to stimulate an immediate sale. Incentives take on various forms, including coupons, price reductions, gift-with-purchase, purchase-with-purchase, refunds, rebates, opportunities to enter a contest or sweepstakes, or an extra amount of the product. Cosmetic companies give away free samples of fragrances and other products to encourage purchase of the sampled product. Producers may couple sunscreen and after-sun moisturizing lotions in specially priced promotional packages of other products to stimulate sales of both products.

Incentives should be relevant, useful, and long-lasting. If the incentive is a cheap, flimsy T-shirt that falls apart after the first washing, customers will think of the company giving it away as cheap and flimsy too. Would you want your logo on such a poorly developed premium? A top-tier incentive was used with the *Milk Your Diet, Lose Weight* campaign for the Milk Processor Education Program. The promotion, created by the sales promotion agency Draft, distributed milk-white water bottles shaped like women's curves at events and through the MilkPEP's website (Duttge, 2006). These water bottles produced a long-term, positive impression for the client.

Incentives have become so important to trade consumers in corporate America that a trade group, the Incentive Marketing Association, was formed to represent incentive merchandise and service providers and expand the incentive market customer base.

Sales promotion activities may also be used to encourage the consumer to purchase an image. Image is a strategy used to position a company as completely different from the competition. Many companies include image development in their corporate mission statement. Sales promotions designed to promote an image may include opportunities for the consumer to purchase a specific image-oriented gift.

Manufacturers and retailers may also promote a corporate image through contributions to nonprofit causes, such as the Children's Miracle Network or Save the Rainforest. Jones New York created the nonprofit In the Classroom, Inc., to improve the quality of education for children through recruitment, retention, and support of teachers in America's public schools. In addition to committing dollars, Jones Apparel Group's employees are encouraged to volunteer (Johannes, 2005). Retailers may use their willingness to contribute to the cause as an incentive for consumers to purchase certain items or make an additional contribution at the point-of-sale. These retailers may use point-of-purchase displays to sell merchandise specially manufactured for the promotion, or ask consumers to add an additional amount to their payment. In both cases, the contributed amount would go to the nonprofit cause. In a third scenario, retailers promote their image as a good community partner by contributing a percentage of sales during a one-day or several-hour sale to the nonprofit cause. This is used as an incentive to encourage consumers to buy during these times.

Sales promotion activities are designed to encourage buyers to make purchases. For example, extra incentives are used to encourage consumers to purchase larger quantities of the product. By encouraging the consumers to buy immediately, the vendor is shortening the purchase cycle. The **purchase cycle** is the interval of time between acquisition and replacement of the same or a similar product in a routine manner. The purchase cycle of health and beauty products may be several months, whereas the purchase cycle of a winter coat may be two or three years. Certain sales promotion techniques boost the consumer to replace a product before he or she has completely finished the current supply. Coupons with an expiration date or limited time offer are examples of sales promotions used to accelerate the purchase process.

Sales promotion is also used in simplified selling situations. **Simplified selling** allows the customer direct contact with the merchandise through "self-service" (Fig. 12.2). In these situations, sales promotion displays and incentives can provide consumers with information and encourage them to make purchases. Retail forms that concentrate on the sale of convenience goods, items purchased at the most convenient acceptable outlet, will use the simplified method of selling. A sales incentive such as a coupon or a bonus pack can influence the purchase, causing the customer to change brands or purchase a larger quantity of the item. Most items purchased at a grocery store are considered convenience goods. Convenience goods are often lower-priced merchandise and the simplified method of selling allows retailers to reduce their selling costs associated with these items.

FIGURE 12.2 Self-service display units encourage consumers to buy by simplifying the selection of merchandise.

Both retailers and customers find simplified selling to be more efficient for merchandise categories that are already packaged and presold through extensive sales promotion generally at the national level. Hosiery is always prepackaged and displayed in units that allow for easy access to the product. Lingerie manufacturers Playtex and Maidenform box their products. Brand-loyal customers trust the product to be consistent from purchase to purchase.

──o sales promotion growth

While sales promotion has been part of marketing communication practices for a long time, its position within an integrated marketing communications program is growing and becoming more significant. Consumer-oriented sales promotion has grown from $56 billion in 1991 to nearly $343 billion in 2005, whereas trade-oriented sales promotion directed toward retailers and wholesalers are estimated to be $150 billion each year (Belch & Belch, 2007). Consumer goods dominate the sales promotion industry, but trade promotion is expected to grow as well.

The use of promotional products in 2005, from coffee mugs, logo T-shirts, to other trinkets distributed as part of a promotion campaign, is part of an increasing $17.8 billion industry (Duttge, 2006). The sales promotion industry has been continually growing, outshining other advertising and promotional campaigns. In comparison that year, $8.3 billion was paid toward Internet display ads, and $15.9 billion was paid for cable TV ads (2006). This reflects a rising trend toward spending promotional budgets on nontraditional media.

Of the marketing and agency executives who took part in the *PROMO Industry Trends Report*, 64 percent say that they develop promotion as part of an overall marketing strategy, compared to 55 percent the previous year and 52 percent two years before (Joyce, 2006). This report also documented the movement toward more integrated marketing communications as they are being demanded by their clients. Nearly 70 percent of the agency executives said that clients are asking for greater integration of their marketing communication, with just 16 percent saying clients were not looking for higher integration (2006). Internal definitions of traditional media advertising spending versus promotional spending have an impact on these "slice-of-the-pie" relationships. But these definitions, once firm, are now breaking down and being redefined.

Many traditional promotion executives, who view creative advertising strategies coupled with media placement as the primary method for developing a brand, have been concerned about the changing direction of promotional spending. But they recognize there is a shift away from established methods.

There are several reasons why more promotional budgets are being taken away from advertising expenditures and directed toward sales promotion. First, the promotion industry has matured. Among the other reasons promotion budgets continue to grow: Retailers are gaining marketplace power, brand loyalty is declining, promotional sensitivity is increasing, and decision-makers are taking a short-term focus.

Promotion Industry Maturation

With growth of the spending on sales promotion over the past decades, the promotion industry has gained sophistication as well as maturity with a more strategic role in many promotion communication programs. Historically, the strategic branding decisions were made before the promotion specialists were brought into the program. Promotion specialists, who were supposed to create a contest, coupon, or sampling program, were considered to be tacticians rather than strategists. As more companies are using promotional techniques, promotion specialists with knowledge of sales promotion techniques are more likely to be part of the strategy development.

In a move to recognize the movement toward an integrated approach, Ogilvy & Mather changed the way it operates in the United States, by combining its advertising, direct marketing, public relations, health-care, and sales promotion agencies into a single reporting structure and profit-and-loss statement (Creamer, 2006). The changes were brought about by the clients' desire for a wider range of promotional solutions. As consumers are moving away from the 30-second spot and turning away from traditional media, budgets are being directed toward digital or nontraditional media. By realigning the company, integrated work will happen faster with more synergy.

Growth of Retailers' Power

There has been a transfer of power from manufacturers to retailers. Consumer product manufacturers for many years had power over retailers in the form of information. Manufacturers knew which brands sold well because they created demand for these brands by using advertising and consumer-oriented promotions, such as coupons. Retailers relied on the manufacturers to provide sales analysis and did very little research on their own to determine which brands were good performers and which were poor performers in the marketplace. With the development of optical checkout scanners and computers, however, sales analysis information became available to retailers. Retailers have the tools within their stores to track good and poor performance of products. Roles have reversed and retailers are now in a position to tell manufacturers which products they will carry instead of accepting the manufacturer-determined product assortment. A manufacturer who is able to provide discounts and promotional support will be given shelf space; a manufacturer who does not comply will have less space or may even be dropped. The advertising budget that a manufacturer once used to promote a specific brand to the consumer has now been replaced with a trade discount to the retailer.

Brand Loyalty Declines

Second, branding, discussed in Chapter 5, is another big influence on the shift from advertising expenditures to sales promotion expenditures. Individuals within an organization responsible for managing the marketing program for a specific brand use sales promotion techniques in an attempt to keep loyal customers and to gain new customers. Using the focus group method, Langer Associates conducted research on consumer preferences for branded merchandise (Shermach, 1997). Results clustered consumers into several categories based on their loyalty to branded merchandise. The clusters include steadfast consumers, loyalty minimizers, category contingent consumers, and image rejectors.

- **Steadfast consumers** declare their loyalty to a brand as a sign of character. It is highly unlikely that sales promotion will change the attitude of a steadfast consumer.
- **Loyalty minimizer consumers** consider themselves free agents willing to shop for the best price. However, they will return to their favorite brand if price is not substantially different. Sales promotion techniques aimed at price reduction have an opportunity to influence loyalty minimizers.
- **Category contingent consumers** are semiloyal based on the product category. If a product is important to them and they perceive a difference among brands, the

category contingent consumer will be loyal to his or her preferred brand. Sales promotions may be used to reinforce to the consumer the perceived difference between brands.

- **Image rejector consumers** have no loyalty to brands and base every buying decision on product characteristics and price.

Two concurrent phenomena concerning branded products have influenced the growth of sales promotion. First, the number of new brands introduced by manufacturers has saturated the marketplace. Often these brands have no distinguishable attributes in the minds of consumers. This causes advertising to be less effective. Second, the saturation of branded merchandise within the marketplace has caused consumers to become less brand loyal. Modern consumers are more interested in price, value, and convenience. As a result, advertising dollars that in the past were used to persuade a customer to purchase a specific brand name product are now being transferred to sales promotion to persuade consumers to try new brands. This is because the added value of a sales incentive has more influence in creating sales than do advertising messages.

Promotion Sensitivity

As marketers increase use of sales promotion, consumers respond positively to the incentives and perceived value. Then, consumers demand incentives as part of their purchase decision. If they have a chance to save money by using coupons or a store loyalty card, they want to use them in the future.

By using a coupon for a discount or gift at a retailer such as Macy's or Bath & Body Works, the customer perceives value. When a purchase is made, another coupon to use in the future is frequently presented. If that occurs, the consumer has future opportunity to shop with a price reduction or another free product. Buying a brand on sale, displayed prominently or with a gift coupon, makes the decision-making process easier for a time-strapped consumer.

Short-Term Focus

Increasing sales quickly is a benefit associated with the use of sales promotion techniques. As sales promotion activities become more common to introduce new products or to meet sales goals, retailers have become dependent upon sales promotion tactics. Thus, retailers and wholesalers are asking for manufacturers and brand managers to help move products with price-related incentives. Many channel members fear that manufacturers, wholesalers, and retailers have become too dependent upon sales promotion.

The growth of sales promotion affected both consumer-oriented and trade-oriented sales promotion. Next, we discuss these two types of sales promotion.

———o CONSUMER-ORIENTED SALES PROMOTION

The ultimate consumer or product user is the target of consumer-oriented sales promotion. These activities include contests, coupons, gift-with-purchase, purchase-with-purchase, point-of-sale displays, refunds, rebates, sweepstakes, and sampling. These activities encourage prompt purchase of products and improve short-term sales.

Objectives of Consumer-oriented Sales Promotion

There are many different sales promotion techniques to encourage consumer purchase of products and services. Each technique or incentive is established with a specific objective in mind. Objectives of consumer-oriented sales promotion include trial and repurchase of a new or existing product, increasing consumption of an existing brand, defending current consumers from the competition, and strengthening advertising and marketing efforts.

Trial

Influencing a consumer to make a **trial purchase** of a new or improved product is the objective of many sales promotion techniques. When a new brand does not have distinguishable attributes in the mind of the consumer, the manufacturer must use techniques other than advertising to encourage purchase of the new products. The consumer is encouraged to test a trial-size portion of the new product. The trial size is often free or discounted significantly to avoid risk on the part of the consumer.

Repurchase

Increasing consumption of an established brand through repurchase is a major objective of sales promotion. Competition between established brand names is strong. Consumers have tried different products and are content with their choice. With established brands, advertising as part of the integrated marketing communications approach is used to maintain brand awareness. Sales promotion can also be used to increase sales of the established brand and defend the brand against competitors.

Increasing Consumption of an Existing Brand

Increased sales of an established product may be generated through showing the consumer a new way to use the product. Recipes or other materials identifying the new use may be accompanied by a sales promotion coupon. Increased sales of an established brand may also be generated by attracting nonusers of the product. Sales promotions used to attract nonusers must be designed to change the mind of a nonuser who sees no need for the product. It is often easier for a brand manager to attract customers who use the competition than it is to attract nonusers.

Defending Current Consumers from Competition

The best way for a brand manager to dissuade current customers from purchasing competing brands is to keep the consumer stocked with the manager's brand at all times. Special incentives may load consumers up with the product before they have a chance to buy the competing brand. Additionally, brand managers may offer to redeem a competitor's coupon to defend against the competition. Sales promotion techniques encourage consumers to buy the product early and often to ensure that a brand will keep its current customer base.

Strengthening Advertising and Marketing Efforts

A successful IMC promotion package will use sales promotion techniques to strengthen the advertising and marketing efforts that are already in place. These sales promotions may include sweepstakes or contests in which the consumer is asked to read an advertisement in order to learn the rules or fill out an entry blank. Forcing the consumer to read the advertisement will reinforce the message. Sweepstakes and contests are only two of many techniques used in consumer-oriented sales promotion that are discussed next.

Tactics

Various sales promotion techniques are used to accomplish the consumer-oriented sales promotion objectives discussed in the previous section. These appeals include sampling, coupons, premiums, gift-with-purchase or purchase-with-purchase programs, contests and sweepstakes, refunds and rebates, bonus packs, price-off deals, reward programs and frequent-buying clubs, and deferred billing.

Sampling

Sampling is a sales promotion technique in which a small quantity of a product is given to a consumer at no charge to coax a trial use. Companies evaluate the possibility for sampling of a product based on three factors:

1. The product has a relatively low unit cost so that samples will not be too expensive for the producer to manufacture.
2. The product is easily divided into small sample sizes that are adequate to demonstrate the brand's features and benefits.

FIGUre 12.3 A magazine insert with a fragrance sample. Fragrance samples are not limited to women's scents.

3. The purchase cycle of the product is short so that the consumer will consider an immediate purchase of the sampled product.

Samples are distributed through direct-response marketing efforts, at in-store demonstrations, or on the packaging of other products. Mailed samples are generally small, lightweight, and nonperishable. Sampling through the mail is controlled through the use of segmentation tools described in Chapter 2. Zip code and income level are common segmentation factors for mailed samples. Increasing postal rates and expanded postal restrictions are detriments to mailed samples.

Fragrance strips are a common product sample inserted in magazines (Fig. 12.3). In 1965, 3M developed the first scratch-and-sniff test strip, called Microfragrance. Arcade, an international scent sampling manufacturer, introduced Scent Strips into magazine advertisements in 1979. The Scent Strip allowed mass distribution of fragrances away from the retail fragrance counter for the first time by developing an accurate rendition of the fragrances between two sheets of paper. Arcade has produced more than 20 billion scented samples in various forms since the first Scent Strip. The samples can be inserted in magazines, store handouts, catalogs, envelopes, direct mail, hang tags, postcards, and other formats. Air France put fragrance samples in its ticket jackets. The American fragrance industry has tripled retail sales volume to an estimated $6 billion since the introduction of the Scent Strip (Larson, 1997), showing a correlation between sampling and industry growth.

Sampling is a technique in which samples are distributed in the retail environment. In-store sampling has become increasingly popular to test food products. Consumers are becoming aware of this sales promotion technique and depend on certain retailers to always have samples available. Benefits of in-store sampling include immediate availability of the product if the consumer decides to purchase the sampled item. In-store sampling requires planning to ensure that tables, trash receptacles, and electricity are available if needed. Selling space must be used to accommodate the demonstration.

On-packaging sampling refers to a trial-size sample that is placed on the product or within another product. On-package sampling is very effective for a specific target market that already uses the accompanying product.

More than other sales promotion techniques, sampling works cross-culturally, because the product, such as a fragrance or a lipstick color, does not have to rely on language to represent it. The scent or the color and the vendor logo provide enough information and do not have to be translated into other languages. Because of this, sampling is on the rise internationally.

Sampling is the most successful sales promotion technique used to encourage the use of a new product, because it offers a risk-free opportunity for a nonuser to try the product. However, the cost to produce trial samples, including product and packaging, and the fact that trial samples given away provide no revenue cause sampling to be a very expensive sales promotion technique. This may prevent some retailers and manufacturers from using this technique.

Coupons

Coupons are printed forms or vouchers that entitle the bearer to certain benefits, such as a cash refund or a gift when redeemed. A coupon may also be attached to a product and be redeemed for a cash discount. C. W. Post Company began using this price-reduction technique in 1895, by offering a penny-off coupon for breakfast cereal (Belch & Belch, 2007).

Manufacturer coupons are a very popular sales promotion technique for both new and established products. Coupons controlled by the manufacturer do not rely on the retailer for cooperation. Coupons allow the price-sensitive consumer to purchase a product at a reduced cost, while not decreasing the cost to all consumers. Those consumers who are not as price-sensitive will overlook the coupon but will still buy the product at the producer's regular marked price. As with sampling, a coupon can reduce the perceived risk to the consumer, encouraging the consumer to try a new product. Coupons are also incentives for the repurchase of a product once a sample has been tried.

Retail-sponsored coupons are becoming popular to entice consumers to shop at their store during busy selling seasons. During the high-volume selling period between Thanksgiving Day and Christmas Day, department stores use coupons to encourage customers to shop during two-hour, one-day, or weekend-only sales. Advertisements complete with coupons may invite customers to shop at the *biggest sale of the year when you bring in this coupon,* or may tell customers, *You will receive the lowest prices of the year with this coupon.* Catalog retailers use coupons as direct-response media to stimulate buyers who have not made recent purchases. Promotional messages may state, *We haven't heard from you in a while . . . use the attached coupon to receive 15% off your next purchase.*

Coupons are distributed through newspapers, magazines, and direct-response, or are enclosed in product packaging. A popular distribution channel is through freestanding inserts within newspapers. Newspaper distribution causes brand awareness in consumers who purposely look for coupons in Sunday editions or on "food day," the day in which all grocery store ads appear in the paper, usually Tuesday or Wednesday.

Manufacturers also place coupons in or on the packaging of the same or similar products. This method is popular because there are no additional distribution costs. A coupon that is good for redemption of the same product is called a **bounce-back coupon**. It encourages the consumer to repurchase the same brand. A **cross-ruff coupon** encourages the consumer to buy a different product manufactured by the same producer. An **instant coupon** is a form placed on the outside of a package to encourage the consumer to immediately redeem the coupon.

The advantage of coupons is the ability to offer price reductions to those targeted customers who need this incentive to purchase the product. By searching for and using a coupon, consumers self-identify their need for the incentive. Consumers who would purchase the product anyway do not need the incentive and are less likely to use the coupon, and the cost associated with the promotion is not wasted on these consumers.

A disadvantage to coupon is tracking. It is impossible to know when a consumer is going to use a coupon. Although expiration dates are printed on some coupons to accelerate the purchase of the product, response is rarely immediate. Additionally, coupons that are intended to attract new buyers are often redeemed by current users of the product. Instead of increasing market share with new users, coupons decrease profit margins when redeemed by current users.

Premiums

Have you ever been offered a free travel clock when you renewed a subscription? Or been offered a free T-shirt if you present a card at a new store opening? The travel clock and the T-shirt are premiums. **Premiums,** also known as ad specialties, are gifts or merchandise offered free or at a reduced price as an inducement to buy something else. We are all familiar with the prizes that appear in Cracker Jacks. These were the first premiums, developed in 1912. Premiums can be almost anything from logo coffee mugs, mousepads, pens, book bags, caps, and T-shirts to other novelty items. They may be given away or included in a package or sent to consumers, who mail in a request and a proof of purchase. The Advertising Specialty Institute, a company serving the promotional products industry, reports a 5.1 percent increase in promotional product sales in 2005, which is the third year of growth in this industry (Duttge, 2006). Firms are interested in premiums that include URLs in addition to the company name and logo to drive traffic to the firm's website. They are also interested in improving response rates for direct mail campaigns, estimated to be 30 percent with a premium. Promotional products have come a long way since mousepads in the mid-1990s, bobble-head dolls in 2003, and USB memory sticks in 2005. A few of the most unique premium items include toasters that burn logos on bread, roses with logos on the petals, or vibrating soap embossed with a logo (2006).

Premiums can be expensive for a vendor to produce and to package within a product. Children are more enticed by premiums than adults. A particularly poor premium, because of selection or quality, targeted to adults may do more harm for a product than good. Sales promotion premiums play an important role in encouraging consumers to buy a product. But a business must be careful that the premium does not backfire, either by being too costly or turning off the consumer.

Direct premiums are attached to or placed inside the promoted item and available immediately to the consumer upon purchase. **Mail-in premiums** require the consumer to send in a proof-of-purchase to receive the gift (Fig. 12.4). Generally they require more than one proof-of-purchase. These premiums encourage repeat purchases and brand loyalty. However, the consumer must take the initiative to send away for the premium and the immediate reward for the consumer is lost.

FIGURE 12.4 Celestial Seasonings is supporting the National Coalition for Women with Heart Disease by offering a mail-in premium for a Red Dress Pin with a minimum purchase of tea.

Self-liquidating premiums require the consumer to pay for the cost of the premium. Payment may be money, or points earned from purchasing the product. Points are commonly printed inside packages, bottle caps, beverage cups, or game cards. Generally, self-liquidating premiums are higher-priced goods, such as sports figure posters, jackets or hats, or sporting equipment. Vendors usually do not attempt to make a profit but do want to cover costs. Pepsi Stuff is a self-liquidating premium intended to enforce brand positioning of Pepsi products.

Gift-with-Purchase or Purchase-with-Purchase Programs

Gift-with-purchase or **purchase-with-purchase** programs are incentives used by retailers to create immediate or limited-time sales. Customers are offered a special gift or bonus package if they buy merchandise over a certain dollar amount. They may receive the gift free or be given the opportunity to purchase an item from the product line at a discounted price. Cosmetic companies use this sales technique extensively (see Box 12.1). Estée Lauder originated this promotional device. Many cosmetic lines offer

○ BOX 12.1

Adding Up Beauty: Federated Rewrites GWP Rules

Last fall—which was unseasonably warm, mind you—department store beauty shoppers were turned off by the sight of tweed. Their disinterest in the heavy fabric did not bode well for the Estée Lauder brand, which had built its fall gift-with-purchase [gwp] promotion around a tweed bag, chock-full of color cosmetics.

The trend misstep and warm temperatures drove the brand's sales down 11 percent and the Estée Lauder Cos. sales down 3 percent in August versus the prior year, noted Morgan Stanley analyst William Pecoriello in a recent research note.

When it comes to a trend-driven business like beauty, misses happen. Only now the stakes are higher, and beauty firms have an even greater obligation to hone in on a must-have bag and cross their fingers for decent weather and consumer confidence. The reason? Federated Department Stores Inc., having morphed Macy's into a coast-to-coast chain, has assigned beauty brands a national date for their seasonal gwp promotions.

Prior to last month, when the shift took hold, brands would stagger their gwp's across a host of major department stores. As a result, 10 weeks out of the season, consumers could likely find a top brand's gwp at a number of retailers. Now, under Federated's watch, brands get one shot a season in its two retailers, Macy's and Bloomingdale's.

Beauty companies began bracing for the change last year when Federated completed its acquisition of May Co. and announced plans to shutter a number of doors and convert 400 former May stores to the Macy's nameplate.

It's a change that Wall Street analysts said will affect department stores' most established beauty brands, including Clinique, Estée Lauder, Lancôme, and Elizabeth Arden.

"It puts more risk on execution and on the weather," said William Chappell, an analyst with SunTrust Robinson Humphrey Capital Markets. "The company could have big [sales] swings if it doesn't get the best weekend or if there is a snowstorm that week."

One beauty executive cautioned that it will take some time to align in-store execution across Macy's 400 stores. "Long term, it's a good business decision, shorter term, it's a mess. Right now it's difficult to get a true read on the business," the executive said, adding that it will be nearly a year until beauty companies are able to compare monthly sales data.

"Harmonizing gwp's within Macy's is likely increasing quarterly volatility for Lauder and Clinique—two-thirds of the Estée Lauder Cos. portfolio—as approximately 35 percent of each brand is sold under gwp's," according to the Morgan Stanley research note, which stated that Lancôme's sales benefited from its August gwp time slot in Macy's, increasing 16 percent.

Elizabeth Arden was also one of the first out of the gate, launching its national gwp on Aug. 22, before Federated had officially converted its acquired May stores to Macy's. Elizabeth Arden's spring gwp is slated for January. To fete the promotion, Elizabeth Arden broke a national advertising campaign, an effort that included an ad in *Vogue* magazine, noted Elizabeth Park, executive vice president, global marketing and general manager for Elizabeth Arden U.S.

Laurie Dowley, the company's vice president, national sales manager, said that while there were certainly logistical challenges to rolling out on "such a big scale," the change worked in the brand's favor because its entire field force was focused on one time period. Park added, "Rolling out over an entire season can be distracting." Both executives acknowledged the risks of one date. "Should anything go wrong, you can't make up that business," said Park. However, she added that the benefits of the move, such as national advertising, outweigh any initial logistical hiccups. Industry sources estimate that Elizabeth Arden's two gwp's drive roughly 24 percent of sales.

Lancôme's Dalia Chammas, general manager, also commented that the one date prompted greater focus. "Having one date means you can be more efficient in so many respects," said Chammas. "We can focus the field force on a specific time frame to achieve high volume."

Referring to inherent risk of a national gwp, Edgar Huber, president of the luxury products division of L'Oreal USA, declared, "The bigger the operation, the bigger the win and the bigger the risk. But we live with these things every day, with every product launch," said Huber. "It's just part of the business." He added that Lancôme has been working to enhance the quality of its gwp's, and that the promotions often require a lead time of 16 months.

Huber nodded to the logic of Federated's decision, and offered that companies work with Federated to integrate regional peculiarities, such as a Spanish holiday, to maximize their promotional efforts.

Clinique has spent the last year readying for the national rollout of its fall gwp, which launched Wednesday and will run for 18 days. "It took some coordinating and some thinking," said Lynne Greene, global president for Clinique. "There's a good deal of merchandise going out the door at once." She expects to iron out much of the wrinkles of the first go around before Clinique's next gwp in April.

But like her peers, Greene acknowledged the vulnerability to external factors, such as weather. She offered that should Clinique's fall promotion be significantly hampered by mother nature, the brand would attempt to launch an anecdotal promotion later on that season. "It would have to be on an exceptional basis," she added.

Clinique has prime time slots for its two yearly gwp promotions, but under the new system, all brands had to jockey for a window on Federated's calendar. Federated executives could not be reached for comment.

"It's mutually beneficial for Macy's to work with its resources in an orderly fashion, and to determine where those resources rank," said Greene. "Clinique happens to be number one."

Estée Lauder launched its gwp on Sept. 13 in all Macy's stores, said Thia Breen, president, Estée Lauder America and Global Business Development, adding that prior to the change, the brand would roll out its three seasonal promotions on 15 dates.

"From an execution standpoint, it really simplifies the approach. For 18 days, everybody—from the retail buyer to the company—is totally focused on Estée Lauder's gwp," said Breen.

She acknowledged that with the nameplate change taking place only a week before, some consumers may not have been aware that "Filene's no longer exists," but said the transition did not cause a disruption in sales. Breen said it's a great benefit because of the amount of promotional and advertising activity taking place.

Industry sources said Federated is spending $90 million to $100 million on the ad campaign to introduce its new national reach.

For its part, Estée Lauder also advertised its gwp in national publications, including *People* magazine, for the first time.

The shift from 15 dates to three a year did require ramping up the supply chain. "We have planned for this [change] for six months" to ensure all promotional merchandise arrived at all Macy's doors on the same date, said Breen. "It was silly not to leverage that national nameplate before," said Breen. "For as much as it is a big gulp," she added, "it will mobilize the company's resources."

Source: Prior, M. (2006, October 6). Adding up beauty: Federated rewrites GWP rules. *Women's Wear Daily*, p. 14.

gift-with-purchase opportunities biannually in selected department stores. The cosmetic companies promote the gift-with-purchase through co-op ads in print media, and the retailers send preferred clients direct-response mail to inform them of the incentive.

Gift-with-purchase incentives have long been used as a sales promotion technique in the moderate-priced market. However, Karl Lagerfeld introduced the gift-with-purchase concept to haute couture ("Scoop," 1997). Haute couture shoppers on the Rue Cambon were given a little quilted handbag adorned with a nameplate in solid gold. The quilted handbag has become a signature piece for the House of Chanel.

Contests and Sweepstakes

Contests are promotions in which consumers compete for a prize based on skill and ability; winners are determined by judging entries and determining the best match based on predetermined criteria. Contests generally require a proof-of-purchase or entry form that a consumer acquires from a vendor's website or advertisement to enter. **Sweepstakes** are promotions in which winners are determined solely by chance and a proof-of-purchase is not required as a condition of entry. Because no skill or proof-of-purchase is required, sweepstakes are more popular than contests with many consumers. Contests and sweepstakes are beneficial in getting the consumer involved with a specific brand. Consumers like sweepstakes and contests because they have the opportunity to win something. Vendors like contests and sweepstakes because they increase brand awareness and relationship with the consumer. More important, they allow the vendor an opportunity to collect data about the consumer using the registration card.

A growing number of companies are using sweepstakes in their online ads. The strategy is to attract consumers with big prizes such as trips, laptop computers, or large sums of money, hooking them with promotional offers, and then use any information gleaned from the registration process to bring consumers back again. The sweepstakes work for two reasons. First, the firm establishes relationships with consumers by encouraging them to invest their time. Second, the firm is more likely to receive accurate data for its database because consumers will provide accurate information if they might win something. Contests and sweepstakes are a good way for companies to start a relationship with consumers. However, consumers want value and convenience more than anything else, so contests and sweepstakes should be replaced with incentives such as samples, rebates, or free shipping if the firm wants to build customer loyalty.

The downside of contests and sweepstakes is the fact that in some cases a consumer is more interested in the contest or the prize than the product being promoted. In these circumstances, the game has not generated any after-promotion effectiveness. Additionally, there are numerous legal considerations that must be followed when designing and administrating contests and sweepstakes. Specific laws within each state and several federal agencies regulate contests and sweepstakes. The Federal Trade Commission (FTC) has rendered various decisions concerning contests and games of chance, relating to the disclosure of the number of prizes to be awarded plus the odds of winning each prize, in addition to other regulations. Advertisers should make certain any contest or sweepstakes conforms to FTC requirements as well as to local and state laws.

Refunds and Rebates

Refunds and rebates are offers by the manufacturer to return a portion of the product purchase price. A **refund** is money given directly to the consumer at the point-of-purchase. Vendors use refunds to entice consumers to try a new product or encourage a consumer to switch brands.

A **rebate** is a price deduction given upon proof-of-purchase. Rebate requests are generally mailed in by the consumer. Rebates are often perceived by the consumer to be an immediate price savings, although the consumer has to mail in proof-of-purchase in order to receive the incentive. As with premiums, the rebate must be worth the time and effort of the consumer because immediate reward for the consumer is lost. The time between the mailing of the offer and the return of the incentive is a detriment to many consumers.

Bonus Packs

Bonus packs are extra amounts of a product, given in addition to what is expected. Manufacturers offer consumers a larger quantity of a product at the regular price. Products may claim *25 percent more free* or *get one free, when you buy two* in specially wrapped packages. Bonus packs may include a larger volume of a consumer good such as hosiery, socks, or other staple items, or an extra item in specially packaged goods. By receiving a larger portion of the product at the point-of-purchase, a consumer sees an immediate value to the incentive.

Manufacturers use bonus packs as leverage against a competitor's promotions, using value to reinforce loyalty of a known brand to the consumer. This is an advantage of the technique. A disadvantage of the technique is that bonus packs are more attractive to current users than to nonusers, who are not sure if they will like an item that is purchased in bulk.

Price-off Deals

Price-off deals reduce the price of the offered item, offering an immediate incentive to the consumer. Price-off deals differ from rebates because the consumer does not have to mail in a proof-of-purchase to receive the price-off deal. It is the marked-down price of the item. The price-off reductions are offered on the package of specially marketed items. Reductions generally come from the manufacturer's profit margin to keep the retailer's margin at the appropriate level, which encourages cooperation from the retailer for current and future promotions. The advantage to using price-off deals is their immediacy. Price-off deals are immediately evident to the consumer, who can view the price reduction along with the regular-priced merchandise from the competition. Price-off deals may also encourage the consumer to buy a larger volume of the merchandise, diminishing possible sales from the competition. A disadvantage of price-off deals is the reduced profit margin for the manufacturer.

Reward Programs

Reward programs, also known as **loyalty programs**, reward frequent buyers for their purchases with incentives of money-off coupons, gifts, invitations to special members-only events, or other benefits. The concept of reward programs was first used in the airline industry, rewarding frequent flyers with free flights or upgrades. In the past few years retailers have adopted this incentive strategy to increase customer loyalty. Neiman Marcus, Saks Fifth Avenue, Sears, and numerous other retailers have programs that reward loyal customers with gifts or discounts good for future purchases, based upon customer spending.

Customers present a frequent-buyer card at the point-of-sale and earn points. For each dollar they spend, they earn an increment of one or more points. When consumers have earned a certain number of points, they receive the incentive. Retailers include discount coupons for their establishment and for other noncompeting industries to encourage repurchase from their store. Examples of incentives are airline or restaurant discounts, discounts on floral bouquets, or free phone cards. Nordstrom offers members gift certificates after the accumulation of points. Additional benefits include member-only advance notice of new products and sales events, and points toward reduced-priced merchandise. Points may be earned by making in-store or catalog purchases.

The increased interest in loyalty programs is based on widely held beliefs about customer loyalty. Dowling (1997) documented these beliefs:

- Many customers want a relationship with the brands they buy.
- A portion of these buyers are loyal to the core and buy only one brand.
- The hard-core, loyal buyers are a profitable group because there are many of them and they are heavy or frequent buyers.
- It should be possible to reinforce these buyers' loyalty and encourage them to be even more loyal.
- With database technology, marketers can establish personalized dialogues with customers, resulting in more loyalty. See Box 12.2 for additional discussion of how stores work to earn customer loyalty.

Consumers, choosing to participate in a rewards program, may increase their opportunities for incentives by using a credit card issued by the retailer. For example, L.L. Bean offers an Outdoor Advantage Program. Members who choose to participate in the program use an L.L. Bean Visa card to earn points towards L.L. Bean products and services. Points are issued on coupons, which are redeemable at stores, through

◯ BOX 12.2
Retailers Go the Extra Mile to Earn Customer Loyalty

Many consumers, who expect little in the way of service, anticipate even less during the holiday season. Now some retailers have created initiatives in an effort to reverse that attitude and win customer loyalty by providing more convenience, attention, and amenities at the busiest time of the year.

"I definitely think service will make an appreciable difference in share of shoppers this holiday," said Candace Corlett, principal at WSL Strategic Retail. "I've absolutely seen an uptick in service this year and an increase in attention to keeping the store tidy, which is a huge undertaking."

Macy's is trying to alleviate long checkout lines with mobile point-of-sale scanners for credit card and gift card transactions, and express checkout carts on wheels in gift-giving areas at the Herald Square flagship in Manhattan. That store has also installed 26 express registers.

Sears is offering customers who purchase gifts at sears.com a guaranteed five-minute in-store pickup option. Shoppers choosing to pick up their online orders at a nearby Sears will receive a $5 coupon if their waiting time exceeds five minutes.

Wal-Mart has a similar service at some stores and the retailer has also tried to ease congestion at checkout by opening extra registers devoted to gift card purchases.

J. Crew is distributing chocolate chip cookies or brownies and hot chocolate at select stores such as the unit on Madison Avenue and 45th Street in Manhattan. If a customer is weighed down with packages, individual stores have the discretion to deliver them locally, a spokeswoman said.

J. Crew is taking some of the anxiety out of choosing the right gift with its Giftfinder feature on jcrew.com. Suggestions include cashmere cable gloves for $38 and enamel bangles for $30. New for the holidays is a cashmere-of-the-month club. Recipients receive a different sweater style and color for each of 12 months for $1,850, including shipping. If shoppers can't find an item in a store they can pick up the red "We'll Find It For You" phone and get connected to a catalog representative, who will search the entire company.

Customers who spend $250 or more through Dec. 24 at Henri Bendel can arrange to have their packages delivered for free in Manhattan in a Mini Cooper, which has been painted in Bendel's signature brown-and-white stripes.

At Target in Nanuet, N.Y., on a recent afternoon, red-vested sales associates were never far from sight. When a shopper couldn't find a dinnerware set on the shelf, a Target employee took out his cell phone and entered the item number. A flash on his phone told him there was a box in the stockroom. Just as quickly, he was able to tell a customer that a coffeemaker was out of stock.

If finding products in stock is a measure of service, retailers are lacking in some areas. A limited amount of featured Target's Go International! designer Behnaz Sarafpour's styles were on display. Only a single black patent leather jacket remained, a few ivory silk lace georgette layered dresses were to be had, and a taffeta dress with black lace waist was available in plum only, not white.

A newly renovated Kmart in Westwood, N.J., looked cleaner and more organized with simple red and gray signage. There were no lines even though there were only three open registers on a Saturday morning.

Of course, the best form of service may be measured in cold, hard savings. Corlett said that retailers this year "have invested heavily in the coupon machine. They've found the motivator to get consumers to use the store card."

Source: Edelson, S. (2006, December 21). Retailers go the extra mile to earn customer loyalty. *Women's Wear Daily*.

---

the mail, or by phone. L.L. Bean also provides free shipping for its credit card customers.

The advantages of reward programs include sustained customer loyalty and less consideration by the consumer to shop at the competition. If, as mentioned earlier in this chapter, brands are becoming less differentiated, reward programs are replacing brand differentiation in the mind of the consumer. The products may be similar but the retailer with the reward program will get the business because of the reward.

Reward programs can be quite costly to a company if participating consumers do not increase their purchasing behavior with program membership. If consumers do not consider the reward certificate to be of great enough value, then the company is out the cost of the program and the opportunity lost with expected sales. These are all disadvantages of the program.

Deferred Billing

Deferred billing is the opportunity for the consumer to postpone or delay payment of a purchase. This incentive is used to accelerate purchases when money is limited. Deferred billing may be promoted on the cover of a catalog or in a print advertising message or a broadcast promotion. Catalogs distributed in August may state, *Buy now, don't pay until next year.* Other slogans may state, *Buy now, no interest charged for the first 6 months.* This incentive is advantageous to a retailer or manufacturer because it gains additional revenue in the form of interest on the sale. However, if a consumer is a credit risk, the retailer may lose interest revenue and the cost of the good if the consumer defaults on the bill.

──o Trade-oriented Sales Promotion

Trade-oriented sales promotion, also referred to as **reseller support**, is directed to distribution intermediaries, including manufacturers, wholesalers, distributors, and retailers, to support the efforts of their resellers. Resellers, motivated by trade sales promotion to carry a product, make an extra effort to promote the product to their customers. Activities aimed at the trade include promotional and merchandising allowances, price deals, sales contests, special counter displays or fixtures, and trade show discounts.

Objectives of Trade-oriented Sales Promotion

There are many different sales promotion techniques used to encourage retailers to carry manufacturer's products. Each incentive is established with a specific objective in mind. Objectives of trade-oriented sales promotion include supporting new products, supporting established brands, encouraging retailers to promote brands, and building inventories.

Supporting New Products

Just as retailers use incentives to encourage consumers to buy certain products, manufacturers use incentives to encourage retailers to buy items for resale. Retailers have limited shelf space where each product category and accompanying brands may be allocated. New products are often considered a risk by retailers who have no sales history on which to base decisions. In order for manufacturers to encourage retailers to stock untested products, trade incentives can be offered to participating retailers to compensate for the financial risk the retailer takes for stocking a new product.

Supporting Established Brands

The support of established brands is as important as the support of new brands. Brands that have established themselves as mature products within the product life cycle are susceptible to losing market share from new products. Mature products are also likely to have fewer advertising dollars. Trade promotions can compensate a retailer for the smaller percentage of sales they are likely to generate with a mature product. They also compensate for decreased sales due to diminished advertising.

Encouraging Retailers to Promote Brands

Sometimes it is not enough to get a retailer to stock a product. Additional trade-oriented sales promotions can be used to encourage the retailer to display the product prominently and actively encourage consumers to buy the product. Incentives may be in the form of money, display fixtures, or other sales promotion tools. Displays that have the greatest chance of generating additional sales are placed away from the regular shelf position in a high-traffic area. At holiday time, department stores set up one-stop shopping displays at the entrance of the store, promoting moderately priced gifts, such as gloves and slippers, cosmetic packages, or plush toys for children and adult consumers. Retailers are encouraged by the manufacturer, through trade incentives, to display the selected items.

Building of Inventories

It is the nature of manufacturers to want retailers to have large inventories of stock. Large inventories will guarantee a retailer the necessary stock during high-volume selling periods and contribute to a more balanced production cycle for the manufacturer. Additionally, a retailer with a large inventory is more likely to push the merchandise to reduce warehousing costs. Manufacturers can encourage retailers to build their inventories through the use of trade-oriented sales promotions.

Tactics

Various sales promotion techniques are used to accomplish the trade-oriented sales promotion objectives discussed previously. These appeals include trade allowances; incentive programs; display and point-of-purchase materials, training programs, contests, and incentives; and cooperative advertising.

Trade Allowances

Trade allowances offer the retailer a discount as an incentive to stock and display merchandise from a specific vendor. Trade allowances include buying allowances, promotional allowances, and slotting allowances. A **buying allowance** is a price reduction on merchandise purchased during a limited time period. The discount may be a certain dollar amount or percentage off the invoice price stated as an off-invoice allowance. Buying allowances may also be extra amounts of merchandise included with the purchase of a certain volume, stated as, *With every purchase of 12 dozen shirts, receive an additional half dozen free.* Buying allowances are well received by retailers and easy to implement by distributors. Retailers are predisposed to expect buying allowances and use them as a factor in selecting merchandise. Trade allowances are frequently negotiated at trade shows or during market weeks to encourage buyers to write orders at the market rather than waiting until they return home.

Promotional allowances are incentives from manufacturers for performing certain promotional activities to support their brand or product. Manufacturers design promotional guidelines that retailers must follow to receive the promotional allowance. The guidelines may specify the location of a sales floor display, directions for an in-store promotional program that may or may not include consumer-oriented sales promotions, or the use of a product in paid advertisements. The allowance must be offered equally to all resellers that carry the merchandise. In return for performing the promotional activities, the retailer receives a fixed amount per case or percentage deduction from the list price for merchandise ordered during the promotional period.

To encourage retailers to stock untested products, manufacturers offer distributors trade incentives called **slotting allowances**, also called stocking allowances, introductory allowances, or street money. These allowances are fees paid to retailers to provide a position or "slot" to accommodate the new product. Slotting allowances are controversial because some marketers believe them to be a form of bribery. Retailers believe they need the money, which can range from a few hundred to several million dollars, to compensate for costs associated with introducing a new product to customers and company employees. Retailers who believe they can get slotting allowances will continue using shelf space as their base of power. Manufacturers with popular brands feel less threatened by slotting allowances and refuse to negotiate, using the power of their brands to assure shelf space.

"We have a p-o-p display for our new perfume. Can we move the beef jerky down a smidge?"

Incentive Programs

Incentive programs, which will be discussed in more detail in Chapter 17, are motivational tools generally designed to increase the sales productivity of sales associates at the retail level. Manufacturers sponsor sales training programs as a trade-oriented sales incentive for the retailer. Sales training assistance may take the form of classes or training sessions to increase the sales associate's product knowledge and usage. Incentive programs may also include sales contests, in which sales associates compete against one another, against other stores within the chain, or against established goals to increase sales. The manufacturer may create the contests and sponsor prizes associated with the contest as a sales incentive for the retailer.

FIGURE 12.5 This cartoon takes a humorous look at the widespread use of POP.

Point-of-Purchase (P.O.P) Materials

An often-used promotional technique at the trade level is point-of-purchase display materials. Point-of-purchase programs use fixtures created by manufacturers for retailers. The trade association Point-of-Purchase Advertising Industry (POPAI) represents this industry. Dick Blatt, POPAI president, defines **point-of-purchase (POP)** merchandising as "displays, signs, structures, and devices that are used to identify, advertise and/or merchandise an outlet, service, or product and which serve as an aid to selling" (Diamond & Diamond, 2004, p. 11). Retailers who use this type of fixturing and signage hope that point-of-purchase promotions and in-store displays developed by manufacturers will motivate shoppers to buy. The cartoon in Figure 12.5 takes a humorous look at the widespread use of POP in the retail setting.

Cooperative Advertising

Cooperative advertising is a sponsored promotion in which the manufacturer works with the retailer to develop an ad and shares in the cost of running that advertisement.

The most common form of cooperative advertising is the trade-oriented form, in which a manufacturer shares the cost of advertising with a retailer as an incentive to carry the product. Cooperative advertising was discussed in detail in Chapter 6 as part of the budgeting process.

Sales promotion activities are very important to retailers and manufacturers to encourage consumers to buy specific products or brands by adding extra value to the product. Branding has become a big influence on the shift from advertising expenditures to sales promotion expenditures. Since brand managers have the responsibility to manage the marketing program for a specific brand, they alone cannot market merchandise effectively. Sales promotion techniques directed at the trade and consumer are most effective when combined with an advertising campaign as part of the IMC promotional package.

Trade-oriented sales promotion is used as an incentive to increase purchasing activity at the retail level. Incentives used at this level in the distribution channel motivate retailers to buy more products. However, as manufacturers and retailers realize that consumers have the final word, the trend is shifting from trade-oriented sales promotion to consumer-oriented programs. Through incentives, consumers are encouraged to try a new product, increase their consumption of an existing brand, or keep from switching to the competition's brand. Traditionally, manufacturers have used sales promotion techniques such as coupons and samples as short-term incentives to encourage consumers. However, in contemporary society, firms are realizing the importance of retaining customers as a long-term investment and are using incentives such as reward programs and frequent buyer clubs to establish long-term relationships with consumers.

summary

- Sales promotion is a set of paid endeavors, other than advertising and personal sales, taken on to encourage buyer action.
- Sales promotions are designed to encourage consumers to buy a specific product or service through a direct incentive, intended to add extra value to a purchase, or to purchase an image.
- Sales promotion activities have grown and advertising expenditures have decreased.
- Objectives of consumer-oriented sales promotion include trial, repurchase, increasing consumption of an existing brand, defending current consumers from competition, and strengthening advertising and marketing efforts.
- Sales promotion techniques used for consumer-oriented appeals include sampling, coupons, premiums, gift-with-purchase or purchase-with-purchase programs, contests and sweepstakes, refunds and rebates, bonus packs, price-off deals, reward programs and frequent-buying clubs, and deferred billing.
- Objectives of trade-oriented sales promotion include supporting new products, supporting established brands, encouraging retailers to promote brands, and building inventories.
- Trade-oriented sales promotion is directed to distribution intermediaries, such as manufacturers, wholesalers, distributors, and retailers to support the efforts of these resellers.
- Sales promotion techniques used for trade-oriented appeals include trade allowances; incentive programs; display and point-of-purchase materials, training programs, contests, and incentives; and cooperative advertising.

KEY TERMS

bonus pack	incentive program	refund
bounce-back coupon	instant coupon	reseller support
buying allowance	loyalty program	reward program
contests	mail-in premium	sales promotion
coupons	point-of-purchase	sampling
cross-ruff coupon	premium	self-liquidating premium
deferred billing	price-off deal	simplified selling
direct premium	promotional allowance	slotting allowance
frequent-buying club	purchase cycle	sweepstakes
gift-with-purchase	purchase-with-purchase	trade allowance
incentive	rebate	trial purchase

QUESTIONS FOR DISCUSSION

1. Why has sales promotion replaced advertising expenditures?
2. What are the advantages and disadvantages of using each type of consumer-oriented sales promotion?
3. What are the advantages and disadvantages of using each type of trade-oriented sales promotion?
4. What role does technology play in sales promotion techniques?

ADDITIONAL RESOURCES

Cummins, J., & Mullins, R. (2003). *Sales promotion: How to create, implement and integrate campaigns that really work.* Philadelphia: Kogan Page.

Neslin, S. A. (2002). *Sales promotion.* Cambridge, M.A.: Marketing Science Institute.

REFERENCES

Belch, G. E., & Belch M. A. (2007). *Advertising and promotion: An integrated marketing communications perspective* (7th ed.). New York: McGraw-Hill/Irwin.

Creamer, M. (2005, October 31). Ogilvy looks to the power of one. *Advertising Age, 76,* p. 8. Retrieved July 6, 2006, from Business Source Premier database.

Diamond, J., & Diamond, E. (2004). *Contemporary visual merchandising and environmental design* (3rd ed.). Upper Saddle River, N. J.: Pearson Education Prentice Hall.

Dowling, G. (1997, June 22). Do customer loyalty programs really work? *Sloan Management Review,* (38) 12, 71.

Duttge, W. (2006, June 8). Give it away now. *Advertising Age, 77,* pp. 4, 87.

Johannes, A. (2005, August 1). Couture finds a cause. *PROMO.* Retrieved July 7, 2006, from www.promomagazine.com

Joyce, K. M. (2006, April 1). Higher gear. *PROMO.* Retrieved July 6, 2006, from www.promomagazine.com

Larson, S. (1997, August 15). Treatment sampling follows scent strips onto magazine pages. *Women's Wear Daily,* pp. 1, 4.

Scoop du jour. (1997, January 22). *Women's Wear Daily,* p. 7.

Shermach, K. (1997, June 9). What consumers wish brand managers knew. *Marketing News. 31,* d. 9. 17.

FIGURE 13.1 Weatherproof
Garment Company.

CHAPTER 13
Public Relations

Outerwear makers are breaking away from traditional marketing to try less proven initiatives—and in some cases are pleased to be reaping the payoff of new customers.

For its second season of sponsoring Bryant Park's ice rink, the Weatherproof Garment Co. dressed the facility's 125 staffers in down coats with its logo embroidered on the front and back. The company hosted a market-week party at the rink, featuring a performance by Olympic skater Johnny Weir. On that day, visitors were encouraged to donate coats for the annual New York Cares coat drive; Weatherproof matched the day's donations with an equal amount of its own coats. It gave free ice skates to the first 100 people who donated coats and a free skating lesson from Weir to the 101st donor.

Source: Feitelberg, R. (2006, December 5). Coat companies liven up ads, marketing.
Women's Wear Daily, p. 8.

After you read this chapter you will be able to:

Describe the purpose of public relations.

Differentiate between advertising, marketing, publicity, and public relations.

Explain the various types of tools used by public relations personnel.

Describe personnel involved with public relations and media.

Identify media outlets available to receive public relations materials.

Create media releases, photographs for the media, and media kits.

Describe methods for evaluating public relations.

A s kate around bryant park is almost guaranteed to make the public feel great about Weatherproof Garment, or so that company hopes. The outerwear manufacturer keeps the skates sharp, the rink smooth, and the staffers warm and comfy in their down coats. Weatherproof helps the public help the homeless, gives away prizes, and introduces them to an Olympic skater. Who wouldn't donate his or her old coat and buy a snug, new Weatherproof parka?

This chapter explores the role of public relations (PR) and the various PR tools used in promotion. We will consider the purpose of public relations and discuss the differences between advertising, marketing, publicity, and public relations. The chapter then focuses on media outlets for publicity. Next, we will look at the vehicles for transmitting PR material from public relations specialists to editors and producers of media outlets. The chapter will conclude with a discussion on the preparation of the elements of media kits, including news releases, photographs for publication, and other communications as part of the promotion strategy.

───○ THE ROLE OF PUBLIC RELATIONS

As we learned in Chapter 1, "Public relations (PR) is the management function that establishes and maintains mutually beneficial relationships between an organization and the public on whom its success or failure depends" (Cutlip, Center & Broom, 2006, p. 5). The role of public relations involves planning and distributing information that will control and manage the image of a firm with a long-range time frame.

Establishing and promoting a favorable public image about the client's event, product, brand, or company, and generating good relations between the business and its customers, are the role of the public relations department. As a unit, the public relations office is responsible for the planned and continual effort to maintain and improve the institution's understanding of its public and conversely, the public's understanding of the institution. The **public** of a company includes customers, potential customers, employees, vendors, educators, the community where the business is located, governments (local, regional, or national), stockholders, and possibly the competition. Another term that comes from marketing, used to describe the public, is **stakeholders**.

Several methods and activities are employed to establish and promote this agreeable relationship with the public. PR analyzes public opinion. By evaluating public opinion, the company defines programs and specific activities to generate and maintain improved relationships with the public and understanding by its public. Allowing customers the opportunity to *tell us what you think* on a comment card is a very common PR program used to improve relationships.

Public relations is an ongoing effort to explain the image of the business through communications designed to create public understanding and acceptance. Public relations is not promotion; however, public relations uses promotion to get the message of image or understanding across to its constituents. A public relations program will use the elements of publicity and other tools to promote the image of the firm and meet objectives established by management. Public relations is a long-range program designed to provide the public with the widest possible overview of the company's policies and activities.

It is also the role of the public relations team to maintain a steady flow of positive information about a firm during times of economic downturn or disaster. Every company should have in place a public relations risk management plan for dealing with a disaster. Disasters may not always be as shattering as terrorist attacks or the murder of Gianni Versace, but they can occur as the result of a designer misjudging a fashion trend, a strike by a primary shipping firm, a safety issue at a manufacturing plant, or damaging public comments by a distraught employee. Public relations specialists must be prepared to address unexpected events, no matter how large or small.

A variety of public relations tools are used by public relations specialists or practitioners to meet the goals and objectives of the firm. Those tools will be explored after we talk about some of the confusion about the terms *advertising, marketing, public relations,* and *publicity*.

Global Public Relations

Public relations is a major part of international communication in the 21st century. With more countries forming trade alliances and increased global production of fashionable goods, public relations is experiencing a more international focus. Working for a *local* company, which meant that a public relations agency worked within a country for a firm that is based in that country, is changing rapidly. Companies are looking beyond their borders for new opportunities.

More than 20 national and international associations were involved in founding the Global Alliance for Public Relations and Communication Management, which was established in 2000 (Global Alliance, n.d.). The alliance is a framework for collaboration to enhance the public relations profession and its practitioners throughout the world. Members of the alliance provide a forum to share ideas, to reveal the best public relations practices, to seek common standards, and provide a better understanding of the cultures where public relations specialists work. The organization also offers access to relevant information and serves to examine ethical standards and accreditation options.

Several global PR trends are emerging as this book is being revised. "Global growth is no longer being driven solely from the U.S. Instead, companies in all parts of the world are looking beyond their own borders" (Hood & Schmelzer, 2006, p. 16). Growth is coming from individual countries, not through expansion of U.S.-based firms.

The PR industry is also concerned about the lack of qualified practitioners, which is a problem throughout the world. According to David Hargreaves of Bite Communications, U.K., "I doubt a single U.K. agency would argue if you said one of the biggest challenges is attracting and retaining the best talent" ("Connecting," 2006, p. 21). Factors influencing this concern include employee burnout as well as finding qualified practitioners in Asia's or India's emerging markets. Another international trend is the power of sport, with World Cup and Olympic events leading the influence on global public spirit.

Dynamic change and growth is taking place in China and Brazil, among other countries. In China there are a lot of opportunities due to the increasing consumer markets. According to David Liu, the managing director for Weber Shandwick, a PR agency in Beijing, "A lot of the opportunities are related to this growing middle class, and increasing wealth and spending" (Hood & Schmelzer, 2006, p. 16).

Public relations growth in Brazil is partially due to industry privatization and an influx of international trade. With growing maturity of business practices in Brazil, clients are much more knowledgeable about public relations practices. According to Valeria Perito, principal and general manager of São Paulo–based Ketchum Estragéria, clients were only interested in little more than news releases when she opened her practice in 1986 (Hood & Schmelzer, 2006). By 2006, the clients were more savvy about objectives, how to position, reposition, and build a brand image.

Global expansion and interaction are just part of the international public relations impact. Agencies are investing in promising markets, and discussions about ethical concerns and business practices are being encouraged by such groups as the Global Alliance for Public Relations and Communication Management. But communication between practitioners in various countries is not the only problem with public relations communication. Next, we look at some of the confusion surrounding public relations terminology.

Terminology Confusion

Many people confuse the roles of advertising, marketing, public relations, and publicity, using the terms synonymously or just using them incorrectly. Each activity actually takes on different and specific roles in the promotion mix. As we learned in Chapter 1, advertising requires the sponsor of the message to pay for the placement of the communication. In this instance, the message sponsor controls what is said and where it is placed. The key here is that the advertiser has authority, and that cannot be taken away by an editor with an opposing viewpoint.

Here is an example showing the basic differences between advertising and publicity. Advertising is a message from the interested party; publicity is a message from a public information medium about the interested party. Figure 13.2 illustrates this concept. In the selected example, *Glamour*, the public communication medium, informs the reader about color selection in women's athletic shoes. Within the story, Foot Locker is complimented for a wide assortment of choices, and Avia and Adidas shoes are pictured. Foot Locker, Avia, and Adidas are represented in the story as the interested parties and benefit from the publicity given to them by *Glamour* in the form of an endorsement. This is an

SOUNDING OFF

brava!
women's sneakers get real

I'D BEEN PUTTING OFF BUYING GYM SHOES FOR months. Sure, my feet throbbed and my knees popped after a workout, but I winced even more at the thought of spending hard-earned dollars on another pair of pink-and-purple athletic shoes that said: "I'm a girl. I don't really sweat." Yet my funk dance instructor had commanded me—on penalty of banishment from her class—to buy new shoes. So here I was in Foot Locker, surrounded by a sea of navy blue, hunter green and black shoes, looking for the women's department. I asked a saleswoman where the women's shoes were. "You're standing in front of them," she said.

Ecstatic, I tried on, oh, 15 different pairs and finally settled on black cross trainers that remind me of my brother's baseball cleats: strong, serious, athletic. As I paid, I asked the saleswoman why turquoise-and-pink shoes weren't sold anymore. She answered, "Times change. Women get normal colors now." Another fashion barrier broken!   —*Caroline Hwang*

Serious shoes in nonsilly colors: Avia lightweight cross trainer, $65, *right,* and Adidas Falcon, $55, *above.*

FIGURE 13.2 Publicity endorsement by *Glamour* for Footlocker, Avia, and Adidas.

example of a publicity endorsement that was not initiated by a media release but rather by news interest of the reporter.

In contrast, advertising is precise and controlled by the paid sponsor. Whatever leaves the advertising department, as approved by the sponsor, is exactly what will be seen on a prearranged date in the periodical or heard on the TV or radio. As long as the advertiser can pay for the ad, and the ad complies with the acceptable standards of the medium, the advertisement or commercial will be printed or broadcast as submitted.

Marketing has a much broader role than public relations. The role of marketing is to plan and execute the creation of pricing, promotion, and distribution of products, ideas, and services. As we also learned in Chapter 1, marketing is involved in the mix of the four Ps—product, price, place, and promotion/communication. Therefore, promotion and communication fall under the umbrella of marketing. What might be confusing some people about the relationship of marketing and public relations is the fact that many marketing-oriented firms are including PR activities as part of their function. In this instance, PR takes on a greater and more marketing-oriented perspective, created to promote the organization in addition to its products and services. In those firms there is a blurring of which employees are part of the marketing function versus which employees are part of the public relations function. Many PR specialists actually work in marketing departments.

Negative Images of Public Relations

The profession of public relations has suffered from a lack of respect from corporate executives as well as private citizens. With its roots in press agentry and getting publicity, one of the original purposes of public relations was getting favorable press, now known as media coverage. In this model, accuracy and truth were not seen as essential. Although this was not the only purpose of public relations, many people associated PR with unethical or unnecessary practices.

Another area for concern comes from a two-way asymmetrical model, which uses research in an effort to influence the public toward a particular point of view. This persuasive or propaganda model promotes a *selfish* opinion by avoiding resolution of conflicting views. This type of public relations leads to mistrust between the public and the message developers. Lobbyists who promote illegal or unethical practices have not alleviated the negative images that some people hold against public relations specialists.

Public relations practitioners frequently work in the political environment. One of the negative images associated with this field is the concept of spin. If spin involves outright lying to hide something that happened, it is in opposition to the proper use of public relations techniques. But **spin** has come to suggest twisting messages to give a favorable meaning to communication, which may or may not be true. Deliberate lies and distortion are among the tools used by spinners. Examples and uses of spin in political, sports, journalism, and business environments have created negative images for public relations professionals.

Faced with a lack of trust and fear of past unethical and illegal practices by PR personnel, workers in the field must work to regain public trust. Public relations practitioners must be sensitive to these concerns and be considerate in order to properly and ethically influence people. Next, we will show the tools of public relations and how public relations is part of the integrated marketing communications package, which includes many other activities as well.

───o PUBLIC RELATIONS TOOLS

Public relations tools include development, internal relationships, investor relations, issues management, lobbying, press agentry, public affairs, and the most well-known tool of public relations—publicity. Next, we will look at each of these tools, and how they support the promotion mix elements.

Development

Development is the tool used to provide support for charitable or nonprofit organizations through fund-raising and membership drives. This activity is also known as advancement, and helps finance the operations of such groups as museums, costume societies, and universities, in addition to many other types of foundations. Many organizations, such as the Phoenix Art Museum, depend upon membership and entrance fees for operating revenues. An annual telethon, 10K run, celebrity auction, or fashion show represent some of the activities to maintain relationships with volunteers, members, donors, in addition to prospective members or participants. Public relations specialists work as development specialists or assist them in making these activities work.

Fund-raising is such an important part of nonprofit and educational institutions that development aspects of public relations are often a major focus. Presenting a student fashion show or producing a museum exhibit frequently have fund-raising as a goal. While not all fashion shows make money, it is a method used by some charitable and educational groups to raise awareness in addition to scholarship or operating funds.

Internal Relations

Internal relations refers to the public relations tool of managing the firm's employees by creating a *corporate culture* that attracts and retains productive workers. Internal specialists work in *internal relations, internal communications,* or *employee relations* departments where internal communication is planned and implemented. This activity keeps employees informed, motivated, and able to support the organization's culture. Building a positive workforce is part of this function, and preparing the firm's newsletter is just one of the internal public relations specialist's jobs.

As apparel, textile, and fashion manufacturers get larger, with expanding operations domestically and overseas in the international marketplace, internal relations becomes more significant. Practitioners of internal public relations coordinate with the human resources department to produce internal communication devices. Print or electronic newsletters let employees know about the state of the firm, its stock, and its relationships with customers. Additionally, newsletters inform employees about career advancement opportunities. For example, Target provides a list of positions that are currently open. If an employee from California is interested in applying for a job in Ohio, he or she can get information and apply from their home store.

Additionally, the internal relationship specialists communicate about benefits, training, safety, and any other topics of interest and concern to employees. They also work with the legal department and communicate with employees about labor relations, contract negotiations, and any work stoppages. When the Prada store and American Eagle offices in New York were abruptly closed after a fire started in the building where the businesses are located, internal relations specialists took control of the internal concerns. The internal relations specialists were responsible for answering employee anxiety about the closure and when they would return to work.

Investor Relations

In publicly held firms, **investor relations** specialists work to enhance the value of the firm. It is the responsibility of the investor relations specialists to keep shareholders informed and, they hope, loyal to the firm. Tracking market trends, providing information about financial data, counseling management about financial trends, and responding to media and stakeholder requests for financial information are the significant parts of the specialist's job.

Firms that trade shares on the stock market are required by law to disclose certain types of financial information at regularly scheduled times. Annual and quarterly reports, SEC-required 10-K forms, and earnings reports are disseminated to analysts, investors, and journalists through e-mails, updated homepages on the Internet, and print media releases, known as news releases.

Information provided by investor relations specialists can have positive or negative impacts upon shareholders and other interested parties. If the news is good, the productivity has improved and the economic outlook is improved, current investors will want to keep the stock and potential investors are more likely to purchase the firm's stock. On the other hand, if the deliveries were late and merchandise was lackluster, the firm might lose investors and fail to obtain new ones. Therefore, in addition to public relations knowledge, investor relations specialists must have a strong background and understanding of financial and economic systems.

Issues Management

Issues management is the proactive process of anticipating, identifying, evaluating, and responding to public policy issues that affect organizations' relationships with their publics (Cutlip et al, 2006). This public relations tool involves two components: (1) identification of concerns that can potentially impact the firm before they become problems, and (2) creation of a strategic response to soften negative impact or benefit the firm from the concerns identified. In other words, the PR specialists try assessing public opinion so that the firm can respond before these opinions create insurmountable conflicts.

At first glance, issues management is not a big concern for the apparel and textiles industry, or is it? The issues related to sweatshop manufacturing are a hot button concern. Does your campus bookstore sell logo sweatshirts and T-shirts? How would the bookstore manager or clothing buyer react to a campus newspaper article about the logo products being manufactured in a sweatshop? Planning how to respond to such campus inquiries can put the bookstore management in a positive position, especially if the goods are manufactured in a humanistic factory.

Lobbying

The public relations tool known as **lobbying** involves a PR specialist building and maintaining relationships with government officials, primarily to influence legislation and government regulation. This is a very specialized and often criticized part of public relations. Some people view lobbying as an attempt to manipulate government for self-interests, even though the right to petition the government is protected by the U.S. Constitution.

The entertainment industry frequently portrays lobbyists as illegally paying off government officials and encouraging unethical behaviors. While there certainly have been instances of unwarranted lavish parties and inappropriate travel, lobbying more often provides an opportunity for open advocacy and discussion on matters of public policy.

Each state determines registration and enforcement practices, but all lobbyists are required to report their activities and expenditures under the Federal Regulation of Lobbying Act. Lobbying remains a legal and acceptable way for citizens, trade associations, labor unions, corporations, or other special-interest groups to influence government decision making.

Both the textile and retailing industries regularly participate in this public relations strategy. Although it is a public relations tool, it is not a primary promotion tool.

Press Agentry

Press agentry or media coverage involves creating newsworthy stories and events to attract attention from the mass media in order to gain public notice. As originally conceived, press agents were concerned about attracting public notice more than building public trust or influencing public understanding. According to some people, the attention does not necessarily have to be positive, basing their approach on the theory that the amount of public exposure in the mass media will subsequently determine public perception about the relative importance of a person, thing, or topic. Because of that role, some press agents have been called "spin doctors" or "flacks" and have not maintained a positive image in the public relations industry.

Press agentry plays a significant role in the entertainment, sports, tourist attractions, and celebrity business industries. For example, press agents have promoted such national event activities as the Super Bowl, entertainment industry award ceremonies and red carpet events, and resorts, including Disneyland or Canyon Ranch Spa. Consumers are made aware of the stars and the wardrobe for a new movie, such as *The Devil Wears Prada* or *The Nanny Diaries*, while it is still being filmed. Merchandise tie-ins, including T-shirts, handbags, and other products are available before the movies premiered. Figure 13.3 shows a product tie-in for *The Devil Wears Prada*.

A good press agent can help mold a musical group's image, try to make a new restaurant or retail store the "in place" to go, or influence the target customer to watch a new

FIGURE 13.3   Movie themes are coordinated with merchandise promotions. This bag is similar to one in The Devil wears Prada.

movie or television show. To be part of public relations, press agents must use professional public relations tools.

Public Affairs

The role of **public affairs** is to build and maintain governmental and local community relations in order to have some bearing on public policy. The military, some governmental organizations, and a few corporations use public affairs as a substitute term for public relations, since federal law prevents federal agencies from spending money on PR, unless authorized by Congress.

Recognizing the need for communication between the government and public, many public relations specialists work for local, state, and federal governments. These people work with titles such as "public affairs," "public information," "communications officer," or "public liaison." These individuals perform communication tasks in an increasingly complex democratic society. Another function is providing information regarding incidents that impact public safety, such as a wildfire or hurricane. Because most public affairs activities focus on government or societal issues, it is rarely a part of the fashion industry.

Publicity

Publicity is communication by the initiating party seeking to tell others about a product, service, idea, or event and delivered to the public at the discretion of the media. The information is disseminated through media to attract public attention, and as a result of public interest, awareness about the event or organization is achieved without the benefit of paid placement in the media, print or broadcast. Every segment and every organization within the fashion industry uses publicity as a short-term promotion strategy. Although it is the intent of every publicity director to promote a positive image of the firm through publicity, media outlets may turn publicity around and use it to further a negative image of the intended subject.

Publicity, if run by the media, may take a form very different from the way it was submitted. Although specific times may be printed on the news release, a newspaper editor may run the publicity when it is most convenient for the newspaper. Perhaps the information is too late to generate an audience for a production.

A publicist may send the same media kit promoting a fashion show to several different print and broadcast outlets. At one outlet, the publicity may be used as a feature article, while at another outlet it may become a small news story in the fashion section. One broadcast outlet may consider the fashion show to be worthy of a live remote broadcast, while another station only reads the news release as a public service announcement, and yet another station may not mention the fashion show at all.

A well-executed publicity campaign will persuade the public to take action as a result of what they have heard or seen from the publicity. Publicity focuses on merchandise, information, events, or is used to build traffic for a specific retailer or department within a store. Common uses of publicity include introducing new products or indicating the depth, range, and variety of product assortments. Fashion information or instruction on product use may be distributed through publicity.

While it may be more difficult to get publicity into media outlets, there is a benefit to the hard work. Publicity is perceived by the public to be a more credible source than advertising. Publicity, although generally written and submitted to the media outlet by a sponsoring firm or organization, is not perceived by the public to be from the firm. Since it is in the media, the media outlet is perceived to be the source of the communication. The public generally has higher regard for the opinion of the media, as an outside objective source, than from the sponsoring firm or organization.

Publicity is not free. While the airtime or column space does not have to be purchased, the effort and materials used to create the publicity must be accounted for in the budgeting process. For example, staff time, volunteer or paid, must be used to write news releases (Fig. 13.4) and create media kits; sponsoring organizations may also have to pay for presentation materials, giveaways, or coupons included in the publicity materials.

Two issues influence the creation of publicity materials. First, we consider how to make the story newsworthy. Next, we consider the differences between created and covered publicity.

FIGURE 13.4 A portion of a press release for CondéNet.

FOR IMMEDIATE RELEASE

Press Contacts:

Lesley Weiner	Jennifer Miller
CooperKatz for CondéNet	CondéNet
212.455.8079	212.790.5198
lweiner@cooperkatz.com	jmiller@condenet.com

CondéNet Launches Flip, New Online Outlet for Teen Girls' Creativity

NEW YORK (February 6, 2007)—CondéNet today announces the launch of Flip (www.flip.com), a new site for teen girls. Flip.com provides teens with an innovative way to express themselves and connect with each other online. More than just another social network, Flip offers its users powerful but easy-to-use interactive tools, inspiration from experts and editors to spark their imagination, and a stage on which to showcase their talents.

At the heart of Flip are Flipbooks—customizable, multimedia scrapbooks/zines/journals that Flip members make and share. Users can upload their own photos, songs, and videos as well as choose from a large collection of stickers, wallpaper, animations, and music provided on the site. Flip members can draw, write, add a sound track, rotate and size elements, add pages, and even choose page transitions. The result is a more powerful and personal way for girls to express themselves than anything else currently online.

"Flip combines social networking with online scrapbooking, and it's clearly an addictive mix," said Jamie Pallot, Editorial Director, CondéNet. "The results so far are amazing—girls have made beautiful, funny, moving Flipbooks about everything from Barack Obama to their favorite indie rock bands. The level of creativity and ingenuity we're seeing is really impressive."

While the majority of the Flip experience is created by its users, CondéNet has developed four channels that reflect key areas of teen girls' lives and interests. These are: My Life; Entertainment; Style; and The World. Each section highlights editorial content, members, Flipbooks, and clubs specific to that category. Another special section of Flip, titled Projects & Contests, gives members ideas, inspiration, and incentives to create Flipbooks and offers the chance to be recognized for their work.

– more –

Newsworthiness

Is the happening of sufficient interest or importance to the public to warrant reporting in the media? This is the question that every editor or producer will ask when reviewing public relations materials, and it is the question every publicist should answer before submitting the public relations materials. A happening of sufficient interest or importance to the public is considered **newsworthy**. It is a subjective evaluation based on what the editor believes to be of value to his or her readers. Fashion stories of genuine interest and value to readers generally fall into the following categories:

- **A fashion trend.** *Red, fashion's favorite color of the moment.*
- **An improvement to a product, product lines, or service.** *Jockey. Let 'em know we're hosiery, too.*
- **A blending of related matters into one story.** *Khakis are becoming a mainstay for all consumer groups.*
- **A response to current lifestyles.** *DKNY appeals to Generation Y.*
- **A major business move.** *Talbot's plans to open a second store in London.*
- **A first or an exclusive.** *Keri Russell has entered into talks with CoverGirl to star as the new face.*
- **Promotion or election of the firm's personnel.** *William Dillard elected president of the National Retail Federation.*

Another factor that editors and producers consider when deciding whether or not to feature PR information is the presence or absence of other news for the day. Publicity has a greater chance of running when no other events of greater importance have occurred on the same day. Publicists cannot plan for unexpected national events, such as a terrorist bombing or fluctuations in the stock market, that take dominant space in newspapers and on broadcasts. However, they can plan around scheduled events and place their publicity in the hands of an editor or news director on a day when other scheduled events are not likely to happen.

We have all heard the saying *she was at the right place at the right time!* The same can be said about PR. It is critically important that media communication materials land on the desk of the right person. The job of a publicist is to determine who the right person is and make the proper contact with that person. Public relations personnel should know each editor or producer for the media outlets they are interested in using. Editors or producers may review all publicity presented for publication or airing, or they may delegate subject areas to specific reporters. Publicists should know which reporter is most likely to want the subject matter they are presenting as well as the most convenient time to contact the reporter. A publicist should make every effort to develop friendly but professional relationships with important reporters and editors within the community. For PR materials to have the greatest chance to be aired or published, it should be written in a professional manner, on a consistent basis, and delivered to the right person at the right time. Here is a list of questions to help direct the news release to the right person:

- **Is the mail addressed to the current editor?** If the release is addressed to a previous editor, the author probably does not read the publication and it is ignored.
- **Does the release give the editor the most important information in the first paragraph?** If the editor does not know why she should be concerned about this product by the second sentence, chances are readers will not care about it either.

- **Does the writer present this news in context?** In other words, how does this new product or service affect the industry? If the release reflects little or no urgency, the editor is likely to let it pass.

Created and Covered Publicity

Within any firm, situations of interest to the general public routinely occur. The construction of a new parking lot at the mall, the implementation of a new service, or personnel changes within a business may be important news to customers of the company. Publicity writers determine the news value of each situation and write about it in a media release. This type of publicity is considered **covered publicity.** Publications may compile several covered media releases into a single column.

Other situations that may by themselves have little news value may be made newsworthy by creating a special event around the situation. For example, a local specialty store may expand their selections of petite and plus size merchandise. A media release simply stating there are new size offerings may not have enough interest to warrant coverage in the local paper. However, a publicist may use this opportunity to plan a fashion show featuring the petite and plus size merchandise, inviting the public to attend. A media release alerting the press about the fashion show will more likely have news value and be passed on to the public. This type of publicity is considered **created publicity.** Created events are of interest to the public and warrant coverage using publicity.

Created publicity may also be corporate sponsorship of special events. By creating publicity for an event, the corporate sponsor has the opportunity to enhance the company image, improve customer relations, increase employee morale, and fulfill its civic responsibilities. Event sponsorship is discussed in more detail in Chapter 14.

Publicity can enhance the advertising budget and marketing efforts of any company that chooses to use this promotion technique. Published articles that incorporate information about brands, products, services, or the firm can raise awareness and interest in the product or firm and give an implied third-party endorsement from the media outlet. Advertising and public relations are often used in coordination with publicity. Mass media are outlets of the public relations effort.

Companies are realizing the important role public relations have in achieving corporate objectives. The key to a successful public relations campaign is the integrated marketing communications approach set forth by management. The company's key product and corporate message, position within the marketplace, image and identity should be coordinated throughout each publicity vehicle and media outlet to present the same message to the public (see Box 13.1). Public relations materials must present the same message as the direct mail campaign; advertising materials should look and feel like the website. The coordinated message should be reflected in sales promotion efforts, visual merchandise presentations, and special events. Effectiveness of the public relations campaign can be measured using public opinion polls and interviews with the targeted market.

──o PUBLIC RELATIONS PERSONNEL

Public relations may be done by an in-house public relations department, by an outside public relations agency, or by a freelance public relations consultant who is hired for a specific job for a limited period of time. The decision to engage an outside firm is usually based on a particular need and circumstance. A top-notch outside agency can be a very powerful tool, bringing specialized expertise, a wealth of new contacts, and a dispassionate assessment of the organization and its public relations strategy, whereas an

BOX 13.1
Wal-Mart Works on Image, Rebutting Critics with Mixed Results

Wal-Mart president and chief executive officer H. Lee Scott appeared on the Rev. Al Sharpton's radio show in July to discuss ways the world's largest retailer is changing corporate practices.

In 45 minutes, Scott answered tough questions from Sharpton, the activist minister and former presidential candidate, and his audience, about the company's stance on unions, its record employing minorities and attempts to build more stores in urban areas.

It was an image-molding move by Scott to go along with Wal-Mart's environmental initiatives, a program offering $4 generic drugs and the retailer's quick response to help in the aftermath of Hurricane Katrina.

Welcome to the new Wal-Mart, which has spent hundreds of millions of dollars in the past three years on a campaign to improve its reputation that experts believe is one of the most ambitious and aggressive in U.S. corporate history. The company has not significantly improved its reputation, but experts and data suggest it hasn't lost ground either, despite well-organized opponents.

December, a make-or-break month because of holiday sales, will test Wal-Mart's effort in the battle for consumers' perceptions. There are indications that, along with merchandise miscues and disruptions because of store remodeling, the ethics issues raised by critics of the world's largest retailer are giving some shoppers pause just when Wal-Mart is trying to kick-start U.S. sales that fell 0.5 in November, the first same-store decline in almost a decade.

"They've been humbled," said Paul Argenti, professor of communications at Dartmouth's Tuck School of Business. "The market has humbled them, and I think they are starting to realize that public relations and reputation is not just window dressing. I think they've seen how deeply it can affect you."

Wal-Mart's image problems have been linked to the company's flat share price, difficulty expanding into potentially lucrative urban markets and, according to the retailer's own data, loss of 2 percent to 8 percent of shoppers turned off by negative press.

"I debated coming here," said Leanne, 47, a homemaker from Beverly, Mass., who did not want to give her last name, as she shopped at the Wal-Mart in Danvers, Mass., outside Boston. A tight family budget keeps her coming back. "My concern is I hear more and more stuff about employees not being treated well with benefits and cutting their hours. I think this may be my last time here." She has begun shopping more often at rival Target.

In northwest Arkansas, near company headquarters in Bentonville, where Wal-Mart employs about 20,000 people, articles in a local newspaper, The Morning News, on the retailer's stricter employment policies and struggles with bad press generated more than 100 postings to the paper's Web site from readers. Most complain about cultural changes at Wal-Mart, and many mention the mistrust engendered by an internal memo leaked to the press . . . in which the retailer proposed cutting health care costs by reducing the number of fulltime and long-tenured workers.

"Our sales are down, and all my friends in Arkansas and Missouri say their sales are down," wrote one reader. "Wal-Mart go back to what you do best—sell merchandise everyday consumers need for the lowest price and quit hiring overpriced p.r. people to tell everyday Americans how great a company you are. It is not working."

Opponents of Wal-Mart are focused and well organized. Union-funded Wake-Up Wal-Mart launched its first television ad campaign Nov. 30, featuring three sales associates complaining about new employment policies that Wake-Up Wal-Mart said penalize working parents, long-term workers and older workers.

"[Company founder] Sam Walton would never have done this," one associate says during the spot. Wake-Up Wal-Mart also started passing out leaflets at Wal-Mart stores in 100 cities labeled "This holiday season, what if Wal-Mart treated your family this way?"

Wal-Mart sees its recent track record differently.

The retailer "is a company in transformation," said spokeswoman Sarah Clark, who manages a 14-member corporate communications staff. "Our reputation work has taught us we can do good, while still doing well for our business."

Once known for an insular culture that viewed public relations as the ultimate corporate frill, Wal-Mart has been re-aligned to play media offense. Members of the corporate communications unit call themselves "reputation warriors." Their mandate runs from Scott, who has plunged into the role of corporate global statesman, down to staffers on a new 800-number media hotline.

Public affairs and government relations staff has tripled to more than 60 people. Store managers use talking points, and senior executives read their speeches off TelePrompTers. Wal-Mart even has consultants dedicated to reading blogs and relaying updates several times a day to headquarters.

Is the strategy working? A consensus appeared to emerge from interviews with financial analysts and retail consultants, as well as experts in public relations, reputation management and crisis management: Wal-Mart's reputation has not gotten substantially better, but by pushing the issue to the top of its agenda, the company may count a small victory in keeping matters from getting worse.

Data seem to bear this out.

Wal-Mart's Reputation Quotient dipped slightly, from 70.6 to 69.9, a measure derived by Rochester, N.Y.-based Harris Interactive, a $216 million market research firm that analyzes factors ranging from social responsibility to financial performance for Fortune 500 companies. Harris considers scores of 75 and above a benchmark for positive reputation.

Wal-Mart is targeted almost daily by Wake-Up Wal-Mart, funded by the Union of Food and Commercial Workers and its counterpart, Wal-Mart Watch, backed by the Service Employees International Union. Both seek to force major change in wages and benefits at the retailer.

"The biggest plus for [Wal-Mart] so far is, they are engaging the enemy rather than rolling over," said Eric Dezenhall, ceo of Washington-based crisis management firm Dezenhall Resources.

Norwalk, Conn.-based media research firm Delahaye, which reviews a half-million articles annually to track Fortune 500 companies' reputations as portrayed by the media, said Wal-Mart's media rating is 3.5 out of 5, or "marginally positive," asserted Mark Weiner, Delahaye president. Target's rating is 3.7; Sears' is 3.9.

Wal-Mart's financial performance, management team and products are generally covered in positive terms, which accounts for the slight positive slant, said Delahaye senior analyst Matt Merlin.

"Organizational integrity has always been their Achilles' heel," Merlin said. "They've always scored fairly low for one of the large companies."

Financial analyst Dana Telsey, founder of Telsey Advisory Group, said Wal-Mart's reputation reached a low point about two years ago and has been stable since.

"The key thing is they are addressing it, and that is making the analyst community more comfortable," she said.

Most experts predicted Wal-Mart will spend the next decade trying to untangle its mistakes. From gender discrimination and wage-and-hour lawsuits to development battles with communities, Wal-Mart in the mid-Nineties built a reputation as a bully. The company was routinely portrayed as exacting a pound of flesh from suppliers and low-paid workers in order to stock its shelves with cheap goods.

"Wal-Mart is the classic example of a company that is transforming and rebuilding its image while there are tremendous challenges going on," said Leslie Gaines Ross, chief reputation strategist at Weber Shandwick public relations. "Every action they take launches a public debate."

Treatment of workers remains the biggest vulnerability, analysts said. As Wal-Mart seeks to rachet down labor costs, its relationship with hourly associates might become a reputation powder keg.

Cost-saving policies instituted by Wal-Mart U.S. ceo Eduardo Castro-Wright, including salary caps, a stricter absenteeism policy and scheduling priority for associates who can be available for second- or third-shift hours over those who need predictable hours, appear to have stirred worker discontent.

Wake-Up Wal-Mart this fall disclosed internal Wal-Mart talking points for managers aimed at handling associate anger over salary caps, something Wal-Mart said . . . it wouldn't institute.

"Wal-Mart is a confused entity right now," said Eli Portnoy, chief brand strategist of The Portnoy Group Inc. "Moving to more part-time employees, cutting back health care while throwing millions of dollars on gleaming stores and ads in Vogue magazine is an image change that's inappropriate."

Opposition groups have exploited benefits as an area of weakness. They've publicized the internal memos that discuss ways to reduce health care costs and touted data that show Wal-Mart associates and their children are often the biggest consumers of state-funded medical aid programs.

Spurred by these figures, several states proposed legislation in the last 12 months that would mandate Wal-Mart spend a certain amount on medical benefits or be forced to contribute to state health care programs. None of the legislation passed, although the topic may be revisited next year in a political climate chillier toward Wal-Mart at the federal level because Democrats will control the House and the Senate.

But history has shown that the giant retailer can be surprisingly adaptable. Wal-Mart's methods have evolved from heavy-handed (running associate "testimonial" television ads, for example) to staging media events, a tactic Target has perfected, to create positive buzz. In October, for instance, the company set up an eco-friendly retail exhibit at the MTV TRL store in Times Square.

Wal-Mart's U.S. stores get 127 million visitors each week, a base it's trying to convince to spend more to maintain earnings growth. The company's same-store sales have lagged those of Target Stores in 39 of the last 40 months.

A McKinsey & Co. study commissioned by Wal-Mart . . . that found between 2 percent and 8 percent of customers had stopped shopping at the retailer because of negative press also concluded that 54 percent of respondents believed Wal-Mart was "too aggressive" and 23 percent said the company was arrogant.

Wal-Mart vice chairman John Menzer signaled a rare strategy shift during a presentation to financial analysts in October, saying the company would slow the pace of expansion, reduce capital expenditures next year and abandon a saturation strategy that saw supercenters placed as close as one mile apart.

In September, Wal-Mart tapped Leslie Dach, former Edelman public relations firm vice chairman and Democratic Party strategist, to be executive vice president of corporate affairs and government relations. Dach promised the company would "play offense every day, because we have a message and a storyline that's persuasive."

Referencing criticisms by union-funded opposition groups, he added, "We want our opponents to react to us because the more they do, the more shrill and out of touch with working families they seem."

Guided by Edelman, Wal-Mart is trying to connect with journalists, academics, politicians and community activists. This fall, the retailer started routing calls, based on area codes, to managers dedicated to servicing that region's journalists.

The retailer's experiments with blogs, another first for Wal-Mart, are seen as progressive, though initial efforts got mixed results. The blog "Wal-Mart-ing Across America," detailing the adventures of a couple's RV adventure, was criticized when it was revealed the retailer had both bloggers on its payroll.

"Lee Scott has gone through a metamorphosis as a leader," said Weber Shandwick's Gaines Ross, who specializes in working with ceo's after major corporate scandals. "He used to be very anti-visibility, but he's realized that when your company is under the gun, there's an obligation to speak up."

Scott comes across as a "very vigorous, neighborly kind of guy," Dezenhall said. "When Lee Scott talks about the environment, Wal-Mart wins on two fronts. It's of great concern to the public, and they have a portfolio to back them up because it's in their corporate interest to reduce waste."

The retailer's credibility was damaged when the . . . internal memo recommending cutting costs by discouraging older and unhealthier workers from working at Wal-Mart was leaked to reporters.

"I would not be shouting from rooftops about workforce benefits until they have a better story to tell," Dezenhall said.

Gaines-Ross said Wal-Mart needs to remember, in an age of instant communication, "everything that's internal is external . . . .[Wal-Mart] should not put anything into a memo that they wouldn't feel comfortable having printed on the front page of a newspaper."

Wal-Mart is changing much about the way it does business in the U.S., and navigating its associate base through these changes is one of the retailer's most immediate reputation challenges. Long term, what may matter more is the company's ability to convince the U.S. public—and eventually consumers worldwide—that Wal-Mart uses its power responsibly.

"It scares people that one entity has so much power," Dezenhall said.

Wal-Mart's Clark sees it differently: "We never liked to talk about our size before. But we're working on sustainability and other ways we can use our size to benefit the world."

Source: Bowers, K. (2006, December 21). Wal-Mart works on image, rebutting critics with mixed results. *Women's Wear Daily,* p. 10.

in-house department is well-versed in the organization's vision, corporate culture, and standard operating procedures.

Public Relations Agency

When a merchandising business, normally a large corporation, hires a public relations agency, they are looking for an outside perspective. It is a detached group that is not involved in the internal politics of the company and can provide a fresh view. Agencies are typically organized by industry and account teams. Larger agency divisions focus on such areas as fashion, sports, entertainment, technology, health care, and so forth. Account teams are assigned to work with specific clients.

Today, public relations firms are huge international businesses with multimillion-dollar revenues, as demonstrated in Table 13.1. Many top public relations firms have been acquired by large advertising agencies. Some practitioners feel this is positive, building on the synergy between advertising and public relations, while others mourn the loss of the traditional client and agency relationships.

ᴛᴀʙʟᴇ 13.1   *Top 10 Public Relations Agencies*

Rank	Agency Name	U. S. Revenues	Staff	Location
1	Edelman	$170,893,272	1,097	Chicago, IL
2	Waggener Edstrom	$79,128,000	546	Bellevue, WA
3	The Ruder Finn Group	$74,402,000	399	New York, NY
4	APCO Worldwide	$41,835,349	186	Washington, DC
5	MWW Group	$41,059,576	218	East Rutherford, NJ
6	Text 100 Public Relations	$25,368,836	162	San Francisco, CA
7	Chandler Chicco Agency	$25,255,668	124	New York, NY
8	Schwartz Communications	$22,184,187	175	Waltham, MA
9	PCGCampbell	$20,906,084	143	Dearborn, MI
10	Zeno Group	$19,610,384	111	New York, NY

Note: 2006 rankings from 2005 data.

Adapted from: PRWeek. (2006). *Agency business report 2006.* http://www.prweek.com/us/features/supplements

In-house Public Relations Department

The structure of in-house departments is as varied as there are firms within the fashion industry. Such a firm will, most likely, have a vice president of promotion, who directs all of the activities for the promotion division, consisting of the advertising, public relations, special events, and visual merchandising departments. This division will have a fashion director, responsible for fashion direction and leadership; a special events director, responsible for directing all special events; a public relations director, responsible for the firm's public relations; and a visual merchandising director, responsible for all store layout and display. Most of these activities are so integrated that the departments cooperate and coordinate fully.

Historically, the fashion director for a fashion retail store, such as Bloomingdales, Henri Bendel, or Neiman Marcus, was considered to be one of the most powerful and high-profile positions in retailing. The late Kal Ruttenstein from Bloomingdales and Joan Kaner, who retired from Neiman Marcus, had enormous impact on their stores' mood and image. Today, each store uses the fashion director in a different manner; some are merchants, some are PR people, while others select fashion trends, direct trend shop creation, promote up-and-coming designers, and plan visual merchandise presentations to coordinate with special events and other image-building activities. This shows the integrated techniques retailers use for promotional strategies in the 21st century.

Macy's, one of the retailers recognizing the important creative and business role a fashion director can play, rebuilt a fashion office after abandoning it for years. Nicole Fischelis, a former fashion director for Saks Fifth Avenue, revitalized Macy's East with fashion forecasting and trend direction presentations for 200 buyers from every division, from sportswear to ready-to-wear and accessories (Moin, 2006). Fischelis does Power-Point fashion trend presentations twice each year for Macy's executives, and she influences the looks that go into Macy's catalogs, promotes designers, and works with private label buyers, in addition to being a visible spokesperson for the store with consumers. While the job does involve spotting trends, it also involves execution. From planning how to present that trend to the consumer, working with the visual merchandising department, putting together a direct mail catalog photo shoot, to inviting a celebrity for a product endorsement, the job of the fashion director has great influence on the promotional plans for the store.

At one time the role of the fashion director was primarily a social one. Today, it is an important job that helps put a retailer one step ahead of the competition in creating promotional opportunities. Without a fashion director, a store is still able to make money, but it risks losing money in a highly competitive environment.

The public relations director will also work very closely with the market research department to understand the perceptions of the public toward the company. In smaller businesses, a public relations or advertising specialist may be responsible for all public relations, publicity, and advertising. A corporate office creates national publicity pieces, while local branch departments are responsible for locally produced events.

All personnel involved with public relations must be completely familiar with the fashion press and incoming trends. They work with fashion editors, subscribe to color and trend services, and use all the fashion forecasting tools introduced in Chapter 4 to understand fashion influences for the season. Based on knowledge of the fashion industry, these individuals create professional news releases, photographs for the media, and media kits that are most likely to create needed publicity for the client or the firm.

Public Relations Professional Organizations

The most well-known and largest domestic professional organization for public relations is the Public Relations Society of America (PRSA). The organization has approximately 20,000 professional and student members organized in 112 chapters (Public Relations Society of America, n.d.). The student division, called Public Relations Student Society of America (PRSSA), has 225 chapters. The vision of the organization is to unify, strengthen, and advance the profession of public relations. The organization attempts to advance the profession through professional development programs and to support professionalism by concentrating on accreditation and maintenance of standards through the Code of Ethics. The organization also is dedicated to strengthening alliances with other public relations organizations throughout the world.

Next, we will focus on the outlets where public relations practitioners direct their mass communication efforts. Media vehicles are spotlighted.

──o Media Vehicles

Media vehicles are any mass communication medium used by a firm or agency to communicate with the public about a product, service, idea, or event. The same outlets that are used for advertising are also used for publicity. Media vehicles include print, broadcast, and online media. A public relations specialist for an outside agency or a public relations director for an internal division of a firm must know where to send materials to assure the greatest opportunity for publication or broadcast.

Materials must be planned and written with the specific medium and type of story in mind. The type of story may be determined by the content, such as fashion product news, fashion collections, institutional information, fashion trends and lifestyle news, or personal interviews. Broadcast materials should be designed for radio or television, as commentary or as a news show. Online media should reflect the latest techniques to capture the interest of the fashionable audience.

Newspapers

National newspapers reach readers throughout the country. Most towns distribute *USA Today*, the *Wall Street Journal*, and the *New York Times*, in addition to regional papers of interest to the local community. Many large metropolitan areas have one or two competing leading daily newspapers with expanded Sunday editions. These papers have a regional readership beyond the metropolitan area. For example, Colorado has two large newspapers, the *Denver Post* and the *Rocky Mountain News*, both published in Denver and have distribution throughout the entire state. News releases sent to large newspapers must be of interest to a larger geographic population in order to get published.

Smaller communities typically have a daily or a weekly local newspaper. The hometown human-interest story is more likely to catch the eye of an editor for community papers. Weekly newspapers may be published for special-interest groups such as a singles population or an ethnic group in a non-English format. Weekly newspapers may also highlight segmented activities, such as arts and entertainment, within a community. Many communities throughout the country publish weekly or quarterly newspapers with information about local cultural events.

Industry newspapers are also published as trade papers. The fashion industry depends on *Women's Wear Daily* to keep designers, manufacturers, suppliers, and retailers informed about the business of fashion on a daily basis. *Women's Wear Daily* targets a selected merchandise classification each day of the week.

- **Monday**—accessories, innerwear, and legwear
- **Tuesday**—ready-to-wear and textiles
- **Wednesday and Thursday**—sportswear
- **Friday**—beauty

In addition to coverage of specific merchandise classifications, *Women's Wear Daily* devotes issues to specific regional markets including Dallas, Chicago, and California. Monthly supplements cover issues of interest such as merchandise associations and consumer market segments. Industry-based newspapers by their nature will create a higher level of interest in publicity for their industry.

Other trade publications include *Daily News Record*, covering news and features on menswear, retailing, apparel, fibers, and fabrics, and WWD *Beauty Biz*, featuring the cosmetic and fragrance industries. *Footwear News* is the leading publication in the international shoe industry. The publication featuring news about furniture, housewares, textiles, consumer electronics, and computers is called *Home Furnishings Network*. Nearly every industry has a trade newspaper that senior managers, buyers, merchandisers, designers, and key executives will use as a resource to know more about their industry.

Newspapers publish two types of stories, news and beat. **News stories** are prepared for the main news section of a paper and include articles about current events, business-related news, announcements, or special events of interest to the general public. **Beat stories** are written as feature stories from the viewpoint of a specific section or column of the newspaper, including fashion, lifestyle, travel, state and local interests, finance, sports, or entertainment, among others. The manner in which the story is written will determine its placement as a general or beat story. Although a story on fashion week might be considered beat news, its significance to the economy in New York made it such a newsworthy event that it appeared on the front page of the *New York Times* as a news story.

Magazines

Magazines predisposed to run fashion and home furnishings news fall into these categories:

- **Trade or business-to-business**—*Stores* and *VM + SD*
- **Consumer fashion**—*W, Vogue, Gentleman's Quarterly,* and *Marie Claire*
- **Women's interest**—*Self, 0,* and *Ladies Home Journal*
- **Shopping**—*Lucky* and *Domino*
- **Shelter and lifestyle**—*Bon Appetit, Architectural Digest,* and *Country Living*
- **News and business weeklies**—*Newsweek, Time,* and *Business Week*
- **Celebrity news**—*People, US Weekly,* and *Star*

Although only a few sample magazines are listed, many more within each of these categories exist and are outlets for fashion public relations.

As with newspapers, it is important to write materials specific to the selective audience of each magazine. As compared with newspapers, magazines are more likely to define an editorial style for the publication. For example, *Glamour*, a Condé Nast publication, and *Cosmopolitan*, a Hearst publication, are both fashion consumer magazines. However, the editorial style for each publication is quite different. *Cosmopolitan* is known for its coverage of relationships and sexual issues, while *Glamour* demonstrates strengths in coverage of careers and young women's issues.

Magazines, and particularly those published in a monthly format, have a longer preparation time for publication than newspapers. The lead time for most magazines is three to four months before the publication date. Therefore, news releases submitted to a magazine should be sent early and will more likely run as editorial matter. Feature stories promoting yearly special events have a better chance at publication than time-specific news articles.

Radio

Radio is one of the outlets for broadcast communication and is similar to newspaper because hometown interest stories are more likely to capture the attention of a local radio news editor. A news release for a radio broadcast is written in the form of a script or delivered as a CD or an audiotape. The public relations writer may have a particular commentator or *personality* in mind when writing the release who may add credibility or validity to the event. The writer may go as far as to suggest the personality to deliver the message.

Broadcast spots that run free of charge to charitable organizations are considered to be **public service announcements (PSAs)**. PSAs are broadcast on television as well as on radio.

Television

The other form of broadcast media is television. Public relations material delivered to television stations may take the form of audio and video-scripted storyboards, slides, clips, DVDs, or film. **Video news releases (VNRs)** are PR pieces created by public relations specialists and delivered to television stations as news stories. A company shoots, edits, and delivers video news releases for broadcast affiliates in professional formats. Neither the television station nor the video news release producer has to mention the firm seeking the publicity or who created the program or story, which causes some ethical concerns.

Online Media

Growth of the Internet has far exceeded initial expectations. Public relations specialists have learned to use the Web and e-mail for distributing information, with many PR practitioners using the Web as their only media vehicle.

In addition to creating corporate websites, many media vehicles have started websites that complement their traditional print or broadcast distribution. Anyone, anywhere in the world, can access the newspapers *New York Times* and *International Herald Tribune* or television networks *CBS* and *BBC* at the websites. Most major retailers, designers, manufacturers and textile producers have corporate websites.

Alternative methods of presenting the point-of-view of the person or company initiating the communication include blogs and podcasts. **Blog**, a word derived from *web log*, allows the creator to present a personal view on public information to anyone willing to look at the website. Blogs have been created on almost any topic, from fashion and shopping to music and celebrity news. For example, a person interested in getting tips about budget apparel can visit the Budget Fashionista website, http://www.thebudgetfashionista.com, where a business can post information about a sale or new product line. Information about beauty products can be found on the web at Glam, http://www.glam.com, where even more blogs are linked.

A **podcast** enables listeners to hear audio files at the time and place of their choosing, as long as the listener has podcasting software installed on a personal computer or synchronized to a portable MP3 player, such as an iPod device. As we put together materials for the second edition of this book, we can only imagine that other alternative methods for distributing publicity are in development stages.

In this discussion we have identified media vehicles that may be suitable for public relations. However, no news organization will accept publicity if it is not submitted to the right people. In the next section of this chapter we discuss the people who work in the media.

──o MEDIA PERSONNEL

Each media vehicle has its own style and ideas on what to report. The people responsible for maintaining the editorial focus for the news organization are called **editors**, and they control the content and subject matter of all stories. Small organizations may have one person responsible for this task while large organizations will have a team. Team members of a print news organization might include the publisher, editor-in-chief, senior, associate, and assistant editors. The **publisher** coordinates all organizational and functional components of the medium. Although he or she generally does not have direct newsroom responsibilities, the publisher is a good communication contact because of his stature in a community. The person in charge of all aspects of reporting the news is titled an **editor-in-chief**. An individual who manages a newspaper section such as business, fashion, or travel will have the title of **senior editor**. These editors are also excellent contacts for fashion- or business-related information. **Associate editors**, often reporters, are assigned to cover certain topics and events. In communities where many events happen on a regular basis, associate editors are good publicity resources because they are likely to consistently cover the same types of events.

Never underestimate the employee at the bottom rung of the ladder. At print media organizations, this is the **assistant editor,** who is responsible for reading all news releases submitted to the organization and reporting the newsworthy pieces to the more senior editors. Often publications will have criteria that news releases must meet to be considered newsworthy. The assistant editor is most likely the person who will know the criteria and be able to assist writers seeking recognition for their event or products in meeting the criteria for publication.

There are similar personnel positions in broadcast organizations. A **producer** is like an editor-in-chief, a top manager. Depending on the size of the news organization, this person may also have responsibilities similar to the publisher of a print medium. The **assignment editor** has control over the flow of information and assignments and, as such, is probably the best connection at a broadcast news outlet. Similar to the senior editors, **associate producers** are specialists in particular subjects and may also be good resources for promotional communication, if they regularly report on fashion or business.

Each public relations specialist maintains a list of specific contacts for each medium in a **media list**. This list is continually updated with key personnel and how to get in touch with them. Figure 13.5 is an example of a media list.

The media can be a friend or a foe. A news release or publicity photo may be run as submitted, cut, rewritten, or ignored completely by the editor or producer of a media vehicle. If a communication piece is used, the producer or editor may use it just as it was presented for publication or develop the item into an article. The news release may result in a news story or a feature story. A news story is information about recent events or happenings, commonly written in an inverted pyramid style. The **inverted pyramid**, used in news stories, puts the most important information first, arranges the paragraphs in descending order of importance, and requires the writer to rank the importance of information. A **feature story** is a prominent or lead article that is original and descriptive.

Media List

Organization	Name	Title	Address	Phone	Email
Lumberjack	Ryan Weaver	Lifestyle Editor	Box 5555 Flagstaff, AZ 86011	928-523-5551	rrw@nau.edu
AZ Daily Sun	Sara Minard	Education Editor	532 Main Street Flagstaff, AZ 86001	928-525-5552	skm@hotmail.com
Mountain Living	Ann Kincaid	Editor	532 Main Street Flagstaff, AZ 86001	928-525-5553	ask@flaglive.com
ASU Press	Jeff Hutchins	Sun Devil Editor	934 Rural Road Tempe, AZ 81502	480-225-5554	jkh@asu.edu
U of A State Press	Kim Wales	Features Editor	1134 Campbell Rd. Tucson, AZ 89100	520-346-5555	ksw@ua.edu
Channel 2 Local NBC	Joan Burg	Morning Anchor	2201 N. Vicky St. Flagstaff, AZ 86001	928-526-5556	jeb@hotmail.com
KJACK	John Allen	News Director	Box 5556 Flagstaff, AZ 86011	928-523-5557	jaa@nau.edu
KNAU	Theresa Bierer	News Director	Box 5557 Flagstaff, AZ 86001	928-523-5558	teb@nau.edu

FIGURE 13.5 An example of a media list.

Feature stories are generally more fluid and resemble short stories. They have distinct beginnings, middles, and ends, which must be read completely to make sense. The editor will base his or her decision about the form on the newsworthiness of the communication.

In this discussion we have identified media personnel who control what information may be suitable for their outlets. However, no news organization will accept news releases if it is not submitted in the correct format. In the next section of this chapter we discuss the proper format for promotion communication submissions.

———o MEDIA KIT COMPONENTS

Public relations communications are presented to media outlets using common delivery vehicles such as media kits, news releases, and photographs, videos, or digital images in addition to other background materials. The format and contents vary, but the essential style remains similar with certain elements common to all instruments.

Media Kits

A **media kit** is a public communication technique used to generate news stories about a company or group through its newsworthy initiatives (Fig. 13.6). Activities including new advertising campaigns, special events, major announcements, press conferences, product launches, fashion shows, trade shows, celebrity appearances, or financial information give the public relations specialist a reason to distribute a media kit. Media kits are prepared to provide important news, background information, facts, perspectives, research, historical information, biographies of people involved, among other items, so that members of the media have information to prepare print, broadcast, or online media stories. It is a reference guide and good source of historical background information for journalists.

Most media kits are prepared for special events, for promotional purposes, or for crisis management. Special event media kits provide details about the event, logistical information, and background material. Promotional media kits include details about the item being promoted along with brochures, advertisements, as well as quotes and reviews from third-party sources. Many promotional media kit writers also provide reprints from newspaper articles. Crisis management media kits allow the communication sponsor to provide up-to-date facts in addition to background data and related critical information. Media kits for critical situations are often presented during a press conference as a means of giving background information about the organization, biographical information about the key individuals involved, or any relevant supporting documentation.

The media kit contains some or all of the following features about the product, service, person, or event being publicized:

- News or feature stories written as a news release
- Photographs with captions
- Biographies of important people
- Company profiles or historical information
- Brochures, samples, or giveaways, such as pencils, buttons, cups, T-shirts, or other promotional items
- DVDs, podcasts, CD-ROMs, or other audio and visual documentation

Media kits are presented in graphically attractive two-pocket folders, representing the theme of the product or event or showing the logo of the message sponsor. This folder is

FIGURE 13.6   A media kit contains a news release, fact sheet, press photographs, or other materials to promote the newsworthy information.

also known as a shell. The front cover clearly identifies that company, event, or theme. It should be an attractive and attention-grabbing cover that expresses the message being conveyed. For a fashion show with the theme *Lights, Camera, Fashion!*, the media kit was placed in a shell that looked like a movie clap-board. It caught the attention of the community editor of a newspaper and resulted in a front-page story and photograph in the local paper. Although the newspaper had been sent a media kit for many years, the clever presentation caught the eye of the editor. The coverage was better than any previous attempt.

Media kits include hard copy of news releases, feature stories, backgrounders, biographical sketches, fact sheets, and the business card of the PR liaison for the firm or the public relations agency representing the firm.

The goal of a media kit is to impress the editor to a greater degree than a single news release or photograph could. The overall theme and graphic design developed for the media kit are used to reinforce the importance of the news. The key to a successful promotional media kit is creativity. Anyone can come up with an idea, but how that idea is promoted and shared with the media and the public will determine how well the idea catches on with the buying public.

The news releases, feature stories, and fact sheets are placed in the right-hand pocket of the shell. The inside pocket on the left side contains supporting documents such as photos, backgrounders, biographies, newspaper articles, reviews, and any additional documentation or product samples.

Cover Letter

A **cover letter** identifies the purpose and the contents of the media kit. It will include the names of the persons to contact for further information and explain why the information is being sent. It should be written with excitement and interest to entice the reader to want more information and review the remaining contents. In essence, the cover letter serves as a pitch to the editor or producer.

News Release

A **news release**, also known as a press release or media release, is the format used to pass information from the sponsoring party to the media outlet. News releases are used independently or as part of a media kit.

Releases were historically known as press releases, because print media, primarily newspapers, were the target media for public communication messages in the early 20th century. When broadcast media became more widespread, the industry started calling this communication tool a news release or a news release, moving away from directing messages exclusively toward traditional print media. You will probably hear all three terms used by various professionals in the field, but now the term news release is widely accepted.

Even though print, broadcast, or online media are the target for news releases, most news releases are written as if they are for print sources. In general, three styles of news releases exist. The first is an announcement, which is a straight news story, commonly written in inverted pyramid style. The second is a feature story, combining information and entertainment. The feature story has more of a human-interest approach. The third type of news release is a hybrid story that is a combination of an announcement and feature story.

While the content of each release differs, the format or layout remains similar with certain common elements. These elements have been established to make reading news releases as easy and as consistent as possible for editors and producers. Many editors use news releases just exactly as they are written, so following desired format for the medium chosen is critical. Figure 13.7 shows an application of the guidelines for writing and formatting a news release:

- Use letterhead stationery, with your organization's or project's logo on the first page.
- Margins should be one to one-and-one half inches.
- Type company name and address, single-spaced, within the margins at the top left-hand corner, when not using letterhead.
- Use plain paper in the same color and quality as the letterhead for the second and any additional pages.
- Type copy on $8\frac{1}{2} \times 11$ inch paper, using only one side of the page.
- Type "News Release" in big bold letters, usually 24-point type.
- Below that, type single spaced headings "FOR IMMEDIATE RELEASE," and the composition date underneath and "FOR MORE INFORMATION" data, which includes a contact person, the contact person's title, a phone number, and an e-mail address.
- Leave about two inches between the headings and the headline.

Organization Letterhead and Logo

News Release

FOR IMMEDIATE RELEASE	FOR MORE INFORMATION:
Provide the actual date	Name of contact person
	Title of contact person
	Phone Number
	Email address

The Newspaper Style Headline

(The headline, bolded, should be placed approximately ⅓ of the way down the page or two inches below the contact information. Capitalize the first word and any proper nouns. Lowercase all other words.)

DATELINE HERE (CITY, STATE abbreviated in all CAPS. The date is optional)—The first paragraph of an announcement news release should contain the *who, what, where, when,* and *how* of the newsworthy event. The news release should be double spaced with margins one to one-and-one-half inches.

Subsequent paragraphs should amplify the information. Quotes from individuals involved should be included. The news release should be written in third person. The word MORE indicates a second page will follow.

If an additional page is necessary, the next pages should contain a condensed two or three word heading repeating important words from the headline. This is called a slug and should be placed in the upper left corner of the page with the page number.

Paragraphs should never be split between pages. News releases should not be more than 2 pages in length. If there are two pages, staple the news release together.

The news release should end with ### or -30- placed on the center of the page to signify the end of the release.

###

FIGURE 13.7 News release format.

- The headline should be a newspaper-style headline, in boldface. Capitalize the first word and any names of people or organizations. Use lowercase for the other words. The headline should present a comprehensive message of the prime news interest of the story.
- The text begins with a dateline, which gives the location of the story written with the name of the city followed by a dash.
- Double-space the text or copy with generous margins that allow for editing and revisions. Begin actual copy approximately halfway down the page.
- Indent first line of each paragraph five spaces.
- Use the word "more" centered at the bottom of any page when copy is continued on the next page.
- If more than one page is necessary, number the page as "Page 2 of 3" at the top left corner as needed.
- At the conclusion of the last page use "####," centered, to signify the end.
- Avoid dividing paragraphs from one page to another.

For an announcement news release, begin actual copy with the lead. The **lead** is one or two sentences that summarize the news, including who, what, where, when, and why. Should an editor or new director need to edit or cut a story, the essence of the message would still remain within the lead. **Amplification** fills out the rest of the story following the lead. All information and facts presented in the amplification section should be written in diminishing order of importance. This is known as inverted pyramid style writing and is frequently used for general news stories.

A feature story or hybrid story news release may start with an anecdote, a question, an image, or another storytelling device to capture interest in the narrative. A feature story highlights something that is not necessarily considered to be immediate or hard news. The feature story is the "softer" side of the media kit, focusing on representatives of the organization using storytelling techniques. The feature story is part of a media kit and is commonly formatted as a news release, using the company's or organization's letterhead. Headings are set up just like a news release with release date, contact information, and headlines. For this format, the most important information may come at the end of the message. This approach differs from the inverted pyramid style used to present an announcement. See Figure 13.8 for a sample feature story created for a media kit.

Organization and clarity of content are essential if the news release is to be read. News releases are written with the editor or producer in mind. The writer should write the news release in an objective manner, in the third person, as if it were a matter-of-fact news story. Subjective opinion based on emotional ties to the product or events should not be evident in the news release. *I, we,* or *you* should never be used. Opinionated words such as *spectacular* or *wonderful* will be rejected by an editor as self-serving to the firm seeking publicity. The writer must determine what the media outlet wants and write in a style as near to those needs as possible. Editors want facts, not opinions, and will trust public relations writers who present professional news releases that do not promote insignificant happenings. A release that allows the editor or producer to immediately grasp the story is a sign of professionalism and is appreciated by the editor.

The timing of a news release should be as close as possible to the actual event. The document may be written in the form of an advance announcement, informing the public of a future event, or in the past tense, sharing the news of a past event. A magazine news release should be sent three to four months in advance of the event, based on the lead time for the magazine. A newspaper or broadcast news release should be sent one to two weeks in advance of the publication date on the news release. Regular contacts at publications or broadcast outlets can provide publicists with exact time lines for news release delivery. It is the responsibility of the writer to determine the timeliness of the story and give a release date that allows the editor to run the story as close to the happening as possible, creating a more newsworthy happening.

Sending news releases and media kits through e-mail is becoming more and more commonplace. An e-mail news release may be typed in single-space, since edits can take place as the material is sent electronically. Even if a news release is sent electronically, enough lead time is still required.

If traditional hard copy is being sent, mail first class or hand deliver the news release. Do not use bulk mail rates because it takes too long for bulk rate to be delivered. While bulk rate delivery time has improved in the last several years, a bulk rate piece may still be held up to three weeks or more during a heavy mail season.

Many media outlets publish **style guides**, which are a set of rules mandated by the outlet so all copy reads the same. Media outlets or firms with established logos or other trademarked symbols also create style guides. The guides help to develop clarity and consistency in a message by providing accurate use of abbreviations and addresses for the firm, accurate reproduction of logos, and other information that may be necessary when writing to a particular media outlet or about a particular firm.

FIGURE 13.8 This is a sample feature story created for the fashion show *Lights, Camera, Fashion.*

NORTHERN ARIZONA UNIVERSITY
College of Social & Behavioral Sciences

School of Communication

Northern Arizona University
PO Box 5619
Flagstaff, AZ 86011-5619

928-523-2232
928-523-1505 fax
www.comm.nau.edu

News Release
FOR IMMEDIATE RELEASE
November 15, 2004

FOR MORE INFORMATION:
Heather Shoop
Promotion Coordinator
928 523.5555
HJShoop@aol.com

NAU Takes Its Turn on the Runway

Strike a pose. There's nothing to it. Except a fashion show is not like a Madonna song. No, there's a lot more to it than a model strutting her stuff on the runway in fashionable clothing.

Lights, Camera, Fashion—the 2004 Fashion Show at Northern Arizona University has been a year in the making. The theme was created during spring semester by the promotion class and students in the fall semester fashion show production class brought the theme to life. The class, consisting of about 30 students, divided into six committees: promotion, stage, merchandise, special events, model, and budget.

The special events committee fits like a glove with Erin Christie's future plans. She wants to be a special events coordinator for fashion shows.

"It's exactly the area I want to be in," she said. "My professor is like my mentor."

For the NAU fashion show, she helped plan the silent and live auctions. The most difficult part was getting donations for the auction, she said.

The day before the show, at the dress rehearsal, the students finally saw how their individual work for the semester came together.

The different categories of clothing were coordinated with well-known television shows or movies. Student designers were in a segment called *Unzipped*, which was based on the documentary about Isaac Mizrahi designing and presenting his fashions at New York Fashion Week.

Most of the student designs are from Phoenix College, although there are several NAU student designers. One NAU student designer, Tommy Elias, made a red velvet evening gown with a fur wrap. "It is fun, extravagant, and a little racy," said Elias, majoring in theater production with an emphasis in costume design. His minor is merchandising.

Lights, Camera, Fashion is being held at the duBois Center ballroom on the NAU campus on Friday, November 19th at 7 P.M. and Saturday, November 20th at 11 A.M. Tickets are $10 at the door.

###

Fact Sheet

There are various methods to communicate factual information. One of the ways is via a **fact sheet** that presents key information as bulleted or numbered lists of significant facts. A glossary of industry terms, typical jargon or specific language is frequently included for journalists unfamiliar with the industry. Fact sheets are rarely presented as narratives in paragraph form, because the writer wants the reader to be able to quickly scan the sheet for pertinent data. A sample fact sheet is illustrated in Figure 13.9.

A basic fact sheet contains fundamental information about the organization or company, including names of officers or administrators, locations of offices with addresses,

NORTHERN ARIZONA UNIVERSITY
College of Social & Behavioral Sciences

School of Communication   Northern Arizona University   928-523-2232
                               PO Box 5619   928-523-1505 fax
                               Flagstaff, AZ 86011-5619   www.comm.nau.edu

**NORTHERN ARIZONA UNIVERSITY
FALL 2006 BI-ANNUAL MERCHANDISING FASHION SHOW
FACT SHEET**

- Show logistics: Friday, November 17, 2006, 7:00 P.M., du Bois Center on the Northern Arizona University campus. Students will sell tickets in the fall.

- Theme: **Model Behavior: Dress Accordingly.**

- Theme influence: Our behavior unifies us as models on the runway of life. We have days when we feel unique, laid-back, spontaneous, confident, or sexy. These are potential scene titles. Students will make final decisions in the fall.

- **Unique:** express what is unique about each of us. Potential merchandise category: Student Designs.

- **Laid-back:** easygoing; having a relaxed or casual atmosphere or character. Potential merchandise category: Casual Wear.

- **Spontaneous:** self-generated; unconstrained; happening arising without apparent external cause. Potential merchandise category: Outerwear.

- **Confident:** self-reliant; characterized by assurance. Potential merchandise category: Businesswear.

- **Sexy:** highly appealing or interesting; attractive. Potential merchandise category: After 5.

- The show is student-produced by the MER 434 Fashion Show Production class. The theme and promotional strategy have been developed by the MER 332 Merchandise Promotion class. Northern Arizona Merchandising Association (NAMA) and student volunteers from across campus model and provide additional assistance.

- All show proceeds go to the *Merchandising Leaders of the 21st Century Scholarship* fund administered through the NAU Foundation.

- The scholarship has been endowed for approximately 15 years. The majority of funds raised for this scholarship have been student-generated through production of fashion events.

FIGURE 13.9 A portion of a fact sheet prepared for the fashion show *Model Behavior.*

telephone numbers and e-mail addresses, and a description of what the group does. Historical information provides background records about where and when the organization was founded in addition to any significant milestones.

A fact sheet for a special event explains the significance of the event as well as the activities. It also provides the date, time, location, and duration of the affair. If the event is sponsored, the role and contributions of the sponsor are listed. If an event is held annually, a brief history about the event is reported. Where and why was the first event held? What significant people have participated? How many people have attended in the past?

A fact sheet should provide enough information for the media to be able to cover the activity in person. Timelines include a chronological list of crucial dates as they relate to current news.

Another popular fact sheet format is a frequently asked questions (FAQ) arrangement. Typical questions are presented and they are followed by the answers in narrative form. Fact sheets are necessary elements of a media kit, providing the media with facts and reference information to help write the stories.

Biography

A **biography** is a historical report about people involved in the project. Biographies of the founder, the officers of the organization, celebrities and their past or current participation, experts in the field, or any other notable individuals involved in the project may be included. Photographs of the significant players may also be included.

A straight biography is factual information, presented as a numbered or bulleted list in descending order of importance. Alternatively, a narrative biography is written in paragraph format, presenting personal details in a more creatively written story. Either method is acceptable, but it is imperative to keep the information up-to-date. Generally, it is best to keep the number of biographies small. If there are several key participants, a series of short, mini-bios can be included on one page.

Backgrounder

A **backgrounder** is an expanded narrative of the history, mission, goals, or purpose of the organization and activity. Primarily driven by factual data, the backgrounder is presented to provide answers to anticipated questions. The media probably will want more comprehensive information. These narratives provide in-depth discussions about the functions of the organization. A backgrounder is rarely used as a stand-alone document, but the information can be included in a news story written by a journalist.

Photographs for the Media

There are two ways to present visual images to the media. First, one to three photographs created from the public relations department specifications are included in the media kit. The second method invites photographers or videographers from the media to create customized visual images.

Publicity photographs are normally sized to 5×7 or 8×10 inches. Alternatively, photographs can be sent as digital images. Photographs of significant people mentioned in the news release, products being presented for a product launch, and window or in-store displays are included for visual stimulation.

Photographs and graphic illustrations for the media that accompany media kits are prepared with the format or visual style of the publication in mind. A drawing may be presented in place of a photograph if it is appropriate to the publication. Figure 13.10 is an example of a publicity photograph from Gap jeans. *Boot Cut Jeans $48.00 rinsed* is the caption on the back of the photograph featured next to the Gap logo.

When inviting media representatives for a photo shoot, a **photo opportunity sheet** is presented in the media kit. Many fashion publications have staff photographers who have developed individualistic styles for the publication.

If the subject matter is of strong interest, a staff photographer from a print publication or a videographer from a broadcast station will be sent to shoot their own images.

As with news releases, photos have specific requirements that should be followed for ease of printing. General requirements that assist the publication of publicity photographs are:

- Black-and-white photography preferred.
- Portraits should be 8"×10" or 5"×7" glossy stock; news photographs should be 4"×5" glossy stock.
- Photographs should emphasize people or fashions, deemphasizing backgrounds.
- Fingerprints should not be left on photographs.
- Photographs should be identified on the back with a preprinted label or a felt-tip pen to avoid making an impression on the photograph.
- Each photograph or drawing should be accompanied by a simple caption, with or without the association of a news release.
- A caption should be five or six lines written following the same stylistic guidelines used for a news release.
- Captions should be typed using the same identification lines as a news release, if accompanying a news release.
- Captions should be attached securely to the back of the bottom of the photograph or drawing with rubber cement.
- People should be identified from left to right with full names, titles, firms, and affiliations.

FIGURE 13.10 Press photograph for Gap jeans.

- Model release forms should be obtained for each individual within a photograph.
- All syndicated or stock news service photos should be credited.
- Press photographs are exclusive to each publication. A news release may be common to several publications.

Other Media Kit Materials

Organizations often include additional materials. These items could include such things as reprints of articles previously published in other publications, position papers describing the organization's stand on specific issues, a personal invitation to the event, or a statement from a spokesperson during a crisis situation. Some firms may also want to include a newsletter, magazine, or other related brochures or publications. If the media kit is for a sponsored event, information about the sponsor and its contributions could be included. More information about sponsorship will be discussed in Chapter 14. Media kits may be supplied for some of the other public relations applications that we introduce in the next section.

──○ OTHER PUBLIC RELATIONS APPLICATIONS

In addition to the public relations applications previously discussed, there are several supplementary techniques available to the promotion specialist. These methods include the press conference, editorial credit, and product placement.

Press Conference

A **press conference,** also known as a news conference, is a gathering held by a firm seeking publicity for an event or happening for news reporters. While other forms of public relations communication have moved toward the use of *media* or *news* instead of *press*, which reflects broadcast as well as print sources, the term press conference has remained the industry standard.

Press conferences are intended to create interest about a newsworthy activity in the media to increase consumer awareness and interest. Frequently fashion editors will receive gifts at press conferences. For example, editors at a Calvin Klein press conference were given shoes, intended to impress the editors so they would give Calvin Klein a favorable mention in their various publications.

A press conference is held when the firm seeking the publicity is confident that the happening or event is of such newsworthiness that journalists and editors will attend the conference. For example, Bob Mackie used press conferences held in various major cities to launch his new fragrance. Media events were held at stores carrying the Bob Mackie line. Models, adorned in Mackie's gowns, provided excitement as they passed through the audience offering fragrance samples. Because it was held in a retail store, customers who happened to be shopping that day were also treated to special samples and giveaways. Media kits were distributed to journalists, and media representatives were given a private meeting with Bob Mackie to answer questions that later could be used in news or feature stories.

Press conferences are also held when a crisis occurs. Part of the public relations responsibility is to keep internal and external stakeholders aware of what is happening and how the crisis is being managed. If an event or public appearance is scheduled, and a natural disaster such as an intense rainstorm floods the venue, participants need to know what will happen. People need to know if the event has been cancelled or postponed, or what?

Editorial Credit

When fashion products appear as part of a story in newspapers or magazines, editors inform the readers where they can purchase the merchandise. The naming of retailers is an **editorial credit**. If the merchandise is featured within the fashion pages of a publication like *Elle* or *Marie Claire* magazine, the accompanying copy lists where the merchandise is available. This is also editorial credit.

In addition to stores, editorial credit may include the name of designers and manufacturers of accessories featured in the shoot. Retailers should be made aware of editorial credit and make necessary arrangements to have the cited merchandise in stock and available to customers who shop as a result of the story.

Product Placement

We have all seen it on television shows or in the movies. The actor drinks a Pepsi or eats a Baby Ruth, or works at a Dell laptop computer. The placement of a branded product versus an unbranded generic product as a prop in a movie or a television show is an example of **product placement**. Product placement has become a popular avenue to increase product or brand publicity. Box 13.2 discusses product placement in entertainment media.

○ BOX 13.2

A Column on (Your Product Here) Placement

Those consumers who prefer their entertainment unbranded—that is, without the products, logos, and other trappings of advertisers embedded in the content—are in for a disappointing decade, according to a new report.

The report, scheduled to be released today, predicts that marketers will remain enamored with placing products wherever they can: in movies, television and radio shows; on websites; in video games; in lyrics; in newspaper and magazine articles; and even in the plots of novels. Product placement is an example of a phenomenon known as ad creep, in which popular culture grows increasingly commercialized. As technology enables consumers to avoid or skip over ads, by using devices like digital video recorders or iPods, marketers are trying to restore the balance in their favor by placing ads where consumers cannot miss them.

The study, from PQ Media, a research company in Stamford, Conn., covers not only the United States, the largest market by far for product placement, but also 14 other countries. It is the first time that PQ has compiled data about—and offered forecasts for—product placement practices overseas.

Placing products in the content offered by entertainment media abroad has lagged for several reasons, including the slower pace of development for commercial television networks in countries where government-run TV has been the norm.

But just as French and British consumers can now shop at American-style convenience stores, the practice of product placement is gaining popularity overseas. In fact, the European Union is considering rules that would liberalize what are now strictures on—and in some instances, virtual prohibitions against—the inclusion of products and brands.

"Product placement has emerged as a key marketing strategy worldwide," said Patrick Quinn, president at PQ, who offered a preview of the report in a telephone interview yesterday.

"There's a new media order emerging," Mr. Quinn said, "fueled by a fear of ad-skipping technology, doubts about traditional advertising's effectiveness and, in some countries, a search for new revenue streams as government subsidies decline.

"As brand marketers are seeking to effectively engage consumers with an emotional connection, product placement is no longer a novel tactic and is increasing dramatically."

The PQ report tracks several types of product placements. One type is paid placements, where marketers spend

money to weave their wares into the plots, scripts, and content of entertainment offerings. Another type is barter, when, for instance, an airline provides tickets to the producers of a TV series in exchange for the airline appearing or being mentioned in an episode.

Spending on paid placements worldwide will reach $3.1 billion this year, the PQ report forecasts, compared with $2.2 billion in 2005. The United States led last year with $1.5 billion in paid placements, the report says, followed by Brazil, Australia, France, and Japan.

By 2010, the report predicts, worldwide paid placements will total almost $7.6 billion.

If the European Union approves the changes under consideration, called the Television Without Frontiers Directive, there could be triple-digit percentage increases in the money that marketers spend in Europe for paid placements, the report says.

Spending on all types of placements, according to the report, will total $7.4 billion this year, compared with just under $6 billion in 2005. The United States was also first last year in all placements, at $4.5 billion, followed by Brazil, Japan, Australia, and France.

By 2010, the report forecasts, all worldwide placements will total almost $14 billion.

Placements are "going to be an integral part of the business" for the foreseeable future, said Dick Lippin, chairman and chief executive at the Lippin Group in Los Angeles, a public relations and marketing agency. Lippin is forming a unit, called Brand to Hollywood, meant to help advertisers forge ties between products and celebrities as well as between products and events in the entertainment industry like award shows.

When Mr. Lippin started his agency in 1986, he said, marketers were content to just run commercials during TV shows; the few ways to dodge the spots included using remote controls or leaving the room.

Today, Mr. Lippin said, because "technology has had a tremendous effect on what consumers watch and don't watch," the marketers "are coming to us asking how to place their products and brands into the entertainment world for maximum effectiveness."

The list of marketers engaged in product placement and branded entertainment is lengthening each week, particularly online. Their ranks were once dominated by makers of packaged foods, soft drinks, and other lower-priced products, which could be easily inserted into the background of a scene.

But that is changing, as illustrated by the five sponsors of *Gold Rush*, a game in the form of a seven-week, online reality series from Mark Burnett Productions, the creator of placement-laden programs like *The Apprentice* on NBC and *Survivor* on CBS.

Gold Rush, which is to begin on Sept. 13 on a website operated by the AOL division of Time Warner (aol.com/goldrush), will have only one packaged-goods sponsor, the Coca-Cola Zero brand sold by the Coca-Cola Company. The others are a retailer, Best Buy; an automaker, the Chevrolet division of General Motors; a wireless carrier, T-Mobile; and a bank, Washington Mutual.

The placements will include using Chevrolet cars and trucks to drive contestants to competitions—and to transport the $2.2 million in gold to be hidden around the country that lends the series its name.

AOL has included product placement in previous online series like *The Biz*, sponsored by Chevrolet and Sprint, but

those were "baby steps" compared with its aggressive pursuit of sponsors for *Gold Rush*, said Kathleen Kayse, executive vice president for sales and partnership alliances at the AOL Media Networks unit of AOL in New York.

The biggest problem with product placement and branded entertainment is how often projects blur or cross the line that traditionally separates editorial content and advertising, potentially alienating the consumers they are meant to woo.

"We've got experience understanding what consumers are willing to accept as entertainment and what they are not willing to accept as commercialization," Ms. Kayse said.

"The last thing we want to do is put the consumer in the position of feeling it's too commercialized," she added.

Source: Elliott, S. (2005, August 16). A column on (your product here) placement. *New York Times*, p.C2. Copyright 2006 The New York Times Company.

Product placement may be planned or unexpected. For example, Laundry, a dress manufacturer, had success with unexpected publicity through product placement when the *New York Times* published a photograph of five bridesmaids wearing the same Laundry dress, in its weddings and engagements column. Loyal Laundry customers immediately recognized the dresses.

Product placement can also be planned. Public relations personnel representing clothing lines promote those lines to set designers and stylists, hoping to put the clothes on movie and television stars. Loyal customers will be validated in their purchase behavior by seeing their favorite brands on television and movie stars. Product placement further promotes brand names to consumers.

With innovative technologies, product placement can occur after the television show or movie is shot. A cereal or shoe box can be digitally entered into the scene. Was that really a Barney's black-and-white logo box on the desk or was it added as product placement?

——o MEASURING PUBLIC RELATIONS EFFECTIVENESS

The methods for evaluating the effectiveness of public relations include evaluating PR programs in relationship to the contributions they make toward attaining communications objectives. Regular evaluation of public relations methods helps management to recognize what these activities have achieved over a period of time. This provides management with quantitative means of measuring achievements as well as a method to judge the quality of the activities and accomplishments.

A variety of methods, from personal observation, evaluation of objectives, evaluation of public opinion to public relations audits, are used to assess public relations effectiveness. With continued expansion into the global market, public relations professionals are looking at the methods for evaluation that work across international boundaries. Any or all of the following means may assist in evaluations.

Personal observation, carefully watching the job done by the PR specialist, can be used for evaluation. A specialist's manager usually provides feedback on the person's contributions. The director reports an annual performance evaluation based upon quantitative and qualitative industry and/or company standards to the practitioner.

As with measuring the effectiveness of advertising, the evaluation of public relations should be led by objectives. Specific objectives for public relations programs should be established early in the planning stages by staff and management. An individual's objectives might include such things as placing a feature story in a specific number of media. This is an objective, quantitative, and measurable goal. Goals are used as the standard to measure accomplishments for individuals as well as teams.

Public opinion, measurement of the beliefs and feelings of the citizens, can also be used to measure public relations effectiveness. If a retail store sets a public relations goal of becoming known for fashion leadership, research in the form of public opinion surveys may be used to evaluate the success of the program. Opinions about the store can be determined through pretesting. Surveys conducted after conclusion of the program can be used to evaluate whether or not the goals were attained.

Public relations practitioners measure success by obtaining public opinion through the media and the public. For example, a company surveys consumers to determine how much attention the media is giving to the company's publicity efforts. One U.S. company held simultaneous media conferences in New York and Paris to introduce six new products. The company then evaluated news coverage in 12 countries in an effort to compare how different media in different sections of the world handled the story ("PR evaluation," 1996). The company was also able to identify the public perception of the product launch in the 12 countries.

Audits are formal reports of activities. Audits may be performed internally or externally. Personnel, superiors, and peers, within the firm conduct an **internal audit** to determine the performance of an employee and his or her programs. Consultants or clients from outside organizations conduct an **external audit**. Audits may focus on such criteria as the percentage of positive and/or negative articles over time, ratios of positive to negative articles, and the percentage of positive and/or negative articles by subject, publication, reporter, or target audience.

summary

- Public relations (PR) is the management function that establishes and maintains mutually beneficial relationships between an organization and the public on whom its success or failure depends.
- Publicity is a public relations tool that nonpaid, unsponsored information initiated by the party seeking to tell others about the product, service, idea, or event and delivered at the discretion of the media.
- Advertising, marketing, publicity, and public relations are distinctly different and have different communication strategies.
- Promotion communication is disseminated through the mass communication media, which includes newspapers, magazines, radio, television, or online media.
- Editors or producers making the decision to cover the story will base their perception on the newsworthiness of the report.
- Media releases may be written after the fact to cover an event or used before an event to create interest about the subject.

- Publicity, along with development, investor relations, internal relations, issues management, lobbying, press agentry, and public affairs, are tools of the public relations effort.
- An in-house department for a large retail organization has a promotion director who is responsible for the public relations staff, which may include the advertising department, the visual merchandising department, and the office of special events.
- Different names for the promotion function are used by retailers. It may be called promotion, marketing, special events, or advertising. The retailer may have a separate fashion director, special events coordinator, and public relations director, or it may combine the roles under one person.
- Specific guidelines are used to create media releases, media kits, and photographs for media usage.
- New technologies for distributing publicity materials include the Internet, CD-ROMs, DVDs, cell phones, and podcasts.

Key Terms

amplification	external audit	podcast
assignment editor	fact sheet	press agentry
assistant editor	feature story	press conference
associate editor	internal audit	producer
associate producer	internal relations	product placement
audit	inverted pyramid	public
backgrounder	investor relations	public affairs
beat story	issues management	public opinion
biography	lead	public service announcement
blog	lobbying	(PSA)
cover letter	media kit	publicity director
covered publicity	media list	publisher
created publicity	news release	senior editor
development	news story	spin
editor	newsworthy	stakeholder
editorial credit	personal observation	style guides
editor-in-chief	photo opportunity sheet	video news release (VNR)

Questions for Discussion

1. Discuss the reasons why a firm may use publicity and public relations.
2. Compare and contrast the roles of publicity and public relations with advertising and marketing.
3. Discuss the differences between created and covered public relations.
4. Discuss ways to make an item newsworthy.
5. Discuss the types of media outlets where publicity can be submitted.
6. Discuss the role technology is playing in distributing public relations materials.
7. Compare some of the positive and negative perceptions about public relations specialists.

Additional Resources

Cutlip, S. M., Center, A. H., & Broom, G. M. (2006). *Effective public relations* (9th. ed.) Upper Saddle River, N.J.: Pearson Prentice Hall.

Diggs-Brown, B. (2007). *The PR styleguide: Formats for public relations practice* (2nd ed.). Belmont, CA: Thomson Wadsworth.

Marsh, C., Guth, D. W., & Short, B. P. (2005). *Strategic writing: Multimedia writing for public relations, advertising, sales and marketing, and business communications.* Boston, MA: Pearson Education.

References

Connecting with the world of PR. (2006, June 26). *PRWeek*, p. 21.

Cutlip, S. M., Center, A. H., & Broom, G. M. (2006). *Effective public relations* (9th. ed.). Upper Saddle River, N.J.: Pearson Prentice Hall.

Global Alliance for Public Relations and Communication Management. (n. d.). *History of the alliance.* www.globalpr.org

Hood, J. & Schmelzer, R. (2006, June 26). Markets of tomorrow. *PR Week.* Retrieved June 27, 2006, from www.prweek.com

Moin, D. (2006, February 6). The new retail world: Fashion director role seen shifting at store. *Women's Wear Daily*, p. 1.

PR evaluation goes global. (1996, July 15). *Marketing News.* 30(15) p. 16.

Public Relations Society of America, (n.d.). *Overview and history.* Retrieved August 16, 2006, from www.prsa.org

FIGURE 14.1 Retailer Henri Bendel and Delta Airlines coordinate store window displays and in-store events that promote travel with the theme *Delta Jet-Set Summer*.

Special Events

New york retailer Henri Bendel and Delta Airlines coordinated their efforts to encourage summer travel with a special event called *Delta Jet-Set Summer* ("Delta Jets," 2006). The theme, created to recall luxury upscale travel during the lazy days of summer, pulled together a range of elements, including airport-inspired window displays, in-store activities, and special events, for an exciting promotion during the month of June. Customers were enticed to come inside Henri Bendel with fake Delta ticket counter signs in the windows, while Delta-branded merchandise was presented at a boutique on the main floor. Shoppers had a chance to win a pair of tickets to Delta's newest international destinations and learn about fashionable traveling must-have items while shopping in the store. By using a shopping passport to purchase items in a variety of departments, a customer could earn a special promotional gift bag.

The special event opened with a kickoff party with celebrities at the store. Beauty tips for jet-set travel were offered by Modelco's beauty team. Dany Levy read from her book, *Daily Candy A–Z*, and travel expert Peter Greenberg signed copies of his book, *The Travelers Diet: Eating Right and Staying Fit on the Road*. Refreshments from Delta's new healthy in-flight menu were served as part of this two-week promotion with 13 different special events.

Source: Delta jets into Henri Bendel's windows. (2006, June 14). *Women's Wear Daily*. Retrieved June 15, 2007, from Business Source Premier database.

> **After you read this chapter you will be able to:**
>
> Explain the purpose of special events.
>
> Examine goals of special events.
>
> Describe the various types of special events.
>
> Incorporate a feasibility study into event planning.
>
> Discuss the personnel involved in special events.
>
> Explain financial considerations for special events.
>
> Evaluate the need for event sponsorship.
>
> Review the evaluation process for special events.

RETAILERS AND MANUFACTURERS put considerable time and money into creating special events that will entice consumers to participate and ultimately buy products from the sponsor. From small events, such as product sampling stations at grocery stores, to large month-long retail celebrations featuring merchandise from other countries, special events play a significant role in promotion strategy.

The creation of special events is an integral part of the promotion mix. This chapter discusses special events in general, and Chapter 15 will discuss the fashion show, a long-established special event specific to the fashion industry. We begin this chapter with a discussion of the role of special events. Special events are produced to fulfill corporate goals, and these goals are the subject of the next section. Then we discuss some of the many types of special events. Next, we focus on the personnel involved in special event planning. It takes many people to put on a special event. The chapter concludes with a discussion of event sponsorship and measuring special event effectiveness.

THE ROLE OF SPECIAL EVENTS IN PROMOTION

If you have never participated in the coordination of a special event, you should—it is one of the most rewarding (and one of the most nerve-racking) promotion strategies you can participate in! As we defined in Chapter 1, a special event is a one-time occurrence with planned activities, focused on a specific purpose, to bring attention to a brand, manufacturer, retailer, or organization, or to influence the sale of merchandise.

Some special events are intended to generate sales, while others are intended to communicate a positive image. They can create a dynamic impression of a sales promotion, team, atmosphere, or shopping season; a product or service; or a business, charity, or community event, or be used for numerous other reasons. Corporate funding or support for a special project may also constitute a special event. All industries use special events as marketing tools to increase awareness of products or services, enhance brand or company image, or raise funds.

As discussed in chapter 13, special events lend themselves to *created* public relations. Situations that, alone, may not be considered newsworthy can be made newsworthy by the attention the special event created. For instance, local newspapers may not find product launches to be newsworthy, but if a celebrity is in town to promote a product launch, the appearance of the guest would be considered newsworthy and be given coverage. Store openings, anniversary celebrations, product launches, community action kickoffs, long-established charity events, and special-interest group recognition events can become special events with a planned promotion as part of the integrated marketing communications mix.

Special events are an effective mechanism to persuade and inform target markets because they can come in any size or shape, frequency or format. Events are designed to promote products by linking them to highly visible activities, issues, or ideas of interest to target audiences. Some events are used as tools to persuade, educate, and provide added value to a particular organization's product or service offering. But behind the glamour, crowds, and product displays, all special events strive to perform the same function: to effectively communicate a message.

Special events are gaining importance as part of an IMC mix. According to IMC expert Don Schultz, the strategically planned use of short-term or long-term events can build links that connect a product or brand to an event of public interest. In turn, these links can help a firm to establish rapport between customers and its product or service. Combining advertising, sales promotion, personal selling, and visual merchandising along with public relations can help create interest, awareness, and acceptance by the target market. For example, Chanel developed an integrated promotion strategy for its men's and women's fragrances. The strategy for Chanel's vendors, outlined in Figure 14.2, included print and television advertising and corporate sponsorship of the U.S. Open Tennis Championship.

Event Ideas

The variety of special events a firm may choose to produce is limitless. Creativity abounds in special event planning and almost any circumstance a firm finds itself in can be turned into a successful event. Just a few of the numerous types of special events are listed here, including:

Anniversary Sale	Brand Awareness	Conference
Athletic Event	Breakfast	Contest
Banquet	Cause Awareness Day	Convention
Beauty Week	Celebrity Appearance	Cook-off
Blood Drive	Civic Responsibility	Festival

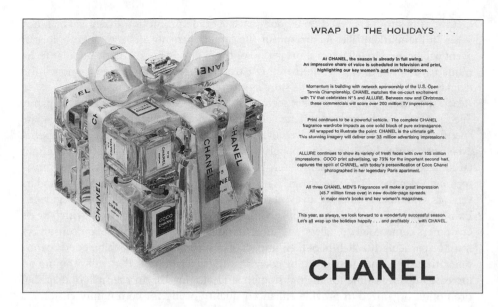

FIGURE 14.2 Chanel's integrated strategy for a fragrance promotion includes event sponsorship.

Employee Training	Product Demonstration	Product Launch
Exhibit	Fund-raiser	Retreat
Extended Hours Sale	Gala	Ribbon Cutting Ceremony
Fair	Gift-with-Purchase	Sidewalk Sale
Fashion Show	Girls' Night Out	Stockholder Meeting
Luncheon	Grand Opening	Tour
Men's Night	Holiday Celebration	Trade Show
Musical Performance	Improvement Project	Workshop
Parade	Informal Modeling	

Event Objectives

Special events are planned to fulfill one or more specified business objectives. Such objectives include the following:

- **Enhance the image of the company to customers or the general public.** Producers, manufacturers, designers, and retailers have had to look beyond their products and focus on their consumers in order to distinguish themselves from the competition (Schultz & Barnes, 1995). Special events are a promotion strategy that can allow a company to distinguish itself from the competition. The event may enhance the image of a company or a brand the company offers to customers, employees, and the general public. These types of events are planned to communicate a positive image or impression of a company. Because retailers, manufacturers, and designers are so heavily dependent on public acceptance, they have become some of the most aggressive and constant users of special events.

- **Sell large quantities of products or services in a short time period while promoting future sales.** The goal of any promotion strategy is to have consumers respond to products, services, and ideas that are for sale. Special events have become a routine technique used to sell products. As part of doing business, retailers purchase large quantities of products based on a good price, a trade promotion incentive, or a hot seller in the marketplace. As a result of the larger-than-normal inventory, a special event will be used to sell it in a short period of time. This is a particularly popular technique used at holidays. During these high-traffic periods, prewrapped items will be displayed on tables throughout the store as gift reminders for consumers.

- **Reach specifically targeted market segments.** Differentiation is the name of the game. Special events can be used to differentiate a firm from its competition, or differentiate specific target consumers who have potential to benefit the organization. Some special events are planned for the whole population, while other events are targeted to certain customers. Men's nights, for example, are popular events hosted by retailers before Christmas and Valentine's Day. A yearly ski swap, hosted cooperatively by a local retailer and its vendors, is another example of an event reaching a specifically targeted market segment.

- **Exhibit good corporate citizenship, giving back to the community from which one's customers come.** Malls, retailers, and supermarkets especially dependent on consumers must be particularly watchful of their impact on a community and exhibit good corporate citizenship. They may do so by coordinating special events that will promote an increased quality of life for their customers and employees. An example of a special promotion organized to provide enhanced quality of life for community customers and employees is illustrated in the following example. A regional supermarket chain has a box display naming each of the local elementary and secondary schools by a specific box. For a specified period of time customers are encouraged to deposit their cash register receipts into one of the boxes as they leave the store. At the conclusion of the time period, the supermarket totals the receipts for each school and makes a monetary donation to each of them. Following the promotion, special events are held at each local school to present the contributions.

- **Enhance customer and VIP relations to preferential and potential customers.** Every firm has special customers, or VIPs, that it wishes to impress. Events may be held for these people to show them how important they are to the firm. Invitation-only events, such as galas or premier showings by designers, illustrate their preferential status. For example, luxury suites sponsored by various international brand names, featuring everything from cosmetic treatments to gowns, jewelry and more, are set up in Los Angeles during the week before the Academy Awards. In addition to gift bags given to nominees and presenters, pampering takes place at such locations as the Estée Lauder Spa in the Four Seasons Hotel and socializing takes place at the Bacardi Lounge in Le Méridien Hotel (Wilson, 2004).

    The Golden Globes Presenter Box and Gift Bag was valued at $52,000 ("Golden Globe Awards," 2006). The gift contained a trip to Antarctica, a Chopard diamond ring, in addition to a sports club membership, fashions from Hugo Boss and Denim for Immortality and many more items. Brands included in the luxury suites and for presenters and nominees at the assorted awards ceremonies hoped to gain celebrities as their clients and recognition from the people that read about these ceremonies.

- **Contribute to community's economic development.** Contributing to the community's economic development is also a goal of special events. Firms cannot exist in a community without contributing back to the economic enrichment of that community. One way for a firm to contribute is to increase sales revenue coming into the community. This can be accomplished by hosting special events that attract certain groups, such as tourists. The tourists will spend money at the event and at other businesses such as hotels and restaurants within the community, thus contributing to economic development. For example, a regional retailer in a resort community may sponsor a juried arts festival over a three-day weekend to attract out-of-town guests. The tourists spend a day at the festival and another day shopping at local shops and boutiques including the retail sponsor. The community benefits from the economic boost from the tourists, and the retailer benefits from increased name recognition and sales. Box 14.1 details a Italian firms' support of art and architecture.

- **Promote a charitable cause.** Increasingly, special events are being used to promote charitable causes. Firms ask their customers, employees, and senior management to get involved and take action in response to a concern or a crisis. Many of the examples that are used in this chapter have a cause associated with them. Causes that have particular support from the fashion industry include AIDS and breast and ovarian cancers, because these diseases have disproportionately affected the industry. Figure 14.3 illustrates Lee's National Denim Day and the international pink ribbon campaign that supports research for breast cancer.

All of these goals are important and a company must consider each goal when planning a special event. A firm may plan an event to accomplish one or more goals. Once a firm has established the goals for a special event, the next step is to determine what type of event to host. We discuss categories of special events in the next section.

FIGURE 14.3 Print advertisement for Lee National Denim Day, displaying the international symbol for breast cancer awareness, the pink ribbon.

─○ special event categories

Special events occur at the primary, secondary, and retail levels of the fashion industry. Raw material producers use events to promote new discoveries in fibers or fabrics to manufacturers and consumers. Manufacturers use events to create interest in buyers to select their line for distribution in retail stores. Retailers use events to encourage consumers to shop at their locations. Figure 14.4 shows an event that promotes both a designer and a retailer.

Special events may be classified into two types—institutional events or merchandise-driven events—based on the intent of the event to influence the sale of merchandise or bring attention to the company. Attention to the company may be promoted through institutional features or attractions, specific customer services, special shows, or celebrity appearances. The sale of merchandise may be promoted through product displays, merchandise clinics or demonstrations, fashion shows, sales inducements, or free samples. These classifications are not mutually exclusive. Many special events may be developed as a combination to sell merchandise and bring recognition to the designer or retailer. In one instance, a store opening may be used to strengthen the image of the firm, in another instance, to sell merchandise.

Italian Fashion Firms Back Cezanne Exhibit

A group of fashion companies here is harking back to the Renaissance with its support for the arts and architecture.

During the men's wear exhibition Pitti Uomo here last week, Partners of Palazzo Strozzi, an association supported by several industry executives and firms, said it would sponsor the "Cézanne in Florence" exhibition, to bow on March 2, among other projects.

The association was created last month; its backers include Leonardo Ferragamo and Ferragamo Finanziaria SpA, Tod's chief executive Diego Della Valle, François Pinault and Gucci Group, Calvin Klein Collection licensee Fingen SpA and Rocco Forte Hotels. It aims to further Florence's cultural life and role as a European cultural center. To support artistic projects at Palazzo Strozzi, the group vows to make a guaranteed contribution over the next three years of about 3 million euros, or $3.8 million at current exchange. The restored medieval Palazzo Strozzi will reopen with the Cézanne show and will, for the first time, also hold a small permanent exhibition on its history and on the Strozzi family.

The prestigious Galleria degli Uffizi, the city's most prominent museum and art gallery, last week unveiled a 17th-century painting by Johann Carl Loth that was restored with the help of Gianfranco Ferré. The Loth painting, "Adam Grieves for Abel," which originally belonged to Ferdinando de'Medici, was put on public display on Saturday in a new section of the expanded Uffizi, which is expected to double its floor space upon completion of a remodeling project next year.

"We should be attentive of what we produce and preserve—after all, these are properties that belong to all of us," said Massimo Macchi, CEO of Gianfranco Ferré. "There is a lot that we can do, and this is a program that we plan to continue."

Macchi noted that Ferré was working with Florentine officials to organize exhibitions at Palazzo Navone, a 16th-century Renaissance building on Via della Vigna Nuova, off central Via Tornabuoni, where the designer opened a boutique last year. (Macchi revealed the company was redoing its Los Angeles boutique in the style of its store in Florence, and that it would open a shop in Hong Kong next month and one in Rome by the summer.)

The restoration of the painting, which was in "dramatic condition," according to restorer Anna Monti, cost 8,400 euros, or almost $11,000.

"Compared to fashion's big sponsorships, this is not a commitment significant in terms of economic obligations, but rather in terms of time and attention," said Macchi. The executive said Ferré, an architect known for his passion for the arts, helped fund the restoration of frescoes by 17th-century artist Guercino in the cathedral of the city of Piacenza in 1983, and donated 300 archival outfits to the Costume Gallery at Palazzo Pitti in 2000.

"Too often, patrons want to finance [the restoration] of major paintings," said Antonio Natale, director of the Uffizi. "The class of a patron such as Mr. Ferré is that he is willing to support a work that does not have a huge resonance," said Natale.

Source: Zargani, L. (2007, January 23) Italian fashion firms back Cezanne exhibit. *Women's Wear Daily*, p. 14.

Institutional Events

Institutional events are planned to enhance the image of the company, through exhibiting good corporate citizenship, embellishing customer relations, contributing to the community economic development, or promoting a charitable cause.

One company that promotes a variety of institutional events is Macy's. In addition to sponsoring the Thanksgiving Day Parade since 1924 in New York and the Passport Event in San Francisco, Macy's also has presented the 4th of July fireworks for over 30 years in New York. Macy's displays the largest fireworks display in America, celebrating the nation's birthday bash with over 120,000 bursts of color, light, and breathtaking pyrotechnics from around the world. Nearly 12 million television viewers and two million live spectators watch in amazement as fireworks burst 1,000 feet in the air to the soundtrack (Macy's, 2006). These events, in addition to others, show Macy's commitment to patriotic, health-, and community-oriented institutional celebrations.

FIGURE 14.4 A special event, the appearance of designer Karen Neuberger at Lord & Taylor for a pajama party, where sales associates join her in modeling her new lines of sleepwear.

Other examples of institutional events include museum exhibits, gallery exhibits, in-store exhibits, musical performances, and anniversary celebrations. These are discussed as a sample of the many kinds of events that can be produced to highlight an institution or brand.

Museum Exhibits

A museum is an institution devoted to the acquisition, conservation, study, exhibition, and educational interpretation of objects having scientific, historical, or artistic value. Fashion items have always had great historical and artistic, as well as scientific, value. Museums may provide a unique exhibit space for clothing or unusual products. A **museum exhibit** is a presentation of fashion items in an interpretive setting at a museum. The opening of a fashion exhibit as a special event at a museum may create excitement and institutional recognition for a designer, retailer, or publisher beyond the walls of the institution. Costume exhibits are among the most popular "art museum" events, drawing people who otherwise would not be exposed to such media. Clothing is displayed on mannequins arranged in attractive vignettes with narrative provided on signage and programs available from the museum. Retrospective books have been sold as part of the event to generate sales and create an ambiance for the showing. The opening night of a museum exhibit is usually a gala party that serves as a fund-raiser for the museum or other charity. Museum exhibits are discussed in Chapter 16 with visual merchandising.

Gallery Exhibits

Museums are not the only locations for fashion-related events; galleries also provide a unique location for special events. Galleries are rooms or buildings designed for the exhibition of artistic work. A **gallery exhibit** is a presentation of fashion items in an artistic setting at a gallery. An exhibit with the theme *Maze, Traps, and Runways* was presented at the Mary Boone Gallery in New York. The gallery exhibit featured Toland Grinnell's artistic interpretation of logomania and fashion's obsession with luggage. One of the featured pieces, *Portable Runway*, was a tiny runway with electric lights tucked into one of his crafted suitcases. The artist Grinnell embraces the synergy between art and fashion, saying that the relationship adds spice to both communities ("Just in case," 2004).

Musical Performances

Musical performances are entertainment presentations hosted by a retailer or manufacturer. A retailer may invite a local musical group to perform in the retail store for the benefit of shoppers to enhance a season or promote a cultural event. Manufacturers may sponsor a musical performance by a well-known popular singer or host a special viewing of a Broadway play to bring name recognition to its firm at a trade show.

With proper public relations and advertising, the retailer may increase traffic and promote goodwill by sponsoring the local musical organization. The simple addition of background music may enhance sales activities. Nordstrom's entertains customers with live piano performances. The success of the pianists in the flagship store was so great that Nordstrom now has piano players in several of its branch locations.

Anniversary Celebrations

Anniversary celebrations are special events used by companies to bring attention to their longevity in the community. Beginnings and endings are often celebrated with anniversaries; these are usually good times to look back and forward at the same time.

"Corporate memory" is used as a marketing tool. According to Phyllis Barr, a New York–based consultant, using a company's past as a promotion tool in the present can bring attention and business to the company by illustrating the one thing that sets the company apart from every other company—its history (2005). History can be used to respond to people's desire for reliability by telling how long a company has been in business and what it has done. History can also be used to bring renewed attention to long-established brand names by capitalizing on their record of reliability. Consumers are also likely to be drawn to history and nostalgia. By using a nostalgic theme for an anniversary event, the audience can look both backward and forward.

For the 85th anniversary of Gucci, designer Frida Giannini revised the iconic Hobo bag, using new materials, a sleeker bit, with brass and enamel plates commemorating the year (Fig. 14.5). Other bags and the 450-page retrospective book *Gucci by Gucci* were among the special projects planned for the anniversary. A special advertising campaign was shot by Craig McDean with models Iselin and Caroline Trintini (Ilari, 2006).

Merchandise Events

Merchandise events are planned to influence the sale of goods. The goals they fulfill include selling large quantities of products in a short time period, reaching specifically targeted market segments, enhancing customer relations, or promoting a charitable cause.

Retailers sponsor activities to attract customers into their stores in order to generate store sales. The activities range from large storewide promotions to small endeavors such as product demonstrations. Special events are an especially important device during off-peak selling seasons. For example, home shows and boat shows at malls are scheduled to bring people in during slower selling seasons. Store anniversary sales are not necessarily celebrated on the actual day of incorporation, but rather during a period in which sales need a boost.

Cosmetic companies use events such as facials or beauty seminars to coincide with gift-with-purchase and purchase-with-purchase sales events to increase traffic and move merchandise. Neiman Marcus took the cosmetic promotion to a new level. The Beauty Event takes place twice each year. This event promotes a variety of well-known beauty brands, not just one. A specially designed seasonal bag is created for Neiman Marcus with samples from various vendors, such as Bobbi Brown, Kiehls, Prada, and Laura Mercier. A customer who makes a minimum purchase will receive the bag and its contents. Many vendors coordinate their gift-with-purchase promotions during this event, making it a huge incentive for customers to buy during this merchandise event. Special events can also increase traffic to dispense merchandise rapidly during peak periods.

FIGURE 14.5 The 85th anniversary of Gucci was celebrated with redesign of some of Gucci's classic handbags.

For example, university bookstores always set up extra checkout lines during the first week of classes to accommodate higher numbers of customers during a rush period. Examples of merchandise events include store openings, celebrity appearances, product launches, vendor or category weeks, and product demonstrations. As with institutional events, this is only a sampling of the different types of events that exist to sell merchandise.

Store Openings

Special events are always planned for a store or boutique opening. **Store openings** are celebrations that introduce customers to a new merchant. The merchant may have the store stocked and ready for sales, or show the space where a future store will be located. Special sales, refreshments, and product demonstrations encourage consumers to shop in the new environment. Some events are planned to show consumers the space, rather than sell merchandise.

Large chains, such as Target, plan several store openings at once across the country and have special store savings at every location. Special events include refreshments, activities for children, and a fireworks display.

Celebrity Appearances

The **celebrity appearance**, featuring an individual from inside or outside the fashion industry to promote a new product or designer line, is a common special event. Nightclub "Social Hollywood" was decorated with giant red lamps and white curtains to look like the Minneapolis-based Target Stores' logo for a launch party for Target Couture. The merchandise, including studded jeans, quilted leather satchels, and diamond pendants were the idea and exclusive property of Los Angeles boutique Intuition's owner Jaye Herswill. Her creations will not be sold in any of the Target stores, because she got permission from the Target Corporation to use the retailer's logo on her products for free (Bowers, 2006). Stars, including Gabrielle Union and Beverly Union, were among the people at the party, wearing Target Couture.

Cosmetic lines often celebrate new fragrances with the designer or celebrity appearing at the product launch. During slower sales periods, malls may invite television stars, particularly soap opera personalities, for one-day guest appearances to sign autographs and lunch with a special winner to increase traffic for the mall.

Product Launches

Product launches are special events planned to set in motion the promotion and sale of new products such as the new line of sleepwear in Figure 14.4. The special event to kick off a new product is the climax of many months of preparation and planning from the inception of the product to release to the consumer. The goal of a product launch is to make sure every promotion element, advertisement, news release, and direct-mail piece has a cohesive sustained message that enhances the brand equity of the product. While many product launches are conducted at retail stores, the events are planned in cooperation with the producers, manufacturers, or designers of the product.

Vendor or Category Weeks

Vendor or **category weeks** are special events that feature a merchandise category or brand. The event may be store-specific, such as Chaps week at Kohls, or the event may be sponsored by a producer and involve several competing retailers. For example, the Intimate Apparel Council sponsors Lingerie Week. During the week, in-store events are held at Bloomingdale's, Macy's, and Nordstrom's to increase the sales of intimate apparel. Events have included fashion shows, celebrity appearances, and musical performances by Broadway stars.

Product Demonstrations

Product demonstrations, which illustrate how consumers can use merchandise, are simple yet effective special events orchestrated to promote new or improved products. Demonstrations are common in accessory and cosmetic departments, and in warehouse retailing (where most product demonstrations require minimal space, perhaps a table or counter as the only requirements). A cosmetic department may offer facials or makeovers for participants who register ahead of time for product demonstrations. The department store may conduct the consultations on the sales floor or have a special room set aside to provide privacy for the customers. Warehouse retailers often have product representatives set up at stations within the store. Food samples or cleaning solutions are often tested before an audience for their reaction. In the case of an environmentally sensitive cleaning product, demonstration of adequate soil removal may cause favorable product evaluation and create increased sales.

———o SPECIAL EVENTS PERSONNEL

People involved in special events range from seasoned professional special event planners and retail executives to volunteers, who are members of charitable organizations or store advisory boards interested in supporting a particular cause or retailer. Whether the event is large or small, certain teams or individuals are needed to accomplish tasks. If the event is a small gathering of 25 to 35 people for an accessory launch at a specialty store, the entire event may be coordinated by one person. But, if the event is as large as the *Chocolate Show*, a three-day festival—including demonstrations by top pastry chefs and chocolate makers, chocolate tastings, exhibits from various chocolate brands, author signings at a cookbook store, and a fashion show with haute couture dresses and accessories made from chocolate—requires a significant staff to handle all of the show planning and execution (Event International, 2004). Although each event function may be given different titles depending upon the situation, the essential tasks of producing an event include administrative, personnel, operations, and marketing.

Administration is handled by the top manager or event director and provides overall leadership at the event control center. Figure 14.6 shows an example of an event request form that the event director will use to put the event on the calendar. The personnel team finds the right people to do each job, and either trains volunteers or finds appropriate outside suppliers and technicians to complete tasks. This function is also known as human resources. Operations personnel get the job done. These people make the event, the venue, and the participants work together. Finally, the marketing team, also known as sales, public relations, or promotion, get people to the event, through selling tickets, finding sponsors, contacting the media, or developing advertising or publicity campaigns. The special events planning checklist (Fig. 14.7) helps keep the staff on track for creating a successful event.

FIGURE 14.6 Escada event request form.

ESCADA (USA) Retail Inc.
Event Request Form

Division: ❐ ESCADA   ❐ LAUREL

Store Number: _____ Location: _____ Manager: _____

Date of Event: _____ Location: _____

Group, Charity, or Organization Having Event
(include background, past events; attach any information):
_____
_____
_____

Contact of Group: _____ Telephone #: _____
Description of Event: _____
_____
_____
_____
_____

Value to the Company: _____
_____
_____

Level of Involvement (marketing support necessary): _____
_____
_____

Approximate Cost (i.e., modeling, catering, staging, invitation): _____
_____

DMM Approval   Date   RMM Approval   Date

FIGURE 14.7 Special events planning checklist.

Special Events Planning Checklist

Event:

Location:

Date:

☐ Plan schedule for events during next promotion cycle and personnel and divisions involved with direction from the Management Team for Special Events.

☐ Identify contact person(s) at each location (volunteer, teen board member, branch manager).

☐ Discuss the type of event, the promotion, and personnel who might be involved with contact person.

☐ Determine the date and location for the special event, taking into consideration other local community events and the schedule of personnel who might be involved with the event.

☐ Contact the facility to discuss cost of using facility, food service, equipment, parking, deposits, RSVP, confirmation dates, and other details. Order a catering menu.

☐ Determine costs for use of facility and food service. Determine reasonable charge for guests, if necessary.

☐ Determine guest list.

☐ Determine timeline for mailing invitations, reminders, and RSVP date.

☐ Draft invitation and RSVP.

☐ Inform accounting department of expenses.

☐ Order invitations and RSVPs, with specific quantity and date to be completed.

☐ Check draft from printer. Sign off. Double-check quantity.

☐ Mail invitations.

☐ Inform all necessary personnel of the event, both verbally and with written details so that they can answer questions.

☐ Have contracts signed and send deposit to facility and/or caterer if necessary.

☐ Develop RSVP list. Have information systems input this data into main database.

☐ Confirm RSVPs, meal selection, and equipment needs.

☐ Confirm number of RSVPs with facility and caterer.

☐ Have checks drafted for payment to caterer/facility/entertainment and other expenses.

☐ Prepare materials for event (gift-with-purchase, name tags, drawing numbers, etc.)

☐ Conduct event.

☐ Submit receipts.

☐ Write thank-yous.

☐ Follow-up payments to vendors.

If an event takes place at a retail store, it is coordinated by the store's special events or public relations director, assisted by members of the promotion and merchandising divisions. Execution may involve everyone from sales associates to department managers as well as personnel from the buying office. In some instances, a retail store may also call on a team of volunteers from the store's teen board, college board, or customer advisory board to assist with an event. These groups advise the retailer about fashion trends and shopping patterns for their particular segment, helping the retailer understand these consumers and establish fashion leadership with them. Youthful shoppers are significant because they develop loyalty as they mature. Members of these boards frequently volunteer to model for fashion shows, participate in personal improvement programs, or attend musical events that are coordinated through the store's special events office.

⎯o EVENT SPONSORSHIP

Event sponsorship has become increasingly popular in recent years. Event sponsorship involves a company supporting an event through monetary or in-kind contributions as a way to meet one or more of its corporate objectives. Throughout this text, we have mentioned event sponsorship many times. It can be used as a consumer-oriented sales promotion technique to entice consumers to buy certain products. Corporations will sponsor events as part of the public relations strategy to enhance their image, improve customer relations, increase employee morale, or fulfill civic responsibilities. Clarifying these objectives will help convince sponsors to participate by answering, "What is in it for me?"

Very few successful large-scale events can be sustained without some form of financial support from the corporate community. The growing trend by corporations is to establish event budgets or use foundation money to sponsor special events or projects. Although event planners often play on the emotions of organization personnel to obtain sponsorship, a company will rarely make a significant contribution unless it can expect to obtain a reasonable business return for the investment.

Sponsorship may take one of two forms. The first form of sponsorship involves advertisers who lend their name to a sporting activity or another type of special event. The *Bay-to-Breakers* is a race held every spring in San Francisco. The event has a number of cosponsors, including retailer Nordstrom, who helps pay for ads, provides event logo merchandise, and generally supports the cross-town run each year. By participating in such activities, Nordstrom hopes that racers will think favorably of them and, therefore, come to their stores to shop.

Secondly, television or radio sponsorship involves an advertiser who underwrites the cost of program production and its commercials. The ads are fit into the program, when and where the advertiser wants them, as the program is broadcast. This is very costly; therefore, single sponsorships are rare and usually limited to special programs. J.C. Penney and Revlon are firms that have been associated with this practice, sponsoring such broadcasts as the Oscar, Grammy, or Emmy award shows. To save costs and reduce risks, many advertisers decide to cosponsor these kinds of programs. Why do they spend so much money on programs and advertising?

There are several important reasons why advertisers sponsor television and radio programs. First, advertisers hope the audience more readily respects the product(s) that are associated with an organization that sponsors high-quality entertainment. This is true when there is prestige attached to programming. Second, the sponsor controls the timing and content of its commercials, so long as they remain within the network's or local station's regulations. If the sponsor wants to run a commercial longer than normal and offer fewer interruptions during the program, they may do so. Consumers, who respect this type of action, are likely to purchase products or services from the sponsor. Moreover, even though sponsorship is expensive, the advertiser is able to reach incredibly large audiences through sponsorship.

Types of Sponsors

Before starting the search for a sponsor, you will need to determine the type of sponsors that will be appropriate for your type of event. There are several types of sponsors, including an exclusive or title sponsor, a segment sponsor, a cosponsor, a media sponsor, or an in-kind sponsor.

An **exclusive sponsor** is also known as the title sponsor that pays a premium to have its name on the title of the event. For example, Mercedes-Benz is the title sponsor for Mercedes-Benz New York Fashion Week and a camera manufacturer is the title sponsor for Canon London Fashion Week. **Segment sponsors,** also known as presenting sponsors, are the major sponsor of a predetermined portion of the event. MAC cosmetics, Pantene hair products, and the *New York Times*, among others, are segment sponsors for New York Fashion Week.

If an event has more than one sponsor, the event is said to be **cosponsored** and expenses are shared by two or more organizations. Cosponsorships exist at every level except at the highest level of exclusive sponsorship.

The **media sponsor** provides a predetermined level of advertising support, and sometimes a media sponsor will also provide some cash support as well. Care must be taken when seeking a media sponsor. If a media outlet becomes the media sponsor, other media outlets may not want to provide any coverage.

In-kind sponsors supply products and services, rather than cash, as a donation to the event. A celebrity may waive normal performance fees and donate his services as an announcer, musician, or host at the event. This will attract an audience interested in seeing or hearing the famous person without huge expenses to the event planners. Other donations may come in the form of food, beverages, or technical skills of photographers, makeup artists, and hairstylists.

The range of sponsor opportunities can come from past and current sponsors, board members, related associations, peers, or professional organizations. Next, we will consider ways to find sponsors.

Locating a Sponsor

Before approaching a potential sponsor, do research about that person or firm. From your local library to the Internet, the first place to start locating a sponsor is by completing research. It is important to know that many corporations have sponsorship requests on a daily basis. How can you locate a sponsor that is interested in your event?

Consider what a potential sponsor wants from participating in an event. Table 14.1 lists the types of things sponsors want versus what events typically offer. The benefits should relate back to the objectives for the event, including enhancing the image of the company to customers or the general public, selling large quantities of products or services in a short time, reaching specifically targeted market segments, exhibiting good corporate citizenship, giving back to the community, enhancing customer and VIP relations to preferential and potential customers, contributing to a community's economic development, and promoting a charitable cause.

Various directories and publications are sources of information about potential sponsors. Industry information can be located in such reports as *Standard & Poor's Industry Surveys, US Industrial Outlook,* and *Forbes Annual Report on American Industry.* Media information can be found in *Editor & Publisher Yearbook International, Broadcasting/Cable Yearbook,* or *Gale's Directory of Publications.* An Internet search can provide information

TABLE 14.1   *Benefits Sought by Event Sponsors*

Benefit	% of Corporations Desiring	% of Events Providing
Signage	70%	89%
Corporate Hospitality	70%	68%
Tickets to Event	70%	75%
Television Coverage / Support	60%	75%
Other Media Coverage / Support	70%	86%
Product Usage	60%	61%
Staff Support	50%	57%
Sampling / Sales Opportunities	20%	50%
Trade-out Possibilities	20%	71%

Source: Schmader, S. W, & Jackson, R. (1990). *Special events: Inside & out.* Champaign, IL: Sagamore Publishing.

about specific companies and their involvement with special events. Looking at peers in professional organizations or employers in related industries may also provide potential sponsors. Having a personal connection with a potential sponsor is always beneficial.

Although United Parcel Service, Motorola, Peroni beer, or faucet maker Kohler are not the type of sponsors normally associated with fashion, these brands have signed on to sponsor fashion events in cities around the globe (Chozick, 2006). IMG, the sports-management giant known for representing stars like Tiger Woods, moved into managing fashion events around the world from Mumbai, India, to Lahore, Pakistan, in addition to many other traditional fashion centers. Firms such as Hershey's York Peppermint Patties that have not been associated with fashion events are participating. York Peppermint Patties became the official candy of Fashion Week in New York. Miller, the producers of Peroni beer, views sponsorship of a fashion event as a way to show popularity with a fashion-forward crowd. Fashion shows have an audience of celebrities, important fashion editors, as well as trendsetters, who influence consumer trends. This has led to the unlikely sponsorship by several nonapparel-oriented manufacturers.

Sponsorship Proposal

Once potential sponsors have been identified and researched, you will put together a **sponsorship proposal**, a document that asks a potential sponsor for contributions to make the event happen. Formatting a sponsorship proposal is up to you and the group you represent. Minimally, a sponsorship proposal should contain a description of the event, background and involvement of other sponsors in the past, objectives for the event and benefits of sponsorship, amount of investment, and the deadline for a decision. Figure 14.8 shows an example of a sponsorship package created for a fashion event.

The event description should explain why the event was created originally, and ties it to the objectives for the current event. It would be appropriate to provide samples of prior media coverage and quotes from event planners as well as members of the audience. Provide a brief history of the event along with evaluations from past participants, sponsors as well as attendees. By identifying the event's objectives, the potential sponsor

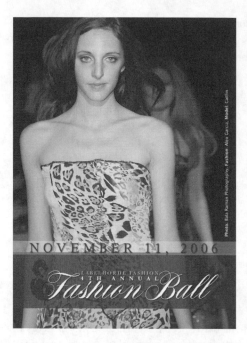

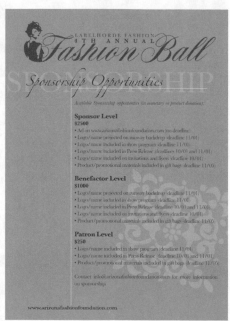

FIGURE 14.8 Labelhorde Fashion put together this sponsorship package for its 4th Annual Fashion Ball.

should be able to find benefits to her company. Ask for a specific amount of money in the investments section of the document. You need to know if the potential sponsor will participate by a certain date. By making that part of the proposal package, you will get an answer in a timely manner.

From an event coordinator standpoint, financial support from a commercial sponsor can help cover expenses, keep patron costs to a minimum, or ensure quality and longevity of the event. From a sponsor's point of view, the event can create publicity, differentiate the sponsor from its competition, complement marketing programs, sell product or services directly, and fulfill responsibilities as a good corporate citizen. By understanding the reasons companies choose to sponsor an event, event planners can be better prepared to approach a potential sponsor.

Many times the content of a special event or project being funded may not be overtly related to the event sponsor, but subtle messages definitely reinforce the idea that the sponsor's products, services, and resources are important to the attendees. For example, Polo Ralph Lauren, which is internationally known as an American fashion design company, is the official outfitter for Wimbledon, the prestigious British tennis tournament. This five-year sponsorship deal with the All England Club, which stages the event each year, identified Polo as the first official apparel outfitter, dressing all on-court personnel, including chair umpires, line judges, and ball people, in the 129-year history of the event. Although the company declined to disclose the terms of the deal, it was estimated that Polo is spending less than $10 million for the sponsorship (Kletter, 2006).

The sponsorship is important to Polo, because the firm wants to build its international presence and its European business. In addition to providing uniforms to umpires, judges (Fig. 14.9), and the young men and women picking up balls on the courts, consumers can purchase the apparel and accessories. An expanded collection is available at special in-store shops at such retailers as Harrods in London, through Polo free-standing stores, or at Polo's website. Box 14.2 describes athletic companies' support of marathons.

FIGURE 14.9 Polo Ralph Lauren adds to his international reputation by sponsoring the apparel worn by umpires, judges, and ball personnel at Wimbledon Tennis Championships.

──○ Measuring Special Event Effectiveness

Evaluation serves important purposes for special event planners and especially for sponsors. When evaluating special events, personnel should determine the strengths and weaknesses of the project, including successes and failures as well as identifying opportunities for potential sponsors in the future. Most important, personnel should secure accurate statistics that will help sell and resell future activities. One of the primary tools used by special event producers is an **event diary,** chronicling all of the planning, budgeting, implementation, and follow-up processes of the activity. Figure 14.10 is a sample event diary.

Both sponsors and production personnel, working as a team, establish benchmarks from which to evaluate the event before the event takes place. Success ascertained by benchmarks can be a tool to measure efficiency and expected outcome of the event before its actual execution. In certain instances an outside firm can be hired to analyze the necessary information for evaluation as an independent third party.

Basic statistical information gathered for evaluation includes attendance records, demographic reach, media coverage, and cash intake, if the event is expected to generate revenue. Broadcast audience reach may be obtained from the station or network providing

○ BOX 14.2

Athletic Companies Hit the Ground Running for NYC Marathon

With a record number of applicants, the ING New York City Marathon is set for what could be its biggest year ever, and athletic companies are racing to keep in step.

"It's amazing when that many people want to run 26.2 miles—and pay to do it," said Ann Hinegardner, senior vice president of business development and marketing strategy for the New York Road Runners Club, the organizer of the event.

About 93,000 people signed up for the 37,000 available spots . . . and although Asics and Footlocker are official sponsors of the race, athletic companies are in their own competition to equip participants and fans with shoes and apparel.

Activewear companies are shipping in treadmills and technicians to offer free gate analysis in order to fit runners with customized shoes. Asics will offer the service at the Jacob K. Javits Convention Center; Nike has bases both at Javits and closer to the race at Nike Town on 57th Street; Adidas is doing it out of its SoHo store—to which it is busing people from Javits—and Fila is using a mobile running unit that will trade a pair of its customized shoes for free in exchange for the shoes the customer is wearing.

As a sponsor of the marathon, Asics runs the 19,000-square-foot Marathon Store at the ING New York City Marathon Health & Fitness Expo at Javits. More than 80,000 people came to the shop last year and bought more than $1 million of goods, according to Asics and the New York Road Runners Club.

"It's an incredible three days of shopping," said Gary Slayton, Asics vice president of marketing. "It's Macy's the day after Thanksgiving times five."

For the first time, official marathon gear will also be sold at Grand Central Terminal on Nov. 3 and 4 and at the finish line in a tent near Tavern on the Green the morning after.

Asics has been involved with the New York Marathon since 1988, but 2006 is "a particularly special year for us," said Slayton. Asics has doubled its marketing funding and peppered the city's subway stations and billboards two months earlier than normal with new "Challenge and Reward" ads.

It cites the formation this year of the "Big Five" series of marathons—New York, Chicago, Boston, London, and Berlin—as one reason for the enthusiasm.

Nike has its own seasoned winner, though chances are he won't place in the marathon. To mark the 10th anniversary of Lance Armstrong's cancer diagnosis, the Tour de France legend kicked off . . . the "Run Like Lance Challenge," which extends through the marathon. As he trained, Armstrong called on his "army" to help him log 50,000 miles via nikeplus.com, for which Nike donated $1 for each mile to the Lance Armstrong Foundation.

When the total was met, Nike extended the challenge for another 10,000 miles. Runners can donate miles to the borough of their choice, and the check is presented in the name of the area with the most miles—Manhattan currently is ahead, according to a Nike spokesman. The company is marketing the alliance with a billboard ad, yellow running shoes, and two old-fashioned taxis in high-traffic running areas.

Fila is also using the race to help those with cancer. Since 2004, the brand has sponsored and outfitted Team Continuum, a group that runs the New York Marathon to raise funds and awareness for cancer care. This year, the team has a record 312 members and projects it will raise more than $1.4 million, according to founder Paul Nicholls. Fila is selling a pink velour track suit, retailing at $90 for the jacket and $70 for the pants, of which 25 percent of the proceeds go to Team Continuum.

Adidas focuses its energy on April's marathon in Boston, which it sponsors.

"[The New York race] is another company's marathon, so we want to be in it in an appropriate way," said an Adidas spokeswoman.

For people inspired by the marathon, Adidas is launching the Urban Running Plan here the week after the marathon, with twice-a-week runs from Chelsea Piers.

Reebok is focusing its New York marathon marketing efforts on promoting the Paris marathon, which it sponsors. Reebok will have a booth at Javits to soft-launch its Pump Paris Trainer, and with each pair of Pump Paris Trainers tried on, consumers can enter to win a trip for two to the Paris marathon.

Source: Beckett, W (2006, October 26). Athletic companies hit the ground running for NYC marathon. *Women's Wear Daily*, p. 10.

Special Event Diary

Name of Event:

Date of Event:

Venue:

Event Sponsor:

Sponsor Contact Information:

Event Planned Objectives:

Were Objectives Met?

Event Personnel and Activities:

    Administration Director

    Personnel Director

    Operations Director

    Marketing Director

Attach Planned and Actual Budget:

Audience Demographics:

Audience Reaction:

Notes for Improvement:

FIGURE 14.10 Evaluation and documentation of a special event is recorded in a special events diary.

coverage. Demographic reach can be measured by surveys or polls conducted over the phone, through direct response media, or in person during the event. Surveys and humanistic observations are good ways to determine the perceptions of the particular event or sponsor by attendees. Publicity can be measured by counting sponsor or event specific mentions and multiplying them by the appropriate circulation or number of viewers or listeners. Newspaper articles or other media mentions should be documented and kept with the event diary.

Surveys are frequently given to audience members attending seminars and workshops. Participants are asked to rate the event and speakers with scores ranging from *strongly like* to *strongly dislike*. The fact that audience members may not be willing to take the time to fill out surveys is the one of the biggest problems for special event planners attempting to document audience reaction. Unless participants are willing to provide positive and negative reactions, planners may have a difficult time assessing the presentation. Event diaries not only document the current event, they are used to plan events in the future.

Special events are planned activities to encourage consumers to come together. A special event may be used to sell merchandise or to promote the image of a brand or a company. Store image is promoted and differentiated through the use of special events. An otherwise ordinary happening is made into a newsworthy milestone when someone plans a special promotion around the happening. Special events are an important ingredient to the promotion mix strategy because of the excitement they create.

summary

- A special event is a one-time occurrence with planned activities, focused on a specific purpose, to bring attention to a brand, manufacturer, retailer, or organization to influence the sale of merchandise.
- Some special events are intended to generate sales by selling large quantities of featured products or services or reaching specifically targeted market segments.
- Special event programs that focus on communicating a positive image of the company have goals such as exhibiting good corporate citizenship, enhancing customer and VIP relations, contributing to community economic development, and promoting a charitable cause.
- Strategically planned short-term and long-term events can build links between a product or brand and the public that can help a firm establish rapport between customers and its product or service.
- Successful special events are those that have been planned in a timely manner.
- While generating increased sales is an important goal behind a special event, other business goals, such as the introduction of a new product, revamping a store image, or offering thanks for continued store loyalty, are additional reasons to stage a special event.
- Special event planners should refer back to the objective of the event and create measurable evaluators to use in judging the success of the event. Intangible factors may be of more importance than the tangible sales figures reflected after the event.
- Adherence to the projected budget is also a measure of success for special events. Adequate preplanning by the event planning team will ultimately decide the success of any special event, large or small.

key terms

anniversary celebration	in-kind sponsor	product launch
category week	institutional event	segment sponsor
celebrity appearance	media sponsor	sponsorship proposal
cosponsor	merchandise event	store opening
exclusive sponsor	museum exhibit	vendor week
event diary	musical performance	
gallery exhibit	product demonstration	

questions for discussion

1. What are the primary and secondary reasons companies stage special events?
2. What is the difference between an institutional and a merchandise special event?
3. Who are the personnel responsible for special event planning and implementation?
4. Why do corporations sponsor events?

additional resources

Allen, J. (2003). *Event planning ethics and etiquette: A principled approach to the business of special event management.* Hoboken, N. J.: Wiley.

Allen, J. (2002). *The business of event planning: Behind-the-scenes secrets of successful special events.* Hoboken, N. J.: Wiley.

Gelhar, M. (2005). *The fashion designer survival guide.* Chicago, I. L.: Dearborn Trade Publishing.

Guerin, P. (2005). *Creative fashion presentations* (2nd ed.). New York: Fairchild Books.

Monroe, J. C. (2006). *Art of the event: Complete guide to designing and decorating special events.* Hoboken, N. J.: Wiley.

references

Bowers, K. (2006). Target's apparel success intensifies challenges from rivals. *Women's Wear Daily,* p. 8.

Chozick, A. (2006, June 8). Sponsors are bit by the fashion bug. *Wall Street Journal,* p. B6.

Delta jets into Henri Bendel's windows. (2006, June 14). *Women's Wear Daily,* p.6.

Event International. (2004). *The chocolate show.* Retrieved July 4, 2006, from http://www.chocolate show.com

Golden Globe Awards Presenter Box. (2006). *InStyle.* Retrieved July 3, 2006, from http://www.instyle .com

Ilari, A. (2006, June 5). Living la vita Gucci. *Women's Wear Daily*, Section II. pp. 18–19.

Just in case. (2004, January 8). *Women's Wear Daily*, p. 4.

Kletter, M. (2006, March 9). Polo aces Wimbledon sponsorship. *Women's Wear Daily,* p. 3.

Macy's. (2006). *Macy's event marketing.* Retrieved August 16, 2006, from http://www.macys.com

Radman, D. (1997, July 1). Show and tell: Using special events to communicate with your market. *Marketing Tools,* 4, (3), p. 58.

Schultz, D., & Barnes, B. (1995). *Strategic advertising campaigns.* Lincolnwood, IL: NTC Business Books.

Wilson, S. (2004, May.) How suite it is. *Lucire*, pp. 48–52, 102.

FIGURE 15.1 Macy's Passport show.

CHAPTER 15

Fashion Shows

The 24th annual Macy's Passport fashion show and auction had a little bit of everything.

The show and auction at Santa Monica airport's Barker Hangar has raised $24 million for AIDS/HIV services, prevention, and research since its inception. The event raised more than $1 million to be donated to 60 Los Angeles organizations.

Sharon Stone returned for her eighth year as host of the live auction, wearing a black satin vintage Gucci dress that she said she would sell if she didn't make her quota. "There's no stopping me, because in my lifetime, AIDS will become a thing of the past," Stone told the audience.

Heatherette designers and Macy's partners Richie Rich and Traver Rains staged a runway presentation combining pieces from their junior and designer lines.

Others on the runway included Lauren Ralph Lauren, Marc Jacobs, and Theory, a favorite of actress Nia Vardalos, who arrived wearing a black velvet dress by Vince and Prada stilettos.

"Passport is about giving," said Bob Mettler, chairman and chief executive officer of Macy's West. "I hope it says that we're committed, as a company, to the people we serve."

Source: Vesilind, E. (2006, October 2). Stars shine at Macy's passport show. *Women's Wear Daily,* p. 32

> **After you read this chapter you will be able to:**
>
> Discuss the purpose of fashion shows.
>
> Describe fashion shows at trade and consumer levels.
>
> List the characteristics of different categories of fashion shows.
>
> Discuss personnel responsibilities for producing fashion shows.
>
> Explain the fashion show planning process.
>
> List the elements of a fashion show.

Ask any executive at an AIDS organization that received a portion of the $24 million why Macy's put on the Passport fashion show and they would probably give you some variation of Sharon Stone's "because in my lifetime, AIDS will become a thing of the past." If you asked a Heatherette designer or Macy's sales representative the same question, they would likely give you a different answer. Like Weatherproof Garment's coat drive for the homeless at the skating rink from the previous chapter, fashion shows can serve as many purposes as any other promotional activity.

This chapter will begin by discussing the role of fashion shows as a promotion tool in the fashion industry and specifically discuss fashion shows created by producers, manufacturers and designers, and retailers. We then look at different categories of fashion shows. Many people are involved in fashion shows, and fashion show personnel will be the topic of the next section. Our focus then moves to planning a fashion show and to differentiating all of the elements necessary to rehearse, conduct, and evaluate a fashion show.

PURPOSE OF FASHION SHOWS

Of all the promotion activities, fashion shows are the most thrilling for many people. A fashion show is a presentation of apparel, accessories, and other products to enhance

FIGURE 15.2 The most famous fashion shows in the world are the
haute couture shows in Paris, including designs by Gaultier (top left),
Lacroix (top right), and Valentino (bottom).

personal attractiveness on live models to an audience. It includes all the elements of a theatrical production—music, lighting, staging, and a script as a performance for a live audience. More than other elements of promotion, a fashion show makes the audience feel influential. It is announced in advance, has a theatrical opening, and creates a sense of exclusivity for the invited audience. An effective show generates a sense of being in on the latest news and hottest trends of the fashion world. Additionally, it reinforces the fashion leadership of the designer or retailer producing the show. The excitement of a fashion show is apparent at all market levels, from the haute couture shows in Paris (Fig.15.2) to the trade shows in major markets, to consumer and charity shows produced in local communities. While the average consumer probably does not buy the fashions shown at a haute couture show, these shows illustrate the pinnacle of fashion-forward design. The trends and inspirations that are forecasted through these shows trickle down to designer ready-to-wear, to bridge, and finally to knockoff merchandise that is available to the mass market.

Although fashion shows are produced for a variety of reasons, the primary one is to sell merchandise. The fashion show helps to make an authoritative visual statement about garments and accessories, thus encouraging a potential customer (manufacturer, designer, retailer, or general public) to buy what has been shown. Shows are also staged for employees and customers to share important fashion information about trends, silhouettes, fabrics, colors, and services. New merchandise, product assortments, special offerings, in-store themes, or sales promotions may be introduced at fashion shows. Firms may also present fashion shows to attract new customers, build traffic, and encourage loyalty from existing customers. This promotion tool enhances a store or brand image and fashion authority, and communicates goodwill to the population.

Fashion shows can play an important role in the overall integrated marketing communications strategy of a firm. For example, a fashion show may be developed with the public relations team as an image-building exercise. As part of the team, the advertising unit suggests the theme for the show as a tie-in to the latest ad campaign. Direct-response mailings inform targeted customers of the show, while the visual merchandising unit creates a comprehensive store image and set design based on the fashions selected for the show. Because fashion shows have the power to influence designers, retailers, buyers, the press, and the public, they are a very important element of promotion.

If you have ever watched the Oscar or Emmy award shows honoring outstanding people in movies and television, you have probably noticed the considerable press coverage given to the clothes worn by the stars. The Oscar ceremony has turned into a fashion show as print and broadcast media report on who designed the outfits, accessories, matching bags, diamond earrings, and so on. The day after the show, the focus of many viewers is not so much on who won the major awards as on who was the best or worst dressed. This is an example of the growing curiosity consumers have for fashion as well as the connection they make between haute couture and the fashions they see in their neighborhood stores. Fashion shows can assist consumers in making this connection.

───o MARKET-LEVEL FASHION SHOWS

Fashion shows are produced by raw materials producers, manufacturers, designers, and retailers. The most consequential reason for staging a show is to sell merchandise to the targeted audience. In Chapter 4, we defined the different market levels within the industry as primary, secondary, and retail. Fashion shows are produced at the primary and secondary levels as trade shows and at the retail level as consumer shows.

FIGURE 15.3 Model at a bridal trade show.

Trade Shows

Textile producers, apparel manufacturers, and trade associations sponsor trade shows. In Chapter 4, we learned that trade shows are an excellent resource for discovering future trends. Many trends are identified on runways at fashion shows sponsored by producers or manufacturers. The typical audience at a trade show is composed of retail buyers and members of the media. Fashion shows produced by textile firms attract audiences of fashion designers and manufacturers looking for fabric and color trends because they are ready to buy the latest fabrics or findings. These trade shows demonstrate the use and versatility of the raw materials, trusting that the audience will like what they see and want to include the fabrication, findings, or piece goods in their next collection.

Shows produced by an apparel manufacturer will draw an audience of retail buyers and professional forecasting agents. In Figure 15.3, a model at a bridal trade show carries a card to tell buyers the style number that can be referenced in the show catalog. At trade shows such as MAGIC, fashion shows are presented three or more times daily throughout the trade show to accommodate the many buyers who comprise the audience and whom the manufacturer wants to influence. The press is invited to trade shows to encourage publicity for the fabrics or piece goods being presented in trade publications and in materials produced by forecasting services.

In 1993, 7th on Sixth was created by the Council of Fashion Designers of America. Participating designers included Ralph Lauren, Donna Karan, Calvin Klein, and Betsey Johnson, among other U.S. designers. The venue for the shows is the tents at the Bryant Park area of New York City at 42nd Street. The original mission of 7th on Sixth was to organize, centralize, and modernize the American fashion collections, and provide a stage for American designers to become players in the global fashion world. State-of-the-art venues, professional production teams, and vast media exposure were among the original goals. Later, I.M.G., the international sports and lifestyle management company, took over 7th on Sixth, creating I.M.G. Fashion, and made it a part of the global sports management corporate family. The I.M.G. Fashion division produces Fashion Week in New York in addition to several other worldwide fashion trade show events, including Los Angeles Fashion Week at Smashbox Studios, Australian Fashion Week in Sydney and Melbourne, and the Singapore Fashion Festival, among others. Fashion shows are produced by I.M.G. Fashion in America, Mexico, Europe, and in the Asia-Pacific regions.

Consumer Shows

Consumer shows are sponsored by retailers and are directed toward retail staff and the consumer market. Consumer shows include in-store shows, community, or charity shows. A consumer show is produced by the retailer to sell ideas and merchandise to the buying public. Consumer shows may feature seasonal, storewide, departmental, designer, private label, or manufacturer-brand merchandise. Manufacturers may cooperatively produce the show or provide elements for the show when their merchandise is shown exclusively or is presented prominently. Sales representatives will be on hand to present the merchandise to customers after the show in special one-day or preseason trunk show events. Consumer fashion shows are a popular magazine tie-in event. Magazines invite readers to attend fashion shows shown throughout the country, which are cosponsored by local retailers.

An **in-store show** is presented for the benefit of store employees, to inform the staff of new and exciting trends for the upcoming season, and is coordinated with the advertising and visual display departments to create a storewide theme. Thus, it stimulates enthusiasm and contributes to suggestion selling. Informed sales associates can, in turn, influence customers by sharing expertise on style characteristics, color combinations, and proper accessories for the latest fashions. Through the use of an in-store fashion show, merchandise trends and the store promotion plan can be conveyed to the entire staff and implemented throughout every department within the store.

A **community** or **charity show** is generally produced by one or more retailers to raise money and awareness for national, local, or fund-raising charities. The retailer may be headlined as a cosponsor or assist behind the scenes by loaning merchandise for the fashion show. In addition to selling merchandise, the retailer is promoting goodwill and building a strong community image. Celebrities, designers, and models often lend their support to these charitable events.

Macy's California has held an annual charity fashion show, called Passport to Global Fashion & Compassion, highlighted in the opening segment of this chapter to benefit AIDS charities since 1982. Fund-raising events have expanded over the years and range from a black-tie V.I.P Gala evening to a series of fashion shows that take place in Los Angeles and San Francisco each fall. Fashion shows present collections from such designers as Calvin Klein and Jennifer Lopez, in addition to student designs from the graduating class of San Francisco-based Academy of Art. Macy's Passport has helped to bring HIV/AIDS-related issues to the center of social concern, as well as raised $24 million to benefit HIV/AIDS research, care, prevention, and education programs ("Macy's Event Marketing," 2006). These programs reach thousands of men, women, youth, and children living with or at risk for HIV to ensure that they can live their lives with dignity.

──○ Fashion Show Categories

Fashion shows are defined by their production style, which includes four categories: production, formal runway, informal, and multimedia production. Show types are not specific to market levels and may be used at trade or consumer levels.

Production Show

The **production show** is the most elaborate and expensive type of fashion shows, loaded with theatrical and dramatic elements. Production shows, also known as spectaculars, feature theatrical backdrops and scenery, lighting effects, live or specially produced music, and dancing or specialized choreography to create a highly energized event. Trends are shown in a presentation format lasting approximately an hour with 15 to 50 models, depending on the needs of the sponsoring organization. High-end fashion-forward merchandise, including couture, eveningwear, bridal, or ready-to-wear collections, are usually the highlights of production shows. Production shows require a great deal of organization and advance planning. A professional show produced by a national magazine or charity will send an advance team to the community prior to the event to ensure all details are in place before the arrival of the merchandise and models. Shows produced locally may be coordinated by a team that plans for the show a year in advance of the event.

Production shows are often promoted as special events for fund-raising purposes and include hor d'oeuvres and cocktails followed by a luncheon or dinner. The Macy's California Passport show discussed earlier in this chapter is an example of a production show.

Paris haute couture shows, which are held twice each year in January and July, are presented as production shows. Karl Lagerfeld for Chanel and John Galliano for Dior, among others, have turned these high-fashion shows into spectacles, the *must-see* fashion shows held for the most influential fashion consumers in the world.

This is where the Dior audience will view creations from John Galliano. His shows can be an unlikely mix of Joan of Arc, Siouxsie Sioux, Botticelli, and forties French film actress Arletty played out against the backdrop of a Renaissance garden, underneath a sky that alternates between bloodred storm clouds and a spinning astrological wheel taken from an illuminated manuscript. These women were represented by a parade of medieval warrior-women in gilded chain mail, copper verdigris gowns, and glass diadems, each equipped with an armored sleeve. It was a bizarre troupe of goth-punks. Designer Galliano's clothes were inspired by the Marcel Carné film *Les Visiteurs du Soir*, in which Arletty wore 1940s interpretations of medieval armor (Fig. 15.4).

Karl Lagerfeld for Chanel came up with a couture statement that might be labeled *Medieval Mod*. In a mostly short collection shown with thigh-high boots, some in distressed denim, Lagerfeld showed abbreviated suits and tunic dresses on a stark-white revolving runway. There was also rich Chanel craftsmanship in every piece. Jeweled buttons and belts, embroideries of exploding stars, pearl and diamond hair decorations, dense patches of appliqué and stones, and black satin bows gave an impression of armor and heraldic pageantry (Fig. 15.5). That is where the sense of futuristic medievalism came into play. It was a fast-moving show, so many of the details were difficult to see, until the very last moment. When the girls finally stood still, the audience, watching from seats facing the circular runway, suddenly found itself revolving leisurely around the models.

In Paris, Italian designer Georgio Armani works to set his Privé collection above his ready-to-wear. He built up the collars of his opening daywear with face-framing furls and finished the look with forward-tilted hats (Fig. 15.6). The stylistic mood hovered somewhere between Poiret-style coats and the peaked-shoulder jacket of old Hollywood silhouettes, cut in complex zigzag patterns and tiny pleats. Armani is a designer in touch with the lifestyles of the super rich in Asia and other far-flung regions where he is extending his reach.

With Cher, Elton John, and Audrey Tatou attending the shows along with such fashion editors as Anna Wintour from American *Vogue* and Carine Roitfeld from French *Vogue*, Paris is the place to see high fashion in January and July. Celebrities, top fashion models, including Stella Tennant, Carmen Koss, and Mariacarla Boscono, and designers attend the fashion shows as well as parties timed to coordinate with them. Such events as Gucci's 85th anniversary party, the preview and opening of the *Balenciaga Paris* exhibition, in addition to private luncheons and cocktail parties, are all part of the couture season for customers, members of the media, and fashion innovators.

FIGURE 15.4 John Galliano for Dior embraces high theatrical design in his Paris haute couture show.

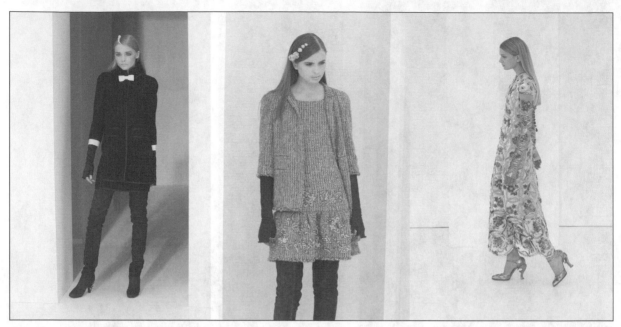

FIGURE 15.5 Karl Lagerfeld's *Medieval Mod* collection for Chanel.

Formal Runway Show

The show type most readers are likely to visualize when thinking about fashion shows is the formal runway show. **Formal runway shows** present merchandise as a parade with the audience seated at the perimeter of the runway. Ready-to-Wear designers and apparel manufacturers use this traditional method almost exclusively to present lines each season.

Formal runway shows may last from 15 minutes to 1 hour and feature models that parade down the runway sequentially, individually, or in groups to present the merchandise. It is very common to have all models come out onto the runway at the conclusion of the show to present a fashion finale and to acknowledge the designer when he or she is present (Fig. 15.7).

A formal runway show is planned around a merchandise theme and held at a special location, such as an auditorium, hotel, restaurant, or on a retail sales floor. Staging, lighting, models, music, and in some cases commentary are all elements of the runway show. Merchandise is generally seasonal, specialty, or ready-to-wear merchandise. A runway show may be directed toward the general public or a specialty market, such as petites, college students, or career women.

The ready-to-wear fashion shows that are held twice each year during the international collections in London, Paris, Milan, and New York, discussed in chapter 4, are presented as formal runway shows. During these events, models wear the latest fashion-forward garments created by the world's most famous fashion designers. Supermodels and up-and-coming models strut the prestigious catwalks, one at a time to show the direction that fashion is moving. Celebrities, members of the media, and the designer's private customers sit in the audience, while photographers document the newest styles and the people sitting in the front row.

FIGURE 15.6 Georgio Armani brings his signature style to the Paris Haute Couture shows.

FIGUre 15.7 Ralph Lauren takes a walk down the runway after showing his line at New York Fashion Week.

Informal Fashion Show

Informal fashion shows present merchandise on models in a casual environment. Lighting, music, staging, and other special elements are not used. A model walks around a sales floor, manufacturer's showroom, or restaurant showing the merchandise and answering questions about the product. Models may carry a sign or distribute business cards, coupons, or handouts to the audience as a teaser, hoping the audience will buy merchandise from the retailer after the presentation. Types of informal fashion shows include tearoom modeling, trunk shows, and mannequin modeling.

Tearoom modeling is a specific type of informal modeling that takes place in a restaurant on a regularly scheduled day. Models walk from table to table showing the merchandise to interested dining guests. Models are discouraged from interrupting the guests unless they are specifically asked about a feature or detail of the merchandise.

Trunk shows feature garments from a single manufacturer or designer and are presented as informal fashion shows in retail stores. A manufacturer or designer ships the complete line to the retail store in "trunks," or sales representative's cases. A sales representative or designer accompanies the fashions and, during an in-store event, answers questions about the products and takes orders from invited guests.

Trunk shows are advantageous to the retailer because the complete line can be presented to the customers without inventory risk to the retailer; rarely will retailers buy an entire line from a manufacturer or designer. Trunk shows also allow the retailer and the manufacturer or designer to gather immediate feedback about the merchandise. By listening to customers, designers and manufacturers can incorporate customers' desires into next season's line. Trunk shows that feature personal appearances by designers also increase the reputation of the retailer as a fashion leader.

With many retailers stocking less inventory and manufacturers limiting the amount of extra merchandise produced, there is new life to the traditional trunk show. Trunk shows focus on the needs of customers, providing unique items with custom characteristics for time-strapped consumers. Retailers and vendors are able to cooperatively show an entire line and cater to customers who need special sizes or want colors not carried by the retailer. Some retailers, such as Roz & Sherm, a 15,000-square-foot better women's apparel store in Bloomfield Hills, Michigan, have weekly trunk shows for their customers, whereas Gloria Fox, owner of Harpers, a 1,700-square-foot boutique in Alpharetta, Georgia, limits trunk shows to three a year ("Packing it in," 2004).

In an attempt to modernize the *trunk show*, Mary K. Dougherty & Associates, a Philadelphia wholesale rep for Nicole Miller, does a *truck show*, logging 75,000 miles a year in a travel trailer. The Nicole Miller Truck Show, which included a cocktail party with pampering by a manicurist and cosmetologist in addition to wardrobe planning services, generated an average sale per customer of $1,200 at Le Montage in Raleigh, N.C., where a goodie bag was included with purchases ("Packing it in," 2004).

Many trunk shows are coordinated with a charity. When Planned Parenthood, the Junior League, or private schools and garden clubs, among others, benefit from a donation of 15 to 20 percent of sales, customers attending trunk shows are given more reason to purchase on that day.

In the past, trunk show customers had to be able to attend a live presentation. But some retailers, recognizing the growing significance of the Internet and that many customers are crunched for time, have started online trunk shows. Retailers, including Saks Fifth Avenue, Neiman Marcus, and Bergdorf Goodman, turned to online trunk shows to give sales a boost and to help predict what the fashion trends will be ahead of time. Bergdorf Goodman held its first online trunk show in 2002, partnered with Style.com, before the retailer created its own website. The online trunk show featured 12 looks and 21 items from Marc Jacobs, bringing in $100,000 in sales during the four days it was online, compared to $350,000 in orders generated from a three-day trunk show at the store on Fifth Avenue (Corcoran, 2005). This gave the retailer time to react and place reorders, because orders came in before the merchandise arrived at the store. That allowed the retailer to capture sales that would otherwise be lost, increasing sales by as much as 5 percent. Box 15.1 gives more information about trunk shows.

Mannequin modeling is a form of informal modeling in which the model acts as a live mannequin in a store window or on a display platform. Live models strike poses similar to a stationary display form. These models must pose in stiffened positions and possess a great discipline and composure to remain perfectly still as the audience inevitably tries to make the models laugh or move.

Multimedia Show

Multimedia shows are specifically produced digitally and distributed to sales representatives or retailers. These fashion shows include point of purchase, instructional, and documentary videos. Multimedia fashion shows are also featured on television and online entertainment programs.

Point-of-purchase DVDs are used as sales promotion tools on the sales floor. Customers are given the opportunity to see the original runway show or an action view of how to wear the presented merchandise. Instructional videos are created for in-store training of sales personnel in place of a formal runway show. The videos demonstrate current information on fashion trends and illustrate special features of the products. A cosmetic line may use a demonstration video to present the new seasonal color palette and show how to creatively apply makeup. Documentary videos focus on the designer or behind-the-scenes activities of a manufacturer. They may be used as training films for company employees, produced for television shows, or used as a point-of-purchase sales promotion item. Immediately following the deaths of Gianni Versace and Diana, Princess of Wales, documentary videos were produced highlighting the lives of both these influential fashion figures.

Fashion shows are widely available on television, through the Style network and E! Entertainment, among other shows. Fashion leaders can even watch shows via podcasts and websites. Newer technologies allow anyone, almost anywhere in the world, with an Internet-enabled device, such as a computer, cell phone, or PDA, to watch live fashion shows via Fashion TV. Information about fashion, beauty, and style, including live events from Paris, Milan, or anywhere else around the world, is available through Fashion TV,

○ BOX 15.1

Shopping Advisor: Trunk Shows Demystified

Do expensive stores and designer departments intimidate you? Believe me, I know the feeling.

It's as though we've got this weird idea that salespeople who work in the high-end retail world come equipped with a special radar that tells them, "She can't possibly afford anything we sell."

All my shopping life, which is roughly since I started walking, I've felt this way. So for most of those years, I've stayed away from swanky stores filled with items I can only yearn for.

But it's time for us to get over it, and I have a suggestion on how to do just that.

For the past month or so I've been looking into designer trunk shows, a concept I didn't quite understand but sounded way too exclusive for us budget-minded types. I've since learned that going to a trunk show is a good way to conquer the intimidation factor. It lets you get up close and personal with designers or their representatives and—this is important—they don't make you feel lousy if you don't buy anything.

Presuming that most of you are like me and don't know anything about trunk shows, let me start by explaining what they are.

Better yet, let expert Julia Knier tell you. A former department store and Gap employee who now owns one of my favorite boutiques, Public I in Wicker Park, Knier says:

"The classic definition of a trunk show is where a store brings in the entire line of a designer's clothes a season ahead and you get the chance to special order anything you want. No store can carry an entire designer's collection, so what you see in stores is the store buyer's interpretation of what best suits their customer." April and May are big trunk show months for fall; September and October for spring fashions.

(If you're wondering, it's called a trunk show because traditionally the clothes were transported from the designer's studio to the store in giant, strapped trunks—although now large garment bags packed in cardboard boxes are often used instead.)

Last week I went to a Zac Posen trunk show at Neiman Marcus (737 N. Michigan Ave.). Posen is a young (25!) New York–based designer and a favorite of fashion insiders; his ready-to-wear collection starts at $300 for a polo shirt and leaps upward from there.

If I hadn't been looking for this show, I would have walked right past it. It basically consisted of two local models walking around the store in Posen's designs and a rack of about 80 pieces of fall clothing tucked into the second-floor designer section of the store, near the Chanel.

Posen wasn't there, but his rep, an enthusiastic acolyte named Stephanie Cozzi, was on hand to point out what's great about the clothes and which ones would look good on me—or you.

These are the actual dresses and pants and coats that the models (a scary size 0-to-2 assortment of glamazons with messy ponytails) wore on the runway at Posen's show last February in New York. So, unless you're impossibly tiny, you can't hope to zip these clothes, but you can try on coats and less fitted garments to get the idea.

And you can touch, feel, and learn about them in a friendly one-on-one (nonthreatening) conversation. Plus, if you love to know what's in, what's new, you get to see the next season's clothes months before they hit the stores or the fashion magazines. I wanted everything starting with the $950 cotton "umbrella blouse" and the sexy linen dress off Cozzi's back.

Cozzi patiently showed me how this collection has pieces edgy enough for young women but also offers twists on classics to appeal to their moms. I gather that snagging mother/daughter shopping duos is like winning the retail lottery.

And it's good for the shoppers too. Not to get all shrink-alodious on you but as Stephanie points out, if you are trying on a designer's offerings alongside your ma, "you get the approval of your mother." This is always a good (if elusive) thing.

While I was wandering around Neiman Marcus I ran into shopper Patrice Missner, who loves trunk shows because "you can see everything for the season" at one time, in one place, rather than the pieces "trickling in" to the store (and, if really popular, immediately selling out). Ordering ahead, "you know you're getting something great in the future" and can sometimes find out if anyone else in the area is ordering the same thing. But beware, you will be paying full price for whatever you order.

Trunk shows, I should add here, are not just for women. I went to one last month at Paul Stuart, the men's clothier in the John Hancock building. The definition of this trunk show is different from the classic. It's a chance to choose fabrics and styles not usually available and have shirts, jackets, and suits made to your exact measure for less than the usual off-the-rack cost.

General manager Margi Godfrey tells me that this twice-a-year event is "unfortunately one of the best-kept secrets in Chicago." Customer David Gross, a Chicago banker, is a regular at the trunk shows. "For Chicago professionals, this is really the best stop in the city," he tells me. He boasted of the savings on his just-ordered, made-to-measure suit for $1,200, where a similar one off the rack is regularly priced at $2,000.

That said, a lot of us can't afford that kind of money for a suit (or a Zac Posen blouse). But Stuart sales director Paul Kelly was happy to answer my dumb questions and I learned a lot about menswear—and you could too.

It's hard at first to plunge into this world, I admit, but once you do, you'll discover that you put on designer pants one leg at a time, just like the $29 pair from Marshalls. And even if you can't afford to buy them, it's wonderful fun to look.

Source: Warren, E. (2006, April 13). Shopping advisor: trunk shows demystified. Retrieved June 11, 2007, from *Chicago Tribune,* http://featuresblogs.Chicagotribune.com

the world's largest 24-hour fashion network, and the website www.ftv.com. FTV broadcasts fashion shows complete with backstage scenes, showing photographers, models, and celebrities to 300 million households in over 202 countries as they occur ("SmartVideo and Fashion TV", 2006). Paris-based Fashion TV chose SmartVideo Technologies to broadcast live, on-demand, and download-and-play television content for Internet-connected consumers. Visual images and communication about fashion trends that used to take months to reach the ultimate consumer are available the instant the fashion shows are presented.

———o Fashion Show Personnel

The key person in any fashion show production is the **fashion show director**. In a retail organization, fashion show production is generally the responsibility of the fashion director. The fashion director produces the show or delegates a member of the fashion office to oversee the production. At the manufacturer's level, a seasoned sales representative or member of the promotion staff will oversee fashion show production or hire an outside production agency.

Leadership qualities of a fashion show director include extensive fashion knowledge, enthusiasm, patience, and good communication skills. The director is ultimately responsible for making sure the show runs smoothly, continually reviewing the progress of the show, meeting deadlines, and staying within the budget.

In most situations a fashion director will have the opportunity to assign staff to assist with the production. An ideal staff will consist of a model coordinator, merchandise coordinator, stage manager, and a promotion coordinator. The **model coordinator** is responsible for hiring, training, and coordinating all activities that involve the models. A **merchandise coordinator** is responsible for collecting and preparing the merchandise, fitting the merchandise to the models, and returning the merchandise to departments after the show. In some cases the merchandise coordinator will select the merchandise to be used; in other situations the fashion director, or a team of managers, or a manufacturer representative will select the merchandise to be presented in the show. In the case of a magazine tie-in show, the fashion editor of the publication will coordinate the merchandise. A **stage manager** oversees the use of the stage and runway, organizes equipment, and supervises people providing behind-the-scenes services, such as sound and lighting technicians. The **promotion coordinator** is responsible for all promotion of the event. This person may work in cooperation with the advertising department.

Many trade shows as well as large consumer shows are produced by fashion show production agencies. These agencies are led by a **fashion show producer** who is hired to

FIGURE 15.8 Every fashion show needs an audience.

bring all of the fashion show elements together, translating the designer's vision into a three-dimensional live show (Everett & Swanson, 2004). The producer is involved with casting the models, overseeing the design and construction of the stage, and directing the technicians in charge of lighting and music. The staff producing the show report to the producer.

One of the important members of a fashion show staff is the stylist. It is the responsibility of the **stylist** to provide creative input to the designer and the show producer, and present the clothes immaculately (Everett & Swanson, 2004). The stylist's creativity pulls the merchandise, props, and most especially the accessories to make an exciting presentation that stands out from every other one. Basically, the stylist interprets the clothes into appropriate groups and sequential order to put the collection in the best light. See Box 15.2 for an example.

──○ PLANNING

Planning a fashion show involves all aspects of preliminary preparation necessary to present a well-executed show. Planning involves organizing the show and working out every detail to avoid unexpected problems. Planning details include audience selection, theme development, venue selection, selection of merchandise, mode fitting, timing of the show, and security issues.

Audience Selection

Every fashion show needs an audience (Fig. 15.8). It is necessary to select the right audience if the show is to be successful as a promotion tool. An audience can be based on merchandise or the merchandise can be selected after a target audience has been determined. In either case, the audience and merchandise must be properly targeted. A fashion show audience may be guaranteed or created. A **guaranteed audience** is established before the show is planned, and is made up of individuals who will attend regardless of the fashions shown. A **created audience** is established after the show is planned as a result of publicity and advertising. The size of the audience should be considered and a location selected that will allow all members of the audience to view the show comfortably. If the primary reason for the fashion show is to sell merchandise, the income level of the audience should be considered. Retailers know the approximate spending habits of their customers and should review this information before selecting merchandise. Demographic and psychographic characteristics of an audience should also be considered when planning a show. A missed detail about the audience can change the atmosphere of the show and decrease the opportunity for sales.

○— BOX 15.2

Who's the Coolest Kid at Fashion Week? Some Say the Stylist

Ms. Goldstein Helps Vera Wang Choose Her Runway Look; A Necklace Gets Nixed

Inspired by the 1999 movie *The Talented Mr. Ripley,* designer Vera Wang wanted to capture the mood of American expatriates in 1950s Italy for her fall 2006 collection.

For advice, she called in a freelance stylist named Lori Goldstein.

Ms. Goldstein, whose job it is to anticipate which way fashion's winds are blowing, was immediately alarmed by a jacket and a skirt that had big buttons. "As soon as I saw them I said, 'We can't show that,'" says Ms. Goldstein, who herself wears layered leggings, boots, and frayed satin jackets. "All those buttons felt like the period, but they don't look modern, and no one is going to wear it with all those buttons."

Ms. Wang sent the garments back to be made with two buttons instead of six.

When her fall 2006 women's fashion collection is presented today, Ms. Wang will take a well-deserved bow. But some of the credit for how Ms. Wang's collection looks should go to Ms. Goldstein.

Operating in the background, stylists are becoming necessary accouterments for fashion designers. Top stylists—many of whom put together editorial photo shoots in the pay of such magazines as *Vogue, Harper's Bazaar, W* and *Elle*—are called in before fashion shows to help choose pieces for the runway, coordinate handbags and shoes and generally decide what looks good. For designers, they act as sounding boards and sometimes cheerleaders.

Ms. Goldstein, who also works for BCBG Max Azria in New York and for Nina Ricci in Paris, first looked in on Ms. Wang's collection in October, helping to select fabrics. When the first sample garments arrived in December, she dropped in again to see how things were going. In the past five days, she has been editing down the 70 outfits in the collection to about 45—discarding, among other things, two ball gowns and several full skirts that "looked too much like last season." She won't say how much she is paid.

She also helped choose 20 models and zeroed in on details like the shade of lipstick they will wear and a soft hairdo "hinting at the 1950s, without being too literal." Yesterday, she was shuffling stacks of Polaroid shots to determine the order and pacing of the show.

As with all stylists, Ms. Goldstein's greatest contribution to the fall collection is much more subtle: She knows what is cutting edge and what isn't.

"Designers want the cool person," explains Sally Singer, fashion news-features director at *Vogue.* "Part of a designer's cool can be validated by the stylist they use."

Although designers have always sought advice, whether it be from elegant customers, fashion models, or magazine editors, such informal consultants never did a whole lot more than toss pearls and scarves on a model or roll up the sleeves of a blouse on the day of the show.

In the past few years—as the job of fashion designer has gotten more complicated—stylists have been in more demand. The best, who can earn as much as $8,000 a day, help designers create an image for product lines that now include handbags, shoes, and watches. More important, these stylists—who aren't to be confused with the people who dress celebrities—can take the heat off of designers' busy schedules.

Designer Nanette Lepore, who operates boutiques in New York, Los Angeles, Las Vegas, and Tokyo, says she and her 14 design assistants are all but burned out trying to keep retail shelves stocked. So when the fashion shows roll around, Ms. Lepore relies on stylist Leah Levin.

"Leah will pick the styles she likes for the show, and she helps us limit our colors. We let her make the decisions," Ms. Lepore says.

Beyond their own good taste, many star stylists, with their ties to photographers, starlets, socialites, and journalists, are big-time networkers. Much as lobbyists wield influence in Washington, stylists can curry favor with the magazines they work for and the fashion crowd they run with.

Fashion publicist Vanessa von Bismarck, who represents designer Richard Chai, says hiring *Vogue* freelance stylist Jessica Diehl last fall provided a boost to the designer. Although he had done two shows in the past without a stylist, he got a lot of requests to borrow his samples for magazine features after Ms. Diehl first styled the collection last fall. One of Mr. Chai's dresses from last fall's show has since appeared in *Vogue.* Ms. Diehl says she had nothing to do with that shoot.

It is impossible to gauge how much Ms. Diehl had to do with Mr. Chai's getting more attention, Ms. von Bismarck says. But in the fashion world, where exclusive cliques reign, it isn't surprising. "It is more likely that people are interested in a designer after he has been endorsed by others," Ms. Diehl allows.

Vogue says it has a policy that only freelance stylists under contract—not full-time staffers—are permitted to work for designers. Because fashion people "travel in packs" and often move between magazine and fashion-house jobs, Ms. Singer acknowledges that they collaborate and "make deals together."

She insists that even those relationships don't guarantee any designer a favored position in *Vogue* editorial spreads. "What gets shot in the magazine is what works from a trend and a story point of view," Ms. Singer says.

Some stylists become so indispensable that their job morphs into that of a designer, as was the case with stylist Venetia Scott, whom designer Marc Jacobs promoted to become the creative director of his casual Marc line. Indeed, some designers think stylists have accumulated too much power. German designer Wolfgang Joop, who will stage his Wunderkind fashion show today, isn't using a stylist this season. "The stylists have become too important in my eyes," Mr. Joop complains. "I am always fighting with my stylist." Last fall, his Italian stylist Daniela Paudice "came in one morning and wanted to rip the sleeves out of my amazingly beautiful dress," Mr. Joop says.

Ms. Paudice, who no longer works for Mr. Joop, was more interested in "being in the movement with the other stylists," he says, than in trying to work with the collection he designed. Ms. Paudice, through her own publicist, declined to comment.

Ms. Wang, who is famous for her bridal gowns and red-carpet creations for such stars as Sharon Stone and Charlize Theron, first hired Ms. Goldstein in 2000. The 56-year-old designer, who has expanded into upscale daywear, china, fine jewelry, and shoes, has become increasingly busy and relies on Ms. Goldstein's fresh eye. Ms. Wang may become even busier soon as she is in contract talks to take on an additional job with St. John Knits Inc. as its new creative director, people close to her company say. Ms. Wang declines to comment. "Having somebody who is out and about and doing shoots to be the devil's advocate here is great," Ms. Wang says.

Ms. Goldstein, 49, has always been obsessed by fashion. After high school, she began as a saleswoman in boutiques, first in her hometown of Cincinnati, and then at Fred Segal in Los Angeles and Fiorucci in New York. In the 1980s, she began styling clothes for catalogs and advertising shoots, before becoming a stylist for *Vanity Fair* photographer Annie Leibowitz and fashion photographer Steven Meisel.

Ms. Goldstein's signature styling flourish is "the unexpected way I put clothes together. I refused to do the full looks from one designer, and I started using a lot of jewelry and mixing things up," she says. "I can't stand when anything matches."

A big part of her job is saying no. Last year, Ms. Goldstein nixed a crocheted necklace of silver lace balls that Ms. Wang planned to use to accent a number of styles. As soon as she saw them, Ms. Goldstein recognized that they were similar to a necklace by Marc Jacobs that Ms. Goldstein herself had used in photo shoots. Ms. Wang relented. "I took them out of the show," the designer recalls.

Through her connections, Ms. Goldstein discovered early on that many designers would be embracing leggings and stretch pants this fall. That validated Ms. Wang's vow to be original with her fifties look. "We heard everybody and his mother is doing the eighties," Ms. Wang says. "Thank god we aren't going there."

Source: Agins, T. (2006, February 9). Who's the coolest kid at Fashion Week? Some say the stylist. *Wall Street Journal*, p. A1.

Theme Development

Fashion shows should have a theme and title, which will tell the audience the nature of the fashion show. The theme may be selected around a targeted audience or a specific merchandise category. Themes may be developed to implement new trends for the season (as discussed in Chapter 4). Theme ideas may come from holidays or seasons, current art or music trends, geographical locations, merchandise categories, or characteristics of the audience. Fashion show themes may also be taken from the fashion theme calendar established by senior management, as discussed in Chapter 5.

Themes should be creative and imaginative for both the staff creating the promotional theme and the audience viewing it. Theme categories include storewide, color, fabrication, lifestyle, and special occasion. The theme should be selected early in the process to allow other details to be coordinated with it. Merchandise selection will be dictated by the theme. Because fashion shows are generally divided into segments, depending on the merchandise selected, each segment or scene can be created to coordinate with the chosen title.

Venue Selection

At the retail level, fashion shows can be held in-store or out-of-store at civic locations, auditoriums, restaurants, or hotels. The advantage of an in-store fashion show is obvious; it allows customers to immediately purchase the items they have just seen, fulfilling the promotional objective to sell merchandise. If, on the other hand, the promotional objective is to create goodwill within the community, an out-of-store location may be desirable for charity or spectacular events in which a large audience is expected.

The international fashion shows are shown in centrally planned locations, as well as at specialized areas, including museums or designer showrooms. The tents at Bryant Park in New York, the Main Tent, Stage One, and the Lightbox at Smashbox Studios, the Natural History Museum in London, and the Carrousel du Louvre and surrounding locations in Paris, all serve as internationally known fashion show venues. Most regional market center structures, like the one at the Dallas Apparel Center, have fashion show production facilities right inside the market building, making it easy for retail buyers to attend fashion shows during market weeks.

Timing of the Show

Determining the day, date, and time of the fashion show as well as confirming the length of the performance are timing elements necessary in show preparation. It is of great importance for a show coordinator to plan shows so they will not conflict with other events in the store or the community. Conflict will diminish the intended audience.

The ideal length of a fashion show is no longer than 45 minutes (Everett & Swanson, 2004). In a well-executed show, 50 to 60 garments can be shown in this time frame. Audiences will be hesitant to attend a show if they perceive it will last longer than an hour.

Once the fashion show location, theme, date, and time have been established, they are posted on a fashion show calendar. The fashion show calendar can then be used by the fashion director and staff to plan, delegate, and follow through with elements of the show production.

Security Issues

The security of merchandise, equipment, the audience, and special guests is a concern when producing a fashion show. Merchandise on loan from either retailers or departments within a retail store are the responsibility of the show staff. The merchandise must be protected from damage while being worn and from theft or vandalism while on loan. In rare instances, merchandise with an extremely high cost might need the added protection of hired security guards. The show staff is responsible for securing the location and protecting borrowed or leased equipment.

To protect all individuals involved, every transferral of merchandise and equipment should be recorded through written agreements signed by show personnel and the leasing agent. Show staff must ensure the safety of the audience and the participants to protect the retailer or sponsoring organization from legal damages resulting from accidents. Celebrities may need hired security personnel to protect them during the show and transport them to and from the fashion show. Protection of people and materials should be reviewed as the show is finalized.

──o SHOW ELEMENTS

A fashion show is made up of many elements that, together, make an exciting show that tells the audience what to wear, when to wear it, and how to accessorize it. Elements of a fashion show include merchandise, models, commentary, set, and music.

Merchandise

Merchandise selection is the designation of apparel, shoes, and accessories for presentation in a fashion show. The fashion director will discuss with department heads, management teams, or manufacturer representatives the appropriate merchandise to be presented in the show. Merchandise must make a clear fashion statement about current trends to stimulate sales after the show. The merchandise must be appropriate to the demographic and psychographic features of the audience, including age, sex, income, and lifestyle, and be priced according to what the audience is projected to spend on clothing. Trade shows will display the best-selling trends of the current season's line to demonstrate the breadth and depth of merchandise. Consumer shows will display merchandise from a specific retailer or selected retailers within a geographical area.

Only merchandise that will be available immediately after the show should be selected for presentation. Trends that will be out-of-season or out-of-fashion by the time the show is presented should be excluded from the selection process. Additionally, if reorders are tight or the merchandise must be back-ordered, a fashion director should eliminate that item.

Ideal charts are tools a fashion director may use to plan merchandise selection. An **ideal chart** lists all categories of merchandise that will be represented in the show. Within each category, the important trends or looks are listed to ensure they will not be missed when selecting merchandise. The ideal chart may also list the number of garments to be included within each merchandise category. Figure 15.9 is an example of an ideal chart.

Once the merchandise is selected, it is pulled from the sales floor and kept in reserve for the show. Extra merchandise should be pulled to avoid last-minute searches of appropriate merchandise when for some reason the selected item does not fit the model or has sold out before the show. Basic seasonal items should be pulled first; newer looks and trends should be left for decision closer to the show. After the merchandise is pulled it should be grouped or coordinated into specific categories that make a series of fashion statements. The merchandise categories should flow from one statement to another, creating excitement for the audience. The first and last categories should make the strongest statements. After completing the merchandise grouping, a lineup should be created. The **lineup** is a listing, in order of appearance, of models and the outfits they will be wearing. The lineup will be used for many different purposes throughout the show, such as planning dressing area organization and scripting the show.

Models

Models are individuals, hired or volunteer, who wear the merchandise and accessories during the show (Fig. 15.10). Models must be able to present merchandise effectively in a believable manner. While models should be attractive, the beauty of the model should not detract from the clothing that they are wearing. The type of show being produced, the targeted audience, and the merchandise selected will determine the type of model to be featured in the show. There are several typical female model types. These include models for sizes 4 to 16 in petite, junior, and misses sizes. Junior models are typically aged 15 to 19.

Lights, Camera, Fashion

Ideal Chart

Segment 1- *Unzipped* **(Student Designers) 30 outfits**

- original designs from 15 students
- approximately 2 garments from each student

Segment 2- *Friends* **(Casual Wear) 20 outfits**

- denim jeans (light and dirty washes)
- sweaters
- sweatshirts/hoodies
- cotton knit shirts
- baseball hats
- coordinated sweat outfits

Segment 3- *Out Cold* **(Outerwear) 20 outfits**

- ski/snowboard coats and pants
- down vests
- peacoats
- leather coats
- tweed coats
- trench coats
- hats, scarves, and gloves

Segment 4- *The Apprentice* **(Business Wear) 20 outfits**

- men's suits
- dress button-up shirts and ties
- women's suits
- women's coordinates
- knee-length skirts

Segment 5- *Coyote Ugly* **(Trendy Date Wear) 20 outfits**

- miniskirts
- black pants
- embellished denim
- trendy shirts
- belt buckles
- trucker and cowboy hats
- halter and tube tops
- slinky skirts
- tank tops

Segment 6- *My Fair Lady* **(Formal/Holiday Wear) 20 outfits**

- cocktail dresses
- tuxedos
- suits with bow ties
- formal dresses
- fur coats and shawls

FIGURE 15.9 Ideal chart for the fashion show *Lights, Camera, Fashion*.

FIGURE 15.10 Fashion show models are chosen according to how well they will show off a particular line of fashion merchandise.

Petite and misses models run the spectrum from young models (teens) with mature looks to mature models (aged 55 and up) with distinguished gray hair and features, and a young appearance. Male and female models should be appropriate to the audience and merchandise. Gender, age (or perceived age), and ethnicity are characteristics that should be evaluated during model selection. Figure 15.11 is an example of a voucher or model release form that all models should sign upon being hired or volunteering for a show.

Amateur or professional models may be used. Amateur models are not professionally trained and are selected from such resources as a retail store's fashion advisory board, customers, and employees; members of the sponsoring organization; or students. Professional models are trained in modeling techniques and are hired through modeling agencies or schools.

Ford Models Incorporated is a premier modeling agency headquartered in New York City, with eight offices worldwide. Eileen and Jerry Ford established the agency in 1947. Their daughter Katie took the helm as president and chief executive officer in 1995. Ford prides itself on turning over rocks to find new and fresh models (Nicholson, 1997). It has a legion of scouts who tour the world, and holds open casting calls in the United States and abroad. A search accomplished through a CBS morning television show procured 20,000 applicants, and the agency interviewed a few thousand of them for possible hire. The agency hires both fit and runway models. According to Katie Ford, it takes six months to two years to get a model's career off the ground, but, she says, it only takes a few weeks to know whether a girl has top model potential.

Television reality shows, including *America's Next Top Model* and *Project Runway*, have created a lot of interest in fashion modeling as a career. In addition to these shows making modeling a high-profile career, supermodels, including Tyra Banks and Heidi Klum, are the subjects of profiles on other television and cable shows. Tyra Banks has progressed from being a top model to becoming a talk show host with her own daytime television show.

Attributes of an excellent model include confidence and poise in walking, timing, turning, and posing for the audience and the camera. A model must move with a

Voucher–Sample

Voucher/Model Release

Bill to:	Requested by:
Customer ID:	Client:
Invoice #:	Product:
Date of first insertion:	Studio/Location:

PO#	JOB#	EMPLOYER	TERMS

MODEL/TALENT:

DATE	TIME FR.	TIME TO	JOB, REH. OR FITTING	TTL HOURS	1ST RATE	2ND RATE	TTL
TRAVEL RATE							
WARDROBE							
MISC. EXP.							
BUYOUT							
BONUS							
SUBTOTAL							

[ ] Billboard   [ ] National Ad   [ ] Point-of-Purchase   [ ] Product Packaging

Photography to be used for any listed use must be checked and pre-negotiated with and signed-off by talent or release is not valid. By my signature below I warrant that I am signing in the official capacity of my company with the intent to bind the undersigned company and that I have read, understand, and accept all the terms herein. The above information is correct.

_____
Client Signature

_____
Talent Signature

In consideration of the sum stated hereon, inclusive of agent's service fee, and valid only upon receipt of full payment (talent fee and service fee), I hereby sell, assign, and grant to above or those for whom they act as indicated above, the right/permission to copyright and/or use, circulate, reuse, and/or publish photographs or other likeness of me in which I may be, in whole or in part, or composites or reproductions thereof, in color or otherwise, still or moving, without restriction as to changes or alterations from time to time, for commercial or print advertising purposes only through any media, trade, or any other similar lawful purpose, except television, billboards, point-of-purchase displays, phone arcades, bus shelters, poster, subway, bus displays, national ads, or other high exposure usages as these require bonuses through special negotiations. Likenesses of me may be used for a period of 12 months, after which reusage fees must be negotiated or rights to use my photograph terminate.

The buyout fee refers to use as purchased. Please note the blocks to the left for separate bonus negotiations.

I hereby waive my right to inspect and/or approve the finished product or the advertising copy that may be used in connection therewith.

I hereby release and discharge the above, its successors and all persons acting under its permission or authority, or those for whom it is acting from any liability by virtue of any blurring, distortion, alteration, optical illusion, or use in composite form that may occur or be produced in the taking of said picture or in any processing thereof through completion of the finished product.

All payments are due in thirty days from date of booking. Talent will receive payment based on payment from client, unless otherwise negotiated by agency.

FOR ALL NEW YORK JOBS ONLY:

You, _____ , as employer of record for this booking, agree that any professional model(s) used in connection with this agreement are employees of _____ for purposes of New York Labor Law.

(W4 info)

THIS RELEASE NOT VALID UNTIL PAYMENT IN FULL IS MADE TO:

FIGURE 15.11 Sample model release form.

smooth, light pace. Body weight should be forward on a straight but not stiff frame. Arms should be loose but not swinging away from the body. Hands should be used to highlight design details such as pockets or accessories. Runway turns are known as pivots. A model should have the ability to pivot in a smooth, graceful, and continuous motion as an individual or simultaneously within a group of models. Models are responsible for the timing of the show. The speed and pace of a model's walk can prolong or shorten the show as dictated by the merchandise lineup or the body language of the audience.

Models are responsible for attending fittings and rehearsals. They should have hair and makeup appropriately applied to accentuate garments and accessories. Garments should be ready for the models when they arrive, and the models should quickly assist show personnel in making necessary alterations or merchandise substitutions. Models should attend the rehearsal and practice the route they will take as they enter and exit the stage. Ideally, the stage and backstage will be adjacent, but in some locales, such as an auditorium or a restaurant, this may not be possible. Models should take note of stairs, doors, and other obstacles that may interfere with their moving to and from the stage. Each model should be fully informed about the outfits and accessories he or she will be wearing and the order in which the garments will be worn. Fittings will have taken place prior to the show, and models will have a clear idea what they are wearing and what is expected of them.

The fashion office should create a file or record on models who have been used for fashion shows. Information should include name and address, sizing information, and personal attributes of the model. Each model should be evaluated on his or her performance after each show to assist the fashion director or model coordinator in selection of future models.

Commentary

Commentary is the oral delivery of information used to identify trends of the season. Commentary should entertain the audience and help interpret clear fashion statements to help sell the merchandise. Good commentary tells something about the merchandise that the audience cannot readily see. Well-executed commentary makes the models and audience feel at ease with one another.

A **commentator** is the individual who is responsible for commentary. Commentary is written from the merchandise lineup, using a detailed fashion vocabulary to highlight important details of the merchandise. Commentary should emphasize trends, feeling, moods, and intrinsic values of the apparel rather than obvious details evident to the audience. As with models, commentary may be used to change the pace of the show.

Commentary is the one optional element of a fashion show. Audiences today are stimulated by music, video presentations, and lighting features as a result of TV exposure and are less likely to require a descriptive or analytical narrative of what they are seeing at a fashion show. Fashion particularly lends itself to visual excitement rather than audio explanation of details. Consumer shows are more likely to use commentary. Spectacular productions will substitute music and video in place of commentary.

Stage Design

Models, merchandise, and commentary all come together as the stage design and runway are planned. The physical layout of the facilities includes the stage, runway, backdrops, lighting, and props. The stage is the background where models enter and exit. The runway is an extension of the stage or a freestanding unit that projects into the audience. The stage and/or runway will vary according to the physical location and needs of the show. When planning a runway show the stage manager should consider the time required of models to enter and exit the runway, the walking route and traffic flow on the runway, and the height, size, and shape of the runway as it relates to the room and audience visibility. Runways may be built in a variety of shapes including the T, I, X, H, Y, U, or Z. The primary limitation to stage shape is the size of the fashion show location. Good lighting and seating should be considered when designing a set to ensure a positive experience by everyone involved in the show.

Set design should also include a model **dressing area** that is behind the scenes yet close to the runway. The dressing area should be large enough to accommodate clothing racks, tables, chairs, full-length mirrors, and all the models and support personnel required for the show. Merchandise should be spaced on racks to prevent wrinkling and allow easy access by the **dressers,** preparation assistants to the models. The dressing room should be organized so that each model has his or her own area. Additionally, model areas should be planned to alternate with busy areas. Models grouped together in the merchandise lineup should be apart in the dressing area to minimize traffic flow problems. Space should also be reserved for hair and makeup. The dressing room should have a clearly defined entrance and exit, preferably through different doors to prevent awkward movements that may be seen by the audience.

Backgrounds are used to enhance the show by creating atmosphere, emphasizing fashion trends, or reinforcing the designer or manufacturer's image through use of a logo. The extent of backdrops or scenery is dependent on the type of show, budget, and personal style of the show producer. Stage backgrounds can range from simple to exotic.

As with backdrops, props can be used to highlight the featured merchandise. Props may be stationary items such as a car, furniture, or a gazebo. Mobile props, such as a briefcase or tennis racket, may also be carried by the model to emphasize a lifestyle characteristic influenced by the fashions. In Figure 15.12 a model uses a prop to accentuate the featured apparel.

Music

Fashions shows produced with or without the use of commentary rely heavily on music to set the mood of the show and appeal to the emotions of the audience. Music is an aesthetically pleasing or harmonious sound or combination of sounds. The right music can prepare an audience to enjoy the show more than any other element of fashion shows. Music is taped or live, and may be instrumental or vocal in nature. Each music category—blues, contemporary, rock, classical, or jazz—can be influential to the audience, causing the members to leave the show excited to buy merchandise. However, the music

FIGURE 15.12 Props accentuate fashions.

must be selected to fit the appropriate target market. Professionals should research preferences and be able to match musicians with the selected audience.

Music is used to set the atmosphere for the audience and set the pace for models. Upbeat, dance-oriented music will cause models to walk at a more rapid speed and may require more outfits to fill the time properly. The music should match the commentary and the merchandise, starting with a strong selection to capture the attention of the audience. Just as the merchandise is presented in a flowing, natural progression, so should the music. During the middle segments, music should not overpower the merchandise but should keep the audience interested. A finishing selection should be strong, with a driving momentum that leaves the audience remembering the show after the finale.

Music directors are in charge of selecting and presenting the audio portion of the show. They and other technicians are generally hired for fashion shows. It is the responsibility of the music director or designated technician to obtain permission to use copyrighted music, mix the music at the event, and prepare the sound system at the show location.

───○ STEPS IN PRODUCING A FASHION SHOW

In addition to show elements, it is necessary to discuss the various stages of fashion show production. These steps include the rehearsal, behind-the-scenes preparations on show day, and evaluation following the show.

Rehearsal

The **rehearsal** is a practice performance, held in private, in preparation for a public performance. The rehearsal is an opportunity for the show coordinator to solve any problems prior to viewing by the public. The rehearsal may be a simple run-through or a full dress rehearsal. A run-through is a rehearsal of the show sequences without the merchandise to show models choreography. A full dress rehearsal consists of a complete walk-through with clothing, music, commentary, and all other technical aspects. The type of show and level of expertise of the participants will dictate the type of rehearsal needed. Dressers, starters, and all other show personnel should be involved with the dress rehearsal to understand the sequence of the show and assist with show timing during the actual performance.

Behind the Scenes

After hours, days, or months of planning, the show is ready to be presented. However, before the models arrive, behind-the-scenes details need to be completed. A complete sound and lighting check should take place to ensure the audio and visual levels are correct for the audience, models, and commentator. The dressing room facilities need to be prepared for the arrival of merchandise. Lineup sheets should be posted at strategic locations and everyone should know the proper entrances, flow of traffic, and exits. Merchandise should be ready for models to wear. Tags are hidden, alterations are finished, and garments are pressed. Programs and/or promotional samples should be placed on audience seats, and hosts should be completely familiar with the seating arrangement for reserved seating.

First impressions by the audience will influence the show's success or failure. All of the preparation will pay off when every element works in concert to present the right fashion to the right audience with all elements correctly executed. As with any performance, it is important to start on time. People grow increasingly impatient when they feel their time is being wasted. Communication between technicians, the fashion director, commentators, and necessary show personnel will influence the smooth running of the show. Show producers should also be aware of the audience's reactions and respond as necessary to make the audience comfortable. Most shows finish with a finale, bringing all models on stage together and acknowledging the designer. When the show is finished, stage strike and cleanup should occur with all participants fulfilling their assigned responsibilities.

─○ Measuring Fashion Show Effectiveness

Evaluation serves an important purpose for fashion show personnel, and as such should not be perceived as a last step of production. Rather, it should be regarded as an ongoing procedure throughout the production. When evaluating fashion shows, personnel should determine the strengths and weaknesses of the project. Most importantly, personnel should secure accurate statistics and reactions that will help future fashion show planners.

One of the primary tools used for evaluation by fashion show producers is a **fashion show diary**, chronicling all of the steps followed in planning, budgeting, and implementing the show as well as evaluating various elements of the show. A fashion show diary also defines the type of show, venue, date and time, theme and title, merchandise presented, audience attendance and reaction, personnel involved, and notes for improvement. This historical record serves as a planning document for the next show. A sample fashion show diary is provided in Figure 15.13.

Basic statistical information gathered for evaluation includes size of the audience, reaction of the attendees, type of media coverage, and profit, taking into consideration revenues and expenses. Attendance that was controlled by ticketing or established seating

---

Fashion Show Diary

Date of Show:

Location:

Show Participants

    Sponsoring Organization:

    Models:

    Commentator:

    Production Staff:

    Audience:

Theme of Show:

Merchandise Presented:

Publicity and Advertising Activities:

Budget:

    Planned Expenses vs. Actual Expenses

    Profit/Loss

Audience Reaction:

Notes for Improvement:

FIGURE 15.13 A fashion show diary template.

capacities can be compared to actual participation. In a noncontrolled situation, attendance estimates are made by counting chairs or counting people as they enter the venue. The audience should be evaluated not only in terms of its size but in terms of its reaction.

Because audience reaction is a primary concern of fashion show planners, surveys are good instruments to determine attendees' perceptions. Audience members may be asked to rate various aspects of the show, such as merchandise selection, music, stage design, theme, models, and so forth, with scores ranging from *strongly like* to *strongly dislike*. But many audience members are not be willing to take the time to fill out surveys, which is one of the biggest problems for fashion show planners attempting to gauge audience reaction. Unless attendees are willing to provide positive and negative reactions, planners may have a difficult time assessing that aspect of the show.

Evidence of media coverage should also be included with the fashion show diary, along with samples of news releases and media kits used to attract media. A copy of the operating statement, with planned revenues and expenses compared to the actual figures, completes the documentation placed in the fashion show diary.

Live fashion shows are a very traditional form of promotion but are no less important to the integrated marketing communications mix. Although the Internet and CD-ROMs have provided an opportunity to enhance the way buyers and consumers view fashion, promotion via a live model, with music, sets, and grand entertainment, will never be completely dismissed, because the audience likes the theatrical spectacular.

summary

- A fashion show is a presentation of apparel, accessories, and other products to enhance personal attractiveness on live models to an audience.
- Fashion shows include all the elements of a theatrical production—music, lighting, staging, and a script as a performance for a live audience.
- The primary reason to produce a fashion show is to sell merchandise.
- Trade shows are sponsored by producers of raw materials to demonstrate the utilization and versatility of these products to buyers at the next market level.
- Consumer shows are sponsored by retailers and are directed toward the retail staff and consumer market; they include in-store, customer, charity, and press shows.
- The most elaborate and expensive fashion show to produce is the production show or spectacular.
- The most familiar fashion show is the formal runway show in which merchandise is presented on models who parade in front of a seated audience.
- Informal fashion shows present merchandise on models in a casual environment, which includes tearoom modeling, trunk shows, and mannequin modeling.
- Fashion shows may be produced digitally for use at point-of purchase, to provide instruction, or as a documentary.
- Fashion shows are produced by fashion show directors or fashion show production companies. The fashion director may delegate responsibilities to staff, including model, merchandise, and promotion coordinators, and a stage manager.
- Fashion shows must be planned. Planning details include audience selection, theme development, merchandise selection, model direction, venue selection, timing, and security.
- Merchandise selection is the designation of apparel, shoes, and accessories for presentation in a fashion show.

- A show may or may not include oral delivery of commentary to identify trends of the season, which are shown through garments and accessories.
- Models and merchandise are displayed on a stage that includes a runway, props, background, music, and lighting.
- Steps of fashion show production include a planning rehearsal and preshow preparation before the event and stage strike and evaluation afterward.

Key Terms

charity show	fashion show producer	models
commentary	formal runway show	multimedia shows
commentator	guaranteed audience	music director
community show	ideal chart	production show
consumer show	informal fashion show	promotion coordinator
created audience	in-store show	rehearsal
dressers	lineup	stage manager
dressing area	mannequin modeling	stylist
fashion show	merchandise coordinator	tearoom modeling
fashion show diary	merchandise selection	trunk show
fashion show director	model coordinator	

Questions for Discussion

1. What are the differences between fashion shows produced for trade and consumer events?
2. In what situations would one use a production show, formal runway show, or multimedia production?
3. What are the primary responsibilities of a model coordinator, merchandise coordinator, stage manager, and promotion coordinator when planning a fashion show?
4. What should happen during the rehearsal, preparation for the show, and show, and at the conclusion of the show?
5. Compare and contrast live, broadcast, and online fashion shows. What are some advantages and disadvantages of each?

Additional Resources

Bean, E., & Bidner, J. (2004). *Complete guide for models: Inside advice from industry pros for fashion modeling*. Asheville, NC: Lark Books.

Esch, N., Gayheart, R., & Walker, C. (1996). *The Wilhelmina guide to modeling*. New York: Fireside.

Everett, J. C., & Swanson, K. K. (2004). *Guide to producing a fashion show* (2nd ed.). New York: Fairchild Books.

Gelhar, M. (2005). *The fashion designer survival guide*. Chicago, IL: Dearborn Trade Publishing.

McMullen, P. (2004). *InTents*. New York: Powerhouse Books.

References

Corcoran, C. T. (2005, January 13). Online trunk shows lift sales, reorders. *Women's Wear Daily*, Retrieved June 30, 2006, from Gale Group database.

Everett, J. C., & Swanson, K. K. (2004). *Guide to producing a fashion show* (2nd ed.). New York: Fairchild Books.

Macy's event marketing. (2006). *Passport*. Retrieved June 29, 2006, from http://wwwl.macys.com/store/marketing.jsp

Packing it in: The designer trunk show has been revamped to appeal to today's busy shopper. (2004, January 14). *Women's Wear Daily*. Retrieved June 30, 2006, from Gale Group database

SmartVideo and Fashion TV premier live streaming worldwide fashion, style, and beauty programming. (2006, May 8). *Business Wire*. Retrieved June 30, 2006, from INFOTRAC database.

FIGURE 16.1 Harrods celebrates the film *Casino Royale.*

Visual Merchandising

Holidays are a time of year when retail mettle is judged for its creativity and ability to separate shoppers from their money. Stores marry whimsy, fantasy, luxury, humor, and originality in their holiday windows. It's art with a touch of commerce. Just how big a touch depends on the store.

At Selfridges in London, there are gold editions of popular designer products, from an Yves Saint Laurent Muse purse and Burberry gold lamé trench to a gold Dualit toaster. They're all exclusives to Selfridges, of course.

The holiday windows of Harrods in London are based on the latest James Bond film, "Casino Royale," showcasing items such as Bond's silver Aston Martin DBS and Sunseeker Yacht, and the one-off gowns that actresses Eva Green and Caterina Murino wear. A window features a roulette table with a mannequin dressed as Solange (Murino), the wife of the villain Alex Dimitrios. She's Bond's first conquest in the film and, naturally, winds up dead.

Le Bon Marché depicted imaginary gardens with products standing in for plants and flowers. There's a scented garden with animated perfume bottles marching like toy soldiers, and a gourmet bower with fruity figurines.

Saks Fifth Avenue uses thousands of Swarovski crystals to create a magical place where cute ice crystals dream of becoming part of the perfect snowflake.

Macy's was also in the mood for a mythical voyage. Its windows follow two elves, Sparkle and Twinkle, on their journey to meet Santa Claus through the "Trees of Wonder." Traveling through different fantasy worlds, they visit landscapes populated by giant animals, dragons, and mermaids.

Source: Edelson, S. (2006, November 22). All the world's a stage at holiday. *Women's Wear Daily*, p. 110

After you read this chapter you will be able to:

Explain the roles visual merchandising and display play in the promotion mix.

Differentiate among the various types of visual merchandising categories.

Discern the component parts of a display.

Explain the importance of store layout and design as a promotion mix tool.

Schedule display changes and store renovations.

WHAT IS IT ABOUT a holiday window display that drives shoppers to buy more? Consumers arrive at stores, and retailer's homepages for that matter, armed with holiday gift lists and already prepared to make purchases before encountering a single golden toaster or itinerant elf. Merchandisers from Macy's to mom-and-pop shops have been creating miracles on 34th Street since Santa Claus was but a glint in Mr. Woolworth's eye. A closer look will reveal the secrets of the appeal of visual merchandising.

We begin this chapter by defining the terms *visual merchandising* and *display*. Next, the importance of visual presentation of merchandise at the different market levels is evaluated. Display locations and categories are presented before the elements of a display are defined. Then, store design and layout are considered as an integral part of creating a pleasant shopping environment. The chapter concludes with an analysis of changing and updating the look of the store as a part of scheduling display installations and store remodeling.

──o THE ROLE OF VISUAL MERCHANDISING

Visual merchandising refers to the physical presentation of products in a nonpersonal approach to promote the image of a firm and the sale of merchandise to the consumer. Displays are the physical exhibits of merchandise and support materials. Although the terms *display* and *visual merchandising* are regularly used synonymously, visual merchandising encompasses a greater number of practices and responsibilities than simply displaying merchandise. When a retailing or manufacturing organization coordinates its visual merchandise presentations with its advertising, direct marketing, and/or sales promotion programs, it is following an integrated marketing communications approach.

In 1949, John Mertes, Chair of Marketing at the University of Oklahoma, defined the responsibilities of visual merchandisers to include store design, planning, store and department identification, customer traffic control, store layout, space-sales analysis, fixturing, window display, interior display, and display research (Marcus, 1978). It became an occupation that was far more demanding than a window *trimmer*, whose job was generally limited to the creation of window displays in previous decades. Although the phrase *visual merchandising* was introduced in the 1940s, the term did not gain widespread acceptance in the industry until the 1970s.

Customers are more likely to respond favorably to merchandise if they are able to view the actual product rather than interpret it from an illustration, photograph, video, or text message. According to a study conducted for Kellwood Company, Baby Boomer women, ages 50 and older, have approximately $26 billion in apparel purchasing power (Seckler, 2006). The research shows that this age group, with significant spending strength, is strongly influenced by in-store displays. Of the media/people most likely to trigger purchases, in-store displays influence 76 percent of the women who took part in the survey. Table 16.1 shows all of the media/people influences on apparel spending, with in-store displays as the

TABLE 16.1   *Top Influences on Apparel Spending: Women 50 and Older*

Ranking	Media/People Most Likely to Trigger Apparel Purchasing	Share of Women Influenced (Age 50 and older)
1	In-store displays	76%
2	Magazine ads, editorial content	41%
3	People on the street	34%
4	Friends	32%
5	Family	15%
6	TV and movies	12%
7	The Internet	9%
8	Celebrities	6%
9	Sales associates	5%
10	None of the above	5%

Note: Percentages are not additive, women could give more than one response.

Adapted from: Seckler, V (2006, February 8). Fickle fiftysomethings vote with their feet. *Women's Wear Daily*, p.19.

most noteworthy. Thus, visual presentation has an advantage over print and broadcast advertisements, which require consumers to interpret what a product looks like. When a garment is shown with suitable accessories in a perfect setting, the shopper's urge to buy the merchandise is stimulated. Visual merchandising is used to enhance the image of a product, demonstrate how the consumer can use it, and create an enjoyable shopping experience. We begin by looking at the different settings in which merchandise is presented through displays.

──○ FIRMS THAT USE VISUAL MERCHANDISING

Visual merchandising takes place in many different locations both inside and outside of the traditional marketing channel. The most obvious place where physical presentation of merchandise occurs is in a retail store. In addition to retailers, manufacturers visually merchandise products in their showrooms and at trade shows. Other firms that use visual merchandise presentation are museums, historical societies, trade associations, tourism groups, and educational institutions. First, we examine merchandise presentation in the retail environment, then its use by manufacturers and other types of organizations.

Retailers

With the consolidation of department stores, retailers such as Macy's, Nordstrom, and Dillard's carry very similar merchandise. Customers often complain that there is little if any difference between merchandise sold by one store and another. What makes a customer choose merchandise in one store and ignore the same merchandise in another is often some intangible factor such as how the merchandise is arranged or how easy the merchandise is to find within the store. The task of visual merchandising is first to make the merchandise desirable and then to make it easy to locate in the store.

The retail visual merchandising professional attempts to bring the customer into the store with creative and interesting displays that incorporate aesthetic principles with basic merchandising techniques to inform and educate potential buyers about the products and/or services carried by the business. Displays utilize products, props, backdrops, and fixtures to sell merchandise. An attractive store layout also brings patrons to the selling areas where sales personnel can close the sale.

Consumers are spending less time in retail stores than ever before, and men are spending less time in stores than women. According to Paco Underhill, urban geographer and retail anthropologist, women shopping with other women are more likely to stay in a shop longer (8 minutes and 15 seconds) than women shopping with men (4 minutes and 41 seconds) (Samson, 2006). And keeping the consumers in the store longer helps convert consumers to customers.

With more and more Americans indicating that they are time-starved, and shopping as a leisure activity is becoming less of a priority, retailers are concerned how to attract customers into their stores. Women spend about one hour a day in stores, while men shop 45 minutes daily on average (Ramey, 2005). But those shopping estimates also included time spent buying basics in supermarkets. With lack of time a big issue, Lars Perner, a consumer psychologist and professor at San Diego State University, says, "There really is more of a need to stand out and give people a reason to look at your merchandise" (Ramey, 2005, p. 6). A strong visual merchandising program can help set a retailer's product apart from others.

In addition to creating stimulating and inspiring presentations, retail visual merchandisers use their craft to introduce and explain new products. A display may be the first three-dimensional representation of a new silhouette or a feature of an electronic gadget. This type of display can be used to educate the consumer about how to wear, accessorize, or use new products.

A window display can promote a store image and entice a shopper to enter the store. Displays featuring the latest fashion trends or lifestyle products can pique the interest of the shopper. Turning a passerby into a *browser* inside the store can greatly increase the possibility of patronage from that person. Displays can show the type of merchandise assortment, stage of fashion leadership, and brand names carried by the store. This enables a store to establish and promote the image and products of the store.

Fashion retailers with limited promotional budgets may use visual merchandising as their only form of nonpersonal promotion. Stores may not have the budget to purchase advertising, launch fashion shows, or distribute direct mail catalogs, but they almost always will use window or interior displays to strengthen sales activities. The article in Box 16.1 shows how to use store planning to create positive first impressions for retail clients. Figure 16.2 illustrates population density analysis, which can assist retailers with floor presentation.

Retail firms are not the only businesses that use visual merchandising as an important promotional strategy. Next, we consider the role of visual merchandising by manufacturers as a promotional strategy.

Manufacturers

Fashion designers and manufacturers use display techniques at their showrooms, which may or may not have window displays. Showrooms in the Chicago Apparel Mart and Dallas Apparel Center have windows inside the marts that serve a function similar to a store window on the street or inside a mall. This type of window display serves to inform the retail buyer about products carried and promote the image of the firm. Once the buyer is inside the showroom, interior displays can help the designer or the manufacturer's sales representative sell the line by making products look coordinated and attractive.

Manufacturers and designers may also develop an assortment of display aids for fashion retailers to use in their stores. These supports, featured in their showrooms or through catalogs, may include signs, props, banners and decals, counter signs, counter racks, and wall and floor fixtures. These items may be provided to retailers free or on a fee basis.

Manufacturers also show merchandise to retailers at trade shows. Vendor exhibits are set up in convention centers and hotels. Events, such as MAGIC, the men's apparel trade show previously discussed, and WWDMagic, its counterpart featuring women's apparel that is also held in Las Vegas twice each year, attract retail buyers and manufacturer's representatives from all over the world. Large international firms, such as Tommy Hilfiger, Levi's, and Calvin Klein, set up huge showrooms at trade shows, whereas small vendors such as True Grit or the House of Dereon, created by Beyonce Knowles and her mother, Tina, set up **exhibit booths,** small exhibit spaces with temporary walls and fixtures, to sell their trendy clothing. Figure 16.3 shows the Sigrid Olsen exhibit space at the WWDMagic show. Firms that specialize in building trade show exhibits can create selling spaces for vendors. Exhibit booths are moved from vendors' headquarters to trade shows, and therefore must be transportable. Channel-Kor,

BOX 16.1
Making First Impressions Count

One of the dangers in store planning is the romance with presentation drawings. Somehow the art form that is a mix of technical skill and surrealistic vision is seen as the hallmark of a good design and designer. From the standpoint of the consumer or businessman, it is important to recognize that any architectural rendering is a means of getting to a three-dimensional end. One of the first drawings you see in a store planner's presentation is the front view of the store.

The assumption that a front view has anything to do with the customer's first or ongoing perception of a store is hogwash. Generally, the only person that sees a store entrance, from the perspective of most presentation drawings, is the random policeman who happens to be in the middle of the street directing traffic in front of the building.

First impressions for any retail site are critical, particularly for stores that depend on impulse purchases. The front of a store and the first 10 to 20 paces into the store are the most seminal elements in forming the consumer's perception of that business and setting up the disposition to make a purchase.

A good retailing team is advised to think about the entrancing experience from the consumer's perspective. In setting the stage for that understanding, it is important to start by reviewing some prevailing retail myths.

Myth No. 1, which we hear often in American retailing circles, is the right product, at the right price, at the right location. The truth is that in the 1990s, we can accept all of those conditions as givens.

Myth No. 2 is about competition. Again, we hear retailers comparing themselves to other retailers in their specialty area. The truth is that retailers, from dress shops to electronics stores, are competing with one another in the big scramble for the same piece of the public's discretionary income. The dollar spent on fashion might just as well be spent on almost anything else, from fast food to auto accessories.

In the broad scope of things, most stores can segment their customer base into two groups: those that need portals and those that need doorways.

Portal shoppers are presold or predirected and make up a large portion of the business for some lucky retailers. For example, in the word of booksellers, some customers are book lovers. For them the entrance to a bookstore does not have to be enticing or seductive.

Book lovers walk in knowing more than many of the employees. They are comfortable asking questions, and price point may very well make no difference at all. The store can be a mess, with stacks of books in the aisles and dirty windows, and they could not care less—all of those elements are part of the ambiance they are willing to accept. For book lovers, the entrance is not a door but a portal into the world of books.

While portal shoppers may be a strong element of retail business, store owners pay rent to attract the shopper that needs doorways.

Although advertising dollars can build public awareness of a shop and announce a sale, the retailer heeds the on-site recognition to close the marketing loop. High consumer awareness does not necessarily translate into customers walking in the door. Advertising only reinforces predisposition—the process of bringing the consumer through the entrance is a design and merchandising issue. That is why store designers and planners exist.

The process of tickling the shopping impulse in the passing consumer is based on time. The longer customers have to think about possibly entering a store, the more likely they will. Our work has shown that often the most important view of the store may be a side or approaching view. The first chance that most shops get to start their impulse tickle may be 25 paces before the customer reaches the doorway. On main streets and in shopping malls, progressive planners have been allowing stores to build out their storefronts to enhance pedestrians' view as they move down the sidewalk or mall concourse. In the same spirit, windows featuring displays that the consumer can recognize or identify with at a 20- to 25-pace distance do a better job of pulling the customer in the door. From our research, we have established a number of general rules concerning windows.

First, it is better to get two messages across positively than five messages possibly—keep it simple. In many retail locations, you can count on the fact that your customer base will pass your window with a certain regularity, be it biweekly, or in some cases, daily. Simple windows that change often may very well be a better use of the display budget than elaborate windows that remain in place for longer periods of time.

Consumer interest is motivated by change. Window spaces that are easy to work with are creative marketing decisions—the small amount of floor space that may be lost is a small trade-off.

When designing a window display, it is important to take into account the way a consumer is going to live with the product and allow passing shoppers to view the product from that distance.

For example, some years ago I saw a window display on New York City's Fifth Avenue, where a small department store had an elegant arrangement of silver flatware on the floor of the window casement. The only shoppers who looked at that section of the window were middle-aged women, who did so from a bent-over position. Their interest was terminated, however, when someone brushed past their protruding rear ends on the busy sidewalk behind them.

Our research also has shown that there is a dominant direction from which people pass almost any storefront. That dominance may be created by the location of the parking lot, a public transportation terminus, or some other physical feature. We have found that displays canted or slanted to that dominant direction of traffic will get more serious attention.

And finally, if graphic information is part of the storefront's message, make sure that it can be read as shoppers walk past; do not expect them to stop to get the message, because they very well may not.

Modern graphics theory has pointed out that people read differently than they did in 1960. Americans and Europeans no longer read letter by letter but have graduated to reading letter clump by letter clump—one reason why typefaces that allow for closer positioning of letters are used much more often than 30 years ago.

One common flaw of store entrances is that they do not take people into account. For many department stores and main street locations, a common flaw is not planning a transition zone. Consider that people have many different walking speeds. The pace at which they move down a rainy street or across a hot parking lot is very different from the pace at which they move through a store. It takes time for people to slow down once they get through the store's entrance.

Directional and promotional signage and displays can be more effective when placed deeper into the store. For one of our clients, we were able to triple the number of customers shopping with in-store circulars by adjusting where, and at what height, the circulars were presented to the customer. Poor placement of information systems not only translates into consumers who may walk out of the store because they do not want to commit to finding their way, but it also means headaches for sales associates, as they are asked the same series of questions over and over.

Aisles and entrances need to be stroller accessible. Even if babies and toddlers are not a store's primary market, the consumers they bring with them are. In reviewing film data for a client, we discovered the comedy of mothers trying to negotiate their baby strollers around a lease-line table. Appearing clumsy becomes one more reason for a customer to leave the store. In this case, almost nothing was sold from the lease-line table—the job of getting around that fixture took precedence.

Good retailers can work magic if they can get people in the door. A good store involves an ongoing dialogue between store designers, merchants, and consumers. Modern retailing history is littered with stores that failed for the most mundane reasons. The difference between stores that work well and look great in the flesh and those that do not often has nothing to do with price points and inventory, and everything to do with a well-executed strategy based on human needs.

Adapted from: Underhill, P. (1999, February). Making first impressions count. *Display & Design Ideas* (On-line). Available: http://www.envirosell.com/articles/dispdes.html. Reprinted with permission from *Display & Design Ideas*, © Shore-Varrone, Inc.

an exhibit manufacturing firm, creates modular systems that may be adjusted in size, so that booths may be used in large or small exhibit spaces and/or updated regularly. The trade publication for designers and builders of exhibits for trade shows, museums, theater sets, visual merchandisers, and retail interior designers is *Exhibit Builder* magazine.

Merchandise Presentation by Other Organizations

Museums, historical societies, trade associations, tourism groups, and educational institutions create displays for enhancing costume knowledge, scholarship, information, fashion details, and trend directions. The Whitney Museum of American Art and Metropolitan Mueseum of Art in New York, the Los Angeles County Museum, London's Victoria and Albert Museum, and the Musée de la Mode et du Costume in Paris are among the international museums that exhibit important historical and contemporary fashion designs.

Regional museums, such as the Phoenix Art Museum, are emerging as places that present unique fashion exhibitions. These exhibitions included retrospectives of designers and artists, such as Christian Dior and Chanel, works by Tiffany and Cartier, and themes such as *AngloMania: Tradition and Transgression in British Fashion*, *Bravehearts: Men in Skirts*, and *Goddess*. Museum curators and assistants use display techniques to feature costumes and accessories for these popular presentations. *The Warhol Look: Glamour, Style, Fashion*, was a traveling exhibit organized by the Andy Warhol Museum in Pittsburgh. The exhibit recreated window displays by Warhol and his display mentor, Gene Moore. Thus, the exhibit featured a display of displays (Fig. 16.4).

The Arizona Office of Tourism established a *Welcome Center* near the Arizona and New Mexico border. Representatives from seven geographical regions in Arizona were asked to set up displays featuring products and events relating to their areas. The Flagstaff Convention and Visitor's Bureau sent representatives to this remote site to create a display depicting the arts and events occurring in that city. Displays featured Native American jewelry, pottery, and rugs in showcases that identified the stores where visitors could purchase similar items when they arrived in Flagstaff.

Educational institutions, such as the Fashion Institute of Technology (FIT), also launch exhibits of historical and contemporary clothing. *The Tailor's Art, Love and War: The Weaponized Woman*, and *FABULOUS! Fashions of the 1940s* are among the costume exhibits promoted by FIT. Exhibits such as these assist designers and manufacturers in reviving fashion trends and creating new ones. Consumer interest in these shows provides an audience for the manufacturer's latest innovations as well as merchandise, such

Population Density Map

FIGURE 16.2 Environsell's population density map.

FIGURE 16.3 This Sigrid Olsen exhibit at WWDMagic is typical of the space set up to display fashion merchandise at a trade show.

FIGURE 16.4 Display for Tiffany's from the late 1950s from *The Warhol Look: Glamour, Style, Fashion.*

as books, fashion, or home accessories, created exclusively for the exhibit. Educational institutions also set up exhibit booths, similar to trade show booths, designed for use at new student orientations, college recruitment fairs, and exhibitions at academic conferences.

The primary trade publication for the visual merchandising industry is *Visual Merchandising & Store Design (VM + SD)*. The articles in the publication cover a wide range of topics related to lighting, store renovations, new store designs, fixtures, and so forth. *VM + SD* selects a store of the year in each of several categories and devotes an issue of the magazine to the winners. The publisher also features a website with highlights from the publication. Another popular visual merchandising magazine is *Display & Design Ideas* (DDI) magazine. It is also available on the Internet. Next, we will look at display categories.

───○ DISPLAY CATEGORIES

There are four basic categories of display: window, exterior, interior, and remote. Which type of display category is used, and how, depends upon the architecture of the building in which the business or organization is located. Retailers use all four categories, whereas manufacturers primarily use window, interior, and remote formats.

Window Display

Window displays are used in large cities with downtown shopping districts and in some mall stores that use conventional windows. Although downtown shopping has declined in many cities because consumers prefer to go to suburban malls, window displays continue to be a source of entertainment and information for workers in cities such as New York, Chicago, Kansas City, and San Francisco. Christmas windows at such retailers as Tiffany's, Lord and Taylor, and Saks Fifth Avenue attract numerous consumers who visit the downtown store only once a year to see these elaborate presentations. Celebrities and a variety of performances often accompany the launch of holiday windows. Hal Linden, dressed in Victorian-era clothing, appeared at the Lord and Taylor store in New York when the Charles Dickens Christmas Windows were unveiled. This festive occasion brought many shoppers to the Fifth Avenue store.

Windows serve as the eyes to the interior of the retail store. The image of the store is portrayed in the window. Several clues are given to persons walking past the store window. If the display contains wallets, handbags, jewelry, and belts, the consumer is assured that the store sells a range of accessories. The look and fashion image of the merchandise serves as an introduction to the consumer. When the window is used effectively the potential customer is attracted into the selling space. Windows can strengthen a store's traffic and sales volume.

Store windows are either closed-back or open-back. **Closed-back windows** are completely contained display spaces. These windows have walls on three sides. There is a door or sliding panel, which can be moved to bring in merchandise, mannequins, and props. The advantage for the visual merchandiser is that he or she will not have to contend with background distractions. But this type of window may serve as a barrier to the customer, who might be intimidated and afraid to enter. A smaller store with this type of window may seem insignificant or claustrophobic.

In contrast, **open-back windows** do not have a back wall. The customer can see into the store, viewing not only the display but also the store itself. This may be an advantage since the customer can see merchandise other than that on display. The disadvantage of an open-backed window is distraction from store merchandise in the background. Display professionals may use screens, curtains, banners, or plants to create a backdrop for this type of window to minimize the problems.

Straight Front Window

Straight front windows are parallel to the road or sidewalk. A store with a straight front may have a single window or several windows, called a **bank of windows.** The entrance may be on one side or in the middle of two or more straight front windows (Fig. 16.5a). Large retailers, such as New York–based Bloomingdale's, Chicago-based Carson Pirie Scott, or Seattle-based Nordstrom, in downtown locations frequently use this type of window. Visual merchandisers like to work with this type of window because they are typically working with a closed back, which does not have visual interference from the store interior. The stagelike settings are ideal for elaborate displays.

Angled Front Window

The entrance to a store with an **angled front window** is recessed from the sidewalk, providing more exposure to display space. There are large display windows on one or both sides of the storefront, creating an aisle for the consumer to walk through to the door. The display windows may be on an angle or parallel to the back wall of the display space. The aisle is frequently covered and serves as a lobby, which leads the shopper to the store's entrance (Fig. 16.5b).

Arcade Front Window

The **arcade front window** is a spacious display space with a variety of configurations, normally found in downtown shopping districts. There are several windows with islands or peninsulas made from glass extending out from the sides. Arcade windows may take on unusual shapes from concave or slanted glass. The shopper may have to take a circuitous route to enter the store. This type of window also has a covered entry that serves as a lobby and a transition zone. The arcade front window, like the angled front, requires the entrance to be set back from the sidewalk. This extends the display area, but limits the store's interior selling space (Fig. 16.5c).

Corner Front Window

The **corner front window** is located where the window faces two streets that are perpendicular to each other; as a result it can be viewed from either street (Fig. 16.5d). The corner window may be next to the store entrance or it may be next to a series of straight windows. The floor plan for this type of window is triangular. It offers special problems for the display professional, who may find it difficult to eliminate distractions from the

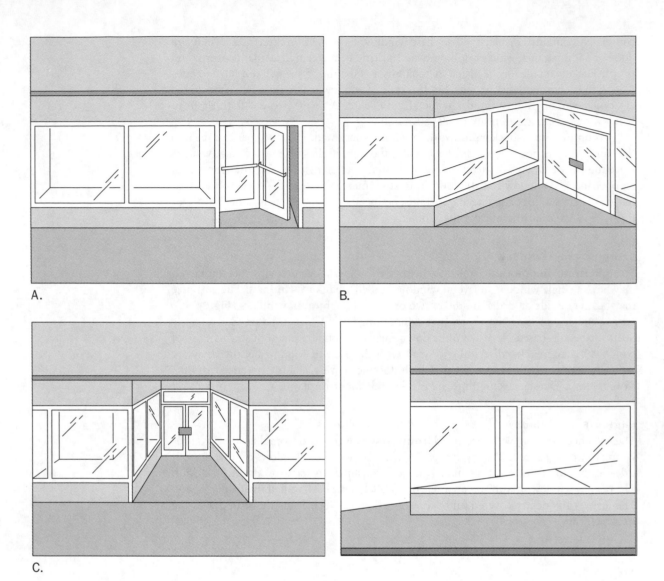

A.

B.

C.

FIGURE 16.5 Illustrations of (a) straight, (b) angled, (c) arcade, and (d) corner windows.

other side. On the other hand, the corner front window can take advantage of passersby from two different directions.

Shadow Box Window

The **shadow box window** is a small closed-back window, dimensioned on a much smaller scale than the previously discussed window styles (Fig. 16.6). The shadow box is used for small, yet relatively expensive items. Typically, shadow box windows are used for fine jewelry, cameras, cosmetics, books, or shoes. Tiffany's uses the shadow box window to attract customers into its famous Fifth Avenue store.

Windowless Window

Stores in enclosed shopping malls often choose to construct their stores without conventional windows. Mall retailers use the **windowless window** or no-window concepts as

FIGUre 16.6 A shadow box window (top) and a windowless storefront in a mall (bottom).

the entrance to their stores (Fig. 16.6). They believe that wide openings at the front of the store will bring consumers in to shop for merchandise easily visible to the passerby. Security is the greatest risk with this concept, because shoplifters can easily steal merchandise from stores with wide openings. It is common to see security guards or store greeters at the entrance of mall stores to prevent theft of merchandise.

Exterior Display

Exterior display, also called facade display, is the outside appearance of the storefront. Along with the style of architecture and building location, exterior display has a great impact on the image of a retail business. Exterior display has greatest applicability to main street and downtown stores, which use storefront design to strengthen the store's image. Stores located in enclosed suburban malls may have limited opportunities for exterior display because they have few or no windows; visual merchandising in such locations is focused on interior displays, space planning, and signage, discussed later in this chapter. Exterior display involves such components as signs, seasonal decorative elements, outdoor lights, and awnings.

Exterior Sign

The exterior sign, which consists of words and/or graphic symbols placed on the outside of a store, is often the initial attention grabber seen by a potential customer. It creates the first impression and sets the mood for the store. City and county codes may regulate how signs are used on the exterior of a building. The style and size of lettering can be used as an attention-getting device. TOYS "R" US in bright primary colors sets the youthful and playful mood for the international toy store. Swedish retailer IKEA uses blue and yellow, the colors of the Swedish flag, for its signage.

The sign can be a plus or a minus for the retailer. A neat and well-kept sign invites customers to enter the store, but a sign with chipped paint and burned-out or missing lights in a dirty window shouts another type of message: *Don't shop here!*

The sign should be a store's signature. The logo or graphic symbol used on interior walls and other promotional materials, such as advertising, can be professionally reproduced for the exterior of the store. The exterior sign can be a memorable part of a complete graphic promotional package, which includes shopping bags, sales receipts, and interior signs.

Seasonal Decorative Elements

Seasonal decorative elements include props and symbols to enhance the mood of the time period. Various seasons lend themselves to such time period or theme decorations. An obvious example of seasonal decorations used in exterior display is the Christmas tree. This image creates a feeling of nostalgia and festivity and puts the consumer in a holiday mood, recalling past events. Rotating planters and flower boxes with each season can proclaim other seasonal changes. Tulips set the scene for spring, while pansies and petunias can be used for summer and the Fourth of July. Adding dried corn stalks and colorful leaves to the outdoor planters can show the arrival of fall.

Banners or flags, which are hangings made from paper or cloth with colors and/or symbols that depict nations, states, or other decorative elements, are colorful, eye-catching devices for the store exterior. Flags can depict the store logo, symbol, or a seasonal theme. Using international flags on the outside of the store for a multinational theme helps to promote the global nature of the event. Banners can also convey a special theme, such as *Back to School,* with a crayon package design.

Storewide themes, such as anniversary sales or import fairs, can also suggest exterior decorative elements. During the anniversary sale, a sign that represents a cake with candles can be attached to the outside of the store. An Italian import event may utilize Italian flags, a model of the Coliosseum, or reproductions of Italian paintings at the store entrance.

Outdoor Lights

Outdoor lights, which illuminate the front of the store, not only serve a decorative function but also are essential tools because most stores today are open in the evening. As such, outdoor lighting serves a security and safety function. Outdoor lights can fit the historical architectural style of a building or emphasize the contemporary nature of the merchandise carried. Lighting can also be used to call the consumer's attention to seasonal or merchandise themes promoted at the store. For example, a menorah with lightbulbs can be lit during each of the eight days of Hanukkah.

Awnings

Awnings are another element that can serve both a functional and a decorative purpose. The awning is a structure that is frequently made from canvas and extends from a window or entrance, providing protection from rain, snow, or sun. Windows with direct exposure to the sun will fade valuable merchandise; the awning can protect merchandise from deteriorating and cut down on the window glare. Awnings may also be used to emphasize the store name or a seasonal theme. Additionally, awnings may be used to cluster independent stores into a grouping with greater impact in an outdoor setting.

Interior Display

Store **interior display,** practiced by both downtown and mall stores, consists of presenting merchandise attractively on a variety of architectural forms, fixtures, and furniture. Although an architect or interior designer created the actual interior design of the store, the visual merchandiser suggests how to best feature the store's merchandise. The style of fixtures, flooring, lighting, mirrors, interior signs, and other decorative elements can reinforce the mood and image of the store.

Architects, interior designers, and visual merchandisers work with **floor plans,** which are scale drawings of the walls, fixtures, and other architectural elements. These floor plans (Fig. 16.7) show the placement of permanent and temporary items. The first consideration with interior space planning is how customers enter and move through a store. If a customer does not have a specific target department to visit, research indicates that most consumers will turn to the right as they enter a store. It is estimated that 80–90 percent of people, or more, will do this (Weishar, 1998). To counteract this behavior, the designer should use aisle and fixture placement to move the customer through the store. A well-planned traffic pattern will bring the customer in contact with as much appropriately placed and attractively presented merchandise as possible.

The selling floor of the store is a functional environment that should also provide a pleasant shopping experience for the consumer. At the same time, visual merchandisers must carefully assess where fixtures will be placed, what merchandise will be put on them, and how to move customer traffic through the store. The components of the store interior display are perimeter walls, trend shops, island displays, fixtures, and interior signs.

Perimeter Walls

The walls that surround the selling area are called perimeter walls. They are among the first merchandising spaces viewed by a potential consumer. This area should be attractively presented, featuring coordinated merchandise. It serves as an invitation for the customer to come into the area to browse. The perimeter wall can be attractively displayed using waterfalls, hanging bars, shelves, and/or pin-up boards. Retailers should avoid using this area as a place to put sale or clearance items, because sale items rarely have the visual impact of a color-coordinated merchandise group.

A **T-wall** is a type of perimeter wall used to separate one department from another. It has a flat end, near an aisle, that is converted to display space by using a panel to cover

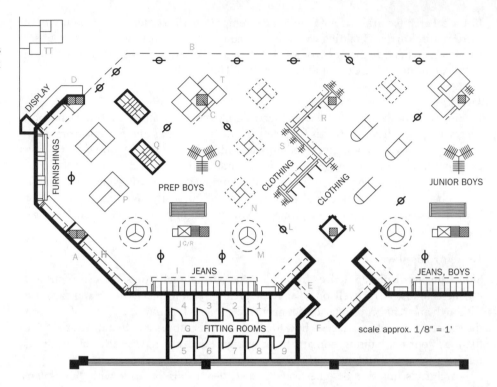

the end of the unit. The panel is the top of the "T." A platform, a raised stagelike surface, may be used in front of the wall to highlight merchandise.

Trend Shop

The **trend shop**, also known as a *highlight shop*, is a merchandising area set apart by special flooring, walls, or ceiling treatments. At a mall store it may be at the retailer's entrance, set apart by a contrasting sales floor. In a traditional downtown department store, it may be an area close to an escalator or elevator. This space is converted into a theme shop based upon whatever merchandise promotions or seasonal events are going on. In April the theme shop might be a *Spring Showers Shop*. This trend shop emphasizes raincoats, boots, umbrellas, and floral accessories. Figure 16.8 illustrates a trend shop request form that gives all of the pertinent information required to implement a special shop.

Island Display

The **island display** is a three-dimensional display space, frequently located at the mall entrance or in a central location where several aisles come together. The island display may be set off by a raised or multilevel platform. A ceiling crown or special lighting or other details may help to stress the importance of this merchandise. Several showcases pulled together are used to form an island display for cosmetics or accessories. These showcases may be enclosed for security or open to encourage self-service.

Fixtures

Cabinets covered in green slime? Garbage can–styled endcaps? The system included several eye-popping pieces, such as a large, orange-colored cash wrap accented with green

---

Trend Shop Request

Shop Name:

Shop Type

❏ Classification

❏ Fashion Theme

❏ Seasonal

Date of Request:

Parent Department(s):

General Merchandise Description:

Opening Date:

Locations:

General Design Suggestions:

Signs needed:

Planned Stock by Unit and Dollar Amounts:

Planned Advertising:

Staffing:

Approved by:

FIGUre 16.8 Blank trend shop request form.

"slime," and a kidney-shaped tiered table with yellow metal stripping and exposed screw heads. Selfridges, the British department store, created display fixtures that looked like Scrabble tiles, which were used as display platforms in the children's department. Fixtures such as these support merchandise and create an entertaining atmosphere.

Fixtures include a wide variety of furniture and equipment to hold and display merchandise. Fixtures include display tables, cubes, counters, showcases, ledges, and racks. Each type of fixture holds a particular category of merchandise.

Display tables are used as a self-service selling activity. Display tables house a large quantity of apparel, such as sweaters, or nonapparel, such as boxed costume jewelry. Customers are allowed to touch and feel the stock, selecting the size or color they desire.

Cubes are box-style display fixtures used for self-selection. Cubes are ideal for flat folded apparel, home textile products such as towels and sheets, and children's clothing. Actually ringing up the sale and handing over merchandise takes place at a counter called a **cash wrap**. Money or credit cards are used to purchase products at this space, which may have an all-glass or partial-glass surface where additional merchandise is displayed. These products include high-impulse items like jewelry, accessories, or hosiery.

Showcases are fixtures used to enclose groupings of similar merchandise. These types of display cases are used in cosmetic, jewelry, and accessory departments. During most of the year, shelves in showcases can be pleasingly presented with seasonal or theme displays. But, in the middle of the busy Christmas holiday season, shelves can be mass merchandised or heavily stocked with coordinated groups of merchandise.

Ledges are located behind islands created by showcases, generally in the cosmetic and accessory departments or behind cash wrap desks. Ledges are traditionally raised about 5 feet above the selling floor. They can be used for back stock, promotional packages, or major theme displays. Some ledges may be large enough to hold standing mannequins, but sitting mannequins or other decorative elements may also be used. Showcases and ledges prevent customers from touching products, making this location ideal for merchandise requiring security.

Racks are wooden or metal futures, ranging from simple T-stands for small quantities of merchandise to large round racks, which hold hundreds of garments. T-stands are used for new or color-coordinated merchandise. These racks are often found near an aisle, at the entrance to a department, or near a T-wall display. Four-way racks are also used to hold coordinated merchandise groups, consisting of a collection of skirts, pants, blouses, and jackets from one vendor.

Interior Signs

Company policy determines how signs are used inside stores. One firm might use manufacturer-created signs, while another retailer bans such signs and produces its own signage. A variety of signs are used as interior signs; these include marks that identify the department, type of merchandise, advertised products, special events, sales promotions, storewide themes, prices, guest appearances, and so forth. Interior sign categories include the following:

- **Banners** and **flags** are used inside the store in a manner similar to the way they are used as decorative elements for window and exterior displays.
- **Countertop signs** are placed on top of showcases to highlight merchandise displayed.
- **Easels,** upright artists' frames used to hold a painting, are also used by retailers and manufacturers to hold signs.
- **Elevator** and **escalator signs** may be attached to the wall as a permanent sign or may be placed as a freestanding unit near an elevator or escalator. These signs are used to help consumers find their way through a store.
- **Fixture toppers** are signs that are placed on top of various fixtures, such as round racks, T-stands, and four-ways. These signs promote a particular category of merchandise, brand, or theme.
- **Hanging signs** are hung from the ceiling. They may be permanent signs that identify a department or provide directions, but they also could be temporary signs signifying a special theme or event, such as a gift-with-purchase promotion.
- **Posters** are placards that offer reinforcement to a merchandising theme or act as an artistic decoration on a wall or in a display.

No matter how attractive or creative an interior display is, effectiveness is lost unless a customer enters the store. This limitation of interior display may be overcome by attracting customers to the store by window displays, advertising, or publicity designed to increase store traffic. In addition to these practices, store designers are asked to renovate and redesign departments or entire stores, to make the shopping experience more desirable.

Renovation and Revitalization

Consumers tend to categorize specific stores as places where they would or would not want to shop due to the stores' physical appearance. Housekeeping, layout, and overall appearance are just as important as the merchandise. Consumers choose which retailer to visit by convenience and such details as well-lit parking lots and cash register locations. Keeping customers interested in coming back to the store requires diligent upkeep and updating fixtures, walls, and merchandise presentation.

With the needs of the consumer in mind, major global retailers consistently are remodeling and refurbishing the interior design and selling space layout through **renovations.** One example is the Japanese department store Sogo. Other examples include the nkstore expansion in São Paulo, Brazil and the redesign of the Shanghai Tang store in London.

After coming out from bankruptcy, Sogo completed a renovation project at the flagship in Osaka, signaling a revival in the company. The 16-level, 28,000-square-foot store (Fig. 16.9) was given the architectural grandeur of a traditional downtown department store, energized into 16 distinct and compelling sales floors (Moin, 2006). Each floor is created with a particular theme in mind. Floor three has a crystalline theme, decorated with glass beads and Swarovski crystals, to highlight cosmetics and jewelry. By contrast, floor five showcases premium denim and contemporary sportswear in an atmosphere inspired by an elegant Paris apartment. Menswear on the eighth floor has a club effect, with Louis Vuitton trunks set upon pool tables serving as display tables for accessories. While much of the revival has international themes, the flagship is also decorated with painted screens and art saved from the original store, integrating traditional Japanese motifs with 21st-century merchandising techniques. In order to accomplish this ambitious project, the original store, built in 1935, was torn down and redesigned and rebuilt by Seattle-based retail design firm Callison Architure Incorporated, at twice the original height at a cost of $228 million (2006). Design and merchandising concepts at the Osaka store will serve as the prototype for redesign at other Sogo locations.

Owner Natalie Klein of the nkstore in São Paulo's fashionable Jardins shopping district wanted to keep her signature look as the store was expanded to 16,000 square feet, double its original size when it originally opened in 1997 (Kepp, 2006). Klein bought a 6,450-square-foot, three-story building on an adjacent street, which shared a common wall with the original store, which allows a seamless flow after

FIGURE 16.9 Sogo in Osaka is redesigned and rebuilt from the bottom to the top.

FIGURE 16.10 The entrance to the nkstore in São Paulo includes a relaxing footbridge over a pool.

the wall was demolished. The store has a black-and-white color theme, with the store's logo written in small black letters on a glossy, black reflective glass façade. The colors were planned so that they would not interfere with the colorful clothing carried. The idea for the footbridge over a pool that leads into the store came from the spa industry (Fig. 16.10), creating a relaxing feeling for customers as they enter the store.

The Sloan Street branch of Shanghai Tang in London (Fig. 16.11) became the first European unit to undergo refurbishment with a prototype design that will be introduced into the 20 boutiques worldwide. The ceilings were raised to give an impression of greater space in the 3,500-square-foot store. Moving from the original cluttered living room design, created by the founder David Tang, to a more streamlined and space environment was the task of Swedish architect Johannes Tüll (Conti & Jones, 2006). The store still maintains a Chinese mood, but it is more modern with Western influences. Tüll designed black lacquered wood cabinets, shelves, and showcases. An abstract design of the Chinese symbol for longevity was used in the showcases.

These renovations show just how quickly the world of retailing and promotion are growing globally. With a Swedish architect renovating a Chinese retail store in London, or an American architectural firm responsible for rebuilding a Japanese department store, the international barriers have certainly been broken.

Remote Display

Remote display is the only category of display where products are featured away from the point-of-purchase. A **remote display** is a physical presentation of merchandise by a retailer or manufacturer placed in such locations as hotel lobbies, exhibit halls, or public transportation terminals. Another type of remote display involves a mall retailer that places a merchandise display in a case at the shopping center entrance, a location that is away from the store, to encourage consumers to visit the store. The display can attract attention and create interest, but in order to purchase the product the customer must travel to the place where the merchandise is sold or make a phone call.

FIGURE 16.11   Shanghai Tang shows its new store concept in London.

Remote display is effective for products relating to travel. A unique suitcase design may be featured in a display located in the waiting area of an airport. Customers waiting for a flight might view the display, understand advantages of the product, and order it from a cell phone.

──○ DISPLAY COMPONENTS

Each display, regardless of its location or the type of business that creates it, consists of several common components. Universal to every display is the merchandise being offered for sale, functional and/or decorative props, backgrounds, lighting, signage, and three-dimensional arrangements. Display themes are based on themes identified by the fashion trend forecasts.

Merchandise

The products selected are the most important component of a display. The merchandise will determine all other elements of the display, from the theme to supporting elements. Merchandise is the focus of the display and the primary purpose for creating the display.

Selection of merchandise and timing of the display are essential to the success of displays. Sometimes unexpected events trigger desires in consumers. For example, a swimwear display featured in a store window immediately after a February snowstorm led to big sales of swimwear to winter-weary customers planning a cruise or a trip to a resort. People passing by the store fantasized about spring and days at the beach.

Props

Props are functional structures used to lean or place merchandise on or decorative elements used symbolically to create a mood. **Functional props** are the physical supports, such as mannequins and furniture, used to hold merchandise. **Mannequins** are body forms that wear apparel. Because mannequins may cost several thousand dollars, they represent a major investment and are a major portion of a visual merchandiser's budget. Other functional props include such standard fixtures as cubes, steps, and racks that may be used for either interior or window displays.

Decorative props, used to establish a mood or theme for the merchandise, include baskets, plants, flags, banners, and musical instruments. There are almost unlimited styles and items that may be used as decorative props. Furniture can be used to create the illusion of a room or soft-sculpture forms can be used to create the image of a southwestern desert.

Backgrounds

The **background** is the foundation, real or implied, where the display is built. A back wall can serve as the base for a background. If the display space does not have a wall, the illusion of a wall can be created with another material. Banners, screens, partial walls, or seamless paper are examples of elements that can be used to create backdrops. In most cases, it is easier for the visual merchandiser to create a stronger visual merchandise impact if the display has some type of background that prevents the viewer's eye from being distracted by other things.

Lighting

Proper **lighting,** or illumination, of the display or selling area is vital to the selling environment. Lighting is used to draw attention to the merchandise or the entire display. Moreover, it can be used to direct consumers through the store. A spotlight or track lighting can be used to draw the eye to the specific merchandise featured. Consumers are attracted toward well-lit areas. Therefore, lighting on a display should be two to five times stronger than the general room lighting (Mills, Paul, and Moorman, 1995).

Lighting plays a significant role in directing consumers through the store and to desired products.

In addition to highlighting the merchandise and directing customers through the store, light can also be used to create a mood. Twinkling Christmas lights can establish a festive holiday spirit, whereas strobe lights, which turn on and off rapidly, can be used to achieve dramatic effects. Color can be introduced into a display by using overlays, called acetate gels, or by using colored, round glass filters. Using templates projected by a pattern and framing projector can also create special effects. Such images are used to simulate scenery, create atmosphere, or apply additional depth to a display setting.

Signage

Signs used in a display convey information about the merchandise or emphasize the theme. Signs may also be used to provide information for the person walking past a window. Details such as the name of the designer or manufacturer and where to find the merchandise in the store are common informational signs.

Many European retailers incorporate prices of the merchandise in the window display. This helps to inform the potential customer about the expense and status of the products in the store. The practice of including the price of merchandise is not common in the United States.

Display Arrangements

Because displays are three-dimensional designs incorporating merchandise and props, some commonly used arrangements can help to effectively handle space. These proportional arrangements include the pyramid, step, zigzag, and repetition.

The **pyramid** is a triangular geometric shape, in which the base of the pyramid is the widest space and the sides rise to a center point or peak in the middle. A **step** arrangement is a series of elevations similar to a stair step. This leads to a high end on one side or the other. The pyramid is an example of formal balance, while the step arrangement makes use of informal balance. **Zigzag** is based on a reversing step design. It consists of a series of short, sharp angles in alternating directions. This design uses the diagonal lines in reaching its objectives.

Repetition is a type of arrangement that uses the same merchandise and/or props in a style that occurs again. Repetition arranges all items in the same way. Although repetition can be considered monotonous and boring, it can be used to emphasize a particular product. A good example of effective use of repetition involves placing several T-shirts or sweaters in a rainbow of colors. Repetition accentuates the product and the color variation not only adds interest but shows the range of available colors.

─o PLANNING VISUAL PRESENTATIONS

Ideally, the planning and scheduling of visual presentations are coordinated into the integrated marketing communications planning process. This is appropriate because displays are often created to feature merchandise that is advertised, featured in a fashion show, or part of another promotion event. A visual merchandising calendar identifies what merchandise will be displayed in which locations during each month. Window and interior display changes can be scheduled on a regular basis using the calendar as a guideline.

How frequently to change displays is an important question for the visual merchandising staff. There are several issues relevant to establishing a display schedule that influence display changes.

- Will the displays be tied to other promotional activities such as advertising or special events?
- Will the same people pass by the display area every day?
- Is the merchandise likely to be damaged by sunlight, lamps, or dust if it is left in the display area too long?
- Are there skilled visual merchandise personnel on staff to facilitate change?
- Are the displays in a high-traffic area of the store where they should be kept up-to-date?
- Is the budget large enough to change the displays frequently?
- Where is the display area located?

The store should establish a policy regarding display change frequency. Change may occur once a week or once a month, depending upon the needs of the individual store. Department stores tend to schedule display changes every seven to 14 days. Specialty stores, with limited stock in particular sizes or colors, change display more frequently as determined by customer demand. Once a schedule is set, it should be followed. The biggest problem with changing displays is the failure to make any changes. Because retailers in tourist areas attract out-of-town visitors, they do not need to change their displays as frequently as other stores. However, displays start to look old and merchandise becomes outdated if displays are not changed. One rural retailer became so lazy about display that the windows were not changed in six months. Needless to say, that retailer is no longer in business.

Some visual merchandising conditions are within the control of the store, while others are not. Planning an audit of the visual spaces for the store will give a retailer guidelines for scheduling a visual merchandising program. Tips for performing this activity are given in Box 16.2.

──○ VISUAL MERCHANDISING PERSONNEL

There is a wide variety of career opportunities and working environments for a person interested in careers in visual merchandising. Although the most prominent career path for

---

○ BOX 16.2

Conduct Your Own Internal "Visual Audit"

As retailers, we routinely conduct end-of-the-month assessments of our financial health, usually through month-end bookkeeping procedures. In addition, an annual physical count of inventory is essential to maintain correct internal financial records. You could call this procedure your own internal financial audit.

Obviously, the financial health of your company is extremely important. However, retailers should also conduct an annual "audit" of their store's visual appeal to customers, because the visual image of a store will have significant impact on a customer's buying decisions.

So, what are the important elements of a visual merchandising (VM) audit? First, start by making a list of the different areas of your store—exterior parking, exterior signage, exterior entry, cash wrap, traffic flow/store layout, store fixtures, and more. Make sure your list includes every area that impacts the overall "character" of your store.

Next, identify those areas over which you have total control, some control, or no control. A "no-control" area might be the overall exterior visual style of the building or mall in which your store is located. Building managers or landlords may place other restrictions on signage, window displays, and so on.

Defining Your Store's Criteria

Before you actually start your VM audit, you need to define your criteria for what would be acceptable or unacceptable visually. For example, you cannot give yourself low marks on an exterior sign if the lease agreement prohibits you from changing it, no matter what you personally think about the sign.

Also, consider the pricing strategy of your store. A store's price orientation should be reflected in how the store looks. Are there other constraints? Be sure to consider these, too.

Now that you have the basics of your audit form prepared, it is time to get going. As you walk through your store, try to see it through your customers' eyes. Pretend that this is the first time you have ever been inside your store. What makes sense? What does not? You may know why it is reasonable to put a certain fixture in a certain spot, but your customer does not. Make sure the store layout makes sense to your customer first, even if it means it is not quite as convenient for you.

Some retailers actually enlist the help of trusted customers or friends. They walk through the store together, and the owner asks, "What do you see?" "What does this say about the store?"

Gaining an Edge over the Competition

Evaluating your store in this manner provides you with two significant benefits: (1) you identify areas in which you can gain an advantage over competitors; and (2) you get a head start on identifying those aspects of the store that should change the next time you remodel.

If you conduct these evaluations on a regular basis, you can compare them to each other over a period of time. That way you can see the progress you have made in the store's overall design—and see where to go next.

To sum up, make your once-a-year appointment with yourself to complete the visual merchandising audit. After all, a set of well-organized financial records is not likely to affect a customer's impression of your store, but your store's image will certainly have a dramatic impact on your customer—and your bottom line.

Adapted from: Dyches, B. (1998, January). Conduct your own internal "visual audit." WWD Specialty Stores: *A Special Report,* 17–18. *Brian Dyches is president of Retail Resource Group.*

merchandise presentation personnel is working for retailers, we have seen there are several other types of firms that hire individuals with skill and training in visual merchandising.

Whether a store is a large multibranch operation or a small single proprietor, a business that sells consumer goods is involved in the processes of merchandise layout, presentation, and display. Employees of a small store may be given the task of displaying merchandise as one of many different duties assigned. A sales associate with a flair for fashion and an interest in display may fulfill the needs of a specialty retailer.

In corporate department stores, such as Macy's, or specialty retailers, such as Holister, the Promotion Division has responsibility for the visual merchandising department. Figure 16.12 shows an organization chart for a visual merchandising department of a large retailer. The department head is a vice president or director of visual merchandising. This person serves as the administrative manager, overseeing the planning, budgeting, and communication about store layout and merchandise presentation. Much coordination takes place with advertising, publicity, special events, and merchandising departments. This administrative manager must be able to communicate with his or her peers and subordinates about the visual image of the store. This supervisor must also be able to translate merchandising and fashion trends into window and interior displays as well as set up special retailing shops as needed by the merchandising staff.

Multibranch chain stores usually have a display person at each location, whereas larger branches may have more than one visual merchandiser. This person has the responsibility of creating displays according to the corporate visual merchandising plan, delivered to the branches as a planogram. The **planogram** is a detailed plan or map that serves as a guide for setting up window, exterior, and interior displays. It has descriptions about merchandise quantities, fixtures, and placements. This type of planning system provides continuity between the various locations.

A person interested in visual merchandise presentation may work for a store or independently. Individuals who prefer to work alone may find career opportunities as a freelancer. This person may be hired to complete a specific job on a one-time basis. Some rural or small-town freelancers may set up contracts with several retailers to change window or interior displays on a regular schedule.

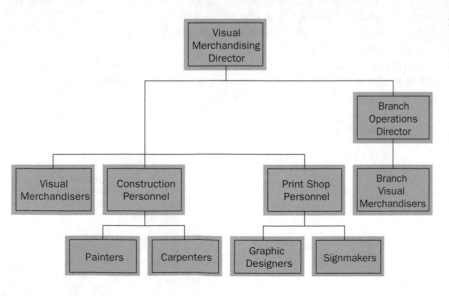

FIGURE 16.12 An organization chart of a visual merchandising department for a large retail company.

In addition to creating displays for retailers or manufacturers, visual merchandisers may find work in comparable fields. The visual merchandiser may find work in trade show exhibition, museum exhibit installation, architecture, and interior, fixture, industrial, or point-of-purchase design.

No matter what size or type of firm the visual merchandiser is working for, he or she is expected to be creative, aware of current fashion directions and display trends. And, the visual merchandiser must be able to execute the plans within the assigned budget. The visual merchandiser may be called upon to work with store advertising, public relations, graphic design, and fashion show personnel. He or she will be expected to communicate with other store personnel, management, and customers. Communication skills, both oral and written, are a necessity.

Visual merchandising involves much more than creating pleasing window and in-store displays. The objective of the visual merchandising staff is to create an attractive, interesting, yet functional merchandising and selling environment. Activities such as store planning and design, traffic flow management, and signage complement the window and interior display projects. The visual merchandising staff typically is part of the retail store's promotion division. Coordination and balance should exist among the advertising, public relations, and fashion offices to produce a cohesive and organized fashion and promotional statement to the public.

summary

- Visual merchandising refers to the physical presentation of products in a nonpersonal approach to promote the image of the firm and the sale of merchandise to the consumer, whereas displays are the physical exhibits of merchandise and support materials.
- Firms that use visual merchandising techniques include retailers, manufacturers, museums, historical societies, trade associations, tourism groups, and educational institutions.
- The four basic categories of display are window, exterior, interior, and remote. Universal to every display is the merchandise being offered for sale, functional and/or decorative props, backgrounds, lighting, signage, and three-dimensional arrangements.
- Planning and scheduling of visual presentations are coordinated into the integrated marketing communications planning process, because displays are often created to feature merchandise that is advertised.
- A visual merchandising calendar identifies what merchandise will be displayed in which locations during each month.
- The most prominent career path for visual merchandising personnel is working for retailers, but other types of firms, such as manufacturers, museums, and other firms, hire individuals with skill and training in the field.

key terms

angled front window	exhibit booth	mannequin
arcade front window	exterior display	open-back window
background	fixtures	planogram
bank of windows	floor plan	prop
cash wrap	functional prop	pyramid
closed-back window	interior display	rack
corner front window	island display	remote display
cube	ledge	renovation
decorative prop	lighting	repetition

shadow box window   straight front window   visual merchandising
showcase   trend shop   windowless window
step   T-wall   zigzag

QUESTIONS FOR DISCUSSION

1. How do the professional responsibilities of a window trimmer differ from those of a visual merchandiser?
2. How does the practice of visual merchandising differ in a retail store, a manufacturer's showroom, a museum, and a trade show?
3. What types of elements can be used to enhance a consumer's shopping experience?
4. What types of firms use visual merchandisers?
5. How does visual merchandising relate to the other promotion mix techniques?

ADDITIONAL RESOURCES

Bell, J., & Ternus, K. (2006). *Silent selling: Best practices and effective strategies in visual merchandising.* New York: Fairchild Books.

Dean, C. (2005). *The inspired retail space: Attract customers, build brands, increase volume.* Gloucester, M. A.: Rockport.

Diamond, J., & Diamond, E. (2004). *Contemporary visual merchandising and environmental design* (3rd ed.). Upper Saddle River, N. J.: Pearson Education Prentice Hall.

Pegler, M. M. (2006). Visual merchandising & display (5th ed.). New York: Fairchild.

Underhill, P. (1999). *Why we buy: The science of shopping.* New York: Simon & Schuster.

Underhill, P. (2004). *Call of the mall.* New York: Simon & Schuster.

Weishar, J. (2005). *The aesthetics of merchandise presentation.* Cincinnati, OH: S. T. Media Group International.

ANNUAL PUBLICATIONS

Pegler, M. M. (Published annually). *Stores of the year.* New York: Visual Reference Publications, Inc.

Editors of *VM + SD Magazine.* (Published annually). *Stores and Retail Spaces.* Cincinnati, OH: S.T. Media Group International.

Editors of Point-of-Purchase Advertising Institute. (Published annually). *Point-of-Purchase Design Annual.* New York: Visual Reference Publications, Inc.

REFERENCES

Conti, S., & Jones, N. (2006, April 26). Shanghai Tang sets new store concept. *Women's Wear Daily*, p. 8.

Cotton Incorporated. (1997, March 27). Show me the clothes: Store displays are the primary source of clothing ideas. *Lifestyle monitor.* Retrieved June 14, 2006 from http://www.cottoninc.com/Ismarticles/?articleID= 364

Diamond, J., & Diamond, E. (2004). *Contemporary visual merchandising and environmental design* (3rd ed.). Upper Saddle River, NJ : Pearson Education Prentice Hall.

DiNardo, A. (2006, May 30). Selfridges' Children's Department, *Visual Store.* Retrieved June 13, 2006 from, http://visualstore.com

Kepp, M. (2006, May 8). Nkstore expansion maintains essence. *Women's Wear Daily*, (Section II), p. 11.

Marcus, S. (1974). *Minding the store.* New York, NY: Signet.

Mills, K. H., Paul, I. E., & Moormann, K. B. (1994). *Applied visual merchandising* (3rd ed.). Upper Saddle River, NJ: Prentice Hall.

Moin, D. (2006, May 8). Japan's Sogo is reimagined on 16 levels. *Women's Wear Daily*, (Section II), p. 10.

Ramey, J. (2005, June 20). No time to shop? *Women's Wear Daily*, (Section II), p.4.

Samson, A. R. (2006, May 5). Fence sitter: Buying pattern. *Business World.* Retrieved June 13, 2006. from the LexisNexis database.)

Seckler, V. (2006, February 8). Fickle fiftysomethings vote with their feet. *Women's Wear Daily*, p. 19.

Weishar, J. (1998, December/January). Moving targets: Customer Traffic flow patterns. *Fashion Group International Bulletin*, pp. 1–2.

FIGURE 17.1 Express storefront.

Personal Selling

Leslie H. Wexner, chairman and CEO of Limited Brands, Inc., came to deliver a seemingly simple message: that he looks at the world as a shopkeeper—and that's not easy [Fig. 17.1].

Often viewed as a master of vertical retailing in apparel, lingerie, and beauty, Wexner humbly portrayed his groundbreaking track record as one driven simply by a desperate need for survival. In retelling the now familiar anecdote about starting his first Limited store with $5,000 borrowed from an aunt, he showed a little-seen side of himself. "I wanted to be a shopkeeper, and on Aug. 10, 1963 [when the store opened], the summary of my life's ambition was, 'Don't go broke,'" he admitted, as a wave of laughter welled up. "It wasn't funny at all," he responded. "I didn't sleep for weeks. I developed stomach ulcers because I just didn't want to go broke. I don't know if I wanted to be a success, but I really didn't want to go broke."

Wexner pointed out, "I did not invent the beauty cosmetics specialty store."

"But we could take our shopkeeping skills and our customer skills and begin to get started.

"The shopkeeper's view is to spend all your time in the shop, spend all your time with the customer and know them like you know a friend. Not know about them, don't research them, just know 'em. Watch their eyes, the way I did in the first store.

"The obsession that the shopkeeper has with the shop and the store is our full-time job. . . . We'll never be as smart in product development, we'll never be as smart in marketing, we'll never be as smart in efficiencies. . . . We have this important, dumb skill of knowing about stores and customers."

Source: Born, P. (2006, May 26). Leslie H. Wexner: Shopkeeper's view. *Women's Wear Daily*, p. 4.

> **After you read this chapter you will be able to:**
>
> Discuss the importance of personal selling.
>
> Explain the buying and selling process.
>
> Demonstrate elements of a sale.
>
> Provide closure after a sale.
>
> Differentiate between personal selling opportunities in the marketing channel.
>
> List attributes of successful selling.
>
> Handle various customer types.

"DON'T GO BROKE." Such hand-to-mouth necessity drives the Wexnerian shopkeeper and can certainly lend an inspirational kick in the pants to a corporate executive. But Wexner's axiom has a practical application as well: What kind of promotional activity occurs every day right down on the sales floor?

In Chapter 1, promotion was defined as all activities initiated by the seller to inform, persuade, and remind the consumer about the products and services offered by the seller, including personal and nonpersonal approaches. Personal selling can be used to promote sales by informing, persuading, and reminding the consumer about products or services. Thus, using this definition, personal selling is a form of promotion.

This chapter begins by discussing the importance of personal selling and its place in the retail and wholesale marketing channels. We then examine the buying and selling process, discuss elements of the sale, and explain how to handle customer problems. The chapter concludes with a discussion about evaluating performance of sales personnel.

──o SIGNIFICANCE OF PERSONAL SELLING

Communication experts believe the first contact is the most important contact two people can make. First impressions make or break lines of communication almost immediately. If a first impression is less than polished, a second encounter may never happen. This is especially true in buying and selling environments.

Personal selling is the direct interaction between the customer and the seller for the purpose of making a sale. This person-to-person communication encourages the seller to assist, and even persuade, a prospective buyer to make a purchase or act upon an idea. Through personal selling the seller can see or hear the potential buyer's reaction and assess the success or failure of the sales message. This feedback allows the seller to adapt the message to the client's needs. Personal selling allows more direct and accurate feedback about the sales message than any other promotion mix technique.

Many promotion mix techniques discussed in this text concentrate on the activities and procedures of nonpersonal selling, including advertising, direct marketing and interactive media, sales promotion, public relations, special events, fashion shows, and visual merchandising. The purpose of nonpersonal selling is to bring customers to the point-of-sale. Nonpersonal selling (or simplified selling, as we discussed in Chapter 12) is very effective in certain selling environments, such as grocery stores. While we do need assistance occasionally in these environments, we would not want a sales associate to assist us through person-to-person communication with every item on our grocery list.

However, in other shopping environments, personal selling is often necessary to close the sale. Clothing and electronics departments are just two of many retail environments where sales associates assist customers in purchase decisions. Sales associates should have complete knowledge of their product, have a high level of self-confidence, and be personable, polite, and outgoing.

To a customer, the salesperson represents the entire organization and is responsible for building customer loyalty and creating customer satisfaction. If a salesperson projects a positive impression to the customer, the customer will likely return to do business with that firm and tell friends and colleagues to buy from that firm as well.

Personal selling is often a function of the marketing process and at times falls short in its effectiveness. Salespeople often cannot answer questions about the merchandise or may not be available at the right moment to assist an impatient customer. A retail salesperson or a manufacturer's rep who is poorly trained or has a bad attitude will likely cause customers to find alternative shopping environments and share their bad experiences with their friends and associates.

Developing and maintaining a successful sales staff is one of the most difficult challenges facing retailers, but this does not mean all salespeople are inadequately trained. Retailers such as Nordstrom and Neiman Marcus have built retailing empires based in part on excellent customer service. In his book, *Minding the Store,* Stanley Marcus stated, "We have one inviolable rule in our organization—that the customer comes first—and any staff meeting can be interrupted to meet the call of a customer" (Marcus, 1974, p.107).

Sales associates provide customer service, stimulate sales, generate add-on sales, encourage repeat business, and control inventory shrinkage. The key to a successful personal selling team is the integrated marketing communications approach set forth by the management. Sales associates should have access to all advertising and public relations materials and tell the same story to create a uniform image of the firm in the customer's mind. The company's key product and corporate messages, positioning, image, and identity should be articulated by each sales associate to present the same message to the public.

──○ Personal Selling in the Marketing Channel

Within the fashion industry, personal selling exists at all levels of the marketing channel. Retailers rely heavily on the selling skills of their sales staffs to close sales within each department. At the manufacturing level, personal selling exists through wholesale representatives, who use their selling skills to sell clothing and accessory lines to potential retail buyers.

Retail Selling

Retail firms that focus on specialty goods will incorporate personal selling into the promotional mix. **Specialty goods** are products aimed at a narrowly defined target market. The target market is generally very knowledgeable about the product in question, has strong brand preferences, and is unlikely to accept merchandise substitutes. Specialty store customers most often prefer personalized selling and use the criteria of personal service in store selection. Department stores use personal selling for staple goods to help customers find what they want in a quick and efficient manner. Through personalized selling, salespeople can close sales and more readily suggest additional purchases, such as accessories or coordinating items. Table 17.1 points out how important sales associates and employees are to customers at luxury department stores.

There are many reasons a customer may need the assistance of a sales associate. Schmidt (1996) has developed several general categories of customer contact situations. They include the following:

- **Customers seek items with little specificity.** These customers do not know what they want so they ask a sales associate for assistance or an opinion.
- **Customers are especially particular about what they want.** They ask a sales associate for assistance in finding the item or for an opinion about the specific item.

TABLE 17.1   *Top 10 Retail Attributes Desired by Luxury Department Store Customers*

Rank	Attribute	Score
1	Courteous, respectful employees	4.54
2	Quick, hassle-free merchandise returns	4.53
3	Staff expertly addresses customer needs	4.48
4	Staff treats customers like they're valued	4.44
5	Staff proficiently wraps purchases	4.36
6	Short wait for purchases	4.29
7	Well-groomed staff	4.01
8	Visually appealing store	4.00
9	Employee dress complements store	3.88
10	Information is easily attainable by phone	3.85

Adapted from: Gustke, C. (2006, July 13). The luxe experience, *Women's Wear Daily*, p. 17.

- **Customers ask for items that are not available.** These items may not be made or carried by the particular firm or may be available only through catalog sales or the Internet.
- **Customers have unusual needs or make request for unusual items.** These requests may be for special sizes, colors, or styles of clothing.
- **Customers request services beyond the scope of services ordinarily provided by the sales associate.** These may include special assistance outside of the department, special deliveries, or just to spend time talking with the sales associate.
- **Customers need assistance overcoming personal problems that make it difficult to shop.** Examples include physical, mental, or language barriers or unruly children.
- **Customers want to negotiate a transaction with the sales associate that is not normally considered legitimate under store policy.** Returning merchandise under questionable circumstances or buying flawed items at a discount represent this type of contact situation.
- **Customers are upset, angry, irritated, or complaining.**
- **Customers are caught in illegal acts.**

Personal selling is a very successful form of sales promotion, as it enables the salesperson to promote the characteristics of a product and overcome any objections the customer may have about the product or service. Customers in some instances see the personal attention they receive as validating their selection and decision to purchase the product. Sales initiated through other sales promotion activities, such as displays, advertising, special events, or fashion shows, are more likely to be completed through personal selling by a sales associate.

In addition to creating a positive first impression with the customer, sales staffs that participate in personal selling have the opportunity to gain feedback about customer needs and wants. Sales associates are in a unique position because they have knowledge of the product, the retail environment, and the consumer. They know why decisions were made to carry certain merchandise and why certain store policies are established. The sales associate is able to ask questions about specific brands, styles, and color preferences that appeal to or are rejected by the customer. The sales associate can ask customers if they were drawn into the store by advertising or other special promotions. Sales associates also know the clientele of the store because they interact with customers on an ongoing basis. By having knowledge of all three components, sales associates are able to view how different customers react to different products or management policies and, in turn, report this information back to the buying office or the management staff. This firsthand knowledge passed to retail management can help determine future directions in merchandise selection and the promotion mix.

Historically, sales associates have not had as much direct contact with customers in discount and drugstores where items such as cosmetics or personal care products were prepackaged. However, drugstore chains have started adding sales staff to the previously "self-service" format in beauty and photo departments as a tool to differentiate themselves from their competitors. The addition of sales associates in these departments allows retailers to enhance service and in some cases increase the opportunity to stock upscale product lines.

Personal Shoppers

In an effort to provide increased customer service and retain store loyalty, some retailers have introduced personal shoppers into the store service program. **Personal shoppers** are sales associates who assemble items for specific customers prior to or in place of a visit to the retail store. Some retailers even provide for personal shoppers to visit the customer's home or office with the selected merchandise.

Personal shoppers are also available to accompany customers through the store, offering assistance and identifying suitable merchandise. A personal shopper generally has good knowledge of the specific customer's preferences for brands, styles, and color and will coordinate merchandise groupings that are likely to appeal to the consumer. Personal shoppers may also call customers when new merchandise arrives in the store that may appeal to a specific client.

Direct Sellers

In addition to providing personal service to customers within a retail store, personal selling can take place individually through direct selling channels. Direct sellers are companies that sell directly to the consumer, bypassing a retail distributor. Individuals involved in direct selling often refer to themselves as **image consultants.** Avon, Mary Kay cosmetics, and Beauty Counselor are long-established companies training sales associates to be image consultants. Image consultants are experts who help individuals create a positive self-image. Areas of consultation include skin care, health, fitness, beauty, cosmetics, apparel, color, wardrobe, and personal and professional etiquette. Image consultants may assist customers with basic information through color draping or extensive assistance, including complete wardrobe analysis and makeovers for hair and beauty. In addition to retail selling, sales personnel also work for manufacturers and designers.

Wholesale Selling

Personal selling at the wholesale level commonly is done by a **manufacturer's sales representative (rep).** Representatives may work in manufacturers' showrooms or cover specific geographical territories, traveling to trade shows, or retail establishments (Fig. 17.2). All product categories require representatives to show the manufacturer's products to potential retail buyers. Responsibilities of a manufacturer's sales representative are varied but include many one-on-one communications with clients. Reps meet with buyers in person to show the latest lines. Complete familiarity with the line is essential for sales representatives. Reps and buyers work in close contact, touching the product line, discussing details of the product, which include findings and fabrics, and coordinating color and style features to create the assortment a buyer wishes to have available in his or her retail store. Reps write orders, complete follow-up work, and occasionally model garments for buyers. Reps may also communicate with buyers on the phone or via e-mail to place reorders or discuss a product detail brought to their attention by retail customers. Manufacturing representatives must provide quality service to buyers if they want their lines represented in retail stores.

As the marketplace becomes global in nature, vendors from other countries are looking at the way U.S. sales representatives are trained. Miller contrasts several characteristics of U.S. and Chinese sales representatives and offers solutions to the Chinese way of doing things. Characteristics include:

- **Relationships.** Chinese business relationships are more personal than American business relationships and are not developed with regard to the business potential of either person. Solutions include teaching Chinese sales representatives to ask relevant, business-related, probing questions rather than social questions.

FIGURE 17.2 Manufacturing sales reps meet with clients.

- **Price.** Chinese sales representatives have historically sold products solely on the basis of price, not qualifying potential customers. To qualify a buyer, it is necessary to determine the decision-maker within the firm. This is even more difficult in China than in the United States because for Chinese people to admit they do not make the decisions would involve a loss of face. Chinese vendors must constantly emphasize the necessity of identifying the decision-maker to achieve efficiency.
- **Training.** U.S. sales representatives are often trained through role-playing and problem solving, with heavy emphasis on in-depth knowledge and its use in helping the customer understand product benefits to ensure sales. This is in contrast to the Chinese tendency to resort to price cutting in the face of any objection to making a purchase. The solution to this problem requires constant drills on product benefits and close supervision to ensure these features are emphasized. This solution complements the Chinese education method of rote memorization (1994).

Miller suggests that Chinese vendors adapt training to fit cultural constraints, while working to modify Western techniques to obtain better results from sales representatives. These are just a few of the problems facing cultures as they become members of the global society. While the American way of doing business is not always the right way, it can be used as a model for other countries because we have been at it longer and have had successes.

Retail sales associates and wholesale sales representatives perform important duties for their employees. Before we discuss the attributes that make these sales personnel successful, it is necessary to look at the buying and selling process that involves both the customer and the sales associate.

─○ BUYING AND SELLING PROCESS

When a salesperson becomes involved with a potential customer who is faced with a buying decision, two separate and distinct processes take place:

FIGURE 17.3 The AIDA model of the selling process.

1. The customer becomes occupied with product acquisition.
2. The salesperson becomes concerned with the selling process.

The **selling process,** illustrated in Figure 17.3, is the method used by a salesperson to encourage a customer to reach a buying decision about a product or service. Researchers in sales literature refer to this as the AIDA model, which stands for *a*ttention, *i*nterest, *d*esire, and *a*ction. Some researchers have added a fifth element, satisfaction, because it is necessary for evaluation.

The selling process involves five steps, as follows:

1. Get the *attention* of the consumer.
2. Create the customer *interest* in a product or service.
3. Form *desire* on the part of the customer for the product or service.
4. Stimulate customer *action* to purchase the item or service.
5. Create customer *satisfaction* to ensure continued loyalty in the firm.

All forms of selling include a buying and selling process. The process may be implemented entirely through personal selling or through a combination of personal selling and other elements of the promotion mix, such as advertising or visual merchandising.

Attention

The goal of a salesperson is to match the elements of the acquisition process with the elements of the buying and selling process in order to satisfy customer needs and generate sales. Figure 17.4 shows the interaction between the selling process and the product acquisition process. At the beginning of the process, the customer recognizes the need for a product. The consumer will peruse catalogs, look online, or go shopping at the mall for the item. She may be influenced by a window display or direct-response message. A sales associate makes first contact with the customer as he or she enters a store or by answering an inbound call. In a retail environment, the salesperson should get the consumer's attention by introducing, demonstrating, or offering samples of a product. A customer calling in response to direct marketing efforts has already taken notice of the firm's merchandise, but a sales associate can draw the customer's attention to additional products or services. Through curiosity, or appreciation

Product acquisition process—Customer driven

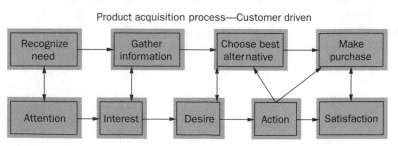

Buying and selling process—Sales associate driven

FIGURE 17.4 Interaction takes place during the acquisition process and the selling process.

of specific features, the customer may consider the product or service for possible examination.

Interest

Following the recognition of a need, the consumer usually wants to know what products might fill his or her need and begins gathering information. During this phase, it is the role of the sales associate to provide enough information about the product to arouse the consumer's interest. A sales associate may explain the expected benefits from the item and describe what the customer will gain by owning the product.

Desire

As the momentum of the acquisition process continues, a consumer will turn interest for a product into conscious desire for the product and begin choosing among alternatives. The sales associate may use the opportunity to explain the enjoyment and satisfaction the product promises in its attainment. The sales associate may also offer extra information about the incentives associated with the product or service that were not evident to the customer.

Action

At a certain point, the sales associate must shift the customer from choosing among alternatives to making a purchase. The sales associate should make every effort to stimulate action in the customer to buy the product through further explanation of specific features or details of the product. The salesperson may speak about or demonstrate the ease of assembly, explain specific care requirements, or explain a convenient feature not previously mentioned. If the client is a regular customer, the sales associate may suggest how the item will complement other items already owned by the customer. Action may also be accomplished by formalizing details of packaging, shipping, or other elements of the transaction. Through personal interaction with a sales associate or service representative, the customer chooses the best item for purchase to satisfy his or her need.

Satisfaction

The last and most important element of the buying and selling process is customer satisfaction. To assure customer satisfaction, the sales associate may offer to exchange the item or take it back in return if the customer is not completely satisfied with the product. Additionally, the sales associate may offer a coupon or free sample to the customer. This is also a good time to distribute customer surveys as a gesture of goodwill by the firm to ensure customer satisfaction and continued patronage. The handshake is a universal symbol of thanks and appreciation for loyalty. A salesperson may not complete each sale with a handshake. However, customers appreciate a friendly smile and a sincere thank-you. The satisfied customer leaves the store and through use or wear of the item begins postpurchase product evaluation.

——○ ELEMENTS OF THE SALE

The buying and selling process is used to persuade customers to reach a buying decision about a product or service. This sounds easy, but just how do sales associates go about making a sale? In this section, we discuss the elements of a sale.

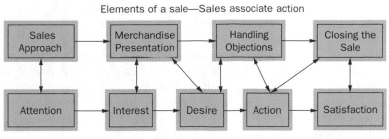

Elements of a sale—Sales associate action

Buying and selling process—Sales associate thought process

There are four steps involved in making a sale. They include (1) sales approach, (2) merchandise presentation, (3) handling objections, and (4) closing the sale. The interaction between the buying and selling process and these elements is illustrated in Figure 17.5.

Sales Approach

The sales approach is the opening recognition and greeting of a customer. At this step, the sales associate is responsible for gaining the attention of the customer. Each customer who makes contact with a firm should be treated as a guest. Whether in person or through phone communication, sales associates should greet customers as friends with respect and courtesy. Mervyn's has trained its sales associates to refer to every customer as a guest. The sales approach may involve personal communication between the salesperson and customer through a greeting such as, *How are you this evening?* or a comment about merchandise such as, *These sweaters have just arrived in new fall colors.*

An incorrect approach can easily bring forth a negative response from the customer. The question, *May I help you?* will almost always be answered with an abrupt no. A sales associate should express simple greetings such as, *Good afternoon,* or ask questions that must be answered in a positive manner such as, *Are you trying to match a particular color?* These are examples of a **greeting approach,** a pleasant salutation expressing good wishes to the individual.

The alternative to a greeting approach is a **merchandise approach**, which directly makes reference to the merchandise at hand. Phone representatives are experts at this method when they ask customers what page they are referring to when ordering merchandise. In most cases, the merchandise approach is more effective than using the greeting approach in getting the attention of the customer since it gives each party something positive to discuss.

During the sales approach, the salesperson should become aware of the customer's reaction to the merchandise. The salesperson should listen to the customer, asking minimal questions to determine specific preferences of the customer, such as color or price, and migrate with the customer toward the described merchandise.

A well-phrased, appropriately timed question is a very effective sales tool. Kahle, president of DaCo Corporation, a firm specializing in systematic approaches to sales, offers the following tips about good questions.

- **Good questions direct customer thinking.** When you use a good question, you penetrate your prospect's mind and direct his or her thinking. For example, instead of asking a customer, *Do you need a new pair of athletic shoes?* ask, *What is more important to* *you, ankle support or a cushioned sole?* The salesperson's question helps customers to direct their thinking about the product they are interested in and conversation naturally proceeds based on the first answer.

- **Good questions will help collect information necessary to construct a sale.** How do you know what a customer thinks, or what his or her situation is, unless you ask a question? For example, if you are selling small kitchen appliances, you need to ask questions to determine whether the customer has counter space for the appliance or needs a spacesaver appliance. You must discover the concerns of the client so you can point out special features of the item to meet those needs.
- **Good questions build relationships.** The act of asking a good question shows you care about the person and his or her problem. The more questions you ask about your customer, the more he or she feels your interest and, therefore, becomes interested in you.
- **Good questions convey the perception of confidence.** Your customer sees you as competent and trustworthy—not necessarily by what you say but rather by what you ask. For example, suppose a potential customer needs calendar refills from an office supply store. The customer asks the salesperson where refills are located in the store. One possible reply would be, *Aisle 3.* A better reply would be, *What is your preferred brand? Day Runner or Daytimer, or something else?* This question conveys the perception to customers that you understand their needs and shows that you are competent at fulfilling their needs. Mastering good questions will increase the likelihood of completing a sale (1997).

Merchandise Presentation

Once a salesperson has recognized the needs of the customer, he or she should begin presenting suitable merchandise to attract interest within the client. The sales associate should lead the customer to the merchandise rather than point to a rack across the room and expect the client to find it. Many successful retail salespeople use the **soft sell** approach, presenting merchandise in a discriminating, not forceful way. Advantages of the product are pointed out to the customer with slight encouragement to purchase the item now rather than postponing the purchase. Most customers are turned off by the **hard sell** approach, which pushes customers to buy a product they may not want.

The salesperson should lead the consumer to the appropriate merchandise, being selective in offerings, careful not to overstimulate or confuse the consumer by presenting too many items. Touching and feeling the merchandise will encourage customers to try on items for fit and color selection. The customer should be told what he most wants to hear about the product. If the customer has asked about price, do not continue to speak about product features. A salesperson should always be alert to tell clients what the product or service will do for them, fulfilling unmet needs.

The presentation should begin with medium-priced merchandise and, upon reaction from the customer, move up or down to fit the budget. Merchandise presentation is the perfect time for a sales associate to learn the tastes of the client and offer appropriate merchandise for the customer's consideration. **Trading up** is the process of substituting higher-priced merchandise from lower-priced merchandise during presentation. Upon assurance from the customer, verbal or nonverbal, that the price is not too high, the salesperson should begin to trade up, showing the customer similar but higher-priced merchandise with more fashion-forward appeal.

Handling Objections

As customers move from interest to desire, they may develop questions or objections that the sales associate must be ready to handle. Consumers often attempt to object to a sales associate's offer for assistance by replying they are "just looking." Other common objections by consumers include requests for out-of-stock merchandise, or for merchandise not carried, or resistance to the price of selected merchandise. It is important for the salesperson to answer objections before they are raised, by watching the customer and preparing an answer to the possible question. If a customer is looking for a certain size, the sales associate should come to his or her assistance by showing the correct location for the size or by offering to find the correct size in reserve inventories. If it is necessary, agree with the customer about the objection and point out a superior feature or alternative product. A sales associate should never argue with the customer. By arguing, sales associates leave a negative impression about themselves and the retail establishment, influencing the customer's decision not to return to the establishment in the future.

Closing the Sale

Either a sales associate or a customer can determine when it is time to take action and close a sale. A customer will often signal he or she is ready to close the sale by a statement or action called a **buying signal.** A buying signal may be a question such as, *Can I charge this?* Or a statement, *This will look great in my apartment.* Customers may also show they are ready to close the sale through nonverbal actions such as appearing restless when additional merchandise is shown, setting one item aside from a group of items, or nodding approval to the sales associate. If several customers are shopping together, a companion may suggest the close of a sale by reaffirming the buyer's decision or moving to a different department within the store.

A sales associate may close the sale by stopping the presentation of additional merchandise, narrowing the selection of items, and concentrating on those in which the customer has shown the greatest interest. This may be done by asking the customer which item he or she prefers. Promptly remove merchandise that has proven to be unsatisfactory to the customer. Ask the customer how he or she intends to pay for the merchandise and reassure the customer about the decision through a statement such as, *Those earrings are a perfect match with your dress.* The sales associate should be conscious of the customer and avoid hurrying the decision of the customer or pressuring the customer into a sale.

Once the decision to buy has been reached, getting the customer through the checkout quickly is critical to closing the sale. In a study conducted by *Women's Wear Daily*, 62 percent of specialty and department store customers indicated that they sought a salesperson for fast checkout. The study concluded that 19 percent of the consumers surveyed said they would leave the store empty-handed if the checkout lines were too long. Positive interaction was also rewarded; 39 percent of the shoppers said if a salesperson was helpful and friendly they often ended up spending more (Schneiderman, 1997).

At the close of a sale it is appropriate for sales associates to suggest additional items or accessories for the customer to consider, but they should avoid suggesting alternative merchandise. **Suggestion selling** includes offering related merchandise, such as accessories, large quantities of the same merchandise in other colors or styles, promotional merchandise, or advertised merchandise. The customer always receives suggestions better if the salesperson shows the merchandise rather than asking if he or she wants to see additional items or directing the customer to another area of the store to search for it without assistance from the salesperson. More than any other selling technique, successful suggestion selling can increase the profitability of the store and the productivity of the sales associate. These benefits cannot be overstated.

─○ AFTER THE SALE

A common practice used by sales associates in specialty and department stores is to keep **customer directories** for future sales opportunities. Each salesperson develops his or her own customer directory with names, addresses, telephone numbers, and important details about the customer's purchases and preferences. Details may include sizes, color preferences, and style details that are of particular interest to the client, and any other information that might be helpful in creating potential future sales. The directory may also include anniversary and birthday dates as reminders to the sales associates and other appropriate people including spouses, other relatives, and friends. An accurate directory can be a valuable resource to a sales associate when new merchandise arrives, assisting the associate in identifying a potential customer. Many retailers send follow-up notes, make phone calls, and sends gifts to clients to show appreciation for their customer's business.

─○ ATTRIBUTES OF SUCCESSFUL SELLING

When making a purchase by phone, have you ever been asked by the customer service representative, *Can this phone conversation be recorded for quality assurance?* If you have, you should be pleased that the firm thought enough of customer service to want to improve its methodology and training. Retailers and manufacturers put a great deal of time and money into establishing store image through the promotion mix. This image is wasted if a customer is met by an uninformed or disinterested sales associate. Here are just a few of the many reasons retail sales are lost by sales associates:

- No salesperson in sight.
- Salesperson chatting with coworkers.
- Salesperson not available at the checkout.
- Salesperson's bad attitude or physical appearance.
- Customer has to ask for assistance.
- Salesperson jumps too quickly to close the sale.
- Salesperson unable to locate advertised merchandise.
- Salesperson ignores a complaint or concern.
- Salesperson has insufficient product knowledge.
- Customers do not feel comfortable in the store.
- Salesperson attempts to serve more than one customer at a time.
- Salesperson is busy with something else.
- Salesperson services a customer on the phone before the customer on the sales floor.

Sales are also lost during phone transactions for various reasons, including:

- Customer put on hold for too long.
- Sales associate has insufficient product knowledge.
- Sales representative unable to make immediate decisions regarding a consumer's question about the merchandise.
- Sales representative lacks good listening skills.

Identifying quality individuals and training them properly is extremely important to retailers and others in the distribution channel. A successful business must incorporate a planned program of sales training into its marketing plan. A training program should educate the employee on store policies and procedures, interpersonal communications, and the goals and objectives of management. Quality training programs include role playing, active listening, feedback, videos, quizzes, and team exercises.

The National Retail Federation (NRF) determined that sales training is so important, the organization developed a certification program to measure and acknowledge the professional skills and competencies of incumbent or prospective sales associates (Figure 17.6). One of more than 500 assessment and certification sites where this certification is available is located at the King of Prussia Retail Skills Center in Pennsylvania (RSC). The RSC provides recruitment, assessment, training, and certification programs and is a partnership among the NRF, Kravco Company, American Express Foundation, and the State of Pennsylvania to raise standards for the retail industry. The center was established to help retailers find, select, and motivate professional retail employees. Workers are trained to increase their employability, raise their retail skills, and improve their knowledge of the industry. Additionally, educators have teamed up with the retail industry to develop programs to help students gain real-life job training.

After the successful creation of the Retail Skills Center in Pennsylvania, additional skills centers opened in over 20 additional locations in 14 states (National Retail Federation, n. d.). Typical retail skills programs include:

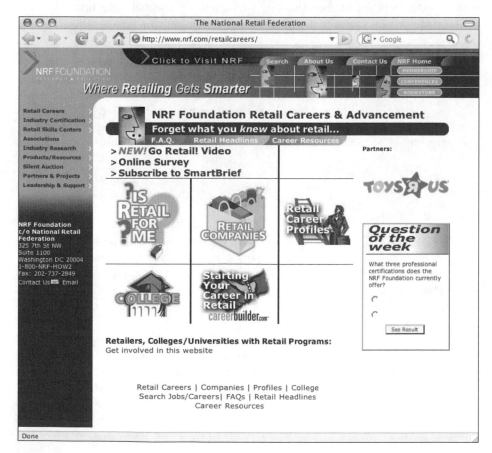

FIGURE 17.6 The National Retail Federation website is a good source for information about retail sales training and learning about career advancement.

- Retail Readiness Assessment
- Assessment for National Professional Certification in Customer Service
- Literacy-based customer service training
- Computer-based learning programs
- Career counseling
- English as a Second Language (ESL) training
- Moderate to intensive classroom training (one day to six weeks)
- Job placement assistance
- Retention and follow-up programs
- Job fairs
- Internships

Providing high-quality service is a mind-set that has long been used by U.S. companies to differentiate products. In Europe, however, recognition of customer service to differentiate products is just emerging as a strategic option. Stewart-Allen highlighted several characteristics fundamental to customer service in the United States that can have positive results in Europe, as follows:

- Realize the importance of customers.
- Survey customers' attitude and behaviors.
- Take ownership at the front line for customer problems.
- Take a proactive approach to suggesting solutions to customer problems.
- Make a statement to customers that they are valued and essential to the firms.
- Give customers the option to provide feedback about the firm (1996).

Knowing what good customer service looks like and surveying customers' and clients' opinions regularly will help European vendors raise the standards of customer service. Effective sales associates broadcast the following positive attributes to each customer they meet: They are well groomed and attractive; have a good working knowledge of the merchandise and retailing environment; have a good rapport with customers; and are motivated and persistent in creating opportunities for sales and excitement in selling. Box 17.1 expands on the importance of good customer service.

○ BOX 17.1

Service, Product Differentiation Key to Success

Industry consolidation often raises concerns over product sameness and limited shopping choices, yet many firms manage to thrive through varying retail cycles.

During a panel discussion called "Meeting Customer Needs," hosted and moderated by Emanuel Weintraub of his eponymous consulting firm, he observed: "This period of consolidation goes to the story of sameness of buying issue, and which stores consumers will frequent. Their number one complaint is long waits at the checkout line. Next is nonresponsive sales help."

Participants in the panel included Coach Inc.'s Jody Kuss, senior vice president of merchandising worldwide; and David Duplantis, senior vice president of retail, Internet and catalogue; Talbots Inc.'s Michele Mandell, executive vice president of stores; Andrew Jennings, former president; and chief operating officer of Saks Fifth Avenue Enterprises; and Lori Holliday Banks, fashion editor at Tobe, an international fashion retail consulting service best known for the Tobe Report.

Holliday Banks noted, "It really does start and end with the customer. The consumer is more demanding than ever before. She is clearly in control."

Holliday Banks said there is tremendous fragmentation in the marketplace. As a result, Tobe's trend research service emphasizes to its clients that customer loyalty must be earned and that the successful retailers are those that "deliver what they promise," whether that's service, product, selection, or value.

So how do companies in retail and apparel stay uppermost in the minds of their customers? At Coach Inc., the 65-year-old handbag and accessories firm, listening to the customer is key.

"We like to think about usage point in our business. Because we're a handbag and accessories firm, we think about our customer in multiple ways. We have a very broad consumer base. To capture her and know her, we are a very consumer-centric organization. We live and breathe by our market research, by our piloting, and by our consumer feedback. A great percentage of what we do we really vet through our market research. We are lucky we can do that because we are a vertical operation and we are close to our customers," Kuss said.

Case in point is the evolution of Coach's Hamptons Weekend collection, with the aim to be youthful in spirit, but not necessarily in age. The initial test of the totes in the stores included questions to customers regarding function, strap length, and weight of the tote, as well as internal pockets and opening price point. Now, three years later, volume is 12 times the tote's initial introduction.

"We try to give consumers exactly what they need and really try to be ahead of them. A lot of the things we do also is to absolutely listen to our customer, and be in a position to dictate some things such as showing the customer what is the must-have product," Kuss said.

"Our service objective is to be as well known for service as we are for the product. We want to create a magical moment for the customer, one that engages her in a way to make her more comfortable to trust us and come back," Duplantis said.

Last year the company began a store-service initiative that includes requiring customers to be greeted with a smile when they enter the stores, an introduction by the store associate and perhaps a lifestyle question so the associate can better service the customer. Handwritten thank-you notes are sent to customers spending more than $250.

Coach also makes sure that its best sales associates are in the stores at peak selling times. "It sounds very simple but it was not necessarily the case before. It meant finding out the peak traffic times and the peak volume times," Duplantis said.

Talbots' Mandell said that, while the heart of the business may be product, the retailer's soul is on service. "We remind each other that if the heart of our brand is fine-quality, classic fashion, then the soul of our brand is really our commitment to outstanding customer service," she said.

Store management teams file weekly comments that are sent to regional offices and corporate headquarters listing what customers say about product, service, and the competition. From that come the ideas for changes to product or store design, or even a new service.

"We do a seasonal shopping panel with our customers asking how to do things better and what they're changing in their wardrobes. This year we asked about our advertising campaigns, [such as] did we convey what we thought was important," Mandell said. She added that the company makes sure its interactions with the customer are personalized to ensure that service is "distinctive and memorable."

Jennings, who will leave Saks at the end of the month and join Cape Town–based Woolworths as group managing director in December, discussed how to navigate the dual pull of consumers who shop for the greater price and the convenient format and those who shop for the total experience and unique finds. "We are looking at creating memorable moments. At Saks, our aim is to transform our stores into exciting destinations. We want to break away from the pack. We call it a category of one," he said.

Jennings said all the good purveyors of style have a special vibe, or energy, in their stores that provide the consumers with a sense of discovery as they move through the store, building their wardrobes while creating a great shopping experience.

"Today's customer no longer shops head-to-toe, wearing either Armani, Prada, or Dolce & Gabbana. It is the Chanel jacket with the Theory pant, with the private label T-shirt. It is all about personal style," Jennings said.

According to Jennings, Saks spent 12 months developing and researching three new customer profiles to better target its merchandising and marketing: the classic "Park Avenue" customer, the modern "Uptown" consumer and the contemporary "SoHo" customer.

"We've learned that, in order to be successful, it is not about keeping up with our customers, it is about keeping ahead of the customer. It is not about predicting where customers are going, but identifying where they want to be," Jennings said.

Source: Young, V.M. (2006, September18). Service, product differentiation key to success. *Women's Wear Daily*, p. 4.

Personal Appearance

Personal qualities required of individuals in a personal selling situation include excellent appearance and grooming, strong fashion sense, outgoing personality, poise, articulateness, quick thinking, social ease, and self-confidence. Research has shown that personal attractiveness enhances personal communication and contributes to persuasiveness. Sales associates at all levels must have immaculate grooming and appearance. This does not mean sales associates must be beautiful or take on the image of a fashion model. They must, however, dress in a professional manner appropriate to their environment and have the restraint not to wear unattractive or inappropriate clothing.

Individuals must have a standard of cleanliness. Hair for both men and women should be clean and styled, and men with beards or mustaches should keep them trimmed and neat. Fingernails should be groomed. Polish, if worn, should be in good taste and not chipped or otherwise unattractive. Colognes and fragrances, if used, should be subtle, not overwhelming. Clothes should be clean, pressed, and in good shape, not tattered and worn. Sales personnel must be in good health and have the stamina necessary to stand for long hours and be able to lift and move merchandise.

Knowledge

Knowledge of the merchandise, the retail policies, and the customer is critical in a good salesperson. Based on the assumption that customers want help in choosing the right merchandise, merchants and vendors should improve the product knowledge of sales associates.

With the volume of advertisements and promotions transmitted through print media, broadcast media, and the Internet, it is rare when a customer knows nothing about the product he or she is purchasing. Knowing more about the product and understanding the qualities of the merchandise that are particularly critical to the consumer are essential if a salesperson is to make a positive impression on the consumer. Salespeople should be familiar with every detail of the product, what the product does and does not do, the merits of particular items, and the benefits each item has to the purchaser.

Sales associates should be able to answer frequently asked questions concerning brands and manufacturers, sizes and colors available, fabric and fiber contents, and care requirements of merchandise, and should be able to use these features as selling points. In addition, a sales associate should be aware of the competition's product and the overall market so she can respond to concerns of the consumer who may be comparing products. The sales staff should be fully aware of fashion information concerning the current trends and know where coordinating accessories, jewelry, shoes, and other items are available in the store. A salesperson who is perceived by the customer as an expert about the merchandise or service being offered has a much greater chance of making a sale. Figure 17.7 shows the Cyber Beauty Advisor, a point-of-purchase interactive video prepared by the cosmetics firm English Ideas. While waiting to be served by a live sales associate, a customer can access a mini-lesson about common makeup problems by touching the screen. The image of Rebecca Pflueger, the company president, presents information about products for lips, face, brows, or eyes. Both customer and sales associate can save time when the Cyber Beauty Advisor imparts this product knowledge. Then the sales associate can supplement this information with answers to specific questions and advice tailored to the customer's needs.

A good sales associate will be aware of store promotions, point-of-purchase displays, advertised merchandise in print media, billing inserts, and catalogs, and be ready

FIGURE 17.7 The point-of-purchase interactive device supplements the service of a knowledgeable sales associate.

to assist customers who have questions. He should be aware of merchandise displayed in windows or remote locations and where the customer may find the merchandise in-house or at branch locations. Buyers and merchandisers should meet regularly with sales associates to share their enthusiasm for the merchandise. Accessories and coordinating pieces should be shown to sales associates with information on where the pieces are located within the store. Reliable communication from the buying office should inform sales associates of ordered stock and estimated time of arrival in the store so they will be able to answer potential questions from customers.

Customer Savvy

Have you ever heard someone exclaim, *She has a lot of savvy!* This compliment means the person is well informed and perceptive, a shrewd businesswoman. Sales associates who can obtain this trait are invaluable to selling firms. A credible salesperson is believable, trustworthy, and honest in dealing with customers and has a good sense of **salesmanship,** the ability to sell goods in a fair, sincere, and distinctive manner. The purpose of salesmanship is to provide assistance to customers during the buying and selling process so they will be satisfied with their purchase decisions. The viewpoint of the customer, not the salesperson, should be the driving force behind good salesmanship. Customers should be given reasons why, and encouraged to purchase because of what the product or service can do for them. Customers are not dumb and should not be treated as such by the use of a mechanical "canned" sales pitch. Salespeople should approach customers with genuine interest and not persuade customers to purchase merchandise that they really do not want. Figure 17.8 alludes to the importance placed on the customer in Japan: *Never, ever is the buyer put in*

FIGURE 17.8 Saturn's commitment to personal service is illustrated in this advertisement.

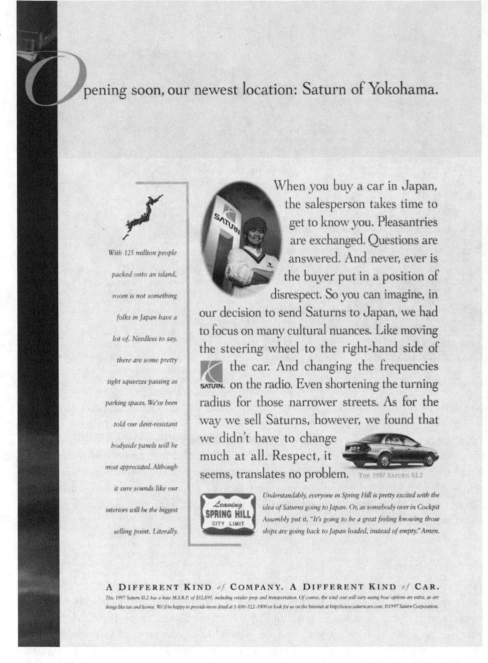

Opening soon, our newest location: Saturn of Yokohama.

With 125 million people packed onto an island, room is not something folks in Japan have a lot of. Needless to say, there are some pretty tight squeezes passing as parking spaces. We've been told our dent-resistant bodyside panels will be most appreciated. Although it sure sounds like our interiors will be the biggest selling point. Literally.

When you buy a car in Japan, the salesperson takes time to get to know you. Pleasantries are exchanged. Questions are answered. And never, ever is the buyer put in a position of disrespect. So you can imagine, in our decision to send Saturns to Japan, we had to focus on many cultural nuances. Like moving the steering wheel to the right-hand side of the car. And changing the frequencies on the radio. Even shortening the turning radius for those narrower streets. As for the way we sell Saturns, however, we found that we didn't have to change much at all. Respect, it seems, translates no problem.

The 1997 Saturn SL2

Leaving SPRING HILL CITY LIMIT

Understandably, everyone in Spring Hill is pretty excited with the idea of Saturns going to Japan. Or, as somebody over in Cockpit Assembly put it, "It's going to be a great feeling knowing those ships are going back to Japan loaded, instead of empty." Amen.

A DIFFERENT KIND *of* COMPANY. A DIFFERENT KIND *of* CAR.

This 1997 Saturn SL2 has a base M.S.R.P. of $12,895, including retailer prep and transportation. Of course, the total cost will vary seeing how options are extra, as are things like tax and license. We'd be happy to provide more detail at 1-800-522-5000 or look for us on the Internet at http://www.saturncars.com. ©1997 Saturn Corporation.

a position of disrespect. It has been beneficial for U.S. companies such as Saturn to adopt this philosophy, because they have reaped the rewards of satisfied customers in a product category that was known for less-than-positive customer experiences in the past.

Savvy sales associates also take advantage of the power of personalization. The easiest way to do this is by using a customer's name. A specialty store sales associate who keeps a list of loyal customers will have easy access to this information. Stores that participate in loyalty programs or frequent-buyer programs also have immediate access to the names of customers who participate in these programs. Addressing customers by name is also becoming more common by mass merchandisers. Sales personnel in these environments have access to the customer's name when the customer's credit card is swiped through the point-of-purchase system. This allows the clerk to conclude the transaction by saying, *Thank you, Ms. Smith.*

Today's customers are increasingly sophisticated in their needs and rushed in the time they can devote to satisfying their needs. They know what they want and have less store loyalty than previous generations. A professional salesperson will understand the demographic and lifestyle nature of his or her customers and offer merchandise to the customer's liking. Customers should not be stereotyped in terms of price, probable intentions to buy, or other characteristics that may be false assumptions. A salesperson should know the customer and the service expectations of the customer. A successful salesperson will help spend the customer's time profitably for both parties by offering merchandise that fits his or her consumer profile.

Motivation

Motivation of sales personnel is vital to the well-being of the individual and the retailer. Motivated sales associates will show their enthusiasm for the retailer and for their role within the institution to each customer who enters the store. Unmotivated sales clerks will also convey their boredom and disrespect for their employer to customers who, in turn, are less likely to make a purchase.

George Gillen, executive vice president of Management Horizons, a consulting division of Price Waterhouse, has suggested the following strategies for transforming associates into "charming, efficient, and persuasive salespeople" (Emerson, 1995). According to Gillen, "great customer service is more than a list of do's and don'ts. It's an attitude—a state of mind—carried by the sales associate and fostered by the store environment itself." Here are just a few of the recommendations made by Gillen for a successful sales staff:

- The easiest way to mobilize your store to provide great customer service is to hire people who are truly customer-oriented, which will show through during an interview and discussions about the business.
- The best way to encourage sales associates to provide excellent customer service is to treat them with respect.
- Have sales associates think in terms of the potential value a single customer can bring to the store. Staff will find that customers can bring in more profit if they are treated as they expect to be treated. These customers will return to the store.
- Provide response cards to the customer. If associates know customers are encouraged to give feedback, they will be motivated to provide the best possible service.
- Encourage sales associates to build relationships with customers and reward the associate who is responsible for bringing customers back.

Sales personnel motivation is the responsibility of management. It may take the form of training sessions and incentive programs designed to generate sales. Sales meetings should be regularly scheduled with sales associates to inform them about new merchandise, specific promotions, and store services.

Incentive Programs

Incentive programs are motivational tools generally designed to increase the sales productivity of each sales associate. Incentive programs can take the form of training sessions, sales contests, or salary enhancements.

Training Sessions

Well-executed training sessions are one of the best motivational tools a company can participate in. As we discussed in Chapter 12, sales training may be a trade-oriented incentive offered by manufacturers. Regardless of who sponsors the training program, it is an excellent resource for sales associates. Training sessions may take the form of a breakfast or luncheon meeting that focuses on product knowledge or usage. All sales associates are encouraged to attend to view the latest trends, hear comments from senior management, or learn about the firm's most recent promotion campaign.

A typical training session to introduce new trends may include a fashion show or display of new merchandise. The buyer will be the spokesperson, discussing each item of merchandise and answering questions from sales associates about the item. Discussion points may include new fabrications and colors, coordinating pieces, determining the correct size, and proper accessories for the item. Certain merchandise categories, such as shoes or bras, require hands-on fitting demonstrations to train associates. These can also be incorporated into a training session.

Training sessions are important for sales representatives, too. A training session with a fun focus on negotiation skills, time management, presentation skills, and the customer experience creates a lot of excitement. Senior management wants to energize the team and create enthusiasm about the merchandise.

Spiffs

PM, which stands for push money or prize money, are salary supplements used to reward sales associates for pushing the sales of certain merchandise and often are used to encourage multiple sales. **Spiffs,** as they are also called, may be given to employees in the form of extra money, additional discounts, or merchandise whenever sales of specific items are made. Incentive rewards may be designed to increase the number of sales, the dollar volume of each sale, or multiple sales. PMs can have a negative effect on the retailer if the sales associates use the incentive to push unwanted merchandise onto customers. When this occurs, the customer loses confidence in the retailer and the retailer loses a return customer.

Sales Contests

Incentives may also take the form of **sales contests** in which sales associates compete against one another, against other stores within the chain, or against established goals to increase sales. The winning employee or store may receive monetary or merchandise rewards. Sometimes these rewards are generous vacations or other large-ticket items. Sales contests are generally designed to increase total sales for a salesperson during a given time or the sale of a particular item during a given time. Sales contests designed to promote competition between branch stores have the advantage of team building among associates within the same branch.

Salary Enhancements

Employers may use salary enhancements to motivate sales associates. **Salary enhancements** are special bonuses, merit pay, or salary incentives used to motivate employees.

Bonus. A sum of money or the equivalent given to an employee in addition to the employer's usual compensation is considered a **bonus.** Bonuses are commonly distributed at the end of the calendar year or the end of a fiscal year to employees and are based on length of service with the organization, not sales. Bonuses are often given as a reward to a team, a department, or the entire staff.

Merit Pay. **Merit pay** is extra pay awarded to an employee for outstanding past performance. Merit pay may take the form of a one-time payment, an increase in base salary, or a percentage of commissions earned. Merit pay is usually distributed on an individual basis as a way for the company to recognize superior performance by the employee.

Profit Sharing. Some companies use profit sharing as a motivation for the sales staff. **Profit sharing** is a plan that offers employees a chance to purchase stock in the company and an opportunity to receive shares of any profits earned by the company. With profit sharing, employees receive payment in addition to their regular salary when the company shows a profit increase. Profit sharing encourages employees to build long-term loyalty and work hard for the company, since they share directly in the profits.

Salary Plus Commission. **Salary plus commission** is an incentive used by some retailers or departments in which employees are given a base salary plus an additional percent based on sales generated. Salary plus commission guarantees a minimum level of income and also allows the salesperson to increase his or her earnings on the basis of sales performance. Macy's department store uses this sales incentive to stabilize earnings for its sales associates and cultivate a better-informed team of sales personnel ("Department Stores," 1996). Nordstrom has long used this incentive as a way to encourage salespeople to work as a team as compared with straight commission, which encourages competition and can result in poor customer service.

Human resources expert Wilfred Roy has found that a good reward system should be based on the following characteristics:

- It should be a reflection of the corporate culture of the firm. In the case of Nordstrom, the company culture stands behind the salesperson and will support satisfying the customer, sometimes even at a substantial cost.
- It should take a linear direction from the sales floor up so that everyone has the same focus.
- It should be at least 20 percent of the base pay to change behavior.
- It should have safeguards to prevent windfalls from events extraneous to efforts. ("Department Stores," 1996).

But even the best trained and most motivated sales associate will occasionally come into contact with a difficult customer. We discuss some of the typical customer types in the next section.

○ HANDLING VARIOUS CUSTOMER TYPES

The selling environment is dynamic and ever changing. No two customers are the same, and a salesperson must be ready for any situation, routine or unusual, that may occur. Customers may be anxious to buy and pleasant to the sales associate or unfriendly toward the sales associate and not satisfied with any solution offered. A sales associate must be persistent and attempt to fulfill the needs and wants of each customer, using the positive energy while brushing off the negative stigma of the previous customer.

Every customer is different and should be treated as such. However, certain types of behavior among customers become recognizable to salespeople once they have familiarized themselves with the buying population.

Eccentric Shopper

The eccentric shopper compulsively shops, but never buys. Eccentric shoppers visit retail stores regularly and become known to the sales associates, who learn quickly that the eccentric shopper is not likely to make a purchase. They will find some excuse to put off the purchase, sometimes waiting until the sales associate has written up the sale. Sales associates should acknowledge the eccentric shopper and show him or her a few pieces and then politely move to the next customer where a sale is more likely to occur.

Browser

The browser is a shopper who will peruse merchandise in a leisurely and casual way. Browsers may be considered bothersome or beneficial, contingent upon their inclination to buy. A nonbuying browser may just be killing time with no intention of making a purchase. However, a browser may enjoy shopping and spending money, and thus is capable of making a purchase if the merchandise is appealing. The disinterested browser will have a detached attitude recognizable by the sales associate. A sales associate should be watchful to identify the potentially interested browser and provide enticing merchandise.

Bargain Hunter

The bargain hunter can be identified as wanting the best quality for the least amount of money. They show up for sales, but they also shop during nonsale periods looking for value investments. Bargain hunters enjoy saving money as a matter of principle and will not be influenced to purchase items they do not believe are worth the price. Some bargain hunters complain about pricing even after discounts or expect the discounted good to be of the same quality standards as the full-priced merchandise. Because bargain hunters are potential purchasers, sales associates should show them merchandise, pointing out details but refusing to argue or negotiate about price, quality, or other selection factors.

Serious Shopper

The serious shopper wants or needs a specific item and will not be influenced by alternatives. A sales associate should listen carefully to the serious shopper to determine what available items might satisfy his or her needs. A serious shopper who leaves a store without making a purchase is more likely to return to the store if the sales associate has been honest in explaining that the store does not have what the customer wants at the moment and has suggested an acceptable alternative.

Pressured Shopper

The pressured shopper is always in a hurry and pressured to make an immediate purchase. Because time is limited, pressured shoppers are often irritable, distracted, and indecisive in their purchasing decisions. The pressured shopper often expects the sales associate to solve his or her purchasing dilemma with little information or time spent evaluating comparative products. Pressured shoppers may need a gift for a birthday or anniversary; others may need items for a vacation or special occasion. A mindful sales associate can lead pressured shoppers to the correct department, then show merchandise in a rapid manner to help them make a decision.

──o Measuring Personal Selling Effectiveness

From the sales associate on the retail sales floor to the sales manager of a large manufacturing company, it is important to assess the performance of the sales force. The most important tool for evaluating performance is a **performance appraisal system.** An effective appraisal system starts with goal setting, with participation from the salesperson and his or her supervisor. Realistic and measurable goals are set for a specific time period. Not every member of the sales team should have exactly the same goals, but comparative standards of performance within the organization should be considered.

Sales goals are expressed in quantitative terms of sales volume, sales expense, or number of customers. For example, a sales goal might state, *the employee will maintain minimum sales of $95 per hour.* In addition to the quantitative goals, most performance appraisal systems include some qualitative measures. Although these characteristics are subjective in nature, they contribute to the overall success of a sales department. Such characteristics rate the individual on attitude and ability to work well with other employees and customers. Rating scales for the quantitative and qualitative contributions are normally ranked on a three-to-five-point scale from a low of *(U) unsatisfactory or fails to meet expectations,* to a high of *(O) outstanding or has far exceeded expectations.* Figure 17.9 illustrates a performance appraisal report.

Performance appraisal systems are set for a specific period of time, ranging from six months to a year. The sales or department manager should have a good idea of all salespersons within his or her supervision. If there is a problem with a member of the sales team, the manager should not wait until the formal review to implement corrective action. Remedial action and emphasis on *what is expected* should take place when performance is substandard. Rewards and wage increases result when a performance is rated positively.

Personal selling is one-on-one communication between a manufacturer or retailer, and a customer. Although often overlooked as a promotion technique, personal selling is an important tool in communicating a sponsor's message to a customer. Using the elements of the buying and selling process—attention, interest, desire, action, and satisfaction—a sales associate has the opportunity to share a firm's message with the customer and complete a sale through personal communication. Box 17.2 details the fine art of selling.

Good salesmanship does not just happen. It takes dedication from both the company and the salesperson to do a good job. Marketers must combine personal selling with all other elements of the promotion mix to encourage positive, direct interaction between the customer and the seller and to create a homogeneous image of the firm. Sales personnel can have the greatest influence on consumers by interacting in a polished and professional manner. A firm has no greater asset than an effective sales associate.

FIGURE 17.9 Sample sales
performance appraisal form.

Performance Appraisal/Sales Associate

Name:

Branch Location:

Review Period: From   **To**

Wage:

(O) Outstanding. Performance **Far Exceeds** requirements of position and objectives. This level is recognized as excellent and unique in contribution and is rarely achieved.

(CE) Consistently Exceeds. Performance **Consistently Exceeds** requirements of position and objectives.

(E) Exceeds. Performance **Sometimes Exceeds** requirements of position and objectives.

(M) Meets. Performance (on average) **Meets** requirements of position and objectives.

(B) Below Requirements. Performance **Does Not Fully Meet** or consistently maintain requirements of position and objectives. **Improvement Plan Required.**

(U) Unsatisfactory. Performance **Fails to Meet** requirements of the position and objectives and does not meet improvement criteria.

Sales Performance
Actual Sales per Hour:
Selling Center Sales per Hour:
Rating (based upon comparison of actual to selling center sales per hour):
Comments:

Selling Skills (includes approaching guests, determining needs, presenting merchandise, answering questions, using suggestion selling and closing techniques, providing product knowledge, developing clientele relationships)
Comments:

Sales Preparation (includes merchandise presentation, stockwork, housekeeping, etc.)
Comments:

Systems and Procedures (includes POS, exchanges, returns, accuracy of transactions)
Comments:

Shortage Awareness and Prevention (includes price changes, claims, transfers, inventory control, merchandise security):
Comments:

Professional Conduct (includes attendance, punctuality, dress and appearance, work relationships):

Comments:

Summary of Performance:	O	CE	E	M	B	U
Sales Performance	O	CE	E	M	B	U
Selling Skills	O	CE	E	M	B	U
Sales Preparation	O	CE	E	M	B	U
Systems and Procedures	O	CE	E	M	B	U
Shortage Awareness and Prevention	O	CE	E	M	B	U
Professional Conduct	O	CE	E	M	B	U

Strengths:

Improvement Opportunities:

Evaluator's Comments:

Evaluator Signature _____ Date _____

Employee Signature _____ Date _____

FIGURE 17.9 (*Continued*)

○ BOX 17.2

The Fine Art of Selling

In retail, there are sales associates and then there are sales associates. Confusing them would be like mistaking canned tuna for sushi grade.

The first group, according to the U.S. Department of Labor, Bureau of Labor Statistics, earned $8.47 an hour in department stores . . . or less than $18,000 a year. Members of the second group, catering to affluent big spenders, routinely sell $1 million or more worth of luxury goods in designer boutiques and specialty stores for an income of at least $70,000. A handful of elite salespeople sell $5 million a year, earning $300,000 to $350,000 annually.

"It's not unheard of to have associates that sell in the $1 million or $2 million range," said Michael Celestino, executive vice president of store operations at Barneys New York. "As

good as they are, they know they can continue to have more opportunities to build more relationships, sell more and earn more money."

Base salaries at designer stores are $10 to $15 an hour and commissions usually start at 3 percent, said a former retail executive who asked not to be identified. Giorgio Armani, for example, uses a tiered commission system—associates receive 2.5 percent on the first $25,000 worth of sales and 5 percent thereafter.

It's not unusual for different product categories to command different commissions. Gucci, which has a developed accessories business, pays 3 percent commission for sales in that area, but 6 percent in the less developed ready-to-wear sector. Armani, on the other hand, wants to encourage sales of accessories, a business it hopes to grow, so the company offers employees 6 percent commission, while rtw garners 3 percent.

"There is definitely big money to be earned," said Roberto Lorenzini, president and chief operating officer of Versace USA's retail division. "Usually the best associates sell more than $1 million or $2 million a year. An associate can earn from $150,000 to $250,000. The highest I've heard of in the industry is an associate earning $500,000. It depends on the brand and how the commission is structured, but it's easily in the six figures."

Bob Mitchell, co-president of Mitchells, in Westport, Conn., and Richards in Greenwich, Conn., said he employs 30 associates who sell more than $1 million a year, 10 of them selling over $2 million and three selling over $3 million. The two stores specialize in designer and contemporary merchandise.

The elite sales associate, whose so-called black books, or customer lists, are highly valuable, are coveted by the competition and closely guarded by their employers. There's no school to prepare for a career in the sales stratosphere where the air is thin, but some retailers think they've found a formula for hiring productive associates.

"We've developed a sales associate selection tool based on dozens and dozens of interviews with our very top sales associates," Ginger Reeder, vice president of corporate communications at Neiman Marcus. "We believe we've isolated the characteristics those people share. We use the tool, which includes a written test, during the initial hiring process and see how they score."

Reeder cited some common characteristics, such as enthusiasm, optimism, and friendliness, although she declined to discuss more subtle traits. After a candidate passes the written test, he or she is subject to one-on-one interviews. At Neiman's, a first-year sales associate receives 150 hours of training, everything from product information sessions with vendors to how to write thank-you notes.

"In the last six or seven years, everybody has been looking for the associate with the great book," said a former retail executive, who asked not to be identified. "Ten years ago, I could go into the coffee shop and meet a waitress and say, 'She has such a great personality, let's recruit her and train her.' Now companies want results from Day One."

Maria Fei, vice president of Louis Boston, said the store's personality attracts offbeat employees. "We believe style is something they'll grow into," she said. "They have to have an energetic and charming personality. It takes a really special person to sell, someone who's happy and has a way of speaking that makes you listen. Our candidates come from all walks of life. A lot come here right out of school and stay. We love artistic people and people majoring in art because the store is artistic and eclectic."

At Barneys New York, the clothes do make the sales associate. While some stores place a stronger emphasis on a candidate's outlook than outfit, Celestino said, "The individual needs to project an appropriate fashion point of view. It's important for the person to have a true passion for the business. Because they do big business, it's good for them to have a strong business acumen. They need to be entrepreneurial. When they join us, they don't necessarily have to have our fashion point of view, but they have to adapt."

Versace's sales associates must have champagne taste. An understanding and appreciation of their client's lifestyles is key. Lorenzini said associates should be sophisticated, well groomed and well educated. "They need to speak professionally, in a soft way that's not too distant or too friendly. They need to have a lot of common knowledge and refinement. They need to know where their customers go on vacation and what parties they attend. Some clients fly the associates to their homes. They should know how this lifestyle and environment works."

"I don't go out to recruit million-dollar sales associates," said Jeffrey Kalinsky, founder of Jeffrey New York. "I don't generally recruit from my competitors. If somebody comes to us with experience working at a great store, that's great and we got lucky. We also love to hire people who've shown they'll stick with a store even if it's not a luxury store. We can teach them our way of customer service and selling. Having a passion for fashion isn't the only reason a person can be great. What about a person with a passion for people, or a single mom with two kids at home who's motivated to earn money?"

A former executive at a European design house said the sales floor of a luxury brand, while elegant and sophisticated, is often not as genteel behind the scenes. Sales associates don't always behave collegially when $10,000 evening gowns and $4,000 handbags are at stake.

"Sales associates try to get away with things," the former European executive said. "They don't have autonomy. They'll try to take the merchandise that's on hold for another sales associate's client because they need it. There are a lot of people who have $1 million books that get recruited from store to store. As you go up, it's harder to give up a secure environment. Anyway, they're not that heavily recruited because they're prima donnas."

She said the highest-earning associates receive a bonus and participate in merit programs in which they can win prizes. If the store achieves its goals, they earn an extra 1 percent commission. "The companies want to keep them happy, but then it gets out of control," she said. "They get to go to the collections and they get trips to Italy. Uniforms are now the big thing. Associates are given company-mandated uniforms, but if they're part of the merit program, they can select something from the collection."

Lorenzini doesn't believe in sales incentives. "The best incentive we can give them is to really make them feel like they are part of the brand," he said. "That will really retain them. If you offer an incentive once in a while, the associate will always wait for them. We don't want the associates to look for contests. We want them to be part of the team and work together."

Louis Boston's associates' compensation isn't based on commission, which eliminates some of the competitive behavior, Fei said.

"It's teamwork and they get along well," she said. "It's not that cutthroat kind of business. We pay them well. It's about their performance. They each have a section of the store that they're in charge of. Debi [Greenberg, owner] is good at making them feel that they have ownership of the store and ownership of their shops. Knowing that the team needs you makes for a congenial and happy environment."

Every designer has produced a less than stellar collection at one time or another, which should be just a blip for the sales force, Lorenzini said. "The good associate can find the best prices for the customer," he said. "They know it's going to be temporary. Besides, the best associates would never focus

on one season. Without a medium- to long-range view, you can't develop the clientele. You need time. It's part of the game for each brand."

It's not just job security that makes it difficult for associates to jump to another designer firm. Star salespeople have a clientele that's built upon the brand they're selling. An associate working for a designer with an older customer base would have trouble taking his or her book to a more forward company.

"Finding great salespeople is a challenge," Barneys' Celestino said. "They could come from a competitor or from another industry with similar skill sets. We have hired people from the hotel industry, the financial industry, and the art world."

Several retailers, including Saks Fifth Avenue and Holt Renfrew, have turned for insight to the Four Seasons Hotels and Resorts, which has a reputation for superior service.

"You can't teach people to be innately friendly and genuine and service-oriented," said Elizabeth Pizzinato, a vice president at the Four Seasons. "When you have an unhappy customer standing in front of you, that's when the rubber hits the roof. People are hired for attitude first."

Source: Edelson, S. & Moin, D. (2006, August 7).The fine art of selling. *Women's Wear Daily*, p. 24.

summary

- The salesperson represents the entire organization to a customer and is responsible for building customer loyalty and creating customer satisfaction.
- Personal selling involves direct interaction between salesperson and customer, initiated by either party, and finished at the completion of the sale.
- Personal shoppers are available at some retail establishments to shop with or for customers.
- Direct sellers, such as image consultants, offer personal service about beauty and fashion on an individual basis.
- All forms of selling include a buying and selling process: (1) getting the attention of the consumer, (2) creating interest, (3) forming desire, (4) stimulating action, and (5) creating customer satisfaction.
- Elements of a sale include: (1) sales approach, (2) merchandise presentation, (3) handling objections, and (4) closing the sale.
- Personal selling is used at both retail and wholesale levels.
- Qualities of a successful salesperson include excellent personal appearance and grooming, along with knowledge of the merchandise, the retail policies, and the customer.
- Employees are motivated to do a good job through incentive programs such as spiffs, sales contests, or salary enhancements, which include special bonuses, merit pay, profit sharing, and salary plus commission.
- Understanding customer types, such as eccentric shoppers, browsers, bargain hunters, serious shoppers, and pressured shoppers, can aid the salesperson in generating sales.

key terms

bonus	merchandise approach	sales contests
buying signal	merit pay	salesmanship
customer directories	performance appraisal	selling process
greeting approach	system	soft sell
hard sell	personal shoppers	specialty goods
image consultants	profit sharing	spiffs
manufacturer's sales	salary enhancements	suggestion selling
representative	salary plus commission	trading up

questions for discussion

1. What is the importance of personal selling as a promotion strategy?
2. Explain the AIDA model. What fifth element have researchers added to the mode, and why is this element important?
3. What are the elements of a sale?
4. What should a sales associate do after a sale is complete?
5. Discuss positive and negative attributes of sales associates. What solutions can you suggest for the negative attributes that were discussed?
6. What kinds of information should sales associates give and receive from management? Give examples.
7. What are some examples of good incentive programs you have participated in?

additional resources

Anderson, R. E., Dubinsky, A. J., & Mehta, R. (2007). *Personal selling: Building customer relationships and partnerships.* Boston: Houghton Mifflin.

Brooks, W. T. (2004). *The new science of selling and persuasion: How smart companies and great sales people sell.* Hoboken, NJ: Wiley & Sons.

Sherman, G. J. & Perlman, S. (2006). *The real world guide to fashion selling and management.* New York: Fairchild Books.

references

Belch, G. E., & Belch, M. A. (2007). *Advertising and promotion: An integrated marketing communications perspective* (7th ed.). New York: McGraw-Hill Irwin.

Department stores debate sales commission system. (1996, November). *Stores, 37–38.*

Emerson, K. (1995, August 8). How to win customers and influence sales associates. *Women's Wear Daily*, p.38.

Kahle, D. (1997, April 1). Your most powerful sales tool. *American Salesman,* 42, (4), 16.

Marcus, S. (1974). *Minding the store.* New York: Signet.

Miller, C. (1996). U. S. techniques not best for Chinese sales reps. *Marketing News*, p.1.

National Retail Federation, (n.d.). *Retail Skills Centers.* Retrieved July 10, 2006, from http://www.nrf.org

Schmidt, M. (1996, April). Improving sales associate selection with structured interviews. *Stores,* RRI-3.

Schneiderman, I. (1998, July 15). The need for speed at the register. *Women's Wear Daily*, p. 4.

Stewart-Allen, A. (1996, November 18). Customer care. *Marketing News*, p.17.

Glossary

Account management division   Division within an agency that works with the client, interpreting the client's needs to agency personnel.

Action advertising   Sponsored messages that attempt to cause the reader or viewer to take immediate action based on the promotion.

Adjacencies   Radio commercials sold at a premium rate, to run just before or after a program.

Administration   Management of personnel and programs based on marketing plans and budgets.

Advertising   Any nonpersonal message, paid for, placed in the mass media, and controlled by the sponsoring organization.

Advertising agencies   Outside organizations hired to assist a company in achieving promotional goals.

Advertising appeal   Approach advertiser chooses to attract the attention of the consumer and motivate them to take action.

Advertising calendar   Guide that identifies when, where, and what items will be advertised.

Advertising campaign   Series of multiple messages, focused on a central theme or concept, presented in a variety of media.

Advertising department   Department responsible for planning, creating, placing the advertising in the media, and evaluating the effectiveness of ads.

Advertising research   Investigation of all elements of advertising including message, media, and evaluation.

Affiliates   Regional television stations.

Age cohorts   Consumers of the same age who have grown up with similar experiences.

All-one-can-afford   Budgeting method in which the portion of the operational budget allocated to promotional activities is the amount the firm can financially manage to spend.

Alternative media   See support media.

Amplification   Information that fills out the rest of the story following the lead.

Angled front window   Store window that is recessed from the sidewalk, which provides more exposure to display space.

Animation   Production technique that uses illustrated figures, such as cartoon characters or puppets, inanimate objects that come to life.

Anniversary celebration   Occurrences used by companies to bring attention to their longevity in the community.

Arbitrary allocation   Budgeting method in which the budget is determined by management solely on the basis of executive judgment.

Arcade front window   Spacious display space with a variety of configurations, normally found in downtown shopping districts.

Art   System of skills, used in a creative manner, to make things of beauty.

Assignment editor   Individual who has control over the flow of information and assignments and, as such, is probably the best connection at a broadcast news outlet.

Assistant editor   Individual who is responsible for reading all press releases submitted to the organization and reporting the newsworthy pieces to the more senior editors.

Associate editor   Reporters who are assigned to cover certain topics and events.

Associate producer   Specialists in particular subjects working for a producer.

Asymmetrical balance   Items have equal weight on both sides but are not mirror images.

Audit   Formal report of activities, which may be performed internally or externally.

Awareness advertising   Sponsored messages that attempt to build the image of a product or familiarity with the product's name and package.

Background   Foundation, real or implied, where the display is built. A back wall can serve as the base for a background.

Backgrounder   Expanded narrative of the history, mission, goals, and purpose of an organization or activity, included in a media kit.

Balance   Equal distribution of weight through a composition.

Bank of windows   Store with several windows at the front of the building.

Banner ad   Sponsored advertisement that appears on websites by third-party vendors.

Basic merchandise   Functional goods that change infrequently and are generally considered necessities.

Beat story   Feature story written from the point of view of a specific section or column of a newspaper.

Behavioristic segmentation   Method of segmenting markets based on consumer usage, loyalty, or buying responses to a product or service.

Benefit segmentation   Dividing the market based on consumer needs or problems and the benefits they will derive from buying products.

Bias   Research procedure has influenced or prejudiced results because of problems with research methodology design.

Biography   Historical report about people involved with a project, included in a media kit.

Bleed pages   Technical feature of a magazine advertisement that allows the dark or colored background to extend to the edge of the page.

Blinking/bunching   Radio advertising approach scheduling activity over a short period, involving one week on, one week off, and so forth.

Blog   Allows the creator of online content to present a personal view on public information to anyone willing to look at the website.

Body copy   Additional copy created to support and reinforce the headline.

Bonus   Sum of money or the equivalent given to an employee in addition to the employee's usual compensation.

Bonus pack   Extra amounts of a product, given in addition to what is expected.

Bottom-up approaches   Budgeting methods that consider the firm's goals and objectives and assign a portion of the budget to meet those objectives.

Bottom-up planning   Flow of information from managers to upper management.

Bounce-back coupon   Coupon that is good for redemption of the same product.

Branch operations division   Division within a firm that supervises the multistore operations in various regions or districts.

Brand   Any name, trademark, logo, or visual symbol that identifies a product or group of products by a specific manufacturer or identifies a specific retailer and helps to differentiate the product(s) or retailer(s) from competitors.

Broadsheet   Large standard size newspaper format six columns wide.

Brokered list   Customer inventories offered for sale or rent through negotiation of a contract in return for a fee or commission to a list broker.

Budgeting   Determining how much to spend on promotion activities in relationship to anticipated income.

Bursting   Radio advertising scheduling pattern where heavy advertising is concentrated over a short period, placing one week's advertising within a four-day period.

Business plan   Defines the broadest decisions of an organization.

Business-to-business market   Exchange of goods and services between businesses.

Buying allowance   Price reduction on merchandise purchased during a limited time period.

Buying benefit   Performance advantages, interpreted by the consumer, as a result of the selling point.

Buying signal   Customer will often signify that he or she is ready to close the sale with a statement or action.

Buying/selling process   Method used by a salesperson to encourage a customer to reach a buying decision about a product or service.

Cable television   Form of television where signals are carried by wire rather than airways.

Camera ready   Paste-up ready to go to the printer.

Cash wrap   Counter where transactions, such as ringing up the sale and handing over merchandise, take place.

Catalog   Published list of articles for sale, usually including descriptive information or illustrations.

Category week   Occurrences that feature a merchandise category or brand; see *vendor week*.

Celebrity appearance   Physical presence of a well-known individual from inside or outside the fashion industry who promotes a new product or designer line.

Channels   Methods by which the message is translated.

Classic   Trend that endures over a long period of time undergoing only minor changes as it progresses through the product life cycle.

Classified advertisement   Sponsored message that contains only copy.

Clients   Persons seeking recognition for their products or services.

Clipping service   Service that cuts out competitors' advertisements from local or national media to track spending.

Closed-back window   Store windows with completely contained display spaces.

Co-branding   Cooperative effort in which a card issuer that wants to increase volume combines with a consumer company to develop a credit card.

Code of ethics   Procedure of conduct the company intends to follow and expects from its employees, clients, vendors, and/or customers.

Color   Property of reflecting light in a visible wavelength resulting in a visible color spectrum.

Color story   Collection of fashion, staple, warm, cool, neutral, and dark colors, coordinated for the upcoming season, different from the last season.

Color wheel   Chart that organized color relationships according to hue, value, and intensity.

Co-marketing   Creation of cooperative efforts where the manufacturer and retailer join forces to increase the revenue and profits for both parties.

Commentary   Oral delivery of information used to identify trends of the season.

Commentator   Individual who is responsible for commentary.

Commercial advertising   Sponsored messages directed toward the profit-making sector.

Commission   Percentage of money given to an agent who assists in a business transaction.

Communication   A transmission or exchange of information and/or messages.

Communication brief   See *creative strategy.*

Communication objective   Specific communication effect such as creating awareness or developing favorable attitudes as opposed to marketing objectives.

Competitive parity   Budgeting method in which the amount of money that a competitor spends on promotion is used as a guide to set budgets.

Complementary colors   Colors positioned on opposite sides of the color wheel.

Concentrated strategy   Marketing strategy that offers the promotional mix to the target segment with the greatest potential for success regardless of size.

Consumer advertising   Sponsored messages directed toward the ultimate user of the product, service, or idea.

Consumer behavior   Study of consumer decision-making processes, as they acquire, consume, and dispose of goods and services.

Consumer jury   Group of 50 to 100 target customers who are interviewed individually or in small groups to evaluate promotional effectiveness.

Consumer market   People who will buy and use merchandise or services.

Consumer research   The investigation of people who want a product or service in terms of their characteristics motives, attitudes, and interests.

Consumer show   Fashion show produced by the retailer to sell ideas and merchandise to the buying public.

Consumerism   Set of activities monitored by government, businesses, and independent organizations designed to protect the rights of consumers.

Consumption   Process of acquiring, using, and discarding products.

Content sponsorship   Sponsor provides advertising dollars in return for name association and provides content on a website.

Contests   Promotions in which consumers compete for a prize based on skill and ability.

Continuity   Scheduling method using a steady placement of advertisements over a designated period of time.

Contract   Legal agreement establishing a fee for limited services based upon specific activities.

Contrast   Using a difference as a presentation point.

Control ads   Sponsored messages that have been extensively evaluated over a period of time and to provide a basis to compare the effectiveness of test ads.

Cool colors   Colors projecting a sensation of calmness; blue, green, and violet.

Cooperative advertising   Agreement in which a manufacturer works with the retailer to develop an ad and shares in the cost of running that advertisement.

Coordination   Balancing all activities and personnel to make sure functional areas are working toward the same goals and objectives.

Copy   Verbal component of a print advertisement.

Copy platform   See *creative strategy.*

Copyright   Legal right granted to an author, a composer, a playwright, a publisher, or a distributor to exclusive publication, production, sale, or distribution of a literary, musical, dramatic, or artistic work.

Corner front window   Store window is located where the window faces two streets that are perpendicular to each other; as a result, it can be viewed from either street.

Corporate advertising   See *institutional advertising.*

Co-sponsored   Event expenses are shared by two or more organizations.

Cost-plus agreement   Pay rate based upon cost of the work plus an agreed-on profit margin, normally a percentage of total costs.

Coupons   Printed forms or vouchers that entitle the bearer to certain benefits, such as a cash refund or a gift when redeemed.

Cover letter   Document that identifies the purpose and content of a media kit.

Cover position   First page, the inside back cover, and the back cover sold at a premium advertising rate.

Coverage   Potential audience that might receive the message through a media outlet.

Covered publicity   Situations of interest to the general public written as a publicity release.

Created audience   Group that is established after the show is planned as a result of publicity and advertising.

Created publicity   Situations that may by themselves have little news value are made newsworthy by creating a special event around the situation.

Creation Process of development and implementation of a unique and inventive promotion program.

Creative boutique An agency that provides only creative services, such as innovative layout, logo, or graphic design.

Creative brief See *creative strategy*.

Creative execution Way in which an advertising appeal is presented and turned into an advertising message.

Creative services division Division of a full service agency responsible for the creation and the execution of the advertisements.

Creative strategy Outcome of the promotion plan explaining consumer insight and summarizing the basic strategy decisions.

Creativity Quality manifested in individuals that enables them to generate clever or imaginative approaches to new solutions to problems.

Cross-ruff coupon Coupon good for redemption of a different product manufactured by the same producer.

Cross-selling The sale of additional products and services to the same customer.

Cube Box style fixtures used for consumer self-selection of merchandise.

Culture Set of socially acquired behavior patterns of a particular society of people.

Cumulative audience Total number of different people who are exposed to a schedule of commercials.

Customer directories Directory created and used by sales associates to record customer preferences and purchases for future sales opportunities.

Data mining In-depth analysis of data in database to gain insights about customers, products, and vendors.

Data warehousing Locating multiple databases within a firm in one location and allowing accessibility to employees at any location.

Database Collection of data arranged for ease and speed of search and retrieval.

Dayparts Television time periods used in buying and selling advertisements.

Decode Process by which a receiver transforms a message back into thought.

Decorative props Items used to establish a mood or theme for the merchandise, including such things as baskets, plants, flags, banners, and musical instruments.

Decorative roles A man, woman, or child is placed in an advertisement with no purpose other than to look attractive.

Deferred billing Opportunity for the consumer to postpone or delay payment of a purchase.

Demographic segmentation Dividing the market using statistical characteristics of the population.

Demographics Statistics used to study a population.

Demonstration Advertising execution showing the consumer how to use a product.

Deprived consumer Value-oriented consumers who purchase during the regression stage of the fashion cycle.

Descriptive research See *quantitative research*.

Design division Division headed by a designer and responsible for designing and producing a minimum of four collections or lines of garments each year.

Design elements Core components of design: color, shape, texture, and line.

Design principles Standards for visually organizing all design elements into a unified composition.

Designated market areas (DMAs) 210 local markets used by Nielsen Media Research to measure viewing audiences for broadcast media.

Development Public relations tool used to provide fund-raising and membership drive support to nonprofit organizations.

Differentiated strategy A marketing strategy that offers a different promotion mix to two or more select target markets.

Digital video effects units Production units that are able to manipulate graphics, music, and sound.

Diminishing returns curve Concave-downward shape that demonstrates that advertising expenditures will increase sales to a point, then the benefits of additional advertising expenses will diminish.

Direct mail All direct response communications delivered through the mail.

Direct marketing Process by which organizations communicate directly with target customers to generate a response or transaction.

Direct marketing agencies Agencies that provide services necessary to conduct direct marketing activities including research, database management, creative assistance, direct mail, media services, and production capabilities.

Direct Marketing Association (DMA)

Direct premium Gifts attached to or placed inside the promoted item and available immediately to the consumer upon purchase.

Direct sellers Companies that sell directly to the consumer.

Direct-response media Mail, telephone, magazines, the Internet, radio, or television messages aimed directly to the target consumer.

Discretionary income Personal income available after taxes and necessities have been paid for.

Display advertisement Sponsored message that features slightly larger type sizes and may include photos, artistic borders, white space, and possibly color.

Disposable income   Personal income available after taxes.

Domain names   Unique Internet names assigned on a first-come, first-served basis by a company called InterNIC.

Dramatization   Advertising execution that focuses on telling a story about the product or brand.

Dressers   Preparation assistants for the models.

Dressing area   Place where models get ready before and change during the show.

Drive time   Period when radio listenership is the highest, usually between 6:00 A.M. and 9:00 A.M. and 4:00 P.M. and 7:00 P.M.

Early majority   Earlier adopters who purchase during acceleration of the fashion cycle.

E-commerce   Selling of goods to the consumer via an interactive computer network.

Editor   Person responsible for maintaining the editorial focus for a news organization.

Editorial content   Feature stories and fashion spreads controlled by the magazine editors, staff writers, and photographers.

Editorial credit   Acknowledgment given to manufacturers and retailers within fashion articles.

Editor-in-chief   Person in charge of all aspects of reporting the news.

Emotional appeal   Appeal that spotlights a consumer's psychological or sociological need for a product.

Emphasis   Giving certain features in a composition more importance than other features.

Encoding   Combination of words or symbols to be presented orally or in written/visual form by the sender.

Ethics   Rules or standards governing the conduct of a person or the members of a profession.

Ethnicity   Description of a group bound together by ties of cultural homogeneity often based around national origins.

Evaluation   Process of judging the worth or value of any activity.

Event bonus   Premium paid above the fixed fee, if the attendance goal of the event is exceeded.

Event diary   A tool used by event producers to chronicle the planning, budget, implementation and follow-up processes of the event.

Exchange   Ambition and interest to give up something in replacement for something else.

Exclusive sponsor   Title sponsor that pays a premium to have its name on the title of an event.

Execution   Implementation of the promotional project or activity after planning has been completed.

Executive summary   A brief summary of the key elements of a written document.

Exhibit booth   Small exhibit spaces with temporary walls and fixtures used by manufacturers to sell their products at trade shows.

Experimental research   Research used in new product development consisting of laboratory testing in which a cause-and-effect relationship is sought.

Exploratory research   See qualitative research.

Exterior display   Outside appearance of the storefront, also known as facade display.

External audit   Document to evaluate an organization from consultants or clients outside of the organization.

External information   Material and facts from outside sources, often beyond the control of the firm including knowledge about the economic, social, political, technological, and competitive environments in which the firm operates.

Fact sheet   Detailed glossary of significant facts contained in the press kit.

Factor   Finance company that buys a manufacturer's accounts receivables.

Fad   Very short-lived trend.

Fashion count   Research method used to survey what people are currently wearing.

Fashion cycle

Fashion department   Department involved in developing the fashion image for the company.

Fashion director   Individual responsible for fashion direction and leadership.

Fashion forecaster   Professionals who work for fashion forecasting services or the forecasting division within retail, manufacturing, or advertising firms.

Fashion forecasting   Specifically looking at fashion trends and attempting to predict what consumers will want to wear during the upcoming season.

Fashion innovators   Early adopters who will adopt a trend at the very earliest opportunity.

Fashion lagger   Earlier adopters within the regression stage of the fashion cycle.

Fashion leader   Later adopters who will accept the trend as it begins to rise in popularity.

Fashion merchandise   Aesthetically appealing products that change frequently and are generally considered non-necessities.

Fashion report   Business document that supports the oral presentations and storyboards or website presentation of a fashion forecast.

Fashion show   Presentation of apparel, accessories, and other products to enhance personal attractiveness on live models to an audience.

Fashion show calendar   Guide that identifies locations, themes, dates, and times for planned fashion shows used by fashion and sales staffs to plan and perform the various steps in fashion show production.

Fashion show diary   Document chronicling all of the planning, budgeting, and implementation processes for a fashion show.

Fashion show director   Key person in fashion show production responsible for all aspects of the show.

Fashion show producer   Agency employee with responsibilities similar to fashion show director.

Fashion show production agencies   Agencies that provide services necessary to present fashion shows.

Fashion theme calendar   Guide that indicates fashion trends and creative interpretations of basic categories.

Fashion trend   Visible direction in which fashion is moving such as a color, a fabric, or a style characteristic apparent for the coming season.

Fashion trend portfolio   Series of visual boards, slides, videos, or kits, projecting major trends in silhouettes, fabrics, colors, patterns, accessory treatments, catchphrases, and theme ideas.

Feature story   A prominent or lead article that is original and descriptive.

Federal Trade Commission Act   Legislation responsible for controlling and regulating antitrust and consumer protection laws.

Fee-commission combination   Fee system in which media commissions are credited against a fee.

Feedback   Receiver's response to a sender.

Financial control division   Division of an organization responsible for administering the budget and handling all of the financial functions, such as payroll, accounts receivable, accounts payable, and inventory control.

Fixed-fee rate   Basic monthly rate charged by an agency for all its services.

Fixture   Wide variety of furniture and equipment to hold and display merchandise.

Flighting   Scheduling method using periods with moderate to heavy exposure followed by a hiatus or lapse prior to restarting the advertising schedule.

Floor plan   Scale drawings of the walls, fixtures, and other architectural elements of a selling space.

Focus group   Carefully planned discussions designed to obtain perceptions of a defined area of interest in a nonthreatening environment.

Font   Complete range of capitals, small capitals, lowercase letters, numerals, and punctuation marks for a particular typeface and size.

Forecaster   Nonspecific title given to any individual within an organization who is responsible for trend identification and image.

Forecasting   Activity of anticipating what will happen next.

Formal balance   See *symmetrical balance.*

Formal runway show   Fashion shows that present merchandise as a parade with the audience seated at the perimeter of the runway.

Frequency   Number of times the receiver is exposed to the media outlet within a specified period of time.

Frequent-buying club   See *reward program.*

Full-service agency   Firm that offers a full range of marketing, communications, and promotional services.

Functional prop   Physical supports, such as mannequins and furniture, used to hold merchandise.

Fur Products Labeling Act   Legislation (1951) that governs fur product labeling to specify, among other things, the English name of the animal from which the fur was taken.

Futurists   Professionals who make long-range forecasts for many industries.

Gallery exhibit   A presentation of fashion items in an artistic setting at a gallery.

Gatefold   Special kind of insert, created by extra-long paper with the sides folded into the center to match the size of the other pages.

Gender   Sexual identity of an individual.

Geographic segmentation   Strategy based on geographic breakdowns such as regions, metropolitan statistical area (MSA) size, density of population, and climate.

Gift-with-purchase   Incentive program in which consumers are offered a special gift if they buy merchandise over a certain dollar amount.

Global advertising   Sponsored messages available throughout the world.

Global brand   Brands broadly distributed worldwide.

Global marketing   International marketing activities.

Globalization   Integration of international trade and foreign investment resulting in worldwide trade of merchandise and resources.

Glocalization   Combination of global branding practices and localized marketing.

Goals   End results that a business wants to achieve usually in the long term.

Greeting approach   Pleasant salutation expressing good wishes to the individual.

Gross domestic product (GDP)   Amount of goods and services produced by a country in one year.

Gross ratings points (GRPs)   Sum of all ratings delivered by a commercial schedule.

Guaranteed audience   Group that is established before the show is planned, and is made up of individuals who will attend regardless of the fashions shown.

Halftone illustration   Drawings using shades or tones created by watercolor, chalk, pencil, markers, or other art medium to illustrate the image with tonal qualities.

Hard sell   Sales approach that forces customers to buy a product they really do not want.

Harmony   Using all design components to make a coordinated composition.

Haute couture   French word that refers to high sewing or dressmaking, results in made-to-measure clothing for a specific customer.

Headline   Boldest statement of an advertisement.

Hierarchy of needs theory   Motivation theory based on five levels of needs: basic physiological, safety and security, love and belonging, esteem, self-actualization.

Homeshopping   Television networks that broadcast direct-response programs in a manner similar to a talk show.

Hue   Color name.

Human resources   Division of an organization responsible for hiring, training, monitoring legal issues, and, if necessary, firing personnel.

Hypothesis   Educated guess about the relationship between things, or predictions about the future.

Ideal chart   List of all categories of merchandise that will be represented in the show.

Image advertising   Sponsored messages that create an identity for a product or service by emphasizing a symbolic association with certain values, lifestyles, or an ideal.

Image consultants   Individuals who sell products to enhance personal attractiveness in a direct sales approach.

Imagery   Advertising execution that is nearly all visual with very little information presented.

Impulse buying   Buying that occurs when no previous need recognition has taken place before the purchase is made.

Inbound call   Phone response initiated by the consumer.

Incentive   Something put in place to induce action or motivate effort.

Incentive program   Motivational tools generally designed to increase the sales productivity of sales associates at the retail level.

Incentive-based compensation   Compensation system that ties payment to performance.

Infomercial   30- to 60-minute program-length product demonstration that often looks like a TV show.

Informal balance   See *asymmetrical balance.*

Informal fashion show   Fashion shows that present merchandise on models in a casual environment.

Information technology division   Division within a firm that manages technology and computer applications.

Informational appeal   Appeal that spotlights a consumer's utilitarian, functional, practical need for a product.

In-house list   Customer inventories developed, owned, and maintained by the company participating in direct marketing activities.

In-kind sponsor   Sponsor that provides products or services rather than a cash donation.

Insert   Advertisement printed on high-quality paper stock

Instant coupon   A form placed on the outside of a package to encourage the consumer to immediately redeem the coupon.

Institutional advertising   Sponsored messages geared toward building the reputation of the firm, enhancing civic sponsorship and community involvement, and developing long-term relationships between customers and the firm.

Institutional event   Occurrence produced to enhance the company image, exhibit good corporate citizenship, embellish customer relations, contribute to the community economic development, or promote a charitable cause.

In-store show   Fashion show presented for the benefit of store employees, in order to inform the staff of new and exciting trends for the upcoming season.

Integrated marketing communication (IMC)   Concept of marketing communications planning that recognizes the added value of a comprehensive plan that evaluates the strategic roles of a variety of communication disciplines.

Integrity pledge   Statement that prohibits employees from accepting any gifts.

Intensity   Purity, brightness, or saturation of a color, ranging from bright to dull.

Interactive media   Back-and-forth flow of information whereby users can participate in and modify the form and content of the information they receive in real time.

Interior display   Technique used to present merchandise attractively on variety of architectural forms, fixtures, and furniture inside of a store.

Internal audit   Report to determine the performance of an employee and his or her programs.

Internal information   Data available from within the firm including information that comes from employees or firm records.

Internal relations   Public relations tool for managing a firm's employees by creating a corporate culture that attracts and retails productive workers.

Internet   Global data communications system.

Intuition   Basing decisions on subjective feelings or instinct.

Inverted pyramid   Used in news stories where the most important information is presented first, arranging paragraphs in descending order of importance.

Investor relations   Public relations with the responsibility to keep shareholders informed and loyal to the firm.

Island display   Three-dimensional display space, frequently located at the mall entrance or in a central location where several aisles come together.

Issues management   Proactive process of anticipating, identifying, evaluating, and responding to public policy issues that affect organizations' relationships with their public.

Jingle   Catchy verse or song with an easy rhythm that is used to create a verbal link to a product.

Key fact   Problem or opportunity that can be solved with promotion.

Key item   Best-selling trend with strong customer demand.

Knockoffs   Products that copy either the shape or design created by a well-known company, but do not bear that company's name.

Late majority   Later adopters who purchase items during the general acceptance phase of a trend.

Laws   Body of rules and principles governing the actions of individuals or organizations and enforced by a political authority.

Layout   Arrangement of the physical elements of art, copy, and white space within the boundaries of the print advertisement.

Lead   One or two sentences that summarize the news, including who, what, where, when, and why.

Ledge   Display areas located behind islands created by showcases, generally in the cosmetic and accessory departments or behind cash wrap desks.

Lighting   Illumination of the display or selling area.

Line   Direction eye moves through an advertisement or garment.

Line drawing   Illustrations made using lines to represent the pictorial image.

Lineup   List of models in the order they will appear and the outfits they will be wearing.

Live action   Production technique that portrays people, animals, and objects as lifelike in everyday situations.

Lobbying   Public relations tool involving building and maintaining relationships with government officials, primarily to influence legislation and government regulation.

Local advertising   Sponsored messages developed for an immediate trading area.

Localized strategy   Marketing approach that recognizes each culture is unique and the strategy must be tailored to meet the sensibilities and needs of each specific country.

Logo   Graphic symbol or distinctive typeface that represents a company's name, mark, or emblem.

Long-term plan   Strategic plan covering more than two years into the future.

Loyalty program   See *reward program*.

Mail-in premium   Gifts that require the consumer to send in a proof-of-purchase to receive the item.

Major selling idea   Central theme or concept that is the focus of the advertising campaign.

Management and finance division   Division of a full-service agency that handles commercial operations including managing the office, billing clients, making payments to the various media, and controlling personnel issues.

Mannequin   Body forms that wear apparel.

Mannequin modeling   Form of informal modeling in which the model acts as a live mannequin in a store window or on a display platform.

Manufacturer's sales representative (rep)   Personal sales associate at the wholesale level.

Market research   Investigation of product, price promotion, place, and other details in order to understand the environment in which a product or service competes.

Market research companies   Research firms that gather information about a firm's clients to enable the advertiser to plan and evaluate their advertising and promotion programs.

Market segment   Homogeneous subset of consumers.

Market situation analysis   Detailed investigation that assesses the external and internal environment that affects marketing operations.

Marketing   Process of planning and executing the conception, pricing, promotion, and distribution of ideas, goods, and services to create exchanges that satisfy individual and organizational objectives.

Marketing mix   Coordination of the four P's—product, price, place, and promotion/communication.

Marketing objectives   Statements that specify what is to be accomplished by the overall marketing program within a short time period and are expressed as part of the planning process.

Marketing plan   Document that describes the overall marketing strategy developed for the company, line, product, or brand.

Marketing strategy   Describes how the company plans to meet marketing objectives.

Mass market   Large group of consumers with similar needs.

Mean income   Average value of all incomes within a sample.

Mechanical   See *paste-up*.

Media   Broad term for mass communication organizations that provide entertainment to viewers or readers and furnish advertisers an environment to reach audiences through promotional messages.

Media buyer   Executive in charge of media placement who must deliberate the pros and cons of each medium in relationship to the advertising budget.

Media buying services   Independent firms that exclusively handle purchasing media time, primarily for radio and television.

Media cost   Expense associated with the placement of an advertisement in a print or broadcast outlet.

Media division   Division of a full-service agency that analyzes, selects, and contracts for space or time in the media.

Media kit   Communication technique used to generate news stories about a company or group through newsworthy initiatives. The collection of publicity materials is delivered to the media as a single unit.

Media list   List of specific contacts for each medium used in public relations.

Media objectives   Goals to be attained by the media program and should be accomplished by media strategies.

Media organizations   Mechanism for communication and advertising messages to be distributed to large audiences.

Media plan   Formalizes the planning process into a plan for selecting the best method for getting an advertiser's message to the market.

Media planner   Executive designated with the responsibility for developing the media plan.

Media planning   Task of deciding when, where, and how the advertising message will be delivered.

Media representatives   Personnel hired to sell space for print and/or electronic communication sources.

Media research   Investigation that attempts to determine the size of advertising outlets and their ability to attract the target audience.

Media savings   Share of the money saved by one agency over another in media placement.

Media sponsor   Sponsor that provides a predetermined level of advertising support.

Media vehicle   Specific newspaper, magazine, television show, or radio program, used to communicate an advertising message.

Median income   Middle value in the income distribution with an equal number of incomes above and below the midpoint.

Medium   Singular form of the word *media,* describing a particular mass communication category such as newspapers.

Merchandise approach   Sales technique that directly makes reference to the merchandise at hand.

Merchandise coordinator   Person who is responsible for collecting, preparing the merchandise, fitting the merchandise to the models, and returning the merchandise to departments after the show.

Merchandise event   Occurrence planned to influence the sale of goods.

Merchandise selection   Designation of apparel, shoes, and accessories for presentation in a fashion show.

Merchandising   Forecasting what customers want to buy, investigating where to find that merchandise, determining the price the customer is willing to pay, and making it available through outlets where the customer is willing to buy the merchandise.

Merchandising division   Division of the retail store responsible for locating, buying, and reselling products.

Merchandising environment   All of the products and services relating to personal and home surroundings, also known as fashion products.

Merit pay   Extra pay awarded to an employee for outstanding past performance.

Message research   Inquiry that is done to evaluate effectiveness of the creative message, from copy and ingenuity to the visual impact of the advertisement.

Middle class   Members of society positioned socioeconomically between the lower working class and the wealthy.

Mission statement   Formalization of the company's mission that usually covers a discussion of the company's products, services, and target consumers.

Model coordinator   Person who is responsible for hiring, training, and coordinating all activities that involve the models.

Models   Individuals, hired or volunteer, who wear the merchandise and accessories during the show.

Modified undifferentiated strategy   Positioning strategy targeted at the largest target market within a population.

Motives   Reasons why consumers buy.

Multimedia shows   Fashion shows specifically produced digitally and distributed to sales representatives or retailers, or on television or online entertainment programs.

Museum exhibit   Presentation of fashion items in an interpretive setting at a museum.

Music director   Person in charge of music selection, permissions, and sound at the show.

Musical performance   Music presentations hosted by a retailer or manufacturer.

Narrative dramatization   Form of radio commercial with actors portraying individuals in real-life situations.

National advertising   Sponsored messages for consumer products or retail stores that are widely available throughout the United States.

National brands   Brands distributed throughout the United States.

News release   Form used to pass information from the sponsoring party to the media outlet, also known as publicity, press, or media release.

News story   Article written about recent events or happenings.

Newsworthy   Happening of sufficient interest or importance to the public to generate a print or broadcast story.

Niche market   Small group of consumers with characteristics noticeably different from the mass market.

Noise   Outside factors that interfere with the reception of information or lead to distortion of a message.

Noncommercial advertising   See *nonprofit advertising*.

Nonmeasured media   See *support media*.

Nonproduct advertising   See *institutional advertising*.

Nonprofit advertising   Sponsored messages used by nonprofit organizations.

Nontraditional media   See *support media*.

Objective and task   Budgeting method in which a budget is created based on planning objectives.

Objectives   Outcomes desired by the firm within a short time period, typically one year or less.

One-step approach   Appeal that directly obtains an order.

On-premises signage   Signage used to promote goods or services offered by businesses on the property where the sign is located.

On-screen entertainment   The slide show that previews before the movie.

Open-back window   Store windows without a back wall.

Operations division   Branch of the store responsible for sales support functions such as facilities management, security, customer service, merchandise processing, and warehousing.

Opportunity   An area for the company's marketing process to move where the company could enjoy a competitive advantage.

Opportunity loss   A missed possibility or a penalty associated with poor communications.

Organizational chart   Structure of a firm showing how responsibilities and authority are delegated within a firm.

Outbound call   A phone appeal initiated by the vendor.

Out-of-home media   Advertising messages that reach consumers away from their homes.

Paid search   Where an advertiser only pays when a customer clicks on their ad or link from a search engine page.

Participations   Advertisers pay for commercial time during one or more programs.

Paste-up   Format of the art, copy, and logo in its presentation layout.

Payout planning   Budgeting strategy used for the introduction of new products requiring 1.5 to 2 times as much promotional expenditures as an existing product.

Penetration   Total number of persons or households that can physically be exposed to a medium by the nature of that medium's geographical circulation or broadcast signal.

Percentage charges   Method of compensating an agency by adding a markup to costs for work done by outside suppliers.

Percentage of sales   A budgeting method in which the promotion budget is based upon a specific percentage of anticipated annual sales.

Performance appraisal system   System for measuring the performance of a sales associate.

Performance evaluation   Investigation of the effects of a program such as promotion or a product such as textiles.

Personal observation   Watching the job done by a public relations specialist for purposes of evaluation.

Personal selling   Direct interaction between the customer and the seller for the purpose of making a sale.

Personal shoppers   Sales associates who assemble items for specific customers prior to or in place of, a visit to the retail store.

Personality symbol   Advertising execution that uses a central character or personality symbol to deliver the advertising message.

Photo opportunity sheet   Document included in a media kit that describes photography needs.

Photography   Process for visual reproduction of a pictorial image.

Physiological profile   Technique for measuring the involuntary reactions to ads.

Plagiarism   Act of using or passing off as one's own an idea, writing, or the creative thought of another.

Planning   Continual process of defining, refining, and explaining promotional goals and objectives.

Planogram   Detailed plan or map that serves as a guide for setting up window, exterior, and interior displays.

Podcast   Enables listeners to hear audio files at the time and place of their choosing, as long as the listener has podcasting software installed on a personal computer or synchronized portable player.

Point-of-purchase (POP)   Merchandise presentations of products at the point where the sale is made, such as a checkout line or a cosmetic or jewelry counter.

Pop-under advertisement   Advertisements that appear under a Web page and only become visible when the user leaves a site.

Pop-up advertisement   Advertisements that appear on screen when the Internet is accessed.

Portfolio test   Participants are exposed to a series of test and control advertisements.

Positioning   Use of the promotion mix to cause consumers to perceive a particular company's product as completely different from other brands of the same product or competing products.

Posttests   Measurements are taken after an advertisement has been placed in the media.

Precollections   Line previews presented to key retail buyers, fashion editors, and private customers three months ahead of the official start of the season.

Premium   Gifts or merchandise offered free or at a reduced price as an inducement to buy something else.

Press agentry   Creating newsworthy stories and events to attract attention from the mass media in order to gain public notice.

Press conference   Gathering held by a firm seeking publicity for an event or happening for news reporters.

Prestige advertising   Sponsored messages created for a long-term effort to build and maintain a fashionable reputation.

Pretests   Tests that are administered prior to the implementation of the advertising campaign.

Price-off deal   Price reductions offered on the package of specially marketed items.

Primary colors   Hues of red, yellow, and blue.

Primary market   (1) Essential target group identified for communication; (2) producers of raw materials including textile fiber firms, fabric manufacturers, and other producers of raw materials.

Primary research   Original research carried out by a company in order to answer a very specific question.

Prime time   Television programming broadcast between 8 P.M. and 11 P.M.

Private label brand   Merchandise manufactured for a specific retailer.

Producer   Top manager of a broadcast organization.

Product acquisition   Process of searching, evaluating, and choosing among alternative items.

Product advertising   Sponsored messages promotion of specific goods or services.

Product demonstration   Occurrences orchestrated to show how new or improved products can be used by consumers.

Product launch   Occurrences planned to set in motion the promotion and sales of new products.

Product placement   Positioning of a branded product versus an unbranded generic product as a prop in a movie or a television show.

Production division   Division responsible for mass-producing merchandise and filling orders placed by retailers.

Production show   Most elaborate and expensive fashion show, loaded with theatrical and dramatic elements; see *spectacular*.

Professional   Person engaged in a profession worthy of high standards.

Professionalism   An approach that infers work of the highest quality or standards.

Profit sharing   Plan that offers employees a chance to purchase stock in the company and an opportunity to receive shares of any profits earned by the company.

Program sponsorship   Advertising time sold for a specific radio show that will include an opening mention, commercials during the show, and a closing credit.

Promotion   Comprehensive term for all communication activities initiated by the seller to inform, persuade, and remind the consumer about products, services, and/or ideas offered for sale.

Promotion calendar   Set of calendars that assist manufacturers, retailers, and advertising agencies in achieving their promotional goals.

Promotion coordinator   Person who is responsible for all promotional activities for the event.

Promotion division   (1) Division responsible for promotion mix of activities including advertising, direct marketing, public relations, sales promotion, event coordination, fashion shows, and visual merchandising; (2) personnel employed by the designer, manufacturer, or retailer that assist clients in achieving promotional goals.

Promotion mix   Basic tools used for achieving a firm's communication and marketing goals.

Promotion objectives   Common and universally accepted objectives of promotion aimed at the consumer including informing, arousing interest, persuading, encouraging purchase, and gaining loyalty.

Promotion plan   Document that describes the overall promotion strategy developed for a company, line, product, or brand.

Promotion planning   Development of objectives, strategies, and tactics to communicate to consumers about a company, line, product, or brand.

Promotion situation analysis   Detailed investigation that assesses the external and internal environment that affects issues relevant to promotion/communication.

Promotional allowance   Incentives from manufacturers for performing certain promotional activities to support their brand or product.

Prop   Functional structures used to lean or place merchandise on or decorative elements used symbolically to create a mood.

Proportion   Ratio of one feature in a design to any other feature.

Psychographic segmentation   Method of profiling markets based on consumer lifestyles including activities, interests, and opinions.

Public   Customers, potential customers, employees, vendors, educators, the community where the business is located, governments (local, regional, or national), stockholders, and possibly the competition who are interested in a particular company or its products.

Public affairs   Public relations tool to build and maintain governmental and local community relations in order to have some bearing on public policy.

Public opinion   Measurement of the beliefs and feelings of citizens.

Public relations (PR)   Management function that establishes and maintains mutually beneficial relationships between an organization and the public on whom its success or failure depends.

Public relations department   Department responsible for developing broad-range policies and programs to create a favorable public opinion of the firm.

Public relations director   Individual in charge of a firm's public relations.

Public relations firm   Agencies hired to manage the client's public image, the client's relationships with consumers, and any other services related to publicity.

Public service announcement (PSA)   Print or broadcast spots that run free of charge to charitable organizations.

Publicity   Information with news value, used in the mass media, that is uncontrolled by the source because the source does not pay the media for placement.

Publicity director   Individual in charge of a firm's public relations; see *public relations director*.

Publicity writer   Individual who writes media releases to seek recognition for their event or products.

Publisher   Individual who coordinates all organizational and functional components of the media.

Pulsing   Method of scheduling combining continuity and flighting scheduling.

Purchase cycle   Interval of time between acquisition and replacement of the same or similar product in a routine manner.

Purchase-with-purchase   Incentive program in which consumers are offered a special purchase price for an additional item if they buy merchandise over a certain dollar amount.

Pyramid   Triangular geometric shaped display arrangement, where the base is the widest space.

Quantitative models   Techniques involving multiple regression analysis used to analyze the relationship of variables to the relative contributions of promotional activities to sales.

Race   Biological heritage of an individual.

Rack   Wooden or metal fixtures, ranging from simple T-stands for small quantities of merchandise to large round racks, which hold hundreds of garments.

Radio   Broadcast medium that allows sound to travel via electrical impulses called signals.

Radio frequency   Number of radio waves a transmitter produces in a second.

Rate cards   Documents that list the costs for space, production (mechanical and copy) requirements, deadlines, and other publication information.

Ratings   Audience for a program; an estimate of the total number of homes reached as a percentage of the total population.

Rational appeal   See *informational appeal*.

Reach   Percentage of target audience, homes or individuals, exposed to an advertiser's message at least once in a period of time.

Readability test   Evaluation technique that depends upon the Flesch formula, which focuses on the human-interest appeal in the material, the length of sentences, and the familiarity of words.

Really simple syndication (RSS)   Method used to send product alerts to Internet users who have set up personalized Web pages on Yahoo, Google, or other search engine sites.

Rebate   Deduction from the amount to be paid or a refund of part of an amount paid upon proof-of-purchase.

Refund   Money directly given back to the consumer at the point-of-purchase.

Regional advertising   Sponsored messages distributed within a limited geographic region.

Regional brands   Brands distributed to one region of the United States.

Regular sponsorship   When a company pays to sponsor a section of a website.

Reliability   Research procedure is free from random error, and the measure is consistent and accurate.

Remote   Live broadcast on location.

Remote display   Physical presentation of merchandise by a retailer or manufacturer placed in such locations as hotel lobbies, exhibit halls, or public transportation terminals.

Renovation   Remodeling and refurbishing the interior design and layout of a selling space.

Repetition   Type of display arrangement that uses the same merchandise and/or props in a style that occurs again.

Research   Investigation of subject in order to understand it in a detailed, accurate manner.

Research division   Division of a full-service agency responsible for gathering, analyzing, and interpreting information used to develop promotional activities.

Reseller support   Also referred to as trade-oriented sales promotion. Sales promotion to support the efforts of intermediaries including manufacturers, wholesalers, distributors, and retailers.

Retail calendar   Guide that indicates what merchandise is currently available in the retail store.

Retail market   Businesses responsible for communicating trends, developed from the primary and secondary markets, to the ultimate consumer.

Return-on-investment   Budgeting method in which advertising and promotion are considered investments that will lead to some type of long-term return.

Reward program   Incentive in which frequent buyers are compensated for their purchases.

Rhythm   Using reoccurring motifs to draw the eye through a composition.

Robinson-Patman Act   Legislation that authorizes the FTC to prevent specified practices involving discriminatory pricing and product promotion.

Rough   Workups of the chosen thumbnails, rendered in actual size to represent where the art, headlines, copy, and logos will be placed.

Rough cut   Film or videotape edited for review or testing prior to making the final commercial.

Salary enhancements   Salary incentives used to motive sales associates.

Salary plus commission   Incentive used by some retailers or departments in which employees are given a base salary plus an additional percent based on sales generated.

Sales contests   Sales associates compete against one another, against other stores within the chain, or against established goals to increase sales.

Sales division   Division responsible for selling the line or collection of merchandise.

Sales promotion   Activities that provide extra value or incentives to the sales force, distributors, or ultimate consumer.

Sales promotion agencies   Agencies hired to develop and manage sales promotion programs, such as contests, refunds or rebates, premium or incentive offers, sweepstakes, or sampling programs.

Salesmanship   Ability to sell goods in a fair, sincere, and distinctive manner.

Sampling   Sales promotion technique in which a small quantity of a product is given to a consumer at no charge to coax a trial use.

Scheduling   Setting the time for advertisements or commercials to run.

Scientific method   A decision-making process focused on objective and orderly testing of ideas before they are accepted.

Secondary colors   Combination of two primary colors; orange, green, and violet.

Secondary market   (1) Auxiliary target group identified for communication; (2) manufacturers of finished goods, such as clothing, shoes, accessories, home furnishings, or cosmetics.

Segment sponsor   Known as presenting sponsors, major sponsor of a predetermined portion of an event.

Segmentation   Subdivision of the marketplace into relatively homogeneous subsets of consumers.

Self-liquidating premium   Items in which the consumer must pay for the cost of the gift.

Self-regulation   An entity voluntarily controls or directs itself according to rules, principles, or laws without outside monitoring.

Selling point   Features and characteristics of the merchandise that make it desirable.

Senior editor   Individual who manages a news section such as business, fashion, or travel.

Shade   Adding black to a hue.

Shadow box window   Small closed-back window, dimensioned on a much smaller scale than other window styles.

Shape   Physical form of a product.

Share   Size of an audience for any given time period.

Short-term plan   Plan for a period of six months to one year.

Showcase   Fixtures used to enclose groupings of similar merchandise.

Simplified selling   Direct contact with merchandise by the consumer with no sales personnel.

Slice of life   Advertising execution that presents a problem consumers have in daily life and how the advertiser's product will solve the problem.

Sliding   Radio advertising schedule in which the frequency of advertising is changed over the course of the advertising campaign.

Slogan   Repeated selling points or appeals that are primarily associated with the product, brand, or company.

Slotting allowance   Fees paid to retailers to provide a position or "slot" to accommodate the new product.

Soft sell   Sales approach that presents merchandise in a discriminating not forceful way.

Special effects   Production techniques such as moving titles, whirling logos, and dissolve images.

Special event   One-time occurrence with planned activities, focused on a specific purpose, to bring attention to a brand, manufacturer, retailer, or organization, or to influence the sale of merchandise.

Special events calendar   Guide that identifies guest appearances, product demonstrations, vendor promotions, and other special activities coordinated by the promotion department or fashion office.

Specialty goods   Products aimed at a narrowly defined target market.

Spiffs   Sales incentives that may be given to employees in the form of extra money, additional discounts, or merchandise whenever sales of specific items are made.

Spin   Twisting messages to give a favorable meaning to communication that may or may not be true.

Split-run advertising   Paid messages run in one or more geographic editions depending upon the advertiser's needs.

Sponsorship   A company supporting an event through monetary and/or in-kind contributions as a way to meet one or more of their corporate objectives.

Sponsorship proposal   Document that asks a potential sponsor for contributions to make an event happen.

S-shaped curve   S-shape that demonstrates that initial outlays of advertising will have little or no impact on consumers in the early stages of sales.

Stage manager   Person who oversees the use of the stage and runway, organizes equipment, and supervises people providing behind-the-scenes services, such as sound and lighting technicians.

Stakeholders   Term used to describe the public.

Standard advertising unit (SAU)   Measurement used to sell advertising space.

Standardized strategy   One marketing approach for multiple international markets.

Step   Display arrangement that is a series of elevations similar to a stair step.

Store opening   Celebration that introduces customers to a new merchant.

Storyboard   Graphic presentations, part advertising layout and part script, that describe television commercials of any length.

Straight front window   Store windows that are parallel to the road or sidewalk.

Straight sell   Advertising execution presenting information as a straightforward or factual message using an informational appeal.

Strategic alliance   Partnership between a manufacturer and a retailer working in a particular supply chain that leverages the core competencies of each firm.

Strategic marketing plan   See *marketing plan*.

Strategic planning   Process of determining goals, setting objectives, and implementing strategies and tactics to realize goals.

Strategies   Plans, methods, or designs by which to accomplish objectives.

Style guides   Written set of rules mandated by the outlet so all copy reads the same.

Stylist   Fashion show staff member with the responsibility of providing creative input to the designer and show producer, and present clothes immaculately.

Subheadline   Secondary statements used to further clarify the primary headline.

Suggestion selling   Offering related merchandise, such as accessories, larger quantities of the same merchandise in other colors or styles, promotional merchandise, or advertised merchandise.

Suppliers   Personnel that assist clients and advertising departments or agencies in preparing promotional materials.

Support media   Less dominant forms of advertising that supplement primary media.

Sweepstakes   Promotions in which winners are determined solely by chance and a proof-of-purchase is not required as a condition of entry.

SWOT analysis   Analysis of strengths, weaknesses, opportunities, and threats.

Symmetrical balance   Items are identical on both sides.

Tabloid   Newspaper format, approximately half the size of a broadsheet format with five columns.

Tactics   Specific ways in which a promotion strategy is executed.

Target market   Homogeneous subset of consumers.

Target ratings points (TRPs)   The number of people in the primary target audience the media buy will reach.

Targeting   Identifying the group most likely to respond to communication messages.

Tearoom modeling   Specific type of informal modeling that takes place in a restaurant on a regularly scheduled day.

Telemarketing   Selling of products or services, or fund-raising for an organization or institution, using the telephone to contact prospective customers.

Television   Broadcast medium where sight is combined with sound and motion to provide the most realistic reproduction of life.

Tertiary colors   Combination of a primary and secondary color; yellow-green, green-blue, blue-violet, red-violet, red-orange, and yellow-orange.

Test ads   Advertisements being pretested or measured for their potential effectiveness.

Test market   Geographic area that has been selected as representative of the target market.

Testimonial Advertising execution presenting information from a user of the product.

Textile Fiber Products Identification Act (TFPIA) Legislation (1960) that requires that a tag or label with certain information relating to the fiber content of textile products be attached to the item at the time of sale and delivery to the consumer.

Texture Uniformity or variation in the surface of an object.

Theme Reoccurring idea seen in color, silhouette, fabric, and other design components.

Third shift manufacturing Producer making unauthorized products, without permission from the brand owner, and selling these goods to an unauthorized distributor.

Thumbnail Preliminary unpolished designs produced in a small size so several versions can be tried.

Tint Adding white to a hue.

Tone Adding gray to a hue.

Top-down approaches Budgeting methods in which the highest management level of the firm establishes the amount for the entire retail corporation or manufacturing concern.

Top-down planning Translation of goals and objectives by the corporate management team to lower levels of management.

Trade advertising Business-to-business directed sponsored messages.

Trade allowance Discount offered to a retailer as an incentive to stock and display merchandise from a specific vendor.

Trade calendar Monthly guide to events occurring at the manufacturing level.

Trade dress Features of a product that comprise its overall look or image and include a product's packaging, labeling, display, product design, and configuration.

Trade market See business-to-business market.

Trademark Word or symbol that indicates a source of origin and can be protected based on actual use.

Trademark counterfeiting Development and sale of imitative products bearing deliberately copied trademarks.

Trading area The city, county, state, or region a company services.

Trading up Process of substituting lower-priced merchandise for higher-priced merchandise during merchandise presentation.

Traffic department

Traffic time See *drive time*.

Transit media Printed advertising messages at bus stops, train stations, or along commuter highways, above the seats in subways, buses, or trains.

Trend General direction that something is moving.

Trend map Identifies which trends are on the rise, continuing to grow, or reaching maturity on the fashion cycle as well as strength of the trend.

Trend shop Merchandising area set apart by special flooring, walls, or ceiling treatments, also known as a highlight shop.

Trend storyboards Boards that accompany fashion trend reports that include illustrations, fabrics, and color cards representing the spirit, mood, and theme of the fashion report.

Trial purchase Test a trial-size portion of a new product.

Trunk show Fashion presentations that feature garments from a single manufacturer or designer and are presented as informal fashion shows in retail stores.

TV spots Short-form, direct-response programs less than 30 minutes in length.

T-wall Type of perimeter wall used to separate one department from another

Two-step approach Appeal that first qualifies potential buyers and then follows up with a second request to generate a response.

Typeface Style of type.

Typography Selection and setting of a typeface.

Undifferentiated strategy Marketing strategy that offers the same promotional mix to the entire population without regard to market segments.

Unique selling proposition (USP) Most important reason for a consumer to prefer one product over all others.

Unit sales incentive Base fee and a bonus for unit sales above the goal or target sales.

Unity See *harmony*.

Validity Testing procedure is free from both random and systematic error.

Value Lightness or darkness of a color.

Vendor week Occurrence that features a merchandise category or brand; see *category week*.

Video news release (VNR) Publicity pieces created by publicists and delivered to television stations as news stories.

Vision statement Positive and inspiring statement that draws upon the mission statement to address where the company wants to be in the future.

Visual merchandising Physical presentation of products in a nonpersonal approach to promote the image of the firm and the sale of merchandise to the consumer.

Visual merchandising calendar Guide developed to organize visual presentations for the business.

Visual merchandising department Department responsible for the visual presentation of the store image and its merchandise.

Warm colors   Colors projecting sensations of warmth; red, orange, and yellow.

Website   Place where providers make information available on the Internet.

White space   Space on an advertisement that is not occupied with artwork or copy.

Windowless window   No-window concepts used as the entrance to mall stores.

Wool Products Labeling Act   Legislation (1939) that governs the labeling of wool and wool-blended textiles.

Word-of-mouth   Direct or face-to-face communication.

World Wide Web (WWW)   Business components of the Internet.

Yellow Pages   Volume or section of a telephone directory that lists businesses, services, or products alphabetically according to field.

Zapping   Consumers use the remote control to change channels during a commercial.

Zigzag   Display arrangement based on a reversing step design.

Zipping   Consumers fast-forward commercials during the playback of a previously recorded program.

Zone editions   Newspapers that provide news and advertising focused to an area within a city.

○ CreDITs

Chapter 1

1.1 Photo © Stephane Fuguere/Courtesy Fairchild Publications, Inc.; 1.2 Courtesy Gap; 1.3 Courtesy IKEA; 1.7 Courtesy Urban Outfitters; 1.8 Photo © Francois Guillot/AFP/Getty Images

Chapter 2

2.1 (top) Photo © Thomas Iannaccone/Courtesy Fairchild Publications, Inc.; 2.1 (bottom) Courtesy Fairchild Publications, Inc.; 2.3 Courtesy L'Oreal; Courtesy The Home Depot; Courtesy Estee Lauder; Courtesy Yoplait, Courtesy the Milk Processor Education Program; 2.8, 2.10, and 2.11 Source: U.S. Census Bureau, 2000 Census

Chapter 3

3.1 Photo © Tim Jenkins/Courtesy Condé Nast Publications; 3.2 Courtesy Cotton Incorporated; 3.5 Photo © Erin Fitzsimmons; 3.9 Courtesy The Association for Women in Communications; 3.10 Courtesy the National Retail Federation; 3.11 Courtesy Unilever

Chapter 4

4.1 (top) Photo © Steve Eichner/Courtesy Fairchild Publications, Inc.; 4.1 (bottom) Photo © WWD Staff/Courtesy Fairchild Publications, Inc.; 4.2 Photo © Robert Mitra/Courtesy the Doneger Group; 4.4 Courtesy Fashion Group International; 4.5 Source: Brannon, E.L. (2005). "Fashion Forecasting" (2nd ed.). New York: Fairchild Books. p. 33; 4.7 Photo © Pascal Le Segretain/Getty Images; 4.11 Courtesy Cotton Incorporated.; 4.12 Source: Brannon, E.L. (2005). "Fashion Forecasting" (2nd ed.). New York: Fairchild Books. p. 72; 4.13 Courtesy Pantone

Chapter 5

5.1 Photo © Yukie Kasuga/Courtesy Fairchild Publications, Inc.; 5.2 Courtesy Fairchild Publications, Inc.; 5.5 Courtesy Fashion Group International; 5.7 Adapted from: Belch, G. E. & Belch, M. A. (2007). Advertising and promotion (7th ed.). New York: McGraw-Hill/Irwin

Chapter 6

6.1 Courtesy Fairchild Publications, Inc.; 6.6 and 6.7 Source: International Journal of Advertising, 2005, 24(3). p. 414

Chapter 7

7.1 Courtesy Fairchild Publications, Inc.; 7.3 Courtesy Victoria's Secret; 7.9 Courtesy Nikon, Inc.; 7.12 Courtesy the Milk Processor Education Program

Chapter 8

8.1 Courtesy Clinique; 8.5 Courtesy Cover Girl

Chapter 9

9.1 Photo © Steve Eichner/Courtesy Fairchild Publications, Inc.; Reprinted with permission of *The New York Times;* 9.7 Courtesy Fairchild Publications, Inc.; 9.10 Courtesy Condé Nast Publications; 9.11 Courtesy www.magazine.org; 9.15 Source: Brannon, E.L. (2005). "Fashion Forecasting"(2nd ed.). New York: Fairchild Books. p.164

Chapter 10

10.1 Photo © Mike Mergen/*The New York Times*/Redux; 10.2 and 10.3 Courtesy Neilsen Media Research; Courtesy DSW; 10.6 and 10.7 Source: Book, A.C. and Schick, C.D. (1997). Fundamentals of Copy and Layout. Lincolnwood, IL: NTC Books

Chapter 11

11.1 Courtesy JCPenney.com; 11.2 Courtesy Cotton Incorporated; 11.6 Sources: Sherwood Outdoor (left) and © New York Convention & Visitors Bureau (right); 11.7 Courtesy Advertising Age. © 2006 Yellow Pages Association; 11.8 Courtesy © Google, Inc.; 11.9 Courtesy Fairchild Publications, Inc.

Chapter 12

12.1 Photo © Frances Roberts/*The New York Times*/Redux; 12.4 Courtesy Hain Celestial Group; 12.5 Source: © The Toos Studio/drewtoos@aol.com

Chapter 13

13.1 Courtesy Weatherproof® Garment Co.; 13.3 Courtesy Condé Nast Publications; 13.4 and 13.10 Courtesy Fairchild Publications, Inc.

Chapter 14

14.1 Photo © Talaya Centeno/Courtesy Fairchild Publications, Inc.; 14.5 Courtesy Gucci; 14.8 Courtesy Angela Johnson

Chapter 15

15.1 Photo © 2006 Robert Bengston/Courtesy Macy's Passport; 15.2, 15.4-15.6 Photo © Giovanni Giannoni/Courtesy Fairchild Publications, Inc.; 15.8 Courtesy Condé Nast Publications; 15.10 Photo © J. Estrin/NYT Pictures; 15.12 Photo © Giovanni Giannoni/Courtesy Fairchild Publications, Inc.

Chapter 16

16.1 Photo © Tim Jenkins/Courtesy Condé Nast Publications; 16.4 Source: The Archives of The Andy Warhol Museum, Pittsburgh. Founding Collection, Contribution, The Andy Warhol Foundation for the Visual Arts, Inc.; 16.6 Photo © Steve Eichner/Courtesy Fairchild Publications, Inc. and Everett Collection; 16.9 Courtesy Fairchild Publications, Inc.; 16.10 Photo © Mike Kepp/Courtesy Fairchild Publications, Inc.; 16.11 Courtesy Fairchild Publications, Inc.

Chapter 17

17.1 Courtesy Fairchild Publications, Inc.; 17.6 Courtesy National Retail Federation; 17.7 Photo © S. Farley/NYT Pictures

Color Plates

CP01 Photo © Donato Sardella/Courtesy Fairchild Publications, Inc.; CP03 Photos © Giovanni Giannoni/Courtesy Fairchild Publications, Inc.; CP04 Photos © Emanuele Scorcelletti/Courtesy Fairchild Publications, Inc. and Photos © Zoe Cassavetes/Courtesy Fairchild Publications, Inc.; CP05 Photos © Courtesy of The Heart Truth, National Heart, Lung, and Blood Institute; CP06 Photos © Courtesy of Sara Lee Corporation; CP08 Photos © Dominique Maitre/Courtesy Fairchild Publications, Inc.

INDEX

note: *f* indicates page with figure; *t* indicates page with table